T0364945

Owners Workshop Manual
for BMW 3-Series

Martynn Randall

(5901 - 352)

Models covered

BMW 3-Series Saloon (E90) & Touring (E91)
318i & 320i petrol and 316d, 318d, 320d, 325d and 330d diesel

Petrol: 2.0 litre (1995cc)

Turbo-Diesel: 2.0 litre (1995cc) & 3.0 litre (2993cc)

Does NOT cover 325i, 330i, 335i, 335d, M3, 'Alpina' versions, Coupe or Convertible
Does NOT cover new 'F-series' model range introduced February 2012

© Haynes Group Limited 2015

ABCDE
FGHIJ
KLMNO
PQ

A book in the **Haynes Owners Workshop Manual Series**

ISBN **978 0 85733 901 0**

British Library Cataloguing in Publication Data
A catalogue record for this book is available from the British Library.

Printed in India

Haynes Group Limited
Sparkford, Yeovil, Somerset BA22 7JJ, England

Haynes North America, Inc
2801 Townsgate Road, Suite 340, Thousand Oaks, CA 91361

Disclaimer

There are risks associated with automotive repairs. The ability to make repairs depends on the individual's skill, experience and proper tools. Individuals should act with due care and acknowledge and assume the risk of performing automotive repairs.

The purpose of this manual is to provide comprehensive, useful and accessible automotive repair information, to help you get the best value from your vehicle. However, this manual is not a substitute for a professional certified technician or mechanic.

This repair manual is produced by a third party and is not associated with an individual vehicle manufacturer. If there is any doubt or discrepancy between this manual and the owner's manual or the factory service manual, please refer to the factory service manual or seek assistance from a professional certified technician or mechanic.

Even though we have prepared this manual with extreme care and every attempt is made to ensure that the information in this manual is correct, neither the publisher nor the author can accept responsibility for loss, damage or injury caused by any errors in, or omissions from, the information given.

Contents

Contents

The BMW 3-Series range covered by this manual was introduced in October 2008 and was available with a choice of 2.0 litre (1995 cc) DOHC petrol engines, and 2.0 litre (1995 cc) or 3.0 litre (2993 cc) diesel engines. Saloon (E90) and Tourer (E91) models are covered by this manual.

All engines are derived from the well-proven engines which have appeared in many BMW vehicles. The engines covered by this manual are of four- and six-cylinder double-overhead camshaft design, mounted longitudinally with the transmission mounted on its rear. Both manual and automatic transmissions are available.

All models have fully-independent front and rear suspension, with anti-roll bars fitted to the front and rear.

A wide range of standard and optional equipment is available within the BMW 3-Series range to suit most tastes, including central locking, electric windows, air conditioning, an electric sunroof, an dynamic stability control, and numerous airbags.

Provided that regular servicing is carried out in accordance with the manufacturer's recommendations, the BMW should prove reliable and very economical. The engine compartment is well-designed, and most of the items requiring frequent attention are easily accessible.

BMW 3-Series manual

The aim of this manual is to help you get the best value from your vehicle. It can do so in several ways. It can help you decide what work must be done (even should you choose to get it done by a garage). It will also provide information on routine maintenance and servicing, and give a logical course of action and diagnosis when random faults occur. However, it is hoped that you will use the manual by tackling the work yourself. On simpler jobs it may even be quicker than booking the car into a garage and going there twice, to leave and collect it. Perhaps most important, a lot of money can be saved by avoiding the costs a garage must charge to cover its labour and overheads.

The manual has drawings and descriptions to show the function of the various components so that their layout can be understood. Tasks are described and photographed in a clear step-by-step sequence.

References to the 'left' and 'right' of the vehicle are in the sense of a person in the driver's seat facing forward.

Acknowledgements

Thanks are also due to Draper Tools Limited and Auto Service Tools Limited (asttools.co.uk), who provided some of the workshop tools, and to all those people at Sparkford who helped in the production of this manual.

Working on your car can be dangerous. This page shows just some of the potential risks and hazards, with the aim of creating a safety-conscious attitude.

General hazards

Scalding

• Don't remove the radiator or expansion tank cap while the engine is hot.
• Engine oil, transmission fluid or power steering fluid may also be dangerously hot if the engine has recently been running.

Burning

• Beware of burns from the exhaust system and from any part of the engine. Brake discs and drums can also be extremely hot immediately after use.

Crushing

• When working under or near a raised vehicle, always supplement the jack with axle stands, or use drive-on ramps. *Never venture under a car which is only supported by a jack*.

• Take care if loosening or tightening high-torque nuts when the vehicle is on stands. Initial loosening and final tightening should be done with the wheels on the ground.

Fire

• Fuel is highly flammable; fuel vapour is explosive.
• Don't let fuel spill onto a hot engine.
• Do not smoke or allow naked lights (including pilot lights) anywhere near a vehicle being worked on. Also beware of creating sparks (electrically or by use of tools).
• Fuel vapour is heavier than air, so don't work on the fuel system with the vehicle over an inspection pit.
• Another cause of fire is an electrical overload or short-circuit. Take care when repairing or modifying the vehicle wiring.
• Keep a fire extinguisher handy, of a type suitable for use on fuel and electrical fires.

Electric shock

• Ignition HT and Xenon headlight voltages can be dangerous, especially to people with heart problems or a pacemaker. Don't work on or near these systems with the engine running or the ignition switched on.

• Mains voltage is also dangerous. Make sure that any mains-operated equipment is correctly earthed. Mains power points should be protected by a residual current device (RCD) circuit breaker.

Fume or gas intoxication

• Exhaust fumes are poisonous; they can contain carbon monoxide, which is rapidly fatal if inhaled. Never run the engine in a confined space such as a garage with the doors shut.
• Fuel vapour is also poisonous, as are the vapours from some cleaning solvents and paint thinners.

Poisonous or irritant substances

• Avoid skin contact with battery acid and with any fuel, fluid or lubricant, especially antifreeze, brake hydraulic fluid and Diesel fuel. Don't syphon them by mouth. If such a substance is swallowed or gets into the eyes, seek medical advice.
• Prolonged contact with used engine oil can cause skin cancer. Wear gloves or use a barrier cream if necessary. Change out of oil-soaked clothes and do not keep oily rags in your pocket.
• Air conditioning refrigerant forms a poisonous gas if exposed to a naked flame (including a cigarette). It can also cause skin burns on contact.

Asbestos

• Asbestos dust can cause cancer if inhaled or swallowed. Asbestos may be found in gaskets and in brake and clutch linings. When dealing with such components it is safest to assume that they contain asbestos.

Special hazards

Hydrofluoric acid

• This extremely corrosive acid is formed when certain types of synthetic rubber, found in some O-rings, oil seals, fuel hoses etc, are exposed to temperatures above 4000C. The rubber changes into a charred or sticky substance containing the acid. *Once formed, the acid remains dangerous for years. If it gets onto the skin, it may be necessary to amputate the limb concerned.*
• When dealing with a vehicle which has suffered a fire, or with components salvaged from such a vehicle, wear protective gloves and discard them after use.

The battery

• Batteries contain sulphuric acid, which attacks clothing, eyes and skin. Take care when topping-up or carrying the battery.
• The hydrogen gas given off by the battery is highly explosive. Never cause a spark or allow a naked light nearby. Be careful when connecting and disconnecting battery chargers or jump leads.

Air bags

• Air bags can cause injury if they go off accidentally. Take care when removing the steering wheel and trim panels. Special storage instructions may apply.

Diesel injection equipment

• Diesel injection pumps supply fuel at very high pressure. Take care when working on the fuel injectors and fuel pipes.

⚠ *Warning: Never expose the hands, face or any other part of the body to injector spray; the fuel can penetrate the skin with potentially fatal results.*

Remember...

DO

• Do use eye protection when using power tools, and when working under the vehicle.

• Do wear gloves or use barrier cream to protect your hands when necessary.

• Do get someone to check periodically that all is well when working alone on the vehicle.

• Do keep loose clothing and long hair well out of the way of moving mechanical parts.

• Do remove rings, wristwatch etc, before working on the vehicle – especially the electrical system.

• Do ensure that any lifting or jacking equipment has a safe working load rating adequate for the job.

DON'T

• Don't attempt to lift a heavy component which may be beyond your capability – get assistance.

• Don't rush to finish a job, or take unverified short cuts.

• Don't use ill-fitting tools which may slip and cause injury.

• Don't leave tools or parts lying around where someone can trip over them. Mop up oil and fuel spills at once.

• Don't allow children or pets to play in or near a vehicle being worked on.

The following pages are intended to help in dealing with common roadside emergencies and breakdowns. You will find more detailed fault finding information at the back of the manual, and repair information in the main chapters.

If your car won't start and the starter motor doesn't turn

- ☐ If it's a model with automatic transmission, make sure the selector is in P or N.
- ☐ Open the right-hand storage tray in the luggage compartment and make sure that the battery terminals are clean and tight.
- ☐ Switch on the headlights and try to start the engine. If the headlights go very dim when you're trying to start, the battery is probably flat. Get out of trouble by jump starting using a friend's car.

If your car won't start even though the starter motor turns as normal

- ☐ Is there fuel in the tank?
- ☐ Is there moisture on electrical components under the bonnet? Switch off the ignition, then wipe off any obvious dampness with a dry cloth. Spray a water-repellent aerosol product (WD-40 or equivalent) on ignition and fuel system electrical connectors like those shown in the photos.

A Check the security of the throttle body connector

B Check the airflow meter wiring connector with the ignition switched off

C Check the security and condition of the battery terminals (located in the luggage compartment).

Check that electrical connections are secure (with the ignition switched off) and spray them with a water dispersant spray like WD-40 if you suspect a problem due to damp. The plastic covers on the engines either pull up from place, or are retained by easily visible bolts – check with the relevant part of Chapter 2.

D Check the glow plug control unit wiring connector(s) (diesel engines only – behind or under the oil filter housing).

Jump starting

HAYNES HiNT

Jump starting will get you out of trouble, but you must correct whatever made the battery go flat in the first place. There are three possibilities:

1 *The battery has been drained by repeated attempts to start, or by leaving the lights on.*

2 *The charging system is not working properly (alternator drivebelt slack or broken, alternator wiring fault or alternator itself faulty).*

3 *The battery itself is at fault (electrolyte low, or battery worn out).*

When jump-starting a car, observe the following precautions:

✓ Before connecting the booster battery, make sure that the ignition is switched off.

Caution: Remove the key in case the central locking engages when the jump leads are connected

✓ Ensure that all electrical equipment (lights, heater, wipers, etc) is switched off.

✓ Take note of any special precautions printed on the battery case.

✓ Make sure that the booster battery is the same voltage as the discharged one in the vehicle.

✓ If the battery is being jump-started from the battery in another vehicle, the two vehicles MUST NOT TOUCH each other.

✓ Make sure that the transmission is in neutral (or PARK, in the case of automatic transmission).

HAYNES HiNT

Budget jump leads can be a false economy, as they often do not pass enough current to start large capacity or diesel engines. They can also get hot.

1 Unclip the plastic cover from the jumpstart terminal (+) on the right-hand side inner wing in the engine compartment, and connect the red jump lead to the terminal.

2 Connect the other end of the red lead to the positive (+) terminal of the booster battery.

3 Connect one end of the black jump lead to the negative (-) terminal of the booster battery

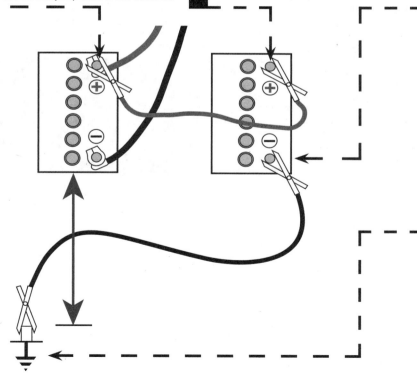

4 Connect the other end of the black jump lead to jump start negative terminal located on the right-hand inner wing in the engine compartment.

5 Make sure that the jump leads will not come into contact with the fan, drive-belts or other moving parts of the engine.

6 Start the engine using the booster battery and run it at idle speed. Switch on the lights, rear window demister and heater blower motor, then disconnect the jump leads in the reverse order of connection. Turn off the lights etc.

Wheel changing

All models covered by this manual are equipped with Run-flat tyres. In the event of a puncture, the structure and construction of the tyre, allows the vehicle to be driven deflated at a maximum speed of 50 mph.

Due to the standard fitment of Run-flat tyres, no spare wheel or vehicle jack is provided.

The maximum distance to be covered with a deflated tyre is:
Low load (1 to 2 people without luggage)   *150 miles*
Moderate load (2 people with luggage,
4 people without luggage)   *90 miles*
Full load (4 or more people with luggage)   *30 miles*

Towing

When all else fails, you may find yourself having to get a tow home – or of course you may be helping somebody else. Long-distance recovery should only be done by a garage or breakdown service. For shorter distances, DIY towing using another car is easy enough, but observe the following points:

☐ Use a proper tow-rope – they are not expensive. The vehicle being towed must display an ON TOW sign in its rear window.

☐ Always turn the ignition key to the 'on' position when the vehicle is being towed, so that the steering lock is released, and the direction indicator and brake lights work.

☐ Only attach the tow-rope to the towing eyes provided. The towing eye is supplied as part of the tool kit which is fitted in the base of the right-hand storage area in the luggage compartment. To fit the eye, press-in the upper section of the access cover from the front/rear bumper (as applicable). Screw the eye into position and tighten it securely **(see illustration)**.

☐ Before being towed, release the handbrake and select neutral on the transmission.

☐ On models with automatic transmission, set the selector lever to position N. Maximum towing speed is 43 mph, and maximum distance is 90 miles.

☐ Note that greater-than-usual pedal pressure will be required to operate the brakes, since the vacuum servo unit is only operational with the engine running.

☐ Greater-than-usual steering effort will also be required.

☐ The driver of the car being towed must keep the tow-rope taut at all times to avoid snatching.

☐ Make sure that both drivers know the route before setting off.

☐ Only drive at moderate speeds and keep the distance towed to a minimum. Drive smoothly and allow plenty of time for slowing down at junctions.

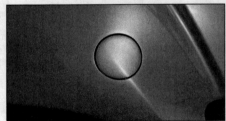

Identifying leaks

Puddles on the garage floor or drive, or obvious wetness under the bonnet or underneath the car, suggest a leak that needs investigating. It can sometimes be difficult to decide where the leak is coming from, especially if an engine undershield is fitted. Leaking oil or fluid can also be blown rearwards by the passage of air under the car, giving a false impression of where the problem lies.

 Warning: Most automotive oils and fluids are poisonous. Wash them off skin, and change out of contaminated clothing, without delay.

 The smell of a fluid leaking from the car may provide a clue to what's leaking. Some fluids are distinctively coloured. It may help to remove the engine undershield, clean the car carefully and to park it over some clean paper overnight as an aid to locating the source of the leak. Remember that some leaks may only occur while the engine is running.

Sump oil

Engine oil may leak from the drain plug...

Oil from filter

...or from the base of the oil filter.

Gearbox oil

Gearbox oil can leak from the seals at the inboard ends of the driveshafts.

Antifreeze

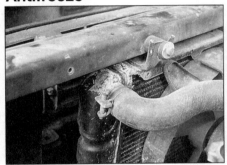

Leaking antifreeze often leaves a crystalline deposit like this.

Brake fluid

A leak occurring at a wheel is almost certainly brake fluid.

Power steering fluid

Power steering fluid may leak from the pipe connectors on the steering rack.

Introduction

There are some very simple checks which need only take a few minutes to carry out, but which could save you a lot of inconvenience and expense.

These checks require no great skill or special tools, and the small amount of time they take to perform could prove to be very well spent, for example:

☐ Keeping an eye on tyre condition and pressures, will not only help to stop them wearing out prematurely, but could also save your life.

☐ Many breakdowns are caused by electrical problems. Battery-related faults are particularly common, and a quick check on a regular basis will often prevent the majority of these.

☐ If your car develops a brake fluid leak, the first time you might know about it is when your brakes don't work properly. Checking the level regularly will give advance warning of this kind of problem.

☐ If the oil or coolant levels run low, the cost of repairing any engine damage will be far greater than fixing the leak, for example.

Underbonnet check points

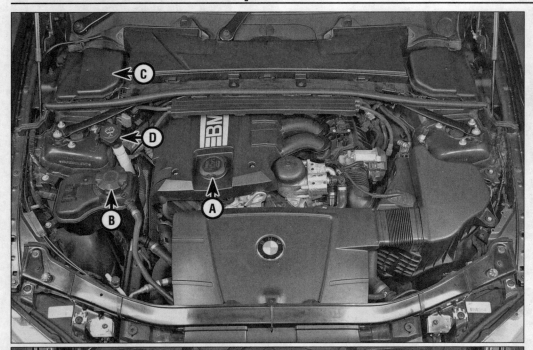

◀ **2.0 litre petrol (N43) engine**

A *Engine oil filler cap*

B *Coolant expansion tank*

C *Brake and clutch fluid reservoir (under the plastic cover)*

D *Screenwasher fluid reservoir*

◀ **2.0 litre diesel (N47T) engine**

A *Engine oil level dipstick*

B *Engine oil filler cap*

C *Coolant expansion tank*

D *Brake and clutch fluid reservoir (under the plastic cover)*

E *Screenwasher fluid reservoir*

Engine oil level

Before you start

✔ Make sure that the car is on level ground.
✔ Check the oil level before the car is driven, or at least 5 minutes after the engine has been switched off.

The correct oil

Modern engines place great demands on their oil. It is very important that the correct oil for your car is used (see *Lubricants and fluids*).

Car care

● If you have to add oil frequently, you should check whether you have any oil leaks. Remove the engine undershield, place some clean paper under the car overnight, and check for stains in the morning. If there are no leaks, the engine may be burning oil, or the oil may only be leaking when the engine is running. Note that petrol models, and some 4-cylinder diesel engines, do not have a traditional oil level dipstick. Instead the level is shown on the instrument cluster. On other engines, the oil level is checked using a traditional dipstick.

Models without a dipstick

● Start the engine, lightly push the button on the indicator stalk up or down until the word OIL is shown in the instrument cluster display. Press the button on the end of the indicator stalk and the oil level will be displayed. If necessary, stop the engine and add engine oil until the level is correct. Refer to the owners handbook for details of the electronic oil level monitor.

Models with a dipstick

● Always maintain the level between the upper and lower dipstick marks, shown in photo 3. If the level is too low, severe engine damage may occur. Oil seal failure may result if the engine is overfilled by adding too much oil.

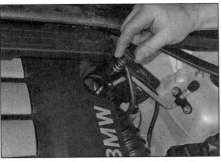

1 The dipstick top is often brightly-coloured for easy identification (see *Underbonnet check points* for exact location). Withdraw the dipstick.

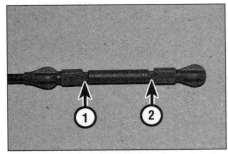

3 Note the oil level on the end of the dipstick, which should be between the upper maximum mark (1) and lower minimum mark (2). Approximately 1.0 litre of oil will raise the level from the lower mark to the upper mark.

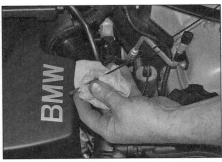

2 Using a clean rag or paper towel remove all oil from the dipstick. Insert the clean dipstick into the tube as far as it will go, then withdraw it again.

4 Oil is added through the filler cap. Unscrew the cap and top-up the level; a funnel may help to reduce spillage. Add the oil slowly, checking the level on the dipstick often. Don't overfill (see *Car care*).

Power steering fluid level

✔ Park the vehicle on level ground.
✔ Set the steering wheel straight-ahead.
✔ The engine should be turned off.

HAYNES HiNT *For the check to be accurate, the steering must not be turned while the level is being checked.*

Safety first!

● The need for frequent topping-up indicates a leak, which should be investigated immediately.

1 The reservoir is located near the front of the engine compartment (see Underbonnet check points for exact location). Wipe clean the area around the reservoir filler neck and unscrew the filler cap/dipstick from the reservoir.

2 Insert the dipstick into the reservoir (without screwing on the cap), then remove it. The fluid level should be between MIN and MAX. When topping-up, use the specified type of fluid and do not overfill the reservoir. When the level is correct, securely refit the cap.

Brake and clutch fluid level

Warning:
• *Brake fluid can harm your eyes and damage painted surfaces, so use extreme caution when handling and pouring it.*
• *Do not use fluid that has been standing open for some time, as it absorbs moisture from the air, which can cause a dangerous loss of braking effectiveness.*

The fluid level in the reservoir will drop slightly as the brake pads wear down, but the fluid level must never be allowed to drop below the MIN mark.

Before you start
✔ Make sure that your car is on level ground.

Safety first!
● If the reservoir requires repeated topping-up this is an indication of a fluid leak somewhere in the system, which should be investigated immediately.
● If a leak is suspected, the car should not be driven until the braking system has been checked. Never take any risks where brakes are concerned.

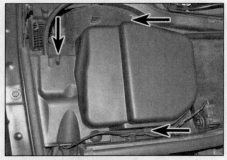

1 Release the three clips and remove the lid from the driver's side lower pollen filter housing.

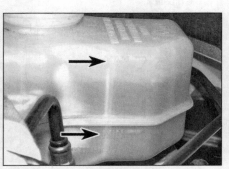

2 The MAX and MIN marks are indicated on the side of the reservoir.

3 If topping-up is necessary, first wipe clean the area around the filler cap to prevent dirt entering the hydraulic system.

4 Unscrew the reservoir cap and carefully lift it out of position, taking care not to damage the level switch float. Inspect the reservoir, if the fluid is dirty the hydraulic system should be drained and refilled (see Chapter 1A or 1B).

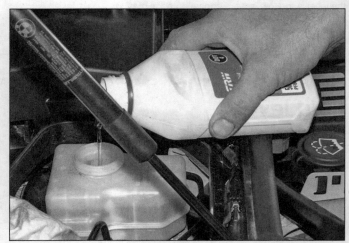

5 Carefully add fluid, taking care not to spill it onto the surrounding components. Use only the specified fluid; mixing different types can cause damage to the system. After topping-up to the correct level, securely refit the cap and wipe off any spilt fluid.

Coolant level

Warning: Do not attempt to remove the expansion tank pressure cap when the engine is hot, as there is a very great risk of scalding. Do not leave open containers of coolant about, as it is poisonous.

Car care

● With a sealed-type cooling system, adding coolant should not be necessary on a regular basis. If frequent topping-up is required, it is likely there is a leak. Check the radiator, all hoses and joint faces for signs of staining or wetness, and rectify as necessary.

● It is important that antifreeze is used in the cooling system all year round, not just during the winter months. Don't top up with water alone, as the antifreeze will become diluted.

1 The coolant expansion tank incorporates a float device which indicates the level of coolant. When the upper end of the float protrudes no more than 20 mm above the filler neck, the level is correct. See the information on the expansion tank adjacent to the filler neck.

2 If topping-up is necessary, wait until the engine is cold. Slowly unscrew the expansion tank cap, to release any pressure present in the cooling system, and remove it.

3 Add a mixture of water and antifreeze to the expansion tank until the level of the coolant is just below the Kalt/Cold mark on the expansion tank, or until the top of the indicator float protrudes no more than 20 mm above the filler neck. Refit the cap and tighten it securely.

Screenwasher fluid level*

* On models with a headlight washer system, the screenwash is also used to clean the headlights

● Screenwash additives not only keep the windscreen clean during bad weather, they also prevent the washer system freezing in cold weather – which is when you are likely to need it most. Don't top-up using plain water, as the screenwash will become diluted, and will freeze in cold weather.

Caution: On no account use engine coolant antifreeze in the screen washer system – this may damage the paintwork.

1 The screenwasher fluid reservoir is located at the right-hand side.

2 Unclip the cap. When topping-up, add a screenwash additive in the quantities recommended by the manufacturer.

Tyre condition and pressure

It is very important that tyres are in good condition, and at the correct pressure - having a tyre failure at any speed is highly dangerous. Tyre wear is influenced by driving style - harsh braking and acceleration, or fast cornering, will all produce more rapid tyre wear. As a general rule, the front tyres wear out faster than the rears. Interchanging the tyres from front to rear ("rotating" the tyres) may result in more even wear. However, if this is completely effective, you may have the expense of replacing all four tyres at once!

Remove any nails or stones embedded in the tread before they penetrate the tyre to cause deflation. If removal of a nail does reveal that the tyre has been punctured, refit the nail so that its point of penetration is marked. Then immediately change the wheel, and have the tyre repaired by a tyre dealer.

Regularly check the tyres for damage in the form of cuts or bulges, especially in the sidewalls. Periodically remove the wheels, and clean any dirt or mud from the inside and outside surfaces. Examine the wheel rims for signs of rusting, corrosion or other damage. Light alloy wheels are easily damaged by "kerbing" whilst parking; steel wheels may also become dented or buckled. A new wheel is very often the only way to overcome severe damage.

New tyres should be balanced when they are fitted, but it may become necessary to re-balance them as they wear, or if the balance weights fitted to the wheel rim should fall off. Unbalanced tyres will wear more quickly, as will the steering and suspension components. Wheel imbalance is normally signified by vibration, particularly at a certain speed (typically around 50 mph). If this vibration is felt only through the steering, then it is likely that just the front wheels need balancing. If, however, the vibration is felt through the whole car, the rear wheels could be out of balance. Wheel balancing should be carried out by a tyre dealer or garage.

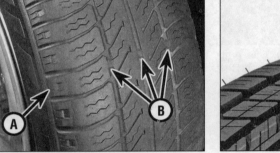

1 *Tread Depth - visual check*
The original tyres have tread wear safety bands (B), which will appear when the tread depth reaches approximately 1.6 mm. The band positions are indicated by a triangular mark on the tyre sidewall (A).

2 *Tread Depth - manual check*
Alternatively, tread wear can be monitored with a simple, inexpensive device known as a tread depth indicator gauge.

3 *Tyre Pressure Check*
Check the tyre pressures regularly with the tyres cold. Do not adjust the tyre pressures immediately after the vehicle has been used, or an inaccurate setting will result.

Tyre tread wear patterns

Shoulder Wear

Underinflation (wear on both sides)
Under-inflation will cause overheating of the tyre, because the tyre will flex too much, and the tread will not sit correctly on the road surface. This will cause a loss of grip and excessive wear, not to mention the danger of sudden tyre failure due to heat build-up.
Check and adjust pressures
Incorrect wheel camber (wear on one side)
Repair or renew suspension parts
Hard cornering
Reduce speed!

Centre Wear

Overinflation
Over-inflation will cause rapid wear of the centre part of the tyre tread, coupled with reduced grip, harsher ride, and the danger of shock damage occurring in the tyre casing.
Check and adjust pressures

If you sometimes have to inflate your car's tyres to the higher pressures specified for maximum load or sustained high speed, don't forget to reduce the pressures to normal afterwards.

Uneven Wear

Front tyres may wear unevenly as a result of wheel misalignment. Most tyre dealers and garages can check and adjust the wheel alignment (or "tracking") for a modest charge.
Incorrect camber or castor
Repair or renew suspension parts
Malfunctioning suspension
Repair or renew suspension parts
Unbalanced wheel
Balance tyres
Incorrect toe setting
Adjust front wheel alignment
Note: *The feathered edge of the tread which typifies toe wear is best checked by feel.*

Wiper blades

Check the condition of the wiper blades; if they are cracked or show any signs of deterioration, or if the glass swept area is smeared, renew them. Wiper blades should be renewed annually.

1 To remove a wiper blade, pull the arm away from the screen until it locks. Release the clip (arrowed) . . .

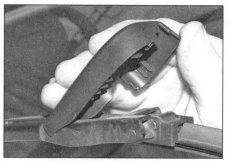

2 . . . and remove the plastic cover.

3 Rotate the blade 90° and disengage it from the arm.

Electrical systems

✔ Check all external lights and the horn. Refer to Chapter 12 Section 2 for details if any of the circuits are found to be inoperative.

✔ Visually check all accessible wiring connectors, harnesses and retaining clips for security, and for signs of chafing or damage.

HAYNES HiNT *If you need to check your brake lights and indicators unaided, back up to a wall or garage door and operate the lights. The reflected light should show if they are working properly.*

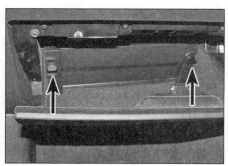

1 If a single indicator light, stop-light or headlight has failed, it is likely that a bulb has blown and will need to be renewed. Refer to Chapter 12 for details. If both stop-lights have failed, it is possible that the switch has failed (see Chapter 9).

2 If more than one indicator light or tail light has failed check that a fuse has not blown or that there is a fault in the circuit (see Chapter 12). The fuses are located in the fusebox in the passenger side glovebox. Details of the circuits protected by the fuses are shown on the card in the fusebox. Open the glovebox, rotate the fasteners 90° anticlockwise and remove the fusebox cover from the front of the glovebox.

3 To renew a blown fuse, simply pull it out using the tweezers clipped to the fusebox, and fit a new fuse of the correct rating (see Chapter 12). If the fuse blows again, it is important that you find out why – a complete checking procedure is given in Chapter 12.

Battery

Caution: Before carrying out any work on the vehicle battery, read the precautions given in 'Safety first!' at the start of this manual.

✔ Make sure that the battery tray is in good condition, and that the clamp is tight. Corrosion on the tray, retaining clamp and the battery itself can be removed with a solution of water and baking soda. Thoroughly rinse all cleaned areas with water. Any metal parts damaged by corrosion should be covered with a zinc-based primer, then painted.

✔ Periodically (approximately every three months), check the charge condition of the battery, as described in Chapter 5A, Section 3.

✔ If the battery is flat, and you need to jump start your vehicle, see *Roadside repairs*.

Battery corrosion can be kept to a minimum by applying a layer of petroleum jelly to the clamps and terminals after they are reconnected.

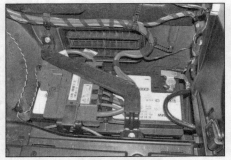
1 The battery is located in the right-hand rear corner of the luggage compartment.

2 On Saloon models, release the clip and open the right-hand storage tray.

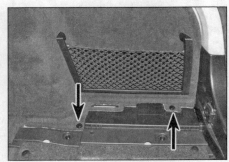
3 On Touring models, lift out the luggage compartment floor, rotate the fastener 90° anti-clockwise, and remove the right-hand side luggage compartment panel . . .

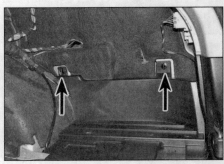
4 . . . then rotate the fasteners anti-clockwise and lift out the storage tray.

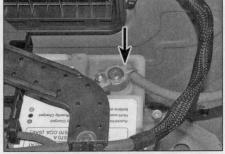
5 Check the tightness of battery clamps to ensure good electrical connections. You should not be able to move them. Also check each cable for cracks and frayed conductors.

6 If corrosion (white, fluffy deposits) is evident, remove the cables from the battery terminals, clean them with a small wire brush, then refit them. Automotive stores sell a tool for cleaning the battery post . . .

7 . . . as well as the battery cable clamps

Lubricants and fluids

Engine:

Petrol engines . . . . BMW Long-life 01, 01-FE or 04. SAE 0W-40 or SAE 5W-30 (fully synthetic)

Diesel engines:

    M57TU 6-cylinder engines . . . . BMW Long-life 01 or 04. SAE 0W-40 or SAE 5W-30 (fully synthetic). The lower viscosity oil is recommended in countries where the outside temperature frequently falls below -20° C

    N47 (4-cylinder) and N57 (6-cylinder) engines . . . . BMW Long-life 04. Note: This oil is specifically designed for engines with a particulate filter. SAE 0W-40 or SAE 5W-30 (fully synthetic)

Cooling system . . . . Long-life ethylene glycol based antifreeze*

Manual transmission:

With yellow or green label adjacent to the filler plug . . . . BMW Lifetime transmission oil MTF-LT-2

With blue label adjacent to the filler plug (from 03/2007) . . . . BMW Lifetime transmission oil MTF-LT-3

Automatic transmission . . . . BMW Lifetime transmission oil*

Final drive unit . . . . SAE 75W/90 EP*

Final drive unit:

Up to 07/11 model year . . . . BMW differential oil SAF-XO/OSP

From 07/11 model year. . . . . Castrol SAF-XO, Esso NLS 75W-90

Braking system . . . . Hydraulic fluid to DOT 4

Power steering . . . . Dexron II* or Pentosin CHF11S (marked as ATF or CHF on the reservoir filler cap)

* Refer to your BMW dealer for brand name and type recommendations

Tyre pressures

The tyre pressures are given on a label affixed to the driver's door aperture.

Chapter 1 Part A:
Routine maintenance and servicing – petrol models

Contents

Degrees of difficulty

| Easy, suitable for novice with little experience | Fairly easy, suitable for beginner with some experience | Fairly difficult, suitable for competent DIY mechanic | Difficult, suitable for experienced DIY mechanic | Very difficult, suitable for expert DIY or professional |

1   Servicing specifications

Capacities

Engine oil (including filter)	4.25 litres

Cooling system:

Manual transmission	8.4 litres
Automatic transmission	9.2 litres

Transmission:

Manual transmission (approximate)	1.4 litres
Automatic transmission (approximate)	3.0 litres
Final drive unit (approximate)	1.2 litres
Fuel tank (all models approximate)	63 litres

Cooling system

Antifreeze mixture:

50% antifreeze	Protection down to -30°

Note: *Refer to antifreeze manufacturer for latest recommendations.*

Ignition system

Spark plugs	NGK ZKBR7A-HTU or Bosch ZGR 6 STE 2
Spark plug electrode gap	Not adjustable

Brakes

Brake pad friction material minimum thickness	2.0 mm
Handbrake shoe friction material minimum thickness	1.5 mm

Note: *The wear warning symbol will illuminate when the pad wears down to 3.7 mm thick.*

Torque wrench settings

	Nm	lbf ft
Cylinder block coolant drain plug	25	18
Engine oil filter cover	25	18
Engine sump oil drain plug:		
M12 plug	25	18
M18 plug	35	26
M22 plug	60	44
Roadwheel bolts	120	89
Spark plugs:		
M12 thread	23	17
M14 thread	30	22

2 Maintenance schedule

The service intervals are tailored according to the operating conditions, driving style, time elapsed and mileage covered, instead of set distance/time limits. These factors are taken into account, and the maintenance requirements are calculated by the vehicles on-board systems, then a symbol representing the item requiring attention is displayed in the instrument cluster. The urgency of the attention is indicated by a colour-coding system – green, yellow or red. Consequently, the intervals listed below are guidelines, starting values/interval forecasts, or our recommendations. For more details, refer to the Owners Handbook supplied with the vehicle.

When the vehicle is new, it should be serviced by a dealer service department (or other workshop recognised by the vehicle manufacturer as providing the same standard of service) in order to preserve the warranty. The vehicle manufacturer may reject warranty claims if you are unable to prove that servicing has been carried out as and when specified, using only original equipment parts or parts certified to be of equivalent quality.

Every 250 miles or weekly
☐ Refer to *Weekly checks*

Every 15 000 miles or 2 years, whichever comes first
☐ Oil service (Section 6)
Note: *This includes engine oil renewal, handbrake check and pollen filter renewal.*
☐ Reset the service interval display (Section 7)

Every 25 000 miles
☐ Front brake service (Section 8)
☐ Reset the service interval display (Section 7)

Every 30 000 miles
☐ Rear brake service (Section 9)
☐ Reset the service interval display (Section 7)

Every 30 000 miles or 4 years, whichever comes first
☐ Vehicle check (Section 10)
☐ Reset the service interval display (Section 7)

Every 45 000 miles or 6 years, whichever comes first
☐ Renew the air filter (Section 11)
☐ Renew the spark plugs (Section 12)
Note: *The spark plugs should be renewed at every 3rd oil service.*
☐ Reset the service interval display (Section 7)

Every 2 years
☐ Renew the brake fluid (Section 13)
☐ Reset the service interval display (Section 7)

Every 4 years
Note: *These items have no specific recommendation concerning their inspection or renewal. However, we consider it prudent to carry out these tasks at least every 4 years.*
☐ Check the condition of the auxiliary drivebelt, and adjust/renew if necessary (Section 14)
☐ Renew the fuel filter (Section 15)
☐ Coolant renewal (Section 16)

Underbonnet view of a 320i

1 *Engine oil filler cap*
2 *Oil filter cover*
3 *Brake and clutch fluid reservoir (under cover)*
4 *Air cleaner housing*
5 *Coolant expansion tank*
6 *Washer fluid reservoir*
7 *Pollen filter cover*
8 *Strut braces*

Front underbody view

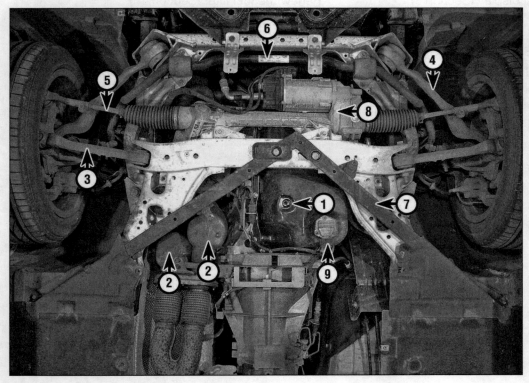

1 *Engine oil (sump) drain plug*
2 *Catalytic converters*
3 *Control arm*
4 *Tension strut*
5 *Steering track rod*
6 *Anti-roll bar*
7 *Reinforcement frame*
8 *Steering rack*
9 *Oil level sensor*

Rear underbody view

1 Fuel tank
2 Exhaust tail box
3 Final drive unit
4 Driveshaft
5 Handbrake cable
6 Camber arm
7 Trailing arm

4 Introduction

General information

1 This Chapter is designed to help the home mechanic maintain his/her vehicle for safety, economy, long life and peak performance.
2 The Chapter contains a master maintenance schedule, followed by Sections dealing specifically with each task in the schedule. Visual checks, adjustments, component renewal and other helpful items are included. Refer to the accompanying illustrations of the engine compartment and the underside of the vehicle for the locations of the various components.
3 Servicing your vehicle in accordance with the service indicator display and the following Sections will provide a planned maintenance programme, which should result in a long and reliable service life. This is a comprehensive plan, so maintaining some items but not others at the specified service intervals will not produce the same results.
4 As you service your vehicle, you will discover that many of the procedures can – and should – be grouped together, because of the particular procedure being performed, or because of the proximity of two otherwise-

unrelated components to one another. For example, if the vehicle is raised for any reason, the exhaust can be inspected at the same time as the suspension and steering components.
5 The first step in this maintenance programme is to prepare yourself before the actual work begins. Read through all the Sections relevant to the work to be carried out, then make a list and gather all the parts and tools required. If a problem is encountered, seek advice from a parts specialist, or a dealer service department.

Remote control battery

6 The remote control battery is recharged every time the key is inserted into the ignition switch. Battery renewal is therefore not necessary. Should the battery fail, the complete key will require renewing. Refer to a BMW dealer or specialist.

5 Regular maintenance

1 If, from the time the vehicle is new, the routine maintenance schedule is followed closely, and frequent checks are made of fluid levels and high-wear items, as suggested throughout this manual, the engine will be

kept in relatively good running condition, and the need for additional work will be minimised.
2 It is possible that there will be times when the engine is running poorly due to the lack of regular maintenance. This is even more likely if a used vehicle, which has not received regular and frequent maintenance checks, is purchased. In such cases, additional work may need to be carried out, outside of the regular maintenance intervals.
3 If engine wear is suspected, a compression test (refer to the relevant Part of Chapter 2) will provide valuable information regarding the overall performance of the main internal components. Such a test can be used as a basis to decide on the extent of the work to be carried out. If, for example, a compression test indicates serious internal engine wear, conventional maintenance as described in this Chapter will not greatly improve the performance of the engine, and may prove a waste of time and money, unless extensive overhaul work is carried out first.
4 The following series of operations are those most often required to improve the performance of a generally poor-running engine:

Primary operations

a) Clean, inspect and test the battery (See ' Weekly checks).

6.3 Rotate the fastener and open the sump plug access flap

6.6a Unscrew the oil filter cover with a filter removal tool...

6.6b... or strap wrench

b) *Check all the engine-related fluids (See 'Weekly checks').*
c) *Check the condition and tension of the auxiliary drivebelt (Section 14).*
d) *Renew the spark plugs (Section 12).*
e) *Check the condition of the air filter, and renew if necessary (Section 11).*
f) *Check the fuel filter (Section 15).*
g) *Check the condition of all hoses, and check for fluid leaks (Section 10).*

5 If the above operations do not prove fully effective, carry out the following secondary operations:

Secondary operations

6 All items listed under Primary operations, plus the following:

h) *Check the charging system (see Chapter 5A).*
i) *Check the ignition system (see Chapter 5B).*
j) *Check the fuel system (see Chapter 4A).*

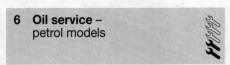

6   Oil service –
    petrol models

Note: *This includes engine oil renewal, handbrake check and pollen filter renewal.*

Oil service

1 The oil service is made up of 5 elements: Engine oil and filter change, handbrake check, pollen filter renewal, air filter element renewal and spark plug change. The handbrake check and pollen filter renewal should be carried out every time the engine oil and filter are changed, whilst the air filter element and spark plugs should be renewed at every 3rd engine oil and filter change. Refer to Section 11 for air filter renewal and Section 12 for spark plug renewal.

Engine oil and filter change

2 Frequent oil and filter changes are the most important preventative maintenance work which can be undertaken by the DIY owner. As engine oil ages, it becomes diluted and contaminated, which leads to premature engine wear.

3 Before starting this procedure, gather together all the necessary tools and materials. Also make sure you have plenty of clean rags and newspapers handy, to mop-up any spills. Ideally, the engine oil should be warm, as it will drain better, and more built-up sludge will be removed with it. Take care, however, not to touch the exhaust or any other hot parts of the engine when working under the car. To avoid any possibility of scalding, and to protect yourself from possible skin irritants and other harmful contaminants in used engine oils, it is advisable to wear gloves. Access to the underside of the car will be improved if it can be raised on a lift, driven onto ramps, or jacked up and supported on axle stands (see *Jacking and vehicle support*). Whichever method is chosen, make sure the car remains level, or if it is at an angle, so that the drain plug is at the lowest point. Access to the sump plug is via a removable flap in the plate (**see illustration**).

4 Working in the engine compartment, locate the oil filter housing on the left-hand side of the engine, in front of the intake manifold.

5 Place a wad of rag around the bottom of the housing to absorb any spilt oil.

6 Using a special oil filter removal tool or socket, unscrew and remove the cover complete with the filter cartridge (**see illustrations**). The oil will drain from the housing back into the sump as the cover is removed.

7 Pull the old filter element from the cover, and remove the O-rings from the cover.

8 Using a clean rag, wipe the mating faces of the housing and cover.

9 Fit new O-rings to the cover (**see illustration**). New O-rings are normally supplied with the new filter – check with your parts supplier.

10 Fit the new filter cartridge to the cover (**see illustration**).

11 Smear a little clean engine oil on the O-rings, refit the cover and tighten it to 25 Nm (18 lbf ft) if using the special filter removal tool, or securely if using a strap wrench (**see illustrations**).

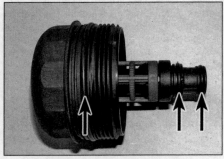

6.9 Renew the filter cover O-rings

6.10 Slide the new filter element past the O-rings into the filter cover

6.11a Lubricate the O-rings with a little clean engine oil...

6.11b... then refit it to the filter housing

6.12 Slacken the sump drain plug

6.15a Fit a new sealing washer to the sump drain plug...

6.15b... then refit the plug

6.19 Oil level indicator in the instrument cluster

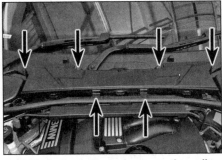

6.22 Undo the bolts and remove the pollen filter cover

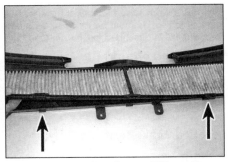

6.23 Release the clips and lift out the pollen filter element

12 Working under the car, slacken the sump drain plug about half a turn **(see illustration)**. Position the draining container under the drain plug, then remove the plug completely. If possible, try to keep the plug pressed into the sump while unscrewing it by hand the last couple of turns.

13 Recover the drain plug sealing ring.

14 Allow some time for the old oil to drain, noting that it may be necessary to reposition the container as the oil flow slows to a trickle.

15 After all the oil has drained, wipe off the drain plug with a clean rag. Fit a new sealing washer to the sump plug (normally supplied with the new filter). Clean the area around the drain plug opening, then refit and tighten the plug to the specified torque **(see illustrations)**.

16 Remove the old oil and all tools from under the car, then lower the car to the ground (if applicable).

17 Add a little less than the correct amount of oil (see Capacities at the start of this Chapter) to the engine through the oil filler cap orifice, using the correct grade and type of oil (see *Lubricants and fluids*). An oil can spout or funnel may help to reduce spillage.

18 Start the engine and run it for 3 minutes; check for leaks around the oil filter seal and the sump drain plug. Note that there may be a delay of a few seconds before the oil pressure warning light goes out when the engine is first started, as the oil circulates through the engine oil galleries and the new oil filter before the pressure builds-up.

19 Press the 'select' button (on the indicator stalk) up or down until OIL is displayed in the instrument cluster display. Press the button on the end of the indicator stalk and the oil level will be displayed. If necessary, stop the engine and add engine oil until the level is correct **(see illustration)**. Refer to the owner's handbook for details of the electronic oil level monitor.

20 Dispose of the used engine oil safely, with reference to General repair procedures in the Reference section of this manual.

Handbrake check

21 Check and, if necessary, adjust the handbrake as described in Chapter 9. Check that the handbrake cables are free to move easily and lubricate all exposed linkages/cable pivots.

Pollen filter renewal

22 Undo the bolts and remove the upper section of the pollen filter housing **(see illustration)**.

23 Release the catches at the front edge, and remove the filter element **(see illustration)**.

24 Fit the new element into the housing, ensuring it's correctly seated.

25 Refit the upper housing and securely tighten the retaining bolts.

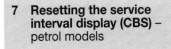

7   Resetting the service interval display (CBS) – petrol models

1 Ensure that all electrical items are switched off then turn on the ignition switch. **Note:** *Do not start the engine*.

2 Ensure the on-board time and date

are correctly set in accordance with the instructions in the owner's handbook.

3 Each service item that appears on the instrument cluster display can be reset. Note that it is only possible to reset an item if the service life of the item is below 80%.

4 Press the trip odometer button for approximately 10 seconds until the first CBS (Condition Based Service) item appears in the instrument cluster display. Note that the most urgent item is displayed first. If this is not the item required, select the item to be reset by briefly pressing the button again.

5 When the required item is selected, press the button again until 'Reset?' appears in the display. Note that the reset process is cancelled by not pressing the button to confirm, and waiting for the display to return to its normal state.

6 Press the button again for approximately 3 seconds to confirm the reset. Note that it is only possible to reset the brake pad display if the pad sensors are working properly.

7 Turn off the ignition switch.

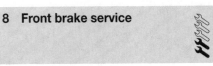

8   Front brake service

Brake pads

1 When this CBS item is displayed, the thickness of the front brake pads friction material should be checked, and if any are approaching the minimum thickness, all four front pads should be renewed.

2 Firmly apply the handbrake, then jack up the front of the car and support it securely on axle stands (see *Jacking and vehicle support*). Remove the front roadwheels.

3 The brake pad warning symbol in the CBS display indicates that the pad friction material thickness is worn and that the pads require renewal. However, the warning will also be given if the wiring to and from each pads sensor is damaged or the connections are poor, dirty, etc. Check the wiring to and from the sensor for poor connections/breaks before renewing the pads.

4 The thickness of friction material remaining on each brake pad can be measured through the top of the caliper body. If any pad's friction material is worn to the specified thickness or less, all four pads must be renewed as a set. Pad renewal is described in Chapter 9.

Brake disc check

5 Check the front brake disc condition, and measure the thickness of the disc as described in Chapter 9. Renew both front discs if necessary.

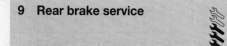

9   Rear brake service

Brake pads

1 When this CBS item is displayed, the thickness of the rear brake pads friction material should be checked, and if any are approaching the minimum thickness, all four rear pads should be renewed.

2 Chock the front wheels, then jack up the rear of the car and support it on axle stands (see *Jacking and vehicle support*). Remove the rear roadwheels.

3 The thickness of friction material remaining on each brake pad can be measured through the top of the caliper body. If any pad's friction material is worn to the specified thickness or less, all four pads must be renewed as a set. Pad renewal is described in Chapter 9.

Brake disc check

4 Check the front brake disc condition, and measure the thickness of the disc as described in Chapter 9. Renew both front discs if necessary.

10.13 Use a hydrometer to check the strength of the antifreeze

Handbrake shoe lining check

5 Inspect and the handbrake shoes lining material as described in Chapter 9. If any of the shoe's lining material has worn below the minimum thickness, renew all four shoes as described in Chapter 9.

10   Vehicle check

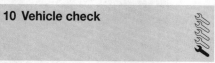

1 The vehicle check consists of several tasks. Before the CBS display can be reset, all of the following tasks must be complete.

Instruments and electrical equipment

2 Check the operation of all instruments and electrical equipment.

3 Make sure that all instruments read correctly, and switch on all electrical equipment in turn, to check that it functions properly.

Seat belt check

4 Carefully examine the seat belt webbing for cuts or any signs of serious fraying or deterioration. Pull the belt all the way out, and examine the full extent of the webbing.

5 Fasten and unfasten the belt, ensuring that the locking mechanism holds securely and releases properly when intended. Check also that the retracting mechanism operates correctly when the belt is released.

6 Check the security of all seat belt mountings and attachments which are accessible, without removing any trim or other components, from inside the car.

Wash/wipe system check

7 Check that each of the washer jet nozzles are clear and that each nozzle provides a strong jet of washer fluid. Renew as necessary – refer to Chapter 12.

8 Check the condition of each wiper blade for damage of wear. As time passes the blades will become hardened, wipe performance will deteriorate, and noise will increase. Renew the blades as necessary – see *Weekly checks*.

Bodywork corrosion check

9 This work should be carried out by a BMW dealer in order to validate the vehicle warranty. The work includes a thorough inspection of the vehicle paintwork and underbody for damage and corrosion.

Tyre check

10 Check the tread depth, external condition and inflation pressure of the tyres. See *Weekly checks* for details of the procedures and tyre pressure information.

Initialise tyre check system

11 Initialisation of the tyre pressure checking system must be carried out after the tyre pressures have been corrected, or a tyre/wheel renewed. The system is initialised as follows:

Models with iDrive

a) *Press the iDrive controller to call up the i menu.*
b) *Select 'Settings' and press the controller.*
c) *Select 'Car/Tyres' and press the controller.*
d) *Turn the controller until 'Tyres: RPA' is selected, then press the controller.*
e) *Start the engine, but do not drive off.*
f) *Select 'Confirm tyre pressure' and press the controller.*
g) *Drive off. Initialisation is completed during the journey.*

Models without iDrive

a) *Start the engine, but do not drive off.*
b) *Press the direction indicator stalk up or down until the tyre pressure symbol and RESET appear in the instrument cluster display.*
c) *Press the button on the end of the indicator stalk to confirm the selection of the Run Flat Indicator.*
d) *Press the button again for approximately 5 seconds, until a check/tick appears after RESET.*
e) *Drive off. Initialisation is completed during the journey.*

Battery check

12 Check the condition of the battery, and recharge if necessary – refer to Chapter 5A.

Coolant concentration check

13 Use a hydrometer to check the strength of the antifreeze **(see illustration)**. Follow the instructions provided with your hydrometer. The antifreeze strength should be approximately 50%. If it is significantly less than this, drain a little coolant from the radiator (see this Chapter), add antifreeze to the coolant expansion tank, then recheck the strength.

Hose and fluid leak check

14 Visually inspect the engine joint faces, gaskets and seals for any signs of water or oil leaks. Pay particular attention to the areas around the camshaft cover, cylinder head, oil filter and sump joint faces. Bear in mind that, over a period of time, some very slight seepage from these areas is to be expected – what you are really looking for is any indication of a serious leak. Should a leak be found, renew the offending gasket or oil seal by referring to the appropriate Chapters in this manual.

15 Also check the security and condition of all the engine-related pipes and hoses. Ensure that all cable-ties or securing clips are in place and in good condition. Clips which are broken or missing can lead to chafing of the hoses, pipes or wiring, which could cause more serious problems in the future.

16 Carefully check the radiator hoses and heater hoses along their entire length. Renew any hose which is cracked, swollen or deteriorated. Cracks will show up better if the hose is squeezed. Pay close attention to the hose clips that secure the hoses to the cooling system components. Hose clips can pinch and puncture hoses, resulting in cooling system leaks.

17 Inspect all the cooling system components (hoses, joint faces, etc) for leaks **(see Haynes Hint)**. Where any problems of this nature are found on system components, renew the component or gasket with reference to Chapter 3.

18 Where applicable, inspect the automatic transmission fluid cooler hoses for leaks or deterioration.

19 With the car raised, inspect the petrol tank and filler neck for punctures, cracks and other damage. The connection between the filler neck and tank is especially critical. Sometimes a rubber filler neck or connecting hose will leak due to loose retaining clamps or deteriorated rubber.

20 Carefully check all rubber hoses and metal fuel lines leading away from the petrol tank. Check for loose connections, deteriorated hoses, crimped lines, and other damage. Pay particular attention to the vent pipes and hoses, which often loop up around the filler neck and can become blocked or crimped. Follow the lines to the front of the car, carefully inspecting them all the way. Renew damaged sections as necessary.

21 Closely inspect the metal brake pipes which run along the car underbody. If they show signs of excessive corrosion or damage they must be renewed.

22 From within the engine compartment, check the security of all fuel hose attachments and pipe unions, and inspect the fuel hoses and vacuum hoses for kinks, chafing and deterioration.

23 Check the condition of the power steering fluid hoses and pipes.

Suspension and steering check

24 Raise the front of the car, and securely support it on axle stands (see *Jacking and vehicle support*).

25 Visually inspect the balljoint dust covers and the steering rack-and-pinion gaiters for splits, chafing or deterioration. Any wear of these components will cause loss of lubricant, then dirt and water entry, resulting in rapid deterioration of the balljoints or steering gear.

26 Check the power steering fluid hoses for chafing or deterioration, and the pipe and hose unions for fluid leaks. Also check for signs of fluid leakage under pressure from the steering gear rubber gaiters, which would indicate failed fluid seals within the steering gear.

27 Grasp the roadwheel at the 12 o'clock and 6 o'clock positions, and try to rock it **(see illustration)**. Very slight free play may be felt, but if the movement is appreciable, further investigation is necessary to determine the source. Continue rocking the wheel while an assistant depresses the footbrake. If the

A leak in the cooling system will usually show up as white- or antifreezecoloured deposits on the area adjoining the leak.

movement is now eliminated or significantly reduced, it is likely that the hub bearings are at fault. If the free play is still evident with the footbrake depressed, then there is wear in the suspension joints or mountings.

28 Now grasp the wheel at the 9 o'clock and 3 o'clock positions, and try to rock it as before. Any movement felt now may again be caused by wear in the hub bearings or the steering track rod balljoints. If the inner or outer balljoint is worn, the visual movement will be obvious.

29 Using a large screwdriver or flat bar, check for wear in the suspension mounting bushes by levering between the relevant suspension component and its attachment point. Some movement is to be expected as the mountings are made of rubber, but excessive wear should be obvious. Also check the condition of any visible rubber bushes, looking for splits, cracks or contamination of the rubber.

30 With the car standing on its wheels, have an assistant turn the steering wheel back-and-forth about an eighth of a turn each way. There should be very little, if any, lost movement between the steering wheel and roadwheels. If this is not the case, closely observe the joints and mountings previously described, but in addition, check the steering column universal joints for wear, and the rack-and-pinion steering gear itself.

Strut/shock absorber check

31 Check for any signs of fluid leakage around the suspension strut/shock absorber

body, or from the rubber gaiter around the piston rod. Should any fluid be noticed, the suspension strut/shock absorber is defective internally, and should be renewed. Note: Suspension struts/shock absorbers should always be renewed in pairs on the same axle.

32 The efficiency of the suspension strut/ shock absorber may be checked by bouncing the car at each corner. Generally speaking, the body will return to its normal position and stop after being depressed. If it rises and returns on a rebound, the suspension strut/shock absorber is probably suspect. Examine also the suspension strut/shock absorber upper and lower mountings for any signs of wear.

Exhaust system check

33 With the engine cold (at least an hour after the car has been driven), check the complete exhaust system from the engine to the end of the tailpipe. The exhaust system is most easily checked with the car raised on a hoist, or suitably supported on axle stands, so that the exhaust components are readily visible and accessible.

34 Check the exhaust pipes and connections for evidence of leaks, severe corrosion and damage. Make sure that all brackets and mountings are in good condition, and that all relevant nuts and bolts are tight **(see illustration)**. Leakage at any of the joints or in other parts of the system will usually show up as a black sooty stain in the vicinity of the leak.

35 Rattles and other noises can often be traced to the exhaust system, especially the brackets and mountings. Try to move the pipes and silencers. If the components are able to come into contact with the body or suspension parts, secure the system with new mountings. Otherwise separate the joints (if possible) and twist the pipes as necessary to provide additional clearance.

Hinge and lock lubrication

36 Lubricate the hinges of the bonnet, doors and tailgate with a light general-purpose oil. Similarly, lubricate all latches, locks and lock strikers. At the same time, check the security and operation of all the locks, adjusting them if necessary (see Chapter 11). Lightly lubricate the bonnet release mechanism and cable with a suitable grease.

10.27 Check for wear in the hub bearings by grasping the wheel and trying to rock it

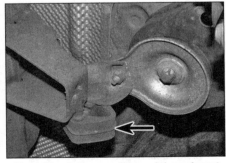

10.34 Check the condition of the exhaust mountings

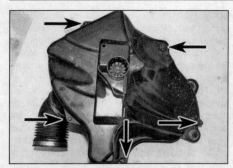

11.2 Undo the bolts and remove the lower section

Road test

Steering and suspension

37 Check for any abnormalities in the steering, suspension, handling or road 'feel'.

38 Drive the car, and check that there are no unusual vibrations or noises.

39 Check that the steering feels positive, with no excessive 'sloppiness', or roughness, and check for any suspension noises when cornering and driving over bumps.

Drivetrain

40 Check the performance of the engine, clutch (where applicable), gearbox/ transmission and driveshafts.

41 Listen for any unusual noises from the engine, clutch and gearbox/transmission.

42 Make sure that the engine runs smoothly when idling, and that there is no hesitation when accelerating.

43 Check that, where applicable, the clutch action is smooth and progressive, that the drive is taken up smoothly, and that the pedal travel is not excessive. Also listen for any noises when the clutch pedal is depressed.

44 On manual gearbox models, check that all gears can be engaged smoothly without noise, and that the gear lever action is smooth and not abnormally vague or 'notchy'.

45 On automatic transmission models, make sure that all gearchanges occur smoothly, without snatching, and without an increase in engine speed between changes. Check that all the gear positions can be selected with the car at rest. If any problems are found,

12.4a Tools required for spark plug removal, gap adjustment, and refitting

11.5 Slide the new filter element into place. Note the locating lug

they should be referred to a BMW dealer or suitably-equipped specialist.

Check the braking system

46 Make sure that the car does not pull to one side when braking, and that the wheels do not lock when braking hard.

47 Check that there is no vibration through the steering when braking.

48 Check that the handbrake operates correctly without excessive movement of the lever, and that it holds the car stationary on a slope.

49 Test the operation of the brake servo unit as follows. With the engine off, depress the footbrake four or five times to exhaust the vacuum. Hold the brake pedal depressed, then start the engine. As the engine starts, there should be a noticeable 'give' in the brake pedal as vacuum builds-up. Allow the engine to run for at least two minutes, and then switch it off. If the brake pedal is depressed now, it should be possible to detect a hiss from the servo as the pedal is depressed. After about four or five applications, no further hissing should be heard, and the pedal should feel much harder.

11 Air filter element renewal – petrol models

Air filter element renewal

1 Remove the air cleaner housing as described in Chapter 4A Section 2.

12.4b Unscrew the spark plugs from the cylinder head using a deep socket and extension bar

2 Undo the 5 bolts and remove the lower section of the air cleaner assembly **(see illustration)**.

3 Pull the filter element from place.

4 Clean the air filter housing, removing all debris.

5 Slide the new filter element into place, ensuring it locates correctly with the housing **(see illustration)**.

6 The remainder of refitting is a reversal of removal.

12 Spark plugs renewal

Note: *The spark plugs should be renewed at every 2nd oil service.*

1 The correct functioning of the spark plugs is vital for the correct running and efficiency of the engine. It is essential that the plugs fitted are appropriate for the engine (the suitable type is specified at the beginning of this Chapter). If this type is used, and the engine is in good condition, the spark plugs should not need attention between scheduled renewal intervals. Spark plug cleaning is rarely necessary, and should not be attempted unless specialised equipment is available, as damage can easily be caused to the firing ends.

2 Remove the ignition coils as described in Chapter 5B.

3 It is advisable to remove the dirt from the spark plug recesses, using a clean brush, vacuum cleaner or compressed air before removing the plugs, to prevent dirt dropping into the cylinders.

4 Unscrew the plugs using a spark plug spanner, suitable box spanner, or a deep socket and extension bar **(see illustrations)**. Keep the socket aligned with the spark plug – if it is forcibly moved to one side, the ceramic insulator may be broken off. As each plug is removed, examine it as follows.

5 Examination of the spark plugs will give a good indication of the condition of the engine. If the insulator nose of the spark plug is clean and white, with no deposits, this is indicative of a weak mixture or too hot a plug (a hot plug transfers heat away from the electrode slowly, a cold plug transfers heat away quickly).

6 If the tip and insulator nose are covered with hard black-looking deposits, then this is indicative that the mixture is too rich. Should the plug be black and oily, then it is likely that the engine is fairly worn, as well as the mixture being too rich.

7 If the insulator nose is covered with light tan to greyish-brown deposits, then the mixture is correct, and it is likely that the engine is in good condition.

8 When buying new spark plugs, it is important to obtain the correct plugs for your specific engine (see *Specifications*).

9 The recommended spark plugs are of the multi-electrode type, and the gap between

12.9 Multi-electrode spark plugs are recommended

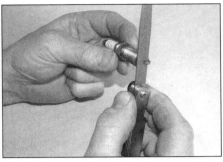

12.10a Measure the spark plug gap with a feeler gauge...

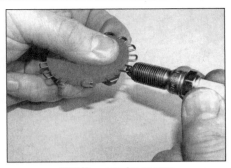

12.10b... or wire gauge

the centre electrode and the earth electrodes cannot be adjusted **(see illustration)**. However, if single electrode plugs are being fitted, the gap between the earth and centre electrode must be correct. If it is too large or too small, the size of the spark and its efficiency will be seriously impaired. The gap should be set to the value given by the spark plug manufacturer.

10 To set the gap on single electrode plugs, measure it with a feeler blade or wire gauge, then bend the outer plug electrode until the correct gap is achieved **(see illustrations)**. The centre electrode should never be bent, as this may crack the insulator and cause plug failure, if nothing worse. If using feeler blades, the gap is correct when the appropriate-size blade is a firm sliding fit.

11 Special spark plug electrode gap adjusting tools are available from most motor accessory shops, or from some spark plug manufacturers.

12 Before fitting the spark plugs, check that the plug exterior surfaces and threads are clean. It is very often difficult to insert spark plugs into their holes without cross-threading them. To avoid this possibility, fit a short length of hose over the end of the spark plug **(see Haynes Hint)**.

13 Remove the rubber hose (if used), and tighten the plug to the specified torque (see Specifications) using the spark plug socket and a torque wrench. Refit the remaining plugs in the same way.

14 Refit the ignition coils as described in Chapter 5B.

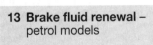

13 Brake fluid renewal – petrol models

Brake fluid renewal

⚠️ **Warning: Brake hydraulic fluid can harm your eyes and damage painted surfaces, so use extreme caution when handling and pouring it. Do not use fluid that has been standing open for some time, as it absorbs moisture from the air. Excess moisture can cause a dangerous loss of braking effectiveness.**

1 The procedure is similar to that for the bleeding of the hydraulic system as described in Chapter 9, except that the brake fluid reservoir should be emptied by siphoning, using a clean poultry baster or similar before starting, and allowance should be made for the old fluid to be expelled when bleeding a section of the circuit.

2 Working as described in Chapter 9, open the first bleed screw in the sequence, and pump the brake pedal gently until nearly all the old fluid has been emptied from the master cylinder reservoir.

3 Top-up to the MAX level with new fluid, and continue pumping until only the new fluid remains in the reservoir, and new fluid can be seen emerging from the bleed screw. Tighten the screw, and top the reservoir level up to the MAX level line.

4 Work through all remaining bleed screws in the sequence until new fluid can be seen at all of them. Be careful to keep the master cylinder reservoir topped-up to above the MIN level at all times, or air may enter the system and increase the length of the task.

HAYNES HiNT

It is often difficult to insert spark plugs into their holes without cross-threading them. To avoid this possibility, fit a short length of 8 mm internal diameter rubber/plastic hose over the end of the spark plug. The flexible hose acts as a universal joint to help align the plug with the plug hole. Should the plug begin to cross-thread, then hose will slip on the spark plug, preventing thread damage to the cylinder head.

HAYNES HiNT *Old hydraulic fluid is usuallymuch darker in colour thanthe new, making it easy todistinguish the two.*

5 When the operation is complete, check that all bleed screws are securely tightened, and that their dust caps are refitted. Wash off all traces of spilt fluid, and recheck the master cylinder reservoir fluid level.

6 Check the operation of the brakes before taking the car on the road.

14 Auxiliary drivebelt check and renewal – petrol models

Drivebelt checking – general

Note: *These items have no specific recommendation concerning their inspection or renewal. However, we consider it prudent to carry out these tasks at least every 4 years.*

1 Due to their function and construction, the belts are prone to failure after a period of time, and should be inspected periodically to prevent problems.

2 To improve access for belt inspection, if desired, remove the cooling fan and shroud as described in Chapter 3 Section 6.

3 With the engine stopped, using your fingers (and an electric torch if necessary), move along the belts, checking for cracks and separation of the belt plies. Also check for fraying and glazing, which gives the belt a shiny appearance. Both sides of the belts should be inspected, which means the belt will have to be twisted to check the underside. If necessary turn the engine using a spanner or socket on the crankshaft pulley bolt so that the whole of the belt can be inspected.

Drivebelt renewal

4 Open the bonnet. Undo the bolts and remove the air intake hood from the bonnet slam panel **(see illustration)**.

5 If the drivebelt is to be re-used, mark the running direction of the belt before removal.

6 Using a spanner or socket, rotate the tensioner pulley clockwise to compress the

14.4 Undo the bolts and remove the intake hood

14.6 Rotate the drivebelt tensioner clockwise

14.7 Insert a drill bit (arrowed) into the holes to lock the tensioner in the compressed position

H48331

14.9 Auxiliary drivebelt routing – N43 engines

1 Air conditioning compressor
2 Crankshaft pulley
3 Tensioner pulley
4 Alternator
5 Idler pulley

tensioner, and slide the drivebelt from the pulleys **(see illustration)**.

7 To aid refitting, the tensioner can be compressed fully and locked in position using a metal rod engaged with the holes in the tensioner and backplate – note that the tensioner has a powerful spring, so a strong rod will be required **(see illustration)**.

8 If the original belt is being refitted, observe the running direction mark made before removal.

9 If the tensioner has not been locked in position, compress the tensioner, and

engage the belt with the pulleys, ensuring that it is routed as noted before removal **(see illustration)**. Make sure that the belt engages correctly with the grooves in the pulleys.

10 Where applicable, compress the tensioner until the locking rod can be removed, then withdraw the rod and release the tensioner.

11 Refit the intake hood to the bonnet slam panel.

15 Fuel filter renewal – petrol models

Note: *An external fuel filter is only fitted to models in markets where fuel quality may be poor.*

1 Depressurise the fuel system (Chapter 4A).

2 Where fitted, the fuel filter is located on a bracket bolted to the left-hand chassis member adjacent to the transmission.

3 Jack up the car and support on axle stands (see *Jacking and vehicle support*). Remove the transmission undershield.

4 Note their fitted locations, and clamp the hoses to and from the fuel filter. Release the retaining clips and disconnect the hoses from the filter. Be prepared for fluid spillage.

5 Slacken the filter clamp bolt or nut, and slide the filter down from under the car.

6 Refitting is a reversal of removal, but make sure that the flow direction arrow on the filter points in the direction of fuel flow (ie, towards the engine), and on completion pressurise the fuel system with reference to Chapter 4A.

16 Coolant renewal – petrol models

Coolant renewal

⚠️ *Warning: Wait until the engine is cold before starting this procedure. Do not allow antifreeze to come in contact with your skin, or with the painted surfaces of the car. Rinse off spills immediately with plenty of water. Never leave antifreeze lying around in an open container, or in a puddle in the driveway or on the garage floor. Children and pets are attracted by its sweet smell, but antifreeze can be fatal if ingested.*

Cooling system draining

1 With the engine completely cold, cover the expansion tank cap with a wad of rag, and slowly turn the cap anti-clockwise to relieve the pressure in the cooling system (a hissing sound may be heard). Wait until any pressure in the system is released, then continue to turn the cap until it can be removed.

2 Unscrew the bleed screw from the top of the hose junction above the expansion tank. Some models are equipped with a bleed screw adjacent to the oil filter cap **(see illustrations)**.

3 Undo the retaining bolts/clips and remove the undershields from beneath the engine and radiator **(see illustrations)**.

4 Position a suitable container beneath the drain plug(s) on the base of the radiator (where fitted). Unscrew the drain plug(s) and allow the coolant to drain into the container **(see illustration)**. On models without a radiator drain plug, release the clamp and disconnect the radiator lower hose.

5 To fully drain the system, also unscrew the coolant drain plug from the right-hand side of the cylinder block and allow the remainder of the coolant to drain into the container **(see illustration)**. Note that access to the drain plug is extremely limited.

6 BMW insist that cooling system must not be refilled with used coolant.

7 Once all the coolant has drained, fit a new

16.2a Slacken the bleed screw on the expansion tank...

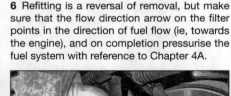

16.2b... and the one adjacent to the oil filter cap

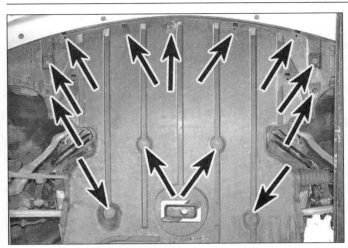

16.3a Undershield fasteners

16.3b Undo the bolts and remove the splash shield under the radiator

sealing washer to the block drain plug and tighten it to the specified torque.

Cooling system flushing

8 If coolant renewal has been neglected, or if the antifreeze mixture has become diluted, then in time the cooling system may gradually lose efficiency, as the coolant passages become restricted due to rust, scale deposits, and other sediment. The cooling system efficiency can be restored by flushing the system clean.

9 The radiator should be flushed independently of the engine, to avoid unnecessary contamination.

Radiator flushing

10 To flush the radiator, disconnect the top and bottom hoses and any other relevant hoses from the radiator, with reference to Chapter 3.

11 Insert a garden hose into the radiator top inlet. Direct a flow of clean water through the radiator, and continue flushing until clean water emerges from the radiator bottom outlet.

12 If after a reasonable period the water still does not run clear, the radiator can be flushed with a good proprietary cooling system cleaning agent. It is important that their manufacturer's instructions are followed

carefully. If the contamination is particularly bad, insert the hose in the radiator bottom outlet, and reverse-flush the radiator.

Engine flushing

13 To flush the engine, remove the thermostat as described in Chapter 3, then temporarily refit the thermostat cover. On models where the thermostat is integral with the housing, remove the housing to allow the water to flow out.

14 With the top and bottom hoses disconnected from the radiator, insert a garden hose into the radiator top hose. Direct a clean flow of water through the engine, and continue flushing until clean water emerges from the radiator bottom hose.

15 On completion of flushing, refit the thermostat and reconnect the hoses with reference to Chapter 3.

Cooling system filling

16 Before attempting to fill the cooling system, make sure that all hoses and clips are in good condition, and that the clips are tight and the radiator and cylinder block drain plugs are securely tightened. Note that an antifreeze mixture must be used all year round, to prevent corrosion of the engine components (see following sub-Section).

17 Slacken the bleed screw(s) **(see illustrations 13.2a and 13.2b)**.

18 Turn on the ignition (without starting the engine), and set the heater control to maximum temperature, with the fan speed set to 'low'. This opens the heating valves.

19 Remove the expansion tank filler cap. Fill the system by slowly pouring the coolant into the expansion tank to prevent airlocks from forming.

20 If the coolant is being renewed, begin by pouring in a couple of litres of water, followed by the correct quantity of antifreeze, then top-up with more water.

21 As soon as coolant free from air bubbles emerges from the radiator bleed screw(s), tighten the screw(s) securely.

22 Once the level in the expansion tank starts to rise, squeeze the radiator top and bottom hoses to help expel any trapped air in the system. Once all the air is expelled, top-up the coolant level until the float in the expansion tank rises to indicate the maximum level, then refit the expansion tank cap **(see illustration)**.

23 Start the engine and run it until it reaches normal operating temperature, then stop the engine and allow it to cool.

24 Check for leaks, particularly around disturbed components. Check the coolant level in the expansion tank, and top-up if necessary. Note that the system must be cold before an accurate level is indicated in the

16.4 Slacken the radiator drain plug

16.5 The cylinder block drain plug is located on the right-hand side

16.22 The float indicates the coolant level. Refer to the markings on the top of the expansion tank

expansion tank. If the expansion tank cap is removed while the engine is still warm, cover the cap with a thick cloth, and unscrew the cap slowly to gradually relieve the system pressure (a hissing sound will normally be heard). Wait until any pressure remaining in the system is released, then continue to turn the cap until it can be removed.

Antifreeze mixture

25 Always use an ethylene-glycol based antifreeze which is suitable for use in mixed-metal cooling systems. The quantity of antifreeze and levels of protection are indicated in the Specifications.

26 Before adding antifreeze, the cooling system should be completely drained, preferably flushed, and all hoses checked for condition and security.

27 After filling with antifreeze, a label should be attached to the expansion tank, stating the type and concentration of antifreeze used, and the date installed. Any subsequent topping-up should be made with the same type and concentration of antifreeze.

Caution: Do not use engine antifreeze in the windscreen/tailgate washer system, as it will damage the vehicle paintwork. A screenwash additive should be added to the washer system in the quantities stated on the bottle.

Chapter 1 Part B:
Routine maintenance and servicing – diesel models

Contents

Degrees of difficulty

Easy, suitable for novice with little experience Fairly easy, suitable for beginner with some experience Fairly difficult, suitable for competent DIY mechanic Difficult, suitable for experienced DIY mechanic Very difficult, suitable for expert DIY or professional

1 Servicing specifications

Capacities

Engine oil (including filter)
4-cylinder engines (approximately) . . . . 5.2 litres
6-cylinder engines (approximately) . . . . 7.5 litres

Cooling system
4-cylinder engines:
  Manual transmission. . . . . 7.5 litres
  Automatic transmission . . . . 7.9 litres
6-cylinder models:
  Manual transmission. . . . . 7.8 litres
  Automatic transmission . . . . 8.2 litres

Transmission
Manual transmission (approximate) . . . . 1.4 litres
Automatic transmission (approximate). . . . . 3.0 litres

Final drive unit
All models (approximate): . . . .
  4-cylinder models. . . . . 1.1 litres
  6-cylinder models . . . . 1.7 litres

Fuel tank
All models (approximate) . . . . 61 litres

Cooling system

Antifreeze mixture:
  50% antifreeze . . . . Protection down to -30°C
Note: *Refer to antifreeze manufacturer for latest recommendations.*

Brakes
Brake pad friction material minimum thickness. . . . . 2.0 mm
Handbrake shoe friction material minimum thickness . . . . 1.5 mm
Note: *The wear warning symbol will illuminate when the pad wears down to 3.7 mm thick.*

Torque wrench settings	Nm	lbf ft
Cylinder block coolant drain plug.	25	18
Engine oil filter cover	25	18
Engine sump oil drain plug:		
M12 plug.	25	18
M18 plug.	35	26
M22 plug.	60	44
Suspension turret/tension braces*:		
M10 (outer bolts):		
Stage 1	40	30
Stage 2	Angle-tighten a further 60°	
M12 (centre bolt):		
Stage 1	100	74
Stage 2	Angle-tighten a further 100°	
Strut/bracket nuts* (Version B)	34	25
Roadwheel bolts.	120	89

*Do not re-use

Maintenance schedule – diesel models 1B•3

2 Maintenance schedule – diesel models

The service intervals are tailored according to the operating conditions, driving style, time elapsed and mileage covered, instead of set distance/time limits. These factors are taken into account, the maintenance requirements are calculated by the vehicle's on-board systems, and a symbol representing the item requiring attention is displayed in the instrument cluster. The urgency of the attention is indicated by a colour-coding system – green, yellow or red. Consequently, the intervals listed below are guidelines, starting values/interval forecasts, or our recommendations. For more details, refer to the Owners Handbook supplied with the vehicle.

When the vehicle is new, it should be serviced by a dealer service department (or other workshop recognised by the vehicle manufacturer as providing the same standard of service) in order to preserve the warranty. The vehicle manufacturer may reject warranty claims if you are unable to prove that servicing has been carried out as and when specified, using only original equipment parts or parts certified to be of equivalent quality.

Every 250 miles or weekly
☐ Refer to *Weekly checks*

Every 15 000 miles or 2 years, whichever comes first
☐ Oil service (Section 6)
Note: *This includes engine oil renewal, handbrake check and pollen filter renewal.*
☐ Reset the service interval display (Section 7)

Every 25 000 miles
☐ Front brake service (Section 8)
☐ Reset the service interval display (Section 7)

Every 30 000 miles
☐ Rear brake service (Section 9)
☐ Reset the service interval display (Section 7)

Every 30 000 miles or 4 years, whichever comes first
☐ Air filter element renewal (Section 11)
☐ Main fuel filter renewal (Section 12)
☐ Vehicle check (Section 10)
☐ Reset the service interval display (Section 7)

Every 125 000 miles
☐ Renew the diesel particulate filter (Section 13)
☐ Reset the service interval display (Section 7)

Every 2 years
☐ Renew the brake fluid (Section 14)
☐ Reset the service interval display (Section 7)

Every 4 years
Note: *These items have no specific recommendation concerning their inspection or renewal. However, we consider it prudent to carry out these tasks at least every 4 years.*
☐ Check the condition of the auxiliary drivebelt(s), and adjust/renew if necessary (Section 15)
☐ Coolant renewal (Section 16)

Underbonnet view of a 4-cylinder N47T engine – others are similar

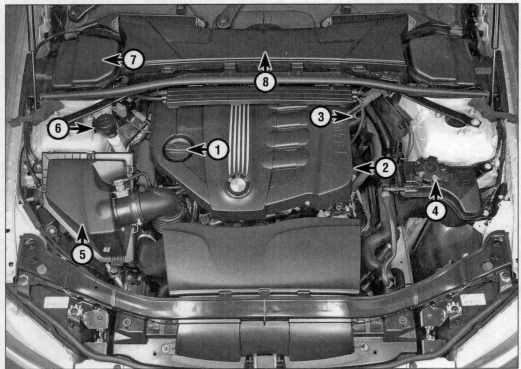

1 Engine oil filler cap
2 Engine oil filter cover
3 Engine oil level dipstick
4 Coolant expansion tank
5 Air filter assembly
6 Washer fluid reservoir
7 Brake and clutch fluid
   reservoir (under cover)
8 Pollen filter housing

Front underbody view – N47 engine shown, others are similar

1 Engine oil (sump) drain
   plug
2 Catalytic converter/
   particulate filter
3 Control arm
4 Tension strut
5 Steering track rod
6 Anti-roll bar
7 Reinforcement frame
8 Steering rack electric
   motor
9 Starter motor

Rear underbody view

1 Fuel tank
2 Exhaust tail box
3 Final drive unit
4 Driveshaft
5 Handbrake cable
6 Camber arm
7 Trailing arm
8 Shock absorber lower
 mounting

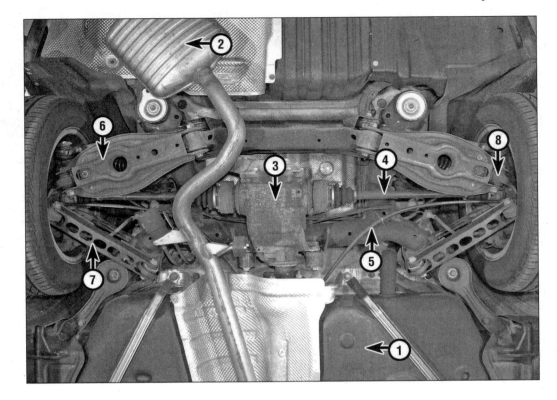

4 Introduction

1 This Chapter is designed to help the home mechanic maintain his/her vehicle for safety, economy, long life and peak performance.
2 The Chapter contains a master maintenance schedule, followed by Sections dealing specifically with each task in the schedule. Visual checks, adjustments, component renewal and other helpful items are included. Refer to the accompanying illustrations of the engine compartment and the underside of the vehicle for the locations of the various components.
3 Servicing your vehicle in accordance with the service indicator display and the following Sections will provide a planned maintenance programme, which should result in a long and reliable service life. This is a comprehensive plan, so maintaining some items but not others at the specified service intervals will not produce the same results.
4 As you service your vehicle, you will discover that many of the procedures can – and should – be grouped together, because of the particular procedure being performed, or because of the proximity of two otherwise-unrelated components to one another. For example, if the vehicle is raised for any

reason, the exhaust can be inspected at the same time as the suspension and steering components.
5 The first step in this maintenance programme is to prepare yourself before the actual work begins. Read through all the Sections relevant to the work to be carried out, then make a list and gather all the parts and tools required. If a problem is encountered, seek advice from a parts specialist, or a dealer service department.

Remote control battery

6 The remote control battery is recharged every time the key is inserted into the ignition switch. Battery renewal is therefore not necessary. Should the battery fail, the complete key will require renewing. Refer to a BMW dealer or specialist.

5 Regular maintenance

1 If, from the time the vehicle is new, the routine maintenance schedule is followed closely, and frequent checks are made of fluid levels and high-wear items, as suggested throughout this manual, the engine will be kept in relatively good running condition, and the need for additional work will be minimised.
2 It is possible that there will be times when

the engine is running poorly due to the lack of regular maintenance. This is even more likely if a used vehicle, which has not received regular and frequent maintenance checks, is purchased. In such cases, additional work may need to be carried out, outside of the regular maintenance intervals.
3 If engine wear is suspected, a compression test (refer to the relevant Part of Chapter 2) will provide valuable information regarding the overall performance of the main internal components. Such a test can be used as a basis to decide on the extent of the work to be carried out. If, for example, a compression test indicates serious internal engine wear, conventional maintenance as described in this Chapter will not greatly improve the performance of the engine, and may prove a waste of time and money, unless extensive overhaul work is carried out first.
4 The following series of operations are those most often required to improve the performance of a generally poor-running engine:

Primary operations

a) Clean, inspect and test the battery (See Weekly checks).
b) Check all the engine-related fluids (See Weekly checks).
c) Check the condition and tension of the auxiliary drivebelt(s) (Section 15).

6.3 Rotate the fastener to access the sump drain plug

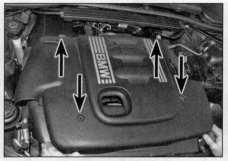

6.4a On M57T2 engines, undo the 2 bolts and lift and pull the plastic cover from the top of the engine. Note the locating lugs at the rear (arrowed)

6.4b On N47 and N57 engines, pull up the front edge, and slide the plastic cover forwards

d) *Renew the main fuel filter (Section 12).*
e) *Check the condition of the air filter, and renew if necessary (Section 11).*
f) *Check the condition of all hoses, and check for fluid leaks (Section 10).*

5 If the above operations do not prove fully effective, carry out the following secondary operations:

Secondary operations

6 All items listed under *Primary operations*, plus the following:
g) *Check the charging system (see Chapter 5A).*
h) *Check the glow plug system (see Chapter 5A).*
i) *Check the fuel system (see Chapter 4B).*

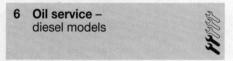

6 Oil service – diesel models

Note: *This includes engine oil renewal, handbrake check and pollen filter renewal.*

Oil service

1 The oil service is made up of 5 elements: engine oil and filter change, handbrake check, pollen filter renewal, air filter element renewal and main fuel filter change. The handbrake check and pollen filter renewal should be carried out every time the engine oil and filter are changed, whilst the air filter element and main fuel filter should be renewed at every 3rd

engine oil and filter change. Refer to Section 11 for air filter renewal and Section 12 for main fuel filter renewal.

Engine oil and filter change

2 Frequent oil and filter changes are the most important preventative maintenance work which can be undertaken by the DIY owner. As engine oil ages, it becomes diluted and contaminated, which leads to premature engine wear.

3 Before starting this procedure, gather together all the necessary tools and materials. Also make sure you have plenty of clean rags and newspapers handy, to mop-up any spills. Ideally, the engine oil should be warm, as it will drain better, and more built-up sludge will be removed with it. Take care, however, not to touch the exhaust or any other hot parts of the engine when working under the car. To avoid any possibility of scalding, and to protect yourself from possible skin irritants and other harmful contaminants in used engine oils, it is advisable to wear gloves. Access to the underside of the car will be improved if it can be raised on a lift, driven onto ramps, or jacked up and supported on axle stands (see *Jacking and vehicle support*). Whichever method is chosen, make sure the car remains level, or if it is at an angle, so that the drain plug is at the lowest point. Where necessary remove the undershield from under the engine. On vehicles equipped with front reinforcement plate between the front suspension lower control arms, access to the

sump plug is via a removable flap in the plate **(see illustration)**.

4 Working in the engine compartment, locate the oil filter housing on the left-hand side of the engine, in front of the intake manifold. Undo the bolts (M57T2 engines only) and remove the plastic acoustic cover from the top of the engine **(see illustrations)**.

5 Place a wad of rag around the bottom of the oil filter housing to absorb any spilt oil.

6 Using a spanner or socket, unscrew and remove the cover, complete with filter cartridge **(see illustration)**. The oil will drain from the housing back into the sump as the cover is removed.

7 Recover the O-rings from the cover.

8 Using a clean rag, wipe the mating faces of the housing and cover.

9 Fit new O-rings to the cover **(see illustration)**.

10 On M57T2 engines, fit the new filter cartridge into the cover **(see illustration)**. On N47 and N57 engines, fit the new filter element into the filter housing, ensuring the lug on the base of the element aligns with the locating hole in the housing **(see illustration)**.

11 Smear a little clean engine oil on the O-rings, refit the cover and tighten it to 25 Nm (18 lbf ft) if using the special filter removal tool, or securely if using a strap wrench.

12 Working under the car, slacken the sump drain plug about half a turn **(see illustration 6.3)**. Position the draining container under the drain plug, then remove the plug completely.

6.6 Unscrew the cover and remove it complete with filter element

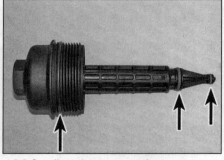

6.9 On all engines, renew the cover cap O-ring seal. Where applicable, also renew the cover centre O-rings

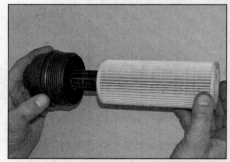

6.10a Fit the new element to the cover – M57T2 engines

6.10b Align the lug on the base of the filter element with the locating hole in the housing – N47 and N57 engines

If possible, try to keep the plug pressed into the sump while unscrewing it by hand the last couple of turns. Note that on some models, it will be necessary to rotate the fastener and open the drain plug access flap in the engine undershield.

13 Recover the drain plug sealing ring.

14 Allow some time for the old oil to drain, noting that it may be necessary to reposition the container as the oil flow slows to a trickle.

15 After all the oil has drained, wipe off the drain plug with a clean rag. Renew the plug sealing washer. Clean the area around the drain plug opening, then refit and tighten the plug (see illustration).

16 Remove the old oil and all tools from under the car, then lower the car to the ground (if applicable).

Models without a dipstick

17 Add a little less than the correct amount of oil (see Capacities at the start of this Chapter) to the engine through the oil filler cap orifice, using the correct grade and type of oil (see *Lubricants and fluids*). An oil can spout or funnel may help to reduce spillage.

18 Start the engine and run it for 3 minutes; check for leaks around the oil filter seal and the sump drain plug. Note that there may be a delay of a few seconds before the oil pressure warning light goes out when the engine is first started, as the oil circulates through the engine oil galleries and the new oil filter, before the pressure builds-p.

19 Lightly push the button on the indicator up or down until the work OIL is shown in the

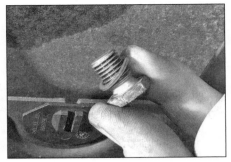

6.15 Renew the sump drain plug washer

instrument cluster display. Press the button on the end of the indicator stalk and the oil level will be displayed. If necessary, stop the engine and add engine oil until the level is correct (see illustration). Refer to the owners handbook for details of the electronic oil level monitor.

Models with a dipstick

20 Remove the dipstick then unscrew the oil filler cap from the cylinder head cover. Fill the engine, using the correct grade and type of oil (see *Lubricants and fluids*). An oil can spout or funnel may help to reduce spillage. Pour in half the specified quantity of oil first, then wait a few minutes for the oil to run to the sump. Continue adding oil a small quantity at a time until the level is up to the lower mark on the dipstick. Finally, bring the level up to the upper mark on the dipstick. Insert the dipstick, and refit the filler cap.

21 Start the engine and run it for a few minutes; check for leaks around the oil filter seal and the sump drain plug. Note that there may be a delay of a few seconds before the oil pressure warning light goes out when the engine is first started, as the oil circulates through the engine oil galleries and the new oil filter, before the pressure builds-up.

22 Switch off the engine, and wait a few minutes for the oil to settle in the sump once more. With the new oil circulated and the filter completely full, recheck the level on the dipstick, and add more oil as necessary.

All models

23 Dispose of the used engine oil safely, with reference to General repair procedures in the Reference section of this manual.

6.19 Oil level display in the instrument cluster

Handbrake check

24 Check and, if necessary, adjust the handbrake as described in Chapter 9. Check that the handbrake cables are free to move easily and lubricate all exposed linkages/ cable pivots.

Pollen filter renewal

25 Undo the bolts and remove the upper section of the pollen filter housing (see illustration).

26 Release the catches at the front edge, and remove the filter element (see illustration).

27 Fit the new element into the housing, ensuring it's correctly seated.

28 Refit the upper housing and securely tighten the retaining bolts.

7 Resetting the service interval display (CBS) – diesel models

1 Ensure that all electrical items are switched off then turn on the ignition switch. **Note:** *Do not start the engine.*

2 Ensure the on-board time and date are correctly set in accordance with the instructions in the owner's handbook. In order for the CBS display to function correctly, the on-board time and date must be correct.

3 Each service item that appears on the instrument cluster display can be reset. Note that it is only possible to reset an item if the service life of the item is below 80%.

4 Press the trip odometer button for approximately 10 seconds until the first CBS (Condition Based Service) item appears in the instrument cluster display. Note that the most urgent item is displayed first. If this is not the item required, select the item to be reset by briefly pressing the button again.

5 When the required item is selected, press the button again until 'Reset?' appears in the display. Note that the reset process is cancelled by not pressing the button to confirm, and waiting for the display to return to its normal state.

6 Press the button again for approximately 3 seconds to confirm the reset. Note that it is only possible to reset the brake pad display if the pad sensors are working properly.

7 Turn off the ignition switch.

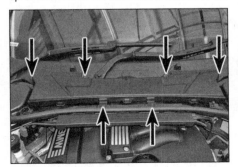

6.25 Undo the bolts and remove the pollen filter cover

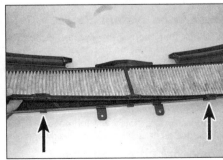

6.26 Release the clips and lift the pollen filter element from place

8 Front brake service

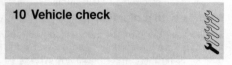

Brake pads

1 When this CBS item is displayed, the thickness of the front brake pads friction material should be checked, and if any are approaching the minimum thickness, all four front pads should be renewed.

2 Firmly apply the handbrake, then jack up the front of the car and support it securely on axle stands (see *Jacking and vehicle support*). Remove the front roadwheels.

3 The brake pad warning symbol in the CBS display indicates that the pad friction material thickness is worn and that the pads require renewal. However, the warning will also be given if the wiring to and from each pads sensor is damaged or the connections are poor, dirty, etc. Check the wiring to and from the sensor for poor connections/breaks before renewing the pads.

4 The thickness of friction material remaining on each brake pad can be measured through the top of the caliper body. If any pad's friction material is worn to the specified thickness or less, all four pads must be renewed as a set. Pad renewal is described in Chapter 9.

Brake disc check

5 Check the front brake disc condition, and measure the thickness of the disc as described in Chapter 9. Renew both front discs if necessary.

9 Rear brake service

Brake pads

1 When this CBS item is displayed, the thickness of the rear brake pads friction material should be checked, and if any are approaching the minimum thickness, all four rear pads should be renewed.

2 Chock the front wheels, then jack up the rear of the car and support it on axle stands

10.13 Use a hydrometer to check the strength of the antifreeze

(see *Jacking and vehicle support*). Remove the rear roadwheels.

3 The thickness of friction material remaining on each brake pad can be measured through the top of the caliper body. If any pad's friction material is worn to the specified thickness or less, all four pads must be renewed as a set. Pad renewal is described in Chapter 9.

Brake disc check

4 Check the front brake disc condition, and measure the thickness of the disc as described in Chapter 9. Renew both front discs if necessary.

Handbrake shoe lining check

5 Inspect and the handbrake shoes lining material as described in Chapter 9. If any of the shoe's lining material has worn below the minimum thickness, renew all four shoes as described in Chapter 9.

10 Vehicle check

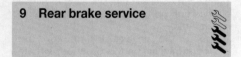

1 The vehicle check consists of several tasks. Before the CBS display can be reset, all of the following tasks must be complete.

Instruments and electrical equipment

2 Check the operation of all instruments and electrical equipment.

3 Make sure that all instruments read correctly, and switch on all electrical equipment in turn, to check that it functions properly.

Seat belt check

4 Carefully examine the seat belt webbing for cuts or any signs of serious fraying or deterioration. Pull the belt all the way out, and examine the full extent of the webbing.

5 Fasten and unfasten the belt, ensuring that the locking mechanism holds securely and releases properly when intended. Check also that the retracting mechanism operates correctly when the belt is released.

6 Check the security of all seat belt mountings and attachments which are accessible, without removing any trim or other components, from inside the car.

Wash/wipe system check

7 Check that each of the washer jet nozzles are clear and that each nozzle provides a strong jet of washer fluid. Renew as necessary – refer to Chapter 12.

8 Check the condition of each wiper blade for damage of wear. As time passes the blades will become hardened, wipe performance will deteriorate, and noise will increase. Renew the blades as necessary – see Weekly checks.

Bodywork corrosion check

9 This work should be carried out by a BMW dealer in order to validate the vehicle warranty.

The work includes a thorough inspection of the vehicle paintwork and underbody for damage and corrosion.

Tyre check

10 Check the tread depth, external condition and inflation pressure of the tyres. See Weekly checks for details of the procedures and tyre pressure information.

Initialise tyre check system

11 Initialisation of the tyre pressure checking system must be carried out after the tyre pressures have been corrected, or a tyre/wheel renewed. The system is initialised as follows:

Models with iDrive

j) Press the iDrive controller to call up the i menu.
k) Select 'Settings' and press the controller.
l) Select 'Car/Tyres' and press the controller.
m) Turn the controller until 'Tyres: RPA' is selected, then press the controller.
n) Start the engine, but do not drive off.
o) Select 'Confirm tyre pressure' and press the controller.
p) Drive off. Initialisation is completed during the journey.

Models without iDrive

q) Start the engine, but do not drive off.
r) Press the direction indicator stalk up or down until the tyre pressure symbol and RESET appear in the instrument cluster display.
s) Press the button on the end of the indicator stalk to confirm the selection of the Run Flat Indicator.
t) Press the button again for approximately 5 seconds, until a check/tick appears after RESET.
u) Drive off. Initialisation is completed during the journey.

Battery check

12 Check the condition of the battery, and recharge if necessary – refer to Chapter 5A.

Coolant concentration check

13 Use a hydrometer to check the strength of the antifreeze **(see illustration)**. Follow the instructions provided with your hydrometer. The antifreeze strength should be approximately 50%. If it is significantly less than this, drain a little coolant from the radiator (see this Chapter), add anti-freeze to the coolant expansion tank, then recheck the strength.

Hose and fluid leak check

14 Visually inspect the engine joint faces, gaskets and seals for any signs of water or oil leaks. Pay particular attention to the areas around the camshaft cover, cylinder head, oil filter and sump joint faces. Bear in mind that, over a period of time, some very slight seepage from these areas is to be expected – what you are really looking for is any indication of a serious leak. Should a leak be found, renew the offending gasket or oil seal by referring to the appropriate Chapters in this manual.

15 Also check the security and condition of all the engine-related pipes and hoses. Ensure that all cable-ties or securing clips are in place and in good condition. Clips which are broken or missing can lead to chafing of the hoses, pipes or wiring, which could cause more serious problems in the future.

16 Carefully check the radiator hoses and heater hoses along their entire length. Renew any hose which is cracked, swollen or deteriorated. Cracks will show up better if the hose is squeezed. Pay close attention to the hose clips that secure the hoses to the cooling system components. Hose clips can pinch and puncture hoses, resulting in cooling system leaks.

17 Inspect all the cooling system components (hoses, joint faces, etc) for leaks **(see Haynes Hint)**. Where any problems of this nature are found on system components, renew the component or gasket with reference to Chapter 3.

18 Where applicable, inspect the automatic transmission fluid cooler hoses for leaks or deterioration.

19 With the car raised, inspect the petrol tank and filler neck for punctures, cracks and other damage. The connection between the filler neck and tank is especially critical. Sometimes a rubber filler neck or connecting hose will leak due to loose retaining clamps or deteriorated rubber.

20 Carefully check all rubber hoses and metal fuel lines leading away from the petrol tank. Check for loose connections, deteriorated hoses, crimped lines, and other damage. Pay particular attention to the vent pipes and hoses, which often loop up around the filler neck and can become blocked or crimped. Follow the lines to the front of the car, carefully inspecting them all the way. Renew damaged sections as necessary.

21 Closely inspect the metal brake pipes which run along the car underbody. If they show signs of excessive corrosion or damage they must be renewed.

22 From within the engine compartment, check the security of all fuel hose attachments and pipe unions, and inspect the fuel hoses and vacuum hoses for kinks, chafing and deterioration.

23 Check the condition of the power steering fluid hoses and pipes.

Suspension and steering check

24 Raise the front of the car, and securely support it on axle stands (see *Jacking and vehicle support*).

25 Visually inspect the balljoint dust covers and the steering rack-and-pinion gaiters for splits, chafing or deterioration. Any wear of these components will cause loss of lubricant, then dirt and water entry, resulting in rapid deterioration of the balljoints or steering gear.

26 Check the power steering fluid hoses for chafing or deterioration, and the pipe and hose unions for fluid leaks. Also check for signs of fluid leakage under pressure from the steering gear rubber gaiters, which would indicate failed fluid seals within the steering gear.

27 Grasp the roadwheel at the 12 o'clock and 6 o'clock positions, and try to rock it **(see illustration)**. Very slight free play may be felt, but if the movement is appreciable, further investigation is necessary to determine the source. Continue rocking the wheel while an assistant depresses the footbrake. If the movement is now eliminated or significantly reduced, it is likely that the hub bearings are at fault. If the free play is still evident with the footbrake depressed, then there is wear in the suspension joints or mountings.

28 Now grasp the wheel at the 9 o'clock and 3 o'clock positions, and try to rock it as before. Any movement felt now may again be caused by wear in the hub bearings or the steering track rod balljoints. If the inner or outer balljoint is worn, the visual movement will be obvious.

29 Using a large screwdriver or flat bar, check for wear in the suspension mounting bushes by levering between the relevant suspension component and its attachment point. Some movement is to be expected as the mountings are made of rubber, but excessive wear should be obvious. Also check the condition of any visible rubber bushes, looking for splits, cracks or contamination of the rubber.

30 With the car standing on its wheels, have an assistant turn the steering wheel back-and-forth about an eighth of a turn each way. There should be very little, if any, lost movement between the steering wheel and roadwheels. If this is not the case, closely observe the joints and mountings previously described, but in addition, check the steering column universal joints for wear, and the rack-and-pinion steering gear itself.

Strut/shock absorber check

31 Check for any signs of fluid leakage around the suspension strut/shock absorber body, or from the rubber gaiter around the piston rod. Should any fluid be noticed, the suspension strut/shock absorber is defective

A leak in the cooling system will usually show up as white- or antifreezecoloured deposits on the area adjoining the leak.

internally, and should be renewed. Note: Suspension struts/shock absorbers should always be renewed in pairs on the same axle.

32 The efficiency of the suspension strut/ shock absorber may be checked by bouncing the car at each corner. Generally speaking, the body will return to its normal position and stop after being depressed. If it rises and returns on a rebound, the suspension strut/shock absorber is probably suspect. Examine also the suspension strut/shock absorber upper and lower mountings for any signs of wear.

Exhaust system check

33 With the engine cold (at least an hour after the car has been driven), check the complete exhaust system from the engine to the end of the tailpipe. The exhaust system is most easily checked with the car raised on a hoist, or suitably supported on axle stands, so that the exhaust components are readily visible and accessible.

34 Check the exhaust pipes and connections for evidence of leaks, severe corrosion and damage. Make sure that all brackets and mountings are in good condition, and that all relevant nuts and bolts are tight **(see illustration)**. Leakage at any of the joints or in other parts of the system will usually show up as a black sooty stain in the vicinity of the leak.

35 Rattles and other noises can often be traced to the exhaust system, especially the brackets and mountings. Try to move the pipes and silencers. If the components are

10.27 Check for wear in the hub bearings by grasping the wheel and trying to rock it

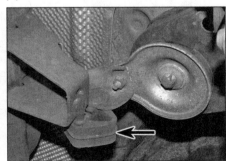

10.34 Check the condition of the exhaust mounting rubbers

11.1 Release the 3 retaining clips

11.2 Lift the cover and remove the element

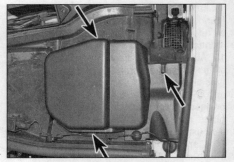

11.7 Release the clips and remove the plastic cover each side

able to come into contact with the body or suspension parts, secure the system with new mountings. Otherwise separate the joints (if possible) and twist the pipes as necessary to provide additional clearance.

Hinge and lock lubrication

36 Lubricate the hinges of the bonnet, doors and tailgate with a light general-purpose oil. Similarly, lubricate all latches, locks and lock strikers. At the same time, check the security and operation of all the locks, adjusting them if necessary (see Chapter 11). Lightly lubricate the bonnet release mechanism and cable with a suitable grease.

Road test

Steering and suspension

37 Check for any abnormalities in the steering, suspension, handling or road 'feel'.
38 Drive the car, and check that there are no unusual vibrations or noises.
39 Check that the steering feels positive, with no excessive 'sloppiness', or roughness, and check for any suspension noises when cornering and driving over bumps.

Drivetrain

40 Check the performance of the engine, clutch (where applicable), gearbox/transmission and driveshafts.
41 Listen for any unusual noises from the engine, clutch and gearbox/transmission.
42 Make sure that the engine runs smoothly

when idling, and that there is no hesitation when accelerating.
43 Check that, where applicable, the clutch action is smooth and progressive, that the drive is taken up smoothly, and that the pedal travel is not excessive. Also listen for any noises when the clutch pedal is depressed.
44 On manual gearbox models, check that all gears can be engaged smoothly without noise, and that the gear lever action is smooth and not abnormally vague or 'notchy'.
45 On automatic transmission models, make sure that all gearchanges occur smoothly, without snatching, and without an increase in engine speed between changes. Check that all the gear positions can be selected with the car at rest. If any problems are found, they should be referred to a BMW dealer or suitably equipped specialist.

Check the braking system

46 Make sure that the car does not pull to one side when braking, and that the wheels do not lock when braking hard.
47 Check that there is no vibration through the steering when braking.
48 Check that the handbrake operates correctly without excessive movement of the lever, and that it holds the car stationary on a slope.
49 Test the operation of the brake servo unit as follows. With the engine off, depress the footbrake four or five times to exhaust the vacuum. Hold the brake pedal depressed, then start the engine. As the engine starts,

there should be a noticeable 'give' in the brake pedal as vacuum builds-up. Allow the engine to run for at least two minutes, and then switch it off. If the brake pedal is depressed now, it should be possible to detect a hiss from the servo as the pedal is depressed. After about four or five applications, no further hissing should be heard, and the pedal should feel much harder.

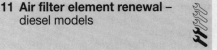

11 Air filter element renewal – diesel models

Air filter element renewal

Note: *The air filter element should be renewed at every 2nd engine oil and filter change.*

N47 4-cylinder and N57 6-cylinder engines

1 Undo the 3 fasteners and lift the filter cover **(see illustration)**.
2 Note its fitted position, and lift the filter element from the housing **(see illustration)**.
3 Clean the air filter housing, removing all debris.
4 Fit the new filter element into place, ensuring it locates correctly with the housing.
5 The remainder of refitting is a reversal of removal.

M57T2 6-cylinder engines

6 Undo the bolts and remove the upper section of the pollen filter housing from the rear of the engine compartment (see illustration 6.25).
7 Release the clips and remove the left- and right-hand plastic covers behind the suspension turrets in the engine compartment **(see illustration)**.
8 Release the clips and pull the cable guide from the front edge of the pollen filter housing **(see illustration)**.
9 Release the clip and bolt on each side, and pull the lower section of the pollen filter housing forwards and upwards **(see illustrations)**.
10 Undo the bolts and remove the plastic cover from the top of the engine **(see illustration)**.
11 Prise out/undo the cap from the centre

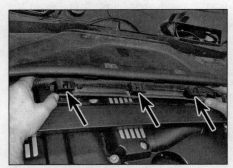

11.8 Release the clips and pull the cable guide forwards

11.9a Rotate the temperature sensor and remove it from the bracket. On the passenger's side, disconnect the bonnet switch

11.9b Undo the bolt and release the clip each side...

11.9c... then pull the pollen filter lower housing forwards

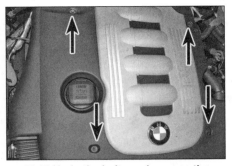

11.10 Undo the bolts and remove the plastic cover

of the scuttle trim panel, undo the exposed bolt, then undo the bolt at each end of the tension brace. Carefully pull each brace from the grommets at the centre of the scuttle **(see illustrations)**. Note that new bolts are required.

12 Undo the bolts securing the plastic cover at the rear of the cylinder head **(see illustration)**. Note that it's not necessary to remove the cover, merely move it a little to the left-hand side.

13 Disconnect the intake hose from the air cleaner housing.

14 Undo the 3 bolts and slide the air filter intake neck forwards **(see illustration)**.

15 Unscrew the oil filler cap, then undo the 5 bolts and remove the air filter cover **(see illustration)**.

16 Lift the filter element from place, noting how the support at the end of the filter element locates in the housing **(see illustrations)**.

17 Clean the air filter housing, removing all debris.

18 Slide the new filter element into place, ensuring it locates correctly with the housing.

19 The remainder of refitting is a reversal of removal.

11.11a Remove the plastic cap from the centre of the scuttle trim panel

11.11b Undo the bolt at the end of each tension brace

12 Main fuel filter renewal – diesel models

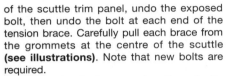

Note: *The main fuel filter should be renewed at every 3rd engine oil and filter change.*

1 Ensure the ignition is switched off, then raise the rear of the vehicle and support it securely on axle stands (see *Jacking and vehicle support*).

2 Undo the bolts and remove the underbody

protection panel to the left-hand side of the transmission **(see illustration)**.

3 Cut off the clamp securing the fuel hose to the front of the filter, and disconnect the hose **(see illustrations)**. Be prepared for fuel

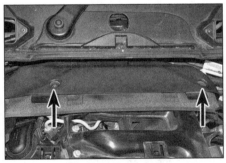

11.12 Undo the bolts and move the cover to the left-hand side

11.14 Undo the bolts and slide the intake neck forward

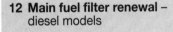
11.15 Air filter cover bolts

11.16a Lift the filter element from place...

11.16b... noting how the rear locating lug engages

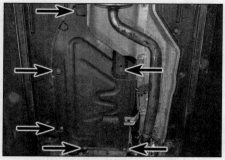

12.2 Undo the fasteners and remove the panel beneath the transmission

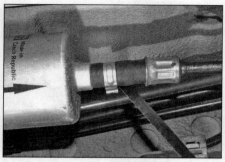

12.3a Cut off the original hose clamp

12.3b When refitting, update the original with a screw-type clamp

12.4 Undo the clamp retaining bolts

12.5a Slide out the retaining clip...

12.5b... and pull the preheater from the filter

spillage. Update the clamp with a screw-type clamp.

4 Undo the bolts securing the filter unit clamp to the vehicle body **(see illustration)**. The clamp must be transferred to the new filter.

5 Slide out the clip and detach the fuel preheater from the rear of the filter **(see illustrations)**.

6 Refitting is a reversal of removal. Turn on the ignition and leave it for approximately 1 minute. The pre-supply pump in the tank is activated, and the fuel pipe to the high-pressure pump is vented. Start the engine and check for leaks.

13 Diesel particulate filter – renewal

1 Renewal of the diesel particulate filter is described in Chapter 4C.

14 Brake fluid renewal – diesel models

Brake fluid renewal

⚠ **Warning: Brake hydraulic fluid can harm your eyes and damage painted surfaces, so use extreme caution when handling and pouring it. Do not use fluid that has been standing open for some time, as it absorbs moisture from the air. Excess**

moisture can cause a dangerous loss of braking effectiveness.

1 The procedure is similar to that for the bleeding of the hydraulic system as described in Chapter 9, except that the brake fluid reservoir should be emptied by siphoning, using a clean poultry baster or similar before starting, and allowance should be made for the old fluid to be expelled when bleeding a section of the circuit.

2 Working as described in Chapter 9, open the first bleed screw in the sequence, and pump the brake pedal gently until nearly all the old fluid has been emptied from the master cylinder reservoir.

3 Top-up to the MAX level with new fluid, and continue pumping until only the new fluid remains in the reservoir, and new fluid can be seen emerging from the bleed screw. Tighten the screw, and top the reservoir level up to the MAX level line.

4 Work through all remaining bleed screws in the sequence until new fluid can be seen at all of them. Be careful to keep the master cylinder reservoir topped-up to above the MIN level at all times, or air may enter the system and increase the length of the task.

5 When the operation is complete, check that all bleed screws are securely tightened, and that their dust caps are refitted. Wash off all traces of spilt fluid, and recheck the master cylinder reservoir fluid level.

6 Check the operation of the brakes before taking the car on the road.

15 Auxiliary drivebelt(s) check and renewal – diesel models

Note: *These items have no specific recommendation concerning their inspection or renewal. However, we consider it prudent to carry out these tasks at least every 4 years.*

Drivebelt(s) checking

1 Due to their function and construction, the belts are prone to failure after a period of time, and should be inspected periodically to prevent problems.

2 The number of belts used on a particular car depends on the accessories fitted. Drivebelts are used to drive the coolant pump, alternator, power steering pump and air conditioning compressor (where applicable).

3 To improve access for belt inspection, if desired, remove the cooling fan and shroud as described in Chapter 3.

4 With the engine stopped, using your fingers (and an electric torch if necessary), move along the belts, checking for cracks and separation of the belt plies. Also check for fraying and glazing, which gives the belt a shiny appearance. Both sides of the belts should be inspected, which means the belt will have to be twisted to check the underside. If necessary turn the engine using a spanner or socket on the crankshaft pulley bolt to that the whole of the belt can be inspected.

15.7 Rotate the tensioner clockwise using a socket on the hexagonal lug

15.8 Lock the tensioner using a drill bit/rod

4-cylinder engines

5 Remove the cooling fan and shroud as described in Chapter 3.
6 If the drivebelt is to be re-used, mark the running direction of the belt before removal.
7 Rotate the tensioner (clockwise), and slide the drivebelt from the pulleys (see illustration).
8 If desired to aid refitting, the tensioner can be compressed fully and locked in position using a metal rod engaged with the holes in the tensioner and backplate – note that the tensioner has a powerful spring, so a strong rod/drill bit will be required (see illustration).
9 If the original belt is being refitted, observe the running direction mark made before removal.
10 If the tensioner has not been locked in position, compress the tensioner, and engage the belt with the pulleys, ensuring that it is routed as noted before removal (see illustrations). Make sure that the belt engages correctly with the grooves in the pulleys.
11 Where applicable, compress the tensioner until the locking rod can be removed, then withdraw the rod and release the tensioner.

All 4-cylinder engines

12 Refit the cooling fan and shroud as described in Chapter 3.

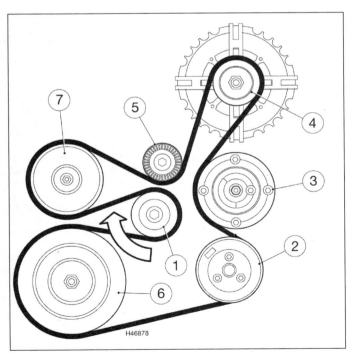

15.10a Auxiliary belt routing – N47 engines

1 Tensioner pulley
2 Power steering pump pulley
3 Air conditioning compressor pulley
4 Alternator pulley
5 Idler pulley
6 Crankshaft pulley
7 Coolant pump pulley

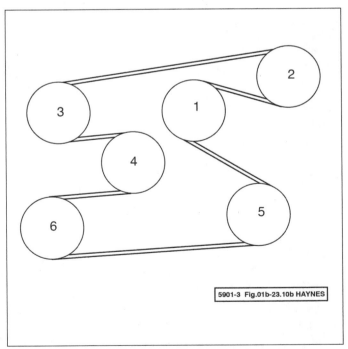

15.10b Auxiliary belt routing – N47T engines

1 Tensioner pulley
2 Alternator pulley
3 Coolant pump pulley
4 Idler pulley
5 Air conditioning compressor pulley
6 Crankshaft pulley

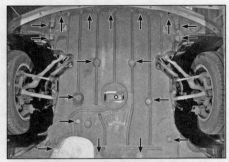

15.13 Undo the fasteners (arrowed) and remove the engine undershield

15.15 Use a flat bar to remove the air conditioning compressor belt

6-cylinder engines

M57T2 engine

13 Raise the front of the vehicle and support

15.20a The BMW tool fits into the centre of the pulley, and feeds the belt into place as it's rotated

15.20c Position the socket into the pulley, the tool in the socket, and fit the belt to the upper edge of the tool...

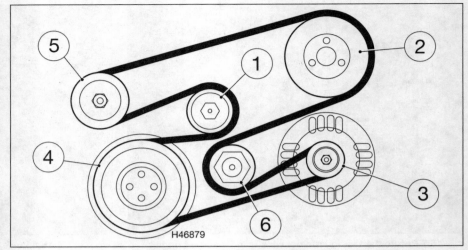

15.19 Auxiliary belt routing – M57T2 engine

1 Tensioner pulley
2 Power steering pump pulley
3 Alternator pulley

4 Crankshaft pulley
5 Coolant pump pulley
6 Idler pulley

it securely on axle stands (see *Jacking and vehicle support*). Undo the fasteners, remove the engine undershield, then remove the splash shield under the radiator **(see illustration)**.

14 Remove the cooling fan and shroud as described in Chapter 3.

15 If the drivebelt is to be re-used, mark the running direction of the belt prior to

15.20b Our tool uses strip steel, a couple of bolts, some studding and a large socket

15.20d... then rotate the tool clockwise and seat the belt in the pulley grooves

removal. Using large flat bar, lever the lower edge of the air conditioning compressor drivebelt forwards, rotate the crankshaft pulley clockwise and remove the belt from the pulleys **(see illustration)**.

16 If the main drivebelt is to be re-used, mark the running direction of the belt before removal.

17 Using a spanner or socket, rotate the tensioner pulley (clockwise) to compress the tensioner, and slide the drivebelt from the pulleys.

18 If the original belt is being refitted, observe the running direction mark made before removal.

19 Compress the tensioner, and engage the belt with the pulleys, ensuring that it is routed as noted before removal **(see illustration)**. Make sure that the belt engages correctly with the grooves in the pulleys.

20 Position the air conditioning compressor drivebelt around the pulley, and the upper half of the crankshaft pulley. Position BMW special tool No. 11 0 330 on the crankshaft pulley, then rotate the pulley clockwise. As the pulley rotates, the belt will be pulled into place. We made an alternative tool using strips of steel **(see illustrations)**.

21 Refit the cooling fan and shroud as described in Chapter 3.

N57 engine

22 Remove the cooling fan and shroud as described in Chapter 3.

23 If the drivebelt is to be re-used, mark the running direction of the belt before removal.

24 Using a spanner or socket, rotate the tensioner pulley (anti-clockwise) to compress the tensioner, and slide the drivebelt from the pulleys **(see illustration)**.

25 If desired to aid refitting, the tensioner can be compressed fully and locked in position using a metal rod engaged with the holes in the tensioner and backplate – note that the tensioner has a powerful spring, so a strong rod will be required **(see illustration)**.

26 If the original belt is being refitted, observe the running direction mark made before removal.

27 If the tensioner has not been locked in position, compress the tensioner, and engage the belt with the pulleys, ensuring that it is routed as noted before removal **(see illustration 15.10a)**. Make sure that the belt engages correctly with the grooves in the pulleys.

28 Where applicable, compress the tensioner until the locking rod can be removed, then withdraw the rod and release the tensioner.

29 Refit the cooling fan and shroud as described in Chapter 3.

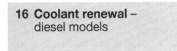

16 Coolant renewal – diesel models

Coolant renewal

Note: *These items have no specific recommendation concerning their inspection or renewal. However, we consider it prudent to carry out these tasks at least every 4 years.*

⚠️ *Warning: Wait until the engine is cold before starting this procedure. Do not allow antifreeze to come in contact with your skin, or with the painted surfaces of the car. Rinse off spills immediately with plenty of water. Never leave antifreeze lying around in an open container, or in a puddle in the driveway or on the garage floor. Children and pets are attracted by its sweet smell, but antifreeze can be fatal if ingested.*

Cooling system draining

1 With the engine completely cold, cover the expansion tank cap with a wad of rag, and slowly turn the cap anti-clockwise to relieve the pressure in the cooling system (a hissing sound may be heard). Wait until any pressure in the system is released, then continue to turn the cap until it can be removed.

2 On N47 and N57 engines, remove the intercooler as described in Chapter 4B.

3 On N47T engines, remove the engine

16.4c... and the EGR cooler according to model

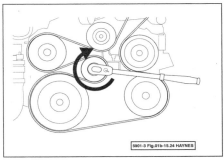

15.24 Rotate the tensioner pulley anti-clockwise

undershield, and panel beneath the intercooler/radiator. No drain plug/tap is fitted to the radiator.

4 Bleed screws may be fitted to the EGR cooler, the coolant return hose and the coolant expansion tank **(see illustrations)**. Undo the screws (where applicable), remove the plastic cover from the top of the engine **(see illustrations 6.4a or 6.4b)** and open the bleed screws.

5 Position a suitable container beneath the drain plug(s) on the base of the radiator (where fitted). Unscrew the drain plug(s) and allow the coolant to drain into the container **(see illustration)**. On models without a radiator drain plug, release the clamp and disconnect the radiator lower hose.

6 To fully drain the system, also unscrew the coolant drain plug from the right-hand side of the cylinder block and allow the remainder of the coolant to drain into the container **(see**

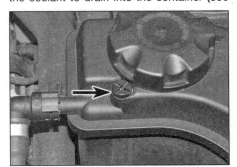

16.4a Coolant bleed screws may be located on the coolant expansion tank...

16.5 Slacken the radiator drain plug

15.25 Lock the tensioner using a drill bit/rod

illustration). Access to the plug is extremely limited.

7 BMW insist that the cooling system is not filled with used coolant.

8 Once all the coolant has drained, fit a new sealing washer to the block drain plug and tighten it to the specified torque.

Cooling system flushing

9 If the antifreeze mixture has become diluted, then in time the cooling system may gradually lose efficiency, as the coolant passages become restricted due to rust, scale deposits, and other sediment. The cooling system efficiency can be restored by flushing the system clean.

10 The radiator should be flushed independently of the engine, to avoid unnecessary contamination.

Radiator flushing

11 To flush the radiator, disconnect the top

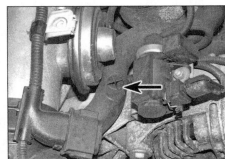

16.4b... the return hose...

16.6 The cylinder block drain plug is located on the right-hand side

16.23 The float indicates the coolant level. Refer to the markings on the top of the expansion tank

and bottom hoses and any other relevant hoses from the radiator, with reference to Chapter 3.

12 Insert a garden hose into the radiator top inlet. Direct a flow of clean water through the radiator, and continue flushing until clean water emerges from the radiator bottom outlet.

13 If after a reasonable period, the water still does not run clear, the radiator can be flushed with a good proprietary cooling system cleaning agent. It is important that their manufacturer's instructions are followed carefully. If the contamination is particularly bad, insert the hose in the radiator bottom outlet, and reverse-flush the radiator.

Engine flushing

14 To flush the engine, remove the thermostat as described in Chapter 3, then temporarily refit the thermostat cover. On models where the thermostat is integral with the housing, remove the housing to allow the water to flow out.

15 With the top and bottom hoses disconnected from the radiator, insert a garden hose into the radiator top hose. Direct a clean flow of water through the engine, and continue flushing until clean water emerges from the radiator bottom hose.

16 On completion of flushing, refit the thermostat and reconnect the hoses with reference to Chapter 3.

Cooling system filling

17 Before attempting to fill the cooling system, make sure that all hoses and clips are in good condition, and that the clips are tight and the radiator and cylinder block drain plugs are securely tightened. Note that an antifreeze mixture must be used all year round, to prevent corrosion of the engine components (see following sub-Section).

18 Slacken the bleed screw(s) **(see illustrations 16.4a, 16.4b and 16.4c)**.

19 Turn on the ignition, and set the heater control to maximum temperature, with the fan speed set to 'low'. This opens the heating valves.

20 Remove the expansion tank filler cap. Fill the system by slowly pouring the coolant into the expansion tank to prevent airlocks from forming.

21 If the coolant is being renewed, begin by pouring in a couple of litres of water, followed by the correct quantity of antifreeze, then top-up with more water.

22 As soon as coolant free from air bubbles emerges from the bleed screw(s), tighten the screw(s) securely.

23 Once the level in the expansion tank starts to rise, squeeze the radiator top and bottom hoses to help expel any trapped air in the system. Once all the air is expelled, top-up the coolant level until the float in the expansion tank rises to indicate the maximum level, then refit the expansion tank cap **(see illustration)**.

24 Start the engine and run it until it reaches normal operating temperature, then stop the engine and allow it to cool.

25 Check for leaks, particularly around disturbed components. Check the coolant level in the expansion tank, and top-up if necessary. Note that the system must be cold before an accurate level is indicated in the expansion tank. If the expansion tank cap is removed while the engine is still warm, cover the cap with a thick cloth, and unscrew the cap slowly to gradually relieve the system pressure (a hissing sound will normally be heard). Wait until any pressure remaining in the system is released, then continue to turn the cap until it can be removed.

Antifreeze mixture

26 Always use an ethylene-glycol based antifreeze which is suitable for use in mixed-metal cooling systems. The quantity of antifreeze and levels of protection are indicated in the Specifications.

27 Before adding antifreeze, the cooling system should be completely drained, preferably flushed, and all hoses checked for condition and security.

28 After filling with antifreeze, a label should be attached to the expansion tank, stating the type and concentration of antifreeze used, and the date installed. Any subsequent topping-up should be made with the same type and concentration of antifreeze.

Caution: Do not use engine antifreeze in the windscreen/tailgate washer system, as it will damage the vehicle paintwork. A screenwash additive should be added to the washer system in the quantities stated on the bottle.

Chapter 2 Part A:
Petrol engine in-car repair procedures

Contents

Degrees of difficulty

Easy, suitable for novice with little experience 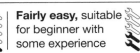	**Fairly easy,** suitable for beginner with some experience	**Fairly difficult,** suitable for competent DIY mechanic	**Difficult,** suitable for experienced DIY mechanic	**Very difficult,** suitable for expert DIY or professional

Specifications

General

Engine code:

2008 to 2011 – 105 kW.	N43 B20AY
2010 to 2012 – 105 kW.	N43 B20UO
2008 to 2012 – 125 kW.	N43 B20A/AA
Capacity	1995 cc
Bore.	84.00 mm
Stroke.	90.00 mm
Direction of engine rotation	Clockwise (viewed from front of vehicle)
No. 1 cylinder location	Timing chain end
Firing order	1-3-4-2
Minimum compression pressure	10.0 bar
Maximum compression difference between cylinders.	2.0 bar
Compression ratio	12.0 : 1

Camshafts

Endfloat	0.065 to 0.150 mm

Lubrication system

Minimum oil pressure:

At idle speed.	1.0 bar
At 2200 to 3500 rpm.	2.2 bar

Torque wrench settings

	Nm	lbf ft
Adjustment unit to camshaft: *		
Stage 1	20	15
Stage 2	Angle-tighten a further 90°	
Stage 3	Angle-tighten a further 90°	
Big-end bearing cap bolts: *................................		
Stage 1	20	15
Stage 2	Angle-tighten a further 120°	
Camshaft bearing cap nuts	10	7
Crankshaft pulley hub/sprocket bolt*......................	300	221
Crankshaft vibration damper/pulley-to-hub bolts	34	25
Cylinder head bolts: *		
M9 bolts:		
Stage 1	30	22
Stage 2	Angle-tighten a further 90°	
Stage 3	Angle-tighten a further 45°	
M10 bolts:		
Stage 1	30	22
Stage 2	Angle-tighten a further 90°	
Stage 3	Angle-tighten a further 90°	
Stage 4	Angle-tighten a further 45°	
To timing cover M9*		
Stage 1	10	7
Stage 2	Angle-tighten a further 90°	
Cylinder head cover bolts:		
M6 bolts	10	7
M7 bolts	15	11
Engine mountings:		
Mounting to subframe:		
M8	28	21
M10	38	28
Mounting to support arm	56	41
Support arm to engine	38	28
Flywheel/driveplate bolts*.................................	130	96
Front subframe bolts: *		
M12	108	78
M10:		
Stage 1	56	41
Stage 2	Angle-tighten a further 90°	
Lower crankcase-to-cylinder block:		
M8 x 40 mm	40	30
M8 x 26 mm	22	15
M10: *		
Stage 1	20	15
tage 2	Angle-tighten a further 70°	
Oil intake manifold bolts...................................	9	7
Oil level sensor..	9	7
Oil pressure sensor......................................	27	20
Oil pump to cylinder block:		
M8	25	18
M6	10	7
Oil pump cover..	10	7
Oil pump sprocket†	30	22
Oil spray pipe banjo bolt*.................................	10	7
Oil spray nozzle	10	7
Steering column lower universal joint pinch-bolt	21	15
Sump	30	22
Sump oil drain plug	25	18
Suspension turret/tension braces: *		
M8*	34	25
M10 (outer bolts):		
Stage 1	40	30
Stage 2	Angle-tighten a further 60°	
M12 (centre bolt):		
Stage 1	100	74
Stage 2	Angle-tighten a further 100°	
Timing chain cover upper..................................	25	18

Torque wrench settings (continued)

	Nm	lbf ft
Timing chain guide pins:		
M7	15	11
M8	20	15
Timing chain guide-to-cylinder head (M6)	8	6
Timing chain tensioner cover plug...........................	32	24
Timing chain tensioner cylinder/piston.........................	65	48
Thermostat housing	10	7
Vanos solenoid bolts	10	7

*Do not re-use
† Left-handed thread

1 General Information

How to use this Chapter

1 This Part of Chapter 2 describes the repair procedures that can reasonably be carried out on the engine while it remains in the vehicle. If the engine has been removed from the vehicle and is being dismantled as described in Part D, any preliminary dismantling procedures can be ignored.

2 Note that, while it may be physically possible to overhaul items such as the piston/connecting rod assemblies while the engine is in the car, such tasks are not usually carried out as separate operations. Usually, several additional procedures are required (not to mention the cleaning of components and oilways); for this reason, all such tasks are classed as major overhaul procedures, and are described in Part D of this Chapter.

3 Part D describes the removal of the engine/transmission from the car, and the full overhaul procedures that can then be carried out.

Engine description

4 The 4-cylinder petrol engine in this Chapter is of double overhead camshaft 16 valve design, direct petrol injection, mounted in-line, with the transmission bolted to the rear end.

5 On all engines, the timing of both the exhaust and intake valves is variable by means of hydraulic adjustment units on the end of each camshaft – BMW refer to this as a 'Vanos' system. These units vary the relationship of the timing chain and sprockets to the camshafts.

6 The crankshaft is supported in five main bearings of the usual shell-type. Endfloat is controlled by thrust bearing shells on No. 4 main bearing (depending on model). All engines are fitted with contra-rotating crankshaft-driven balancer shafts.

7 The pistons are selected to be of matching weight, and incorporate fully-floating gudgeon pins retained by circlips.

8 The rotor-type oil pump is located at the front of the engine, and is driven directly by the crankshaft.

Operations with engine in car

9 The following operations can be carried out without having to remove the engine from the vehicle:

a) Removal and refitting of the cylinder head.
b) Removal and refitting of the timing chain and sprockets.
c) Removal and refitting of the camshafts.
d) Removal and refitting of the sump.
e) Removal and refitting of the big-end bearings, connecting rods, and pistons*.
f) Removal and refitting of the oil pump.
g) Renewal of the engine/transmission mountings.
h) Removal and refitting of the flywheel/driveplate.

* Although in theory it is possible to remove these components with the engine in place, for reasons of access and cleanliness it is recommended that the engine is removed.

Caution: On models with the automatic stop/start function (MSA), ensure the system is deactivated prior to working on the engine by means of the button on the facia centre panel. Refer to the owners handbook if necessary.

2 Compression test – description and interpretation

1 When engine performance is down, or if misfiring occurs which cannot be attributed to the ignition or fuel systems, a compression test can provide diagnostic clues as to the engine's condition. If the test is performed regularly, it can give warning of trouble before any other symptoms become apparent.

2 The engine must be fully warmed-up to normal operating temperature, the battery must be fully-charged, and all the spark plugs must be removed (Chapter 1A Section 12). The aid of an assistant will also be required.

3 Fit a compression tester to the No. 1 cylinder spark plug hole – the type of tester which screws into the plug thread is to be preferred.

4 Have the assistant fully depress the throttle pedal, and crank the engine on the starter motor. After one or two revolutions, the compression pressure should build-up to a maximum figure, and then stabilise. Record the highest reading obtained.

5 Repeat the test on the remaining cylinders, recording the pressure in each.

6 All cylinders should produce very similar pressures; a difference of more than 2 bars between any two cylinders indicates a fault. Note that the compression should build-up quickly in a healthy engine; low compression on the first stroke, followed by gradually-increasing pressure on successive strokes, indicates worn piston rings. A low compression reading on the first stroke, which does not build-up during successive strokes, indicates leaking valves or a blown head gasket (a cracked head could also be the cause). Deposits on the undersides of the valve heads can also cause low compression.

7 BMW-recommended values for compression pressures are given in the Specifications.

8 If the pressure in any cylinder is low, carry out the following test to isolate the cause. Introduce a teaspoonful of clean oil into that cylinder through its spark plug hole, and repeat the test.

9 If the addition of oil temporarily improves the compression pressure, this indicates that bore or piston wear is responsible for the pressure loss. No improvement suggests that leaking or burnt valves, or a blown head gasket, may be to blame.

10 A low reading from two adjacent cylinders is almost certainly due to the head gasket having blown between them; the presence of coolant in the engine oil will confirm this.

11 If one cylinder is about 20 percent lower than the others and the engine has a slightly rough idle, a worn camshaft lobe could be the cause.

12 If the compression reading is unusually high, the combustion chambers are probably coated with carbon deposits. If this is the case, the cylinder head should be removed and decarbonised.

13 On completion of the test, refit the spark plugs (Chapter 1A Section 12) and refit the fuse.

3 Top Dead Centre (TDC) for No. 1 piston – locating

Note: To lock the engine in the TDC position, and to check the position of the camshafts, special tools will be required. Some of these tools can be improvised – see text.

1 Top Dead Centre (TDC) is the highest point in the cylinder that each piston reaches as

3.4 The camshaft lobes for No. 1 cylinder should be pointing upwards and slightly towards each other

3.5 Undo the banjo bolts and unclip the oil supply pipes

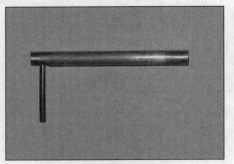

3.6 Pull out the blanking plug from beneath the starter motor (removed for clarity)

3.7 Crankshaft locking tool

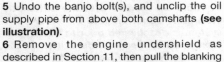

3.8 Insert the locking tool

it travels up and down when the crankshaft turns. Each piston reaches TDC at the end of the compression stroke and again at the end of the exhaust stroke, but TDC generally refers to piston position on the compression stroke. No. 1 piston is at the timing chain end of the engine.

2 Positioning No. 1 piston at TDC is an essential part of many procedures, such as timing chain removal and camshaft removal.

3 Remove the cylinder head cover as described in Section 4.

4 Using a spanner or socket on the crankshaft pulley bolt, turn the crankshaft clockwise until the slots in the rear ends of the camshaft flanges are vertical. In this position, the lobes on No. 1 cylinder intake and exhaust camshafts should be pointing upwards and slightly towards each other (see illustration).

5 Undo the banjo bolt(s), and unclip the oil supply pipe from above both camshafts (see illustration).

6 Remove the engine undershield as described in Section 11, then pull the blanking plug (where fitted) from the timing hole in the left-hand rear corner flange of the cylinder block below the starter motor. Access to the flange is very limited. If necessary, remove the intake manifold (see Chapter 4A Section 11) and access the flange from above (see illustration).

7 To 'lock' the crankshaft in position, a special tool will be required. BMW tool No. 11 5 120 can be used, but an alternative can be made up by using an 8 mm diameter rod, approximately 80 mm in length. In order to be able to extract the rod from the timing hole, we drilled into the rod at one end, and tapped in a roll-pin (see illustration).

8 Insert the rod through the timing hole. If necessary, turn the crankshaft slightly until the rod enters the TDC hole in the flywheel (see illustration). Note: On models equipped with automatic transmission, it is possible to mistakenly insert the rod into a larger hole in the driveplate. Ensure that when the rod is inserted, it is not possible to rotate the crankshaft at all.

9 The crankshaft is now 'locked' in position with No. 1 piston at TDC.

10 Due to the camshaft timing adjustment facility, it is necessary to check that the camshafts are in their 'initial' positions, by attempting to rotate both camshafts in their normal direction of rotation (clockwise viewed from the front of the engine). Use a spanner on the hexagonal section of each camshaft. When the engine stops, both camshafts should be locked in their 'initial' positions automatically. If either camshaft can be rotated, continue turning until it comes to a stop. When the camshaft(s) stop turning, or cannot be turned in the first place, they are in their 'initial' positions, and the adjustment units are locked in place.

11 In this position, it should be possible to fit BMW special tool No. 11 8 691/2/3 over the intake and exhaust camshaft flanges. With the camshaft correctly positioned, the tools should contact the cylinder head upper surface with no air gap below them, or the tool over the intake camshaft is raised by up to 0.5 mm on the intake side, or the exhaust camshaft tool is raised by up to 1.0 mm on the intake side. A home-made alternative can be fabricated using the dimensions given (see illustrations).

12 Do not attempt to turn the engine with the flywheel or camshaft locked in position, as engine damage may result. If the engine is to be left in the 'locked' state for a long period of time, it is a good idea to place suitable warning notices inside the vehicle, and in the engine compartment. This will reduce the possibility of the engine being cranked on the starter motor.

3.11a Fit BMW tool No. 11 8 691/2/3 over the square ends of the camshafts

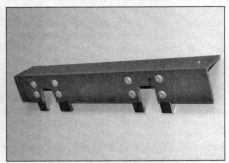

3.11b It is possible to fabricate and alternative to the BMW tool, using 3.0 mm thick angle iron...

Not to scale

All dimensions in mm

H48327

3.11c... to the dimensions shown

3.11d Home-made tool fitted

4 Cylinder head cover – removal and refitting

Removal

1 Remove the ignition coils as described in Chapter 5B Section 3.
2 Remove the high-pressure fuel pump and fuel injectors as described in Chapter 4A.

3 Squeeze together the sides of the collar and disconnect the breather hose from the cylinder head cover **(see illustration)**.
4 Unclip the injector/ignition coil wiring loom guide from the cylinder head cover, and undo the nuts securing the earth connections **(see illustrations)**.
5 Undo the bolts around the edge of the cover, and the 7 bolts in the centre **(see illustrations)**. Lift the cover off. Note that some of the spark plug tubes may come out

with the cover. Remove the remaining ones by pulling them from place.

Refitting

6 Renew the cover gasket/seal if it shows any signs of damage or deterioration **(see illustration)**.
7 Ensure the cylinder head surface is clean and free from debris. Fit the cover and tighten the bolts evenly and gradually to the specified torque.

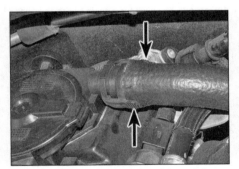

4.3 Squeeze together the sides of the collar

4.4a Release the clips securing the injector/coil wiring loom and guide to the cylinder head cover

4.4b Undo the earth connections (front connection arrowed)

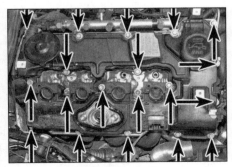

4.5a Undo the bolts...

4.5b... and remove the cylinder head cover

4.5c Pull any remaining spark plug tubes from the cylinder head

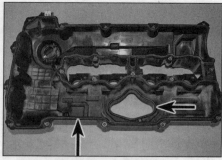

4.6 Renew the main cylinder head cover seal, and the seal around the fuel pump location

8 Push the spark plug tubes into place, aligning the square hole at the top of the tube aligns with the lug on the cylinder head cover **(see illustration)**. Use screwdriver on the upper edge of the tube, and push them fully home using a sharp blow with your hand. The remainder of refitting is a reversal of removal.

5 Crankshaft vibration damper/pulley and pulley hub – removal and refitting

Note: If the pulley hub is removed, a new securing bolt will be required on refitting, and a torque wrench capable of providing 300 Nm (221 lbf ft) of torque will be required.

Removal

1 Remove the alternator drivebelt as described in Chapter 1A Section 14.

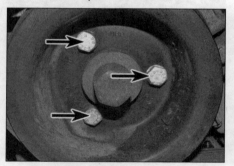

5.2 Vibration damper/pulley bolts

5.4b... and a commercially available tool

4.8 Align the square hole in the spark plug tube with the lug in the cylinder head cover

2 Unscrew the securing bolts, and remove the vibration damper/pulley from the hub. If necessary, counterhold the hub using a socket or spanner on the hub securing bolt **(see illustration)**.
3 To remove the hub, the securing bolt must be unscrewed.

⚠ *Warning: If the crankshaft pulley securing bolt is slackened, the timing chain/oil pump/balancer shaft sprockets will no longer be locked to the crankshaft and can rotate independently. Consequently, once the hub bolt is slackened, lock the crankshaft and camshafts in position as described in Section 3.*

⚠ *Warning: The crankshaft pulley hub securing bolt is very tight. A tool will be required to counterhold the hub as the bolt*

5.4a Holding the crankshaft hub stationary using a home-made tool...

6.8 Vanos solenoids retaining bolts

is unscrewed. A special tool (No. 11 8 180) is available from BMW. Do not attempt the job using inferior or poorly-improvised tools, as injury or damage may result.
4 Make up a tool to hold the pulley hub. A suitable tool can be fabricated using two lengths of steel bar, joined by a large pivot bolt. Bolt the holding tool to the pulley hub using the pulley-to-hub bolts. If using the BMW tool, insert the tool through the hole in the base of the gearbox bell housing. An alternative tool may be available that bolts to the hub **(see illustrations)**.
5 Using a socket and a long swing-bar, loosen the pulley hub bolt. Note that the bolt is very tight. We recommend the help of an assistant
6 With the bolt removed, slide the hub from the end of the crankshaft and detach it from the chains. Discard the bolt, a new one must be fitted. It is advisable to take the opportunity to renew the oil seal in the lower timing chain cover, with reference to Section 15.

Refitting

7 Refitting is a reversal of removal, remembering to tighten all fasteners to the specified torque where given.

6 Timing chain – removal, inspection and refitting

Removal

1 Remove the air filter housing with the mass airflow sensor as described in Chapter 4A.
2 Ensure the engine is set to TDC as described in Section 3.
3 Remove the crankshaft vibration damper/pulley and hub as described in Section 5. **Note:** *Once the hub bolt is slackened, the crankshaft is no longer locked to the timing chain/oil pump/balancer shaft sprocket. Do not rotate the camshafts or crankshaft once the bolt is slackened.*
4 Jack up the front of the vehicle, and support it securely on axle stands (see *Jacking and vehicle support*).
5 Using an engine support beam located on the inner wings, or an engine hoist, attach lifting chains to the lifting eye at the front of the engine, and take the weight of the engine.
6 Lower the front subframe as described in Section 12. Note there is no need to detach the steering rack from the subframe, undo the steering column universal joint pinch-bolt and separate the pinion from the column.
7 Remove the sump as described in Section 10.
8 Disconnect the wiring plug, undo the retaining bolts and pull both Vanos solenoids from the timing cover **(see illustration)**. Discard the O-ring seals – new ones must be fitted.
9 With the camshafts locked in place as described in Section 3, slacken the exhaust

6.9 Undo the camshaft adjustment bolts

6.10 Undo the chain tensioner

6.11 Note that the camshaft adjusting units are marked EX or IN

6.12 Unscrew the cover plug and undo the timing chain guide lower pin

6.13a Undo the cover plug...

6.13b... then unscrew the timing chain upper guide pin

and intake camshaft adjustment unit bolts **(see illustration)**.

10 Working on the front right-hand side of the engine block, undo the chain tensioner **(see illustration)**. Be prepared for oil spillage. Discard the sealing washer, a new one must be fitted. If the piston is to be re-used, holding it vertical slowly compress the piston to evacuate all the oil.

11 Completely unscrew the exhaust camshaft adjustment unit bolt, and remove the unit complete with the camshaft sensor ring and sprocket. Repeat this procedure for the intake camshaft. Note that the units are marked EX and IN. Do not mix up the parts **(see illustration)**. Note that new bolts are required.

12 Using an Allen key, remove the plug to the right and above the front crankshaft oil seal, and unscrew the timing chain guide lower pin **(see illustration)**.

13 Undo the cover plug and remove the timing chain guide upper pin **(see illustrations)**. Renew the plug seal. **Note:** *On some engines, it may be necessary to remove the engine lifting bracket to access the plug.*

14 Remove the chain guide upper bolts from the cylinder head **(see illustration)**.

15 Pull up on the timing chain, and remove it along with the guides and crankshaft sprocket.

16 Pull the chain down from the guides and manoeuvre the crankshaft sprocket from the chain.

17 Carefully prise apart the lower edges of the timing chain guide, and pull the chain free **(see illustration)**.

Inspection

18 The chain should be renewed if the sprockets are worn or if the chain is worn (indicated by excessive lateral play between the links, and excessive noise in operation). It is wise to renew the chain in any case if the engine is dismantled for overhaul. Note that the rollers on a very badly worn chain may be slightly grooved. To avoid future problems, if there is any doubt at all about the condition of the chain, renew it.

19 Examine the teeth on the sprockets for wear. Each tooth forms an inverted V. If worn, the side of each tooth under tension will be slightly concave in shape when compared with the other side of the tooth (ie, the teeth will have a hooked appearance). If the teeth appear worn, the sprockets must be renewed. Also check the chain guide and tensioner rail contact

6.14 Remove the chain guide upper bolts

surfaces for wear, and renew any worn components as necessary.

Refitting

20 Carefully prise apart the lower edges of the timing chain guide, and feed the chain through **(see illustration 6.17)**.

21 Position the crankshaft sprocket in the lower loop of the chain. Note that the collar on the sprocket must face towards the crankshaft **(see illustration)**.

22 Pull the timing chain up through the guide, until the lower edge of the guide traps the sprocket in position. Keep the chain/guide/sprocket in this position.

23 Undo the bolts and remove the oil intake manifold from the base of the balancer shaft assembly. Renew the suction tube O-ring seal.

24 Rotate the balance shafts until BMW

6.17 Prise apart the lower edges, and remove the chain from the guide (using welding rods)

6.21 Position the crankshaft sprocket in the chain, with the sprocket collar towards the crankshaft

tool No. 11 8 700 can be inserted across the flats at the flywheel end of the shafts **(see illustration)**. Alternatively, obtain a tool from an automotive tool specialist.

25 Lower the assembly down through the timing chain tunnel, and install the sprocket over the end of the crankshaft.

26 Install the lower timing chain guide pin though the hole in the front of the timing cover, and tighten it to the specified torque. Using a new sealing ring, refit the cover plug and tighten it to the specified torque.

27 Install the upper timing chain guide pin through the hole in the timing cover, and tighten it securely. Using a new sealing ring, refit the cover plug and tighten it to the specified torque.

28 Refit the crankshaft pulley hub, only finger-tighten the bolt at this stage.

29 Ensure that the crankshaft locking tool is still in place, and tighten the crankshaft hub bolt to 60 Nm (44 lbf ft) only. If more torque is applied to the bolt, damage may occur to the tool and/or the engine block.

30 Remove the special tool aligning the balancer shafts in place.

31 Refit both intake and exhaust camshaft adjuster unit solenoids to the front of the cylinder head using new O-ring seals. Tighten the retaining bolts securely, and reconnect the wiring plugs

32 Refit the timing chain upper guide retaining bolt(s), and tighten them securely. Renew the sealing ring of the lower bolt cover plug, refit and tighten it to the specified torque.

6.24 Insert the special tool across the flats of the balancer shafts

33 Lift the timing chain and hold it under tension. Engage the intake camshaft adjustment unit with the chain, and position it on the end of the camshaft complete with the sensor ring. Retain the unit/ring with a new bolt, screwing it in sufficiently to eliminate any free play, but no tighter. Repeat the procedure on the exhaust camshaft adjustment unit. Note that although the adjustment units are marked IN and EX, the sensor rings are identical.

34 Ensure that the timing chain rests correctly against the tensioner blade. Install BMW tool No. 11 9 340 into the tensioner piston hole, then turn the adjuster screw on the tool until the end of the screw just touches the tensioner rail without tensioning the chain **(see illustration)**.

35 Fit BMW tool No. 11 8 711 to the end of the cylinder head, ensuring that the locating pins of the tool engage correctly with the corresponding holes in the sensor rings **(see illustrations)**. Screw the tool to the cylinder head using the two bolts supplied.

36 Using a suitable socket, slacken the bolts securing the adjustment units/sensor rings to the camshafts half a turn, then retighten them until they just touch the sensor ring surface without any play.

37 Pretension the chain tensioner guide by screwing in the tool adjusting screw with a torque wrench to a value of 0.6 Nm (0.4 lbf ft). If no suitable torque wrench is available, turn in the adjusting screw by hand just enough to eliminate all free play in the chain.

38 Tighten both camshaft adjustment units retaining bolts to the specified torque.

6.34 Fit tool No. 11 9 340 into the tensioner hole

39 Undo the retaining bolts and remove tool No. 11 8 711 from the end of the cylinder head.

40 Slacken the adjusting screw, and remove tool No. 11 9 340 from the tensioner piston aperture.

41 Ensure the timing chain tensioner piston has been drained completely, then refit it to the aperture in the engine block with a new sealing ring. Tighten it to the specified torque.

42 Remove the crankshaft and camshafts locking tools, and using spanner or socket on the crankshaft pulley hub bolt, rotate the crankshaft 720° clockwise and check that the camshaft and crankshaft locking tools can be refitted. Note that it is permissible to have a gap of up to 1.0 mm (exhaust camshaft tool) or 0.5 mm (intake camshaft tool) between the intake manifold sides of the camshaft locking tools and the cylinder head upper gasket face **(see illustration)**.

43 With the timing correct, remove the locking tools, and tighten the crankshaft pulley hub bolt to the specified torque, counterholding it using the method employed during removal.

44 The remainder of refitting is a reversal of removal.

7 Timing chain sprockets and tensioner – removal and refitting

Timing chain sprockets

1 The procedure is described as part of the timing chain removal procedure in Section 6.

6.35a Fit tool No. 11 8 711 to the end of the cylinder head

6.35b Ensure the pins of the tool engage correctly with the holes in the sensor rings

6.42 The exhaust camshaft timing is correct if the gap is less than 1.0 mm

Timing chain tensioner

2 The timing chain tensioner is a hydraulically-operated piston that acts upon the right-hand chain tensioner guide. Working of the right-hand front side of the cylinder block, unscrew the piston **(see illustration 6.10)**. Be prepared for fluid spillage. Discard the sealing ring, a new one must be fitted.

3 If the piston is to be refitted, hold the assembly vertically, with the hexagonal head in the palm of your hand, and slowly compress the piston against a hard, flat surface to evacuate any oil. Repeat this procedure.

4 With a new sealing ring, refit the piston and tighten it to the specified torque.

8 Camshafts and followers – removal and refitting

Intake or exhaust camshaft

Removal

1 Set the engine in the TDC on No. 1 cylinder position, as described in Section 3.

2 With the camshafts locked in place as described in Section 3, slacken the exhaust and intake camshaft adjustment unit bolts **(see illustration 6.9)**.

3 Working on the front right-hand side of the engine block, undo the chain tensioner piston **(see illustration 6.10)**. Be prepared for oil spillage. Discard the sealing washer, a new one must be fitted. If the piston is to be re-used, holding it vertical slowly compress the piston to evacuate all the oil.

4 Completely unscrew the exhaust camshaft adjustment unit bolt, and remove the unit complete with the camshaft sensor ring and sprocket. Repeat this procedure for the intake camshaft. Note that the units are marked EX and IN. Do not mix up the parts **(see illustration)**. Ensure that tension is kept on the chain – tie the chain up or support it using wire to prevent it from dropping into the timing chain cover.

5 Undo the banjo bolts and unclip the oil spray pipes above the camshafts **(see illustration)**.

6 Remove the camshaft locking tools.

7 Undo the timing chain guide upper bolt(s) **(see illustration 6.14)**.

8 Undo the 4 nuts and remove the intake/exhaust camshaft bearing cap from the timing chain end of the engine.

9 The remaining camshaft bearing caps are marked 1 to 4, starting at the timing chain end of the engine – A for exhaust, and E for intake. Undo the nuts and remove the oil pipe retaining clips from the camshaft bearing caps at locations E1, E4, A1 and A4 **(see illustration)**.

10 Gradually and evenly, undo the remaining retaining nuts and remove the camshaft bearing caps. Note that they must be refitted to their original positions.

8.4 Unscrew the bolt and remove the exhaust camshaft adjustment unit

11 Lift the camshafts from the cylinder head, and store then in a clean, dry location.

12 If required, lift the rocker arms complete with hydraulic adjusters from above the exhaust valves. Separate the rockers from the adjusters. Store them in order, and refit them to their original positions if re-used. The hydraulic adjusters should be stored in containers and immersed in clean engine oil.

Inspection

13 Clean all the components, including the bearing surfaces in the bearing castings and bearing caps. Examine the components carefully for wear and damage. In particular, check the bearing and cam lobe surfaces of the camshaft(s) for scoring and pitting. Examine the surfaces of the cam followers for signs wear or damage. Renew components as necessary.

Refitting

14 Lubricate the camshaft bearing surfaces with clean engine oil.

15 Where removed, refit the rocker arms and hydraulic adjusters to their original locations.

16 Lay the camshafts in position, with the lobes on No. 1 cylinder pointing upwards and slightly inwards **(see illustration 3.4)**.

17 Ensure that the ends of the compression rings at the front end of the camshafts point upwards **(see illustration)**.

18 Lubricate the bearing caps with clean engine oil, and lay the caps in place over the camshaft. Note the markings and orientation of the caps.

19 Fit the oil feed pipe retaining clips to the Nos. 1 and 4 bearing caps, then fit the nuts

8.9 Note the oil spray pipe retaining clips

8.5 Undo the banjo bolt and unclip the oil spray pipes

and tighten the nuts gradually and evenly until the underside of the caps touches the cylinder head.

20 Working from the inside out, tighten the nuts half-a-turn at a time, until the specified torque is obtained.

21 Refit the intake/exhaust camshaft bearing cap at the timing chain end of the engine, and tighten the nuts to the specified torque.

22 Refit the oil spray pipe to the clips, and tighten the banjo bolt securely.

23 Refit the timing chain guide upper bolt and tighten it to the specified torque.

24 The remainder of refitting is a reversal of removal.

9 Cylinder head – removal and refitting

Note: *New cylinder head bolts and a new cylinder head gasket will be required on refitting.*

Removal

1 Drain the cooling system and cylinder block as described in Chapter 1A Section 16, and disconnect the battery negative lead as described in Chapter 5A Section 4.

2 Set the engine in the TDC on No. 1 cylinder position, as described in Section 3.

3 With the camshafts locked in place as described in Section 3, slacken the exhaust and intake camshaft adjustment unit bolts **(see illustration 6.9)**.

4 Working on the front right-hand side of

8.17 The ends of the rings must be at the top

9.8 Squeeze together the sides of the collar and disconnect the hose from the vacuum pump

the engine block, undo the chain tensioner piston **(see illustration 6.10)**. Be prepared for oil spillage. Discard the sealing washer, a new one must be fitted. If the piston is to be re-used, hold it vertical and slowly compress the piston to evacuate all the oil.

5 Completely unscrew the exhaust camshaft adjustment unit bolt, and remove the unit complete with the camshaft sensor ring and sprocket **(see illustration 8.4)**. Repeat this procedure for the intake camshaft. Note that the units are marked EX and IN. Do not mix up the parts **(see illustration 6.11)**. Ensure that tension is kept on the chain – tie the chain up or support it using wire to prevent it from dropping into the timing chain cover.

6 Remove the intake and exhaust manifolds, as described in Chapter 4A Section 11. Note that it may be possible to detach the exhaust manifold from the cylinder head and lay it to one side without completely removing it. This depends to great extent on whether or not the manifold mounting studs come out the cylinder head as the retaining nuts are removed.

7 Undo the bolts and remove the Vanos solenoids from the front face of the cylinder head. Renew the O-ring seals.

8 Disconnect the vacuum hose from the pump at the rear of the cylinder head **(see illustration)**.

9 Disconnect all electrical connections and coolant hoses to the cylinder head, taking note of their fitted locations and harness routing. Note the earth connection on the right-hand side of the cylinder head.

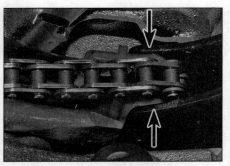

9.11 Carefully spread apart the edge of the chain guide

10 Undo the plug then unscrew and remove the upper timing chain guide pin from the left-hand, front face of the cylinder head **(see illustration 6.13a and 6.13b)**. If necessary, undo the bolts and remove the engine lifting bracket. Renew the plug seal.

11 Remove the upper timing chain guide bolts **(see illustration 6.14)**, carefully spread apart the top of the left-hand chain guide, and release the lower part of the upper guide. Remove the upper timing chain guide **(see illustration)**.

12 Remove the camshaft locking tools.

13 Undo the two bolts in the timing chain tunnel securing the cylinder head to the cylinder block.

14 Working from the outside inwards, in the reverse of the sequence shown in illustration 9.28, evenly and gradually unscrew the cylinder head bolts. Bolts in positions 7 to 10 have an M9 thread with an E10 head, whilst bolts 1 to 6 have an M10 thread with an E12 head. Note that the bolt in position 8 is shorter than all others.

15 Release the cylinder head from the cylinder block and locating dowels by rocking it. Do not prise between the mating faces of the cylinder head and block, as this may damage the gasket faces.

16 Ideally, two assistants will now be required to help remove the cylinder head. Have one assistant hold the timing chain up, clear of the cylinder head, making sure that tension is kept on the chain. With the aid of another assistant, lift the cylinder head from the block – take care, as the cylinder head is heavy. Support

the timing chain from the cylinder block using wire.

17 Recover the cylinder head gasket. Note that the bolts securing the bearing bridge adjacent to the vacuum pump location must not be slackened.

Inspection

18 The mating faces of the cylinder head and block must be perfectly clean before refitting the head. Use a scraper to remove all traces of gasket and carbon, and also clean the tops of the pistons. Take particular care with the aluminium cylinder head, as the soft metal is easily damaged. Also make sure that debris is not allowed to enter the oil and water passages. Using adhesive tape and paper, seal the water, oil and bolt holes in the cylinder block. To prevent carbon entering the gap between the pistons and bores, smear a little grease in the gap. After cleaning each piston, rotate the crankshaft so that the piston moves down the bore, then wipe out the grease and carbon with a cloth rag.

19 Check the block and head for nicks, deep scratches and other damage. If very slight, they may be removed from the cylinder block carefully with a file. More serious damage may be repaired by machining, but this is a specialist job.

20 If warpage of the cylinder head is suspected, use a straight-edge to check it for distortion, with reference to Chapter 2D Section 7.

21 Clean out the bolt holes in the block using a pipe cleaner or thin rag and a screwdriver. Make sure that all oil and water is removed, otherwise there is a possibility of the block being cracked by hydraulic pressure when the bolts are tightened.

22 Examine the bolt threads and the threads in the cylinder block for damage. If necessary, use the correct size tap to chase out the threads in the block.

23 At the front edge of the cylinder block are located the intake and exhaust camshaft oil supply non-return valves and rubber spacers. If the valves are heavily fouled or contaminated, prise the spacers and valves out and renew them (use a small magnet to extract the valve sleeves). Note that when correctly fitted, the top of the spacers should be slightly proud of the cylinder block gasket surface **(see illustrations)**.

Refitting

24 Ensure that the mating faces of the cylinder block, timing chain housing, and head are spotlessly clean, that the cylinder head bolt threads are clean and dry, and that they screw in and out of their locations.

25 Check that the cylinder head locating dowels are correctly positioned in the cylinder block.

 Warning: To avoid any possibility of piston-to-valve contact when refitting the cylinder head, it is necessary to ensure that none of

9.23a Oil supply non-return valves

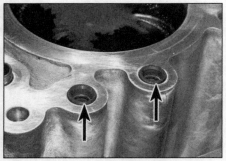

9.23b The oil non-return valve seals should be slightly proud of the gasket surface

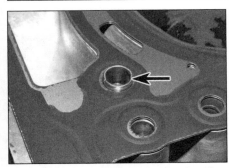

9.26 Fit the new gasket over the dowels

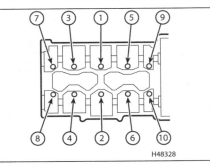

9.28 Cylinder head bolt tightening sequence

9.34 Press the upper guide into the locating holes in the lower guide

the pistons are at TDC. Before proceeding further, if not already done, turn the crankshaft to position No. 1 piston at TDC (check that the locking rod can be engaged with the flywheel, then remove the locking rod and turn the crankshaft approximately 45° anti-clockwise using a spanner or socket on the crankshaft pulley hub bolt.

26 Fit a new cylinder head gasket to the block, locating it over the dowels (see illustration). Make sure that it is the correct way up. Note that 0.3 mm thicker-than-standard gaskets are available for use if the cylinder head has been machined (see Chapter 2D Section 7).

27 With the new gasket in place, lower the cylinder head into position.

28 Apply a thin coat of clean engine oil to the new cylinder bolt threads and washer contact area, then insert the bolts and washers into their correct locations. Note that bolts in positions 1 to 6 have M10 thread and an E12 Torx head, whilst the bolts in positions 7 to 10 have an M9 thread with E10 Torx heads. The bolt in position 8 is shorter than the others. Tighten the bolts in the order shown (see illustration), and in the stages given in the Specifications – ie, tighten all bolts in sequence to the Stage 1 torque, then tighten all bolts in sequence to the Stage 2 torque, and so on.

29 Insert the two bolts in the timing chain tunnel at the front of the cylinder head, and tighten them to the specified torque.

30 Align the left-hand chain guide, and insert the upper retaining pin. Tighten the pin securely. Refit the cover plug with a new seal, and tighten it to the specified torque.

31 Refit the camshaft locking tools – see Section 3.

32 Rotate the crankshaft back to TDC, and refit the crankshaft locking tool.

33 With new O-ring seals, refit the camshaft adjustment solenoids to the front of the engine. Pulling the timing chain up and apart, insert the solenoids though the chain. Refit the solenoid retaining brackets, and tighten the bolts securely. Reconnect the solenoid wiring plugs.

34 Pull up the timing chain, and refit the upper chain guide. Carefully prise apart the top of the left-hand guide and press the upper guide to engage correctly with the locating holes (see illustration).

35 Refit the upper timing chain guide upper retaining bolts, and only finger-tighten it at this stage.

36 Where applicable, refit the upper timing chain guide lower bolt, and tighten both the chain guide upper and lower bolts securely. Refit the bolt cover plug to the casing and tighten it to the specified torque.

37 Refit the timing chain, sprockets and camshaft adjustment units as described in Section 6.

38 The remainder of refitting is a reversal of removal.

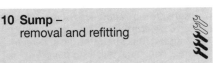

10 Sump – removal and refitting

Removal

1 Drain the engine oil (see Chapter 1A Section 6).

2 Remove the air cleaner housing as described in Chapter 4A Section 2.

3 Lower the front subframe as described in Section 12.

4 On models with an oil level dipstick, unclip any hoses from the dipstick guide tube ad support bracket. Unscrew the support bracket mounting bolt, and using a clockwise twisting motion, pull the guide tube from the sump. Inspect the O-ring seal and renew if necessary.

5 Disconnect the oil level sensor wiring plug.

6 Disconnect the wiring plug/loom from the suspension height sensor (where applicable).

10.10 Fit a new sump gasket

7 Undo the sump retaining bolts. Lower the sump, and manipulate it out towards the rear of the vehicle. If necessary, lower the subframe further, using the jack, to give sufficient clearance. Similarly, if necessary, unbolt the oil pick-up pipe to ease sump removal.

8 Recover the sump gasket, and discard it.

Refitting

9 Commence refitting by thoroughly cleaning the mating faces of the sump and cylinder block.

10 Position a new gasket on the sump (see illustration).

11 Refit the sump, insert the retaining bolts and tighten them to the specified torque.

12 The remainder of refitting is a reversal of removal, noting the following points:
a) Tighten all fasteners to the specified torque where given.
b) Refill the engine with oil as described in Chapter 1A Section 6.

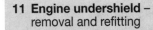

11 Engine undershield – removal and refitting

Removal

1 Apply the handbrake, then jack up the front of the vehicle and support securely on axle stands (see *Jacking and vehicle support*).

2 Undo the various bolts (see illustration).

3 Pull the undershield forwards, over the front bumper, then pull the rear edge of the

11.2 Engine undershield fasteners

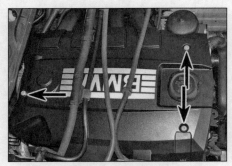

12.2 Acoustic cover retaining bolts

12.6 Steering column lower universal joint pinch-bolt

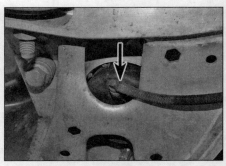

12.8 Disconnect the vacuum hose from the underside of the engine mountings

undershield downwards, slide it to the rear and remove it.

Refitting

4 Check the condition of the nuts that the undershield bolts fit into, and renew as necessary.
5 Slide the front edge over the bumper, then lift the rear edge, and slide it back into position.
6 Tighten the bolts securely.
7 Lower the vehicle to the ground.

12 Front subframe – lowering, removal and refitting

Lowering

1 The front subframe must be lowered in order to carry out various procedures, including sump removal. Begin by removing the engine undershield as described in the previous Section.
2 Undo the bolts and remove the acoustic cover from the top of the engine **(see illustration)**.
3 Position a hoist and lifting tackle over the engine compartment, and connect the lifting tackle to the front engine lifting bracket.
4 Unscrew the nuts securing the left- and right-hand engine support brackets to the engine mountings on the subframe.
5 Fully extend the steering column and move the steering wheel to the highest position.
6 Undo the steering column lower universal joint pinch-bolt and slide the shaft upwards

from the steering rack **(see illustration)**. Note that a new bolt will be required.
7 Disconnect the wiring plug from the front ride height sensor (where applicable).
8 Disconnect the vacuum hose from the engine mountings **(see illustration)**.
9 On models with EPS (Electric Power Steering), cut through the cable-tie securing the wiring loom to the subframe.
10 Support the centre of the subframe, using a jack and a block of wood.
11 Unscrew the subframe securing bolts, then lower the subframe a maximum of 10 cm using the jack **(see illustrations)**.
Caution: Do not allow the power steering hoses to be stretched.
12 Refitting the subframe is a reversal of lowering, noting the following points.
a) *Tighten the subframe front mounting bolts first, followed by the middle ones, then the rear ones.*
b) *Use new subframe bolts.*
c) *Tighten all fasteners to the specified torque where given.*
d) *On models with AFS (Active Front Steering) it may be necessary to carry out the steering angle adjustment procedure after refitting the subframe. As this task requires BMW diagnostic equipment, entrust this task to a BMW dealer or suitably-equipped specialist.*

Removal

Note: *After refitting the front subframe, it is essential that the alignment of the wheels is checked by a BMW dealer or suitably-equipped specialist.*

13 Proceed as described in Paragraphs 1 to 11 in this Section.
14 Remove the front anti-roll bar as described in Chapter 10 Section 7.
15 Disconnect the control arms and tension struts from the front subframe as described in Chapter 10 Section 5.
16 Undo the nuts and detach the steering track rod ends from the hub carriers as described in Chapter 10 Section 25.
17 Note their fitted positions and release any hoses/wiring looms from the front subframe.
18 Slacken the steering rack mounting bolts.
19 Support the centre of the subframe, using a jack and a block of wood.
20 Remove the mounting bolts, and lower the subframe a little **(see illustrations 12.11a and 12.11b)**.
21 Completely remove the mounting bolts, and secure the steering rack in place using string/cable, etc.
22 With the help of an assistant, carefully lower the subframe to the ground.

Refitting

23 Refitting the subframe is a reversal of lowering, noting the following points.
a) *Tighten the subframe front mounting bolts first, followed by the middle ones, then the rear ones.*
b) *Use new subframe bolts.*
c) *Tighten all fasteners to the specified torque where given.*
d) *On models with AFS (Active Front Steering) it may be necessary to carry out the steering angle adjustment procedure after refitting the subframe. As this task requires BMW diagnostic equipment, entrust this task to a BMW dealer or suitably-equipped specialist.*
e) *Have the wheel alignment checked by a BMW dealer or specialist as soon as possible.*

13 Balancer shafts – information

1 These engines are equipped with balancer shafts to smooth out any engine vibration. These contra-rotating shafts are driven be a chain from the crankshaft sprocket, and are integral with the oil pump. For details

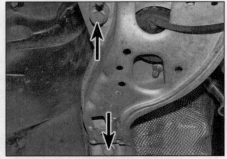

12.11a Front subframe rear, middle...

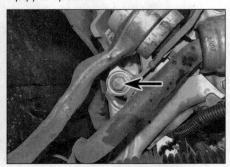

12.11b... and front mounting bolts

14.2 Undo the bolts and remove the oil pump pick-up tube

of the balancer shaft removal and refitting procedure, refer to the Section regarding oil pump removal.

14 Oil pump – removal, inspection and refitting

Removal

1 The oil pump is integral with the balancer shaft housing. The two must not be separated or dismantled. Remove the sump as described in Section 10.
2 Unscrew the retaining bolts, rotate the oil pick-up tube out of the oil pump, and pull it downwards **(see illustration)**. Discard the O-ring seal, a new one must be fitted.
3 Using a socket on the crankshaft pulley bolt, rotate the crankshaft to TDC (see Section 3), and lock it in place with the crankshaft locking tool.
4 Undo the oil pump sprocket retaining nut. **Note:** *This nut has a left-hand thread.*
5 Push the oil pump chain tensioner away from the chain, and lock it in place with a length of rod inserted through the hole in the guide **(see illustration)**.
6 Undo the bolts securing the chain lower guide to the oil pump/balancer shaft housing **(see illustration)**.
7 Using a length of wire or rod, pull the sprocket from the oil pump shaft, and disengage it from the shaft splines **(see illustration)**.
8 Have an assistant support the housing, undo the bolts, and pull the housing down slightly at the rear, then manoeuvre backwards from place **(see illustration)**. Ease the chain tensioner guide from its locating pin as the assembly is removed. No dismantling of the assembly is recommended.
9 In order to renew the oil pump drive chain, remove the timing chain as described in Section 6, Unscrew the cover plug to the right of the crankshaft, and undo the bolt securing the upper section of the oil pump drive chain tensioner/guide **(see illustration)**.
10 Slide the chain tensioner/guide down from its location and lift the chain from its location. Note that the tensioner can only be removed from the guide once the assembly has been removed.

Refitting

11 Where removed, refit the oil pump drive chain to the crankshaft, and the timing chain (see Section 6).
12 Slide the chain guide/tensioner into place and finger-tighten the retaining bolt at this stage.
13 Check that the locating dowels are still in place, and insert the balancer shaft/oil pump housing shaft into the chain sprocket, and manoeuvre it onto the locating dowels. Oil the threads and insert the new retaining bolts. Tighten the bolts to the specified torque.
14 Using a length of wire or rod, pull the sprocket away from the pump and off from the shaft splines **(see illustration 14.7)**.
15 Rotate the balance shafts until BMW tool No. 11 8 700 can be inserted across the flats at the flywheel end of the shafts **(see illustration 6.24)**.
16 Check that the crankshaft is still locked in the TDC position (see Section 3), and push

14.7 Use a length of wire to pull the sprocket from the splines

14.9 Undo the cover plug and unscrew the guide bolt

14.6 Undo the lower chain guide retaining bolt

the sprocket over the splines on the shaft. Pull out the rod locking the chain tensioner in place and check the balancer shafts still align. If they do not, or the sprocket splines do not align, pull the sprocket from the shaft, and rotate the balancer shafts 360° and try again. In some circumstances, it may take 7 attempts to align the sprocket and shaft.
17 With the shafts aligned and the sprocket over the splines, if not already done so, refit the bolts retaining the tensioner/guide, and tighten them securely. Refit the cover plug to the engine front casing.
18 Refit the sprocket nut, and tighten it to the specified torque. **Note:** *The nut has a left-hand thread.*
19 Refit the oil pump pick-up tube with a new O-ring seal **(see illustration)**. Tighten the retaining bolt(s) securely.
20 Remove the crankshaft locking tool, and refit the sump as described in Section 10.

14.8 Oil pump/balancer shaft housing Torx socket head bolts

14.19 Renew the pick-up tube O-ring seal

14.5 Use a length of rod to lock the tensioner blade in place

15.3 Screw the BMW tool into the inner edge of the seal, then tighten the bolt and pull the seal from place – it may take several attempts to fully extract the seal

15.6a Align the two grooves in the edge of the seal with the joint in the engine casing...

15.6b... then drive it into the original depth using a tubular drift

15 Crankshaft oil seals – renewal

Front seal

1 Remove the crankshaft vibration damper/ pulley as described in Section 5. Do not remove the hub.
2 Note the fitted depth of the oil seal in the cover. On the engine we examined, the outer edge of the seal was flush with the front edge of the seal bore in the cylinder block.
3 Due to the extra depth of the seal, we found it essential to remove the seal using using BMW tool No. 11 0 371 to extract the seal **(see illustration)**.
4 Clean the oil seal housing and the hub sealing surface. Apply a little clean engine oil to the surface of the hub.
5 New seals are supplied with a support sleeve to aid fitment. Slide the sleeve with the oil seal fitted, over the hub.
6 Align the two grooves in the outer edge of the seal with the horizontal joint in the engine casing. Carefully drive the seal into the housing until it is at the same depth as the original, using a tubular spacer that bears evenly on the hard, outer edge of the seal **(see illustrations)**.
7 Using the sealing kit available from BMW (comprising of Loctite sealing compound, primer and injector), push the integral brush

into the grooves in the oil seal to coat the surfaces with primer.
8 Use the injector in the kit to fill both grooves with sealing compound **(see illustration)**. Then coat the end of the grooves with primer.
9 Refit the crankshaft vibration damper/pulley as described in Section 5.

Rear seal

10 Remove the flywheel/driveplate as described in Section 16.
11 Measure and note the fitted depth of the oil seal.
12 Drill several small holes in the oil seal, and screw in self-tapping screws. Pull the screws, complete with seal, from the housing.
13 Clean the oil seal housing and the crankshaft sealing surface. Apply a light coat of clean engine oil to the crankshaft sealing surface.
14 New seals are supplied with a support sleeve to aid fitment. Slide the sleeve with the seal fitted, over the crankshaft.
15 Align the two grooves in the outer edge of the seal with the horizontal joint in the engine casing **(see illustration 15.6a)**. Carefully drive the seal into the housing until it is at the same depth as the original, using a tubular spacer that bears evenly on the hard, outer edge of the seal **(see illustration 15.6b)**.
16 Using the sealing kit available from BMW (comprising of Loctite sealing compound, primer and injector), push the integral brush into the grooves in the oil seal to coat the surfaces with primer.

17 Use the injector in the kit to fill both grooves with sealing compound **(see illustration 15.8)**. Then coat the end of the grooves with primer.
18 Refit the flywheel/driveplate as described in Section 16.

16 Flywheel/driveplate – removal, inspection and refitting

Flywheel

Note: *New flywheel retaining bolts must be used on refitting.*

Removal

1 Remove the clutch assembly as described in Chapter 6 Section 2.
2 Prevent the flywheel from turning by locking the ring gear teeth with a similar arrangement to that shown **(see illustration)**. Alternatively, bolt a strap between the flywheel and the cylinder block/crankcase.
3 Slacken and remove the retaining bolts and remove the flywheel, noting its locating dowel. Do not drop it, as it is very heavy. Discard the bolts, they must be renewed whenever they are disturbed.

Inspection

4 If the flywheel-to-clutch mating surface is deeply scored, cracked or otherwise damaged, then the flywheel must be renewed, unless it is possible to have it surface ground. Seek the advice of a BMW dealer or engine reconditioning specialist.
5 If the ring gear is badly worn or has missing teeth, then it must be renewed. This job is best left to a BMW dealer or engine reconditioning specialist.
6 Some of these vehicles are fitted with dual mass flywheels. Whilst BMW do not publish any checking procedures, some clutch and flywheel manufacturers publish information concerning rotational and lateral movement.
7 In order to check the rotational movement, lock the flywheel in place as previously described. Rotate the flywheel secondary element (drive surface) by hand anti-

15.8 Inject sealant into both grooves

16.2 We fabricated a metal hook and bolted it to the engine block flange

clockwise, mark its position in relation to the primary flywheel element (bolted to the crankshaft), then rotate it by hand clockwise and mark its position. Bear in mind, that the free rotational movement is being measured here – do not use excessive force to rotate the secondary element. Mark the limits of the rotational movement in relation to the number of flywheel starter ring gear teeth (see illustrations).

8 The number of starter ring gear teeth travelled by the flywheel secondary element should be noted and compared to the flywheel manufacturer's specification. The permissible travel varies enormously, and differs from one flywheel part number to the next. If in any doubt, consult a BMW dealer or transmission specialist as to whether a new unit is needed.

9 In order to check the lateral movement of the flywheel, attach a length of steel strip to the flywheel secondary element (drive surface), and mount a DTI gauge so that it measures in-line with the edge of the secondary flywheel element (see illustrations). Pull the steel strip away from the flywheel, zero the DTI gauge, then push the strip towards the flywheel and read off the measurement. Again, the permissible amount of lateral movement varies from one flywheel part number to the next. Compare the measurement taken with the manufacturer's specification. If in any doubt, consult a BMW dealer or transmission specialist as to whether a new unit is needed.

Refitting

10 Clean the mating surfaces of the flywheel and crankshaft and remove all traces of locking compound from the crankshaft threaded holes.

11 Fit the flywheel to the crankshaft, engaging it with the crankshaft locating dowel, and fit the new retaining bolts. **Note:** *If the new bolts are not supplied pre-coated with locking compound, apply a few drops prior to fitting the bolts.*

12 Lock the flywheel using the method employed on dismantling then, working in a diagonal sequence, tighten all the retaining bolts to the specified torque setting.

13 Refit the clutch assembly as described in Chapter 6 Section 2.

Driveplate

Note: *New driveplate retaining bolts must be used on refitting.*

Removal

14 Remove the automatic transmission and torque converter as described in Chapter 7B Section 5.

15 Prevent the driveplate from turning by locking the ring gear teeth with a similar arrangement to that shown (see illustration 16.2). Alternatively, bolt a strap between the driveplate and the cylinder block/crankcase.

16 Slacken and remove the retaining bolts and remove the driveplate, noting its locating dowel. Discard the bolts, they must be renewed whenever they are disturbed.

16.7a Turn the flywheel secondary element anti-clockwise and mark the limit of its travel on the starter ring gear teeth...

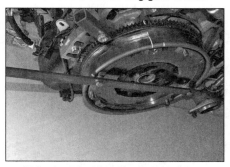
16.9a Attach a length of steel strip to the flywheel secondary element (drive surface)...

17.3 Drive the flywheel pilot bearing out the from the engine side

16.7b... then turn the secondary element clockwise, and mark its travel limit again

16.9b... and mount a DTI gauge in-line with the edge of the secondary element

Inspection

17 If the ring gear is badly worn or has missing teeth, then it must be renewed. This job is best left to a BMW dealer or engine reconditioning specialist.

Refitting

18 Clean the mating surfaces of the driveplate and crankshaft and remove all traces of locking compound from the crankshaft threaded holes.

19 Fit the driveplate to the crankshaft, engaging it with the crankshaft locating dowel, and fit the new retaining bolts. **Note:** *If the new bolts are not supplied pre-coated with locking compound, apply a few drops prior to fitting the bolts.*

20 Lock the driveplate using the method employed on dismantling then, working in a

diagonal sequence, tighten all the retaining bolts to the specified torque setting.

21 Refit the torque converter and automatic transmission as described in Chapter 7B Section 5.

17 Crankshaft pilot bearing – renewal

Inspection

1 The pilot bearing is fitted into the centre of the dual mass flywheel or the end of the crankshaft, and provides support for the free end of the gearbox input shaft on manual transmission vehicles. It can only be examined once the clutch (Chapter 6 Section 2) or flywheel (Section 16) has been removed. Using a finger, rotate the inner race of the bearing and check for any roughness, binding or looseness in the bearing. If any of these conditions are evident, the bearing must be renewed.

Removal

2 Remove the flywheel as described in Section 16.

Flywheel-mounted bearing

3 The bearing must be pressed out using a hydraulic press, with a drift that bears only on the inner bearing race. The bearing is pressed from the engine side of the flywheel and out of the clutch side (see illustration). Note that

17.4 Extract the bearing using a suitable puller

17.5a Position the bearing...

17.5b... then fit it using a tubular spacer or socket

the act of pressing the bearing out will render it unusable – it must be renewed.

Crankshaft-mounted bearing

4 Remove the bearing from the crankshaft using suitable bearing extractor **(see illustration)**.

Refitting

5 Using a suitable tubular spacer that bears only on the hard outer edge of the bearing, press the new bearing into the flywheel/ crankshaft until it contacts the shoulder **(see illustrations)**.
6 Refit the flywheel as described in Section 16.

18 Engine mountings – inspection and renewal

Inspection

1 Two engine mountings are used, one on either side of the engine.
2 If improved access is required, remove the engine undershield as described in Section 11.
3 Check the mounting rubber to see if it is cracked, hardened or separated from the metal at any point. Renew the mounting if any such damage or deterioration is evident.
4 Check that all the mounting fasteners are securely tightened.
5 Using a large screwdriver or a crowbar, check for wear in the mounting by carefully

levering against it to check for free play. Where this is not possible, enlist the aid of an assistant to move the engine/transmission back and forth, or from side to side, while you observe the mounting. While some free play is to be expected, even from new components, excessive wear should be obvious. If excessive free play is found, check first that the fasteners are correctly secured, then renew any worn components as required.

Renewal

6 Support the engine, either using a hoist and lifting tackle connected to the engine lifting brackets (refer to Engine – removal and refitting in Part D of this Chapter), or by positioning a jack and interposed block of wood under the sump. Ensure that the engine is adequately supported before proceeding.
7 Unscrew the nuts securing the left- and right-hand engine support brackets to the mounting rubbers, then unbolt the support brackets from the cylinder block, and remove the mountings. Disconnect any engine earth straps from the mountings (where fitted) **(see illustration)**. If improved access is required, remove the intake manifold as described in Section.
8 Unscrew the nuts securing the mountings to the subframe, then withdraw the mountings. Disconnect the vacuum hoses from the mountings as they are withdrawn (where applicable)
9 Refitting is a reversal of removal. Tighten all fasteners to their specified torque where given.

19 Oil pressure and level sensors – removal and refitting

Oil pressure sensor

1 The oil pressure sensor is located on the left-hand side of the engine block behind the alternator. Remove the alternator as described in Chapter 5A Section 7.
2 Disconnect the wiring plug, and unscrew the sensor from the engine block **(see illustration)**. Be prepared for oil spillage.
3 Refitting is a reversal of removal, using a new sealing washer, and tightening the sensor to the specified torque.

Oil level sensor

4 Drain the engine oil as described in Chapter 1A Section 6.
5 Remove the engine undershield as described in Section 11.
6 Disconnect the wiring plug, undo the three retaining nuts and remove the level sensor **(see illustration)**.
7 Ensure that the sump mating surface is clean.
8 Install the oil level sensor, complete with a new seal, apply a little thread-locking compound and tighten the retaining nuts to the specified torque.
9 Refit the engine undershield, and replenish the engine oil as described in Chapter 1A Section 6.

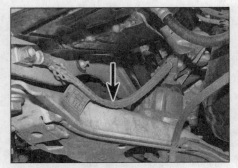

18.7 An earth strap is fitted between the left-hand engine mounting and vehicle body

19.2 Oil pressure warning sensor

19.6 Undo the 3 nuts and remove the oil level sensor

Chapter 2 Part B:
Diesel engine (M57TU2) in-car repair procedures

Contents

Degrees of difficulty

Easy, suitable for novice with little experience	Fairly easy, suitable for beginner with some experience	Fairly difficult, suitable for competent DIY mechanic	Difficult, suitable for experienced DIY mechanic	Very difficult, suitable for expert DIY or professional

Specifications

General

Engine type:

M57T2	Six-cylinder in-line, double overhead camshaft, 16-valve, four-stroke, liquid cooled
Bore	84.00 mm
Stroke	90.00 mm
Capacity	2993 cc
Direction of crankshaft rotation	Clockwise (seen from the front of the engine)

Compression ratio:

D25	16.5 : 1
D30	17.0 : 1

Compression pressure:

Minimum.	10 bar

Lubrication system

Minimum system pressure:

Idle speed (hot).	1.3 bar
3500 rpm (hot)	4.0 to 6.0 bar

Torque wrench settings

	Nm	lbf ft
Acoustic cover-to-engine bolts	8	6
Camshaft bearing cap bolts:		
M6	10	7
M7	15	11
Camshaft cover bolts:		
M6	10	7
M7	15	11
Camshaft sprocket to gearwheel (intake camshaft)*	14	10
Connecting rod big-end bearing cap bolts:		
Stage 1	5	4
Stage 2	20	15
Stage 3	Angle-tighten a further 70°	
Crankshaft pulley/vibration damper bolts: *		
Stage 1	40	30
Stage 2	Angle-tighten a further 120°	
Crankshaft rear oil seal housing bolts:		
M6	10	7
M8	22	16
Cylinder head bolts: *		
Stage 1	80	59
Stage 2	Slacken 180°	
Stage 3	50	37
Stage 4	Angle-tighten a further 90°	
Stage 5	Angle-tighten a further 90°	
Cylinder head-to-timing cover bolts:		
M7	15	11
M8	20	15
Engine mountings:		
Mounting to front subframe:		
M8	28	21
M10	56	41
Mounting-to-support bracket:		
M10	56	41
M12	68	49
Flywheel/driveplate bolts*	120	89
Front subframe mounting bolts:		
M10:		
Stage 1	56	41
Stage 2	Angle-tighten a further 90°	
M12	108	80
Fuel injection pump sprocket retaining nut	65	48
Main bearing cap bolts: *		
Stage 1	50	37
Stage 2	Angle-tighten a further 90°	
Oil cooler-to-oil filter housing bolts	22	16
Oil feed guide rail bolts	10	7
Oil filter cap	25	18
Oil filter housing bolts	25	18
Oil level switch	8	6
Oil pressure switch	28	19
Oil pump:		
Drive sprocket to driveshaft:		
M6	10	7
M7	25	18
Retaining bolts:		
M6	14	10
M7	25	18
Intake pipe (M8)	19	14
Piston oil spray jet bolts	10	7
Power steering pump bolts:		
M6	10	7
M8	25	18
Power steering pump pulley bolts	32	24
Reinforcement brace to subframe: *		
Stage 1	56	41
Stage 2	Angle-tighten a further 90°	
Roadwheel bolts	120	89

Torque wrench settings

	Nm	lbf ft
Steering column lower joint pinch bolt*	21	15
Suspension turret/tension braces: *		
M10 (outer bolts):		
Stage 1	40	30
Stage 2	Angle-tighten a further 60°	
M12 (centre bolt):		
Stage 1	100	74
Stage 2	Angle-tighten a further 100°	
Strut/bracket nuts* (Version B)	34	26
Sump bolts:		
M6	10	7
M8	19	14
Sump drain plug:		
M12	25	18
M18	35	26
Timing chain cover bolts:		
M6	10	7
M7	15	11
M8	22	16
Timing chain cover bolt plug:		
M30	70	52
M40	30	22
Timing chain tensioner bolts	10	7
Turbocharger-to-exhaust manifold bolts	50	36
Vacuum pump bolts*	22	16

*Do not re-use

Caution: All aluminium fastenings must be renewed. If in doubt, try to attract the bolt/stud with a magnet. Aluminium is not magnetic.

1 General information and precautions

How to use this Chapter

1 This Part of the Chapter describes those repair procedures that can reasonably be carried out on the engine whilst it remains in the vehicle. If the engine has been removed from the vehicle and is being dismantled as described in Part D of this Chapter, any preliminary dismantling procedures can be ignored.

2 Note that whilst it may be possible physically to overhaul items such as the piston/connecting rod assemblies with the engine in the vehicle, such tasks are not usually carried out as separate operations and usually require the execution of several additional procedures (not to mention the cleaning of components and of oilways). For this reason, all such tasks are classed as major overhaul procedures and are described in Part D of this Chapter.

Engine description

3 This Chapter covers 6-cylinder M57TU2 diesel engines fitted to the E90 and E91 3-Series range from October 2008.

4 The cast-iron cylinder block is of the dry-liner type. The crankshaft is supported within the cylinder block on five shell-type main bearings. Thrustwashers are integral with the No 6 main bearing shells to control crankshaft endfloat.

5 The cylinder head is of the double overhead camshaft, 4-valve per cylinder design – two intake and two exhaust valves per cylinder. The valves are operated by one intake camshaft and one exhaust camshaft, via rocker fingers. One end of each finger acts upon the valve stem, whilst the other end pivots on a support pillar. Valve clearances are maintained automatically by hydraulic compensation elements (tappets) incorporated within the support pillars. In order to achieve high levels of combustion efficiency, the cylinder head has two intake ports for each cylinder. One port is tangential, whilst the other is helical.

6 The connecting rods rotate on horizontally-split bearing shells at their big-ends. The pistons are attached to the connecting rods by gudgeon pins which are secured in position with circlips. The aluminium alloy pistons are fitted with three piston rings, comprising two compression rings and an oil control ring.

7 The intake and exhaust valves are each closed by coil springs and operate in guides pressed into the cylinder head. Valve guides cannot be renewed.

8 A timing chain, driven by the crankshaft, drives the high-pressure fuel pump sprocket, which in turn drives the intake camshaft. The camshafts are geared together. The vacuum pump is fitted to the front of the cylinder head, and is driven by the exhaust camshaft. The coolant pump is driven by the auxiliary drivebelt.

9 Lubrication is by means of an eccentric-rotor type pump driven by the crankshaft via a Simplex chain. The pump draws oil through a strainer located in the sump, and then forces it through an externally-mounted full-flow paper element type oil filter into galleries in the cylinder block/crankcase, from where it is distributed to the crankshaft (main bearings), timing chain (sprayed by a jet), and camshafts. The big-end bearings are supplied with oil via internal drillings in the crankshaft, while the camshaft bearings and the followers receive a pressurised supply via drillings in the cylinder head. The camshaft lobes and valves are lubricated by oil splash, as are all other engine components. An oil cooler (integral with the oil filter housing) is fitted to keep the oil temperature stable under arduous operating conditions.

Operations with engine in car

10 The following work can be carried out with the engine in the vehicle:
a) Compression pressure – testing.
b) Camshaft cover – removal and refitting.
c) Crankshaft pulley – removal and refitting.
d) Balance shaft housing – removal and refitting.
e) Camshafts and rocker arms – removal, inspection and refitting.
f) Cylinder head – removal and refitting.
g) Cylinder head and pistons – decarbonising.
h) Sump – removal and refitting.
i) Oil pump – removal, overhaul and refitting.
j) Oil filter housing/cooler – removal and refitting.
k) Crankshaft oil seals – renewal.
l) Engine/transmission mountings – inspection and renewal.
m) Flywheel/driveplate – removal, inspection and refitting.

Note: Although in theory it is possible to remove the timing cover and timing chains with the engine fitted, in practice access is extremely limited, special BMW tools are needed, and the cylinder head and sump must be removed. Consequently, it is recommended that the engine is removed prior to timing cover and chains removal.

3.5 Pull out the blanking plug from the timing pin hole in the engine block

2 Compression test – description and interpretation

Compression test

Note: *A compression tester specifically designed for diesel engines must be used for this test.*

1 When engine performance is down, or if misfiring occurs which cannot be attributed to the fuel system, a compression test can provide diagnostic clues as to the engine's condition. If the test is performed regularly, it can give warning of trouble before any other symptoms become apparent.

2 A compression tester specifically intended for diesel engines must be used, because of the higher pressures involved. The tester is connected to an adapter which screws into the glow plug or injector hole. It is unlikely to be worthwhile buying such a tester for occasional use, but it may be possible to borrow or hire one – if not, have the test performed by a garage.

3 Unless specific instructions to the contrary are supplied with the tester, observe the following points:

a) *The battery must be in a good state of charge, the air filter must be clean, and the engine should be at normal operating temperature.*

b) *All the glow plugs should be removed before starting the test (see Chapter 5A).*

c) *Disconnect the wiring plugs from the fuel injectors.*

3.8 Fit the special tool over the flats on the intake camshaft collar. The tool must contact both sides of the camshaft cover gasket face on the cylinder head

3.7 Insert the timing pin through the engine block flange into the indent in the flywheel

4 There is no need to hold the accelerator pedal down during the test, because the diesel engine air intake is not throttled.

5 Crank the engine on the starter motor; after one or two revolutions, the compression pressure should build-up to a maximum figure, and then stabilise. Record the highest reading obtained.

6 Repeat the test on the remaining cylinders, recording the pressure in each.

7 All cylinders should produce very similar pressures; a difference of more than 2 bars between any two cylinders indicates a fault. Note that the compression should build-up quickly in a healthy engine; low compression on the first stroke, followed by gradually-increasing pressure on successive strokes, indicates worn piston rings. A low compression reading on the first stroke, which does not build-up during successive strokes, indicates leaking valves or a blown head gasket (a cracked head could also be the cause). Deposits on the undersides of the valve heads can also cause low compression. Note: The cause of poor compression is less easy to establish on a diesel engine than on a petrol one. The effect of introducing oil into the cylinders ('wet' testing) is not conclusive, because there is a risk that the oil will sit in the swirl chamber or in the recess on the piston crown instead of passing to the rings.

8 Refer to a BMW dealer or other specialist if in doubt as to whether a particular pressure reading is acceptable.

9 On completion of the test, refit the glow plugs as described in Chapter 5A.

3.9 Use the clamp to lock the camshaft tool in place

Leakdown test

10 A leakdown test measures the rate at which compressed air fed into the cylinder is lost. It is an alternative to a compression test, and in many ways it is better, since the escaping air provides easy identification of where pressure loss is occurring (piston rings, valves or head gasket).

11 The equipment needed for leakdown testing is unlikely to be available to the home mechanic. If poor compression is suspected, have the test performed by a suitably-equipped garage.

3 Engine assembly/valve timing settings – general information and usage

Note: *BMW tool No 11 6 080 or suitable home-made equivalent will be required to lock the crankshaft in position, and access to BMW tool No 11 6 321 and 11 6 322 or home-made equivalents are required to position the camshafts.*

1 The flywheel is equipped with an indent, which aligns with a hole in the engine block when No 1 piston is at TDC (top dead centre). In this position, if No 1 piston is at TDC on its compression stroke, it will be possible to fit a BMW special tool (No 11 6 321) or home-made equivalent over the square sections of the intake camshaft (with all four No 1 cylinder camshaft lobes pointing towards the right-hand side). Note: As explained in the front of this manual, all references to left and right are in the sense of a person in the driver's seat facing forward.

2 Firmly apply the handbrake then jack up the front of the vehicle and support it securely on axle stands (see *Jacking and vehicle support*).

3 Undo the retaining bolts/clips and remove the engine undershield (where fitted)

4 Remove the camshaft cover and gasket, as described in Section 4.

5 Pull out the blanking plug from the timing pin hole in the engine block **(see illustration)**. The plug is more easily accessible from underneath.

6 Using a socket and extension bar on the crankshaft pulley centre bolt, turn the crankshaft clockwise whilst keeping an eye on the No 1 cylinder camshaft lobes. Note: Do not turn the engine anti-clockwise.

7 Rotate the crankshaft clockwise until the No 1 cylinder camshaft lobes approach the point where all four lobes are pointing upwards. Have an assistant insert BMW Tool No 11 6 080 or home-made equivalent into the timing pin hole, and press the pin gently against the flywheel. Continue to turn the crankshaft slowly until the pin is felt to engage in the indent in the flywheel and the crankshaft locks **(see illustration)**.

8 With the crankshaft in this position, all four camshaft lobes of No 1 cylinder should be pointing to the right-hand side. Fit BMW tool No 11 6 321 over the flats on the intake camshaft collar, adjacent to No 1 camshaft bearing cap. If the camshaft is timed correctly, the tool will contact both sides of the camshaft cover gasket face on the cylinder head **(see illustration)**.

9 To lock the intake camshaft in this position, fit BMW tool No 11 6 322. This tool clamps tool No 11 6 321 in place, preventing the tool from moving. Note that the exhaust camshaft is geared to the intake camshaft, and adjustment is not possible **(see illustration)**.

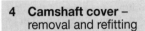

4 Camshaft cover –
removal and refitting

Removal

1 Disconnect the battery negative lead (refer to Chapter 5A).
2 Remove the cooling fan and shroud as described in Chapter 3 Section 6.
3 With reference to Chapter 4B, remove the fuel injectors.
4 Undo the bolts and detach the air intake ducting from the air filter housing.
5 Undo the 4 bolts and remove the air filter housing cover **(see illustration)**. Remove the air filter element.
6 Undo the 2 bolts and pull the air duct forwards from the air filter housing **(see illustration)**.
7 Disconnect the wiring plugs from the camshaft position, and mass airflow/intake air temperature sensors **(see illustrations)**.
8 Undo the bolts securing the fuel common rail to the cylinder head.
9 Slide out the rectangular wiring connector, then use a small flat-bladed screwdriver to lift the retaining clips, and pull the wiring harness guide plate upwards, and detach it from the right-hand edge of the camshaft cover. Similarly, lift the clip and slide out the harness retaining clip at the rear of the edge **(see illustration)**.
10 Working from the outside-in, evenly slacken and remove the bolts securing the camshaft cover to the cylinder head. Note the bolt at the front left-hand corner of the cover, under the oil filler cap surround insulation **(see illustrations)**.
11 Gently ease the common rail away, and remove the cover and discard its gasket. Note that when the gasket is removed, the bolts will fall from the cover.

Refitting

12 Ensure the mating surfaces are clean and dry then fit the new gasket to the cover. Insert the bolts into the gasket.
13 Apply a 3 mm bead of sealant (Drei Bond 1209) to the cylinder head mating surface as shown **(see illustration)**.
14 Refit the cover to the cylinder head,

4.5 Undo the air filter housing cover bolts

4.6 Air duct retaining bolts

4.7a Disconnect the wiring plug from the mass airflow sensor...

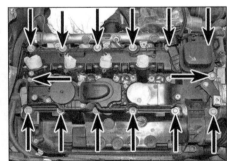
4.7b... and the camshaft position sensor

ensuring that the gasket remains correctly seated.
15 Insert the cover retaining bolts and tighten them all by hand. Once all bolts are in position,

tighten them to the specified torque setting starting from the inside, working outwards.
16 The remainder of refitting is a reversal of removal.

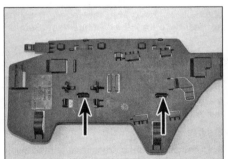
4.9 Lift the two clips and slide the harness guide plate upwards from the right-hand edge of the camshaft cover

4.10a Camshaft cover bolts

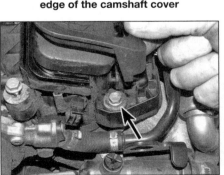
4.10b Note the bolt under the filler cap surround

4.13 Apply a bead of sealant to the areas shown

5.4a We fabricated a tool...

5.4b... which is bolted to the bellhousing, and locates through a hole, engaging with the flywheel starter ring gear

5.4c The part of the tool which engages with the ring gear is an old bolt, ground at the end to match the profile of the ring gear teeth. The bolt must be a good fit in the bellhousing hole

5.5a Unscrew the retaining bolts...

5.5b... and remove the crankshaft pulley

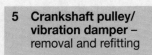

5 Crankshaft pulley/ vibration damper – removal and refitting

Removal

1 Firmly apply the handbrake then jack up the front of the vehicle and support it securely on axle stands (see *Jacking and vehicle support*).
2 Remove the auxiliary drivebelt(s) as described in Chapter 1B.
3 If further dismantling is to be carried out (beyond pulley removal), align the engine assembly/valve timing settings as described in Section 3.
4 Slacken the crankshaft pulley retaining bolts. The pulley retaining bolts are extremely tight. The crankshaft must be prevented from rotating using BMW tool No 11 8 182/183 (or

6.4 With all the camshaft lobes of No 1 cylinder pointing downwards...

equivalent), fitted through the hole in the base of the transmission bellhousing, and engages with the teeth of the starter ring gear on the flywheel/driveplate – the vibration damper is retained by 4 bolts **(see illustrations)**. If the engine is removed from the vehicle it will be necessary to lock the flywheel (see Section 12).
Caution: Do not be tempted to use the crankshaft locking pin (see Section 3) to prevent rotation as the centre bolts are slackened.
5 Unscrew the retaining bolts, and remove the pulley from the crankshaft **(see illustrations)**.

Refitting

6 Fit the pulley to the crankshaft and screw in the new retaining bolts.
7 Lock the crankshaft by the method used on removal, and tighten the pulley retaining bolts to the specified Stage 1 torque setting then

6.5... remove the camshaft sprocket upper bolt

angle-tighten the bolts through the specified Stage 2 angle, using a socket and extension bar. It is recommended that an angle-measuring gauge is used during the final stages of the tightening, to ensure accuracy. If a gauge is not available, use paint to make alignment marks between the bolt heads and pulley prior to tightening; the marks can then be used to check that the bolt has been rotated through the correct angle.
8 Refit the auxiliary drivebelt(s) as described in Chapter 1B.
9 Refit the roadwheel then lower the vehicle to the ground.

6 Camshafts, rocker arms and hydraulic tappets – removal, inspection and refitting

Removal

1 Remove the camshaft cover as described in Section 4, and the vacuum pump as described in Chapter 9.
2 Firmly apply the handbrake, then jack up the front of the vehicle and support it securely on axle stands (see *Jacking and vehicle support*).
3 Undo the fasteners and remove the engine undershield (where fitted).
4 Using a socket and ratchet, rotate the crankshaft pulley clockwise until the lobes of the No 1 cylinder intake camshaft are pointing downwards **(see illustration)**.
5 Undo and remove the upper bolt securing the sprocket to the camshaft **(see illustration)**.
6 Remove the plug in the timing chain cover **(see illustration)**.
7 Fit an open-ended spanner to the hexagonal section of the exhaust camshaft, and rotate the camshaft anti-clockwise slightly, to force the timing chain tensioner to compress **(see illustration)**.
8 Whilst the tensioner is compressed, insert a 4.0 mm diameter rod/drill bit through the plug hole in the timing cover to lock the tensioner in place **(see illustration)**.
9 Pull out the blanking plug from the timing

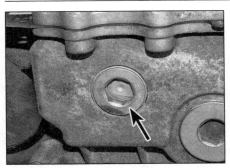

6.6 Unscrew the plug from the timing chain cover

6.7 Use an open-ended spanner on the hexagonal section of the exhaust camshaft

6.8 Insert a 4.0 mm drill bit/rod into the tensioner

pin hole in the engine block **(see illustration 3.5)**.

10 Using a socket and extension bar on the crankshaft pulley centre bolt, turn the crankshaft clockwise whilst keeping an eye on the No 1 cylinder camshaft lobes.

11 Rotate the crankshaft clockwise until the No 1 cylinder camshaft lobes approach the point where all four lobes are pointing upwards. Have an assistant insert BMW tool No 11 6 080 or home-made equivalent into the timing pin hole, and press the pin gently against the flywheel – see Section 3. Continue to turn the crankshaft slowly until the pin is felt to engage in the indent in the flywheel and the crankshaft locks **(see illustration 3.7)**.

12 Undo the 2 bolts securing the sprocket to the intake camshaft **(see illustration)**.

13 Unscrew and remove the timing chain guide bearing pins from the timing cover **(see illustration)**. Where necessary, undo the bolts and remove the lifting eye bracket to access the left-hand pin.

14 Pull the sprocket from the intake camshaft, hold it across to the right-hand side, then pull the left-hand timing chain guide upwards from the timing cover **(see illustrations)**.

15 Disengage the sprocket from the timing chain, then lay the chain to the left-hand side of the cylinder head. Secure the chain in place with tape, etc, to prevent it falling into the timing cover.

16 Identify the camshaft bearing caps, to ensure they are refitted to their original positions. The exhaust camshaft is marked A,

6.12 Remove the remaining camshaft sprocket bolts

so mark the exhaust camshaft bearing caps as A1, A2, A3, etc, starting with the cap nearest the timing chain. The intake camshaft is marked E, so repeat the procedure for the intake camshaft starting with E1 adjacent to the timing chain **(see illustration)**.

17 Evenly and progressively, slacken and remove the retaining bolts, and remove the camshaft bearing caps. Note: Do not undo the bolts securing the vacuum pump guide to the cylinder head.

18 Remove the camshafts from the cylinder head.

19 Lift the rocker arms from the cylinder head, and lay them out in order on a clean surface, so that they can be fitted into their original positions – if they are to be re-used.

20 Obtain 24 small, clean plastic containers, and label them for identification. Alternatively, divide a larger container into compartments.

6.13 Unscrew the timing chain guide bearing pins

Withdraw each hydraulic tappet in turn, and place it in its respective container, which should then be filled with clean engine oil. *Caution: Do not interchange the tappets, and do not allow the tappets to lose oil, as they will take a long time to refill with oil on restarting the engine, which could result in incorrect valve clearances. Absolute cleanliness is essential at all times when handling the tappets.*

Inspection

21 Examine the camshaft bearing surfaces and cam lobes for signs of wear ridges and scoring. Renew the camshaft if any of these conditions are apparent. Examine the condition of the bearing surfaces both on the camshaft journals and in the cylinder head. If the head bearing surfaces are worn excessively, the cylinder head will need to be renewed.

6.14a Pull the sprocket from the camshaft, hold it to the right-hand side...

6.14b... then pull the left-hand chain guide upwards

6.16 The camshaft bearing caps are marked E for intake, A for exhaust, and numbered from the timing chain end

6.23 Refit each hydraulic tappet to its original location

6.24 Refit the rocker arms, ensuring they locate on the top of the tappets correctly

6.26a The 2 dots on the rear of the exhaust camshaft gear must align with the dot on the intake gear

6.26b The dots on the gears must be approximately flush with the upper surface of the cylinder head

22 Examine the rocker bearing surfaces which contact the camshaft lobes for wear ridges and scoring. If the engine's valve clearances have sounded noisy, particularly if the noise persists after initial start-up from cold, then there is reason to suspect a faulty tappet. If any tappet is thought to be faulty or is visibly worn it should be renewed.

Refitting

23 Where removed, lubricate the tappets with clean engine oil and carefully insert each one into its original location in the cylinder head **(see illustration)**.
24 Refit the rocker arms to their original locations, ensuring that they are correctly orientated **(see illustration)**.
25 Remove the crankshaft locking tool, and rotate the crankshaft 45° anti-clockwise (if not already done so) to prevent any accidental

piston-to-valve contact. Ensure the timing chain does not fall into the timing cover, or jam on the crankshaft sprocket.
26 Engage the gear on the exhaust camshaft with the gear on the intake camshaft, so the 2 dots on the rear of the exhaust camshaft gear are each side of the dot on the intake camshaft gear, then lay the camshafts in place on the cylinder head so the dots are flush with the upper surface of the cylinder head **(see illustrations)**.
27 Lubricate the bearing surfaces of the camshaft with clean engine oil, then refit the bearing caps to their original positions.
28 Insert the bearing cap bolts, then evenly and progressively tighten the retaining bolts to draw the bearing caps squarely down into contact with the cylinder head. Once the caps are in contact with the head, tighten the retaining bolts to the specified torque.

6.32 Align the sprocket with the bolts holes

7.6 Common rail mounting bolts

Caution: If the bearing caps bolts are carelessly tightened, the caps might break. If the caps are broken then the complete cylinder head assembly must be renewed; the caps are matched to the head and are not available separately.

29 With the camshafts in this position, it should be possible to fit BMW tool No 11 6 321 (or equivalent) over the flat in the collar on the intake camshaft, as described in Section 3. If it is not, adjust the position of the camshafts slightly using an open-ended spanner on the hexagonal section of the exhaust camshaft.
30 With the camshafts held in position, rotate the crankshaft 45° clockwise (back to TDC) so the flywheel locking tool can be reinserted. Ensure the timing chain doesn't fall inside the cover, or jam on the crankshaft sprocket.
31 Lower the left-hand timing chain guide into position.
32 Engage the timing chain with the sprocket, and position the sprocket on the end of the intake camshaft so the bolt holes align **(see illustration)**. Fit the new retaining bolts, but only finger-tighten them at this stage – the sprocket must be able to rotate independently of the camshaft.
33 Apply a little thread-locking compound, then refit and tighten the timing chain guide bearing pins.
34 Remove the rod/drill bit locking the timing chain tensioner
35 Tighten the new sprocket retaining bolts to the specified torque.
36 Remove the flywheel and camshaft locking tools, then rotate the crankshaft so the remaining sprocket bolt can be inserted and tightened.
37 Refit and tighten the plug to the timing chain cover.
38 Rotate the crankshaft clockwise until the third camshaft sprocket bolt can be installed, and tightened.
39 The remainder of refitting is a reversal of removal.

---

7 Cylinder head –
removal and refitting

Removal

1 Remove the camshafts, rocker arms and tappets as described in Section 6, then lift out the right-hand upper timing chain guide.
2 Drain the cooling system, as described in Chapter 1B.
3 Remove the EGR cooler as described in Chapter 4C.
4 Disconnect the fuel pressure sensor wiring plug, and release the harness grommet from the cylinder head.
5 Disconnect the engine coolant temperature sensor wiring plug.
6 Undo the high-pressure fuel pipe unions, remove the pipe from the pump to the common rail, then undo the bolts and remove

7.9a The coolant rail is secured by a bolt at the front...

7.9b... and one at the rear

7.13 Undo the bolts securing the cylinder head to the timing chain cover

the common rail. Disconnect the wiring plugs and return hose as the common rail is withdrawn **(see illustration)**. Note that a new high-pressure fuel pipe must be fitted.

7 Gently pull the connectors from the glow plugs.

8 Release the retaining clips, and disconnect the various coolant hoses from the cylinder head.

9 Unscrew the bolts securing the coolant rail, release the clips and manoeuvre the coolant rail to one side **(see illustrations)**.

10 Slacken the bolts securing the turbocharger to the cylinder block.

11 Slacken the clamp securing the turbocharger to the exhaust manifold. Once the cylinder head has been removed, refit the clamp.

12 Undo the 2 bolts securing the wiring guide and bracket to the rear of the cylinder head.

13 Unscrew the bolts securing the cylinder head to the timing cover **(see illustration)**.

14 Make a final check to ensure that all relevant hoses, pipes and wires, etc, have been disconnected.

15 Working in the reverse of the tightening sequence **(see illustration 7.33)**, progressively slacken the cylinder head bolts by a third of a turn at a time until all bolts can be unscrewed by hand. Withdraw and discard the bolts, new ones must be fitted.

16 Lift the cylinder head from the cylinder block. If necessary, tap the cylinder head gently with a soft-faced mallet to free it from the block, but do not lever at the mating faces.

17 When the joint is broken, lift the cylinder head away then remove the gasket. Note the fitted positions of the two locating dowels, and remove them for safe-keeping if they are loose. Keep the gasket for identification purposes (see paragraph 23).

Caution: Do not lay the head on its lower mating surface; support the head on wooden blocks, ensuring each block only contacts the head mating surface not the glow plugs. The glow plugs protrude out the bottom of the head and they will be damaged if the head is placed directly onto a bench.

18 If the cylinder head is to be dismantled, refer to the relevant Sections of Part D of this Chapter.

Preparation for refitting

19 The mating faces of the cylinder head and block must be perfectly clean before refitting the head. Use a scraper to remove all traces of gasket and carbon, and also clean the tops of the pistons. Take particular care with the aluminium surfaces, as the soft metal is damaged easily. Also, make sure that debris is not allowed to enter the oil and water channels – this is particularly important for the oil circuit, as carbon could block the oil supply to the camshaft or crankshaft bearings. Using adhesive tape and paper, seal the water, oil and bolt holes in the cylinder block. To prevent carbon entering the gap between the pistons and bores, smear a little grease in the gap. After cleaning the piston, rotate the crankshaft so that the piston moves down the bore, then wipe out the grease and carbon with a cloth rag. Clean the piston crowns in the same way.

20 Check the block and head for nicks, deep scratches and other damage. If slight, they may be removed carefully with a file. More serious damage may be repaired by machining, but this is a specialist job.

21 If warpage of the cylinder head gasket surface is suspected, use a straight-edge to check it for distortion. Refer to Part D of this Chapter if necessary.

22 Ensure that the cylinder head bolt holes in the crankcase are clean and free of oil. Syringe or soak up any oil left in the bolt holes. This is most important in order that the correct bolt tightening torque can be applied and to prevent the possibility of the block being cracked by hydraulic pressure when the bolts are tightened.

23 On these engines, the cylinder head-to-piston clearance is controlled by fitting different thickness head gaskets. The piston protrusion is represented by the number of holes in the gasket next to the timing chain area **(see illustration)**.

Holes in gasket	Largest piston protrusion
One hole	0.77 to 0.92 mm
Two holes	0.92 to 1.03 mm
Three holes	1.03 to 1.18 mm

24 Select the new gasket which has the same thickness/number of holes as the original, unless new piston and connecting rod assemblies have been fitted. In that case, the correct thickness of gasket required is selected by measuring the piston protrusions as follows.

25 Remove the locking pin from the flywheel and mount a dial test indicator securely on the block so that its pointer can be easily pivoted between the piston crown and block mating surface.

26 Ensure No 1 piston is at exactly TDC then zero the dial test indicator on the gasket surface of the cylinder block. Carefully move the indicator over No 1 piston, taking measurements in line with the gudgeon pin axis, measure the protrusion on both the left-hand and right-hand side of the piston **(see illustration)**. Note: When turning the crankshaft, ensure that the timing chain does not jam in the timing cover.

27 Rotate the crankshaft to bring the remaining pistons to TDC in turn. Ensure the crankshaft is accurately positioned then measure the protrusions of the remaining pistons, taking two measurements for each

7.23 Cylinder head gasket identification holes

7.26 Measure the piston protrusion with a DTI gauge

7.29 Ensure the dowels are in position

7.32 Insert the new bolts and washers into place

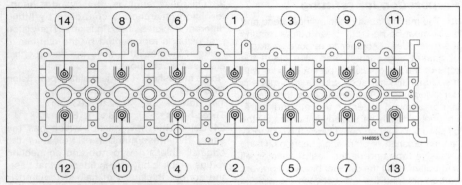

7.33 Cylinder head bolt tightening sequence

piston. Once all the pistons have been measured, rotate the crankshaft to bring No 1 piston back to TDC. Then rotate it 45° anti-clockwise.

28 Use the table in paragraph 23 to select the appropriate gasket.

Refitting

29 Wipe clean the mating faces of the head and block and ensure that the two locating dowels are in position on the cylinder block/ crankcase surface **(see illustration)**.

30 Fit the new gasket to the cylinder block, ensuring that it fits correctly over the locating dowels.

31 Carefully refit the cylinder head, locating it on the dowels. Make sure the timing chain can be pulled up through the cylinder head tunnel.

32 The new cylinder head bolts are supplied pre-coated – do not wash the coating off, or apply grease/oil to them. Carefully enter the main bolts (1 to 14) into the holes and screw them in, by hand only, until finger-tight **(see illustration)**.

Caution: Do not drop the bolts into their holes.

33 Working progressively and in sequence, first tighten all the cylinder head bolts to the Stage 1 torque setting **(see illustration)**.

34 Slacken all the bolts half a turn (180°), then tighten them in sequence to the Stage 3 setting.

35 Again, in sequence, angle-tighten them 90° (Stage 4), and another 90° (Stage 5), using an angle-measuring gauge **(see illustration)**.

36 Refit and tighten the bolts securing the cylinder head to the timing cover, to the specified torque. Note: Take great care not to drop the inner bolt down the timing chain tunnel **(see illustration 7.13)**.

37 The remainder of refitting is a reversal of removal, noting the following points:
a) *Renew all gaskets/seals disturbed during the removal procedure.*
b) *Refit the right-hand upper timing chain guide before installing the camshafts.*
c) *Tighten all fasteners to their specified torque where given.*
d) *Refill the cooling system as described in Chapter 1B.*

8 Sump –
removal and refitting

Removal

1 Drain the engine oil and remove the oil filter as described in Chapter 1B. Refit the sump plug with a new washer and tighten the plug to the specified torque.

2 On all models, it's necessary to lower the front subframe as follows:

3 Jack up the front of the vehicle and support it securely on axle stands (see *Jacking and vehicle support*). Remove the retaining bolts and fasteners and remove the engine undershield **(see illustration)**.

4 Undo the bolts and remove the front section of the acoustic cover from the top of the engine **(see illustration)**.

Models with suspension turret braces

5 Remove the plastic cap from the centre of the scuttle trim panel. Two different types of the cap are fitted: one with a central slot, removed by rotating it 45° anti-clockwise, and one without a central slot, which is prised from place **(see illustration)**. Note, if the cap or seal are damaged, they must be renewed. Failure to do so may result in water ingress.

6 Undo the bolt in the centre of the scuttle, exposed by the cap removal **(see illustration)**. Discard the bolt – a new one must be fitted.

Version A

7 Undo the bolt at each outer end of the braces, then hold the rubber grommet in place and slide the braces outwards from place **(see**

7.35 Use and angle gauge to accurately tighten the cylinder head bolts

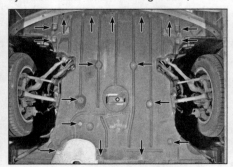

8.3 Undo the fasteners and remove the engine undershield

8.4 Undo the bolts and pull the acoustic cover forwards

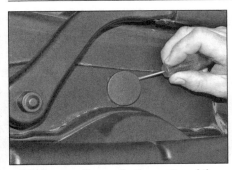

8.5 Remove the cap in the centre of the scuttle trim...

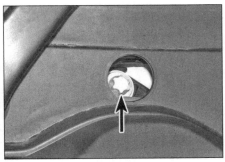

8.6... and undo the bolt in the centre

8.7 Undo the bolt at each end

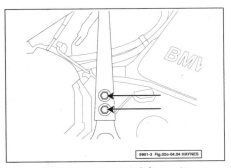

8.8 Strut brace retaining nuts

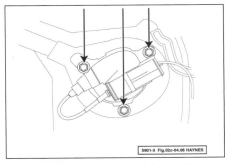

8.9 Strut bracket retaining nuts

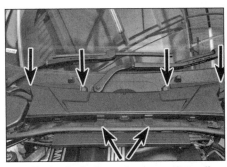

8.10 Undo the bolts and remove the pollen filter upper cover

illustration). Do not allow the grommet to be displaced. Discard the bolts – new ones must be fitted.

Version B

8 Undo the nuts and remove the strut brace **(see illustration)**.

9 If required, undo the nuts and remove the bracket from the top of the suspension turret each side **(see illustration)**. Renew the nuts.

All models

10 Working at the rear of the engine compartment, undo the bolts and remove the pollen filter upper cover **(see illustration)**. Slide the filter from the housing. If necessary, refer to Chapter 1B.

11 Release the catches and remove the left- and right-hand plastic covers from behind the suspension turret each side of the engine compartment **(see illustration)**.

12 Depress the clips and pull the cable guide forwards from the pollen filter lower housing **(see illustration)**.

13 Release the catch and undo the bolt each

side, then slide the pollen filter lower housing forwards and manoeuvre it from place **(see illustrations)**.

14 Undo the 2 bolts and remove the rear

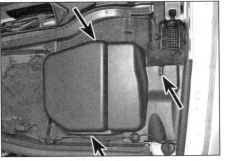

8.11 Release the clips and remove the cover each side

8.12 Release the clips (arrowed) and pull the cable guide forwards

8.13a Rotate the temperature sensor and detach it from the bracket

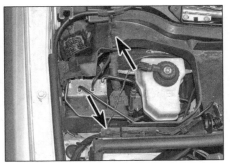

8.13b Undo the bolt and release the clip each side

8.13c Pull the pollen filter lower housing forwards

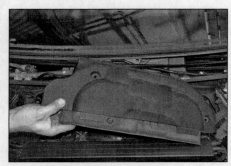

8.14 Remove the rear section of the engine cover

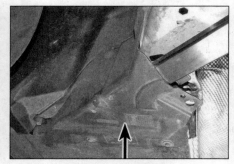

8.18 Remove the panelling

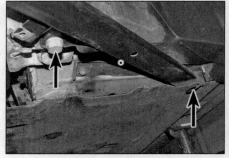

8.19a Remove the bolts each side (arrowed) of the reinforcement brace...

8.19b... and the two in the centre

8.20 Steering column pinch-bolt

section of the acoustic cover on the top of the engine **(see illustration)**.

15 Remove the intake manifold as described in Chapter 4B.

16 The engine must be supported in position using an engine hoist or engine crossbeam. Attach the hoist/crossbeam to the engine lifting eyes at the front and rear of the cylinder head. Take the weight of the engine.

17 Undo the nut each side securing the engine mounting support brackets to the mountings, then raise the engine approximately 10 mm.

18 Undo the fasteners, and remove the underbody panelling each side in the area of the reinforcement brace under the subframe **(see illustration)**.

19 Undo the nuts/bolts and remove the reinforcement brace each side under the front subframe **(see illustrations)**. Discard the nuts/bolts – new ones must be fitted.

20 Remove the steering column lower universal joint pinch-bolt and lift the column shaft upwards from the steering rack pinion **(see illustration)**. Discard the pinch-bolt – a new one must be used.

Caution: Ensure the steering wheel/ column is not rotated with the universal joint disconnected from the steering rack pinion. Damage to the column could result.

21 Disconnect the wiring plugs from the ride height sensors (where fitted), then disconnect the vacuum hoses (where fitted) from the engine mountings.

22 On models with electric power steering, cut the cable tie securing the wiring harness to the subframe.

23 Support the front subframe using a work- shop jack and lengths of wood, etc, then undo the 3 bolts each side and carefully lower the subframe a maximum of 10 cm **(see illustrations)**. Pay attention to the power steering

hoses/pipes as the subframe is being lowered – do not allow them to be bent or stretched. Note that the subframe bolts at the front are 90 mm long, the middle bolts are 145 mm long, and the rearmost bolts are 53 mm long. When refitting, tighten down the front bolts first.

24 Undo the bolts securing the oil level dipstick guide tube and pull the tube from the sump. Renew the guide tube O-ring seal.

25 Disconnect the wiring plug from the engine oil level sensor.

26 Slacken and remove the bolts securing the transmission casing to the sump.

27 Progressively slacken and remove the bolts securing the sump to the base of the cylinder block.

28 Break the sump joint by striking the sump with the palm of the hand, then lower the sump away from the engine. Remove the gasket and discard it, a new one should be used on refitting.

29 While the sump is removed, take the opportunity to check the oil pump pick-up/ strainer for signs of clogging or splitting. If necessary, unbolt the pick-up/strainer, and remove it from the engine along with its gasket **(see illustration)**. The strainer can then be cleaned easily in solvent. Inspect the strainer mesh for signs of clogging or splitting and renew if necessary. If the pick-up/strainer bolts are damaged they must be renewed.

Refitting

30 Clean all traces of gasket from the mating surfaces of the cylinder block and sump, then use a clean rag to wipe out the sump and the engine interior.

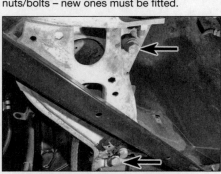

8.23a Front subframe rear bolts...

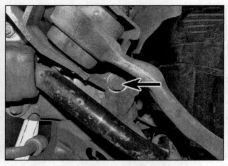

8.23b... and front bolt

8.29 Oil pump pick-up/strainer bolts

31 Where necessary, fit a new gasket to the oil pump pick-up/strainer then carefully refit the pipe. Refit the retaining bolts, and tighten them to the specified torque setting.

32 Apply a bead of suitable sealant (Drei Bond 1209 is available from your BMW dealer) to the cylinder block/timing cover mating surface in the areas shown **(see illustration)**.

33 Fit the gasket to the sump then offer up the sump to the cylinder block/crankcase **(see illustration)**. Refit the sump retaining bolts, and tighten the bolts finger-tight only.

34 Fit the bolts securing the sump to the gearbox. In order to align the rear sump flange with the gearbox, lightly tighten the bolts, then slacken them. If the sump is being refitted to the engine with the gearbox removed, use a straight-edge to ensure that the sump casting is flush with the end of the engine block **(see illustration)**.

35 Tighten the sump-to-engine block bolts, and then the sump-to-transmission bolts to the specified torque.

36 Refit the oil dipstick tube, with a new O-ring, and tighten the bolts securely.

37 The remainder of refitting is a reversal of removal, noting the following points:
a) *Renew all gaskets/seals where disturbed.*
b) *Tighten all fasteners to their specified torque where given.*
c) *Renew the engine oil and filter as described in Chapter 1B.*
d) *If necessary, have the front wheel alignment checked by a BMW dealer or suitably-equipped specialist.*

9 Oil pump –
removal, inspection and refitting

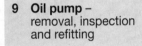

Removal

1 Remove the sump as described in Section 8.
2 Undo the bolt securing the sprocket to the pump shaft **(see illustration)**.
3 Undo the bolts and remove the oil pick-up assembly. Discard the O-ring seal, a new one must be fitted.
4 Undo the four bolts and remove the oil pump.

Inspection

5 At the time of writing, no parts are available for the oil pump. If defective, the complete assembly must be renewed. Consult a BMW dealer or parts specialist.

Refitting

6 Offer the pump into position and engage the sprocket (with the chain still in place) with the pump driveshaft.
7 Insert the pump retaining bolts and tighten them to the specified torque.
8 Refit the sprocket retaining bolt and tighten it to the specified torque.
9 Fit a new O-ring seal to the pick up tube and refit it. Tighten the bolts securely.
10 Refit the sump as described in Section 8.

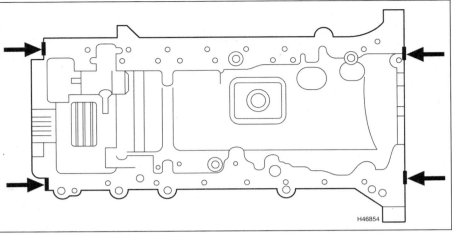

8.32 Apply a 2 mm wide bead of sealant to the areas arrowed

8.33 Offer the sump up into position and insert a couple of the retaining bolts

8.34 Use a straight-edge to ensure the sump casting is flush with the end of the engine block

10 Oil cooler –
removal and refitting

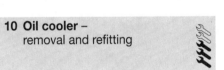

Removal

1 Drain the engine coolant, engine oil, and remove the oil filter as described in Chapter 1B.
2 Release the clamp and disconnect the coolant hose from the oil cooler.
3 Disconnect the wiring plug, then undo the bolts and remove the oil filter housing from the left-hand side of the cylinder block **(see illustration)**.
4 Undo the bolts and detach the oil cooler from the filter housing. Renew the gasket.

Refitting

5 Ensure the mating surfaces of the oil cooler and oil filter housing are clean and dry, and with a new gasket fit the cooler to the housing. Tighten the bolts to the specified torque.
6 The remainder of refitting is a reversal of removal.

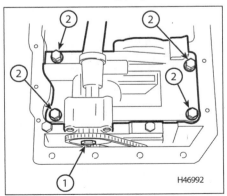

9.2 Oil pump sprocket bolt (1) and mounting bolts (2)

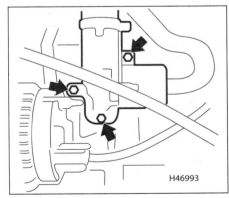

10.3 Oil filter housing retaining bolts

11.2 Remove the crankshaft oil seal using a self-tapping screw

11.4 Press the seal squarely into position until it's flush with the timing chain cover

11.7 Remove the cap from the end of the crankshaft

11 Crankshaft oil seals – renewal

Timing chain end seal

1 Remove the crankshaft pulley/vibration damper as described in Section 5.
2 Very carefully punch or drill two small holes opposite each other in the oil seal. Screw a self-tapping screw into each and pull on the screws with pliers to extract the seal **(see illustration)**.
Caution: Great care must be taken to avoid damage to the crankshaft.
3 Clean the seal housing and polish off any burrs or raised edges which may have caused the seal to fail in the first place.
4 Ease the new seal into position on the end

of the shaft – do not oil the seal lips. Press the seal squarely into position until it is flush with the housing. If necessary, a suitable tubular drift, such as a socket, which bears only on the hard outer edge of the seal can be used to tap the seal into position. Take great care not to damage the seal lips during fitting and ensure that the seal lips face inwards **(see illustration)**.
5 Refit the crankshaft pulley as described in Section 5.

Flywheel/driveplate end oil seal

6 Remove the flywheel or driveplate as described in Section 12.
7 Carefully remove the cap from the end of the crankshaft **(see illustration)**.
8 Undo the bolt and pull the crankshaft position sensor from the oil seal housing **(see illustration)**.
9 Undo the retaining bolts, then carefully detach the oil seal housing from the cylinder

block, without damaging the sump gasket **(see illustration)**. If the gasket is damaged, the sump will have to be removed as described in Section 8. Note that oil seal is integral with the housing.
10 The new seal and housing assembly is supplied with a seal protector installed. Position the seal protector, complete with seal, over the end of the crankshaft, and ease the seal and housing over the crankshaft shoulder **(see illustrations)**.
11 Refit the oil seal housing bolts, and tighten them to the specified torque.
12 Refit the crankshaft position sensor and tighten the bolt securely.
13 Ensure the dowel is correctly fitted in the end of the crankshaft, and refit the end cap.
14 Wash off any oil then refit the flywheel/driveplate as described in Section 12.

12 Flywheel/driveplate – removal, inspection and refitting

Flywheel

Note: *New flywheel retaining bolts must be used on refitting.*

Removal

1 Remove the clutch assembly as described in Chapter 6.
2 Prevent the flywheel from turning by locking the ring gear teeth with a similar arrangement to that shown **(see illustration)**. Alternatively, bolt a strap between the flywheel and the cylinder block/crankcase.

11.8 Undo the bolt and pull the crankshaft position sensor from place

11.9 Undo the bolts and pull the seal housing from the engine block. Take care not to damage the sump gasket

11.10a With the seal protector installed...

11.10b... position the assembly over the end of the crankshaft

12.2 Lock the flywheel using a similar tool

3 Slacken and remove the retaining bolts and remove the flywheel, noting its locating dowel **(see illustration)**. Do not drop it, as it is very heavy. Discard the bolts, they must be renewed whenever they are disturbed.

Inspection

4 If the flywheel-to-clutch mating surface is deeply scored, cracked or otherwise damaged, then the flywheel must be renewed, unless it is possible to have it surface ground. Seek the advice of a BMW dealer or engine reconditioning specialist.

5 If the ring gear is badly worn or has missing teeth, then it must be renewed. This job is best left to a BMW dealer or engine reconditioning specialist.

6 These vehicles are fitted with dual mass flywheels. Whilst BMW do not publish any checking procedures, rotate the inner mass by hand anti-clockwise, mark its position in relation to the outer mass, then rotate it by hand clockwise and measure the travel. As a general rule, if the movement is more than 30 mm or less than 15 mm, consult a BMW dealer or transmission specialist as to whether a new unit is needed.

Refitting

7 Clean the mating surfaces of the flywheel and crankshaft and remove all traces of locking compound from the crankshaft threaded holes.

8 Fit the flywheel to the crankshaft, engaging it with the crankshaft locating dowel, and fit the new retaining bolts. Note: If the new bolts are not supplied pre-coated with locking compound, apply a few drops prior to fitting the bolts.

9 Lock the flywheel using the method employed on dismantling then, working in a diagonal sequence, tighten all the retaining bolts to the specified torque setting.

10 Refit the clutch assembly as described in Chapter 6.

Driveplate

Note: *New driveplate retaining bolts must be used on refitting.*

Removal

11 Remove the automatic transmission and torque converter as described in Chapter 7B.

12 Prevent the driveplate from turning by locking the ring gear teeth with a similar arrangement to that shown **(see illustration 12.2)**. Alternatively, bolt a strap between the driveplate and the cylinder block/crankcase.

13 Slacken and remove the retaining bolts and remove the driveplate, noting its locating dowel. Discard the bolts, they must be renewed whenever they are disturbed.

Inspection

14 If the ring gear is badly worn or has missing teeth, then it must be renewed. This job is best left to a BMW dealer or engine reconditioning specialist.

Refitting

15 Clean the mating surfaces of the

12.3 Note the locating dowel

driveplate and crankshaft and remove all traces of locking compound from the crankshaft threaded holes.

16 Fit the driveplate to the crankshaft, engaging it with the crankshaft locating dowel, and fit the new retaining bolts. Note: If the new bolts are not supplied pre-coated with locking compound, apply a few drops prior to fitting the bolts.

17 Lock the driveplate using the method employed on dismantling then, working in a diagonal sequence, tighten all the retaining bolts to the specified torque setting.

18 Refit the torque converter and automatic transmission as described in Chapter 7B.

13 Engine mountings – inspection and renewal

Inspection

1 Two engine mountings are used, one on either side of the engine.

2 If improved access is required, raise the front of the vehicle and support it securely on axle stands (see *Jacking and vehicle support*). Undo the fasteners and remove the engine undershield.

3 Check the mounting rubber to see if it is cracked, hardened or separated from the metal at any point. Renew the mounting if any such damage or deterioration is evident.

4 Check that all the mounting fasteners are securely tightened.

5 Using a large screwdriver or a crowbar,

13.7a Disconnect the earth strap from the mounting bracket

check for wear in the mounting by carefully levering against it to check for free play. Where this is not possible, enlist the aid of an assistant to move the engine/transmission back-and-forth, or from side-to-side, while you observe the mounting. While some freeplay is to be expected, even from new components, excessive wear should be obvious. If excessive freeplay is found, check first that the fasteners are correctly secured, then renew any worn components as required.

Renewal

6 Support the engine, either using a hoist and lifting tackle connected to the engine lifting brackets (refer to Engine – removal and refitting in Part D of this Chapter), or by positioning a jack and interposed block of wood under the sump. Ensure that the engine is adequately supported before proceeding.

7 Unscrew the nuts securing the left- and right-hand engine mounting brackets to the mounting rubbers, then unbolt the mounting brackets from the cylinder block, and remove the mounting brackets. Disconnect any engine earth straps from the mountings (where fitted) **(see illustrations)**.

8 Unscrew the nuts securing the mountings to the subframe, then withdraw the mountings. Disconnect the vacuum hoses from the mountings as they are withdrawn (where applicable)

9 Refitting is a reversal of removal. Tighten all fasteners to their specified torque where given.

14 Flywheel pilot bearing – inspection, removal and refitting

Inspection

1 The pilot bearing is fitted into the centre of the dual mass flywheel, and provides support for the free end of the gearbox input shaft on manual transmission vehicles. It can only be examined once the clutch (Chapter 6) has been removed. Using a finger, rotate the inner race of the bearing and check for any roughness, binding or looseness in the bearing. If any of these conditions are evident, the bearing must be renewed.

13.7b Engine mounting bracket retaining bolts (3 bolts arrowed – 1 bolt hidden)

14.3 Drive the flywheel pilot bearing out from the engine side

14.4a Position the bearing...

14.4b... then fit it using a tubular spacer or socket

Removal

2 Remove the flywheel as described in Section 12.

3 Ideally the bearing should be pressed out using a hydraulic press. However, we managed to remove the old bearing and fit the new one using a hammer, drift and socket. Position the flywheel over a 27 mm socket that bears on the flywheel centre immediately surrounding the bearing. Then drive the bearing from the flywheel with a drift. The bearing is driven from the engine side of the flywheel and out of the clutch side **(see illustration)**. Note that the act of pressing the bearing out will render it unusable – it must be renewed.

Refitting

4 Using a suitable tubular spacer that bears only on the hard outer edge of the bearing, press/drive the new bearing into the flywheel until it contacts the shoulder **(see illustrations)**.

5 Refit the flywheel as described in Section 12.

15 Timing chains and cover – removal and refitting

Removal

1 Remove the cylinder head as described in Section 7.

2 Remove the sump as described in Section 8.

3 Remove the crankshaft timing chain end oil seal as described in Section 11.

4 On models with conventional power steering, undo the 3 bolts securing the pulley to the power steering pump, then undo the 3 mounting bolts and move the pump to one side. There's no need to disconnect the hoses/pipes.

5 Remove the alternator as described in Chapter 5A.

6 Undo the bolt and remove the alternator drivebelt tensioner **(see illustration)**.

7 Remove the coolant pump as described in Chapter 3.

8 Undo the 2 bolts securing the EGR solenoid valve bracket to the timing cover.

9 Undo the bolts and pull the timing cover from place **(see illustration)**.

10 In order to renew the timing cover gasket, the timing chain from the crankshaft to the fuel injection pump must be removed as follows:

11 Compress the timing chain tensioner by hand, and lock it in place using a 4.0 mm drill bit **(see illustration)**.

12 Undo the bolts and remove the chain tensioner, followed by the upper guide rail **(see illustrations)**.

13 Undo the nut securing the sprocket to the fuel injection pump **(see illustration)**.

15.6 Drivebelt tensioner bolt

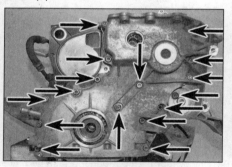

15.9 Timing chain cover bolts

15.11 Push back the tensioner piston, then lock it in place with a 4.0 mm drill bit

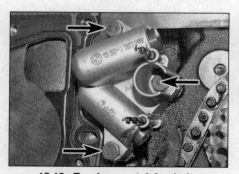

15.12a Tensioner retaining bolts

15.12b Slide the upper guide rail from place

15.13 Undo the fuel injection pump sprocket nut

15.14a Remove the chain sprockets and lower guide rail

15.14b If necessary, use a puller to extract the fuel pump sprocket

15.17 Locate the new gasket over the dowels on the engine block

14 Carefully pull the timing chains, the sprockets from the crankshaft and fuel injection pump shaft, and the lower guide rail from place. If necessary, use a two-legged puller to release the fuel pump sprocket from the shaft taper **(see illustrations)**.

15 Remove the old gasket.

Refitting

16 Ensure the timing chain cover and cylinder block mating surfaces are clean and free from oil and debris. Ensure the dowels in the cylinder block are undamaged and in place.

17 Locate the new gasket over the dowels on the cylinder block **(see illustration)**.

18 Refit the timing chains and sprockets, and lower guide rail as an assembly to the crankshaft and fuel injection pump shaft. Ensure the crankshaft sprocket locates correctly over the shaft key **(see illustration)**.

19 Tighten the fuel injection pump sprocket retaining nut to the specified torque.

20 Refit the upper timing chain guide rail and tensioner. Tighten the fasteners to the specified torque, then pull out the tensioner locking drill bit.

21 Apply a little sealant (Drei Bond 1209) to the base of the gasket each side **(see illustration)**, then refit the timing chain cover over the dowels in the cylinder block.

22 Insert the timing chain cover bolts and tighten them evenly to their specified torque.

23 Fit a new crankshaft/timing cover oil seal as described in Section 11.

24 The remainder of refitting is a reversal of removal.

16 Oil pressure and level switches – removal and refitting

Oil pressure switch

1 The oil pressure switch is located on the left-hand side of the engine block behind the

15.18 Ensure the sprocket locates over the crankshaft key

16.2 Oil pressure switch

oil filter housing. Remove the oil filter element as described in Chapter 1B. This allows the oil to drain from the housing, preventing excessive oil leakage as the switch is removed.

2 Disconnect the wiring plug, and unscrew the switch **(see illustration)**. Be prepared for oil spillage.

3 Refitting is a reversal of removal, using a new sealing washer, and tightening the switch to the specified torque. Top-up the engine oil.

Oil level switch

4 Drain the engine oil as described in Chapter 1B.

15.21 Apply a little sealant to the base of the gasket each side

16.6 The oil level switch is retained by 3 nuts

5 Undo the fasteners and remove the engine undershield.

6 Disconnect the wiring plug, undo the three retaining nuts and remove the switch **(see illustration)**.

7 Ensure that the sump mating surface is clean.

8 Complete with a new seal, install the switch, apply a little thread-locking compound and tighten the retaining nuts to the specified torque.

9 Refit the engine undershield, and replenish the engine oil as described in Chapter 1B.

Chapter 2 Part C:
Diesel engine (N47 and N57) in-car repair procedures

Contents

Degrees of difficulty

Easy, suitable for novice with little experience	**Fairly easy,** suitable for beginner with some experience	**Fairly difficult,** suitable for competent DIY mechanic	**Difficult,** suitable for experienced DIY mechanic	**Very difficult,** suitable for expert DIY or professional

Specifications

General

Engine type:

N47	Four-cylinder in-line, double overhead camshaft, 16-valve, four-stroke, liquid-cooled
N57	Six-cylinder in-line, double overhead camshaft, 16-valve, four-stroke, liquid cooled
Bore	84.00 mm
Stroke	90.00 mm
Capacity:	
Four-cylinder engines.	1995 cc
Six-cylinder engines.	2993 cc
Direction of crankshaft rotation	Clockwise (seen from the front of the engine)
Compression ratio:	
N47	16.0 : 1
N47T	16.5 : 1
N57	16.5 : 1
Compression pressure:	
Minimum.	16 bar

Lubrication system

Minimum system pressure:	
Idle speed (hot).	1.3 bar
3500 rpm (hot)	4.0 to 6.0 bar

Torque wrench settings

	Nm	lbf ft
Auxiliary belt guide pulley bolt	20	15
Camshaft bearing cap bolts	10	7
Camshaft carrier to cylinder head	13	10
Camshaft cover bolts:		
M6	10	7
M7	15	11
Camshaft sprocket to gearwheel (intake camshaft)	14	10
Connecting rod big-end bearing cap bolts:		
Stage 1	5	4
Stage 2	20	15
Stage 3	Angle-tighten a further 70°	
Crankshaft pulley/vibration damper bolts: *		
Stage 1	40	30
Stage 2	Angle-tighten a further 120°	
Cylinder block drain plug	25	18
Cylinder block reinforcement plate (N57 only)	19	14
Cylinder head bolts: *		
Stage 1	70	52
Stage 2	Slacken 180°	
Stage 3	50	37
Stage 4	Angle-tighten a further 120°	
Stage 5	Angle-tighten a further 120°	
Cylinder head-to-timing cover bolts:		
M7	15	11
M8	20	15
Engine mountings:		
Mounting to front subframe:		
M8	28	21
M10	56	41
Mounting to engine support bracket	56	41
Engine support bracket to engine	38	28
Flywheel/driveplate bolts*	120	89
Front subframe mounting bolts:		
M10:		
Stage 1	56	41
Stage 2	Angle-tighten a further 90°	
M12	108	80
Fuel injection pump sprocket retaining bolt	65	48
Main bearing cap bolts: *		
Stage 1	25	18
Stage 2	50	37
Stage 3	Angle-tighten a further 60°	
Stage 4	Angle-tighten a further 60°	
Oil cooler-to-oil filter housing bolts	22	16
Oil filter cap	25	18
Oil filter housing bolts	25	18
Oil level switch	8	6
Oil pressure switch	28	19
Oil pump:		
N47 engine:		
M7	25	18
M8: *		
Stage 1	15	11
Stage 2	Angle-tighten a further 90°	
N57 engine	20	15
Oil pump intake pipe	20	15
Oil pump sprocket (left-hand thread):		
Stage 1	5	4
Stage 2	Angle-tighten a further 50°	
Piston oil spray jet bolts	10	7
Reinforcement brace to subframe: *		
Stage 1	56	41
Stage 2	Angle-tighten a further 90°	
Roadwheel bolts	120	89

Torque wrench settings (continued)

	Nm	lbf ft
Suspension turret/tension braces: *		
M10 (outer bolts):		
Stage 1	40	30
Stage 2	Angle-tighten a further 60°	
M12 (centre bolt):		
Stage 1	100	74
Stage 2	Angle-tighten a further 100°	
Sump bolts:		
M6	10	7
M8	25	18
Sump drain plug.	25	18
Timing chain cover bolts:		
M6:		
Stage 1	8	6
Stage 2	Angle-tighten a further 90°	
Timing chain cover bolt plug:		
M34	20	15
M40	30	22
Timing chain cover to fuel pump:		
M6	10	7
M7	15	11
M8	22	16
Timing chain lower guide pins	20	15
Timing chain tensioner:		
Lower bolts.	10	7
Upper bolts.	70	52

*Do not re-use
Caution: All aluminium fastenings must be renewed. If in doubt, try to attract the bolt/stud with a magnet. Aluminium is not magnetic.

1 General information and precautions

How to use this Chapter

1 This Part of the Chapter describes those repair procedures that can reasonably be carried out on the engine whilst it remains in the vehicle. If the engine has been removed from the vehicle and is being dismantled as described in Part D of this Chapter, any preliminary dismantling procedures can be ignored.

2 Note that whilst it may be possible physically to overhaul items such as the piston/ connecting rod assemblies with the engine in the vehicle, such tasks are not usually carried out as separate operations and usually require the execution of several additional procedures (not to mention the cleaning of components and of oilways). For this reason, all such tasks are classed as major overhaul procedures and are described in Part D of this Chapter.

Engine description

3 This Chapter covers 4- and 6-cylinder diesel engines fitted to the E90/91 3-Series range from September 2008. These engines are in most respects, identical to one another, apart from the number of cylinders.

4 The aluminium cylinder block is of the dry-liner type. The crankshaft is supported within the cylinder block on five shell-type main bearings. Thrustwashers are integral

with the No 3 (4-cylinder engine) or No 4 (6-cylinder engine) main bearing shells to control crankshaft endfloat.

5 The cylinder head is of the double overhead camshaft, 4-valve per cylinder design – two intake and two exhaust valves per cylinder. The valves are operated by one intake camshaft and one exhaust camshaft, via rocker fingers. One end of each finger acts upon the valve stem, whilst the other end pivots on a support pillar. Valve clearances are maintained automatically by hydraulic compensation elements (tappets) incorporated within the support pillars. In order to achieve high levels of combustion efficiency, the cylinder head has two intake ports for each cylinder. One port is tangential, whilst the other is helical.

6 The connecting rods rotate on horizontally-split bearing shells at their big-ends. The pistons are attached to the connecting rods by gudgeon pins which are secured in position with circlips. The aluminium alloy pistons are fitted with three piston rings, comprising two compression rings and an oil control ring.

7 The intake and exhaust valves are each closed by coil springs and operate in guides pressed into the cylinder head. Valve guides cannot be renewed.

8 A timing chain at the rear of the engine, driven by the crankshaft, drives the high-pressure fuel pump sprocket, which in turn drives the intake camshaft. The camshafts are geared together. The vacuum pump is integral with the oil pump. The coolant pump is driven by the auxiliary drivebelt.

9 On all engines, lubrication is by means of

an eccentric-rotor type pump driven by the crankshaft via a Simplex chain. The pump draws oil through a strainer located in the sump, and then forces it through an externally-mounted full-flow paper element type oil filter into galleries in the cylinder block/crankcase, from where it is distributed to the crankshaft (main bearings), timing chain (sprayed by a jet), and camshafts. The big-end bearings are supplied with oil via internal drillings in the crankshaft, while the camshaft bearings and the followers receive a pressurised supply via drillings in the cylinder head. The camshaft lobes and valves are lubricated by oil splash, as are all other engine components. An oil cooler (integral with the oil filter housing) is fitted to keep the oil temperature stable under arduous operating conditions.

10 On 4-cylinder engines, the cylinder block is fitted with counter-rotating balance shafts, driven by a gear on the crankshaft.

Repair operations possible with the engine in the car

11 The following work can be carried out with the engine in the vehicle:
a) *Compression pressure – testing.*
b) *Camshaft cover – removal and refitting.*
c) *Crankshaft pulley – removal and refitting.*
d) *Camshafts and rocker arms – removal, inspection and refitting.*
e) *Cylinder head – removal and refitting.*
f) *Cylinder head and pistons – decarbonising.*
g) *Sump – removal and refitting.*
h) *Oil pump – removal, overhaul and refitting.*
i) *Oil filter housing/cooler – removal and refitting.*

3.1 Kits like this from Auto Service Tools Ltd include crankshaft and camshaft setting tools, along with a tool that fits over the pulley bolts to facilitate crankshaft rotation

j) *Crankshaft oil seals – renewal.*
k) *Engine/transmission mountings – inspection and renewal.*
l) *Flywheel/driveplate – removal, inspection and refitting.*

Note: *Although in theory it is possible to remove the timing cover and timing chains with the engine fitted, in practice access is extremely limited, special BMW tools are needed, and the cylinder head and sump must be removed. Consequently, it is recommended that the engine is removed prior to timing cover and chains removal.*

2 Compression test – description and interpretation

Compression test

Note: *A compression tester specifically designed for diesel engines must be used for this test.*

1 When engine performance is down, or if misfiring occurs which cannot be attributed to the fuel system, a compression test can provide diagnostic clues as to the engine's condition. If the test is performed regularly, it can give warning of trouble before any other symptoms become apparent.

2 A compression tester specifically intended for diesel engines must be used, because of the higher pressures involved. The tester is

connected to an adapter which screws into the glow plug or injector hole. It is unlikely to be worthwhile buying such a tester for occasional use, but it may be possible to borrow or hire one – if not, have the test performed by a garage.

3 Unless specific instructions to the contrary are supplied with the tester, observe the following points:

a) *The battery must be in a good state of charge, the air filter must be clean, and the engine should be at normal operating temperature.*
b) *All the glow plugs should be removed before starting the test (see Chapter 5A).*
c) *Disconnect the wiring plugs from the injectors (see Chapter 4B).*

4 There is no need to hold the accelerator pedal down during the test, because the diesel engine air intake is not throttled.

5 Crank the engine on the starter motor; after one or two revolutions, the compression pressure should build-up to a maximum figure, and then stabilise. Record the highest reading obtained.

6 Repeat the test on the remaining cylinders, recording the pressure in each.

7 All cylinders should produce very similar pressures; a difference of more than 2 bars between any two cylinders indicates a fault. Note that the compression should build-up quickly in a healthy engine; low compression on the first stroke, followed by gradually-increasing pressure on successive strokes, indicates worn piston rings. A low compression reading on the first stroke, which does not build-up during successive strokes, indicates leaking valves or a blown head gasket (a cracked head could also be the cause). Deposits on the undersides of the valve heads can also cause low compression. Note: The cause of poor compression is less easy to establish on a diesel engine than on a petrol one. The effect of introducing oil into the cylinders ('wet' testing) is not conclusive, because there is a risk that the oil will sit in the swirl chamber or in the recess on the piston crown instead of passing to the rings.

8 Refer to a BMW dealer or other specialist if in doubt as to whether a particular pressure reading is acceptable.

9 On completion of the test, refit the glow

plugs as described in Chapter 5A, and reconnect the injector wiring plugs.

Leakdown test

10 A leakdown test measures the rate at which compressed air fed into the cylinder is lost. It is an alternative to a compression test, and in many ways it is better, since the escaping air provides easy identification of where pressure loss is occurring (piston rings, valves or head gasket).

11 The equipment needed for leakdown testing is unlikely to be available to the home mechanic. If poor compression is suspected, have the test performed by a suitably-equipped garage.

3 Engine assembly/valve timing settings – general information and usage

Note: *BMW tool No 11 5 320 or suitable equivalent will be required to lock the crankshaft in position, and access to BMW tool No 11 8 760 or equivalent is required to position the camshafts.*

1 The flywheel is equipped with an indent, which aligns with a hole in the engine block when No 1 piston is at TDC (top dead centre). In this position, if No 1 piston is at TDC on its compression stroke, it will be possible to fit a BMW special tool (No 11 8 760) or equivalent, over the square sections of the exhaust camshaft (with all four No 1 cylinder camshaft lobes pointing towards the right-hand side) **(see illustration)**.

2 Firmly apply the handbrake then jack up the front of the vehicle and support it securely on axle stands (see *Jacking and vehicle support*).

3 Undo the retaining bolts/clips and remove the engine undershield (where fitted) **(see illustration)**.

4 Remove the camshaft cover and gasket, as described in Section 4.

5 Pull out the blanking plug from the timing pin hole in the engine block above the starter motor **(see illustration)**. Access is limited – with difficulty, we removed the plug using a length of welding rod. To Improve access, remove the catalytic converter/particulate filter as described in Chapter 4C.

6 Using a socket and extension bar on one

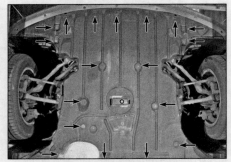

3.3 Undo the fasteners and remove the engine undershield

3.5 Pull the blanking plug from the timing pin hole

3.6 The tools fits over the heads of the pulley bolts

3.7 Insert the crankshaft timing pin and engage it with the indent in the flywheel

3.8a The marks on the sprocket faces must align

3.8b Fit the setting tool over the flats on the exhaust camshaft collar

of the crankshaft pulley centre bolts, turn the crankshaft clockwise whilst keeping an eye on the No 1 cylinder camshaft lobes. BMW tool No 11 6 480 or equivalent is available to rotate the crankshaft pulley bolts. The tool fits over all 4 bolts **(see illustration)**. Note: Do not turn the engine anti-clockwise.

7 Rotate the crankshaft clockwise until the No 1 cylinder camshaft lobes approach the point where all four lobes are pointing upwards. Have an assistant insert BMW Tool No 11 5 320 or equivalent into the timing pin hole, and press the pin gently against the flywheel. Continue to turn the crankshaft slowly until the pin is felt to engage in the indent in the flywheel and the crankshaft locks **(see illustration)**.

8 With the crankshaft in this position, all four camshaft lobes of No 1 cylinder should be pointing to the right-hand side. Check that the 2 marks on the front of the exhaust camshaft sprocket align with the single mark on the front of the intake camshaft sprocket. Fit BMW tool No 11 8 760 or equivalent over the flats on the exhaust camshaft collar, adjacent to No 1 camshaft bearing cap. If the camshaft is timed correctly, the tool will contact both sides of the camshaft cover gasket face on the cylinder head **(see illustrations)**. Note: To avoid confusion, bear in mind that the timing chain and sprockets are fitted at the rear of the engine.

4 Camshaft cover – removal and refitting

Removal

1 Disconnect the battery negative lead (refer to Chapter 5A).
2 Remove the pollen filter housing as described in Chapter 1B Section 6.
3 Pull the engine cover front edge upwards, the forwards from place.
4 Remove the lower pollen filter housing as described in Chapter 1B Section 11.

Models with suspension turret braces

5 Remove the plastic cap from the centre of the scuttle trim panel. Two different types of the cap are fitted: one with a central slot, removed by rotating it 45° anti-clockwise, and

one without a central slot, which is prised from place **(see illustration)**. Note that if the cap or seal are damaged, they must be renewed. Failure to do so may result in water ingress.
6 Undo the bolt in the centre of the scuttle, exposed by the cap removal **(see illustration)**. Discard the bolt – a new one must be fitted.

Version A

7 Undo the bolt at each outer end of the braces, then hold the rubber grommet in place and slide the braces outwards from place **(see illustration)**. Do not allow the grommet to be displaced. Discard the bolts – new ones must be fitted.

Version B

8 Undo the nuts and remove the strut brace **(see illustration)**.
9 If required, undo the nuts and remove the bracket from the top of the suspension turret each side **(see illustration)**. Renew the nuts.

4.5 Remove the cap in the centre of the scuttle trim...

4.6... and undo the bolt in the centre

4.7 Undo the bolt at each end

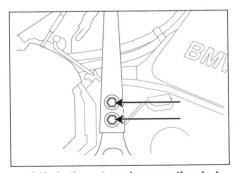

4.8 Undo the nuts and remove the strut brace

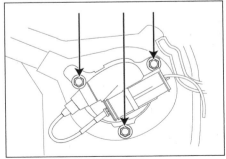

4.9 Strut brace bracket retaining nuts

**4.11a Cable bracket retaining bolts –
4-cylinder engines...**

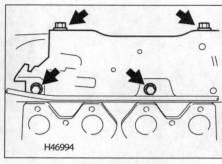

4.11b... and 6-cylinder engines

4.12 Oil filler neck retaining bolt

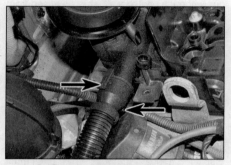

**4.13a Squeeze together the clips and
disconnect the breather hose**

**4.13b Release the wiring harness from the
cover**

**4.14 Undo the bolts and remove the
grommet housing**

**4.18 Don't forget to renew the seals around
the injector apertures**

All models

10 With reference to Chapter 4B, remove the intake manifold, fuel injectors and common rail.

11 Note their fitted positions and routing, then undo the bolts and move the wiring harness and cable holders to one side **(see illustrations)**. Disconnect the wiring plugs as necessary, and place the wiring harness assembly over the left-hand side of the engine compartment.

12 On 6-cylinder engines, and some 4-cylinder engines, undo the bolt, rotate the oil filler neck anti-clockwise to the stop, and remove it from the camshaft cover **(see illustration)**.

13 Release the clips and detach the engine breather hose from the camshaft cover, and the wiring harness from the cover **(see illustrations)**.

6-cyilnder engines

14 Undo the 3 bolts, press the bulkhead grommet housing down and pull it forwards to remove it **(see illustration)**.

15 Working in the reverse of the sequence shown in illustration 4.19, gradually unscrew the retaining bolts, and remove the camshaft cover. Discard the gaskets.

4-cylinder engines

16 Working from the outside-in, evenly slacken and remove the bolts securing the camshaft cover to the cylinder head.

17 Remove the cover and discard its gaskets.

Refitting

18 Ensure the mating surfaces are clean and dry then fit the new gaskets to the cover **(see illustration)**.

19 Refit the cover to the cylinder head, ensuring that the gaskets remain correctly seated.

4-cylinder engines

20 Insert the cover retaining bolts and tighten them all by hand. Once all bolts are in position, tighten them to the specified torque setting starting from the inside, working outwards.

6-cylinder engines

21 Insert the cover retaining bolts and tighten them all by hand. Once the bolts are in position, tighten them to the specified torque in sequence **(see illustration)**.

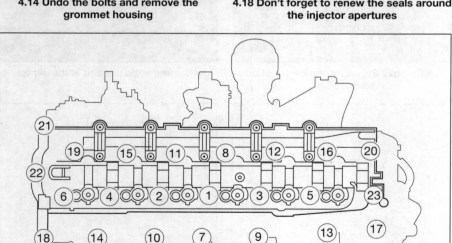

4.21 Camshaft cover bolt tightening sequence – 6-cylinder engines

5.5a Prise out the guide pulley cap and undo the retaining bolt

All engines

22 The remainder of refitting is a reversal of removal.

5 Crankshaft pulley/ vibration damper – removal and refitting

Removal

1 Firmly apply the handbrake then jack up the front of the vehicle and support it securely on axle stands (see *Jacking and vehicle support*).
2 Remove the cooling fan and shroud as described in Chapter 3.
3 Remove the auxiliary drivebelt(s) as described in Chapter 1B.
4 If further dismantling is to be carried out (beyond pulley removal), align the engine assembly/valve timing settings as described in Section 3.
5 Slacken the crankshaft pulley retaining bolts. To prevent crankshaft rotation (the pulley retaining bolts are extremely tight) prise out the guide pulley cap, undo the retaining bolt and remove the pulley. Align BMW special tool No. 11 7 221 with the cut-outs in the centre of the crankshaft pulley, and secure it in place by screwing the locking rod provided into the guide pulley hole **(see illustrations)**. If the engine is removed from the vehicle it is possible to lock the flywheel as described in Section 13.
Caution: Do not be tempted to use the crankshaft locking pin (see Section 3) to prevent rotation as the centre bolt is slackened.
6 Unscrew the retaining bolts, and remove the pulley from the crankshaft **(see illustration)**. Discard the bolts, new ones must be fitted.

Refitting

7 Fit the pulley to the crankshaft and screw in the new retaining bolts.
8 Lock the crankshaft by the method used on removal, and tighten the pulley retaining bolts to the specified Stage 1 torque setting then angle-tighten the bolts through the specified Stage 2 angle, using a socket and extension bar. It is recommended that an angle-measuring gauge is used during the final stages of the tightening, to ensure accuracy. If a gauge is not available, use paint to make

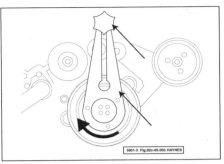

5.5b Align the BMW tool with the damper cut-outs, and secure it with the fastener provided in the guide pulley hole

alignment marks between the bolt heads and pulley prior to tightening; the marks can then be used to check that the bolt has been rotated through the correct angle.
9 The remainder of refitting is a reversal of removal.

6 Camshafts, rocker arms and hydraulic tappets – removal, inspection and refitting

Removal

1 Remove the cylinder head cover as described in Section 4.
2 Firmly apply the handbrake, then jack up the front of the vehicle and support it securely on axle stands (see *Jacking and vehicle support*).
3 Undo the fasteners and remove the engine undershield (where fitted) **(see illustration 3.3)**.

6.5 Unscrew the timing chain tensioner

6.6b... then remove the sprocket and secure the chain to one side

5.6 Crankshaft pulley retaining bolts

4 Set the engine to TDC on No 1 cylinder as described in Section 3. Insert the flywheel locking tool, but do not fit the camshaft locking tool.
5 Undo and release the timing chain tensioner **(see illustration)**. Discard the seal, a new one must be fitted.
6 Undo and remove the bolts securing the sprocket to the camshaft. Pull the sprocket from the camshaft, disengage it from the chain, then use welding rod (or similar) to secure the chain and prevent it from falling into the timing chain cover **(see illustrations)**.
7 Identify the camshaft bearing caps, to ensure they are refitted to their original positions. The exhaust camshaft is marked A, so mark the exhaust camshaft bearing caps as A1, A2, A3, etc, starting with the cap at the front of the engine. The intake camshaft is marked E, so repeat the procedure for the intake camshaft starting with E1 at the front of the engine (furthest from the timing chain) **(see illustration)**.

6.6a Undo the sprocket retaining bolts...

6.7 The camshaft bearing caps are marked A for exhaust, and E for intake. No 1 is at the front of the engine, the timing chain is at the rear

6.10 Working from the outside-in, undo the camshaft carrier bolts

6.15 Refit the hydraulic tappets and rocker arms to their original positions

6.17 Renew the seals between the camshaft carrier and the cylinder head

8 Evenly and progressively, slacken and remove the retaining bolts, and remove the camshaft bearing caps.

9 Remove the camshafts from the cylinder head.

10 Working from the outside towards the centre, undo the bolts and remove the camshaft carrier **(see illustration)**. Recover the seals between the carrier and the cylinder head.

11 Lift the rocker arms from the cylinder head, and lay them out in order on a clean surface, so that they can be fitted into their original positions – if they are to be re-used. Note that the rocker arms are clipped to the tappets – unless required, there is no need to separate the two – lift the rockers and tappets together.

12 Obtain 16 (4-cylinder engines) or 24 (6-cylinder engines) small, clean plastic containers, and label them for identification. Alternatively, divide a larger container into compartments. Withdraw each hydraulic tappet in turn, and place it in its respective container, which should then be filled with clean engine oil.

Caution: Do not interchange the tappets, and do not allow the tappets to lose oil, as they will take a long time to refill with oil on restarting the engine, which could result in incorrect valve clearances. Absolute cleanliness is essential at all times when handling the tappets.

Inspection

13 Examine the camshaft bearing surfaces and cam lobes for signs of wear ridges

and scoring. Renew the camshaft if any of these conditions are apparent. Examine the condition of the bearing surfaces both on the camshaft journals and in the cylinder head. If the head bearing surfaces are worn excessively, the cylinder head will need to be renewed.

14 Examine the rocker bearing surfaces which contact the camshaft lobes for wear ridges and scoring. If the engine's valve clearances have sounded noisy, particularly if the noise persists after initial start-up from cold, then there is reason to suspect a faulty tappet. If any tappet is thought to be faulty or is visibly worn it should be renewed.

Refitting

15 Where removed, lubricate the tappets with clean engine oil and carefully insert each one into its original location in the cylinder head **(see illustration)**.

16 Refit the rocker arms to their original locations, ensuring that they are correctly orientated, and clipped onto the tappets (if removed).

17 Ensure the mating surfaces of the camshaft carrier and cylinder head are clean, then refit the camshaft carrier using new seals. Tighten the bolts to the specified torque working from the centre to the outside **(see illustration)**.

18 Remove the crankshaft locking tool, and rotate the crankshaft 45° anti-clockwise to prevent any accidental piston-to-valve contact. Ensure the timing chain does not fall into the timing cover, or jam on the crankshaft sprocket.

19 Engage the gear on the exhaust camshaft with the gear on the intake camshaft, so the 2 dots on the front of the intake camshaft gear are each side of the dot on the exhaust camshaft gear, then lay the camshafts in place on the camshaft carrier so the dots are flush with the upper surface of the cylinder head **(see illustration 3.8a)**.

20 Lubricate the bearing surfaces of the camshaft with clean engine oil, then refit the bearing caps to their original positions.

21 Insert the bearing cap bolts, then evenly and progressively tighten the retaining bolts to draw the bearing caps squarely down into contact with the cylinder head. Once the caps are in contact with the head, tighten the retaining bolts to the specified torque.

Caution: If the bearing caps bolts are carelessly tightened, the caps might break. If the caps are broken then the complete cylinder head assembly must be renewed; the caps are matched to the head and are not available separately.

22 With the camshafts in this position, it should be possible to fit BMW tool No 11 8 760 (or equivalent) over the square section on the exhaust camshaft, as described in Section 3. If not, rotate the camshafts using a 10 mm Allen key in the hexagonal section in the centre of the exhaust camshaft **(see illustrations)**.

23 With the camshafts held in position, rotate the crankshaft 45° clockwise (back to TDC) so the flywheel locking tool can be reinserted. Ensure the timing chain doesn't fall inside the cover, or jam on the crankshaft sprocket.

24 Engage the timing chain with the sprocket,

6.22a Rotate the exhaust camshaft using a 10 mm Allen bit/key...

6.22b... in the hexagonal section in the centre of the camshaft

6.24 The sprocket bolts holes should be almost in the centre of the slots

and position the sprocket on the end of the intake camshaft so the bolt holes are in the centre of the slots (see illustration).

25 Fit the sprocket retaining bolts into the holes and tighten them to 10 Nm (7 lbf ft), then slacken them 90° each.

26 The oil within the chain tensioner must be evacuated. Hold the tensioner on a hard, level surface and slowly compress to squeeze out the oil (see illustration). Repeat this procedure twice. With a new seal fitted, refit the chain tensioner and tighten it to the specified torque.

27 Make a final check to ensure the camshaft and flywheel locking tools are correctly fitted, then tighten the camshaft sprocket bolts to the specified torque.

28 Remove the camshaft and flywheel locking tools, then rotate the crankshaft two complete revolutions clockwise, and check the camshaft and flywheel tools can still be installed. If they cannot, repeat the fitting procedure from paragraph 24 onwards.

29 The remainder of refitting is a reversal of removal.

7 Cylinder head – removal and refitting

Removal

1 Remove the camshafts, rocker arms and tappets as described in Section 6.

2 Drain the cooling system, as described in Chapter 1B.

3 Remove the turbocharger as described in Chapter 4B.

4 Remove the EGR cooler as described in Chapter 4C.

5 Release the retaining clips, and disconnect the various coolant hoses from the cylinder head (see illustration).

6 Undo the plug on the right-hand side of the cylinder block and drain the coolant (see illustration). Fit a new sealing washer and tighten the drain plug to the specified torque.

7 Undo the 2 bolts at the rear of the cylinder head (see illustration). Where applicable, undo the 3 bolts and remove the wiring harness support bracket from the cylinder head and right-hand engine mounting bracket.

8 Undo the 3 bolts at the rear, left-hand corner or the cylinder head (see illustration).

9 Make a final check to ensure that all relevant hoses, pipes and wires, etc, have been disconnected.

10 Working in the reverse of the tightening sequence (see illustration 7.28a or 7.28b), progressively slacken the cylinder head bolts by a third of a turn at a time until all bolts can be unscrewed by hand. Withdraw and discard the bolts, new ones must be fitted.

11 Lift the cylinder head from the cylinder block. If necessary, tap the cylinder head gently with a soft-faced mallet to free it from the block, but do not lever at the mating faces.

6.26 Compress the tensioner piston to evacuate any oil

12 When the joint is broken, lift the cylinder head away then remove the gasket. Note the fitted positions of the two locating dowels, and remove them for safe-keeping if they are loose. Keep the gasket for identification purposes (see paragraph 18).

Caution: Do not lay the head on its lower mating surface; support the head on wooden blocks, ensuring each block only contacts the head mating surface not the glow plugs. The glow plugs protrude out the bottom of the head and they will be damaged if the head is placed directly onto a bench.

13 If the cylinder head is to be dismantled, refer to the relevant Sections of Part D of this Chapter.

Preparation for refitting

14 The mating faces of the cylinder head and block must be perfectly clean before refitting

7.5 Prise out the clips and disconnect the various coolant hoses from the cylinder head

7.7 Undo the 2 bolts at the rear of the cylinder head...

the head. Use a scraper to remove all traces of gasket and carbon, and also clean the tops of the pistons. Take particular care with the aluminium surfaces, as the soft metal is damaged easily. Also, make sure that debris is not allowed to enter the oil and water channels – this is particularly important for the oil circuit, as carbon could block the oil supply to the camshaft or crankshaft bearings. Using adhesive tape and paper, seal the water, oil and bolt holes in the cylinder block. To prevent carbon entering the gap between the pistons and bores, smear a little grease in the gap. After cleaning the piston, rotate the crankshaft so that the piston moves down the bore, then wipe out the grease and carbon with a cloth rag. Clean the piston crowns in the same way.

15 Check the block and head for nicks, deep scratches and other damage. If slight, they may be removed carefully with a file. More serious damage may be repaired by machining, but this is a specialist job.

16 If warpage of the cylinder head gasket surface is suspected, use a straight-edge to check it for distortion. Refer to Part D of this Chapter if necessary.

17 Ensure that the cylinder head bolt holes in the crankcase are clean and free of oil. Syringe or soak up any oil left in the bolt holes. This is most important in order that the correct bolt tightening torque can be applied and to prevent the possibility of the block being cracked by hydraulic pressure when the bolts are tightened.

18 On these engines, the cylinder head to piston clearance is controlled by fitting

7.6 The cylinder block drain plug is located on the right-hand side of the block

7.8... and the 3 at the rear, left-hand corner

7.18 Cylinder head gasket identification holes (arrowed – see text)

7.21 Measure the piston protrusion using a DTI gauge

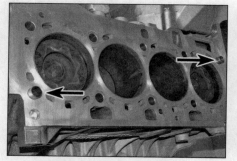

7.24 Ensure the locating dowels are in place

7.25 Apply sealant where the cylinder block meets the timing chain cover

different thickness head gaskets. The piston protrusion is represented by the number of holes in the gasket next to the timing chain area **(see illustration)**.

Holes in gasket	Largest piston protrusion
One hole	Up to 0.92 mm
Two holes	0.92 to 1.03 mm
Three holes	1.03 to 1.18 mm

19 Select the new gasket which has the same thickness/number of holes as the original, unless new piston and connecting rod assemblies have been fitted. In that case, the correct thickness of gasket required is selected by measuring the piston protrusions as follows.

20 Remove the locking pin from the flywheel and mount a dial test indicator securely on the block so that its pointer can be easily pivoted between the piston crown and block mating surface.

21 Ensure the piston is at exactly TDC then zero the dial test indicator on the gasket surface of the cylinder block. Carefully move the indicator over No 1 piston, taking measurements in line with the gudgeon pin axis, measure the protrusion on both the left-hand and right-hand side of the piston **(see illustration)**. Note: When turning the crankshaft, ensure that the timing chain does not jam in the timing cover.

22 Rotate the crankshaft to bring the remaining pistons to TDC in turn. Ensure the crankshaft is accurately positioned then measure the protrusions of remaining pistons, taking two measurements for each piston. Once all the pistons have been measured, rotate the crankshaft to bring No 1 piston back to TDC. Then rotate it 45° anti-clockwise.

23 Use the table in paragraph 18 to select the appropriate gasket.

Refitting

24 Wipe clean the mating faces of the head and block and ensure that the two locating dowels are in position on the cylinder block/crankcase surface **(see illustration)**.

25 Apply a little sealant (Drei Bond 1209) to the area where the timing chain cover meets the cylinder block **(see illustration)**, then fit the new gasket to the cylinder block, ensuring that it fits correctly over the locating dowels.

26 Carefully refit the cylinder head, locating it on the dowels. Make sure the timing chain can be pulled up through the cylinder head tunnel.

27 The new cylinder head bolts are supplied pre-coated – do not wash the coating off, or apply grease/oil to them. Carefully enter the main bolts (1 to 10 on 4-cylinder engines, or 1 to 14 on 6-cylinder engines) into the holes and screw them in, by hand only, until finger-tight. **Caution: Do not drop the bolts into their holes.**

28 Working progressively and in sequence, first tighten all the cylinder head bolts to the Stage 1 torque setting **(see illustrations)**.

29 Slacken all the bolts half a turn (180°), then tighten them in sequence to the Stage 3 setting.

30 Again, in sequence, angle-tighten them to Stage 4, and then Stage 5, using an angle-measuring gauge **(see illustration)**.

31 Refit and tighten the bolts at the rear/corner securing the cylinder head to the timing cover, to the specified torque **(see illustrations 7.7 and 7.8)**.

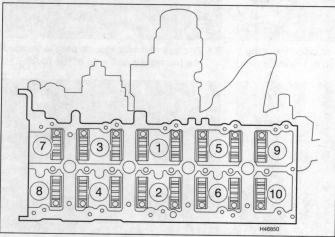

7.28a Cylinder head bolt tightening sequence – 4-cylinder engines

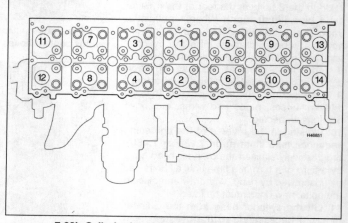

7.28b Cylinder head bolt tightening sequence – 6-cylinder engines

7.30 Tighten the cylinder head bolts using an angle-gauge

32 The remainder of refitting is a reversal of removal, noting the following points:
a) *Renew all gaskets/seals disturbed during the removal procedure.*
b) *Tighten all fasteners to their specified torque where given.*
c) *Refill the cooling system as described in Chapter 1B.*

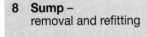

8 Sump –
removal and refitting

Removal

1 Drain the engine oil and remove the oil filter as described in Chapter 1B. Refit the sump plug with a new washer and tighten the plug to the specified torque.
2 Remove the acoustic cover from the top of the engine **(see illustration)**.

8.10 Release the clips and remove the plastic cover each side

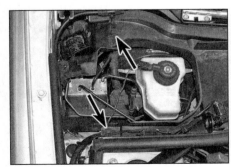

8.12b Undo the bolt, release the clip...

8.2 Pull up the front edge, and slide the acoustic cover forwards

3 Remove the cooling fan and shroud as described in Chapter 3.
4 On 4-cylinder models, it may just be possible to remove the sump without lowering the front subframe. However, we recommend the front subframe is lowered a little as follows:
5 Jack up the front of the vehicle and support it securely on axle stands (see *Jacking and vehicle support*). Remove the retaining bolts and fasteners and remove the engine undershield.
6 Remove the exhaust system as described in Chapter 4B.
7 Remove the bonnet as described in Chapter 11.
8 Remove the wiper arms as described in Chapter 12.
9 Undo the bolts and remove the upper section of the pollen filter housing **(see illustration)**.
10 Release the clips and remove the left-

8.11 Release the clips and slide the cable guide forwards

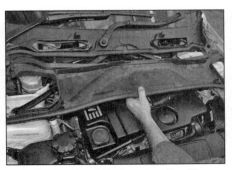

8.12c... and pull the lower pollen filter housing forwards

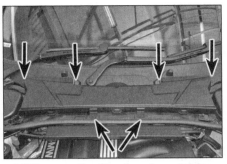

8.9 Upper pollen filter housing retaining bolts

and right-hand plastic covers from the behind the suspension turrets each side **(see illustration)**.
11 Release the clips and detach the cable guide from the front edge of the lower pollen filter housing **(see illustration)**.
12 Undo the bolts, release the clips and slide the pollen filter lower housing forwards and upwards **(see illustrations)**.
13 Disconnect the hose, disconnect the wiring plugs, then remove the windscreen scuttle panel cover.

Models with suspension turret braces

14 Remove the plastic cap from the centre of the scuttle trim panel. Two different types of the cap are fitted: One with a central slot, removed by rotating it 45° anti-clockwise, and one without a central slot, which is prised from place **(see illustrations)**. Note, if the cap or seal are damaged, they must be renewed. Failure to do so may result in water ingress.

8.12a Rotate the temperature sensor and pull it from the bracket. On the passenger's side, disconnect the bonnet switch

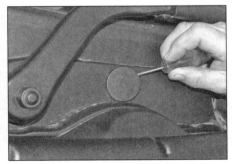

8.14a Prise the cap from place...

8.14b... or rotate it anti-clockwise

8.15 Undo the bolt in the centre of the scuttle trim panel...

8.16... and the bolt at the end of each brace

15 Undo the bolt in the centre of the scuttle, exposed by the cap removal **(see illustration)**. Discard the bolt – a new one must be fitted.

Version A

16 Undo the bolt at each outer end of the braces, then hold the rubber grommet in place and slide the braces outwards from place **(see illustration)**. Do not allow the grommet to be displaced. Discard the bolts – new ones must be fitted.

Version B

17 Undo the nuts and remove the strut brace **(see illustration 4.8)**.
18 If required, undo the nuts and remove the bracket from the top of the suspension turret each side **(see illustration 4.9)**. Renew the nuts.

All models

19 Undo the 3 bolts and remove the grommet

housing from the bulkhead **(see illustration 4.14)**.
20 The engine must be supported in position using an engine hoist or engine crossbeam. Attach the hoist/crossbeam to the engine lifting eyes at the front and rear of the engine. Take the weight of the engine.
21 Undo the nut each side securing the engine mounting support brackets to the mountings, then raise the engine approximately 10 mm.
22 Undo the fasteners, and remove the underbody panelling each side in the area of the reinforcement brace under the subframe **(see illustration)**.
23 Undo the nuts/bolts and remove the reinforcement brace each side under the front subframe **(see illustration)**. Discard the nuts/ bolts – new ones must be fitted.
24 Remove the steering column lower universal joint pinch-bolt and lift the column

shaft upwards from the steering rack pinion **(see illustration)**. Discard the pinch-bolt – a new one must be used.
Caution: Ensure the steering wheel/ column is not rotated with the universal joint disconnected from the steering rack pinion. Damage to the column could result.
25 Disconnect the wiring plugs from the ride height sensors (where fitted), then disconnect the vacuum hoses from the engine mountings (where applicable).
26 On models with electric power steering, cut the cable tie securing the wiring harness to the subframe.
27 Support the front subframe using a workshop jack and lengths of wood, etc, then undo the 3 bolts each side and carefully lower the subframe a maximum of 10 cm **(see illustrations)**. Pay attention to the power steering hoses/pipes as the subframe is being lowered – so not allow them to be bent or stretched. Note that the

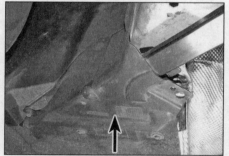

8.22 Remove the underbody panelling each side

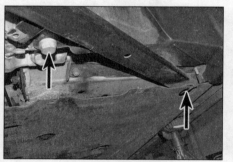

8.23a Undo the bolts each side...

8.23b... and the 2 in the centre of the reinforcement brace

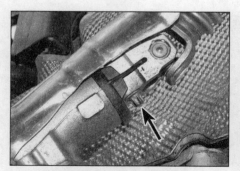

8.24 Steering column universal joint pinch-bolt

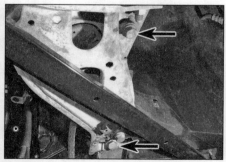

8.27a The front subframe is secured by 2 bolts each side...

8.27b... and one at the front

8.29 The oil level dipstick guide tube is bolted to the oil filter housing

8.34 Oil pump intake pipe bolts

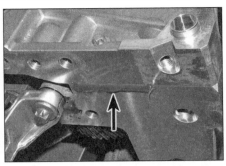

8.37 Apply sealant to the area where the cylinder block meets the timing chain cover

subframe bolts at the front are 90 mm long, the middle bolts are 145 mm long, and the rearmost bolts are 53 mm long. When refitting, tighten down the front bolts first.

28 Remove the starter motor as described in Chapter 5A.

29 Undo the bolt securing the oil level dipstick guide tube and pull the tube from the sump **(see illustration)**. Renew the guide tube O-ring seal.

30 Disconnect the wiring plug from the engine oil level sensor.

31 Slacken and remove the bolts securing the transmission casing to the sump.

32 Progressively slacken and remove the bolts securing the sump to the base of the cylinder block.

33 Break the sump joint by striking the sump with the palm of the hand, then lower the sump away from the engine. Remove the gasket and discard it, a new one should be used on refitting.

34 While the sump is removed, take the opportunity to check the oil pump intake pipe for signs of clogging or splitting. If necessary, unbolt the intake pipe, and remove it from the engine along with its gasket **(see illustration)**. The strainer can then be cleaned easily in solvent. Inspect the strainer mesh for signs of clogging or splitting and renew if necessary. If the intake pipe bolts are damaged they must be renewed.

Refitting

35 Clean all traces of gasket from the mating surfaces of the cylinder block and sump, then use a clean rag to wipe out the sump and the engine interior.

36 Where necessary, fit a new seal to the oil pump intake pipe then carefully refit the pipe. Refit the retaining bolts, and tighten them to the specified torque setting.

37 Apply a bead of suitable sealant (Drei Bond 1209 is available from your BMW dealer) to the area where the cylinder block meets the timing cover **(see illustration)**.

38 Fit the gasket to the sump then offer up the sump to the cylinder block/crankcase **(see illustration)**. Refit the sump retaining bolts, and tighten the bolts finger-tight only.

39 Fit the bolts securing the sump to the gearbox. In order to align the rear sump flange

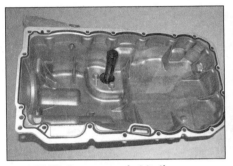

8.38 Fit the new gasket to the sump

with the gearbox, lightly tighten the bolts, then slacken them. If the sump is being refitted to the engine with the gearbox removed, use a straight-edge to ensure that the sump casting is flush with the end of the cylinder block **(see illustration)**.

40 Tighten the sump-to-engine block bolts, and then the sump-to-transmission bolts to the specified torque.

41 Refit the oil dipstick tube, with a new O-ring, and tighten the bolts securely.

42 The remainder of refitting is a reversal of removal, noting the following points:

a) Renew all gaskets/seals where disturbed.

b) Tighten all fasteners to their specified torque where given.

c) Renew the engine oil and filter as described in Chapter 1B.

d) If necessary, have the front wheel alignment checked by a BMW dealer or suitably-equipped specialist.

9.2 Rotate the spacers anti-clockwise and remove them

8.39 Use a straight-edge to ensure the sump is flush with the cylinder block

9   Oil/vacuum pump – removal, inspection and refitting

4-cylinder engines

Note: *BMW insist that a removed oil pump must not be refitted: it must be renewed. The drive gear of the new pump is coated with paint to ensure correct backlash adjustment.*

Removal

1 Remove the sump and oil pump intake pipe as described in Section 8.

2 On N47 engines, undo the 3 bolts down the centre line of the pump, then remove the spacers by rotating them anti-clockwise **(see illustration)**. Discard the bolts – new ones must be fitted.

3 On all 4-cylinder engines, undo the pump retaining bolts.

4 Lift up the front edge of the pump assembly, and manoeuvre the drive sprocket out the from the chain.

Inspection

5 At the time of writing, no new parts are available for the oil/vacuum pump. If defective, the complete assembly must be renewed. Consult a BMW dealer or parts specialist.

Refitting

6 Ensure the mating surfaces of the pump and cylinder block are clean and dry. Ensure all mounting holes are clean and free from oil.

7 Engage the pump drive sprocket with the

11.3 Disconnect the air temperature sensor from the intake pipe

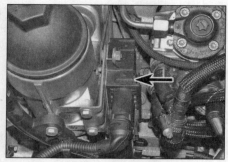

11.4 The glow plug control unit is located behind the oil filter housing

11.7 Oil filter housing bolts

chain and with the pump in place, insert the 8 retaining bolts.
8 Where applicable, refit the 3 spacers to the pump by rotating them clockwise, then refit the 3 pump centre line bolts **(see illustration 9.2)**.
9 Tighten the pump retaining bolts to their specified torque.
10 Refit the sump as described in Section 8.

6-cylinder engines

Removal

11 Remove the sump as described in Section 8.
12 Undo the four retaining bolts and lift the front edge of the pump. Feed the drive sprocket out from the chain, and remove the oil pump.
13 If required, the drive sprocket can be removed from the shaft. Undo the retaining bolt which has a left-hand thread and pull the sprocket from the shaft.
14 If required, undo the 2 bolts and remove the oil pump intake pipe/strainer. Renew the O-ring seal.

Inspection

15 At the time of writing, no new parts are available for the oil pump. If defective, the complete assembly must be renewed. Consult a BMW dealer or parts specialist.

Refitting

16 Where applicable, refit the oil intake pipe and drive sprocket. Tighten the bolts to the specified torque.
17 Engage the drive sprocket with the chain, and position the pump over the locating

11.8a Undo the bolts...

dowels. Insert the pump retaining bolts and tighten them to the specified torque.
18 Refit the sump as described in Section 8.

10 Balance shaft assembly – general information

1 Only the 4-cylinder N47 engine is fitted with balance shafts. These shafts are fitted into the cylinder block each side of the crankshaft, and are gear-driven from the crankshaft. In order to remove the balance shafts, the crankshaft must first be removed. Refer to Chapter 2D.

11 Oil cooler – removal and refitting

Removal

1 Drain the engine coolant, engine oil, and remove the oil filter as described in Chapter 1B.
2 Remove the front section of the acoustic cover from the top of the engine.

N47 and N57 engines

3 Disconnect the intake air temperature sensor wiring plug, then release the clamp at each end and disconnect the air intake duct from the throttle body/intake manifold **(see illustration)**. Check the condition of the seals at each end of the air duct. If the seals or duct sealing lips are in any way damaged/worn, renew them.

11.8b... and pull the cooler from the housing

4 Disconnect the wiring plug from the glow plug control unit **(see illustration)**.
5 Release the cable tie securing the wiring harness, then undo the bolt and pull the engine oil level dipstick guide tube from position **(see illustration 8.29)**. Renew the guide tube O-ring seal.
6 Disconnect the oil pressure switch wiring plug.
7 Undo the bolts and remove the oil filter housing **(see illustration)**. Discard the sealing gasket.

4-cylinder engines

8 Undo the bolts and detach the oil cooler from the oil filter housing. Renew the seals **(see illustrations)**.

6-cylinder engines

9 Release the clips and pull the oil cooler from the filter housing. Renew the seals.

N47T engines

10 Remove the intake manifold as described in Chapter 4B Section 16.
11 Undo the bolts and detach the oil filter housing from the cylinder block.
12 Undo the retaining screws and separate the cooler from the filter housing. Renew the seals/gaskets.

Refitting

13 Ensure the mating surfaces of the oil cooler and oil filter housing are clean and dry, and with a new gasket, fit the cooler to the housing. Tighten the bolts securely or clip the cooler into the housing as applicable.
14 The remainder of refitting is a reversal of removal.

12 Crankshaft oil seals – renewal

Front end oil seal

1 Remove the crankshaft pulley/vibration damper as described in Section 5.
2 Lever out the seal using a flat-bladed screwdriver (or similar).
Caution: Great care must be taken to avoid damage to the crankshaft.
3 Clean the seal housing and polish off any

burrs or raised edges which may have caused the seal to fail in the first place.

4 Do not lubricate the new seal with engine oil or lubricant – the seal must be installed dry. BMW specify a special tool (No 11 8 501) to guide the seal over the crankshaft shoulders. However, with care, it is possible to fit the seal without the tool. Ensure the lips of the seal are around the outer edge of the crankshaft. Press the seal squarely into position until it is flush with the housing. If necessary, a suitable tubular drift, such as a socket, which bears only on the hard outer edge of the seal can be used to tap the seal into position. Take great care not to damage the seal lips during fitting and ensure that the seal lips face inwards.

5 Refit the crankshaft pulley as described in Section 5.

Flywheel/driveplate end oil seal

6 Remove the flywheel or driveplate as described in Section 13, then remove the end cap (where fitted) **(see illustration)**. Avoid touching the outer edge of the end cap with fingers, as the crankshaft position sensor wheel is embedded in the rubber.

7 Lever out the seal using a flat-bladed screwdriver (or similar) **(see illustration)**.
Caution: Great care must be taken to avoid damage to the crankshaft.

8 Do not lubricate the new seal with engine oil or lubricant – the seal must be installed dry. BMW specify a special tool (No 11 8 815) to guide the seal over the crankshaft shoulders. However, with care, it is possible to fit the seal without the tool **(see illustration)**.

9 Press the seal squarely into position until it is flush with the housing. If possible, a suitable tubular drift, such as a socket, which bears only on the hard outer edge of the seal can be used to tap the seal into position. Take great care not to damage the seal lips during fitting and ensure that the seal lips face inwards **(see illustration)**. If available, BMW specify tools No 11 8 11 8 811, 11 8 812, 11 8 813 and 11 8 814 to draw the seal into position in the timing chain cover. Although desirable, the use of these tools is not essential.

10 Refit the end cap, followed by the flywheel/driveplate as described in Section 13.

12.6 Remove the end cap from the crankshaft

12.7 Lever out the seal using a hooked tool or screwdriver

12.8 Guide the seal lips over the crankshaft shoulders...

12.9... then press it into place until it's flush with the housing

13 Flywheel/driveplate – removal, inspection and refitting

Flywheel

Note: New flywheel retaining bolts must be used on refitting.

Removal

1 Remove the clutch assembly as described in Chapter 6.

2 Prevent the flywheel from turning by locking the ring gear teeth with a similar arrangement to that shown **(see illustration)**. Alternatively, bolt a strap between the flywheel and the cylinder block/crankcase.

3 Slacken and remove the retaining bolts and remove the flywheel, noting its locating dowel **(see illustrations)**. Do not drop it, as it is very heavy. Discard the bolts, they must be renewed whenever they are disturbed.

Inspection

4 If the flywheel-to-clutch mating surface is deeply scored, cracked or otherwise damaged, then the flywheel must be renewed, unless it is possible to have it surface ground. Seek the advice of a BMW dealer or engine reconditioning specialist.

5 If the ring gear is badly worn or has missing teeth, then it must be renewed. This job is best left to a BMW dealer or engine reconditioning specialist.

6 These vehicles are fitted with dual mass flywheels. Whilst BMW do not publish any checking procedures, rotate the inner mass by hand anti-clockwise, mark its position in relation to the outer mass, then rotate it by hand clockwise and measure the travel. As a general rule, if the movement is more than 30 mm or less than 15 mm, consult a BMW

13.2 Lock the flywheel using a similar tool

13.3a Note the locating dowel...

13.3b... which corresponds with the hole in the flywheel

13.8a Clean out the crankshaft flywheel bolt threads using an old bolt with a saw cut across it

dealer or transmission specialist as to whether a new unit is needed.

Refitting

7 Clean the mating surfaces of the flywheel and crankshaft and remove all traces of locking compound from the crankshaft threaded holes.

8 Fit the flywheel to the crankshaft, engaging it with the crankshaft locating dowel, and fit the new retaining bolts **(see illustrations)**. **Note:** *If the new bolts are not supplied pre-coated with locking compound, apply a few drops prior to fitting the bolts.*

9 Lock the flywheel using the method employed on dismantling then, working in a diagonal sequence, tighten all the retaining bolts to the specified torque setting.

10 Refit the clutch assembly as described in Chapter 6.

Driveplate

Note: *New driveplate retaining bolts must be used on refitting.*

Removal

11 Remove the automatic transmission as described in Chapter 7B.

12 Prevent the driveplate from turning by locking the ring gear teeth with a similar arrangement to that shown **(see illustration 13.2)**. Alternatively, bolt a strap between the driveplate and the cylinder block/crankcase.

13 Slacken and remove the retaining bolts and remove the driveplate, noting its locating dowel. Discard the bolts, they must be renewed whenever they are disturbed.

14.7 An earth strap is bolted to the left-hand engine mounting bracket

13.8b The new bolts should be pre-coated with thread-locking compound

Inspection

14 If the ring gear is badly worn or has missing teeth, then it must be renewed. This job is best left to a BMW dealer or engine reconditioning specialist.

Refitting

15 Clean the mating surfaces of the driveplate and crankshaft and remove all traces of locking compound from the crankshaft threaded holes.

16 Fit the driveplate to the crankshaft, engaging it with the crankshaft locating dowel, and fit the new retaining bolts. Note: If the new bolts are not supplied pre-coated with locking compound, apply a few drops prior to fitting the bolts.

17 Lock the driveplate using the method employed on dismantling then, working in a diagonal sequence, tighten all the retaining bolts to the specified torque setting.

18 Refit the automatic transmission as described in Chapter 7B.

14 Engine mountings – inspection and renewal

Inspection

1 Two engine mountings are used, one on either side of the engine.

2 If improved access is required, raise the front of the vehicle and support it securely on axle stands (see *Jacking and vehicle support*).

15.3 Drive the flywheel pilot bearing out from the engine side

Undo the fasteners and remove the engine undershield.

3 Check the mounting rubber to see if it is cracked, hardened or separated from the metal at any point. Renew the mounting if any such damage or deterioration is evident.

4 Check that all the mounting fasteners are securely tightened.

5 Using a large screwdriver or a crowbar, check for wear in the mounting by carefully levering against it to check for free play. Where this is not possible, enlist the aid of an assistant to move the engine/transmission back-and-forth, or from side-to-side, while you observe the mounting. While some free play is to be expected, even from new components, excessive wear should be obvious. If excessive free play is found, check first that the fasteners are correctly secured, then renew any worn components as required.

Renewal

6 Support the engine, either using a hoist and lifting tackle connected to the engine lifting brackets (refer to Engine – removal and refitting in Part D of this Chapter), or by positioning a jack and interposed block of wood under the sump. Ensure that the engine is adequately supported before proceeding.

7 Unscrew the nuts securing the left- and right-hand engine mounting brackets to the mounting rubbers, then unbolt the mounting brackets from the cylinder block, and remove the mountings. Disconnect any engine earth straps from the mountings (where fitted) **(see illustration)**.

8 Unscrew the nuts securing the mountings to the subframe, then withdraw the mountings. Disconnect the vacuum hoses from the mountings as they are withdrawn (where applicable)

9 Refitting is a reversal of removal. Tighten all fasteners to their specified torque where given.

15 Flywheel pilot bearing – inspection, removal and refitting

Inspection

1 The pilot bearing is fitted into the centre of the dual mass flywheel, and provides support for the free end of the gearbox input shaft on manual transmission vehicles. It can only be examined once the clutch (Chapter 6) has been removed. Using a finger, rotate the inner race of the bearing and check for any roughness, binding or looseness in the bearing. If any of these conditions are evident, the bearing must be renewed.

Removal

2 Remove the flywheel as described in Section 13.

3 The bearing must be pressed out using a hydraulic press, with a drift that bears only on

15.4a Position the bearing...

15.4b... then fit it using a tubular spacer or socket

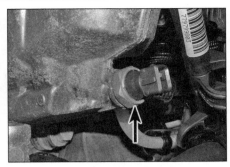

17.2 Oil pressure switch

the inner bearing race. The bearing is pressed from the engine side of the flywheel and out of the clutch side **(see illustration)**. Note that the act of pressing the bearing out will render it unusable – it must be renewed.

Refitting

4 Using a suitable tubular spacer that bears only on the hard outer edge of the bearing, press the new bearing into the flywheel until it contacts the shoulder **(see illustrations)**.
5 Refit the flywheel as described in Section 13.

16 Timing chains and cover –
general information

1 On these engines, the timing chains are fitted at the rear of the engine. In order to remove the timing chains or the timing cover, it is necessary to first remove the engine. Consequently, renewal of the timing chain and covers is described in Chapter 2D.

17 Oil pressure and level switches –
removal and refitting

Oil pressure switch

1 The oil pressure switch is fitted into the base of the oil filter housing. Remove the oil filter element as described in Chapter 1B. This allows the oil to drain from the housing, preventing excessive oil leakage as the switch is removed.
2 Disconnect the wiring plug, and unscrew the switch **(see illustration)**. Be prepared for oil spillage.

3 Refitting is a reversal of removal, using a new sealing washer, and tightening the switch to the specified torque. Top-up the engine oil.

Oil level switch

4 Drain the engine oil as described in Chapter 1B.
5 Undo the fasteners and remove the engine undershield **(see illustration 3.3)**.
6 Disconnect the wiring plug, undo the three retaining nuts and remove the switch from the base of the sump.
7 Ensure that the sump mating surface is clean.
8 Complete with a new seal, install the switch, apply a little thread-locking compound and tighten the retaining nuts to the specified torque.
9 Refit the engine undershield, and replenish the engine oil as described in Chapter 1B.

Chapter 2 Part D:
General engine overhaul procedures

Contents

Degrees of difficulty

Easy, suitable for novice with little experience	Fairly easy, suitable for beginner with some experience	Fairly difficult, suitable for competent DIY mechanic	Difficult, suitable for experienced DIY mechanic	Very difficult, suitable for expert DIY or professional

Specifications

Engine codes
Petrol engines:
    4-cylinder N43
Diesel engines:
    4-cylinder . . . . N47 and N47T
    6-cylinder . . . . M57TU and N57

Cylinder head
Maximum gasket face distortion . . . . 0.050 mm
Cylinder head machining limit:
    Petrol engines . . . . 0.3 mm
    Diesel engines . . . . Not available

Valves
Valve head diameter:
    4-cylinder petrol engines:
        Intake . . . . 29.3 mm
        Exhaust . . . . 26.3 mm
    Diesel engines:
    M57T2:
        Intake . . . . 25.90 mm
        Exhaust . . . . 25.90 mm
    N47 and N57 . . . . Not available

Cylinder block
Cylinder bore diameter:
    Petrol engines . . . . 84.00 mm (nominal)
    Diesel engines . . . . 84.00 mm (nominal)
Maximum cylinder bore ovality . . . . 0.005 mm
Maximum cylinder bore taper . . . . 0.010 mm

Crankshaft

Endfloat (all engines) .... 0.060 to 0.250 mm

Piston rings

End gaps:
  Petrol engines:
    Top compression ring .... 0.15 to 0.30 mm
    Second compression ring................................ 0.20 to 0.40 mm
    Oil control ring .... Not applicable
  Diesel engines:
    M57T2:
      Top compression ring .... 0.20 to 0.35 mm
      Second compression ring........................... 0.30 to 0.45 mm
      Oil control ring................................... Not applicable
    N47 and N57
      Top compression ring .... 0.20 to 0.30 mm
      Second compression ring........................... 0.30 to 0.45 mm
      Oil control ring................................... 0.25 to 0.50 mm

Torque wrench settings

Refer to Chapter 2A, 2B, 2C Specifications, as applicable

1 General Information

1 Included in this Part of Chapter 2 are details of removing the engine/transmission from the car and general overhaul procedures for the cylinder head, cylinder block/crankcase and all other engine internal components.

2 The information given ranges from advice concerning preparation for an overhaul and the purchase of parts, to detailed step-by-step procedures covering removal, inspection, renovation and refitting of engine internal components.

3 After Section 5, all instructions are based on the assumption that the engine has been removed from the car. For information concerning in-car engine repair, as well as the removal and refitting of those external components necessary for full overhaul, refer to Part A, B or C of this Chapter, as applicable and to Section 5. Ignore any preliminary dismantling operations described in Parts A. B or C that are no longer relevant once the engine has been removed from the car.

4 Apart from torque wrench settings, which are given at the beginning of Parts A, B or C, all specifications relating to engine overhaul are at the beginning of this Part of Chapter 2.

2 Engine overhaul – general information

1 It is not always easy to determine when, or if, an engine should be completely overhauled, as a number of factors must be considered.

2 High mileage is not necessarily an indication that an overhaul is needed, while low mileage does not preclude the need for an overhaul. Frequency of servicing is probably the most important consideration. An engine which has had regular and frequent oil and filter changes, as well as other required maintenance, should give many thousands of miles of reliable service. Conversely, a neglected engine may require an overhaul very early in its life.

3 Excessive oil consumption is an indication that piston rings, valve seals and/or valve guides are in need of attention. Make sure that oil leaks are not responsible before deciding that the rings and/or guides are worn. Perform a compression test, as described in Part A, B or C of this Chapter (as applicable), to determine the likely cause of the problem.

4 Check the oil pressure with a gauge fitted in place of the oil pressure switch, and compare it with that specified. If it is extremely low, the main and big-end bearings, and/or the oil pump, are probably worn out.

5 Loss of power, rough running, knocking or metallic engine noises, excessive valve gear noise, and high fuel consumption may also point to the need for an overhaul, especially if they are all present at the same time. If a complete service does not remedy the situation, major mechanical work is the only solution.

6 A full engine overhaul involves restoring all internal parts to the specification of a new engine. During a complete overhaul, the pistons and the piston rings are renewed, and the cylinder bores are reconditioned. New main and big-end bearings are generally fitted; if necessary, the crankshaft may be reground, to compensate for wear in the journals. The valves are also serviced as well, since they are usually in less-than-perfect condition at this point. Always pay careful attention to the condition of the oil pump when overhauling the engine, and renew it if there is any doubt as to its serviceability. The end result should be an as-new engine that will give many trouble-free miles.

7 Critical cooling system components such as the hoses, thermostat and water pump should be renewed when an engine is overhauled. The radiator should be checked carefully, to ensure that it is not clogged or leaking. Also, it is a good idea to renew the oil pump whenever the engine is overhauled.

8 Before beginning the engine overhaul, read through the entire procedure, to familiarise yourself with the scope and requirements of the job. Overhauling an engine is not difficult if you carefully follow all of the instructions, have the necessary tools and equipment, and pay close attention to all specifications. It can, however, be time-consuming. Plan on the car being off the road for a minimum of two weeks, especially if parts must be taken to an engineering works for repair or reconditioning. Check on the availability of parts and make sure that any necessary special tools and equipment are obtained in advance. Most work can be done with typical hand tools, although a number of precision measuring tools are required for inspecting parts to determine if they must be renewed. Often the engineering works will handle the inspection of parts and offer advice concerning reconditioning and renewal.

9 Always wait until the engine has been completely dismantled, and until all components (especially the cylinder block/crankcase and the crankshaft) have been inspected, before deciding what service and repair operations must be performed by an engineering works. The condition of these components will be the major factor to consider when determining whether to overhaul the original engine, or to buy a reconditioned unit. Do not, therefore, purchase parts or have overhaul work done on other components until they have been thoroughly inspected. As a general rule, time is the primary cost of an overhaul, so it does not pay to fit worn or sub-standard parts.

10 As a final note, to ensure maximum life and minimum trouble from a reconditioned engine, everything must be assembled with care, in a spotlessly-clean environment.

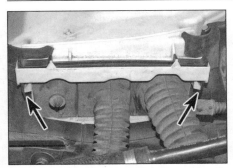

4.8a Press out the retaining clips and pull up the black plastic locking catch at each end...

4.8b... slide the front and rear locking clip to the 'unlock' position

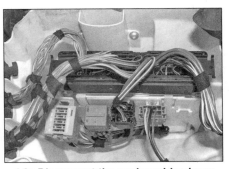

4.8c Disconnect the engine wiring loom plugs

3 Engine removal – methods and precautions

1 If you have decided that the engine must be removed for overhaul or major repair work, several preliminary steps should be taken.
2 Locating a suitable place to work is extremely important. Adequate work space, along with storage space for the car, will be needed. If a workshop or garage is not available, at the very least, a flat, level, clean work surface is required.
3 Cleaning the engine compartment and engine/transmission before beginning the removal procedure will help keep tools clean and organised.
4 An engine hoist or A-frame will also be necessary. Make sure the equipment is rated in excess of the weight of the engine. Safety is of primary importance, considering the potential hazards involved in lifting the engine/transmission out of the car.
5 If this is the first time you have removed an engine, an assistant should ideally be available. Advice and aid from someone more experienced would also be helpful. There are many instances when one person cannot simultaneously perform all of the operations required when lifting the engine out of the vehicle.
6 Plan the operation ahead of time. Before starting work, arrange for the hire of or obtain all of the tools and equipment you will need. Some of the equipment necessary to perform engine/transmission removal and installation safely and with relative ease (in addition to an engine hoist) is as follows: a heavy duty trolley jack, complete sets of spanners and sockets (see *Tools and working facilities*), wooden blocks, and plenty of rags and cleaning solvent for mopping-up spilled oil, coolant and fuel. If the hoist must be hired, make sure that you arrange for it in advance, and perform all of the operations possible without it beforehand. This will save you money and time.
7 Plan for the car to be out of use for quite a while. An engineering works will be required to perform some of the work which the do-it-yourselfer cannot accomplish without

special equipment. These places often have a busy schedule, so it would be a good idea to consult them before removing the engine, in order to accurately estimate the amount of time required to rebuild or repair components that may need work.
8 Always be extremely careful when removing and refitting the engine/transmission. Serious injury can result from careless actions. Plan ahead and take your time, and a job of this nature, although major, can be accomplished successfully.
9 On all models, then engine is removed by first removing the gearbox/transmission, then lifting the engine out from above the vehicle.

4 Engine – removal and refitting

Note: *This is an involved operation. Read through the procedure thoroughly before starting work, and ensure that adequate lifting tackle and jacking/support equipment is available. Make notes during dismantling to ensure that all wiring/hoses and brackets are correctly repositioned and routed on refitting.*

Removal

1 Remove the bonnet as described in Chapter 11.
2 On petrol models, depressurise the fuel system as described in Chapter 4A. Disconnect the battery negative lead (see Chapter 5A) on all models.
3 Drain the cooling system as described in Chapter 1A or 1B.
4 Drain the engine oil, referring to Chapter 1A or 1B.
5 Remove the manual gearbox (Chapter 7A) or the automatic transmission (Chapter 7B), as applicable.
6 Remove the auxiliary drivebelt(s) as described in Chapter 1A or 1B, then unbolt the air conditioning compressor from the engine, release the pipes from the retaining clips, and support the compressor clear of the working area, as described in Chapter 3.

 Warning: Do not disconnect the refrigerant lines – refer to Chapter 3 for precautions to be taken.

7 Remove the alternator as described in Chapter 5A Section 7.
8 Make a note of their fitted locations, then disconnect the engine wiring loom plugs from the electric box **(see illustrations)**.
9 Remove the intake manifold and air cleaner assembly as described in Chapter 4A or 4B.
10 Remove the radiator, cooling fan and shroud as described in Chapter 3.
11 Make a note of their fitted positions, then disconnect the various coolant hoses from the engine.

Diesel engines

12 If not already done so, disconnect and remove the intake and outlet hoses from the intercooler – see Chapter 4B.
13 On N57 6-cylinder engines, remove the wiper arms as described in Chapter 12 Section 15, then disconnect the washer hose/ wiring plug, and unclip the scuttle panel from the base of the windscreen.
14 Working underneath the vehicle, disconnect the fuel feed and return pipes **(see illustration)**. Plug/seal the openings to prevent contamination.
15 Remove the catalytic converter/particulate filter as described in Chapter 4C.
16 On models with conventional power steering, remove the power steering pump as described in Chapter 10. Note there is no need to disconnect the hoses – place the pump to one side.
17 Undo the 3 bolts and remove the heater end panel from the bulkhead. Note that the M6 x 20 mm bolt is fitted in the centre location.

4.14 Depress the release buttons each side and disconnect the fuel pipes

4.19a Disconnect the earth lead from the mounting to the body...

4.19b... and the earth lead from the cylinder head

4.23 Undo the reinforcement bolts (centre bolts arrowed)

All engines

18 Unless a hoist is available which is capable of lifting the engine out over the front of the vehicle with the vehicle raised, it will now be necessary to remove the axle stands and lower the vehicle to the ground. Ensure that the engine is adequately supported during the lowering procedure.

19 Unbolt the earth lead(s) from the engine mounting bracket(s), and the earth lead from the cylinder head to the right-hand inner wing (where fitted) **(see illustrations)**.

20 Make a final check to ensure that all relevant hoses, pipes and wiring have been disconnected from the engine and moved clear to allow the engine to be lifted out.

21 Position the lifting tackle and hoist to support the engine both from the lifting eye at the rear left-hand corner of the cylinder block, and from the lifting bracket at the front of the cylinder head.

22 Raise the hoist to just take the weight of the engine.

Petrol engines

23 Undo the fasteners and remove the underbody protection panels to access the reinforcement frame bolts each side. Undo the bolts and remove the frame **(see illustration)**. Discard the bolts – new ones must be fitted.

24 Unscrew the nuts securing the left-hand engine mounting bracket to the mounting rubber/block, unbolt the mounting bracket from the cylinder block, then the mounting from the subframe, and remove the mounting bracket. Undo the bolts securing the right-hand mounting/block to the subframe

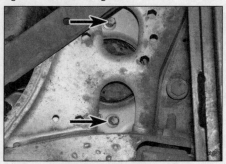

4.24 Undo the bolts securing the mounting to the subframe

(see illustration). Unclip any hoses/pipes from the support brackets.

Diesel engines

25 Undo the nuts securing the engine mountings to the mounting bracket each side, then undo the bolts and remove the right-hand mounting bracket from the cylinder block.

All engines

26 With the aid of an assistant, raise the hoist, and manoeuvre the engine from the engine compartment. Access is limited – take care not to damage and wiring, hoses, etc, as the engine is removed.

Refitting

27 Refitting is a reversal of removal, bearing in mind the following points.
a) Tighten all fixings to the specified torque where given.
b) Ensure that all wiring, hoses and brackets are positioned and routed as noted before removal.
c) Refit the auxiliary drivebelt with reference to Chapter 1A or 1B.
d) Refit the intake manifold as described in Chapter 4A or 4B.
e) Refit the radiator, referring to Chapter 3.
f) Refit the manual gearbox or automatic transmission as described in Chapter 7A or 7B respectively.
g) On completion, refill the engine with oil, and refill the cooling system as described in Chapter 1A or 1B.

5 Engine overhaul – dismantling sequence

1 It is much easier to dismantle and work on the engine if it is mounted on a portable engine stand. These stands can often be hired from a tool hire shop. Before the engine is mounted on a stand, the flywheel/driveplate should be removed, so that the stand bolts can be tightened into the end of the cylinder block/crankcase.

2 If a stand is not available, it is possible to dismantle the engine with it blocked up on a sturdy workbench, or on the floor. Be extra

careful not to tip or drop the engine when working without a stand.

3 If you are going to obtain a reconditioned engine, all the external components must be removed first, to be transferred to the new engine (just as they will if you are doing a complete engine overhaul yourself). These components include the following:
a) Ancillary unit mounting brackets (oil filter, starter, alternator, power steering pump, etc).
b) Thermostat and housing (Chapter 3).
c) All electrical switches and sensors.
d) Inlet and exhaust manifolds – where applicable (Chapter 4A or 4B).
e) Ignition coils and spark plugs – as applicable (Chapter 1A and 5B).
f) Flywheel/driveplate (Part A, B or C of this Chapter).

Note: When removing the external components from the engine, pay close attention to details that may be helpful or important during refitting. Note the fitted position of gaskets, seals, spacers, pins, washers, bolts, and other small items.

4 If you are obtaining a 'short' engine (which consists of the engine cylinder block/crankcase, crankshaft, pistons and connecting rods all assembled), then the cylinder head, sump, oil pump, and timing chain will have to be removed also.

5 If you are planning a complete overhaul, the engine can be dismantled, and the internal components removed, in the order given below, referring to Part A, B or C of this Chapter unless otherwise stated.
a) Inlet and exhaust manifolds – where applicable (Chapter 4A or 4B).
b) Timing chains, sprockets and tensioner(s).
c) Cylinder head.
d) Flywheel/driveplate.
e) Sump.
f) Oil pump.
g) Piston/connecting rod assemblies (Section 9).
h) Crankshaft (Section 11).

6 Before beginning the dismantling and overhaul procedures, make sure that you have all of the correct tools necessary. Refer to Tools and working facilities for further information.

6.2a Compress the valve springs using a spring compressor tool

6.2b Remove the valve stem oil seals

6.5 Place each valve and its associated components in a labelled polythene bag

6 Cylinder head – dismantling

Note: *New and reconditioned cylinder heads are available from the manufacturer, and from engine overhaul specialists. Be aware that some specialist tools are required for the dismantling and inspection procedures, and new components may not be readily available. It may therefore be more practical and economical for the home mechanic to purchase a reconditioned head, rather than dismantle, inspect and recondition the original head. A valve spring compressor tool will be required for this operation.*

1 Remove the cylinder head, camshafts, cam followers/rocker arms and hydraulic adjusters as described in Part A, B or C of this Chapter as applicable.

2 Using a valve spring compressor, compress the spring on each valve in turn until the split collets can be removed. Note that where the springs have a larger diameter at one end, this end must be placed against the cylinder head upon refitting. Release the compressor, and lift off the spring retainer, and spring. Using a pair of pliers, carefully extract the valve stem oil seal/spring seat from the top of the guide **(see illustrations)**.

3 If, when the valve spring compressor is screwed down, the spring retainer refuses to free and expose the split collets, gently tap the top of the tool, directly over the retainer, with a light hammer. This will free the retainer.

4 Withdraw the valve through the combustion chamber.

5 It is essential that each valve is stored together with its collets, retainer, springs, and spring seats. The valves should also be kept in their correct sequence, unless they are so badly worn that they are to be renewed. If they are going to be kept and used again, place each valve assembly in a labelled polythene bag or similar small container **(see illustration)**. Note that No 1 valve is at the front of the engine – the crankshaft pulley end.

7 Cylinder head and valves – cleaning and inspection

1 Thorough cleaning of the cylinder head and valve components, followed by a detailed inspection, will enable you to decide how much valve service work must be carried out during the engine overhaul. Note: If the engine has been severely overheated, it is best to assume that the cylinder head is warped – check carefully for signs of this.

Cleaning

2 Scrape away all traces of old gasket material from the cylinder head.

3 Scrape away the carbon from the combustion chambers and ports, then wash the cylinder head thoroughly with paraffin or a suitable solvent.

4 Scrape off any heavy carbon deposits that may have formed on the valves, then use a power-operated wire brush to remove deposits from the valve heads and stems.

Inspection

Note: *Be sure to perform all the following inspection procedures before concluding that the services of a machine shop or engine overhaul specialist are required. Make a list of all items that require attention.*

Cylinder head

5 Inspect the head very carefully for cracks, evidence of coolant leakage, and other damage. If cracks are found, a new cylinder head should be obtained.

6 Use a straight-edge and feeler blade to check that the cylinder head gasket surface is not distorted **(see illustration)**. If it is, it may be possible to have it machined, provided that the cylinder head is not reduced to less than the specified height. Note: If 0.3 mm is machined off the cylinder head, a 0.3 mm thicker cylinder head gasket must be fitted when the engine is reassembled. This is necessary in order to maintain the correct dimensions between the valve heads, valve guides and cylinder head gasket face.

7 Examine the valve seats in each of the combustion chambers. If they are severely pitted, cracked, or burned, they will need to be renewed or recut by an engine overhaul specialist. If they are only slightly pitted, this can be removed by grinding-in the valve heads and seats with fine valve-grinding compound, as described later in this Section.

8 Check the valve guides for wear by inserting the relevant valve, and checking for side-to-side motion of the valve. A very small amount of movement is acceptable. If the movement seems excessive, renew the valve. Separate valve guides are not available, although different grades (sizes) of valves (stems) are.

9 Examine the bearing surfaces in the cylinder head or bearing castings (as applicable) and the bearing caps for signs of wear or damage.

10 Where applicable, check the camshaft bearing casting mating faces on the cylinder head for distortion.

Valves

⚠️ *Warning: The exhaust valves fitted to some engines are filled with sodium to improve their heat transfer. Sodium is a highly reactive metal, which will ignite or explode spontaneously on contact with water (including water vapour in the air). These valves must NOT be disposed of as ordinary scrap. Seek advice from a BMW dealer or your local authority when disposing of the valves.*

11 Examine the head of each valve for pitting, burning, cracks, and general wear. Check the valve stem for scoring and wear ridges. Rotate the valve, and check for any

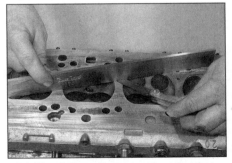

7.6 Check the cylinder head gasket face for distortion

7.12 Measure the valve stem diameter using a micrometer

7.15 Grinding-in a valve

obvious indication that it is bent. Look for pits or excessive wear on the tip of each valve stem. Renew any valve that shows any such signs of wear or damage.

12 If the valve appears satisfactory at this stage, measure the valve stem diameter at several points using a micrometer **(see illustration)**. Any significant difference in the readings obtained indicates wear of the valve stem. Should any of these conditions be apparent, the valve(s) must be renewed.

13 If the valves are in satisfactory condition, they should be ground (lapped) into their respective seats, to ensure a smooth, gas-tight seal. If the seat is only lightly pitted, or if it has been recut, fine grinding compound only should be used to produce the required finish. Coarse valve-grinding compound should not be used, unless a seat is badly burned or deeply pitted. If this is the case, the cylinder head and valves should be inspected

by an expert, to decide whether seat recutting, or even the renewal of the valve or seat insert (where possible) is required.

14 Valve grinding is carried out as follows. Place the cylinder head upside-down on a bench.

15 Smear a trace of (the appropriate grade of) valve-grinding compound on the seat face, and press a suction grinding tool onto the valve head **(see illustration)**. With a semi-rotary action, grind the valve head to its seat, lifting the valve occasionally to redistribute the grinding compound. A light spring placed under the valve head will greatly ease this operation.

16 If coarse grinding compound is being used, work only until a dull, matt even surface is produced on both the valve seat and the valve, then wipe off the used compound, and repeat the process with fine compound. When a smooth unbroken ring of light grey matt

finish is produced on both the valve and seat, the grinding operation is complete. Do not grind-in the valves any further than absolutely necessary, or the seat will be prematurely sunk into the cylinder head.

17 When all the valves have been ground-in, carefully wash off all traces of grinding compound using paraffin or a suitable solvent, before reassembling the cylinder head.

Valve components

18 Examine the valve springs for signs of damage and discoloration. No minimum free length is specified by BMW, so the only way of judging valve spring wear is by comparison with a new component.

19 Stand each spring on a flat surface, and check it for squareness. If any of the springs are damaged, distorted or have lost their tension, obtain a complete new set of springs. It is normal to renew the valve springs as a matter of course if a major overhaul is being carried out.

20 Renew the valve stem oil seals regardless of their apparent condition.

8 Cylinder head – reassembly

Note: *New valve stem oil seals should be fitted, and a valve spring compressor tool will be required for this operation.*

1 Lubricate the stems of the valves, and insert the valves into their original locations **(see illustration)**. If new valves are being fitted, insert them into the locations to which they have been ground.

2 Working on the first valve, dip the new valve stem seal in fresh engine oil. New seals are normally supplied with protective sleeves which should be fitted to the tops of the valve stems to prevent the collet grooves from damaging the oil seals. If no sleeves are supplied, wind a little thin tape round the top of the valve stems to protect the seals. Carefully locate the seal over the valve and onto the guide. Take care not to damage the seal as it is passed over the valve stem. Use a suitable socket or metal tube to press the seal firmly onto the guide **(see illustrations)**.

3 Locate the valve spring on top of the

8.1 Lubricate the valve stem

8.2a Fit the protective sleeve to the valve stem...

8.2b... then fit the oil seal using a socket

8.3a Fit the valve spring...

8.3b... followed by the spring retainer

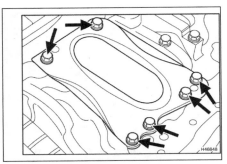

9.2 Undo the bolts and remove the reinforcement plate

9.4 Big end bearing cap marks

9.6 Remove the big-end bearing cap

seat, then refit the spring retainer. Where the spring diameter is different at each end, the larger diameter end of the valve spring fits against the seat on the cylinder head **(see illustrations)**.

4 Compress the valve spring(s), and locate the split collets in the recess in the valve stem. Release the compressor, then repeat the procedure on the remaining valves.

5 With all the valves installed, support the cylinder head on blocks of wood and, using a hammer and interposed block of wood, tap the end of each valve stem to settle the components.

6 Reassemble the cylinder head as described in Part A, B or C of this Chapter.

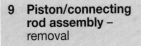

9 Piston/connecting rod assembly – removal

Warning: On engines with oil spray jets fitted to the cylinder block, take care not to damage the jets as the piston/connecting rod assemblies are removed. BMW insist that if the jets are bent, they must be renewed.

1 Remove the cylinder head, sump and balancer shaft/oil/vacuum pump housing (as applicable) as described in Part A, B or C of this Chapter as applicable.

2 On N57 engines, unbolt the reinforcement plate from the bottom of the cylinder block **(see illustration)**.

3 If there is a pronounced wear ridge at

the top of any bore, it may be necessary to remove it with a scraper or ridge reamer, to avoid piston damage during removal. Such a ridge indicates excessive wear of the cylinder bore.

4 Check the connecting rods and big-end caps for identification marks. Both rods and caps should be marked with the cylinder number. Note that No 1 cylinder is at the crankshaft pulley end of the engine. If no marks are present, using a hammer and centre-punch, paint or similar, mark each connecting rod and big-end bearing cap with its respective cylinder number on the flat machined surface provided **(see illustration)**.

5 Turn the crankshaft to bring pistons 1 and 4 (4-cylinder engines) or 1 and 6 (6-cylinder engines), as applicable, to BDC (bottom dead centre).

6 Unscrew the bolts from No 1 piston big-end bearing cap. Take off the cap, and recover the bottom half bearing shell **(see illustration)**. If the bearing shells are to be re-used, tape the cap and the shell together.

7 Using a hammer handle, push the piston up through the bore, and remove it from the top of the cylinder block. Recover the bearing shell, and tape it to the connecting rod for safe-keeping. Take great care not to damage the oil spray jets.

8 Loosely refit the big-end cap to the connecting rod, and secure with the bolts – this will help to keep the components in their correct order.

9 Remove No 4 piston assembly (4-cylinder engines) or No 6 piston assembly (6-cylinder

engines), as applicable, in the same way.

10 Turn the crankshaft as necessary to bring the remaining pistons to BDC, and remove them in the same way.

10 Timing chains (N47 and N57 diesel engines) – removal and refitting

Note: *The engine has to removed to access the timing chains.*

Removal

1 Remove the cylinder head, flywheel and sump as described in Chapter 2C.

2 Undo the bolts and remove the timing cover from the rear of the engine **(see illustration)**.

3 Remove the metal gasket from rear of the cylinder block. Check the locating dowels are in good condition and correctly located.

4 Undo the bolt securing the sprocket to the oil pump shaft. Note that the bolt has a left-hand thread **(see illustration)**. Pull the sprocket and chain from the shaft.

5 Slide the upper timing chain guide rail from the locating pin **(see illustration)**.

6 Secure the crankshaft against rotation and slacken the fuel pump central bolt **(see illustration)**.

7 Using BMW tool No 11 8 740 or a suitable puller, release the fuel pump sprocket from the shaft **(see illustration)**.

8 Press in the chain tensioner piston, and insert a suitable diameter rod/drill bit to lock the piston in place **(see illustration)**.

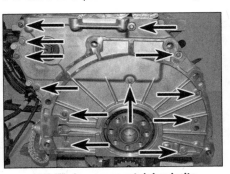

10.2 Timing cover retaining bolts

10.4 The oil pump sprocket bolt has a left-hand thread

10.5 Slide the upper chain guide from the pin

10.6 Slacken the fuel pump sprocket bolt

10.7 Use a puller to remove the fuel pump sprocket

10.8 Push in the piston, then use a drill bit/ rod to secure it in place

9 Slide the guide rails from each side of the fuel pump drive chain, as the chain and fuel pump sprocket are removed **(see illustration)**.

Refitting

N47 engines

10 Position the crankshaft so piston No 1 is 11° after top dead centre (TDC). This can be verified by measuring the distance from the cylinder block upper gasket surface to the top of the piston. When the crankshaft is correctly positioned, the distance should be 0.5 to 1.0 mm. To lock the crankshaft in this position, BMW special tool No. 2 285 671 can be fitted between the cylinder block and the crankshaft **(see illustration)**.

N57 engines

11 Position the crankshaft so piston No 1 at top dead centre (TDC). This can be verified by measuring the distance from the cylinder block upper gasket surface to the top of the piston. To lock the crankshaft in this position, BMW special tool No. 11 4 320 can be fitted between the cylinder block and the crankshaft.

All engines

12 With the crankshaft correctly positioned, the groove in the fuel pump shaft must be aligned with the mark on the cylinder block **(see illustration)**.

13 Fit the fuel pump sprocket into the chain, then fit the chain around the crankshaft sprocket. Position the sprocket on the fuel pump shaft noting the mark and pin on the sprocket (which aligns with the groove on the pump shaft) must align with the mark on the cylinder block **(see illustration)**. Push the sprocket onto the pump shaft, and refit the guide rails at the same time.

14 With the crankshaft held stationary,

tighten the fuel pump shaft bolt to the specified torque.

15 Pull out the locking rod/drill bit from the tensioner to release the tensioner piston.

16 Engage the upper timing chain with the fuel pump sprocket, and the lower chain with the oil pump sprocket and crankshaft sprocket. Fit the sprocket to the oil pump, noting that the flat on the pump shaft must align with the flat in the sprocket mounting hole **(see illustration)**.

17 Prevent the crankshaft from rotating, and tighten the oil pump sprocket retaining bolt to the specified torque. Note that the bolt has a left-hand thread.

18 Fit the new gasket over the locating dowels, then refit the timing cover to the rear of the cylinder block. Tighten the retaining bolts to the specified torque.

19 The remainder of refitting is a reversal of removal.

11 Crankshaft – removal

Note: *On N47 4-cylinder diesel engines, in order to remove the crankshaft, the balance shafts must first be removed. This is a complex task requiring the use of several BMW special tools. Consequently, it is recommended that this task be entrusted to a BMW dealer or suitably-equipped engine overhaul specialist.*

1 On N43 petrol engines, remove the sump, timing chain, balancer shaft housing/oil pump,

10.9 Remove the timing chain, pump sprocket and guide rails together

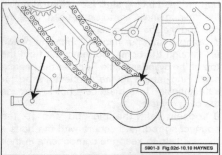
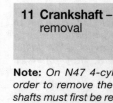

10.10 Bolt the BMW tool to the cylinder block to lock the crankshaft in position

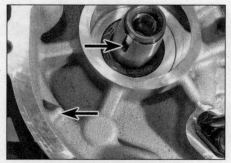

10.12 The groove on the pump shaft must align with the mark on the block

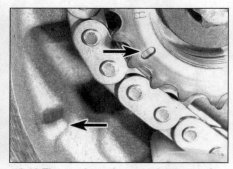

10.13 The mark on the sprocket must also align with the mark on the block

10.16 The flat on the oil pump shaft aligns with the flat in the mounting hole

flywheel/driveplate and crankshaft oil seals as described in Part A of this Chapter.

2 On 6-cylinder diesel engines, remove the sump, the oil pump, the timing chain(s), the flywheel/driveplate and crankshaft oil seals, as described in Part B or C of this Chapter as applicable.

3 Remove the pistons and connecting rods, as described in Section 9. If no work is to be done on the pistons and connecting rods, there is no need to remove the cylinder head, or to push the pistons out of the cylinder bores.

 Warning: If the pistons are pushed up the bores, and the cylinder head is still fitted, take care not to force the pistons into the open valves.

Petrol engines

4 The pistons should just be pushed far enough up the bores so that they are positioned clear of the crankshaft journals.

5 Check the crankshaft endfloat as described in Section 14, then proceed as follows.

6 The bearing shells are fitted into a 'crankcase lower half'. Starting from the outside working inwards, slacken and remove the retaining bolts, and lift away the lower crankcase. Note that new main bearing/crankcase lower half bolts must be fitted.

7 Recover the bearing shells from their locations in the crankcase lower half. Note that the thrustwasher is integral with the bearing shell in the No 4 or No 5 bearing position.

Diesel engines

4-cylinder

8 The pistons should just be pushed far enough up the bores so that they are positioned clear of the crankshaft journals.

9 Check the crankshaft endfloat as described in Section 14, then proceed as follows.

10 The main bearing caps should be numbered 1 to 5 from the timing chain end of the engine. If the bearing caps are not marked, mark them accordingly using a centre-punch.

11 Slacken and remove the main bearing cap retaining bolts, and lift off each bearing cap **(see illustration)**. Recover the lower bearing shells, and tape them to their respective caps for safe-keeping. Note that the main bearing cap bolts must be renewed.

12 Note that the lower thrust bearing shell, which controls crankshaft endfloat, may be fitted to No 4 or No 5 main bearing saddle. The correct location can be identified by the machined area for the thrust bearings to locate.

6-cylinder M57T2

13 Undo the bolts and remove the reinforcement plate from the base of the cylinder block.

14 The pistons should just be pushed far enough up the bores so that they are positioned clear of the crankshaft journals.

15 Check the crankshaft endfloat as described in Section 14, then proceed as follows.

11.11 Carefully remove each cap from the cylinder block

16 The main bearing caps should be numbered 1 to 7 from the timing chain end of the engine. If the bearing caps are not marked, mark them accordingly using a centre-punch.

17 Slacken and remove the main bearing cap retaining bolts, and lift off each bearing cap **(see illustration 11.11)**. Recover the lower bearing shells, and tape them to their respective caps for safe-keeping. Note that the main bearing cap bolts must be renewed.

18 Note that the lower thrust bearing shell, which controls crankshaft endfloat, may be fitted to No 6 main bearing saddle. The correct location can be identified by the machined area for the thrust bearings to locate.

6-cylinder N57

19 The pistons should just be pushed far enough up the bores so that they are positioned clear of the crankshaft journals.

20 Check the crankshaft endfloat as described in Section 14, then proceed as follows.

21 The main bearing caps should be numbered 1 to 7 from the timing chain end of the engine. If the bearing caps are not marked, mark them accordingly using a centre-punch.

22 Slacken and remove the main bearing cap retaining bolts, and lift off each bearing cap **(see illustration 11.11)**. Recover the lower bearing shells, and tape them to their respective caps for safe-keeping. Note that the main bearing cap bolts must be renewed.

23 Note that the lower thrust bearing shell, which controls crankshaft endfloat, may be fitted to No 4 main bearing saddle. The correct location can be identified by the machined area for the thrust bearings to locate.

12.2 Remove the piston oil spray jet tubes from the main bearing locations

11.25 Lift the upper main bearing shells from the cylinder block

All engines

24 Lift the crankshaft from place. Take care as the crankshaft is heavy.

25 Recover the upper bearing shells from the cylinder block **(see illustration)**. Again, note the location of the upper thrust bearing shell.

12 Cylinder block/crankcase – cleaning and inspection

Cleaning

 Warning: On engines with oil spray jets fitted to the cylinder block between the bearing locations, take care not to damage the jets when working on the cylinder block/crankcase. BMW insist that if the jets are bent, they must be renewed.

1 Remove all external components and electrical switches/sensors from the block. For complete cleaning, the core plugs should ideally be removed. Drill a small hole in the plugs, then insert a self-tapping screw into the hole. Pull out the plugs by pulling on the screw with a pair of grips, or by using a slide hammer.

2 Where applicable, pull/unscrew the piston oil jet spray tubes from the bearing locations in the cylinder block **(see illustration)**.

3 On 4-cylinder petrol engines, remove the oil pressure check valve from the top face of the cylinder block. A check valve is fitted, with a rubber-lined spacer sleeve above **(see illustrations)**.

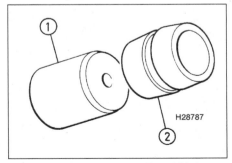

12.3a Oil pressure calibrated jet components

1 Jet   2 Spacing sleeve

12.3b Pull the check valve from the gasket face

12.9 Clean the cylinder block threaded holes using a suitable tap

12.13 When fitted, the tubular spacers should be slightly proud of the cylinder block gasket surface

4 Scrape all traces of gasket from the cylinder block/crankcase, taking care not to damage the gasket/sealing surfaces.
5 Remove all oil gallery plugs (where fitted). The plugs are usually very tight – they may have to be drilled out, and the holes retapped. Use new plugs when the engine is reassembled.
6 If any of the castings are extremely dirty, all should be steam-cleaned.
7 After the castings are returned, clean all oil holes and oil galleries one more time. Flush all internal passages with warm water until the water runs clear. Dry thoroughly, and apply a light film of oil to all mating surfaces, to prevent rusting. Also oil the cylinder bores. If you have access to compressed air, use it to speed up the drying process, and to blow out all the oil holes and galleries.

 Warning: Wear eye protection when using compressed air.
8 If the castings are not very dirty, you can do an adequate cleaning job with hot (as hot as you can stand), soapy water and a stiff brush. Take plenty of time, and do a thorough job. Regardless of the cleaning method used, be sure to clean all oil holes and galleries very thoroughly, and to dry all components well. Protect the cylinder bores as described above, to prevent rusting.
9 All threaded holes must be clean, to ensure accurate torque readings during reassembly. To clean the threads, run the correct-size tap into each of the holes to remove rust, corrosion, thread sealant or sludge, and to restore damaged threads **(see illustration)**. If possible, use compressed air to clear the holes of debris produced by this operation.

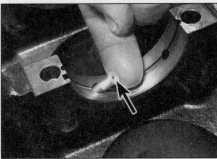

12.14 Clean the holes in the oil spray tubes

HAYNES HINT *A good alternative is to inject aerosol-applied water dispersant lubricant into each hole, using the long spout usually supplied.*
 Warning: Wear eye protection when using compressed air.

Caution: On 6-cylinder petrol engines, the cylinder block is made from a magnesium alloy. All aluminium bolts must be renewed. If thread repairs are necessary, have them carried out by a suitably-equipped specialist.
10 Ensure that all threaded holes in the cylinder block are dry.
11 After coating the mating surfaces of the new core plugs with suitable sealant, fit them to the cylinder block. Make sure that they are driven in straight and seated correctly, or leakage could result.

HAYNES HINT *A large socket with an outside diameter which will just fit into the core plug can be used to drive core plugs into position.*

12 Apply suitable sealant to the new oil gallery plugs, and insert them into the holes in the block. Tighten them securely.
13 Where applicable, thoroughly clean the oil pressure check valve (see paragraph 3), then fit the check valve and spacer to the cylinder block gasket surface **(see illustration)**.

13.2 Remove the piston rings with the aid of a feeler gauge

14 Where applicable, thoroughly clean the piston oil spray tubes which fit in the bearing locations in the cylinder block, then refit the tubes **(see illustration)**.
15 On petrol engines, ensure the sealant grooves in the lower crankcase/bedplate and engine block are clean and free from sealant debris. Discard the sealant groove nozzles, new ones must be fitted.
16 If the engine is not going to be reassembled right away, cover it with a large plastic bag to keep it clean; protect all mating surfaces and the cylinder bores as described above, to prevent rusting.

Inspection

17 Visually check the castings for cracks and corrosion. Look for stripped threads in the threaded holes. If there has been any history of internal water leakage, it may be worthwhile having an engine overhaul specialist check the cylinder block/crankcase with special equipment. If defects are found, have them repaired if possible, or renew the assembly.
18 Check each cylinder bore for scuffing and scoring. Check for signs of a wear ridge at the top of the cylinder, indicating that the bore is excessively worn.
19 Have the bores of the engine block measured by a BMW dealer or automotive engineering workshop. Then if the bore wear exceeds the permitted tolerances, or if the bore walls are badly scuffed or scored, then the cylinders must be rebored. Have the work carried out by a BMW dealer or automotive engineering workshop, who will also be able to supply suitable oversize pistons and rings.

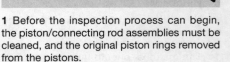

13 Piston/connecting rod assembly – inspection

1 Before the inspection process can begin, the piston/connecting rod assemblies must be cleaned, and the original piston rings removed from the pistons.
2 Carefully expand the old rings over the top of the pistons. The use of two or three old feeler blades will be helpful in preventing the rings dropping into empty grooves **(see illustration)**. Be careful not to scratch the

13.13a Prise out the circlips...

13.13b... and remove the gudgeon pins from the pistons

piston with the ends of the ring. The rings are brittle, and will snap if they are spread too far. They are also very sharp – protect your hands and fingers. Note that the third ring incorporates an expander. Always remove the rings from the top of the piston. Keep each set of rings with its piston if the old rings are to be re-used. Note which way up each ring is fitted.

3 Scrape away all traces of carbon from the top of the piston. A hand-held wire brush (or a piece of fine emery cloth) can be used, once the majority of the deposits have been scraped away.

4 Remove the carbon from the ring grooves in the piston, using an old ring. Break the ring in half to do this (be careful not to cut your fingers – piston rings are sharp). Be careful to remove only the carbon deposits – do not remove any metal, and do not nick or scratch the sides of the ring grooves.

5 Once the deposits have been removed, clean the piston/connecting rod assembly with paraffin or a suitable solvent, and dry thoroughly. Make sure that the oil return holes in the ring grooves are clear.

6 If the pistons and cylinder bores are not damaged or worn excessively, and if the cylinder block does not need to be rebored, the original pistons can be refitted. Measure the piston diameters, and check that they are within limits for the corresponding bore diameters. If the piston-to-bore clearance is excessive, the block will have to be rebored, and new pistons and rings fitted. Normal piston wear shows up as even vertical wear on the piston thrust surfaces, and slight looseness of the top ring in its groove. New piston rings should always be used when the engine is reassembled.

7 Carefully inspect each piston for cracks around the skirt, around the gudgeon pin holes, and at the piston ring 'lands' (between the ring grooves).

8 Look for scoring and scuffing on the piston skirt, holes in the piston crown, and burned areas at the edge of the crown. If the skirt is scored or scuffed, the engine may have been suffering from overheating, and/or abnormal combustion which caused excessively high operating temperatures. The cooling and lubrication systems should be checked

thoroughly. Scorch marks on the sides of the pistons show that blow-by has occurred. A hole in the piston crown, or burned areas at the edge of the piston crown, indicates that abnormal combustion (pre-ignition, knocking, or detonation) has been occurring. If any of the above problems exist, the causes must be investigated and corrected, or the damage will occur again. The causes may include incorrect ignition timing, inlet air leaks, or incorrect air/fuel mixture.

9 Corrosion of the piston, in the form of pitting, indicates that coolant has been leaking into the combustion chamber and/or the crankcase. Again, the cause must be corrected, or the problem may persist in the rebuilt engine.

10 New pistons can be purchased from a BMW dealer.

11 Examine each connecting rod carefully for signs of damage, such as cracks around the big-end and small-end bearings. Check that the rod is not bent or distorted. Damage is highly unlikely, unless the engine has been seized or badly overheated. Detailed checking of the connecting rod assembly can only be carried out by a BMW dealer or engine repair specialist with the necessary equipment. Note that on all engines, the connecting rods can only be renewed as a complete, matched set.

12 The gudgeon pins are of the floating type, secured in position by two circlips. The pistons and connecting rods can be separated as follows. Note that the gudgeon pins are matched to the pistons, they are not available separately.

13 Using a small flat-bladed screwdriver, prise out the circlips, and push out the gudgeon pin **(see illustrations)**. Hand pressure should be sufficient to remove the pin. Identify the piston and rod to ensure correct reassembly. Discard the circlips – new ones must be used on refitting. Note that BMW recommend that gudgeon pins must not be renewed separately – they are matched to their respective pistons.

14 Examine the gudgeon pin and connecting rod small-end bearing for signs of wear or damage. It should be possible to push the gudgeon pin through the connecting rod by hand, without noticeable play. Wear can only be cured by renewing both the pin and piston.

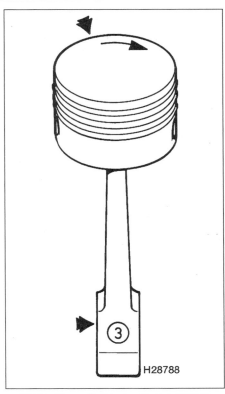

13.17a The cylinder number markings should be on the exhaust manifold side of the engine, and the arrow on the piston crown should point towards the crankshaft pulley end of the engine

15 The connecting rods themselves should not be in need of renewal, unless seizure or some other major mechanical failure has occurred. Check the alignment of the connecting rods visually, and if the rods are not straight, take them to an engine overhaul specialist for a more detailed check.

16 Examine all components, and obtain any new parts from your BMW dealer. If new pistons are purchased, they will be supplied complete with gudgeon pins and circlips. Circlips can also be purchased individually.

17 Position the piston in relation to the connecting rod, so that when the assembly is refitted to the engine, the identifying cylinder

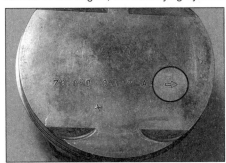

13.17b Installation direction arrow on 6-cylinder engine piston crown

14.2 Measure the crankshaft endfloat using a dial gauge...

14.3... or feeler gauges

15 Main and big-end bearings – inspection

numbers on the connecting rod and big-end cap are positioned on the exhaust manifold side of the engine, and the installation direction arrow on the piston crown points towards the crankshaft pulley end of the engine **(see illustrations)**.

18 Apply a smear of clean engine oil to the gudgeon pin. Slide it into the piston and through the connecting rod small-end. Check that the piston pivots freely on the rod, then secure the gudgeon pin in position with two new circlips. Ensure that each circlip is correctly located in its groove in the piston.

14 Crankshaft – inspection

Checking crankshaft endfloat

1 If the crankshaft endfloat is to be checked, this must be done when the crankshaft is still installed in the cylinder block/crankcase, but is free to move.

2 Check the endfloat using a dial gauge in contact with the end of the crankshaft. Push

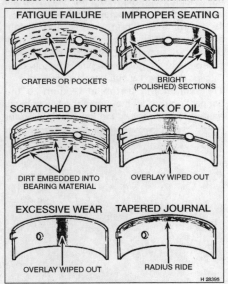

15.2 Typical bearing failures

FATIGUE FAILURE — CRATERS OR POCKETS
IMPROPER SEATING — BRIGHT (POLISHED) SECTIONS
SCRATCHED BY DIRT — DIRT EMBEDDED INTO BEARING MATERIAL
LACK OF OIL — OVERLAY WIPED OUT
EXCESSIVE WEAR — OVERLAY WIPED OUT
TAPERED JOURNAL — RADIUS RIDE

H 28395

the crankshaft fully one way, and then zero the gauge. Push the crankshaft fully the other way, and check the endfloat. The result can be compared with the specified amount, and will give an indication as to whether new thrust bearing shells are required **(see illustration)**.

3 If a dial gauge is not available, feeler blades can be used. First push the crankshaft fully towards the flywheel end of the engine, then use feeler blades to measure the gap between the crankshaft web and the thrust bearing shell **(see illustration)**.

Inspection

4 Clean the crankshaft using paraffin or a suitable solvent, and dry it, preferably with compressed air if available. Be sure to clean the oil holes with a pipe cleaner or similar probe, to ensure that they are not obstructed.
Warning: Wear eye protection when using compressed air.

5 Check the main and big-end bearing journals for uneven wear, scoring, pitting and cracking.

6 Big-end bearing wear is accompanied by distinct metallic knocking when the engine is running (particularly noticeable when the engine is pulling from low speed) and some loss of oil pressure.

7 Main bearing wear is accompanied by severe engine vibration and rumble – getting progressively worse as engine speed increases – and again by loss of oil pressure.

8 Check the bearing journal for roughness by running a finger lightly over the bearing surface. Any roughness (which will be accompanied by obvious bearing wear) indicates that the crankshaft requires regrinding (where possible) or renewal.

9 If the crankshaft has been reground, check for burrs around the crankshaft oil holes (the holes are usually chamfered, so burrs should not be a problem unless regrinding has been carried out carelessly). Remove any burrs with a fine file or scraper, and thoroughly clean the oil holes as described previously.

10 Have the crankshaft journals measured by a BMW dealer or automotive engineering workshop. If the crankshaft is worn or damaged, they may be able to regrind the journals and supply suitable undersize bearing shells. If no oversize shells are available and

the crankshaft has worn beyond the specified limits, it will have to be renewed. Consult your BMW dealer or engine specialist for further information on parts availability.

1 Even though the main and big-end bearings should be renewed during the engine overhaul, the old bearings should be retained for close examination, as they may reveal valuable information about the condition of the engine. The bearing shells are graded by thickness, the grade of each shell being indicated by the colour code marked on it.

2 Bearing failure can occur due to lack of lubrication, the presence of dirt or other foreign particles, overloading the engine, or corrosion **(see illustration)**. Regardless of the cause of bearing failure, the cause must be corrected (where applicable) before the engine is reassembled, to prevent it from happening again.

3 When examining the bearing shells, remove them from the cylinder block/crankcase, the connecting rods and the connecting rod big-end bearing caps. Lay them out on a clean surface in the same general position as their location in the engine. This will enable you to match any bearing problems with the corresponding crankshaft journal. Do not touch any shell's bearing surface with your fingers while checking it, or the delicate surface may be scratched.

4 Dirt and other foreign matter gets into the engine in a variety of ways. It may be left in the engine during assembly, or it may pass through filters or the crankcase ventilation system. It may get into the oil, and from there into the bearings. Metal chips from machining operations and normal engine wear are often present. Abrasives are sometimes left in engine components after reconditioning, especially when parts are not thoroughly cleaned using the proper cleaning methods. Whatever the source, these foreign objects often end up embedded in the soft bearing material, and are easily recognised. Large particles will not embed in the bearing, and will score or gouge the bearing and journal. The best prevention for this cause of bearing failure is to clean all parts thoroughly, and keep everything spotlessly-clean during engine assembly. Frequent and regular engine oil and filter changes are also recommended.

5 Lack of lubrication (or lubrication break-down) has a number of interrelated causes. Excessive heat (which thins the oil), overloading (which squeezes the oil from the bearing face) and oil leakage (from excessive bearing clearances, worn oil pump or high engine speeds) all contribute to lubrication breakdown. Blocked oil passages, which usually are the result of misaligned oil holes in a bearing shell, will also oil-starve a bearing, and destroy it. When lack of lubrication is the cause of bearing failure, the bearing material is wiped or extruded from the steel backing of the bearing. Temperatures may increase to the point where the steel backing turns blue from overheating.

6 Driving habits can have a definite effect on bearing life. Full-throttle, low-speed operation (labouring the engine) puts very high loads on bearings, tending to squeeze out the oil film. These loads cause the bearings to flex, which produces fine cracks in the bearing face (fatigue failure). Eventually, the bearing material will loosen in pieces, and tear away from the steel backing.

7 Short-distance driving leads to corrosion of bearings, because insufficient engine heat is produced to drive off the condensed water and corrosive gases. These products collect in the engine oil, forming acid and sludge. As the oil is carried to the engine bearings, the acid attacks and corrodes the bearing material.

8 Incorrect bearing installation during engine assembly will lead to bearing failure as well. Tight-fitting bearings leave insufficient bearing running clearance, and will result in oil starvation. Dirt or foreign particles trapped behind a bearing shell result in high spots on the bearing, which lead to failure.

9 Do not touch any shell's bearing surface with your fingers during reassembly; there is a risk of scratching the delicate surface, or of depositing particles of dirt on it.

10 As mentioned at the beginning of this Section, the bearing shells should be renewed as a matter of course during engine overhaul; to do otherwise is false economy.

17.5 Measure the piston ring end gaps

16 Engine overhaul – reassembly sequence

1 Before reassembly begins, ensure that all new parts have been obtained, and that all necessary tools are available. Read through the entire procedure to familiarise yourself with the work involved, and to ensure that all items necessary for reassembly of the engine are at hand. In addition to all normal tools and materials, thread-locking compound will be needed. A suitable sealant (available from BMW dealers) will also be required.

2 In order to save time and avoid problems, engine reassembly can be carried out in the following order, referring to the relevant Part of this Chapter unless otherwise stated:

a) Crankshaft (Section 18).
b) Piston/connecting rod assemblies (Section 19).
c) Oil pump/balancer shaft housing.
d) Sump.
e) Flywheel/driveplate.
f) Cylinder head.
g) Timing chain, tensioner and sprockets.

h) Engine external components.

3 At this stage, all engine components should be absolutely clean and dry, with all faults repaired. The components should be laid out (or in individual containers) on a completely clean work surface.

17 Piston rings – refitting

1 Before fitting new piston rings, the ring end gaps must be checked as follows.

2 Lay out the piston/connecting rod assemblies and the new piston ring sets, so that the ring sets will be matched with the same piston and cylinder during the end gap measurement and subsequent engine reassembly.

3 Insert the top ring into the first cylinder, and push it down the bore using the top of the piston. This will ensure that the ring remains square with the cylinder walls. Position the ring near the bottom of the cylinder bore, at the lower limit of ring travel. The top and second compression rings are different. The second ring is easily identified by the step on its lower surface, and by the fact that its outer face is tapered.

4 Measure the end gap using feeler blades.

5 Repeat the procedure with the ring at the top of the cylinder bore, at the upper limit of its travel **(see illustration)**, and compare the measurements with the figures given in the Specifications.

6 If the gap is too small (unlikely if genuine BMW parts are used), it must be enlarged, or the ring ends may contact each other during engine operation, causing serious damage. Ideally, new piston rings providing the correct end gap should be fitted. As a last resort, the end gap can be increased by filing the ring

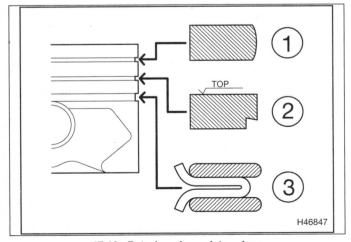

17.10a Petrol engines piston rings

1 Top compression ring
2 2nd compression ring
3 Three-part oil control ring

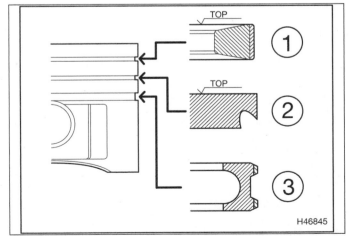

17.10b Diesel engines piston rings

1 Top compression ring
2 2nd compression ring
3 Oil control ring

18.4a Fit the thrust bearing shell to the correct location – see text

18.4b Lubricate the bearing shells

18.11 Drive the new nozzles into place

ends very carefully with a fine file. Mount the file in a vice equipped with soft jaws, slip the ring over the file with the ends contacting the file face, and slowly move the ring to remove material from the ends. Take care, as piston rings are sharp, and are easily broken.

7 With new piston rings, it is unlikely that the end gap will be too large. If the gaps are too large, check that you have the correct rings for your engine and for the particular cylinder bore size.

8 Repeat the checking procedure for each ring in the first cylinder, and then for the rings in the remaining cylinders. Remember to keep rings, pistons and cylinders matched up.

9 Once the ring end gaps have been checked and if necessary corrected, the rings can be fitted to the pistons.

10 Fit the piston rings using the same technique as for removal. Fit the bottom (oil control) ring first, and work up. When fitting a three-piece oil control ring, first insert the expander, then fit the lower rail with its gap positioned 120° from the expander gap, then fit the upper rail with its gap positioned 120° from the lower rail. When fitting a two-piece oil control ring, first insert the expander, then fit the control ring with its gap positioned 180° from the expander gap. Ensure that the second compression ring is fitted the correct way up, with its identification mark (either a dot of paint or the word TOP stamped on the ring surface) at the top, and the stepped surface at the bottom **(see illustrations)**. Arrange the gaps of the top and second compression rings 120° either side of the oil

18.12 Force the sealing compound through the nozzles until it emerges from the grooves alongside the crankshaft oil seals

control ring gap, but make sure that none of the rings gaps are positioned over the gudgeon pin hole. Note: Always follow any instructions supplied with the new piston ring sets – different manufacturers may specify different procedures. Do not mix up the top and second compression rings, as they have different cross-sections.

18 Crankshaft – refitting

Selection of new bearing shells

1 Have the crankshaft inspected and measured by a BMW dealer or automotive engineering workshop. They will be able to carry out any regrinding/repairs, and supply suitable main and big-end bearing shells.

Crankshaft refitting

Note: *New main bearing cap/lower crankcase bolts must be used when refitting the crankshaft.*

2 Where applicable, ensure that the oil spray jets are fitted to the bearing locations in the cylinder block.

3 Clean the backs of the bearing shells, and the bearing locations in both the cylinder block/crankcase and the main bearing caps/ lower crankcase/bedplate.

4 Press the bearing shells into their locations, ensuring that the tab on each shell engages in the notch in the cylinder block/crankcase or bearing cap/lower crankcase. Take care not to touch any shell's bearing surface with your fingers. Note that on petrol engines, the upper bearing shells have an oil groove running along the full length of the bearing surface. On diesel engines, only the shells with a yellow paint mark on the back, or lubrication groove, must be fitted to the crankcase/cylinder block. The thrust bearing shells fit in No 4 or No 5 bearing location on 4-cylinder engines, or No 4 or 6 bearing location on 6-cylinder engines **(see illustration)**. Ensure that all traces of protective grease are cleaned off using paraffin. Wipe dry the shells with a lint-free cloth. Liberally lubricate each bearing shell in the cylinder block/crankcase and cap/lower crankcase with clean engine oil **(see illustration)**.

5 Lower the crankshaft into position so that Nos 1 and 4 cylinder crankpins (4-cylinder engines) or Nos 1 and 6 cylinder crankpins (6-cylinder engines), as applicable, will be at BDC, ready for fitting No 1 piston. Check the crankshaft endfloat as described in Section 14.

Petrol engines

6 Fit the lower main bearing shells to their locations in the lower crankcase/bedplate. Ensure the locating lugs on the shells engage with the corresponding recesses in the caps.

7 Check the locating dowels are in place, and refit the lower crankcase/bedplate. Thoroughly clean the new main bearing bolts, and lightly oil the threads, then insert the bolts, tightening them only loosely at this stage.

8 Tighten the bolts to their specified torque settings, working from the inside out.

9 Fit a new crankshaft oil seals, as described in Part A of this Chapter, as applicable. Ensure the grooves in the front seal aligns with the lower crankcase-to-block joint.

10 Obtain the 'Injection Gasket Service Kit' from a BMW dealer. This kit includes Loctite primer. Use the integral brush to coat the inside of the grooves/joint with primer.

11 Drive the new 'nozzles' into the holes on each side of the lower crankcase/block joint. A BMW tool No 11 9 360 is available for this task, or use a suitably-shaped punch/drift **(see illustration)**.

12 Using the injector supplied, force the sealing compound through the nozzle, until it can be seen to emerge from the grooves in the front and rear crankshaft oil seals **(see illustration)**. Repeat this procedure on the other side.

13 Again, using the integral brush, coat the surface of the sealing compound at the seals with primer to bind the sealant.

Diesel engines

14 Lubricate the lower bearing shells in the main bearing caps with clean engine oil. Make sure that the locating lugs on the shells engage with the corresponding recesses in the caps.

15 Fit the main bearing caps to their correct locations, ensuring that they are fitted the correct way round (the bearing shell tab recesses in the block and caps must be on the same side).

16 Tighten the main bearing cap bolts to the specified torque, in the stages given in the Specifications.

All engines

17 Check that the crankshaft rotates freely.
18 Refit the piston/connecting rod assemblies as described in Section 19.

19 Piston/connecting rod assembly – refitting

Warning: On engines with oil spray jets fitted to the cylinder block between the bearing locations, take care not to damage the jets when working on the cylinder block/crankcase. BMW insist that if the jets are bent, they must be renewed.

Selection of bearing shells

1 There are a number of sizes of big-end bearing shell produced by BMW; a standard size for use with the standard crankshaft, and oversizes for use once the crankshaft journals have been reground.
2 Have the crankshaft inspected and measured by a BMW dealer or automotive engineering workshop. They will be able to carry out any regrinding/repairs, and supply suitable main and big-end bearing shells.

Piston/connecting rod refitting

Note: *New big-end cap bolts must be used when finally refitting the piston/connecting rod assemblies. A piston ring compressor tool will be required for this operation.*

3 Note that the following procedure assumes that the main bearing caps are in place (see Section 18).
4 Press the bearing shells into their locations, ensuring that the tab on each shell engages in the notch in the connecting rod and cap. On 4-cylinder petrol, and M57T2 and N47 diesel engines, fit the shell with the red mark on its back into the bearing cap, and the one with the blue mark (or S mark) in to the connecting rod. On N57 diesel engines, the shells are different for the cap and rod, but will only fit one way. Take care not to touch any shell's bearing surface with your fingers. Ensure that all traces of the protective grease are cleaned off using paraffin. Wipe dry the shells and connecting rods with a lint-free cloth.
5 Lubricate the cylinder bores, the pistons, and piston rings, then lay out each piston/connecting rod assembly in its respective position.
6 Start with assembly No 1. Make sure that the piston rings are still spaced as described in Section 17, then clamp them in position with a piston ring compressor.
7 Insert the piston/connecting rod assembly

19.7a Insert the piston/connecting rod assembly into the cylinder bore...

19.7b... then lightly tap the assembly into the cylinder

into the top of cylinder No 1. Ensure that the arrow on the piston crown points towards the crankshaft pulley end of the engine, and that the identifying marks on the connecting rods and big-end caps are positioned as noted before removal. Using a block of wood or hammer handle against the piston crown, tap the assembly into the cylinder until the piston crown is flush with the top of the cylinder **(see illustrations)**.
8 Ensure that the bearing shell is still correctly installed. Liberally lubricate the crankpin and both bearing shells. Taking care not to mark the cylinder bores, pull the piston/connecting rod assembly down the bore and onto the crankpin. Refit the big-end bearing cap. Note that the bearing shell locating tabs must abut each other.
9 Fit new bearing cap securing bolts, then tighten the bolts evenly and progressively to the Stage 1 torque setting. Once both bolts have been tightened to the Stage 1 setting, angle-tighten them through the specified Stage 2 angle, using a socket and extension bar. It is recommended that an angle-measuring gauge is used during this stage of the tightening, to ensure accuracy. If a gauge is not available, use a dab of white paint to make alignment marks between the bolt and bearing cap prior to tightening; the marks can then be used to check that the bolt has been rotated sufficiently during tightening.
10 Once the bearing cap bolts have been correctly tightened, rotate the crankshaft. Check that it turns freely; some stiffness is to be expected if new components have been fitted, but there should be no signs of binding or tight spots.
11 Refit the remaining piston/connecting rod assemblies in the same way.
12 Where applicable, refit the oil baffle/deflector to the bottom of the cylinder block.
13 On 4-cylinder engines, refit the cylinder head, balancer shaft housing/oil pump/vacuum pump, and sump as described in Part A or C of this Chapter.
14 On 6-cylinder engines, refit the cylinder head, oil pump/vacuum pump and sump as described in Part B or C of this Chapter.

20 Engine – initial start-up after overhaul

1 With the engine refitted in the vehicle, double-check the engine oil and coolant levels. Make a final check that everything has been reconnected, and that there are no tools or rags left in the engine compartment.
2 Disable the ignition and fuel injection systems by removing the engine management relay (located in the engine electrical box), and the fuel pump fuse (located in the main fuse box – see Chapter 12), then turn the engine on the starter motor until the oil pressure warning light goes out.
3 Refit the relays (and ensure that the fuel pump fuse is fitted), and switch on the ignition to prime the fuel system.
4 Start the engine, noting that this may take a little longer than usual, due to the fuel system components having been disturbed.
Caution: When first starting the engine after overhaul, if there is a rattling noise from the valve gear, this is probably due to the hydraulic tappets partially draining. If the rattling persists, do not run the engine above 2000 rpm until the rattling stops.
5 While the engine is idling, check for fuel, water and oil leaks. Don't be alarmed if there are some odd smells and smoke from parts getting hot and burning off oil deposits.
6 Assuming all is well, keep the engine idling until hot water is felt circulating through the top hose, then switch off the engine.
7 After a few minutes, recheck the oil and coolant levels as described in *Weekly checks*, and top-up as necessary.
8 If new pistons, rings or crankshaft bearings have been fitted, the engine must be treated as new, and run-in for the first 500 miles. Do not operate the engine at full-throttle, or allow it to labour at low engine speeds in any gear. It is recommended that the oil and filter are changed at the end of this period.

Chapter 3
Cooling, heating and ventilation systems

Contents

Degrees of difficulty

Easy, suitable for novice with little experience	Fairly easy, suitable for beginner with some experience	Fairly difficult, suitable for competent DIY mechanic	Difficult, suitable for experienced DIY mechanic	Very difficult, suitable for expert DIY or professional

Specifications

General

Expansion tank cap opening pressure:	
Petrol engines	1.5 ± 0.2 bar
Diesel engines	1.4 ± 0.2 bar
Air conditioning refrigerant capacity: *	
Upto 04/2010	590 ± 10g
From 04/2010	620 ± 10g

*Refer to the underbonnet sticker

Thermostat

Opening temperatures	Not available

Torque wrench settings

	Nm	lbf ft
Compressor mounting bolts:		
All models	20	15
M8 x 52 mm:		
Stage 1	10	7
Stage 2	Angle-tighten a further 90°	
M8 x 87 mm:		
Stage 1	10	7
Stage 2	Angle-tighten a further 180°	
Coolant pump nuts/bolts (except petrol engines):		
Diesel engines:		
M6	10	7
M7	13	10
M8	22	16
Coolant pump:		
N43 petrol engines:		
M8	22	16
M10	40	30
M57T2 diesel engine	13	10
N47 and N57 diesel engines	10	7
Coolant temperature sensor:		
Petrol engines and M57T2 diesel engine	13	10
N47 and N57 diesel engines	3.5	2.5
Cooling fan viscous coupling to coolant pump (left-hand thread)	40	30
Facia crossmember:		
End nuts	21	15
To steering column bracket	19	14
Refrigerant pipe unions	20	15
Thermostat cover bolts	10	7
Thermostat housing	10	7

*Do not re-use

Caution: All aluminium fastenings must be renewed. If in doubt, try to attract the bolt/stud with a magnet. Aluminium is not magnetic.

1 General information and precautions

1 The cooling system is of pressurised type, comprising a pump, an aluminium crossflow radiator, cooling fan, and a thermostat. The system functions as follows. Cold coolant from the radiator passes through the hose to the coolant pump where it is pumped around the cylinder block and head passages. After cooling the cylinder bores, combustion surfaces and valve seats, the coolant reaches the underside of the thermostat, which is initially closed. The coolant passes through the heater and is returned through the cylinder block to the coolant pump.

2 When the engine is cold the coolant circulates only through the cylinder block, cylinder head, expansion tank and heater. When the coolant reaches a predetermined temperature, the thermostat opens and the coolant passes through to the radiator. On some models, the thermostat opening and closing is controlled by the engine management ECM by a heating element within the wax capsule of the thermostat. This allows fine control of the engine running temperature, resulting in less emissions, and better fuel consumption. As the coolant circulates through the radiator it is cooled by the inrush of air when the car is in forward motion. Airflow is supplemented by the action of the cooling fan. Upon reaching the radiator, the coolant is now cooled and the cycle is repeated.

3 Two different fan configurations are used, depending on model. On some engines, the fan is electrically-operated, and mounted on the engine side of the radiator. On others, a belt-driven cooling fan is fitted. The belt is driven by the crankshaft pulley via a viscous fluid coupling. The viscous coupling varies the fan speed, according to engine temperature. At low temperatures, the coupling provides very little resistance between the fan and pump pulley so only a slight amount of drive is transmitted to the cooling fan. As the temperature of the coupling increases, so does its internal resistance therefore increasing drive to the cooling fan.

4 On petrol engines, the coolant pump is driven by an integral electric motor, which is under the control of the engine management ECM. On diesel engines the coolant pump is driven by the auxiliary drivebelt from the crankshaft pulley.

5 Refer to Section 11 for information on the air conditioning system.

⚠ **Warning: Do not attempt to remove the expansion tank filler cap or disturb any part of the cooling system while the engine is hot, as there is a high risk of scalding. If the expansion tank filler cap must be removed before the engine and radiator have fully cooled (even though this is not recommended) the pressure in the cooling system must first be relieved. Cover the cap with a thick layer of cloth, to avoid scalding, and slowly unscrew the filler cap until a hissing sound can be heard. When the hissing has stopped, indicating that the pressure has reduced, slowly unscrew the filler cap until it can be removed; if more hissing sounds are heard, wait until they have stopped before unscrewing the cap completely. At all times keep well away from the filler cap opening.**

Do not allow antifreeze to come into contact with skin or painted surfaces of the vehicle. Rinse off spills immediately with plenty of water. Never leave antifreeze lying around in an open container or in a puddle in the driveway or on the garage floor. Children and pets are attracted by its sweet smell. Antifreeze can be fatal if ingested.

Refer to Section 11 for precautions to be observed when working on models equipped with air conditioning.

2 Cooling system hoses – disconnection and renewal

Note: *Refer to the warnings given in Section 1 of this Chapter before proceeding.*

1 If the checks described in Chapter 1A or 1B reveal a faulty hose, it must be renewed as follows.

2 First drain the cooling system (see Chapter 1A or 1B). If the coolant is not due for renewal, it may be re-used if it is collected in a clean container.

3 To disconnect a hose, prise up the wire retaining clip and pull the hose from its fitting (see illustrations). Some hoses may be secured using traditional hose clamps. To disconnect these hoses, slacken the worm-drive screw, then move them along the hose, clear of the relevant inlet/outlet union. Carefully work the hose free. While the hoses can be removed with relative ease when new, or when hot, do not attempt to disconnect any part of the system while it is still hot.

4 Note that the radiator inlet and outlet unions are fragile; do not use excessive force when attempting to remove the hoses. If a hose proves to be difficult to remove, try to release it by rotating the hose ends before attempting to free it (see Haynes Hint).

> **HAYNES HINT** *If all else fails, cut the hose with a sharp knife, then slit it so that it can be peeled off in two pieces. Although this may prove expensive if the hose is otherwise undamaged, it is preferable to buying a new radiator.*

5 To refit a hose, simply push the end over the fitting until the retaining clip engages and lock the hose in place. Pull the hose to make sure its locked in place. When fitting a hose with traditional hose clips, first slide the clips onto the hose, then work the hose into position. If the hose is stiff, use a little soapy water as a lubricant, or soften the hose by soaking it in hot water. Work the hose into position, checking that it is correctly routed, then slide each clip along the hose until it passes over the flared end of the relevant inlet/outlet union, before securing it in position with the retaining clip.

6 Refill the cooling system with reference to Chapter 1A or 1B.

7 Check thoroughly for leaks as soon as possible after disturbing any part of the cooling system.

3 Radiator – removal, inspection and refitting

Removal

> **HAYNES HINT** *If leakage is the reason for wanting to remove the radiator, bear in mind that minor leaks can be often be cured using a radiator sealant with the radiator in situ.*

1 Drain the cooling system as described in Chapter 1A or 1B.

2 Undo the bolts and remove the air intake duct rearwards and upwards from place (see illustration).

2.3a Prise up the wire locking clip...

2.3b... and pull the hose from the fitting

3.2 Undo the bolts and remove the intake duct

3.5a Prise up the clip and disconnect the upper...

3.5b... and lower radiator hoses

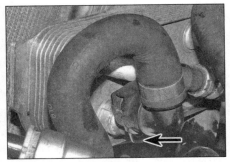

3.5c Prise out the clip and disconnect the coolant hose from the automatic transmission fluid cooler

3.7a Undo the radiator retaining bolt in the left-hand upper corner...

3.7b... and the right-hand upper corner

3 On petrol-engined models, remove the air filter housing as described in Chapter 4A.

4 Remove the electric cooling fan and shroud as described in Section 6.

5 Prise out the wire clips and disconnect the radiator upper and lower coolant hoses **(see illustrations)**. Where applicable, disconnect the coolant hose from the automatic transmission fluid cooler.

6 On diesel models with automatic transmission, undo the bolt and detach the fluid cooler hose from the radiator.

7 Undo the upper mounting bolts, then pull the top of the radiator rearwards and upwards from place **(see illustrations)**.

Inspection

8 If the radiator has been removed due to suspected blockage, reverse flush it as described in Chapter 1A or 1B. Clean dirt and debris from the radiator fins, using an airline (in which case, wear eye protection) or a soft brush. Be careful, as the fins are easily damaged, and are sharp.

9 If necessary, a radiator specialist can perform a 'flow test' on the radiator, to establish whether an internal blockage exists.

10 A leaking radiator must be referred to a specialist for permanent repair. Do not attempt to weld or solder a leaking radiator, as damage may result.

11 Inspect the radiator lower mounting rubbers for signs of damage or deterioration and renew if necessary.

Refitting

12 Refitting is the reverse of removal, noting the following points.

a) *Lower the radiator into position, engage it with the mountings and secure it in position with the retaining bolts.*

b) *Ensure that the fan cowl is correctly located with the lugs on the radiator and secure it in position with the clips.*

c) *Reconnect the hoses and ensure the retaining clips engage securely.*

d) *Check the condition of the O-ring seals in the end of the radiator fittings. Renew any that are defective.*

e) *On completion, refill the cooling system (see Chapter 1A or 1B).*

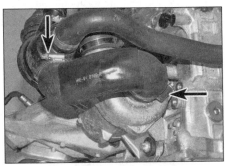

4.2 Slacken the clamps and remove the hose from the coolant pump to the thermostat housing

4 Thermostat – removal and refitting

Note: *A new thermostat sealing ring and (where fitted) housing gasket/seal will be required on refitting.*

Removal

1 Drain the cooling system as described in Chapter 1A or 1B.

Petrol engines

2 Release the clamp and disconnect the hose from the front of the coolant pump **(see illustration)**.

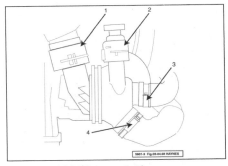

4.3 Thermostat hoses

1 Radiator return hose
2 Heater return hose
3 Cylinder head bypass hose
4 Coolant pump hose

4.4 Thermostat housing retaining bolts

4.9 Thermostat housing bolts

3 Note their fitted positions, then release the clamps securing the coolant hoses to the thermostat housing **(see illustration)**.

1 *Radiator return hose*
2 *Heater return hose*
3 *Cylinder head bypass hose*
4 *Coolant pump hose*

4 Undo the bolts securing the thermostat housing to the coolant pump, and manoeuvre it forwards from position **(see illustration)**.

5 Disconnect the wiring plug from the rear of the coolant pump, and unclip the wiring loom from the front of the engine to allow sufficient slack in the loom for the thermostat to be pulled forwards, then disconnect the thermostat wiring plug and the remaining coolant hoses. No further dismantling of the thermostat housing is recommended.

M57T2 diesel engines

6 Remove the cooling fan as described in Section 5.

7 Remove the EGR cooler as described in Chapter 4C.

8 Lever out the clips and disconnect the coolant hoses from the thermostat housing.

9 Undo the bolts and remove the thermostat housing **(see illustration)**. Note that the thermostat is integral with the housing, and can only be renewed as a complete assembly. Discard the O-ring seal, a new one must be fitted.

N47 diesel engines

10 Remove the alternator drive belt as described in Chapter 1B Section 15.

11 Remove the air filter housing as described in Chapter 4B.

12 Release the clips and remove the turbocharger-to-intercooler air hose on the right-hand side of the engine **(see illustrations)**.

13 Release the clamp and disconnect the coolant hose from the thermostat housing.

14 Undo the 4 bolts and remove the thermostat housing **(see illustrations)**. Pull the thermostat from the housing. Discard the O-ring seal, a new one must be fitted.

N47T diesel engines

15 Remove the cooling fan and shroud as described in Section 6.

16 Release the clamps and disconnect the coolant hoses from the thermostat housing **(see illustration)**.

17 Undo the 3 retaining bolts and manoeuvre the thermostat housing from place **(see illustrations)**. Renew the housing seal.

N57 diesel engines

18 Remove the cooling fan and shroud as described in Section 6.

19 Release the clips and remove the intercooler-to-turbocharger air hose on the right-hand side of the engine **(see illustrations 4.12a and 4.12b)**.

20 Release the clamp and disconnect the coolant hose from the thermostat housing.

21 Undo the 4 bolts and remove the thermostat housing **(see illustrations 4.14a, 4.14b and 4.14c)**. Note that the thermostat is integral with the housing, and can only be renewed as a complete assembly. Discard the O-ring seal, a new one must be fitted.

4.12a To release this type, press the hose onto the connection, then prise out the clip

4.12b Disconnect the turbocharger-to-intercooler hose

4.14a Undo the thermostat housing bolts

4.14b Pull the thermostat from the housing

4.14c Renew the thermostat housing seal

4.16 Prise out the wire clips a little, and disconnect the hoses from the thermostat housing

4.17a Thermostat housing retaining bolts

4.17b Note how the thermostat locates in the housing – renew the seal

Refitting

22 Refitting is a reversal of removal, bearing in mind the following points.
a) *Renew the thermostat cover/housing O-ring seal.*
b) *Tighten the thermostat cover/housing bolts to the specified torque where given.*
c) *On completion refill the cooling system as described in Chapter 1A or 1B.*

5 Cooling fan and viscous coupling – removal and refitting

Note: *This viscous coupling and fan is only fitted to some 6-cylinder diesel models.*

Removal

1 Remove the bolts and remove the plastic cover from above the radiator.

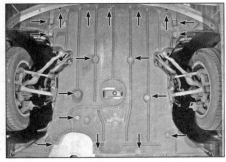

6.2a Undo the fasteners and remove the engine undershield

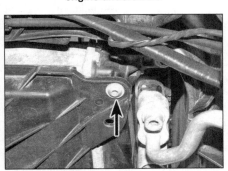

6.4 Undo the bolt in the upper right-hand corner of the shroud

2 Release the fan shroud upper retaining clips by pulling out their centre pins then lift the shroud upwards and out of position.
3 Using a suitable open-ended spanner unscrew the viscous coupling from the coolant pump and remove the cooling fan. **Note:** *The viscous coupling has a left-hand thread. If necessary use a strip of metal bolted to the drive pulley to counterhold the nut.*
4 If necessary, slacken and remove the retaining bolts and separate the cooling fan from the coupling noting which way around the fan is fitted.

Refitting

5 Where necessary, refit the fan to the viscous coupling and securely tighten its retaining bolts. Make sure the fan is fitted correct way around. **Note:** *If the fan is fitted the wrong way around the efficiency of the cooling system will be significantly reduced.*

6.2b Transmission fluid cooler retaining bolt

6.5a Pull back the clip...

6 Refit the fan and shroud. Screw the fan onto the coolant pump and tighten it to the specified torque. Engage the fan shroud with the lugs on the radiator and secure it in position with the retaining clips.
7 Reconnect the auxiliary cooling ducts (where fitted) to the shroud then refit the plastic cover to the bonnet crossmember and securely tighten its retaining bolts.

6 Electric cooling fan and shroud – removal and refitting

Removal

1 Undo the bolts, and remove the air intake hood from the centre of the bonnet slam panel **(see illustration 3.2)**. Disconnect the intake hose as the hood is withdrawn.
2 On automatic transmission models, release the fasteners, remove the engine undershield, then undo the bolt and detach the transmission cooler from the fan shroud **(see illustrations)**. There's no need to disconnect the hoses.
3 Disconnect the fan motor wiring plug, and unclip the coolant hose (where applicable) from the top of the shroud **(see illustration)**.
4 Unclip the wiring harness, then undo the bolt at the right-hand upper edge of the shroud **(see illustration)**.
5 Pull back and release the clip at the left-hand side, and lift the shroud from place **(see illustrations)**.

6.3 Disconnect the fan motor wiring plug

6.5b... then lift the fan and shroud from place

7.5 Radiator outlet thermostatic switch

7.10 The engine coolant temperature sensor is located under the intake manifold

7.17 Coolant temperature sensor

Refitting

6 Refitting is a reversal of removal, ensuring the lugs on the lower edge of the shroud engage in the corresponding slots in the radiator edge.

---

7 Cooling system electrical switches – testing, removal and refitting

---

Testing

1 Testing of the switches/sensors should be entrusted to a BMW dealer or suitably-equipped specialist.

Radiator outlet thermostatic switch

Note: *Not all models are fitted with a radiator outlet thermostatic switch.*

2 The switch is located in the radiator lower hose. The engine and radiator should be cold before removing the switch.

3 Disconnect the battery negative lead (see Chapter 5A).

4 Either drain the cooling system to below the level of the switch (as described in Chapter 1A or 1B), or have ready a suitable plug which can be used to plug the switch aperture in the radiator whilst the switch is removed. If a plug is used, take great care not to damage the radiator, and do not use anything which will allow foreign matter to enter the radiator.

5 Disconnect the wiring plug from the switch **(see illustration)**.

7.21 Pull up the front edge, and slide forwards the engine cover

6 Release the retaining clip, and remove the switch. Recover the sealing ring.

7 Refitting is a reversal of removal using a new sealing washer. On completion, refill the cooling system as described in Chapter 1A or 1B or top-up as described in *Weekly checks*.

8 Start the engine and run it until it reaches normal operating temperature, then continue to run the engine and check that the cooling fan cuts in and functions correctly.

Coolant temperature sensor

Petrol engines

9 Either partially drain the cooling system to just below the level of the sensor (as described in Chapter 1A), or have ready a suitable plug which can be used to plug the sensor aperture whilst it is removed. If a plug is used, take great care not to damage the sensor unit aperture, and do not use anything which will allow foreign matter to enter the cooling system.

10 The sensor is located on the left-hand side of the cylinder block below the intake manifold **(see illustration)**. To access the sensor, remove the alternator as described in Chapter 5A.

11 Disconnect the wiring plug, and unscrew the sensor from the cylinder block. Recover the sealing ring.

12 Renew the sealing ring and refit the sensor, tightening it to the specified torque.

13 Reconnect the wiring connector then refill the cooling system as described in Chapter 1A or top-up as described in *Weekly checks*. Check for leaks.

7.22 Coolant temperature sensor – N47 and N57 diesel engines

M57T2 diesel engines

14 Either partially drain the cooling system to just below the level of the sensor (as described in Chapter 1B), or have ready a suitable plug which can be used to plug the sensor aperture whilst it is removed. If a plug is used, take great care not to damage the sensor unit aperture, and do not use anything which will allow foreign matter to enter the cooling system.

15 The sensor is located under the intake manifold at the rear of the left-hand side of the cylinder head. Remove the intake manifold as described in Chapter 4B.

16 Release the clip, and disconnect the wiring plug from the sensor.

17 Unscrew the sensor from the cylinder head **(see illustration)**.

18 Apply a little sealant to the sensor unit threads and refit the sensor, tightening it to the specified torque.

19 Reconnect the wiring connector then refill the cooling system as described in Chapter 1B or top-up as described in *Weekly checks*. Check for leaks.

N47 and N57 diesel engines

20 Either partially drain the cooling system to just below the level of the sensor (as described in Chapter 1B), or have ready a suitable plug which can be used to plug the sensor aperture whilst it is removed. If a plug is used, take great care not to damage the sensor unit aperture, and do not use anything which will allow foreign matter to enter the cooling system.

21 Lift up the front edge, then slide the acoustic cover forwards from the top of the engine **(see illustration)**.

22 The sensor is located at the front of the cylinder head. Slide up the locking clip and disconnect the wiring plug from the sensor **(see illustration)**.

23 Using a deep socket, unscrew the sensor from the cylinder head.

24 Apply a little sealant to the sensor unit threads and refit the sensor, tightening it to the specified torque.

25 Reconnect the wiring connector then refill the cooling system as described in Chapter 1B or top-up as described in *Weekly checks*. Check for leaks.

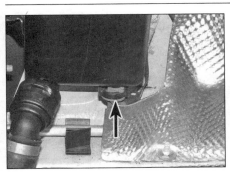

7.26 The level switch is located at the base of the expansion tank

8.3 Coolant pump top hose (1), wiring plug (2) and mounting bolts (3) – N43 engine

8.6 Coolant pump retaining bolts

Coolant level switch

26 The level switch is fitted into the base of the coolant expansion tank. Disconnect the level switch wiring plug **(see illustration)**.
27 Undo the 2 retaining bolts and raise the coolant tank. There's no need to disconnect the hoses.
28 Tilt the expansion tank so the switch is uppermost, then rotate the switch anti-clockwise and pull it from the tank.
29 Refitting is a reversal of removal. If necessary, top-up the coolant as described in *Weekly checks*.

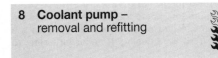

8   Coolant pump – removal and refitting

Note: *A new sealing ring will be required on refitting.*

Removal

1 Drain the cooling system as described in Chapter 1A or 1B.

Petrol engines

2 Remove the thermostat as described in Section 4.
3 Slacken the clamp and disconnect the hose from the top of the pump **(see illustration)**.
4 Disconnect the wiring plug, undo the retaining bolts and remove the pump.
Note: *If the pump is to be re-used, fill it with 50: 50 antifreeze/water mixture and rotate the*

pump impeller one complete revolution before storing it (coolant staying in the pump).

M57T2 diesel engines

5 Remove the thermostat as described in Section 4.
6 Undo the 4 retaining bolts and remove the coolant pump **(see illustration)**.
7 The coolant pump gasket was originally integral with the lower timing cover gasket. In order to remove the pump gasket, cut through where the gaskets join **(see illustration)**.

N47 and N57 diesel engines

8 On N47T engines, remove the EGR cooler as described in Chapter 4C Section 3.
9 Remove the thermostat as described in Section 4.
10 Undo the retaining bolts and remove the pump **(see illustration)**. Discard the pump seal.

Refitting

Petrol engines

11 Position the pump and tighten the retaining bolts to the specified torque.
12 Reconnect the top hose and the wiring plug.
13 Refit the thermostat as described in Section 4.

M57T2 diesel engines

14 Cut the coolant pump gasket from the new lower timing cover gasket. Ensure it locates correctly on the cylinder block. Note that new coolant pump gaskets may now be

available separately from the timing cover gasket.
15 Position the pump, insert the retaining bolts and tighten them to the specified torque.
16 Refit the thermostat as described in Section 4.

N47 and N57 diesel engines

17 Fit a new seal to the pump, then fit the pump and tighten the bolts to the specified torque **(see illustration)**.
18 Refit the thermostat as described in Section 4.

9   Heating and ventilation system – general information

1 The heating/ventilation system consists of a multispeed blower motor, face-level vents in the centre and at each end of the facia, and air ducts to the front and rear footwells.
2 The control unit is located in the facia, and the controls operate flap valves to deflect and mix the air flowing through the various parts of the heating/ventilation system. The flap valves are contained in the air distribution housing, which acts as a central distribution unit, passing air to the various ducts and vents.
3 Cold air enters the system through the grille at the rear of the engine compartment. A pollen filter is fitted to the inlet to filter out dust, spores and soot from the incoming air.
4 The airflow, which can be boosted by the blower, then flows through the various ducts,

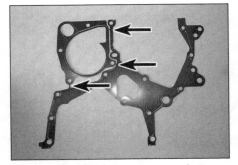

8.7 The original coolant pump gasket was part of the timing chain cover gasket. Cut where arrowed to separate the two

8.10 Coolant pump retaining bolts

8.17 Renew the pump seal

10.2 Carefully prise the decorative trim strip from the facia

10.3a Carefully prise the control unit from the facia

10.3b Lever over the catches and disconnect the wiring plugs

according to the settings of the controls. Stale air is expelled through ducts at the rear of the vehicle. If warm air is required, the cold air is passed through the heater matrix, which is heated by the engine coolant.

5 If necessary, the outside air supply can be closed off, allowing the air inside the vehicle to be recirculated. This can be useful to prevent unpleasant odours entering from outside the vehicle, but should only be used briefly, as the recirculated air inside the vehicle will soon deteriorate.

6 Certain models may be fitted with heated front seats. The heat is produced by electrically-heated mats in the seat and backrest cushions (see Chapter 12). The temperature is regulated automatically by a thermostat, and can be set at one of three levels, controlled by switches on the facia.

10 Heater/ventilation components – removal and refitting

Heater/air conditioning/ventilation control unit

1 Disconnect the battery negative lead (see Chapter 5A).

2 On models with Central Information Computer (CIC)/Car Communication Computer (CCC)/Audio System Controller (ASK), use a flat-bladed blunt tool to carefully prise the passengers side decorative facia trim strip rearwards to release the retaining clips (see illustration). Disconnect any wiring plugs as the trim strip is withdrawn.

3 Using a blunt, flat-bladed tool, carefully prise the control unit from the facia, releasing the clip each side of the unit (see

illustrations). Note their fitted positions and disconnect the wiring plugs as the unit is withdrawn.

4 Carefully unclip the trim surround from the control unit.

5 Refitting is a reversal of removal. Note that if a new control unit has been fitted, it must be programmed using BMW test equipment. Entrust this task to a BMW dealer or suitably-equipped specialist.

Heater assembly

6 Have the air conditioning refrigerant discharged by a suitably-equipped specialist.

7 Working at the rear of the engine compartment, undo the bolts and remove the pollen filter cover (see illustration). Slide the filter from the housing. If necessary, refer to Chapter 1A or 1B.

8 Release the catches and remove the left- and right-hand plastic covers from behind the suspension turret each side of the engine compartment. Unclip the wiring where applicable (see illustration).

9 Depress the clips and pull the cable guide forwards from the pollen filter lower housing (see illustration).

10 Release the catch and undo the bolt each side, then slide the pollen filter lower housing forwards and manoeuvre it from place (see illustrations). Models with suspension turret braces

11 Remove the plastic cap from the centre of the scuttle trim panel. Two different types of the cap are fitted: one with a central slot, removed by rotating it 45° anti-clockwise,

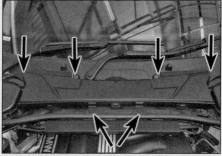

10.7 Undo the bolts and remove the pollen filter cover

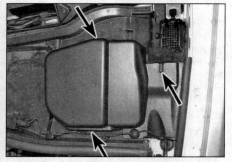

10.8 Release the clips and remove the plastic cover each side

10.9 Release the clips and slide the cable guide forwards

10.10a Rotate the temperature sensor and pull it from the bracket. On the passenger's side, disconnect the bonnet switch

10.10b Undo the bolt, release the clips each side...

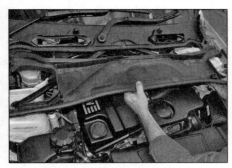
10.10c... and pull the pollen filter lower housing forwards

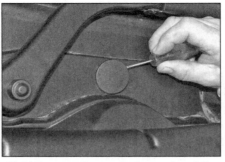
10.11 Remove the cap in the centre of the scuttle trim panel

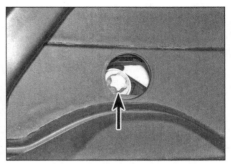
10.12 Undo the bolt (arrowed) in the centre...

and one without a central slot, which is prised from place **(see illustration)**. Note, if the cap or seal are damaged, they must be renewed. Failure to do so may result in water ingress.
12 Undo the bolt in the centre of the scuttle, exposed by the cap removal **(see illustration)**. Discard the bolt – a new one must be fitted.

Version A

13 Undo the bolt at each outer end of the braces, then hold the rubber grommet in place and slide the braces outwards from place **(see illustration)**. Do not allow the bulkhead grommets to be displaced. Discard the bolts – new ones must be fitted.

Version B

14 Undo the nuts securing the strut brace, then undo the nuts securing the strut bracket to the suspension turret **(see illustration)**. Renew the nuts.

All models

15 Undo the 2 bolts and detach the refrigerant pipes from the expansion valve at the engine compartment bulkhead **(see illustration)**. Discard the pipe seals, new ones must be fitted.
16 Undo the 2 bolts and remove the expansion valve **(see illustration)**. Recover the plate behind the valve.
17 Remove the complete facia as described in Chapter 11.
18 On models with the N47 engine, undo the 3 screws and remove the heater end panel from the engine compartment bulkhead.
19 Unclip the plastic cap from the engine compartment bulkhead, then undo the bolt **(see illustration)**.
20 Unclip the left- and right-hand footwell air ducts from the heater assembly.

21 Clamp both heater hoses as close to the bulkhead as possible to minimise coolant loss. Alternatively, drain the cooling system as described in Chapter 1A or 1B.
22 Disconnect the heater hoses at the bulkhead **(see illustrations)**. If possible, use compressed air applied to one of the heater matrix pipes to evacuate coolant from the heater.
23 Undo the 4 nuts securing the heater assembly in the area of the coolant hose connections, then carefully remove the sealing plate and rubber **(see illustration)**.
24 Make a note of their fitted positions and routing, then unclip all wiring harnesses/cable ducts from the facia crossmember.
25 Undo the various nuts and bolts and, with the help of an assistant, manoeuvre the facia crossmember from the passenger cabin **(see illustrations)**.

10.13... and the bolt at each end of the braces

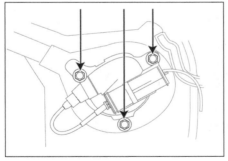
10.14 Undo the nuts securing the bracket to the suspension turret

10.15 Refrigerant pipe retaining bolts

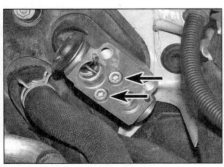
10.16 Expansion valve retaining bolts

10.19 Remove the cap and undo the bolt exposed

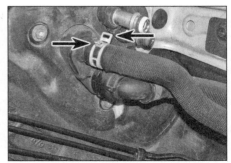
10.22a Squeeze together the tabs and release the upper hose clamp...

10.22b... prise out the wire clip and pull the lower hose from the pipe

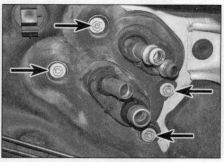

10.23 Undo the nuts then remove the sealing plate and rubber

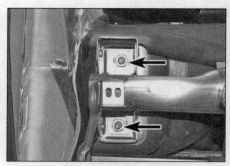

10.25a The facia crossmember is secured by 2 nuts at each end...

10.25b... a bolt beside the fusebox...

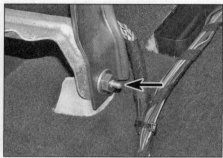

10.25c... a bolt at the floor tunnel...

10.25d... a bolt above the pedals...

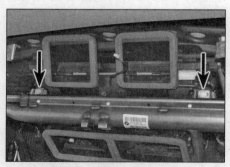

10.25e... 2 bolts in the centre...

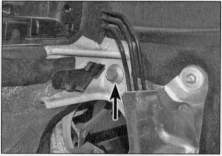

10.25f... a bolt in the engine compartment above the steering column hole...

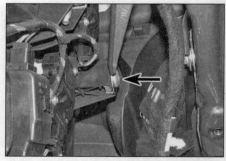

10.25g... a bolt on the right-hand side of the heater housing...

10.25h... 2 bolts above the crossmember on the driver's side...

10.25i... and one each side of the bracket above the steering column

10.26 Evaporator drain grommet

10.29a Peel off the grommet...

10.29b... and undo the plate retaining bolt

10.31a Undo the 3 bolts...

10.31b... and slide the blower motor housing upwards

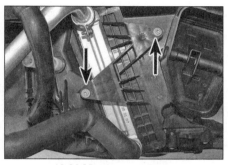
10.32 Matrix cover bolts

10.33 Slide the matrix from the housing

Caution: The facia crossmember has a lot of sharp edges – it would be prudent to wear gloves.

26 Remove the heater assembly from the passenger cabin. Note the evaporator drain grommet in the floor **(see illustration)**.

27 Refitting is a reversal of removal, noting the following points:

a) *Tighten all fasteners to their specified torque, where given.*

b) *Renew all seals and gaskets.*

c) *Have the refrigerant circuit recharged by a suitably-equipped specialist.*

d) *Top-up the coolant system as described in Chapter 1A or 1B.*

Heater matrix

28 Remove the heater assembly as described previously in this Section.

29 Peel off the rubber grommet around the pipes, and undo the bolt securing the mounting plate around the pipes **(see illustrations)**.

30 Disconnect the wiring plug from the air recirculation servo motor on the top of the heater blower motor housing, and release the wiring harness from the retaining clips.

31 Undo the 3 bolts and slide the heater blower motor housing upwards from the main heater housing **(see illustrations)**.

32 Undo the matrix cover bolts and remove the cover **(see illustration)**. On diesel models with an electric auxiliary heating element,

disconnect the wiring plug, and slide out the element **(see illustration 13.4)**.

33 Undo the bolt securing the air conditioning evaporator pipes clamp, then slide the matrix and pipes from the heater assembly **(see illustration)**. Be prepared for coolant spillage.

34 If required, slacken the clamp bolts and detach the pipes from the matrix **(see illustration)**. Discard the sealing rings, new ones must be fitted. BMW insist that the pipes are also renewed.

35 Refitting is a reversal of removal, noting the following points:

a) *Use new sealing rings between the pipes and the matrix.*

b) *When refitting the matrix, the outlet connection (slightly larger – marked with a black dot) must be at the top.*

c) *Top-up the coolant system as described in Chapter 1A or 1B.*

Heater blower motor

36 Undo the 2 bolts, and slide the trim panel under the passenger's glovebox downwards and rearwards **(see illustration)**. Disconnect the footwell light as the panel is withdrawn.

37 Disconnect the blower motor wiring plug.

38 Lift the retaining clip slightly, rotate the

10.34 Slacken the pipe clamp bolts

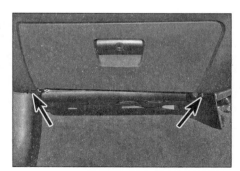
10.36 Panel retaining bolts

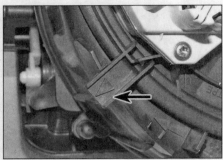

10.38a Lift the retaining clip...

10.38b... rotate the blower motor anti-clockwise and remove it

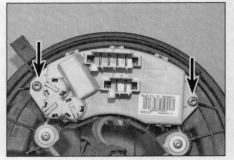

10.41 Blower motor resistor bolts

blower motor anti-clockwise and slide it from the housing (see illustrations).

39 Refitting is a reversal of the removal procedure making sure the motor is correctly clipped into the housing.

Heater blower motor resistor

40 Remove the heater blower motor as described in this Section.

41 Undo the 2 bolts, and remove the resistor (see illustration).

42 Refitting is the reverse of removal.

11 Air conditioning system – general information and precautions

General information

1 An air conditioning system enables the temperature of incoming air to be lowered, and dehumidifies the air, which makes for rapid demisting and increased comfort.

2 The cooling side of the system works in the same way as a domestic refrigerator. Refrigerant gas is drawn into a belt-driven compressor and passes into a condenser mounted in front of the radiator, where it loses heat and becomes liquid. The liquid passes through an expansion valve to an evaporator, where it changes from liquid under high pressure to gas under low pressure. This change is accompanied by a drop in temperature, which cools the evaporator. The refrigerant returns to the compressor and the cycle begins again.

3 Air blown through the evaporator passes to the air distribution unit, where it is mixed with hot air blown through the heater matrix to achieve the desired temperature in the passenger compartment.

4 The operation of the system is controlled by an electronic control module, with a self-diagnosis system. Any problems with the system should be referred to a BMW dealer or suitably-equipped specialist.

5 The air conditioning refrigerant circuit high- and low-pressure service ports are located in the engine compartment (see illustrations).

Precautions

6 When an air conditioning system is fitted, it is necessary to observe special precautions whenever dealing with any part of the system, its associated components and any items which require disconnection of the system. If for any reason the system must be disconnected, entrust this task to your BMW dealer or a suitably-equipped specialist.

7 Do not operate the air conditioning system if it is known to be short of refrigerant, as this may damage the compressor.

⚠ *Warning: The refrigerant is potentially dangerous and should only be handled by qualified persons. If it is splashed onto the skin it can cause frostbite. It is not itself poisonous, but in the presence of a naked flame (including a cigarette) it forms a poisonous gas. Uncontrolled discharging of the refrigerant is dangerous and potentially damaging to the environment.*

11.5a The refrigerant circuit service ports are located on the left-hand inner wing...

11.5b... and behind the right-hand headlight

12.3 Cut through the foam at the points arrowed

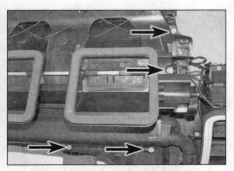

12.4a Undo the bolts on the left-hand side...

12 Air conditioning system components – removal and refitting

⚠ *Warning: Do not attempt to open the refrigerant circuit. Refer to the precautions given in Section 11.*

Evaporator

1 Remove the heater assembly as described in Section 10.

2 Peel off the rubber grommet from the pipes, and undo the bolt securing the pipe clamp (see illustrations 10.26a and 10.26b).

3 Carefully cut through the foam seal at the top of the heater assembly (see illustration).

4 Undo the bolts and remove the upper heater housing (see illustrations). Disconnect

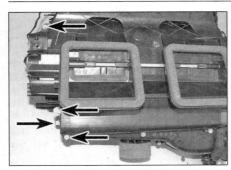

12.4b... and right-hand side of the heater housing...

12.4c... and the 3 in the centre...

12.4d... then lift off the upper heater housing

12.5a Lift out the plastic flap...

12.5b... and remove the evaporator

12.5c Recover the plastic cap from the lower edge

the positioning motor wiring plugs and outlet temperature sensor plug as the housing is removed.

5 Lift out the plastic flap, then lift the evaporator from the housing. Recover the plastic cap from the lower edge of the evaporator **(see illustrations)**.

6 Refitting is a reversal of removal. Have the refrigerant recharged by a BMW dealer or specialist, and top-up the coolant level as described in Chapter 1A or 1B.

Expansion valve

7 Have the air conditioning refrigerant discharged by a suitably-equipped specialist.

Models with suspension turret braces

8 Remove the suspension turret braces as described in Section 10.

All models

9 Working at the rear of the engine compartment, undo the bolts and remove the pollen filter cover. Slide the filter from the housing **(see illustration 10.6)**.

10 Release the catches and remove the left- and right-hand plastic covers from behind the suspension turret each side of the engine compartment. Unclip the hose from the left-hand cover **(see illustration 10.7)**.

11 Depress the clips and pull the cable guide forwards from the pollen filter lower housing **(see illustration 10.8)**.

12 Release the catch and undo the bolt each side, then slide the pollen filter lower housing forwards and manoeuvre it from place **(see illustrations 10.9a and 10.9b)**.

13 Undo the 2 bolts and detach the refrigerant pipes from the expansion valve and the engine compartment bulkhead **(see illustration 10.13)**. Discard the pipe seals, new ones must be fitted.

14 Undo the 2 bolts and remove the expansion valve **(see illustration 10.14)**. Discard the O-ring seals, new ones must be fitted.

15 Refitting is a reversal of removal. Have the refrigerant recharged by a BMW dealer or specialist, and top-up the coolant level as described in Chapter 1A or 1B.

Receiver/drier

16 The receiver/drier should be renewed when:
a) *There is dirt in the air conditioning system.*
b) *The compressor has been renewed.*
c) *The condenser or evaporator has been renewed.*

12.18 Unscrew the cap...

d) *A leak has emptied the air conditioning system.*
e) *The air conditioning system has been opened for more than 24 hours.*

17 Remove the condenser as described in this Section.

18 Unscrew the cap from the condenser **(see illustration)**.

19 Remove the circlip securing the receiver/drier insert.

20 Using an old bolt, pull the insert from the receiver/drier **(see illustration)**.

21 Fit the new desiccant sack into the new insert, and fit it to the condenser **(see illustration)**. The remainder of refitting is a reversal of removal.

Compressor

22 Have the air conditioning refrigerant discharged by a BMW dealer or suitably-equipped specialist.

12.20... remove the circlip and use an old bolt to extract the receiver/drier

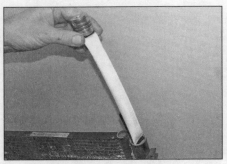

12.21 Fit the desiccant sack into the insert

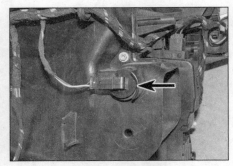

12.36 Evaporator temperature sensor

Pressure sensor

38 The pressure sensor is fitted to the refrigerant pipe on the left-hand side of the engine compartment. Have the air conditioning refrigerant discharged by a BMW dealer or suitably-equipped specialist.

39 Undo the bolts and move the heat shield to one side.

40 Disconnect the sensor wiring plug, and unscrew the sensor. Plug/seal the openings to prevent contamination.

41 Refitting is a reversal of removal, tighten the sensor securely, and have the refrigerant recharged by a BMW dealer or specialist.

Condenser

42 Have the air conditioning refrigerant discharged by a BMW dealer or suitably-equipped specialist.

43 The condenser is located in front of the radiator. Remove the radiator as described in Section 3.

44 Undo the two bolts and disconnect the refrigerant pipes from the condenser **(see illustration)**. Discard the O-ring seals, new ones must be fitted.

45 Undo the retaining bolt, lever out the retaining plate, and pull the right-hand side of the condenser rearwards **(see illustration)**. Manoeuvre the condenser from place.

46 Refitting is a reversal of removal, noting the following points:

a) *Prior to refitting the condenser it is essential that the correct amount of refrigerant oil is added – refer to your dealer for the correct amount and specification.*

b) *Always use new seals when reconnecting the refrigerant pipes.*

c) *Upon completion, have the refrigerant recharged by a BMW dealer or specialist.*

12.44 Refrigerant pipe bolts

12.45 Undo the condenser retaining bolt

23 Remove the air filter housing as described in Chapter 4A or Chapter 4B.

24 On M57T2 diesel engines, remove the cooling fan and shroud as described in Section 5.

25 On N57 diesel engines, disconnect the sensor wiring plug, release the clips and remove the intercooler outlet pipe from the right-hand side of the engine.

26 On N47 and N57 diesel engines, remove the alternator as described in Chapter 5A.

27 On all models, undo the two bolts and disconnect the air conditioning pipes from the compressor. Discard the O-ring seals, new ones must be fitted. Seal/plug the openings to prevent contamination.

28 Remove the auxiliary drivebelt(s) as described in Chapter 1A or 1B (if not already done so).

29 Disconnect the compressor wiring plug.

30 Firmly apply the handbrake, then jack up the front of the car and support it on axle stands. Undo the fasteners and remove the engine undershield.

31 Working underneath the vehicle, undo the mounting bolts, and remove the compressor.

32 Refitting is a reversal of removal, noting the following points:

a) *Prior to refitting the compressor, it is essential that the correct amount of refrigerant oil is added – refer to your dealer for the correct amount and specification.*

b) *Always use new seals when reconnecting the refrigerant pipes.*

c) *Upon completion, have the refrigerant recharged by a BMW dealer or specialist.*

Sunlight sensor

33 Using a blunt, flat-bladed tool, carefully prise the sensor from the centre of the facia. Disconnect the wiring plug, and secure the harness from falling into the facia with tape.

34 Refitting is a reversal of removal.

Evaporator temperature sensor

35 Undo the 3 bolts, then pull the trim panel under the passenger's side of the facia downwards and rearwards **(see illustration 10.36)**. Disconnect the footwell light wiring plug as the panel is withdrawn.

36 Disconnect the sensor wiring plug, then withdraw the sensor from the heater housing **(see illustration)**.

37 Refitting is a reversal of removal.

13.4 Electrical heater element retaining bolts

13 Electric auxiliary heater element – removal and refitting

Note: *The electric auxiliary heater element is only fitted to some diesel models.*

1 Remove the heater assembly as described in Section 10.

2 Disconnect the wiring plug from the air recirculation servo motor on the top of the heater blower motor housing, and release the wiring harness from the retaining clips.

3 Undo the 3 bolts and slide the heater blower motor housing upwards from the main heater housing **(see illustrations 10.31a and 10.31b)**.

4 Undo the 2 bolts and pull the element from the heater assembly **(see illustration)**.

5 Refitting is a reversal of removal.

14.2a Undo the 2 bolts, and remove the 2 plastic expansion rivets

14.2b Prise up the centre pins, and lever out the expansion rivets

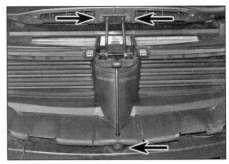

14.3 Undo the Torx bolts and remove the bumper bar stay

14 Radiator airflow control flaps and motor – removal and refitting

1 Remove the front bumper as described in Chapter 11.

2 Prise up the centre pins, lever out the plastic expansion rivets, then undo the two bolts and remove the intake ducting from the bonnet slam panel **(see illustrations)**.

3 Undo the 3 Torx bolts and remove the bumper bar stay **(see illustration)**.

4 Undo the 2 Torx bolts, disconnect the wiring plug and pull the control flap assembly forwards from place **(see illustrations)**.

5 Refitting is a reversal of removal.

14.4a Remove the Torx bolt each side...

14.4b... and remove the control flap assembly

Chapter 4 Part A:
Fuel and exhaust systems – petrol engines

Contents

Degrees of difficulty

Easy, suitable for novice with little experience	**Fairly easy,** suitable for beginner with some experience	**Fairly difficult,** suitable for competent DIY mechanic	**Difficult,** suitable for experienced DIY mechanic	**Very difficult,** suitable for expert DIY or professional

Specifications

System type
N43 engines . . . . DME (Digital Motor Electronics) direct injection engine

Fuel system data
Fuel pump type . . . . Electric, immersed in tank
Fuel pressure regulator rating . . . . 5.0 ± 0.2 bar
Tank level sensor resistance:
    Empty tank . . . . 51 ohms
    Full tank . . . . 993 ohms

Torque wrench settings

	Nm	lbf ft
Camshaft position sensor bolt	7	5
Coolant temperature sensor	13	10
Crankshaft position sensor bolt	10	7
Exhaust manifold nuts: *		
M6 nuts	10	7
M7 nuts	20	15
M8 nuts	22	16
Fuel rail to cylinder head	13	10
High-pressure fuel pipe unions:		
Pipe to injector	23	17
Pipe to fuel rail	23	17
Pump to fuel rail pipe	30	22
High-pressure pump bolts	10	7
High-pressure sensor	30	20
Injector clamp bolts	13	10
Intake manifold:		
M6	10	7
M7	15	11
M8	22	16
Low-pressure sensor	20	15
Rear tension struts: *		
M8	24	18
M12: *		
Stage 1	100	74
Stage 2	Angle-tighten a further 90°	
Throttle body	7	5
Transmission tunnel reinforcement plate	24	18

*Do not re-use

1 General information and precautions

1 The fuel supply system consists of a fuel tank (which is mounted under the rear of the vehicle, with an electric fuel pump immersed in it), a fuel filter, fuel feed and return lines. The fuel pump supplies fuel to the fuel rail, which acts as a reservoir for the fuel injectors which inject fuel into the intake tracts. A fuel filter and pressure regulator is incorporated into the left-hand fuel level sensor. The fuel pump has its own control unit, located behind the rear seat backrest on the right-hand side.

2 Refer to Section for further information on the operation of the fuel injection system, and to Section 12 for information on the exhaust system.

⚠ **Warning: Many of the procedures in this Chapter required the disconnection of fuel lines and connections, which may result in some fuel spillage. Before carrying out any operation on the fuel system, refer to the precautions given in 'Safety first!', and follow then implicitly. Petrol is a highly dangerous and volatile liquid, and the precautions necessary when handling it cannot be overstressed.**

3 Residual pressure will remain in the fuel lines long after the vehicle was last used. When disconnecting any fuel line, first depressurise the fuel system as described in Section 6.

2 Air cleaner assembly – removal and refitting

Removal

1 Undo the 3 bolts, and pull the air intake duct rearwards/upwards and disconnect the intake hose **(see illustrations)**.
2 Lift the rubber cap and disconnect the airflow sensor wiring plug **(see illustrations)**.
3 Release the clamp and disconnect the air outlet hose from the air cleaner assembly.
4 Undo the 2 bolts securing the assembly to the inner wing, then lift it from position **(see illustration)**. Where necessary unclip the coolant hose as the assembly is withdrawn.

Refitting

5 Refitting is a reversal of removal, but ensure that the lower mounting engages with the plastic lug on the body, and where a rubber seal is fitted between the intake hose and the housing, apply a little acid-free grease to the seal to ease refitting.

3 Fuel tank – removal and refitting

Removal

1 Disconnect the battery negative lead as described in Chapter 5A.
2 Before removing the fuel tank, all fuel should be drained from the tank. Since a fuel tank drain plug is not provided, it is preferable to carry out the removal operation when the tank is nearly empty.
3 Remove the rear seat cushion as described in Chapter 11.
4 Jack up the rear of the vehicle, and support it securely on axle stands (see *Jacking and vehicle support*). Remove the right-hand rear wheel.
5 Remove the propeller shaft as described in Chapter 8.
6 Detach the handbrake cables from the hand- brake lever as described in Chapter 9.
7 Pull the handbrake cables from the guide tubes, then undo the bolts and remove the guide tubes **(see illustration)**.
8 The right-hand wheel arch liner is retained by a combination of bolts, plastic nuts, and plastic expansion rivets. Remove these fasteners and manoeuvre the wheel arch liner from place.
9 Working under the vehicle, prise up the

2.1a Undo the bolts...

2.1b... and remove the intake duct

2.2a Prise up the rubber cap...

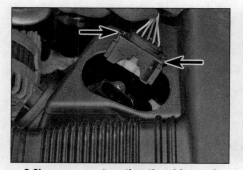
2.2b... squeeze together the sides and disconnect the air flow sensor wiring plug

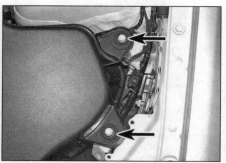
2.4 Air cleaner assembly retaining bolts

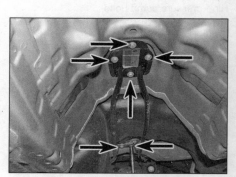
3.7 Undo the bolts and remove the guide tubes

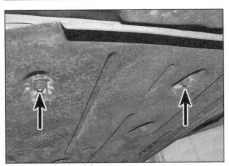

3.9a Undo the nuts and lower the panels in front of the tank

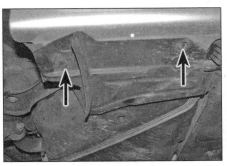

3.9b Remove the fasteners and remove the sill trim panels

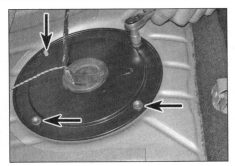

3.10 Undo the 4 nuts and remove the access cover

3.13 Slacken the filler neck hose clip

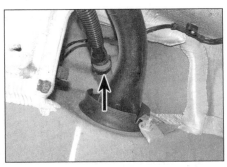

3.14 Squeeze together the sides of the collar and disconnect the vent hose

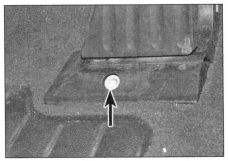

4.1 Undo the bolt at the base of the throttle pedal assembly

centre pins and remove the plastic expansion rivets, release the clips, undo the nuts, then remove the trim panel from under the left-hand side of the tank, and the sill trim **(see illustrations)**. Repeat this procedure on the right-hand side of the tank.

10 Working inside the vehicle, undo the 4 nuts, and remove the fuel tank access covers from the left- and right-hand side of the floor panel beneath the rear seat cushion location **(see illustration)**.

11 Disconnect the wiring plug from the left-hand sensor unit cover, then pull the locking collar away and disconnect the fuel feed pipe **(see illustration 7.15)**.

12 Disconnect the wiring plugs accessible through the right-hand sensor/pump access hole, then depress the release button and disconnect the vent pipe from the sensor/pump unit cover **(see illustrations 7.6a and 7.6b)**.

13 Slacken the hose clip, then disconnect the fuel filler hose from the tank neck **(see illustration)**.

14 Working in the wheel arch area, release the connector, and unclip the vent hose from the filler pipe **(see illustration)**.

15 Support the fuel tank using a trolley jack and an interposed block of wood.

16 Undo the retaining nut in the centre rear of the tank, and the bolts securing the tank retaining straps. Lower the tank, and manoeuvre it from under the vehicle.

Refitting

17 Refitting is a reversal of removal. Note that once the tank is refitted at least 5 litres of fuel must be added to allow the fuel system to function correctly.

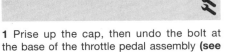

4 Throttle pedal –
removal and refitting

1 Prise up the cap, then undo the bolt at the base of the throttle pedal assembly **(see illustration)**.

2 Lift the throttle pedal assembly upwards, and disconnect the wiring plug. Note that the throttle pedal is only available as a complete assembly, which includes the position sensor. If defective, the complete assembly must be renewed.

3 Refitting is a reversal of removal.

5 Fuel Injection system –
general information

1 An integrated engine management system known as DME (Digital Motor Electronics) is fitted to all models, and the system controls all fuel injection and ignition system functions using a central ECM (Electronic Control Module).

2 On all models, the system incorporates

a closed-loop catalytic converter and an evaporative emission control system, and complies with the very latest emission control standards. Refer to Chapter 5B for information on the ignition side of the system; the fuel side of the system operates as follows.

3 The fuel pump (which is immersed in the fuel tank) supplies fuel from the tank to the fuel rail. Fuel supply pressure is controlled by the pressure regulator, integral with the fuel level sensor module. When the optimum operating pressure of the fuel system is exceeded, the regulator allows excess fuel to return to the tank.

4 On the N43 engine covered by this manual, fuel is injected directly into the combustion chambers, whereas traditionally, fuel is injected into the inlet tracts of the cylinder head.

5 The electrical control system consists of the ECM, along with the following sensors:

a) *Mass airflow/intake temperature sensor – informs the ECM of the quantity and temperature of air entering the engine.*

b) *Throttle position sensor – informs the ECM of the throttle position, and the rate of throttle opening/closing.*

c) *Coolant temperature sensor(s) – informs the ECM of engine temperature.*

d) *Crankshaft position sensor – informs the ECM of the crankshaft position and speed of rotation.*

e) *Camshaft position sensors – informs the ECM of the camshaft(s) positions.*

5.11 Unclip the cover to access the OBD diagnostic plug

f) *Oxygen sensors – informs the ECM of the oxygen content of the exhaust gases (explained in greater detail in Part C of this Chapter).*

g) *Clutch pedal position sensor – informs the ECM of the clutch pedal position.*

h) *Oil temperature – informs the ECM of the engine oil temperature.*

6 All the above signals are analysed by the ECM which selects the fuelling response appropriate to those values. The ECM controls the fuel injectors (varying the pulse width – the length of time the injectors are held open – to provide a richer or weaker mixture, as appropriate). The mixture is constantly varied by the ECM, to provide the best setting for cranking, starting (with a hot or cold engine), warm-up, idle, cruising and acceleration.

7 The ECM also has full control over the engine idle speed, via a motor attached to the throttle body valve.

8 The ECM controls the exhaust and evaporative emission control systems, which are described in Part C of this Chapter.

9 The ECM also controls the following systems:

a) *The engine temperature, via the electric cooling fans and electric thermostat.*

b) *Electric coolant pump.*

c) *Evaporative emissions system (see Chapter 4C Section 2).*

d) *Electric air flap control (radiator grille).*

e) *Fuel pump (via a separate ECM).*

f) *Cruise control.*

g) *Alternator.*

h) *Camshaft position (Vanos system – see Chapter 2A Section 8).*

10 If there is an abnormality in any of the readings obtained from the sensors, the ECM enters its back-up mode. In this event, it ignores the abnormal sensor signal and assumes a pre-programmed value which will allow the engine to continue running (albeit at reduced efficiency). If the ECM enters this back-up mode, the relevant fault code will be stored in the ECM memory.

11 If a fault is suspected, the vehicle should be taken to a BMW dealer at the earliest opportunity. A complete test of the engine management system can then be carried out, using a special electronic diagnostic test unit which is simply plugged into the system's diagnostic connector. The 16-pin OBD socket is located under the facia on the driver's side, whilst the BMW diagnostic socket is located in the right-hand corner of the engine compartment or under the facia on the driver's side **(see illustration)**.

6 Fuel injection system – depressurisation and priming

Depressurisation

1 Remove the fuel pump fuse from the fusebox. The fuse is located in the main fusebox in the passenger glovebox, and the exact location is given on the fusebox cover (see Chapter 12).

2 Start the engine, and wait for it to stall. Switch off the ignition.

3 Remove the fuel filler cap.

4 The fuel system is now depressurised. **Note:** *Place a wad of rag around fuel lines before disconnecting, to prevent any residual fuel from spilling onto the engine.*

5 Disconnect the battery negative lead before working on any part of the fuel system (see Chapter 5A).

Priming

6 Refit the fuel pump fuse, then switch on the ignition and wait for a few seconds for the fuel pump to run, building-up fuel pressure. Switch off the ignition unless the engine is to be started.

7 Fuel pump/fuel level sensors – removal and refitting

Removal

1 There are two level sensors fitted to the fuel tank – one in the left-hand side of the tank, and one in the right-hand side. The pump is integral with the right-hand side sensor, and at the time of writing can only be renewed as a complete unit. Check with a BMW dealer or parts specialist.

Right-hand sensor/fuel pump

2 Before removing the fuel level sensor/pump, all fuel should be drained from the tank. Since a fuel tank drain plug is not provided, it is preferable to carry out the removal operation when the tank is nearly empty.

3 Remove the rear seat cushion as described in Chapter 11.

4 Fold back the insulation material to expose the access cover.

5 Undo the four nuts, and remove the access cover from the floor **(see illustration 3.10)**.

6 Disconnect the two wiring plugs through the access hole, then depress the release button and disconnect the vent hose from the sender/pump cover **(see illustrations)**. Be prepared for fuel spillage.

7 Unscrew the fuel pump/level sensor unit locking ring and remove it from the tank. Although a BMW tool (No 16 1 020) is available for this task, it can be accomplished using a large pair of grips to push on two opposite raised ribs on the locking ring. Alternatively, a home-made tool can be fabricated to engage with the raised ribs of the locking ring or aftermarket collar removal tools are readily available. Turn the ring anti-clockwise until it can be unscrewed by hand. Make an alignment mark between the collar and the tank to aid reassembly **(see illustration)**.

8 Carefully lift the fuel pump/level sensor unit cover from the tank. Disconnect the vent hose and wiring plugs from the base of the cover. Note how the rods in the base of the cover locate in the pump/sensor unit **(see**

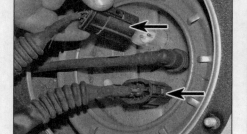

7.6a Disconnect the wiring plugs...

7.6b... then depress the release button and disconnect the vent hose

7.7 Using a home-made tool to unscrew the locking ring

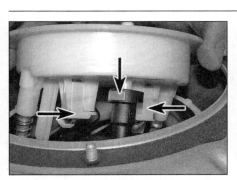

7.8 Disconnect the wiring plugs and vent hose

7.9 Press in the button, disconnect the main hose, then unclip the remaining hoses

7.11 Release the clips and slide the level sensor upwards

illustration). Do not detach the black plastic wire connection between the cover and the pump unit – it's essential to stop the pump unit floating away during reassembly.

9 Note their fitted locations, and disconnect the hoses from the pump unit **(see illustration)**.

10 Carefully manoeuvre the pump/sensor unit from the tank. Take great care not to bend/damage the float arm as the unit is withdrawn.

11 If required, the level sensor can be unclipped from the pump assembly **(see illustration)**. On full deflection the sensor resistance was 993 , and on zero deflection the resistance was 51 .

Left-hand sensor

12 Remove the right-hand sensor/fuel pump as previously described.

13 Fold back the insulation material to expose the access cover.

14 Undo the four nuts, and remove the access cover from the floor **(see illustration 3.10)**.

15 Disconnect the wiring plug from the sensor unit cover, then pull the locking collar away and disconnect the fuel feed pipe **(see illustration)**.

16 Unscrew the fuel pump/level sensor unit locking ring and remove it from the tank. Although a BMW tool (No 16 1 020) is available for this task, it can be accomplished using a large pair of grips to push on two opposite raised ribs on the locking ring. Alternatively, a home-made tool can be fabricated to engage

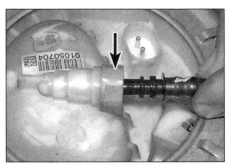

7.15 Pull the locking collar away and disconnect the pipe

with the raised ribs of the locking ring, or aftermarket collar removal tools are readily available. Turn the ring anti-clockwise until it can be unscrewed by hand **(see illustration 7.7)**.

17 Tie a length of string/cable around the disconnected hoses accessible through the right-hand tank access hole, as these hoses will be removed with the left-hand sensor/filter unit **(see illustration)**. The idea is to pull the string/cable into the tank as the sensor/filter unit is removed, then leave it in place to facilitate refitting.

18 Carefully lift the sensor/filter unit from the tank, and remove it **(see illustration)**. Untie the string/cable and leave it in place.

Refitting

19 Refitting is a reversal of removal, noting the following points:

7.17 Fit a cable tie around the hoses, then attach string to the main transfer hose to aid refitting

a) Use a new sealing ring.
b) To allow the unit to pass through the aperture in the fuel tank, press the float arm against the fuel pick-up strainer.
c) When the unit is fitted, the locating lug on the unit must engage with the corresponding slot in the fuel tank collar **(see illustration)**.
d) The locating rods of the right-hand sensor unit cover must align with the corresponding holes in the pump/sensor unit.
e) The locking ring must be tightened until the notch on the ring aligns with the mark on the tank.

8 Fuel injection system – testing and adjustment

Testing

1 If a fault appears in the fuel injection system, first ensure that all the system wiring connectors are securely connected and free of corrosion. Ensure that the fault is not due to poor maintenance; ie, check that the air cleaner filter element is clean, the spark plugs are in good condition and correctly gapped, the cylinder compression pressures are correct, and that the engine breather hoses are clear and undamaged, referring to the relevant parts of Chapters 1A, and 5A for further information.

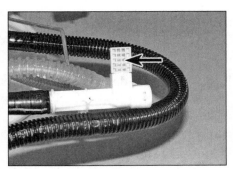

7.18 The fuel pick-up pipe incorporates a coarse filter

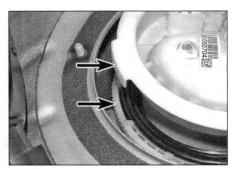

7.19 The lug must engage with the slot on the tank collar

9.3a Throttle body retaining bolts

9.3b Renew the throttle body O-ring seal if necessary

2 If these checks fail to reveal the cause of the problem, the vehicle should be taken to a BMW dealer or suitably-equipped specialist for testing. A wiring block connector is incorporated in the engine management circuit, into which a special electronic diagnostic tester can be plugged. The EOBD (European On-Board Diagnostic) 16-pin socket is located under the driver's side of the facia **(see illustration 5.11)**. The tester will locate the fault quickly and simply, alleviating the need to test all the system components individually, which is a time-consuming operation that also carries a risk of damaging the ECM.

Adjustment

3 Experienced home mechanics with a considerable amount of skill and equipment (including a tachometer and an accurately calibrated exhaust gas analyser) may be able to check the exhaust CO level and the idle speed. However, if these are found to be in need of adjustment, the car must be taken to a BMW dealer or specialist for further testing.

9 Throttle body – removal and refitting

Removal

1 Remove the air cleaner housing as described in Section 2.
2 Release the clamp and detach the air intake hose from the throttle body.
3 Disconnect the wiring plug, undo the four bolts and remove the throttle body **(see illustrations)**.

Refitting

4 Examine the throttle body-to-intake manifold O-ring seal. If it is good condition, it can be re-used. Refit the throttle body to the manifold, and tighten the four bolts to the specified torque.
5 Refit the air intake hose, air cleaner assembly and plastic cover.
6 The remainder of refitting is a reversal of removal. On completion, have a BMW dealer or specialist interrogate the engine management self-diagnosis fault memory, and delete any fault codes stored.

10 Fuel injection system components – removal and refitting

Electronic control module (ECM)

1 Disconnect the battery negative lead, as described in Chapter 5A. Note: *Disconnecting the battery will erase any fault codes stored in the ECM. It is recommended that the fault code memory of the module is interrogated using special test equipment prior to battery disconnection. Entrust this task to a BMW dealer or suitably-equipped specialist.*
2 Remove the pollen filter housing and suspension turret braces (where applicable) as described in Chapter 3 Section 10.
3 Undo the screws/nut and lift out the heater end panel from engine compartment bulkhead.
4 Working in the left-hand corner of the engine compartment, release the locking clips, and remove the cover from the electrical box **(see illustrations)**.
5 Slide out the locking elements, disconnect the module wiring plugs, then disconnect the plugs behind the ECM **(see illustration)**.
6 Release the retaining clips at the front, then slide the ECM upwards from place **(see illustration)**.
7 Refitting is a reversal of removal. After reconnecting the battery, the vehicle must be driven for several miles so that the ECM can learn its basic settings. If the engine still runs erratically, the basic settings may be reinstated by a BMW dealer or specialist using special diagnostic equipment. **Note:** *If a new module has been fitted, it will need to be coded using special test equipment. Entrust this task to a BMW dealer or suitably-equipped specialist.*

Fuel rail and injectors

⚠️ *Warning: Refer to the warning notes in Section 1 before proceeding.*

8 Disconnect the battery negative lead as described in Chapter 5A Section 4.
9 Remove the ignition coils as described in Section 5B Section 3.
10 Use a vacuum cleaner to remove all dirt and debris from the area adjacent to the high-pressure pipes, injectors, etc. It's

10.4a Squeeze together the clips and pull the black plastic clip upwards

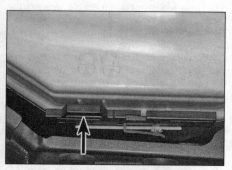

10.4b Slide the catch to the 'unlock' position

10.5 Slide out the locking element

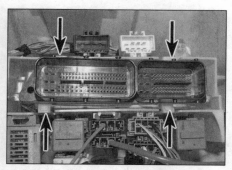

10.6 Release the clips and pull the ECM upwards

10.11 Counterhold the injector port when slackening the pipe union. Note the cylinder identification marking

10.12 Pull the clip aside and disconnect the injector wiring plug

essential that high standards of cleanliness are observed. Do not allow fuel to contact the ignition coils, as the resistance of the silicone material used in the coils is significantly reduced by contact with fuel.

11 Place clean rags to collect any escaping fuel, then, starting with the unions on the fuel rail, slacken and remove the high-pressure fuel pipes from the fuel rail to the injectors. Counterhold the port on the injector whilst slackening the union. It's essential that the pipes be refitted to their original locations, so mark them prior to removal **(see illustration)**. Plug the openings to prevent contamination.

12 Release the clip and disconnect the wiring plug from each injector **(see illustration)**.
13 Undo the retaining bolt and remove the injector clamps **(see illustrations)**.
14 Pull the injectors from place **(see illustration)**. Place close-fitting plastic caps over each injector fuel intake port and injection nozzle. Caps of various sizes are available from BMW dealers or automotive parts stockists. **Note:** *If the injectors are to be re-used, mark their position. It's essential they be refitted to their original positions.*
15 Use a small screwdriver to remove the coupling element from each injector **(see illustration)**. New ones must be fitted.

16 Using a sharp craft knife (or the tools supplied in the BMW special tool kit) carefully cut the PTFE seal from the ends of the injectors. Take great care not to mark the metal of the injector nozzle **(see illustrations)**.
17 Clean the cylindrical part of each injector nozzle using clean, fluff-free rags – don't use any other cleaning agents/tools. Do not attempt to clean the nozzle tip.
18 New injectors are supplied with the PTFE seals already fitted, and secured with plastic caps. Don't remove the caps more than 10 min- utes before fitting the injectors, as once the caps are removed, the seals start to swell.

10.13a Undo the retaining bolt...

10.13b... and remove the injector clamp

10.14 Pull each injector from place

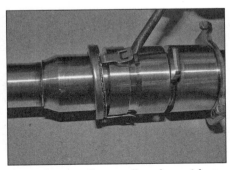

10.15 Remove the coupling element from each injector

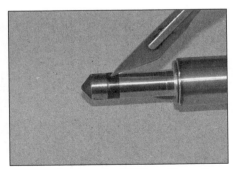

10.16a Remove the PTFE seal from the injector using a sharp knife...

10.16b... or the tools provided in the BMW kit

10.19a Slide the new seal over the tapered fitting tool...

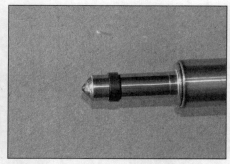

10.19b... and into the groove in the injector

10.19c Slide tool No. 13 0 192 (largest bore) over the PTFE seal to compress it a little...

10.19d... followed by No. 13 0 193 (mid-sized bore), and No. 13 0 194 (smallest bore)

10.20 Slide a new coupling element into place

19 To renew the PTFE seal when refitting used injectors, BMW technicians use a number of special tools (Nos. 13 0 192, 13 0 193, 13 0 194 and 13 0 195) which spreads the seal, and push it into place, and compress it into place afterwards. Equivalent tools may also available from specialist automotive tool manufacturers. In the absence of these tools, it may be prudent to have the rings renewed by a BMW dealer or specialist **(see illustrations)**. Note that the seal must not be lubricated. **Note:** *Do not remove the seal compression tool (No. 13 0 194) more than 10 minutes before fitting the injector, as once the tool is removed, the seal starts to swell.*
20 On re-used injectors, renew the coupling element on each injector **(see illustration)**.
21 Use a nylon brush and a vacuum cleaner to thoroughly clean out the injector holes in

the cylinder head. Take care not to let any debris fall into the combustion chamber.
22 If new injectors are being fitted, their adjustment values must be programmed into the engine management ECM using dedicated diagnostic equipment/scanner. Make a note of the values on each injector before fitting. They are printed on the injector body in 2 rows of 3-digits **(see illustration)**. If this equipment is not available, entrust this task to a BMW dealer or suitably-equipped repairer. Note that it may be possible to drive the vehicle, albeit with reduced performance/increased emissions, to a repairer for the numbers to be programmed, but the engine may run poorly or fail to start.
23 Remove the plastic caps/compressing tool, and install each injector into its original position (where applicable) **(see illustration)**.

24 Fit the clamps between the injectors, with the convex side facing upwards. Only finger-tighten the retaining bolts at this stage – it must be possible to still rotate each injector.
25 Reconnect each injector wiring plug.
26 Refit the high-pressure pipes to their original locations between the injectors and the fuel rail. It's essential that the pipes are fitted without tension – it must be possible to screw on the union nuts easily by hand. If necessary, rotate the relevant injector a little to facilitate this.
27 With each high-pressure pipe union tightened down by hand, tighten then injector clamp bolts to the specified torque.
28 Starting with the union on the rearmost the injector and working forwards, tighten the high-pressure fuel pipe unions to the specified torque, using a crows-foot spanner **(see illustration)**. Note that the unions on the injectors should all be tightened before tightening the unions on the fuel rail.
29 Refit the ignition coils as described in Chapter 5B Section 3.
30 If new injectors have been fitted, have their adjustment values entered into the ECM using BMW diagnostic equipment.

Mass airflow/ intake air temperature sensor

31 Remove the air cleaner filter element as described in Chapter 1A Section 11.
32 Undo the retaining bolt and remove the

10.22 Note the injector adjustment values

10.23 Ensure the lug on the injector aligns with the slot in the cylinder head

10.28 Use a crows-foot spanner to tighten the pipe unions

10.32 Undo the mass airflow sensor retaining bolt

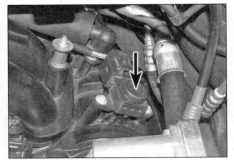

10.36 Air pressure differential sensor

10.40 Crankshaft position sensor

sensor from the air cleaner housing **(see illustration)**.

33 Refitting is a reversal of removal.

Throttle pedal position sensor

34 The throttle pedal position sensor is integral with the throttle pedal, and cannot be renewed separately. Refer to Section 4.

Air pressure differential sensor

35 Undo the bolts/nuts and remove the plastic cover over the engine.

36 Undo the 2 retaining bolts, disconnect the wiring plug, and remove the sensor from the air intake manifold **(see illustration)**.

37 Refitting is a reversal of removal.

Coolant temperature sensor

38 Removal of the sensor is described in Chapter 3.

Crankshaft position sensor

39 The sensor is located below the starter motor. Remove the intake manifold as described in Section 11.

40 Disconnect the sensor wiring plug, undo the retaining bolt and remove the sensor **(see illustration)**. Recover the seal.

41 Check the condition of the sealing ring and renew if necessary. Refit the sensor and tighten the retaining bolt to the specified torque.

42 The remainder of refitting is a reversal of removal.

Camshaft position sensors

43 Undo the bolts and remove the air intake duct from the bonnet slam panel. Disconnect the air hose as the duct is removed.

44 The sensors are located in the front side of the cylinder head, under their respective camshaft ends. Ensure the ignition is switched off.

45 Squeeze together the locking lugs, and disconnect the sensor wiring plug **(see illustration)**.

46 Undo the retaining bolt and remove the sensor. Recover the seal.

47 Refitting is a reversal of removal. Check the condition of the seal and renew it if necessary.

Oxygen sensors

48 Refer to Chapter 4C.

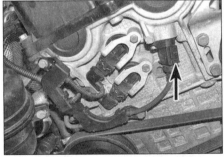

10.45 Depress the clip and disconnect the camshaft position sensor wiring plug

High-pressure fuel pump

49 Disconnect the battery negative lead as described in Chapter 5A Section 4.

50 Remove the ignition coils as described in Section.

51 Use a vacuum cleaner to remove all dirt and debris from the area adjacent to the high-pressure pipes between the pump and the fuel rail. It's essential that high standards of cleanliness are observed. Do not allow fuel to contact the ignition coils, as the resistance of the silicone material used in the coils is significantly reduced by contact with fuel.

52 Place clean rags to collect any escaping fuel, then prise off the clip, push the collar into the coupling, and disconnect the fuel feed pipe at the connection above the intake manifold **(see illustrations)**. Plug the openings to prevent contamination.

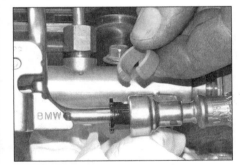

10.52a Remove the clip...

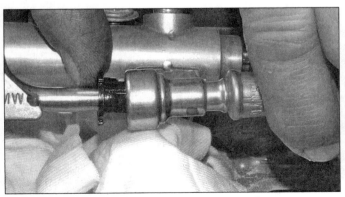

10.52b... push the collar into the coupling...

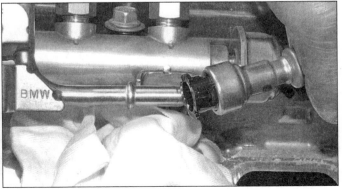

10.52c... and disconnect the fuel feed pipe

10.53a Undo the union nut

10.53b Connection assembly retaining bolt

53 Undo the union nut at the pump, then disconnect the wiring plug, undo the retaining bolt and remove the high-pressure pipe along with the connection assembly **(see illustrations)**. Plug the openings to prevent contamination.
54 Place clean rags to collect any escaping fuel, then slacken the unions and remove the high-pressure fuel pipe from the fuel rail to the pump. Plug the openings to prevent contamination.
55 Disconnect the wiring plug, then undo the bolts and remove the pump from position **(see illustration)**. Recover the seal, a new one must be fitted.
56 Begin refitting by renewing the pump seal. Smear a little clean engine oil on the seal and the pump bore in the cylinder head.

57 Refit the pump, then evenly and gradually tighten the retaining bolts by hand. It must be possible to rotate the pump a little.
58 Refit the high-pressure pipe between the pump and the fuel rail. It's essential that the pipe is fitted without tension – it must be possible to screw on the union nuts easily by hand. If necessary, rotate the pump a little to facilitate this.
59 Tighten the pump retaining bolts to the specified torque, then starting with the union on the pump, tighten the high-pressure pipe unions to their specified torque using a crows-foot spanner.
60 The remainder of refitting is a reversal of removal.

High-pressure sensor

61 Disconnect the battery negative lead as described in Chapter 5A Section 4.
62 Undo the bolts and remove the plastic cover from the top of the engine.
63 Disconnect the sensor wiring plug, then unscrew the sensor from the rear end of the fuel rail **(see illustration)**. Note that BMW insist the sensor can only be fitted to the rail a maximum of 3 times. Mark the sensor with a dot of paint each time it's fitted.
64 Fit the sensor to the fuel rail and tighten it to the specified torque.
65 The remainder of refitting is a reversal of removal.

Low-pressure sensor

66 Disconnect the battery negative lead as described in 5A Section 4.
67 Undo the bolts and remove the plastic cover from the top of the engine.
68 Disconnect the sensor wiring plug, then unscrew the sensor from place **(see illustration)**. Counterhold the connection bracket as the sensor is slackened.
69 Fit the sensor to the connection assembly and tighten it to the specified torque.
70 The remainder of refitting is a reversal of removal.

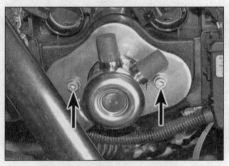

10.55 High-pressure pump retaining bolts

10.63 High-pressure sensor

11 Manifolds – removal and refitting

Intake manifold – removal

1 Ensure the ignition is turned off, and remove the air cleaner housing as described in Section 2.
2 Remove the alternator as described in Chapter 5A Section 7.
3 Disconnect the air intake hose from the throttle body.
4 Squeeze together the sides of the collar and disconnect the breather hose from the cylinder head cover **(see illustration)**.

10.68 Low pressure sensor

11.4 Squeeze together the sides of the breather hose collar

11.5a Disconnect the pressure sensor wiring plug...

11.5b... and the purge valve wiring plug

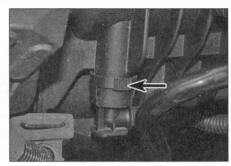

11.6 Squeeze the side of the purge valve hose collar

5 Disconnect the various wiring plugs from the manifold, and unclip the purge valve **(see illustrations)**.

6 Squeeze together the sides of the collar and disconnect the purge valve hose from the manifold **(see illustration)**.

7 Undo the 2 bolts securing the wiring bracket (where fitted) to the top of the manifold **(see illustration)**.

8 Undo the intake manifold retaining bolts **(see illustration)**. Note the bolts on the underside of the manifold require the use of a long extension and universal joint.

9 Lift the manifold slightly, undo the bolts and detach the EGR pipe from the underside of the manifold **(see illustrations)**. Disconnect the sensor wiring plug.

10 With the manifold raised, note their fitted positions and disconnect the vacuum hoses and wiring plug from the DISA valve on the underside of the manifold **(see illustration)**. Make a final check to ensure all necessary wiring/looms have been unplugged/unclipped from the manifold, including the engine mounting vacuum solenoid (under the rear of the manifold), and the wiring from the bracket at the rear.

11 Manoeuvre the manifold from the engine compartment.

Intake manifold – refitting

12 Check the condition of the manifold seals, and renew if necessary.

13 Refitting is a reversal of removal, tightening the retaining bolt to their specified torque.

Exhaust manifold

Removal

14 Remove the exhaust system as described in Section 12.

15 Remove the right-hand engine mounting as described in Chapter 2A Section 18, then unbolt the support arm from the cylinder block.

16 Drain the cooling system as described in Chapter 1A Section 16, then undo the retaining bolts, disconnect the hoses and remove the coolant expansion tank.

17 Remove the pollen filter housing and suspension turret braces (where applicable) as described in Chapter 3 Section 10.

18 Undo the bolts securing the exhaust bracket to the under side of the vehicle **(see illustration)**.

11.7 Undo the bolts securing the wiring bracket

11.8 The two bolts at the base of the manifold require a long extension and universal joint to remove

11.9a The EGR pipe...

11.9b... is secured to the underside of the manifold by 2 bolts. Disconnect the sensor wiring plug

11.10 Disconnect the wiring plug from the DISA valve

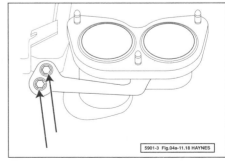

11.18 Undo the bolts securing the exhaust bracket

19 Slacken the clamp and disconnect the EGR pipe from the manifold.

20 Unclip the oxygen sensor cables, and disconnect their wiring plugs.

21 Undo the retaining nuts and manoeuvre the exhaust manifold from place.

Refitting

22 Refitting is a reversal of removal, but use new gaskets and new manifold securing nuts, and coat the mounting studs with high temperature grease.

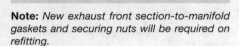

12 Exhaust system – removal and refitting

Note: *New exhaust front section-to-manifold gaskets and securing nuts will be required on refitting.*

Removal

1 Jack up the vehicle and support securely on axle stands (see *Jacking and vehicle support*). Undo the fasteners and remove the engine undershield.

2 On Touring models, undo the bolts, and remove the rear tension struts (where fitted) under the rear axle. Discard the bolts – new ones must be fitted.

3 Unscrew the securing nuts, and disconnect

12.3 Renew the exhaust pipe sealing gasket

the exhaust front section from the manifold. Recover the gasket **(see illustration)**.

4 Support the exhaust system with a trolley jack, etc. It is very heavy.

5 Unscrew the retaining nuts securing the various mounting brackets to the vehicle underside.

6 Undo the bolts, and remove the reinforcement plate (where fitted) from across the transmission tunnel **(see illustration)**.

7 Trace the oxygen/NOx sensors wiring back to the wiring plugs and disconnect them.

8 If required, unscrew the oxygen/NOx sensors from the front exhaust pipe.

9 Withdraw the complete exhaust system from under the vehicle.

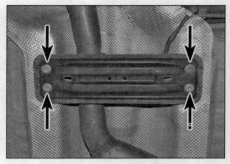

12.6 Transmission tunnel reinforcement plate

10 To remove the heat shield, undo the nuts and bolts, then lower it to the ground.

Refitting

11 Refitting is a reversal of removal, bearing in mind the following points.

a) *Use new gaskets when reconnecting the exhaust front section to the manifold. Also use new nuts, and coat the threads of the new nuts with copper grease.*

b) *Check the position of the tailpipes in relation to the cut-out in the rear valance, and if necessary adjust the exhaust mountings to give sufficient clearance between the system and the valance.*

Chapter 4 Part B:
Fuel and exhaust systems – diesel engines

Contents

Degrees of difficulty

| Easy, suitable for novice with little experience | Fairly easy, suitable for beginner with some experience | Fairly difficult, suitable for competent DIY mechanic | Difficult, suitable for experienced DIY mechanic | Very difficult, suitable for expert DIY or professional |

Specifications

Engine codes
4-cylinder N47/T
6-cylinder . . . . M57T2 and N57

General
System type . . . . Direct injection common rail with Bosch high pressure delivery pump and Electronic Diesel Control with DDE ECM
Fuel delivery pump pressure . . . . 3.5 to 4.5 bar
Injection pressure . . . . 250 to 1600 bar

Torque wrench settings

	Nm	lbf ft
Crankshaft position sensor	8	6
Engine compartment tension braces:		
M10:		
Stage 1	40	30
Stage 2	Angle-tighten a further 60°	
M12:		
Stage 1	100	74
Stage 2	Angle-tighten a further 100°	
Exhaust manifold to cylinder head:		
M57T2 engines*	20	15
N47 and N57 engines*	13	10
Fuel injector clamp bolts (N47 and N57 engines)	26	19
Fuel injector clamp nuts/studs (M57T2 engines)	10	7
Fuel injection pump mounting:		
Nuts	25	18
Bolts:		
M6	8	6
M8	19	14
Fuel injection pump sprocket retaining bolt	65	48
Fuel pipe union nuts	23	17
Fuel pressure regulator:		
M57T2 engines	85	63
N47 engines	85	63
Fuel pressure sensor:		
M57T2 engines	70	52
N47 engines	70	52
Fuel rail-to-cylinder head bolts	25	18
Intake manifold:		
M6	10	7
M7	15	11
M8	22	16
Rear reinforcement plate	45	33
Rear tension braces: *		
M10	50	37
M12:		
Stage 1	100	74
Stage 2	Angle-tighten a further 90°	
Timing cover access plug (fuel pump)	30	22
Turbocharger oil feed banjo bolts	22	16
Turbocharger-to-exhaust manifold bolts:		
M57T2 engines	50	37
N47 engines	25	18

*Do not re-use

1 General information and precautions

1 Fuel is drawn from a tank under the rear of the vehicle by a tank-immersed electric pump, then by a filter assembly mounted under the right-hand rear wheel arch, and then forced through a filter to the injection pump. The chain driven injection pump supplies very high pressure fuel to the common fuel rail, which is connected to each individual injector. The injectors are operated by solenoids/crystals controlled by the ECM, based on information supplied by various sensors. The engine ECM also controls the preheating side of the system – refer to Chapter 5A for more details.

2 The operation of the fuel injection system is described in more detail in Section 5.

3 The EDC (electronic diesel control) system fitted incorporates a 'drive by wire' system, where the traditional accelerator cable is replaced by an accelerator pedal position sensor. The position and rate-of-change of the accelerator pedal is reported by the position sensor to the ECM, which then adjusts the fuel injectors to deliver the required amount of fuel, and optimises combustion efficiency.

4 The exhaust system incorporates a turbocharger, a particulate filter (depending on model) and an EGR system. Further detail of the emission control systems can be found in Chapter 4C.

Precautions

5 When working on diesel fuel system components, scrupulous cleanliness must be observed, and care must be taken not to introduce any foreign matter into fuel lines or components.

6 After carrying out any work involving disconnection of fuel lines, it is advisable to check the connections for leaks; pressurise the system by cranking the engine several times.

7 Electronic control units are very sensitive components, and certain precautions must be taken to avoid damage to these units as follows:

a) When carrying out welding operations on the vehicle using electric welding equipment, the battery and alternator should be disconnected.

b) Although the underbonnet-mounted modules will tolerate normal underbonnet conditions, they can be adversely affected by excess heat or moisture. If using welding equipment or pressure-washing equipment in the vicinity of an electronic module, take care not to direct heat, or jets of water or steam, at the module. If this cannot be avoided, remove the module from the vehicle, and protect its wiring plug with a plastic bag.

c) Before disconnecting any wiring, or

removing components, always ensure that the ignition is switched off.

d) Do not attempt to improvise ECM fault diagnosis procedures using a test lamp or multimeter, as irreparable damage could be caused to the module.

e) After working on fuel injection/engine management system components, ensure that all wiring is correctly reconnected before reconnecting the battery or switching on the ignition.

2 Air cleaner assembly – removal and refitting

2.2 Disconnect the mass airflow sensor wiring plug

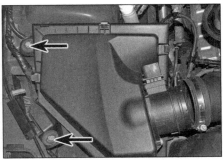

2.4 Air cleaner assembly mounting bolts

M57T2 engine

1 The air cleaner housing is integral with the cylinder head cover – see Chapter 2B.

N47 and N57 engines

2 Disconnect the mass airflow sensor wiring plug (see illustration).
3 Slacken the clamp and pull the air outlet hose from the air cleaner cover.
4 Undo the 2 air cleaner assembly mounting bolts (see illustration).
5 Pull the intake 'snorkel' from the intake hood, then pull the air cleaner assembly upwards from place.
6 Refitting is a reversal of removal.

3 Fuel tank – removal and refitting

Removal

1 Disconnect the battery negative lead as described in Chapter 5A.
2 Before removing the fuel tank, all fuel should be drained from the tank. Since a fuel tank drain plug is not provided, it is preferable to carry out the removal operation when the tank is nearly empty. The remaining fuel can then be siphoned or hand-pumped from the tank.
3 Remove the rear seat cushion as described in Chapter 11.
4 Jack up the rear of the vehicle, and support

it securely on axle stands (see Jacking and vehicle support). Remove the right-hand rear roadwheel.
5 Detach the handbrake cables from the handbrake lever as described in Chapter 9.
6 Pull the handbrake cables from the guide tubes, then undo the bolts and remove the guide tubes.
7 Remove the propeller shaft as described in Chapter 8.
8 The right-hand wheel arch liner is retained by a combination of bolts, plastic nuts, and plastic expansion rivets. Remove these fasteners and manoeuvre the wheel arch liner from place.
9 Working under the vehicle, prise up the centre pins and remove the plastic expansion rivets, release the clips, undo the nuts, then remove the trim panel from under the

left-hand side of the tank, and the sill trim (see illustrations). Repeat this procedure on the right-hand side of the tank.
10 Working inside the vehicle, undo the 4 nuts, and remove the fuel tank access covers from the left- and right-hand side of the floor panel beneath the rear seat cushion location (see illustration).
11 Disconnect the wiring plug from the left-hand sensor unit cover, then unlock the quick-release connectors and disconnect the fuel pipes (see illustration).
12 Disconnect the wiring plugs accessible through the right-hand sensor/pump access hole.
13 Slacken the hose clip, then disconnect the fuel filler hose from the tank neck (see illustration).
14 Working in the wheel arch area, release

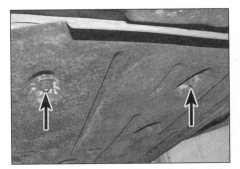

3.9a Undo the nuts and lower the panels in front of the tank

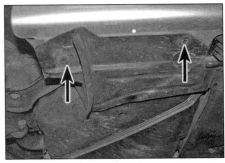

3.9b Remove the fasteners and remove the sill trim panels

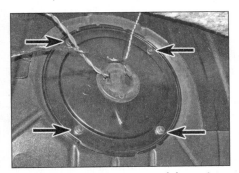

3.10 Tank access cover retaining nuts

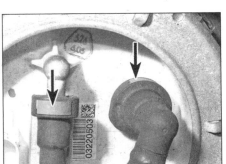

3.11 Depress the release buttons and disconnect the fuel pipes

3.13 Slacken the clip and disconnect the filler hose

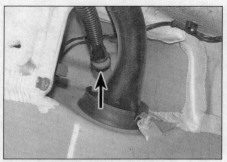

3.14 Squeeze together the sides of the collar and disconnect the vent hose

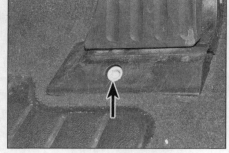

4.1 Accelerator pedal assembly retaining bolt

5.8 Unclip the cover to access the diagnostic plug

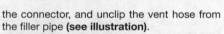

the connector, and unclip the vent hose from the filler pipe **(see illustration)**.

15 Support the fuel tank using a trolley jack and an interposed block of wood.

16 Undo the bolts securing the tank retaining straps. Lower the tank, and manoeuvre it from under the vehicle.

Refitting

17 Refitting is a reversal of removal. Note that once the tank is refitted, at least 5 litres of fuel must be added to allow the fuel system to function correctly.

4 Accelerator pedal – removal and refitting

1 Prise up the cap, then undo the bolt at the base of the accelerator pedal assembly **(see illustration)**.

2 Lift the throttle pedal assembly upwards, and disconnect the wiring plug. Note that the accelerator pedal is only available as a complete assembly, which includes the position sensor. If defective, the complete assembly must be renewed.

3 Refitting is a reversal of removal.

5 Fuel Injection system – general information

1 The system is under the overall control of the Electronic Diesel Control (EDC) system, which also controls the preheating system (see Chapter 5A).

2 Fuel is supplied from the rear-mounted fuel tank, via an electrically-powered lift pump and fuel filter, to the fuel injection pump. The fuel injection pump supplies fuel under high pressure to the common fuel rail. The fuel rail provides a reservoir of fuel under pressure ready for the injectors to deliver direct to the combustion chamber. The individual fuel injectors incorporate solenoids, which when operated, allow the high pressure fuel to be injected. The solenoids are controlled by the ECM. The fuel injection pump purely provides high pressure fuel. The timing and duration of the injection is controlled by the ECM, based

on the information received from the various sensors. In order to increase combustion efficiency and reduce combustion noise (diesel 'knock'), a small amount of fuel is injected before the main injection takes place – this is known as Pre- or Pilot-injection.

3 Additionally, the control module activates the exhaust gas recirculation (EGR) system (see Chapter 4C).

4 The system uses the following sensors.

a) *Crankshaft sensor – informs the ECM of the crankshaft speed and position.*

b) *Coolant temperature sensor – informs the ECM of engine temperature.*

c) *Mass airflow sensor – informs the ECM of the mass of air entering the intake tract.*

d) *Wheel speed sensor – informs the ECM of the vehicle speed.*

e) *Accelerator pedal position sensor – informs the ECM of the accelerator pedal position, and the rate of pedal opening/ closing.*

f) *Fuel pressure sensor – informs the ECM of the pressure of the fuel in the common rail.*

g) *Fuel temperature sensor – informs the ECM of the temperature of the fuel returning to the tank..*

h) *Fuel pressure regulator – controls the pressure produced by the high-pressure fuel pump.*

i) *Camshaft position sensor – informs the ECM of the camshaft position so that the engine firing sequence can be established.*

j) *Stop-light switch – informs the ECM when the brakes are being applied*

k) *Turbocharger boost pressure sensor – informs the ECM of the boost pressure generated by the turbocharger.*

l) *Intake air temperature sensor – informs the ECM of the temperature of the air entering the intake manifold.*

5 The signals from the various sensors are processed by the ECM, and the optimum fuel quantity and injection timing settings are selected for the prevailing engine operating conditions.

6 A catalytic converter and an exhaust gas recirculation (EGR) system is fitted, to reduce harmful exhaust gas emissions. Details of this and other emissions control system equipment are given in Chapter 4C.

7 If there is an abnormality in any of the

readings obtained from any sensor, the ECM enters its back-up mode. In this event, the ECM ignores the abnormal sensor signal, and assumes a preprogrammed value which will allow the engine to continue running (albeit at reduced efficiency). If the ECM enters this back-up mode, the warning light on the instrument panel will come on, and the relevant fault code will be stored in the ECM memory.

8 If the warning light comes on, the vehicle should be taken to a BMW dealer or specialist at the earliest opportunity. A complete test of the Electronic Diesel Control (EDC) system can then be carried out, using a special electronic test unit which is simply plugged into the system's diagnostic connector **(see illustration)**. The connector is located under the driver's side of the facia; to gain access to the connector unclip the socket cover.

6 Fuel system – priming and bleeding

1 The fuel supply system is designed to be self-bleeding. After disturbing the fuel system, proceed as follows.

2 Switch on the ignition, and leave it for approximately 1 minute. Do not attempt to start the engine. During this time the electric fuel pump is activated and the system vented.

3 Depress the accelerator pedal to the floor then start the engine as normal (this may take longer than usual, especially if the fuel system has been allowed to run dry – operate the starter in ten second bursts with 5 seconds rest in between each operation). Run the engine at a fast idle speed for a minute or so to purge any remaining trapped air from the fuel lines. After this time the engine should idle smoothly at a constant speed.

4 If the engine idles roughly, then there is still some air trapped in the fuel system. Increase the engine speed again for another minute or so then recheck the idle speed. Repeat this procedure as necessary until the engine is idling smoothly.

5 On N47 and N57 engines, if the above procedure fails to allow the engine to start, proceed as follows:

6.7 Disconnect the camshaft position sensor wiring plug at the rear of the cylinder head

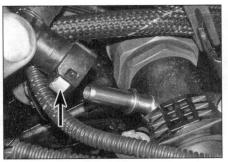

6.8 Depress the button and disconnect the fuel return hose from the common rail

6.9 Attach a hand-held vacuum pump and pull the fuel through

6 Remove the plastic cover from the top of the engine as described in Chapter 2C.

7 Disconnect the camshaft position sensor wiring plug **(see illustration)**.

8 Depress the release button and disconnect the fuel return hose from the common rail **(see illustration)**.

9 Attach a hand-held vacuum pump to the return port on the common rail, and operate the pump until clear, bubble-free fuel emerges **(see illustration)**.

10 Reconnect the fuel return hose to the common rail, and refit the camshaft position sensor wiring plug.

11 Refit the engine cover, and proceed as described in paragraph 2.

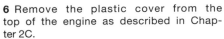

7 Fuel pump/level sensors and control unit – removal and refitting

Fuel pump/level sensors removal

1 There are two level sensors fitted to the fuel tank – one in the left-hand side of the tank, and one in the right-hand side. The pump is integral with the right-hand side sensor, and at the time of writing only the level sensor is available separately. Check with a BMW dealer or parts specialist.

Right-hand sensor/fuel pump

2 Before removing the fuel level sensor/pump, all fuel should be drained from the tank. Since a fuel tank drain plug is not provided, it is preferable to carry out the removal operation when the tank is nearly empty.

3 Remove the rear seat cushion as described in Chapter 11.

4 Fold back the insulation mating to expose the access cover.

5 Undo the four nuts, and remove the access cover from the floor **(see illustration 3.10)**.

6 Disconnect the wiring plug(s) through the access hole.

7 Unscrew the fuel pump/level sensor unit locking ring and remove it from the tank. Although a BMW tool (No 16 1 020) is available for this task, it can be accomplished using a large pair of grips to push on two opposite raised ribs on the locking ring. Alternatively, a home-made tool can be fabricated to engage with the raised ribs of the locking ring, or collar releasing tools are readily available from automotive tool suppliers. Turn the ring anti-clockwise until it can be unscrewed by hand **(see illustration)**.

8 Carefully lift the fuel pump/level sensor unit cover from the tank. Note their fitted positions, then disconnect the fuel hoses at the quick-release connectors **(see illustration)**. Note how the rods in the base of the cover locate in the pump/sensor unit.

9 Carefully manoeuvre the pump/sensor unit

from the tank. Take great care not to bend/damage the float arm as the unit is withdrawn.

10 If required, release the clip and slide the level sensor upwards from place **(see illustration)**. When refitting, the sensor must clip back into place.

11 If required, the level sensor can be unclipped from the pump assembly. On full deflection the sensor resistance was 995 Ω, and on zero deflection the resistance was 52 Ω.

Left-hand sensor

12 Remove the right-hand sensor/fuel pump as previously described.

13 Fold back the insulation mating to expose the access cover.

14 Undo the four nuts, and remove the access cover from the floor **(see illustration 3.10)**.

15 Disconnect the wiring plug from the sensor unit cover, then depress the release buttons and disconnect the fuel pipes.

16 Unscrew the fuel pump/level sensor unit locking ring and remove it from the tank. Although a BMW tool (No 16 1 020) is available for this task, it can be accomplished using a large pair of grips to push on two opposite raised ribs on the locking ring. Alternatively, a home-made tool can be fabricated to engage with the raised ribs of the locking ring. Turn the ring anti-clockwise until it can be unscrewed by hand **(see illustration 7.7)**.

17 Tie a length of string/cable around the

7.7 A home-made tool can be used to unscrew the locking ring

7.8 Depress the release buttons and disconnect the hoses from the pump/sender unit

7.10 Release the clip each side, and slide the sensor upwards

7.17 Use a cable tie to keep the hoses together, then tie a length of string/cable around the hoses to aid refitting – see text

7.19 The lug must engage with the slot in the collar

7.21 Pull the top edge of the side backrest forwards

disconnected hoses accessible through the right-hand tank access hole **(see illustration)**. As these hoses will be removed with the left-hand sensor/filter unit, the idea is to pull the string/cable into the tank as the sensor/filter unit is removed, then leave it in place to facilitate refitting.

18 Carefully lift the sensor/filter unit from the tank, and remove it. Untie the string/cable and leave it in place.

Refitting fuel pump/level sensors

19 Refitting is a reversal of removal, noting the following points:
a) Use a new sealing ring.
b) To allow the unit to pass through the aperture in the fuel tank, press the float arm against the fuel pick-up strainer.
c) When the unit is fitted, the locating lug on the unit must engage with the corresponding slot in the fuel tank collar **(see illustration)**.
d) The locating rods of the right-hand sensor unit cover must align with the corresponding holes in the pump/sensor unit.
e) The locking ring must be tightened until the notch on the ring aligns with the mark on the tank.

Fuel pump control unit

Removal

20 On Saloon models, remove the rear side backrest, as described in Chapter 11.
21 On Touring models, fold down the rear seat backrest, then pull the top edge of

the right-hand side backrest side section forwards to release the clip, and remove it **(see illustration)**. Be prepared for clip breakage – renew it if necessary.
22 Disconnect the wiring plug, undo the 2 retaining nuts and remove the control unit **(see illustration)**.

Refitting

23 Refitting is a reversal of removal. Note that if a new control unit has been fitted, it will need to be programmed using BMW test equipment. Entrust this task to a BMW dealer or suitably-equipped specialist.

---

8 Fuel injection system – testing and adjustment

Testing

1 If a fault appears in the fuel injection system, first ensure that all the system wiring connectors are securely connected and free from corrosion. Ensure that the fault is not due to poor maintenance; ie, check that the air cleaner filter element is clean, that the cylinder compression pressures are correct (see Chapter 2B or 2C), and that the engine breather hoses are clear and undamaged (see Chapter 4C).
2 If the engine will not start, check the condition of the glow plugs (see Chapter 5A).
3 If these checks fail to reveal the cause of the problem, the vehicle should be taken to a BMW dealer or specialist for testing using special electronic equipment which is plugged

into the diagnostic connector (see Section 5). The tester should locate the fault quickly and simply, avoiding the need to test all the system components individually, which is time-consuming, and also carries a risk of damaging the ECM.

Adjustment

4 The engine idle speed and maximum speed are all controlled by the ECM. Whilst in theory it is possible to check the settings, if they are found to be in need of adjustment, the car will have to be taken to a suitably-equipped BMW dealer or specialist. They will have access to the necessary diagnostic equipment required to test and (where possible) adjust the settings.

---

9 Fuel injection pump – removal and refitting

Caution: Be careful not to allow dirt into the injection pump or injector pipes during this procedure.
1 Disconnect the battery negative lead (see Chapter 5A).

M57T2 engines

Removal

2 Refer to Section 16, and remove the intake manifold.
3 Disconnect the wiring plug from the pressure regulator on the pump **(see illustration)**.
4 Release the clamp, and disconnect the fuel feed pipe from the pump **(see illustration)**.

7.22 Fuel pump control unit

9.3 Disconnect the wiring plug from the regulator on the pump

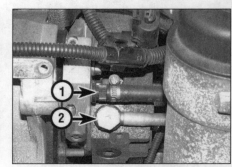

9.4 Fuel feed (1) and return (2) pipes

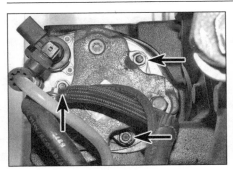

9.7 Pump retaining nuts

9.9 Unscrew the cap from the timing chain cover

9.11a Screw the tool into the timing cover...

Plug or seal the openings to prevent contamination.

5 Undo the banjo bolt and disconnect the fuel return pipe from the pump.

6 Note the position of the rubber mounting, then undo the unions and disconnect the high-pressure fuel pipe from between the pump and the common rail. Discard the pipe – a new one must be fitted.

7 Undo the 3 nuts securing the injection pump to the cylinder block **(see illustration)**.

8 Remove the auxiliary drivebelt as described in Chapter 1B.

9 Undo the cap from the timing chain cover **(see illustration)**. Discard the seal, a new one must be fitted.

10 Slacken and remove the fuel pump sprocket nut.

11 Screw BMW tool No 13 5 192 into the timing chain cover, then screw BMW tool No 13 5 191 into the fuel pump drive sprocket. Carefully tighten the centre bolt of the tool, and free the pump shaft from the sprocket **(see illustrations)**. Do not remove tool No 13 5 192 once the shaft is free from the sprocket or the timing would be lost. If the special BMW tools are not available, the only other alternative is to remove the timing chains and pull the sprocket from the shaft as described in Chapter 2B. Although, in theory it would be possible to free the sprocket from the shaft using a drift or similar, the position of the sprocket, and therefore the tension of the timing chains, would be lost.

12 Remove the fuel pump. Discard the gasket, a new one must be fitted.

Refitting

13 Ensure that the mating surfaces of the pump and engine are clean and dry, and fit the new pump gasket.

14 Unscrew tool No 13 5 191 from the centre of tool No 13 5 192.

15 Position the fuel pump on the cylinder block. Note that the position of the pump shaft in relation to the crankshaft position is not important.

16 Fit the pump retaining nuts and tighten them to the specified torque.

17 Fit the new high-pressure fuel pipe, with the rubber mounting. Tighten the unions to the specified torque.

9.11b... then screw the special tool into the pump sprocket

18 Reconnect the fuel hoses to the pump. Use a new banjo bolt seal.

19 Reconnect the wiring plug to the fuel pump.

20 If the BMW special tools were used to release the fuel pump drive sprocket and hold the sprocket in position, unscrew the tools, fit and tighten the sprocket retaining nut to the specified torque. If the tools were not available, refit the timing chains, sprockets and covers, as described in Chapter 2B.

21 Ensure that the timing cover access plug is clean, fit the new seal, and tighten it to the specified torque.

22 With reference to Chapter 1B, refit the auxiliary drivebelt.

23 Refer to Section 16, and refit the intake manifold.

24 Reconnect the battery negative lead as described in Chapter 5A.

9.28 The glow plug control unit is located on the rear of the oil filter housing – N47 engines

9.11c Tighten the centre bolt to release the pump shaft from the sprocket

25 Bleed the fuel system as described in Section 6.

N47/T engines

Removal

26 Pull up the front edge of the acoustic cover on the top of the engine, then slide it forwards and remove it.

27 Remove the air intake manifold as described in Section 16.

28 Where applicable, disconnect the wiring plug, then remove the glow plug control unit **(see illustration)**.

29 Lock the crankshaft/flywheel at TDC on No 1 cylinder as described in Chapter 2C.

30 Release the locking catch, and disconnect the wiring plug from the metering unit on the injection pump **(see illustration)**.

31 Slacken the clamps and disconnect the

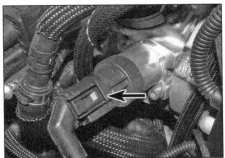

9.30 Disconnect the wiring plug from the metering unit

9.31 Note their positions, then disconnect the fuel feed and return hoses from the pump

9.32 Note the rubber grommets on the high-pressure fuel pipe

9.33 Unscrew the cap at the rear of the engine

fuel feed and return pipes from the pump **(see illustration)**. Plug or seal the openings to prevent contamination.

32 Note the fitted locations of the rubber mountings, then undo the union nuts and remove the high-pressure fuel pipe between the injection pump and the common rail **(see illustration)**.

33 Undo the sealing cap in the timing cover at the rear of the engine **(see illustration)**. Discard the sealing ring – a new one must be fitted.

34 Screw BMW special tool No 11 8 741 into the cap hole in the timing chain cover **(see illustration)**. This tool traps the fuel pump sprocket and chain in place. Failure to secure the sprocket will result in the camshaft timing being lost. If the tool is not available, remove the engine and timing chain as described in Chapter 2D.

35 Undo the retaining bolts and remove the support bracket from the front of the pump **(see illustration)**.

36 Undo the bolts securing the pump to the timing chain cover. Note that it's not necessary to remove the bolts from their locations.

37 Undo the bolt securing the drive chain sprocket to the pump shaft. Note that the bolt remains in place in the sprocket.

38 Remove the pump from position **(see illustration)**.

Refitting

39 Ensure the pump and cylinder block mating surfaces are clean, then align the keyway on the pump shaft with the key in the tapered bore in the pump drive sprocket.

40 Fit a new O-ring seal, then offer the pump into position **(see illustration)**.

41 Engage the shaft with the drive sprocket. Ensure the key and keyway engage correctly.

42 Lightly tighten the bolts securing the pump to the cylinder block/timing chain cover.

43 Refit the pump support bracket, then working in sequence, tighten the bolts hand-tight, then to their specified torque **(see illustration)**.

44 Tighten the drive sprocket retaining bolt to the specified torque.

45 Unscrew the special tool, then refit the sealing cap with a new seal. Tighten the cap to the specified torque.

46 Remove the crankshaft/flywheel locking tool, with reference to Chapter 2C.

47 Fit the new high-pressure fuel pipe between the pump and common rail, tighten the nuts to the specified torque, then refit the rubber mounting.

48 The remainder of refitting is a reversal of removal, noting the following points:
a) *Tighten all fasteners to their specified torque where given.*
b) *Reconnect the battery negative lead as described in Chapter 5A.*
c) *Bleed the fuel system as described in Section 6.*

N57 engines

Removal

49 Remove the air intake manifold as described in Section 16.

50 Disconnect the wiring plug, then remove the glow plug control unit **(see illustration)**.

51 Note the fitted locations of the rubber mountings, then undo the union nuts and remove the high-pressure fuel pipe between the injection pump and the common rail. Plug or seal the openings to prevent contami-nation.

9.34 Screw the special tool into the timing chain cover

9.35 Remove the support bracket from the front of the pump

9.38 Withdrawn the pump from the cylinder block

9.40 Renew the fuel pump O-ring seal

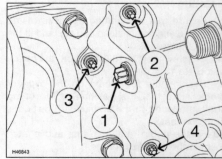

9.43 Injection pump support bracket bolts tightening sequence

9.50 The glow plug control unit is attached to the engine mounting bracket

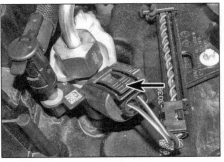

10.5 Depress the retaining clip and pull the wiring plug from the injector

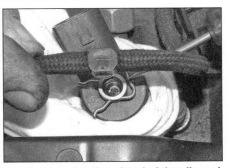

10.6 Push in the closed end of the clip and pull the return hose upwards

52 Remove the transmission as described in Chapter 7A or 7B.
53 Lock the crankshaft/flywheel at TDC on No 1 cylinder as described in Chapter 2C.
54 Release the locking catch, and disconnect the wiring plug from the metering unit on the injection pump (see illustration 9.30).
55 Disconnect the fuel feed and return pipes from the pump (see illustration 9.31). Plug or seal the openings to prevent contamination.
56 Screw BMW special tool No 11 8 741 into the cap hole in the timing chain cover (see illustration 9.34). This tool traps the fuel pump sprocket and chain in place. Failure to secure the sprocket will result in the camshaft timing being lost. If the tool is not available, remove the engine and timing chain as described in Chapter 2D.
57 Undo the retaining bolts and remove the support bracket from the front of the pump (see illustration 9.35).
58 Undo the bolts securing the pump to the timing chain cover/cylinder block. Note that it's not necessary to remove the timing cover bolt from its location.
59 Undo the bolt securing the drive chain sprocket to the pump shaft. Note that the bolt remains in place in the sprocket.
60 Remove the pump from position.

Refitting

61 Ensure the pump and cylinder block mating surfaces are clean, then align the keyway on the pump shaft with the key in the tapered bore in the pump drive sprocket.
62 Offer the pump into position, and engage the shaft with the drive sprocket, ensure the key and keyway engage correctly.
63 Lightly tighten the bolts securing the pump to the cylinder block/timing chain cover.
64 Refit the pump support bracket, then working in sequence, tighten the bolts hand-tight, then to their specified torque (see illustration 9.43).
65 Tighten the drive sprocket retaining bolt to the specified torque.
66 Unscrew the special tool, then refit the sealing cap with a new seal. Tighten the cap to the specified torque.
67 Remove the crankshaft/flywheel locking tool, with reference to Chapter 2C.
68 Fit the new high-pressure fuel pipe

between the pump and common rail, tighten the nuts to the specified torque, then refit the rubber mounting.
69 The remainder of refitting is a reversal of removal, noting the following points:
a) Tighten all fasteners to their specified torque where given.
b) Refit the transmission as described in Chapter 7A or 7B.
c) Reconnect the battery negative lead as described in Chapter 5A.
d) Bleed the fuel system as described in Section 6.

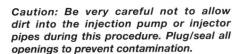

10 Fuel injectors – removal and refitting

Caution: Be very careful not to allow dirt into the injection pump or injector pipes during this procedure. Plug/seal all openings to prevent contamination.

Removal

1 Disconnect the battery negative lead, as described in Chapter 5A.
2 On N47 engines, remove the pollen filter housing as described in Section 11.
3 Where applicable, remove the cover and sound insulation material above the injectors.
4 On M57T2 engines, remove the intake manifold as described in Section 16.
5 Disconnect the wiring plugs from the injectors (if not already done so) (see illustration).

10.7b... and N47 engine

6 Two different types of return hose connections may be encountered. On the first type, push in the closed end of the clips, and remove the fuel return hoses from the injectors (see illustration). If the rubber seals are damaged, the complete return hose assembly must be renewed. Plug/cover the openings to prevent contamination.
7 On the second type of connector, carefully prise up the locking cap, then pull the return hose connection from the top of each injector (see illustrations). Check the condition of the sealing rings and renew if necessary. Plug/cover the openings to prevent contamination.
8 Slacken the pipe unions (where possible, counterhold the union on the common fuel rail and the injector), and remove the relevant injector pipe (see illustration). Plug/cover the openings to prevent contamination.

10.7a Prise up the locking cap and pull the return hose connection upwards – N47T engine...

10.8 If possible, use a crows foot adapter to slacken and tighten the high-pressure pipe unions

10.9a Undo the injector retaining nuts...

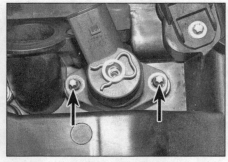

10.9b... undo the Torx studs to force the injector upwards...

10.9c... then remove the clamp jaw and injector

10.9d Store the injectors upright, and label them so they can be refitted to their original locations

10.10a Undo the injector retaining bolt and remove the clamping jaw – N47 and N57 engines...

10.10b... and N47T engines

M57T2 engines

Note: *The high-pressure pipes from the common fuel rail to the injectors and the pump must be renewed.*

10.10c If necessary, use a spanner to rotate the injector a few degrees...

10.13 Common rail clamp bolts

10.10d... and pull it from place

9 Unscrew the two nuts securing each injector clamp. Use a Torx socket to unscrew the mounting studs, and force the injectors upwards from place. Discard the sealing

10.14 Depress the release button and disconnect the return hose

washers – new ones must be fitted. If the injectors are to be refitted, they must be stored upright, and marked/labelled so they can be refitted into their original positions **(see illustrations)**.

N47 and N57 engines

Note: *BMW state the pipes can be re-used 3 times, then renewed.*

10 Undo the retaining bolt, remove the clamping jaw and remove the injectors. If the injectors are reluctant to move, rotate them a few degrees each way to release them **(see illustrations)**. Discard the sealing washers – new ones must be fitted. If the injectors are to be refitted, they must be stored upright, and marked/labelled so they can be refitted into their original positions **(see illustration 10.9d)**.

11 If the common fuel rail is to be removed, the intake manifold must be removed as described in Section 16. Once the manifold is withdrawn, undo the unions and remove the high-pressure fuel pipe between the pump and rail.

12 Disconnect the wiring plugs from the sensors on the common rail.

13 Undo the retaining bolts and remove the common rail clamps **(see illustration)**.

14 Lift the rail from place, depress the release button and disconnect the return hose from the rail **(see illustration)**.

Refitting

15 On N47 and N57 engines, where applicable, refit the common rail and clamps, then tighten the bolts to the specified torque.

10.17a Injector adjustment value – M57T2 engines

10.17b Injector adjustment value – N47 and N57 engines

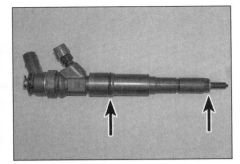

10.18a Renew the injector sealing washers...

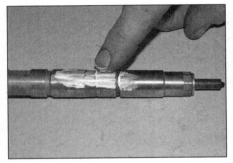

10.18b... and apply a little high-temperature anti-seize grease to the injector stems

10.19 N47 engine shown

10.21 Renew the sealing ring

Fit the new high-pressure pipe (see the Note above) between the pump and rail, and tighten the unions to the specified torque. Note the rubber sleeves fitted to the common rail locations in the camshaft cover and clamps.

16 Ensure that the injectors and seats in cylinder head are clean and dry.

17 If any of the injectors are being renewed, make a note of the 6- or 7- digit adjustment value engraved on the top of injector **(see illustrations)**. In order for the injector to function at maximum efficiency, this number must be programmed into the engine management ECM using BMW diagnostic equipment. Entrust this task to a BMW dealer or suitably-equipped specialist.

18 Fit new sealing washers to the injectors, apply a little high-temperature anti-seize grease (BMW part No 83 23 0441 070 or Copperslip) to the injector stems and refit them with the clamps **(see illustrations)**. If new injectors are not being fitted, it's absolutely essential they are refitted to their original positions. On M57T2 engines, tighten the clamp nuts to the specified torque. On N47 and N57 engines, refit the clamping jaw, insert the retaining bolt, and tighten it to the specified torque.

19 Refit the injection pipe(s), and tighten the unions finger-tight, then to the specified torque. Refit the pipe retaining clips **(see illustration)**.

20 On the first type of return hose connection, squeeze together the open ends of the clips and refit the fuel return hoses to the injectors.

21 On the second type of return hose

connection, with the new sealing rings fitted to the injectors or return pipe fittings (where necessary), press the return hose connections down on to the injectors, then press the locking caps down **(see illustration)**.

22 The remainder of refitting is a reversal of removal.

11 Electronic Diesel Control (EDC) system components – removal and refitting

Crankshaft sensor

M57T2 engines

1 The sensor is mounted on the left-hand side of the engine block. To gain access, remove the starter motor as described in Chapter 5A.

11.3 Crankshaft sensor retaining bolt

2 Disconnect the wiring connector from the sensor.

3 Slacken and remove the retaining bolt and carefully remove the sensor from the engine **(see illustration)**.

4 Refitting is the reverse of removal, tightening the retaining bolt to the specified torque.

N47 and N57 engines

5 Raise the front of the vehicle and support it securely on axle stands (see *Jacking and vehicle support*).

6 Undo the fasteners and remove the engine undershield **(see illustration)**.

7 The sensor is located beneath the fuel injection pump at the rear of the engine. Disconnect the sensor wiring plug.

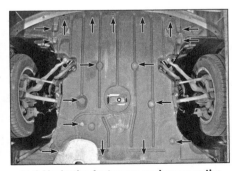

11.6 Undo the fasteners and remove the engine undershield

11.8 Crankshaft sensor retaining bolt

11.13 Undo the bolts and pull the intake pipe forwards

11.15 Undo the bolts and remove the mass airflow sensor

8 Undo the retaining bolt and pull the sensor from position **(see illustration)**.
9 Refitting is a reversal of removal.

Coolant temperature sensor

10 The sensor is screwed directly into the cylinder head. Refer to Chapter 3 for removal and refitting details.

Accelerator pedal position sensor

11 The sensor is integral with the accelerator pedal assembly – see Section 4.

Mass airflow sensor

M57T2 engines

12 Remove the acoustic cover from the top of the engine, by undoing the bolts, pulling up the front edge and sliding it forwards.
13 Undo the 2 bolts, unclip the hose, and pull

the intake pipe forwards from the sensor **(see illustration)**.
14 Disconnect the wiring plug from the sensor.
15 Slacken and remove the two Torx bolts, and withdraw the sensor **(see illustration)**.
16 Refitting is a reversal of removal.

N47 and N57 engines

17 The mass airflow sensor is located on the air filter cover outlet ducting. Disconnect the sensor wiring plug **(see illustration)**.
18 Slacken the air outlet hose clamp and disconnect the hose.
19 Undo the 2 bolts and remove the mass airflow sensor from the filter cover **(see illustration)**.
20 Refitting is a reversal of removal.

Intake air temperature sensor

21 The intake air temperature sensor is

located in the intake ducting on the left-hand side of the engine. Disconnect the sensor wiring plug.
22 Two different types of sensor may be fitted. On the first type, a retaining clip must be pulled from place, before the sensor is removed by rotating it 45° anti-clockwise **(see illustration)**. On the second type, no clip is fitted.
23 Refitting is a reversal of removal.

Stop-light switch

24 The engine control module receives a signal from the stop-light switch which indicates when the brakes are being applied. Stop-light switch removal and refitting details can be found in Chapter 9.

Electronic control module (ECM)

Note: *If a new ECM is to be fitted, it will be necessary to entrust the task to a BMW dealer or specialist. After fitting, it will be necessary to programme the ECM to enable it function correctly. This can only be done using the special BMW equipment which is plugged into the diagnostic connector (see Section 5).*
25 Disconnect the battery negative lead (see Chapter 5A).
26 Undo the bolts and remove the upper section of the pollen filter housing **(see illustration)**.
27 Release the catches and remove the left- and right-hand plastic covers from behind the suspension turret each side of the engine compartment. Unclip any wiring as the covers are removed **(see illustration)**.

11.17 Mass airflow sensor wiring plug

11.19 Undo the bolts and remove the mass airflow sensor

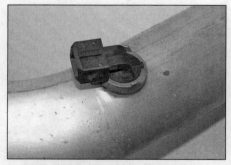

11.22 To remove this type of air temperature sensor, rotate it 45° anti-clockwise

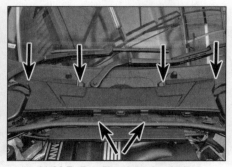

11.26 Pollen filter housing bolts

11.27 Release the clips and remove the plastic cover each side

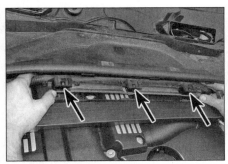

11.28 Release the clips and slide the cable guide forwards

11.29a Rotate the temperature sensor and remove it. On the passenger's side, disconnect the bonnet switch

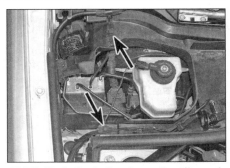

11.29b Undo the bolt, release the clip each side...

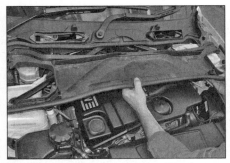

11.29c... then slide the pollen filter lower housing forwards

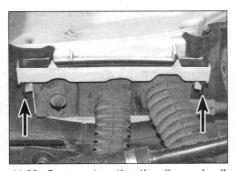

11.30a Squeeze together the clips and pull the black plastic clip upwards

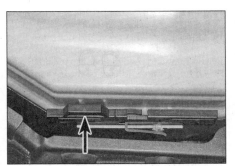

11.30b Slide the catch to the 'unlock' position

28 Depress the clips and pull the cable guide forwards from the pollen filter lower housing **(see illustration)**.

29 Release the catch and undo the bolt each side, then slide the pollen filter lower housing forwards and manoeuvre it from place **(see illustrations)**.

30 Release the clips and remove the electrical box cover, located on the left-hand side of the engine compartment **(see illustrations)**.

31 Note their fitted locations, and disconnect the wiring plugs from the ECM. To release these plugs, slide out the locking element, and disconnect the plugs from the ECM **(see illustration)**.

32 Release the two retaining clips and remove the ECM **(see illustration)**.

33 Refitting is the reverse of removal.

Turbocharger boost pressure sensor – M57T2 engines

34 Undo the bolts and remove the upper section of the pollen filter housing **(see illustration 11.26)**.

35 Release the catches and remove the left- and right-hand plastic covers from behind the suspension turret each side of the engine compartment. Unclip the hose from the left-hand cover **(see illustration 11.27)**.

36 Depress the clips and pull the cable guide forwards from the pollen filter lower housing **(see illustration 11.28)**.

37 Release the catch and undo the bolt each side, then slide the pollen filter lower housing forwards and manoeuvre it from place **(see illustrations 11.29a, 11.29b and 11.29c)**.

38 Undo the bolts and remove the plastic cover from the top of the engine.

39 Disconnect the sensor wiring plug, then pull if from the manifold **(see illustration)**.

40 Check the condition of the seal and renew if necessary.

41 Upon refitting, lubricate the sensor seal with petroleum jelly, then push it into the hole in the manifold.

42 Reconnect the sensor wiring plug.

43 The remainder of refitting is a reversal of removal.

Turbocharger boost pressure sensor – N47 and N57 engines

44 Remove the plastic acoustic cover from the top of the engine by pulling up the front edge, and sliding it forwards.

11.31 Slide out the locking element

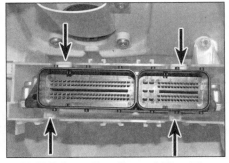

11.32 Release the clips and lift out the ECM

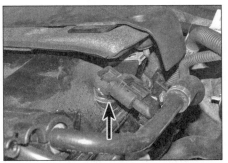

11.39 Boost pressure sensor (arrowed) – M57T2 engine

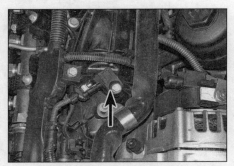

11.45 Boost pressure sensor – N47 and N57 engines

11.55 The fuel pressure sensor is located at the front of the common rail – N47 engine

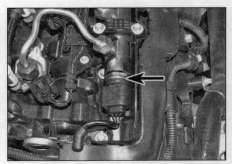

11.63 Fuel pressure sensor – N57 engine

45 The sensor is located at the front of the intake manifold. Disconnect the sensor wiring plug **(see illustration)**.

46 Undo the retaining bolt and pull the sensor from the manifold. Check the condition of the sealing ring, and renew if necessary.

47 Upon refitting, lubricate the sensor seal with petroleum jelly, then fit it to the manifold, and tighten the retaining bolt securely.

Fuel pressure sensor

M57T2 engines

48 Remove the plastic acoustic cover from the top of the engine, by removing the retaining bolts, and sliding it forwards.

49 The fuel pressure sensor is located in the front end of the common fuel rail. Ensure that the ignition is switched off, and disconnect the wiring plug from the sensor.

50 Counterhold the sensor with a spanner to prevent rotation, then undo the locknut.

51 Ensure that the mating surfaces of the sensor and common rail are clean and dry, then bolt the sensor into position, counterhold it with a spanner to prevent rotation, and tighten the locknut to the specified torque.

52 The remainder of refitting is a reversal of removal. Note that if a new sensor has been fitted, the mean value adaptation value stored in the ECM must be reset using BMW diagnostic equipment. Entrust this task to a BMW dealer or suitably-equipped specialist.

N47 engines

53 Remove the plastic acoustic cover from the top of the engine by pulling up the front edge, and sliding it forwards.

54 Slacken the union nuts and remove the pressure fuel pipes from the common fuel rail to the injectors, and to the high-pressure pump. It's essential that all openings are plugged to prevent contamination. Note that the pipes must not be re-used more than 3 times – they must be renewed.

55 Disconnect the wiring plugs from the pressure sensor and regulator on the common fuel rail **(see illustration)**.

56 Depress the release button, and disconnect the fuel return pipe from the common rail **(see illustration 6.8)**.

57 Undo the retaining bolts and remove the common fuel rail.

58 Carefully grip the common rail in a bench vice, then unscrew the sensor from place.

59 Upon refitting, apply a little grease to the sensor threads, then tighten it to the specified torque.

60 The remainder of refitting is a reversal of removal. Note that if a new sensor has been fitted, the mean adaptation value stored in the ECM must be reset using BMW diagnostic equipment. Entrust this task to a BMW dealer or suitably-equipped specialist.

N57 engines

61 Remove the intake manifold as described in Section 16.

62 Slacken the union nuts and remove the high-pressure fuel pipes from the common fuel rail to the injectors, and to the high-pressure pump. It's essential that all openings are plugged to prevent contamination. Note that the pipes can only be used 3 times. After this they must be renewed.

63 Disconnect the wiring plugs from the pressure sensor and regulator on the common fuel rail **(see illustrations)**.

64 Disconnect the fuel return pipe from the common rail **(see illustration 6.8)**.

65 Undo the retaining bolts and remove the common fuel rail.

66 Carefully grip the common rail in a bench vice, then unscrew the sensor from place.

67 Upon refitting, apply a little grease to the sensor threads, then tighten it to the specified torque.

68 The remainder of refitting is a reversal of removal. Note that if a new sensor has been fitted, the mean adaptation value stored in the ECM must be reset using BMW diagnostic equipment. Entrust this task to a BMW dealer or suitably-equipped specialist.

Fuel pressure regulator

M57T2 engines

Note: *BMW insist that the regulator can only be used once. If removed, it must be renewed.*

69 With reference to Section 16, remove the intake manifold.

70 Disconnect the wiring plug from the regulator, located in the rear of the common rail.

71 Use a spanner to counterhold the regulator, then slacken the regulator locknut.

72 Ensure the common rail and regulator mating faces are clean, then screw the regulator into position. Counterhold it with a spanner and tighten the locknut to the specified torque.

73 Refit the manifold as described in Section 16.

N47 engines

Note: *BMW insist that the regulator can only be used once. If removed, it must be renewed.*

74 Remove the plastic acoustic cover from the top of the engine by pulling up the front edge, and sliding it forwards.

75 Slacken the union nuts and remove the high-pressure fuel pipes from the common fuel rail to the injectors, and to the high-pressure pump. It's essential that all openings are plugged to prevent contamination. Note that the pipes must not be re-used – they must be renewed.

76 Disconnect the wiring plugs from the pressure sensor and regulator on the common fuel rail.

77 Depress the release button, and disconnect the fuel return pipe from the common rail.

78 Undo the retaining bolts and remove the common fuel rail.

79 Carefully grip the common rail in a bench vice.

80 Note the fitted position of the regulator is relation to the common rail. Counterhold the regulator with a spanner, then slacken the locknut. Unscrew the sensor from place.

81 Ensure the common rail and regulator mating faces are clean, then screw the regulator into position. Counterhold it with a spanner and tighten the locknut to the specified torque.

82 The remainder of refitting is a reversal of removal. Note that if a new regulator has been fitted, the adaptation value stored in the ECM must be reset using BMW diagnostic equipment. Entrust this task to a BMW dealer or suitably-equipped specialist.

N57 engines

83 Remove the intake manifold as described in Section 16.

84 Slacken the union nuts and remove the high-pressure fuel pipes from the common fuel rail to the injectors, and to the high-pressure

pump. It's essential that all openings are plugged to prevent contamination. Note that the pipes can only be used 3 times. After this they must be renewed.

85 Disconnect the wiring plugs from the pressure sensor and regulator on the common fuel rail.

86 Disconnect the fuel return pipe from the common rail **(see illustration 6.8)**.

87 Undo the retaining bolts and remove the common fuel rail.

88 Carefully grip the common rail in a bench vice.

89 Note the fitted position of the regulator is relation to the common rail. Counterhold the regulator with a spanner, then slacken the locknut. Unscrew the sensor from place.

90 Ensure the common rail and regulator mating faces are clean, then screw the regulator into position. Counterhold it with a spanner and tighten the locknut to the specified torque.

91 The remainder of refitting is a reversal of removal. Note that if a new regulator has been fitted, the adaptation value stored in the ECM must be reset using BMW diagnostic equipment. Entrust this task to a BMW dealer or suitably-equipped specialist.

Camshaft position sensor

M57T2 engines

92 Undo the bolts and remove the plastic acoustic cover from the top of the engine.

93 Disconnect the wiring plug, undo the retaining bolt and pull the sensor from the front of the cylinder head cover. Check the condition of the sealing ring and renew if necessary.

94 Upon refitting, lubricate the sealing ring with petroleum jelly, refit the sensor and tighten the retaining bolt securely.

N47 and N57 engines

95 Remove the plastic acoustic cover from the top of the engine by pulling up the front edge, and sliding it forwards.

96 Undo the bolts and remove the upper section of the pollen filter housing **(see illustration 11.26)**.

97 Release the catches and remove the left- and right-hand plastic covers from behind the suspension turret each side of the engine compartment. Unclip the hose from the left-hand cover **(see illustration 11.27)**.

98 Depress the clips and pull the cable guide forwards from the pollen filter lower housing **(see illustration 11.28)**.

99 Release the catch and undo the bolt each side, then slide the pollen filter lower housing forwards and manoeuvre it from place **(see illustrations 11.29a, 11.29b and 11.29c)**.

100 Prise up the centre pins, lever out the plastic expansion rivets, then remove the insulation material from the rear of the cylinder head (where fitted).

101 Disconnect the wiring plug from the camshaft position sensor, then undo the

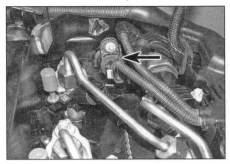

11.101 Camshaft position sensor – N47 and N57 engines

retaining bolt and pull the sensor from place **(see illustration)**.

102 Upon refitting, lubricate the sensor seal with a little petroleum jelly, then refit it and tighten the retaining bolt securely.

103 The remainder of refitting is a reversal of removal.

12 Turbocharger – description and precautions

1 A turbocharger is fitted to all diesel engines. It increases engine efficiency by raising the pressure in the intake manifold above atmospheric pressure. Instead of the air simply being sucked into the cylinders, it is forced in. Additional fuel is supplied by the injection pump in proportion to the increased air intake.

2 Energy for the operation of the turbocharger comes from the exhaust gas. The gas flows through a specially-shaped housing (the turbine housing) and in so doing spins the turbine wheel. The turbine wheel is attached to a shaft, at the end of which is another vaned wheel known as the compressor wheel. The compressor wheel spins in its own housing and compresses the inducted air on the way to the intake manifold.

3 The compressed air passes through an intercooler. This is an air-to-air heat exchanger, mounted with the radiator at the front of the vehicle. The purpose of the intercooler is to remove from the inducted air some of the heat gained in being compressed. Because cooler air is denser, removal of this heat further increases engine efficiency.

4 The turbocharger has adjustable guide vanes controlling the flow of exhaust gas into the turbine. The vanes are swivelled by the boost pressure control motor (integral with the turbocharger), controlled by the engine management ECM. At lower engine speeds, the vanes close together, giving a smaller exhaust gas entry port, and therefore higher gas speed, which increases boost pressure at low engine speed. At high engine speed, the vanes are turned to give a larger exhaust gas entry port, and therefore lower gas speed, effectively maintaining a reasonably constant boost pressure over the engine rev range.

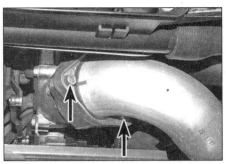

13.2 Undo the charge pressure hose clamp bolts

5 The turbo shaft is pressure-lubricated by an oil feed pipe from the main oil gallery. The shaft 'floats' on a cushion of oil. A drain pipe/hose returns the oil to the sump.

Precautions

- **The turbocharger operates at extremely high speeds and temperatures. Certain precautions must be observed to avoid premature failure of the turbo or injury to the operator.**
- **Do not operate the turbo with any parts exposed. Foreign objects falling onto the rotating vanes could cause excessive damage and (if ejected) personal injury.**
- **Do not race the engine immediately after start-up, especially if it is cold. Give the oil a few seconds to circulate.**
- **Always allow the engine to return to idle speed before switching it off – do not blip the throttle and switch off, as this will leave the turbo spinning without lubrication.**
- **Allow the engine to idle for several minutes before switching off after a high-speed run.**
- **Observe the recommended intervals for oil and filter changing, and use a reputable oil of the specified quality (see 'Lubricants and fluids'). Neglect of oil changing, or use of inferior oil, can cause carbon formation on the turbo shaft and subsequent failure.**

13 Turbocharger – removal and refitting

M57T2 engines

1 Remove catalytic converter/particulate filter as described in Chapter 4C.

2 Slacken the bolts, rotate the clamp and detach the charge pressure hose from the base of the turbocharger **(see illustration)**. Cap/seal the openings to prevent contamination.

3 Unscrew and remove the turbocharger oil feed banjo bolt from the turbocharger. Discard the sealing washers, new ones must be fitted. Plug the hose and block openings to prevent contamination.

13.4 Turbocharger boost control motor wiring plug

13.13 Press the hose onto the turbocharger, and prise out the clip

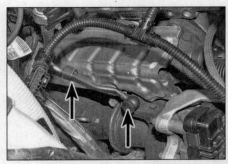

13.17 Undo the banjo bolt and the support bracket bolt

4 Unlock and disconnect the turbocharger boost control motor wiring plug **(see illustration)**.

5 Undo the retaining bolt and detach the oil return hose from the base of the turbocharger. Plug/seal the openings to prevent contamination.

6 Release the two retaining bolts, and disconnect the turbocharger duct from the mass airflow sensor. Remove the duct. Recover the duct seal and breather pipe connector.

7 Slacken the clamp securing the turbocharger to the manifold. Note that a new clamp will be required.

8 Undo the retaining bolts and manoeuvre the turbocharger from place.

9 Refitting is a reversal of removal, noting the following points:
a) Ensure all mating surfaces are clean and dry.
b) Renew all O-rings, seals and gasket.
c) Tighten all fasteners to the specified torque where available.

N47 and N57 engines

10 Remove the plastic acoustic cover from the top of the engine.

11 Remove the cooling fan and shroud as described in Chapter 3.

12 Remove the air cleaner assembly as described in Section 2.

13 Release the clamps and remove the charge pressure hose between the intercooler and the turbocharger **(see illustration)**.

14 Remove the EGR cooler and catalytic

converter/particulate filter as described in Chapter 4C.

15 Prise out the locking clip, undo the bolt and detach the air intake pipe from the turbocharger.

16 Disconnect the wiring plug from the turbocharger boost control motor.

17 On N47T engines, undo the banjo bolt securing the 'exhaust' pipe to the manifold, and the support bracket bolt from the heat shield **(see illustration)**. Discard the banjo bolt sealing washers – new ones must be fitted.

18 Undo the bolts and remove the heat shield from the exhaust manifold. Note the mounting bolt at the rear of the manifold.

19 Undo the banjo bolt and detach the oil feed pipe from the cylinder block **(see illustration)**. Discard the pipe seals, new ones must be fitted. Plug/seal the openings to prevent contamination.

20 Slacken the clamp, undo the 2 retaining bolts and remove the oil return pipe from the base of the turbocharger, then slacken the clamp and detach the pipe from the hose on the cylinder block. Discard the gasket. Plug/seal the openings to prevent contamination.

21 Undo the bolts and remove the support bracket from the base of the turbocharger and the cylinder block.

4-cylinder engines

22 Undo the 3 bolts and detach the turbocharger from the exhaust manifold **(see illustration)**. Renew the gasket.

23 Refitting is a reversal of removal, noting the following points:
a) Ensure all mating surfaces are clean and dry.
b) Renew all O-rings, seals and gasket.
c) Tighten all fasteners to the specified torque where available.

6-cylinder engines

24 Slacken the clamp and detach the turbocharger from the exhaust manifold. Note the locating pin on the turbocharger flange. Discard the seal – a new one must be fitted.

25 Refitting is a reversal of removal, noting the following points:
a) Ensure all mating surfaces are clean and dry.
b) Renew all O-rings, seals and gasket.
c) Tighten all fasteners to the specified torque where available.

14 Turbocharger – examination and overhaul

1 With the turbocharger removed, inspect the housing for cracks or other visible damage.

2 Spin the turbine or the compressor wheel to verify that the shaft is intact and to feel for excessive shake or roughness. Some play is normal since in use the shaft is 'floating' on a film of oil. Check that the wheel vanes are undamaged.

3 The variable vane assembly and actuator are integral with the turbocharger, and cannot be checked or renewed separately. Consult a BMW dealer or other specialist if it is thought that the variable vane assembly may be faulty.

4 If the exhaust or induction passages are oil-contaminated, the turbo shaft oil seals have probably failed. (On the induction side, this will also have contaminated the intercooler, which should be flushed with a suitable solvent.)

5 No DIY repair of the turbo is possible. A new unit may be available on an exchange basis.

13.19 Turbocharger oil feed banjo bolt

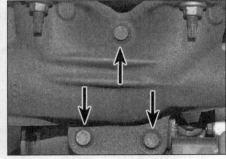

13.22 Turbocharger-to-manifold bolts – N47 engine

15 Intercooler –
removal and refitting

Removal

1 Raise the front of the vehicle and support it securely on axle stands (see *Jacking and vehicle support*). Remove the engine undershield **(see illustration 11.6)**.
2 Undo the fasteners and remove the undershield beneath the radiator.
3 Release the clamps, and disconnect the intercooler intake and outlet hoses **(see illustration)**. Examine the hose seals and renew if necessary.
4 Unscrew the 2 retaining bolts and lower the intercooler from place **(see illustration)**.

Refitting

5 Refitting is the reverse of removal. Apply a little petroleum jelly to the intake and outlet hoses seals to aid refitting.

16 Manifolds –
removal and refitting

Intake manifold

M57T2 engines

1 Disconnect the battery negative lead as described in Chapter 5A.
2 Undo the bolts and remove the upper section of the pollen filter housing **(see illustration 11.26)**.
3 Release the catches and remove the left- and right-hand plastic covers from behind the suspension turret each side of the engine compartment **(see illustration 11.27)**.
4 Depress the clips and pull the cable guides forwards from the pollen filter lower housing **(see illustration 11.28)**.
5 Release the catch and undo the bolt each side, then slide the pollen filter lower housing forwards and manoeuvre it from place **(see illustration 11.29a, 11.29b and 11.29c)**. Detach the ambient temperature sensor, washer hose and bonnet switch wiring plug

15.3 Prise out the clip and disconnect the intercooler hoses

from the housing as it's withdrawn.
6 On models with tension braces at the rear of the engine compartment, remove the plastic cap from the centre of the scuttle trim panel. Two different types of the cap are fitted: one with a central slot, removed by rotating it 45° anti-clockwise, and one without a central slot, which is prised from place **(see illustration)**. Note, if the cap or seal are damaged, they must be renewed. Failure to do so may result in water ingress.
7 Undo the bolt in the centre of the scuttle, exposed by the cap removal **(see illustration)**. Discard the bolt – a new one must be fitted.

Version A

8 Undo the bolt at each outer end of the braces, then hold the rubber grommet in place and slide the braces outwards from place **(see illustration)**. Do not allow the grommet to be displaced. Discard the bolts – new ones must

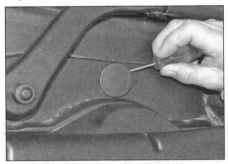

16.6 Remove the plastic cap in the centre of the scuttle panel

15.4 Undo the bolt each side and lower the intercooler

be fitted.

Version B

9 Undo the nuts securing the tension brace brackets to the suspension turrets, and manoeuvre the braces from place **(see illustration)**.

All models

10 Remove the wiper arms as described in Chapter 12.
11 Peel away the rubber seal at the front edge, then pull the scuttle trim panel upwards from the base of the windscreen. Disconnect the washer jet wiring plugs as the panel is withdrawn.
12 Undo the 3 bolts and remove the tension brace grommet housing from the bulkhead **(see illustration)**.
13 Prise off the plastic cover, then undo the nut and disconnect the positive cable

16.7 Undo the bolt in the centre of the panel...

16.8... and the one at the end of each brace

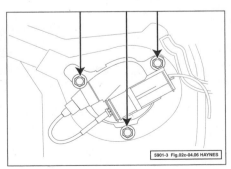

16.9 Tension brace brackets retaining nuts

16.12 Undo the bolts and remove the grommet housing

16.15 Oil level dipstick guide tube retaining bolt

16.16 Injector wiring harness guide bolts

16.27 Remove the clips and lift the panel

connection from the right-hand side inner wing. Depress the clip, disconnect the servo vacuum hose and lay the cable/hose guide to the left-hand side of the engine bay.

14 Undo the bolts and pull up the plastic acoustic cover at the front of the engine, then lift the rear cover from place.

15 Undo the bolt securing the engine oil level dipstick guide tube to the manifold (see illustration).

16 Depress the clips, disconnect the injector wiring plugs, then undo the bolts, release the clip and place the injector wiring harness/guide to one side (see illustration).

17 Note their fitted positions and disconnect the wiring plugs/harnesses/vacuum hoses from the intake manifold/throttle body/EGR valve/map sensor and manifold variable geometry solenoid valve.

18 Slacken the clamp securing the EGR pipe to the throttle body.

19 Prise out the clip and detach the charge air pipe from the throttle body.

20 Undo the nuts/bolts and detach the intake manifold from the cylinder head. Discard the seals.

21 Ensure the mating faces of the intake manifold and cylinder head are clean. Renew the manifold seals.

22 Position the manifold against the cylinder head, refit the nuts/bolts and tighten them to their specified torque.

23 The remainder of refitting is a reversal of removal.

N47 engines

24 Proceed as described in paragraphs 1 to 11.

25 Pull the plastic acoustic cover upwards and forwards from the top of the engine.

26 Undo the nut and disconnect the positive connection from the rear of the alternator, then depress the release catch and disconnect the servo vacuum hose at the left-hand side of the engine. Position the cable guide to one side.

27 Prise up the centre pins, remove the plastic expansion rivets and remove the insulation from the rear of the cylinder head (see illustration).

28 Note their fitted locations, then disconnect the wiring plugs from the mass airflow sensor, turbocharger wastegate control motor, EGR valve position sensor, EGR valve control solenoid, swirl flap control motor, turbo vacuum control solenoid, common fuel rail pressure sensor and the coolant temperature sensor. Undo any harness retaining clips and the bolts securing the harness duct to the front of the cylinder head cover.

29 On N47T engines, disconnect the wiring plug from the glow plug control unit, and manifold changeover valve, then unclip the valve and move it to one side (see illustration).

30 Pull the fuel injectors' wiring harness from the retaining clips, release the clips open the ECM box cover and pull the harness rubber grommet from the box and move it to one side.

31 Disconnect the intake air temperature sensor, then push the charge pressure pipe against the throttle body, prise out the retaining clip until it locks in place and pull the charge air pipe from the throttle body. If required, prise out the clip and disconnect the pipe from the intercooler, then manoeuvre it from the engine compartment (see illustration).

32 Disconnect the wiring plugs from the camshaft position sensor, boost pressure sensor, oil pressure sensor, air conditioning compressor and common fuel rail regulator.

33 Release the wiring harness from the clips above the manifold and move it to one side.

34 Disconnect the wiring plug from the throttle body.

35 Release the wiring harnesses and servo vacuum hose from any retaining clips at the rear/side of the manifold.

36 Undo the 5 bolts and manoeuvre the

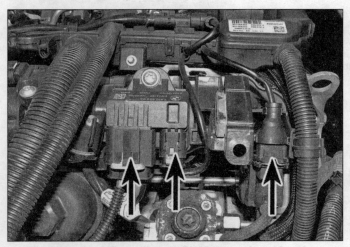

16.29 Glow plug control unit, and changeover valve wiring plugs – N47T engines

16.31 Push the pipe onto the throttle body, then prise out the clip

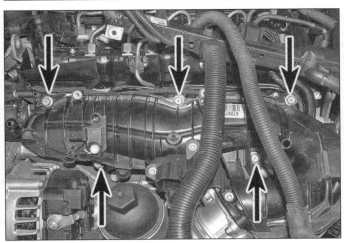

16.36a Manifold retaining bolts – N47 engines

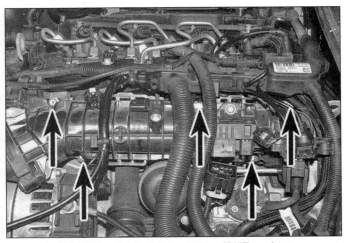

16.36b Manifold retaining bolts – N47T engines

manifold from place **(see illustrations)**. Renew the manifold/EGR pipe seals.

37 Ensure the mating faces of the intake manifold and cylinder head are clean. Renew the manifold seals.

38 Position the manifold against the cylinder head, refit the bolts and tighten them to their specified torque.

39 The remainder of refitting is a reversal of removal.

N57 engines

40 Proceed as described in paragraphs 1 to 12.

41 Remove the plastic acoustic covers from the top of the engine, then prise up the centre pins, remove the plastic rivets, lift up the cover at the rear of the engine, then remove the foam insulation panel from the top of the engine.

42 Undo the 3 bolts and remove the bulkhead grommet housing **(see illustration 16.11)**.

43 Release the clamp and disconnect the air intake pipe from the throttle body.

44 Disconnect the wiring plugs from the throttle valve actuator, turbocharger boost pressure sensor, oil pressure switch and air conditioning compressor.

45 Undo the bolt securing the engine oil level dipstick guide tube to the manifold.

46 Undo the 3 bolts and move the wiring harness guide above the manifold to one side.

47 Release the clamp, undo the 2 bolts and remove the EGR pipe. Undo the 2 bolts securing the pipe to the manifold **(see illustration)**.

48 Gradually and evenly undo the retaining bolts and lift the manifold from position. Release the clip and detach the solenoid valve from the manifold underside as it's withdrawn.

49 Ensure the mating faces of the intake manifold and cylinder head are clean. Renew the manifold seals.

50 Position the manifold against the cylinder head, refit the bolts and tighten them to their specified torque.

51 The remainder of refitting is a reversal of removal.

Exhaust manifold

M57T2 engines

52 Remove the cooling fan and shroud as described in Chapter 3.

53 Remove the air cleaner element as described in Chapter 1B.

54 Remove the catalytic converter/particulate filter as described in Chapter 4C.

55 Undo the 2 retaining bolts and detach the air intake pipe from the air cleaner housing.

56 Slacken the clamp, undo the bolts and remove the EGR pipe from the front of the cylinder head. On engines with an EGR cooler, remove the cooler as described in Chapter 4C.

16.47 EGR pipe retaining bolts

57 Slacken the 2 bolts securing the charge air pipe to the turbocharger, and rotate the retaining collar clockwise.

58 Prise out the clip and disconnect the charge air pipe from the turbocharger at the quick-release coupling on the intercooler, and remove the pipe. Cap/seal the turbocharger openings to prevent contamination.

59 Prise out the sealing caps from the heat shield, then remove the 3 plugs from the cylinder head cover **(see illustrations)**.

60 Undo the 3 retaining bolts securing the turbocharger to the manifold **(see illustration)**.

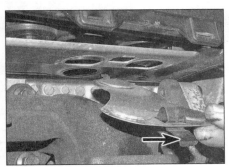

16.59a Depress the clip and slide the shield outwards

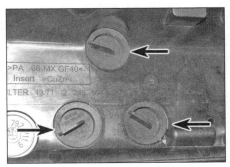

16.59b Prise out the plugs

16.60 Undo the 3 bolts and lower the turbocharger

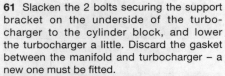

16.68 EGR pipe-to-manifold bolts

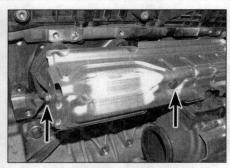

16.70 Heat shield retaining bolts

61 Slacken the 2 bolts securing the support bracket on the underside of the turbocharger to the cylinder block, and lower the turbocharger a little. Discard the gasket between the manifold and turbocharger – a new one must be fitted.

62 Undo the retaining nuts and withdrawn the manifold from the studs. Discard the gaskets and nuts, new ones must be fitted.

63 Examine all the manifold studs for signs of damage and corrosion; remove all traces of corrosion, and repair or renew any damaged studs.

64 Ensure the mating surfaces of the exhaust manifold and cylinder head are clean and dry. Position new gaskets, and refit the exhaust manifold to the cylinder head.

65 Apply a little high-temperature anti-seize grease (Copperslip) to the mounting studs, then tighten the new nuts to the specified torque.

66 The remainder of refitting is a reversal of removal.

N47 and M57 engines

67 Remove the turbocharger as described in Section 13.

68 Undo the bolts and remove the EGR pipe from the exhaust manifold to the EGR valve **(see illustration)**.

69 Undo the bolts, and remove the starter motor wiring harness bracket from the right-hand side of the engine.

70 Undo the bolts and remove the manifold heat shield **(see illustration)**.

71 On 6-cylinder engines, undo the banjo bolt and unclip the exhaust pressure pipe.

72 Undo the retaining nuts and withdraw the exhaust manifold from the cylinder head studs. Recover the gaskets.

73 Examine all the manifold studs for signs of damage and corrosion; remove all traces of corrosion, and repair or renew any damaged studs.

74 Ensure the mating surfaces of the exhaust manifold and cylinder head are clean and dry.

The new manifold-to-cylinder head gaskets have a graphite coating on one side. This side of the gaskets must face the manifold. Position new gaskets and refit the exhaust manifold to the cylinder head.

75 Apply a little high-temperature anti-seize grease (Copperslip) to the mounting studs, then tighten the new nuts to the specified torque.

76 The remainder of refitting is a reversal of removal.

---

17 Exhaust system – general information and renewal

General information

1 The exhaust system consists of several sections, which can be removed individually, or the as a complete system.

2 The tailpipe is a sleeve fit over the end of the intermediate pipe, which is a sleeve fit to the catalytic converter/particulate filter, and the system is suspended throughout its entire length by rubber mountings.

Removal

3 Each exhaust section can be removed

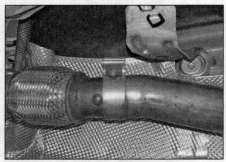

17.5 Spray a little penetrating fluid around the exhaust clamps

individually, or alternatively, the complete system can be removed as a unit. Even if only one part of the system needs attention, it can sometimes be easier to remove the whole system and separate the sections on the bench.

4 To remove the system or part of the system, first jack up the front or rear of the car and support it securely on axle stands (see *Jacking and vehicle support*). Alternatively, position the car over an inspection pit or on car ramps.

5 Spray a little penetrating fluid around the exhaust pipe clamps, then slacken the clamp bolts/nuts **(see illustration)**.

6 Undo the bolts and remove the rear tension braces (where fitted) and reinforcement plate from under the vehicle **(see illustration)**.

7 Have an assistant support the exhaust system, or position a trolley jack appropriately, then undo the bolts/nuts securing the exhaust mounting brackets to the vehicle underside.

8 Manoeuvre the system from under the vehicle.

9 Heat shield(s) are fitted to the underside of the vehicle body. Each shield can be removed once its retaining bolts have been undone.

Refitting

10 Each section is refitted by reversing the removal sequence, noting the following points:

a) Inspect the rubber mountings for signs of damage or deterioration, and renew as necessary.

b) Prior to tightening the exhaust system fasteners to the specified torque, ensure that all rubber mountings are correctly located, and that there is adequate clearance between the exhaust system and vehicle underbody.

c) Where applicable, refit the rear tension braces with new bolts, and tighten them to their specified torque.

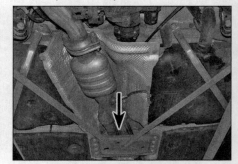

17.6 Remove the reinforcement plate (arrowed – note the tension braces)

Chapter 4 Part C:
Emission control systems

Contents

Degrees of difficulty

Easy, suitable for novice with little experience	**Fairly easy,** suitable for beginner with some experience	**Fairly difficult,** suitable for competent DIY mechanic	**Difficult,** suitable for experienced DIY mechanic	**Very difficult,** suitable for expert DIY or professional

Specifications

Engine codes
Petrol engines.	N43T
Diesel engines:	
4-cylinder	N47/T
6-cylinder	M57T2 and N57

Torque wrench settings
	Nm	lbf ft
Exhaust gas recirculation (EGR) cooler to cylinder head	25	18
Exhaust gas recirculation (EGR) valve/pipe bolts:		
M6 bolts	10	7
M8 bolts	25	18
Oxygen sensors	50	37

1 General Information

1 All petrol engine models use unleaded petrol and also have various other features built into the fuel system to help minimise harmful emissions. They are equipped with a crankcase emission control system, a catalytic converter and an evaporative emission control system to keep fuel vapour/exhaust gas emissions down to a minimum.

2 All diesel engine models are also designed to meet strict emission requirements. They are fitted with a crankcase emission control system, a catalytic converter and an exhaust gas recirculation (EGR) system to keep exhaust emissions down to a minimum. On some models, a combined catalytic converter and particulate filter is fitted.

3 The emission control systems function as follows.

Petrol models

Crankcase emission control

4 To reduce the emission of unburned hydrocarbons from the crankcase into the atmosphere, the engine is sealed and the blow-by gases and oil vapour are drawn from inside the crankcase, through a wire mesh oil separator, into the intake tract to be burned by the engine during normal combustion.

5 Under conditions of high manifold depression (idling, deceleration) the gases will be sucked positively out of the crankcase through a small diameter pipe and into the intake tract 'downstream' of the throttle valve. A larger diameter pipe, 'upstream' of the throttle valve, allows fresh air to be drawn back into the crankcase and mix with the crankcase gases. Under conditions of low manifold depression (acceleration, full-throttle running) the gases are forced out of the crankcase by the (relatively) higher crankcase pressure; and drawn through both pipes 'upstream and downstream' of the throttle valve.

Exhaust emission control

6 To minimise the amount of pollutants which escape into the atmosphere, all models are fitted with a catalytic converter in the exhaust system. The system is of the closed-loop type, in which oxygen sensors in the exhaust system supply a voltage signal to the engine management system ECM, enabling the ECM to adjust the mixture to provide the best possible conditions for the converter to operate. Two oxygen sensors are fitted per catalytic converter. One fitted to the exhaust manifold (pre-catalyst sensor), and one 'downstream' of the catalytic converter (post-catalyst sensor). The oxygen sensor has a built-in heating element which is controlled by the ECM; the heating element is used to warm the sensor when the engine is cold to bring it quickly up to an efficient operating temperature.

7 The oxygen sensor's tip is sensitive to oxygen and sends the ECM a varying voltage depending on the amount of oxygen in the exhaust gases; the leaner the air/fuel mixture, the higher the oxygen content, and the lower the voltage from the sensor(s). If the intake air/fuel mixture is too rich, the exhaust gases are low in oxygen so the sensor sends a higher-voltage signal. Peak conversion efficiency of all major pollutants occurs if the intake air/fuel mixture is maintained at the chemically-correct ratio for the complete combustion of petrol of 14.7 parts (by weight) of air to 1 part of fuel (the 'stoichiometric' ratio). The sensor output voltage alters in a large step at this point, the ECM using the signal change as a reference point and correcting the intake air/fuel mixture accordingly by altering the fuel injector pulse width.

Evaporative emission control

8 To minimise the escape into the atmosphere of unburned hydrocarbons, an evaporative emissions control system is also fitted to all models. The fuel tank filler cap is sealed and a charcoal canister is mounted just behind the right-hand rear roadwheel. The canister collects the petrol vapours generated in the tank when the car is parked and stores them until they can be cleared from the canister (under the control of the engine management system ECM) via the purge valve into the intake tract to be burned by the engine during normal combustion.

9 To ensure that the engine runs correctly when it is cold and/or idling and to protect the catalytic converter from the effects of an over-rich mixture, the purge control valve is not opened by the ECM until the engine has warmed up, and the engine is under load; the valve solenoid is then modulated on and off to allow the stored vapour to pass into the intake tract.

Diesel models

Crankcase emission control

10 To reduce the emission of unburned hydrocarbons from the crankcase into the atmosphere, the engine is sealed and the blow-by gases and oil vapour are drawn from inside the crankcase, through a wire mesh oil separator, into the intake tract to be burned by the engine during normal combustion. Crankcase gases are drawn via a depression

limiting valve. The valve closes progressively as the engine speed increases, so limiting the maximum depression in the crankcase.

Exhaust emission control

11 To minimise the level of exhaust pollutants released into the atmosphere, a catalytic converter is fitted in the exhaust system of all models.

12 The catalytic converter consists of a canister containing a fine mesh impregnated with a catalyst material, over which the hot exhaust gases pass. The catalyst speeds up the oxidation of harmful carbon monoxide, unburned hydrocarbons and soot, effectively reducing the quantity of harmful products released into the atmosphere via the exhaust gases.

Particulate filter

13 This device is designed to trap carbon particulates produced by the combustion process. The particulate filter is combined with the catalytic converter. In order to prevent the filter blocking, pressure and temperature sensors are fitted to the filter. Under the normal, high-speed driving conditions, the soot particulates are burnt off in the filter by the high temperature of the exhaust gases. However, where the driving conditions are such that the exhaust gases are not sufficiently high, the engine management system injects fuel into the cylinders after the point of combustion. These are called post-injections, and raise the temperature of the exhaust gases, causing the soot particulates in the filter to be burnt off.

Exhaust gas recirculation system

14 This system is designed to recirculate small quantities of exhaust gas into the intake tract, and therefore into the combustion process. This process reduces the level of unburnt hydrocarbons present in the exhaust gas before it reaches the catalytic converter. The system is controlled by the engine management system ECM, using the information from its various sensors, via the EGR valve which is fitted to the metal pipe connecting the intake and exhaust manifolds. On some models, the exhaust gases are cooled prior to entering the intake manifold by

passing through a cooler mounted on the side of the EGR valve. Engine coolant circulates through the cooler.

2 Petrol engine emission control systems – testing and component renewal

Crankcase emission control

1 The components of this system require no attention other than to check that the hose(s) are clear and undamaged at regular intervals.

Evaporative emission control

Testing

2 If the system is thought to be faulty, disconnect the hoses from the charcoal canister and purge control valve and check that they are clear by blowing through them. Full testing of the system can only be carried out using specialist electronic equipment which is connected to the engine management system diagnostic wiring connector (see Chapter 4A). If the purge control valve or charcoal canister is thought to be faulty, they must be renewed.

Charcoal canister renewal

3 The canister is located under the vehicle, just behind the right-hand side rear roadwheel. Raise the rear of the vehicle and support it securely on axle stands (see Jacking and vehicle support).

4 Undo the fasteners and remove the cover beneath the canister (see illustration).

5 Note the fitted locations of the pipes. Squeeze together the sides of the collars and disconnect the tank, air and purge pipes from the canister (see illustration).

6 Undo the 2 bolts and remove the canister (see illustration).

7 Refitting is a reverse of the removal procedure, ensuring the hoses are correctly and securely reconnected.

Purge valve renewal

8 The valve is located on a bracket on

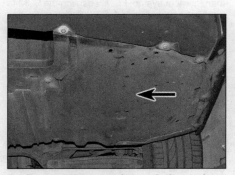

2.4 Remove the cover beneath the canister

2.5 Squeeze together the side of the collars and pull the hose from the canister

2.6 Canister retaining bolts

2.8 The purge valve is located on the side of the intake manifold

2.20a Access to the front oxygen sensors (arrowed) is very limited

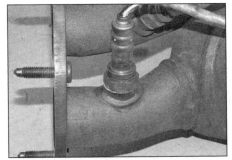

2.20b The post-catalytic converter oxygen sensor is mounted just in front of the joining flange

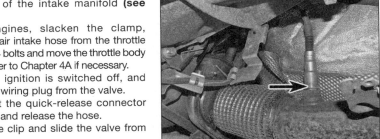

2.20c 'Monitoring' oxygen sensor

2.20d Exhaust temperature sensor

the underside of the intake manifold (see illustration).

9 On N52 engines, slacken the clamp, disconnect the air intake hose from the throttle body, undo the 4 bolts and move the throttle body to one side – refer to Chapter 4A if necessary.

10 Ensure the ignition is switched off, and disconnect the wiring plug from the valve.

11 Disconnect the quick-release connector from the valve, and release the hose.

12 Release the clip and slide the valve from the bracket.

13 Refitting is a reversal of removal. Ensure the valve and hose are securely held by the retaining clips.

Exhaust emission control

Testing

14 The performance of the catalytic converter can be checked only by measuring the exhaust gases using a good-quality, carefully-calibrated exhaust gas analyser.

15 If the CO level at the tailpipe is too high, the vehicle should be taken to a BMW dealer or specialist so that the complete fuel injection and ignition systems, including the oxygen sensor, can be thoroughly checked using the special diagnostic equipment. Once these have been checked and are known to be free from faults, the fault must be in the catalytic converter, which must be renewed.

Catalytic converter renewal

16 The primary catalytic converter is integral with the exhaust manifold(s) – see Chapter 4A.

17 The NOx catalytic converter is integral with the front exhaust pipe. Refer to Chapter 4A Section 12.

Oxygen/NOx sensor(s) renewal

Note: The oxygen/NOx sensor is delicate and will not work if it is dropped or knocked, if its power supply is disrupted, or if any cleaning materials are used on it.

18 Two oxygen sensors are fitted to the exhaust manifold, whilst on models with a NOx catalytic converter are fitted with a NOx sensor fitted to the front exhaust pipe.

19 Ensure the ignition is switched off then trace the wiring back from the oxygen/NOx sensor. Free the connector from its retaining clip and

disconnect the two halves of the connector.

20 Unscrew the sensor and remove it from the manifold/exhaust pipe. Note that the use of a special deep, split socket is recommended (see illustrations). Recover the sensor sealing washer and discard it; a new one must be used on refitting.

21 Refitting is a reverse of the removal procedure, using a new sealing washer. Apply a little high-temperature anti-seize compound (Copperslip) to the threads, then tighten the sensor to the specified torque and ensure that the wiring is correctly routed and in no danger of contacting either the exhaust manifold or the engine.

3 **Diesel engine emission control systems** – testing and component renewal

Crankcase emission control

Testing

1 The components of this system require no attention other than to check that the hose(s) are clear and undamaged at regular intervals. If the system is thought to be faulty, renew the crankcase pressure limiting valve as follows.

Crankcase pressure limiting valve renewal

Note: Not fitted to the N47T engine

2 Remove the plastic cover from the top of the engine.

3 Disconnect the injector wiring plugs,

unscrew the three retaining bolts, and move the injector harness to one side.

4 Unscrew the four bolts, and remove the depression limiting valve complete with filter (see illustration).

5 Ensure the mating surfaces are clean and dry, renew the seals and refit the valve housing. Tighten the Allen bolts securely.

6 The remainder of refitting is a reversal of removal.

Exhaust emission control

Testing

7 The performance of the catalytic converter can be checked only by measuring the exhaust gases using a good-quality, carefully-calibrated exhaust gas analyser.

8 Before assuming that the catalytic converter is faulty, it is worth checking whether the

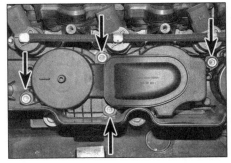

3.4 Undo the bolts and remove the depression limiting valve

3.13a Remove the support bracket underneath – N47 engine...

3.13b... and on some models, the bracket above – N47 engine

3.14 Particulate filter pressure take-off hose(s)

problem is not due to faulty injector(s). Refer to your BMW dealer or specialist for further information.

Catalytic converter/ particulate filter renewal

9 Raise the front of the vehicle and support it securely on axle stands (see *Jacking and vehicle support*). Undo the fasteners and remove the engine and transmission undershields.

10 On N47T engines, remove the air cleaner assembly as described in Chapter 4B Section 2.

11 Slacken the clamp securing the front section of the exhaust to the catalytic converter/particulate filter, undo the exhaust system mounting bolts and slide the system rearwards.

12 Trace the temperature/oxygen sensors' wiring back to their connectors, and unplug

them. Note the wiring harness routing, then release the harness from any retaining clips.

13 Undo the bolts and remove the catalytic converter/particulate filter support bracket(s) **(see illustrations)**.

14 Note their fitted positions, and disconnect the pressure take-off hose(s) from the particulate filter (where applicable) **(see illustration)**.

15 Slacken the clamp securing the catalytic converter/particulate filter to the turbocharger, and manoeuvre the assembly from place **(see illustration)**.

16 Refitting is a reversal of removal. Note that if a new particulate filter has been fitted, the engine management ECM adaption counter must be reset using BMW diagnostic equipment. Entrust this task to a BMW dealer or suitably-equipped specialist.

Turbocharger/Exhaust back pressure sensor (N47T engine only)

17 Remove the plastic cover from the top of the engine.

18 Disconnect the wiring plug from the top of the sensor.

19 Release the clamp, and unclip the sensor from the exhaust sample pipe **(see illustration)**.

20 Refitting is a reversal of removal. Note that if a new sensor is fitted, an adaption procedure must be carried out using BMW diagnostic equipment (or equivalent). Entrust this task to a BMW dealer or suitably equipped repairer.

Exhaust gas recirculation system

Testing

21 Comprehensive testing of the system can only be carried out using specialist electronic equipment which is connected to the injection system diagnostic wiring connector (see Chapter 4B). If the EGR valve or solenoid valve are thought to be faulty, they must be renewed as follows.

22 Remove the cover from the top of the engine.

EGR valve renewal – M57T2 engines

23 Release the retaining clips and disconnect the air intake ducting assembly from the EGR valve **(see illustration)**.

24 Disconnect the vacuum hose from the EGR valve **(see illustration)**.

25 Completely slacken the clamp bolt and disconnect the EGR pipe from the valve **(see illustration)**.

3.15 Catalytic converter/particulate filter-to-turbocharger clamp bolt

3.19 Turbocharger/exhaust back pressure sensor

3.23 Prise out the clip and pull the intake duct from the EGR valve/throttle housing

3.24 Disconnect the vacuum valve

3.25 Slacken the clamp securing the pipe to the EGR valve

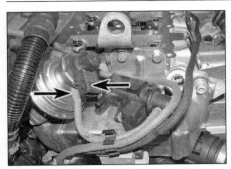

3.28 Disconnect the EGR valve wiring plug and vacuum hose

3.29 EGR valve retaining bolts

3.31 Disconnect the breather hose

3.32 EGR valve retaining screws

3.37a Disconnect the EGR solenoid valve wiring plug – M57T2 engines

3.37b EGR solenoid valve – N47 and N57 engines

26 Unscrew the four retaining bolts, and remove the EGR valve.

27 Refitting is a reversal of removal, using a new seal and tightening the valve retaining bolts to the specified torque.

EGR valve renewal – N47 and N57 engines

28 Disconnect the wiring plug and vacuum hose from the valve **(see illustration)**.

29 Undo the 2 bolts and detach the valve from the pipe **(see illustration)**. Renew the gasket – where fitted.

30 Refitting is a reversal of removal.

EGR valve renewal – N47T engines

31 Release the clips and disconnect the breather hose from the cylinder head cover **(see illustration)**.

32 Undo the EGR valve retaining screws **(see illustration)**.

33 Apply clamps to the hoses, then disconnect the coolant hoses from the EGR valve.

34 Disconnect the wiring plug, then manoeuvre the valve from position.

35 Upon refitting, connect the rear coolant hose prior to fitting the valve.

36 The remainder of refitting is a reversal of removal. If necessary, check and top up the cooling system as described in *Weekly checks*.

EGR solenoid valve renewal

Note: *No EGR solenoid valve is fitted to the N47T engine*

37 Disconnect the wiring plug from the solenoid **(see illustrations)**.

38 Unscrew the two bolts securing the

solenoid bracket to the cylinder block. Note their fitted locations then disconnect the vacuum hoses. If necessary, the solenoid can be separated from the mounting bracket by unscrewing the two retaining nuts.

39 Refitting is a reversal of removal.

EGR cooler renewal – M57T2 engines

40 Remove the plastic cover from the top of the engine.

41 Completely slacken and remove the clamp securing the EGR pipe to the cooler.

42 Undo the bolts securing the EGR cooler to the exhaust manifold

43 Undo the three bolts securing the EGR cooler to the cylinder head **(see illustration)**.

44 Be prepared for coolant spillage, and disconnect the coolant hoses from the cooler. Be prepared for coolant spillage – plug the openings.

45 Refitting is a reversal of removal. Top-up the coolant level as described in *Weekly checks*.

EGR cooler renewal – N47 and N57 engines

46 Undo the 2 bolts securing the EGR pipe to the exhaust manifold.

47 Undo the 2 bolts securing the EGR outlet pipe to the cylinder head.

48 Disconnect the black vacuum hose from the valve above the cooler **(see illustration)**.

49 Undo the 2 bolts securing the vacuum solenoid bracket to the cylinder head above the cooler **(see illustration)**.

50 Remove the remaining mounting bolt

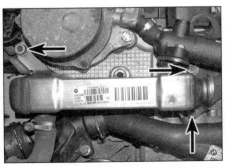

3.43 EGR cooler retaining bolts

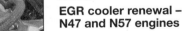

3.48 Disconnect the black vacuum hose from the valve

3.49 Undo the bracket retaining bolts

3.50 Manoeuvre the EGR cooler from position

3.54 EGR cooler-to-intake manifold bolts

and manoeuvre the cooler from place **(see illustration)**. Be prepared for coolant spillage – plug the openings.

51 Refitting is a reversal of removal. Top-up the coolant as described in *Weekly checks*.

EGR cooler renewal – N47T engines

52 Drain the coolant system as described in Chapter 1B Section 16, or apply clamps to the hoses attached to the EGR valve.

53 Remove the plastic cover from the top of the engine.

54 Undo the bolts securing the EGR cooler to the intake manifold **(see illustration)**.

55 Undo the bolts securing the EGR cooler to the turbocharger/manifold.

56 Unclip the changeover valve solenoid from the cooler, and disconnect the vacuum hose **(see illustration)**.

57 Disconnect the coolant hoses to and from the EGR valve.

58 Remove the mounting bolts and manoeuvre the EGR cooler from position.

3.56 Unclip the solenoid valve

59 Refitting is a reversal of removal. Note that the cooler mounting bolts must be tightened in the correct sequence **(see illustration)**.

---

4 Catalytic converter – general information and precautions

---

1 The catalytic converter is a reliable and simple device which needs no maintenance in itself, but there are some facts of which an owner should be aware if the converter is to function properly for its full service life.

Petrol engine

a) *DO NOT use leaded petrol or LRP – the lead will coat the precious metals, reducing their converting efficiency and will eventually destroy the converter.*

b) *Always keep the ignition and fuel systems well-maintained in accordance with the manufacturer's schedule.*

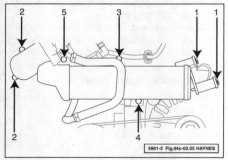

3.59 EGR cooler bolts tightening sequence – N47T engines

c) *If the engine develops a misfire, do not drive the car at all (or at least as little as possible) until the fault is cured.*

d) *DO NOT push- or tow-start the car – this will soak the catalytic converter in unburned fuel, causing it to overheat when the engine does start.*

e) *DO NOT switch off the ignition at high engine speeds.*

f) *DO NOT use fuel or engine oil additives – these may contain substances harmful to the catalytic converter.*

g) *DO NOT continue to use the car if the engine burns oil to the extent of leaving a visible trail of blue smoke.*

h) *Remember that the catalytic converter operates at very high temperatures. DO NOT, therefore, park the car in dry undergrowth, over long grass or piles of dead leaves after a long run.*

i) *Remember that the catalytic converter is FRAGILE – do not strike it with tools during servicing work.*

j) *In some cases a sulphurous smell (like that of rotten eggs) may be noticed from the exhaust. This is common to many catalytic converter-equipped cars and once the car has covered a few thousand miles the problem should disappear.*

k) *The catalytic converter, used on a well-maintained and well-driven car, should last for between 50 000 and 100 000 miles – if the converter is no longer effective it must be renewed.*

Diesel engine

2 Refer to the information given in parts f, g, h and i of the petrol engine information given above.

Chapter 5 Part A:
Starting and charging systems

Contents

Degrees of difficulty

Easy, suitable for novice with little experience 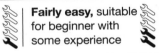	Fairly easy, suitable for beginner with some experience	Fairly difficult, suitable for competent DIY mechanic	Difficult, suitable for experienced DIY mechanic	Very difficult, suitable for expert DIY or professional

Specifications

Engine codes
Petrol engines	N43
Diesel engines:	
4-cylinder	N47/T
6-cylinder	M57T2 and N57

General
System type	12 volt negative earth
Alternator regulated voltage	13.5 to 14.2 volts (at 1500 rpm engine speed with no electrical equipment switched on)

Torque wrench settings

	Nm	lbf ft
Alternator to engine block:		
Petrol engines	19	14
Diesel engines	38	28
Alternator pulley retaining bolt:		
Valeo alternator	75	55
Bosch alternator	65	48
Belt tensioner pulley bolt	55	40
Glow plugs	13	9
Starter motor-to-gearbox/transmission nuts and bolts:		
Petrol engines	47	35
M57T2 diesel engines	45	33
N47 and N57 diesel engines	19	14

*Do not re-use

1 General information and precautions

1 The engine electrical system consists mainly of the charging and starting systems. Because of their engine-related functions, these components are covered separately from the body electrical devices such as the lights, instruments, etc (which are covered in Chapter 12). For information on the ignition system refer to Part B of this Chapter.

2 The electrical system is of the 12 volt negative earth type.

3 The battery is of the low maintenance or 'maintenance-free' (sealed for life) type and is charged by the alternator, which is belt-driven from the crankshaft pulley.

4 The starter motor is of the pre-engaged type incorporating an integral solenoid. On starting, the solenoid moves the drive pinion into engagement with the flywheel ring gear before the starter motor is energised. Once the engine has started, a one-way clutch prevents the motor armature being driven by the engine until the pinion disengages from the flywheel.

Precautions

5 Further details of the various systems are given in the relevant Sections of this Chapter. While some repair procedures are given, the usual course of action is to renew the component concerned.

6 It is necessary to take extra care when working on the electrical system to avoid damage to semi-conductor devices (diodes and transistors), and to avoid the risk of personal injury. In addition to the precautions given in *Safety first!* at the beginning of this manual, observe the following when working on the system:

• *Always remove rings, watches, etc, before working on the electrical system. Even with the battery disconnected, capacitive discharge could occur if a component's live terminal is earthed through a metal object. This could cause a shock or nasty burn.*

• *Do not reverse the battery connections. Components such as the alternator, electronic control modules, or any other components having semi-conductor circuitry could be irreparably damaged.*

• *If the engine is being started using jump leads and a slave battery, make use of the built-in jump lead connections points (see Jump starting, at the beginning of this manual). This also applies when connecting a battery charger.*

• *Never disconnect the battery terminals, the alternator, any electrical wiring or any test instruments when the engine is running.*

• *Do not allow the engine to turn the alternator when the alternator is not connected.*

• *Never 'test' for alternator output by 'flashing' the output lead to earth.*

• *Never use an ohmmeter of the type incorporating a hand-cranked generator for circuit or continuity testing.*

• *Always ensure that the battery negative lead is disconnected when working on the electrical system.*

• *Before using electric-arc welding equipment on the car, disconnect the battery, alternator and components such as the fuel injection/ignition electronic control unit to protect them from the risk of damage.*

7 If an audio unit with a built-in security code is fitted, note the following precautions. If the power source to the unit is cut, the anti-theft system will activate. Even if the power source is immediately reconnected, the audio unit will not function until the correct security code has been entered. Therefore, if you do not know the correct security code for the audio unit do not disconnect the battery negative terminal of the battery or remove the audio unit from the vehicle.

2 Electrical fault finding – general information

1 Refer to Chapter 12.

3 Battery – testing and charging

Note: *The following is intended as a guide only. Always refer to the manufacturer's recommendations (often printed on a label attached to the battery) before charging a battery.*

1 All models are fitted with a maintenance-free battery in production, which should require no maintenance under normal operating conditions.

2 If the condition of the battery is suspect, remove the battery as described in Section 4, and check that the electrolyte level in each cell is up to the MAX mark on the outside of the battery case (about 5.0 mm above the tops of the plates in the cells). If necessary, the electrolyte level can be topped-up by removing the cell plugs from the top of the battery and adding distilled water (not acid).

3 An approximate check on battery condition can be made by checking the specific gravity of the electrolyte, using the following as a guide.

4 Use a hydrometer to make the check and compare the results with the following table. The temperatures quoted are ambient (air) temperatures. Note that the specific gravity readings assume an electrolyte temperature

of 15°C; for every 10°C below 15°C subtract 0.007. For every 10°C above 15°C add 0.007.

	Above 25°C	Below 25°C
Fully-charged	1.210 to 1.230	1.270 to 1.290
70% charged	1.170 to 1.190	1.230 to 1.250
Discharged	1.050 to 1.070	1.110 to 1.130

5 If the battery condition is suspect, first check the specific gravity of electrolyte in each cell. A variation of 0.040 or more between any cells indicates loss of electrolyte or deterioration of the internal plates.

6 If the specific gravity variation is 0.040 or more, the battery should be renewed. If the cell variation is satisfactory but the battery is discharged, it should be charged in accordance with the manufacturer's instructions.

7 In cases where a 'sealed for life' maintenance-free battery is fitted, topping-up and testing of the electrolyte in each cell is not possible. The condition of the battery can therefore only be tested using a battery condition indicator or a voltmeter.

8 Models may be fitted with a battery, with a built-in charge condition indicator. The indicator is located in the top of the battery casing, and indicates the condition of the battery from its colour. If the indicator shows green, then the battery is in a good state of charge. If the indicator turns darker, eventually to black, then the battery requires charging, as described later in this Section. If the indicator shows clear/yellow, then the electrolyte level in the battery is too low to allow further use, and the battery should be renewed. Do not attempt to charge, load or jump start a battery when the indicator shows clear/yellow.

9 Vehicles equipped with 'stop-start' system are fitted with Absorbent Glass Matt (AGM) batteries as standard.

10 If testing the battery using a voltmeter, connect the voltmeter across the battery. A fully-charged battery should give a reading of 12.5 volts or higher. The test is only accurate if the battery has not been subjected to any kind of charge for the previous six hours. If this is not the case, switch on the headlights for 30 seconds, then wait four to five minutes before testing the battery after switching off the headlights. All other electrical circuits must be switched off, so check that the doors and tailgate are fully shut when making the test.

11 Generally speaking, if the voltage reading is less than 12.2 volts, then the battery is discharged, whilst a reading of 12.2 to 12.4 volts indicates a partially-discharged condition.

Note: *Do not charge AGM batteries above 14.8 volts, or the battery may be damaged.*

12 If the battery is to be charged with a trickle charger, locate the charge points in the engine compartment, and connect the charger leads to the connections **(see illustrations)**. If a rapid, or boost charger is used (or if in doubt as to which type of charger you have), remove the battery from the vehicle (Section 4) and charge it in accordance with its maker's instructions.

4	**Battery** – disconnection, removal and refitting

Note: *When the battery is disconnected, any fault codes stored in the engine management ECM memory will be erased. If any faults are suspected, do not disconnect the battery until the fault codes have been read by a BMW dealer or specialist. If the vehicle is fitted with a code-protected audio unit, refer to the Owners handbook.*

Disconnection

1 The battery is located beneath a cover on the right-hand side of the luggage compartment.
2 On Saloon models, lift the catch, and remove the left-hand side luggage compartment side trim above the battery **(see illustration)**. On Touring models, lift out the luggage compartment floor panel, undo the two fasteners and lift out the side panel, then rotate the two fasteners 90° anti-clockwise and lift out the trim above the battery **(see illustrations)**.
3 Slacken the clamp nut, and disconnect the clamp from the battery negative (earth) terminal **(see illustration)**. Position the

3.12a Remove the red cap, and connect the positive lead from the charger

negative lead away from the battery, so there is no risk of accidental contact between it and the battery terminal. For extra protection, cover the disconnected lead clamp with a rag or rubber glove, etc.

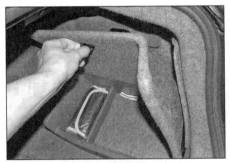
4.2a Rotate the catch and lift out the panel – Saloon models

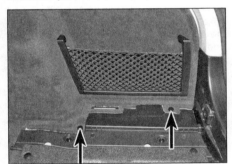
4.2c Rotate the fasteners 90°...

4.2d... and lift the base of the panel inwards to remove it

4.2f... and lift the panel above the battery

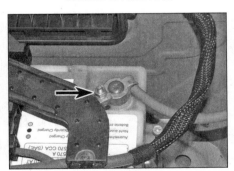
4.3 Slacken the nut and disconnect the negative lead clamp

3.12b Connect the negative lead to the earth point on the inner wing

Removal

4 Disconnect the battery negative lead as described previously.
5 Undo the 2 bolts and remove the support bracket above the battery **(see illustration)**.

4.2b Lift the handle and remove the luggage compartment floor panel

4.2e Rotate the fasteners 90°...

4.5 Undo the 2 bolts and remove the bracket above the battery

4.6 Prise up the cover, undo the nut...

4.7a... lever apart the retaining clip each side...

4.7b... and lift off the connector assembly

6 Prise up the plastic cover, and undo the nut securing the connector assembly to the positive clamp **(see illustration)**.
7 Using a flat-bladed screwdriver, lever apart the retaining clip each side and lift up the connector assembly from the top of the battery **(see illustrations)**. Position the connector assembly to one side.
8 Prise up the plastic cover, slacken the nut and pull the positive clamp assembly from the terminal on the battery **(see illustrations)**.
9 Unscrew the bolt, and remove the battery retaining clamp **(see illustration)**.
10 Lift the battery from its housing, disconnect the vent hose as the battery is removed **(see illustrations)**. Take care as the battery is heavy.

Refitting

11 Refitting is a reversal of removal. Always reconnect the positive lead first, and the negative lead last.

4.8a Prise up the plastic cover, slacken the nut...

4.9 Undo the bolt and remove the battery retaining clamp

12 After reconnecting the battery, several of the vehicles ECMs will require time to relearn certain values. This will normally be complete within a normal driving pattern of 15 miles (approximately). In addition, several systems may require re-initialisation as follows:

Sunroof

a) *With the battery reconnected, and the ignition on, press the sunroof operating switch into the 'tilt' position and hold it there.*
b) *Once the sunroof has reached the 'fully-tilted' position, hold the switch in that position for approximately 20 seconds. Initialisation is complete, when the sunroof briefly lifts at the rear again.*

Electric windows

c) *Operate the button to fully close the window, then continue to hold the button for at least 1 second to 'normalise' the anti-trapping function.*

4.8b... and pull up the positive clamp

4.10a Pull the vent hose from the side of the battery...

13 If a new battery has been installed, the new battery details may need be registered in the vehicles ECM using BMW diagnostic equipment (or equivalent) to enable off the convenience system/functions to operate correctly. Entrust this task to a BMW dealer or suitably equipped specialist.

5 Charging system – testing

Note: *Refer to the warnings given in Safety first! and in Section 1 of this Chapter before starting work.*

1 If the ignition warning light fails to illuminate when the ignition is switched on, first check the alternator wiring connections for security. If satisfactory, check that the warning light bulb has not blown, and that the bulbholder is secure in its location in the instrument panel. If the light still fails to illuminate, check the continuity of the warning light feed wire from the alternator to the bulbholder. If all is satisfactory, the alternator is at fault and should be renewed or taken to an auto-electrician for testing and repair. Note that on some models, the function of the alternator is controlled by the engine management ECM, and is therefore included in the vehicle's self-diagnosis system. Should a fault occur, have the system interrogated using a code reader or scanner.
2 If the ignition warning light illuminates when the engine is running, stop the engine and check that the drivebelt is correctly

4.10b... and lift it from place

7.4 Disconnect the wiring plug, then undo the nut securing the positive lead

7.5 Alternator mounting bolts

7.6a Insert the special tools in to the alternator shaft and pulley centre

tensioned (see Chapter 1A or 1B) and that the alternator connections are secure. If all is so far satisfactory, have the alternator checked by an auto-electrician for testing and repair. See the note in the previous paragraph.

3 If the alternator output is suspect even though the warning light functions correctly, the regulated voltage may be checked as follows.

4 Connect a voltmeter across the battery terminals and start the engine.

5 Increase the engine speed until the voltmeter reading remains steady; the reading should be approximately 12 to 13 volts, and no more than 14.2 volts.

6 Switch on as many electrical accessories (eg, the headlights, heated rear window and heater blower) as possible, and check that the alternator maintains the regulated voltage at around 13 to 14 volts.

7 If the regulated voltage is not as stated, the fault may be due to worn alternator brushes, weak brush springs, a faulty voltage regulator, a faulty diode, a severed phase winding or worn or damaged slip-rings. The alternator should be renewed or taken to an auto-electrician for testing and repair.

7.6b Hold the alternator shaft and slacken the pulley centre...

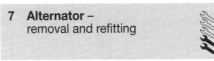

7 Alternator – removal and refitting

Removal
Petrol engines

1 Disconnect the battery negative lead (see Section 4).

2 Remove the alternator drivebelt as described in Chapter 1A or 1B.

3 Remove the air cleaner housing as described in Chapter 4A.

4 Unlock and disconnect the wiring plug, then unscrew the nut and disconnect the battery lead from the rear of the alternator **(see illustration)**.

5 Undo the bolts, and manoeuvre the alternator from the engine compartment **(see illustration)**.

7.6c... and slide the pulley from the shaft

6 To remove the alternator pulley on models with an over-running clutch, prise off the plastic cap, then the pulley can be removed by inserting tool No 12 7 121 into the pulley centre, and holding the alternator shaft with tool No 12 7 122 **(see illustrations)**. Slacken the pulley centre whilst holding the alternator shaft stationary. Suitable alternative tools are available from tool aftermarket tool manufacturers.

M57T2 diesel engines

7 Unlock and disconnect the wiring plug, then unscrew the nut and disconnect the battery lead from the rear of the alternator **(see illustration)**.

8 Undo the bolt and remove the auxiliary drivebelt idler pulley **(see illustration)**.

9 Undo the upper and lower mounting bolt, then remove the alternator **(see illustration)**.

6 Alternator drivebelt – removal, refitting and tensioning

1 Refer to the procedure given for the auxiliary drivebelt(s) in Chapter 1A or 1B.

7.7 Depress the clip, disconnect the wiring plug, and undo the nut and disconnect the battery lead

7.8 Prise off the cap and undo the pulley retaining bolt

7.9 Alternator mounting bolts – M57T2 diesel engines

7.12 Disconnect the wiring from the rear of the alternator

10 To remove the alternator pulley on models with an over-running clutch, grip the alternator in a bench vice, then the pulley can be removed by inserting tool No 12 7 110 into the pulley centre, and slackening the retaining bolt with a suitable Allen, or Torx bit as applicable. Suitable alternative tools are available from tool aftermarket tool manufacturers. Pull the pulley from the alternator shaft.

N47 and N57 diesel engines

11 On N47T engines, remove the intake manifold as described in Chapter 4B Section 16.

12 Unlock and disconnect the wiring plug, then unscrew the nut and disconnect the battery lead from the rear of the alternator **(see illustration)**.

13 On N47T engines, prise out the cap, undo the Torx bolt and remove the belt tensioner pulley **(see illustration)**.

14 Undo the upper and lower mounting bolt, then remove the alternator **(see illustration)**.

15 To remove the alternator pulley on models with an over-running clutch, grip the alternator in a bench vice, prise off the plastic cap, then the pulley can be removed by inserting tool No 12 7 121 into the pulley centre, and holding the alternator shaft with tool No 12 7 122 **(see illustration 7.6a, 7.6b and 7.6c)**.

Slacken the pulley centre whilst holding the alternator shaft stationary. Suitable alternative tools are available from tool aftermarket tool manufacturers.

Refitting

16 Refitting is a reversal of removal, tightening all fasteners to their specified torque where given.

8   Alternator – testing and overhaul

1 If the alternator is thought to be suspect, it should be removed from the vehicle and taken to an auto-electrician for testing. Most auto-electricians will be able to supply and fit brushes at a reasonable cost. However, check on the cost of repairs before proceeding as it may prove more economical to obtain a new or exchange alternator.

9   Starting system – testing

Note: *Refer to the precautions given in Safety first! and in Section 1 of this Chapter before starting work.*

1 If the starter motor fails to operate when the ignition key is turned to the appropriate position, the following possible causes may be to blame.
a) *The battery is faulty.*
b) *The electrical connections between the switch, solenoid, battery and starter motor are somewhere failing to pass the necessary current from the battery through the starter to earth.*
c) *The solenoid is faulty.*
d) *The starter motor is mechanically or electrically defective.*
2 To check the battery, switch on the

headlights. If they dim after a few seconds, this indicates that the battery is discharged – recharge (see Section 3) or renew the battery. If the headlights glow brightly, operate the ignition switch and observe the lights. If they dim, then this indicates that current is reaching the starter motor, therefore the fault must lie in the starter motor. If the lights continue to glow brightly (and no clicking sound can be heard from the starter motor solenoid), this indicates that there is a fault in the circuit or solenoid – see following paragraphs. If the starter motor turns slowly when operated, but the battery is in good condition, then this indicates that either the starter motor is faulty, or there is considerable resistance somewhere in the circuit.

3 If a fault in the circuit is suspected, disconnect the battery leads (including the earth connection to the body), the starter/ solenoid wiring and the engine/transmission earth strap. Thoroughly clean the connections, and reconnect the leads and wiring, then use a voltmeter or test lamp to check that full battery voltage is available at the battery positive lead connection to the solenoid, and that the earth is sound. Smear petroleum jelly around the battery terminals to prevent corrosion – corroded connections are amongst the most frequent causes of electrical system faults.

4 If the battery and all connections are in good condition, check the circuit by disconnecting the wire from the solenoid blade terminal. Connect a voltmeter or test lamp between the wire end and a good earth (such as the battery negative terminal), and check that the wire is live when the ignition switch is turned to the 'start' position. If it is, then the circuit is sound – if not the circuit wiring can be checked as described in Chapter 12.

5 The solenoid contacts can be checked by connecting a voltmeter or test lamp between the battery positive feed connection on the starter side of the solenoid, and earth. When the ignition switch is turned to the 'start'

7.13 Pulley cap and alternator mounting bolts – N47T engines

7.14 Alternator mounting bolts – N47 and N57 diesel engines

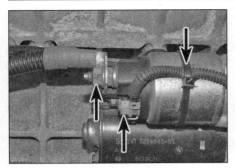

10.3 Disconnect the starter motor leads, and cut the clip

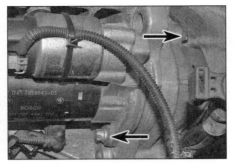

10.4 Starter motor mounting bolts – petrol engines

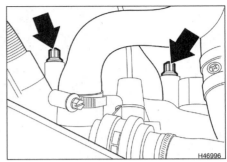

10.8 Starter motor mounting bolts (viewed down the rear of the engine) – M57T2 diesel engines

position, there should be a reading or lighted bulb, as applicable. If there is no reading or lighted bulb, the solenoid is faulty and should be renewed.
6 If the circuit and solenoid are proved sound, the fault must lie in the starter motor. In this event, it may be possible to have the starter motor overhauled by a specialist, but check on the cost of spares before proceeding, as it may prove more economical to obtain a new or exchange motor.

10 Starter motor – removal and refitting

Removal
1 Disconnect the battery negative lead (see Section 4).

Petrol engines
2 Remove the intake manifold as described in Chapter 4A.
3 Note their fitted positions, then undo the nuts and disconnect the leads from the starter solenoid (see illustration).
4 Undo the two bolts and remove the starter motor (see illustration).

M57T2 diesel engine
5 Raise the front of the vehicle and support it securely on axle stands (see *Jacking and vehicle support*).
6 Undo the fasteners and remove the engine/transmission undershield.

10.11 Undo the nuts and disconnect the starter motor wiring

7 Disconnect the wiring plug, then undo the nut securing the wiring to the rear of the starter motor.
8 Undo the 2 bolts and remove the starter motor, lowering it from position (see illustration).

N47 and N57 diesel engines
9 Raise the front of the vehicle and support it securely on axle stands (see *Jacking and vehicle support*).
10 Undo the fasteners and remove the engine/transmission undershield.
11 Undo the nuts securing the wiring to the rear of the starter motor (see illustration).
12 Undo the 3 bolts and remove the starter motor (see illustration). **Note:** *When refitting the starter, tighten the outer mounting bolts before tightening the inner one.*

Refitting
13 Refitting is a reversal of removal. Tighten the starter motor mounting bolts to the specified torque.

11 Starter motor – testing and overhaul

1 If the starter motor is thought to be suspect, it should be removed from the vehicle and taken to an auto-electrician for testing. Most auto-electricians will be able to supply and fit brushes at a reasonable cost. However, check on the cost of repairs before proceeding, as it

10.12 Starter motor mounting bolts – N47 and N57 diesel engines

may prove more economical to obtain a new or exchange motor.

12 Diesel preheating system – description and testing

Description
1 To assist cold starting, diesel engines are fitted with a preheating system, which consists of four of glow plugs (one per cylinder), a glow plug relay unit, a facia-mounted warning lamp, the engine management ECM, and the associated electrical wiring.
2 The glow plugs are miniature electric heating elements, encapsulated in a metal case with a probe at one end and electrical connection at the other. Each combustion chamber has one glow plug threaded into it, with the tip of the glow plug probe positioned directly in line with incoming spray of fuel from the injectors. When the glow plug is energised, it heats up rapidly, causing the fuel passing over the glow plug probe to be heated to its optimum combustion temperature, ready for combustion. In addition, some of the fuel passing over the glow plugs is ignited and this helps to trigger the combustion process.
3 The preheating system begins to operate as soon as the ignition key is switched to the second position, but only if the engine coolant temperature is below 20°C and the engine is turned at more than 70 rpm for 0.2 seconds. A facia-mounted warning lamp informs the driver that preheating is taking place. The lamp extinguishes when sufficient preheating has taken place to allow the engine to be started, but power will still be supplied to the glow plugs for a further period until the engine is started. If no attempt is made to start the engine, the power supply to the glow plugs is switched off after 10 seconds, to prevent battery drain and glow plug burn-out.
4 With the electronically-controlled diesel injection systems fitted to models in this manual, the glow plug relay unit is controlled by the engine management system ECM, which determines the necessary preheating time based on inputs from the various

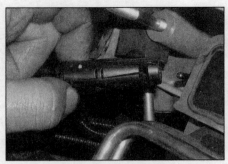

12.12 Squeeze together the ends of the connector and pull it from the glow plug

13.3 Unscrew and remove the glow plug

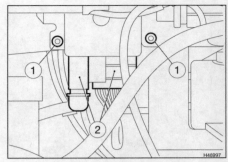

14.1 Glow plug control unit mounting nuts (1) and wiring plugs (2) – M57T2 engine

system sensors. The system monitors the temperature of the intake air, then alters the preheating time (the length for which the glow plugs are supplied with current) to suit the conditions.

5 Post-heating takes place after the ignition key has been released from the 'Start' position, but only if the engine coolant temperature is below 20ºC, the injected fuel flow is less than a certain rate, and the engine speed is less than 2000 rpm. The glow plugs continue to operate for a maximum of 60 seconds, helping to improve fuel combustion whilst the engine is warming-up, resulting in quieter, smoother running and reduced exhaust emissions.

Testing

6 If the system malfunctions, testing is ultimately by substitution of known good units, but some preliminary checks may be made as follows. Note that the preheating system is included in the vehicle's self-diagnosis system. Consequently, have the system interrogated using a fault code reader or scanner, via the vehicle's diagnostic socket – see Chapter 4B.

7 Connect a voltmeter or 12 volt test lamp between the glow plug supply cable and earth (engine or vehicle metal). Make sure that the live connection is kept clear of the engine and bodywork.

8 Have an assistant switch on the ignition, and check that voltage is applied to the glow plugs. Note the time for which the warning light is lit, and the total time for which voltage is applied before the system cuts out. Switch off the ignition.

9 Warning light time will increase with lower temperatures and decrease with higher temperatures.

10 If there is no supply at all, the control unit or associated wiring is at fault.

11 To gain access to the glow plugs for further testing, refer to Chapter 4B Section 16 and remove the intake manifold.

12 Squeeze together the side to release the clips, then pull the electrical connector from each glow plug **(see illustration)**.

13 Use a continuity tester, or a 12 volt test lamp connected to the battery positive

terminal, to check for continuity between each glow plug terminal and earth. The resistance of a glow plug in good condition is very low (less than 1 ohm), so if the test lamp does not light or the continuity tester shows a high resistance, the glow plug is certainly defective.

14 If an ammeter is available, the current draw of each glow plug can be checked. After an initial surge of 15 to 20 amps, each plug should draw 12 amps. Any plug which draws much more or less than this is probably defective.

15 As a final check, the glow plugs can be removed and inspected as described in the following Section. On completion, refit any components removed for access.

13 Glow plugs – removal, inspection and refitting

Caution: If the preheating system has just been energised, or if the engine has been running, the glow plugs will be very hot.

Removal

1 Ensure the ignition is turned off. To gain access to the glow plugs, remove the intake manifold as described in Chapter 4B.

2 Squeeze together the side to release the clips, then pull the electrical connector from each glow plug **(see illustration 12.12)**.

3 Unscrew the glow plug(s) and remove from the cylinder head **(see illustration)**.

Inspection

4 Inspect each glow plug for physical damage. Burnt or eroded glow plug tips can be caused by a bad injector spray pattern. Have the injectors checked if this sort of damage is found.

5 If the glow plugs are in good physical condition, check them electrically using a 12 volt test lamp or continuity tester as described in the previous Section.

6 The glow plugs can be energised by applying 12 volts to them to verify that they heat up evenly and in the required time. Observe the following precautions.

a) Support the glow plug by clamping it carefully in a vice or self-locking pliers. Remember it will become red-hot.

b) Make sure that the power supply or test lead incorporates a fuse or overload trip to protect against damage from a short-circuit.

c) After testing, allow the glow plug to cool for several minutes before attempting to handle it.

7 A glow plug in good condition will start to glow red at the tip after drawing current for 5 seconds or so. Any plug which takes much longer to start glowing, or which starts glowing in the middle instead of at the tip, is defective.

Refitting

8 Refit by reversing the removal operations. Apply a smear of copper-based anti-seize compound to the plug threads and tighten the glow plugs to the specified torque. Do not overtighten, as this can damage the glow plug element.

9 Refit any components removed for access.

10 On N47T engines, if any of the glow plugs are renewed, the preheating control service function must be performed using BMW diagnostic equipment (or equivalent). Entrust this task to a BMW dealer or suitably equipped repairer.

14 Pre/post-heating system control/relay unit – removal and refitting

Removal

M57T2 engine

1 The relay is located just in front of the starter motor. Disconnect the relay wiring plugs **(see illustration)**.

2 Undo the 2 nuts and remove the relay.

N47 engine

3 The relay is located just behind the oil filter housing. Raise the front edge, and pull the plastic cover from the top of the engine.

4 Release the clamp and disconnect the air delivery pipe from the throttle valve.

14.5 The glow plug control unit is located behind the oil filter housing – N47 engine

14.8 Glow plug control unit – N47T engine

5 Disconnect the wiring plug and remove the glow plug control/relay unit **(see illustration)**.

N47T engine

6 Remove the lower section of the pollen filter housing as described in Chapter 5B Section 3.
7 Release the clips at the front and lift up the acoustic cover from the rear of the cylinder head.
8 Slide out the locking catches, disconnect the wiring plugs, undo the retaining bolt and remove the glow plug control unit **(see illustration)**.

N57 engine

9 Raise the front edge, and pull the plastic cover from the top of the engine.
10 Disconnect the intake air temperature sensor wiring plug, prise out the locking clips, and detach the air delivery pipe from the throttle valve.
11 Release the clip and disconnect the wiring plug from the control unit **(see illustration)**.
12 Undo the 2 bolts and remove the control unit.

Refitting

13 Refitting is a reversal of removal, ensuring that the wiring connectors are correctly connected.

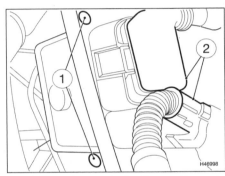

14.11 Glow plug control unit mounting nuts (1) and wiring plugs (2) – N57 engine

Chapter 5 Part B:
Ignition systems

Contents

Degrees of difficulty

Easy, suitable for novice with little experience

Fairly easy, suitable for beginner with some experience

Fairly difficult, suitable for competent DIY mechanic

Difficult, suitable for experienced DIY mechanic

Very difficult, suitable for expert DIY or professional

Specifications

Firing order
All engines 1-3-4-2
Ignition timing. . . . . Electronically-controlled by DME – no adjustment possible

Torque wrench settings	Nm	lbf ft
Spark plugs:		
M12 thread	23	17
M14 thread	30	22
Knock sensor securing bolt	20	15

1 General information and precautions

1 The ignition system is controlled by the engine management system (see Chapter 4A), known as DME (Digital Motor Electronics). The DME system controls all ignition and fuel injection functions using a central ECM (Electronic Control Module).
2 The ignition timing is based on inputs provided to the ECM by various sensors supplying information on engine load, engine speed, coolant temperature sensor and inlet air temperature (see Chapter 4A Section 10).
3 All engines are fitted with knock sensors to detect 'knocking' (also known as 'pinking' or pre-ignition). The knock sensors are sensitive to vibration and detect the knocking which occurs when a cylinder starts to pre-ignite. The knock sensor provides a signal to the ECM which in turn retards the ignition advance setting until the knocking ceases.
4 A distributorless ignition system is used, with a separate HT coil for each cylinder. No distributor is used, and the coils provide the high voltage signal direct to each spark plug.
5 The ECM uses the inputs from the various sensors to calculate the required ignition advance and the coil charging time.

Precautions
• *Refer to the precautions in Chapter 5A.*
• *Testing of ignition system components should be entrusted to a BMW dealer. Improvised testing techniques are time-consuming and run the risk of damaging the engine management ECM.*

2 Ignition system – testing

1 If a fault appears in the engine management (fuel/injection) system, first ensure that the fault is not due to a poor electrical connection, or to poor maintenance, ie, check that the air cleaner filter element is clean, that the spark plugs are in good condition and correctly gapped, and that the engine breather hoses are clear and undamaged.
2 If the engine is running very roughly, check the compression pressures as described in Chapter 2A Section 2.
3 If these checks fail to reveal the cause of the problem, then the vehicle should be taken to a BMW dealer or specialist for testing using the appropriate specialist diagnostic equipment. The ECM incorporates a self-diagnostic function which stores fault codes in the system memory (note that stored fault codes are erased if the battery is disconnected). These fault codes can be read using the appropriate BMW diagnosis equipment. Improvised testing techniques are time-consuming and run the risk of damaging the engine management ECM.

3 Ignition HT coil – removal and refitting

Removal
1 Working at the rear of the engine compartment, undo the bolts and remove the

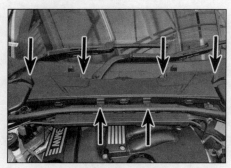

3.1 Undo the bolts and remove the pollen filter cover

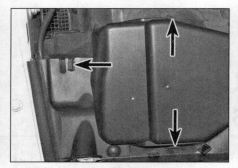

3.2 Release the clips and remove the plastic cover each side

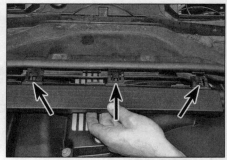

3.3 Release the clips and slide the cable guide forwards

pollen filter cover **(see illustration)**. Slide the filter from the housing. If necessary, refer to Chapter 1A Section 6.

2 Release the clips and remove the plastic cover behind the suspension turret each side. Unclip any wiring/hoses as the covers are removed **(see illustration)**.

3 Depress the clips, and slide the cable guide forwards from the pollen filter lower housing **(see illustration)**.

4 Open the clamps and release the hose at the front of the pollen filter lower housing.

5 Undo the bolt, release the clip each side, and pull the front edge of the pollen filter lower housing forwards and upwards **(see illustrations)**. Unclip any wiring looms as the housing is removed.

6 Remove the plastic cover from the top of the engine.

7 Prise up the edge of the plastic covers over the ignition coils (above the spark plugs), and disconnect the coils' wiring plugs **(see illustrations)**. With the wiring plugs disconnected, pull the coils from the spark plugs.

Refitting

8 Refitting is a reversal of removal, but ensure that any earth leads and brackets are in position as noted before removal.

4 Knock sensor – removal and refitting

Removal

1 Disconnect the battery negative lead as described in Chapter 5A Section 4.

2 Remove the intake manifold as described in Chapter 4A Section 11.

3 Two knock sensors are fitted. The rear knock sensor is obscured by the starter motor. To access the rear sensor, undo the starter motor retaining bolts, pull the starter out from its mounting, and rotate it downwards **(see illustration)**.

4 Trace the wiring back from the sensors, and disconnect the wiring plugs.

5 Undo the bolt(s) and remove the sensor(s) **(see illustration)**.

Refitting

6 Refitting is a reversal of removal, ensuring that the sensor-to-engine block contact area is clean, and tighten the sensor bolt to the specified torque.

3.5a Undo the bolt, release the clip each side...

3.5b... the pull the pollen filter lower housing forwards and upwards

3.7a Lift the cover and disconnect the coil wiring plug

3.7b Pull the coil from above the spark plug

4.3 The rear knock sensor is obscured by the starter motor

4.5 The front knock sensor is adjacent to the coolant temperature sensor

Chapter 6
Clutch

Contents

Degrees of difficulty

Easy, suitable for novice with little experience	Fairly easy, suitable for beginner with some experience	Fairly difficult, suitable for competent DIY mechanic	Difficult, suitable for experienced DIY mechanic	Very difficult, suitable for expert DIY or professional

Specifications

Type . . . . Single dry plate with diaphragm spring, hydraulically-operated

Driveplate

Minimum lining thickness above rivet head . . . . 1.0 mm

Diameter:
 Petrol engines . . . . 228 mm
 Diesel engines . . . . 240 mm

Torque wrench settings	Nm	lbf ft
Note: *On some fixings different grades of bolt can be used; the grade of each bolt is stamped on the bolt head. Ensure that each bolt is tightened to the correct torque for its grade.*		
Clutch master cylinder bolts	22	16
Clutch slave cylinder nuts	22	16
Hydraulic pipe union bolts	20	15
Pressure plate-to-flywheel bolts: *		
M8:		
8.8	24	18
10.9	34	25
ZNS bolts:		
Stage 1	15	11
Stage 2	Angle-tighten a further 90°	

*Do not re-use

1 General Information

1 All models are fitted with a single dry plate clutch, which consists of five main components; friction disc, pressure plate, diaphragm spring, cover and release bearing.

2 The friction disc is free to slide along the splines of the gearbox input shaft, and is held in position between the flywheel and the pressure plate by the pressure exerted on the pressure plate by the diaphragm spring. Friction lining material is riveted to both sides of the friction disc. All models are fitted with a Self-Adjusting Clutch (SAC), which compensates for friction disc wear by altering the attitude of the diaphragm spring fingers by means of a sprung mechanism within the pressure plate cover. This ensures a consistent clutch pedal 'feel' over the life of the clutch.

3 The diaphragm spring is mounted on pins, and is held in place in the cover by annular fulcrum rings.

4 The release bearing is located on a guide sleeve at the front of the gearbox, and the bearing is free to slide on the sleeve under the action of the release arm which pivots inside the clutch bellhousing.

5 The release mechanism is operated by the clutch pedal, using hydraulic pressure. The pedal acts on the hydraulic master cylinder pushrod, and a slave cylinder mounted on the gearbox bellhousing operates the clutch release lever via a pushrod.

6 When the clutch pedal is depressed, the release arm pushes the release bearing forwards, to bear against the centre of the diaphragm spring, thus pushing the centre of the diaphragm spring inwards. The diaphragm spring acts against the fulcrum rings in the cover, and so as the centre of the spring is pushed in, the outside of the spring is pushed out, so allowing the pressure plate to move backwards away from the friction disc.

7 When the clutch pedal is released, the diaphragm spring forces the pressure plate into contact with the friction linings on the friction disc, and simultaneously pushes the friction disc forwards on its splines, forcing it against the flywheel. The friction disc is now firmly sandwiched between the pressure plate and the flywheel, and drive is taken up.

2 Clutch assembly – removal, inspection and refitting

Warning: Dust created by clutch wear and deposited on the clutch components may contain asbestos, which is a health hazard. DO NOT blow it out with compressed air, or inhale any of it. DO NOT use petrol (or petroleum-based solvents) to clean off the dust. Brake system cleaner or methylated spirit should be used to flush the dust into a suitable receptacle. After the clutch components are wiped clean with rags, dispose of the contaminated rags and cleaner in a sealed, marked container.

Removal

1 Remove the gearbox, as described in Chapter 7A.

2 If the original clutch is to be refitted, make alignment marks between the clutch pressure plate and the flywheel, so that the clutch can be refitted in its original position.

3 Progressively unscrew the bolts securing the clutch cover/pressure plate assembly to the flywheel, and where applicable recover the washers.

4 Withdraw the clutch pressure plate from the flywheel. Be prepared to catch the clutch friction disc, which may drop out of the pressure plate as it is withdrawn, and note which way round the friction disc is fitted – the two sides of the disc are normally marked 'Engine side' and 'Transmission side'. The greater projecting side of the hub faces away from the flywheel.

Inspection

5 With the clutch assembly removed, clean off all traces of dust using a dry cloth. Although most friction discs now have asbestos-free linings, some do not, and it is wise to take suitable precautions; asbestos dust is harmful, and must not be inhaled.

6 Examine the linings of the friction disc for wear and loose rivets, and the disc for distortion, cracks, and worn splines. The surface of the friction linings may be highly glazed, but as long as the friction material pattern can be clearly seen, this is satisfactory. If there is any sign of oil contamination, indicated by a continuous, or patchy, shiny black discolouration, the disc must be renewed. The source of the contamination must be traced and rectified before fitting new clutch components; typically, a leaking crankshaft rear oil seal or gearbox input shaft oil seal – or both – will be to blame (renewal procedures are given in the relevant Part of Chapter 2 and Chapter 7A respectively). The disc must also be renewed if the lining thickness has worn down to, or just above, the level of the rivet heads. Note that BMW specify a minimum friction material thickness above the heads of the rivets (see Specifications0).

7 Check the machined faces of the flywheel and pressure plate. If either is grooved, or heavily scored, renewal is necessary. The pressure plate must also be renewed if any cracks are apparent, or if the diaphragm spring is damaged or its pressure suspect.

8 With the clutch removed, it is advisable to check the condition of the release bearing, as described in Section 3.

9 Check the spigot bearing in the end of the crankshaft. Make sure that it turns smoothly and quietly. If the gearbox input shaft contact face on the bearing is worn or damaged, fit a new bearing, as described in Chapter 2A Section 17, Chapter 2B Section 14 or Chapter 2C Section 15.

Refitting

10 If new clutch components are to be fitted, ensure that all anti-corrosion preservative is cleaned from the friction material on the disc, and the contact surfaces of the pressure plate.

11 It is important to ensure that no oil or grease gets onto the friction disc linings, or the pressure plate and flywheel faces. It is advisable to refit the clutch assembly with clean hands, and to wipe down the pressure plate and flywheel faces with a clean rag before assembly begins.

12 Offer the disc to the flywheel, with the greater projecting side of the hub facing away from the flywheel (most friction discs will have an 'Engine side' or Transmission side' marking which should face the flywheel or gearbox as applicable) (see illustration). Using a suitable BMW tool or a suitable alternative manufactured by an automotive tool specialist, centre the friction disc in the flywheel (see illustration).

13 If the original pressure plate and cover is to be refitted, engage the legs of BMW tool 21 2 170 with the cover in the area of the adjusting springs. Screw down the knurled collar to lock the legs in place, then tighten down the spindle to compress the diaphragm spring. Using a screwdriver, reset the self-adjusting mechanism by pushing the adjustment ring thrust pieces fully anti-clockwise, whilst undoing the special tool spindle only enough to allow the adjustment ring to move. With the adjustment ring reset, tighten down the special tool spindle to compress the spring fingers, whilst preventing the adjustment ring thrust

2.12a The friction disc may be marked 'Getriebeseite' meaning 'Gearbox side'

2.12b Use a suitable tool to centre the friction disc

2.13a Use BMW tool 21 2 170 to compress the diaphragm spring

2.13b Push the adjustment ring thrust pieces fully anti-clockwise...

2.13c... and insert metal spacers between the thrust pieces and the cover

2.13d A special BMW tool is available to reset the adjustment ring thrust pieces

2.14 Ensure the cover locates over the flywheel dowels

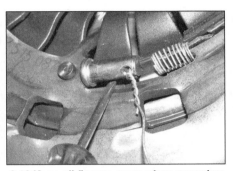

2.16 Keep all fingers away when removing the metal spacers

pieces from moving by inserting metal spacers in the gap between the thrust pieces and the cover. Note that a special tool is available from BMW to reset the adjustment ring **(see illustrations)**.

14 Fit the clutch cover assembly, where applicable aligning the marks on the flywheel and clutch pressure plate. Ensure that the clutch pressure plate locates over the dowels on the flywheel **(see illustration)**. Insert the securing bolts and washers, and tighten them to the specified torque.

15 If a new pressure plate cover was fitted, insert a 14 mm Allen key into the centre of the diaphragm spring locking piece, and turn it clockwise and remove it to release the spring.

16 Where the original pressure plate cover was refitted, undo the spindle and knurled collar, then remove the compression tool from the cover. Prise out the metal spacers holding

the adjustment ring thrust pieces in place **(see illustration)**.
Caution: As the last spacer is withdrawn, the adjustment ring may spring into place. Ensure all fingers are clear of the area.

17 If the BMW centring tool was used, remove the tool by screwing a 10 mm bolt into its end and pulling using a pair of pliers or similar **(see illustration)**.

18 Refit the gearbox as described in Chapter 7A.

3 Clutch release bearing and lever – removal, inspection and refitting

⚠ *Warning: Dust created by clutch wear and deposited on the clutch components may contain asbestos,*

which is a health hazard. DO NOT blow it out with compressed air, or inhale any of it. DO NOT use petrol (or petroleum-based solvents) to clean off the dust. Brake system cleaner or methylated spirit should be used to flush the dust into a suitable receptacle. After the clutch components are wiped clean with rags, dispose of the contaminated rags and cleaner in a sealed, marked container.

Removal

1 Remove the gearbox as described in Chapter 7A.

2 Slide the release lever sideways to release it from the retaining spring clip and pivot, then pull the lever and bearing forwards from the guide sleeve **(see illustration)**.

3 Do not detach the release bearing from the lever. The bearing is only available as a complete assembly with the lever.

Inspection

4 Spin the release bearing, and check it for excessive roughness. Hold the outer race, and attempt to move it laterally against the inner race. If any excessive movement or roughness is evident, renew the bearing. If a new clutch has been fitted, it is wise to renew the release bearing as a matter of course.

5 Inspect the release bearing, pivot and slave cylinder pushrod contact faces on the release lever for wear. Renew the lever if excessive wear is evident.

6 Check the release lever retaining spring clip, and renew if necessary. It is advisable to renew the clip as a matter of course.

2.17 Thread the bolt into the end of the centring tool, and pull it out

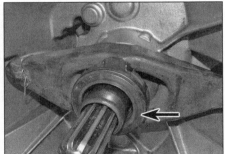

3.2 Slide the release lever sideways to disengage it from the retaining clip

3.8 Ensure the lever engages correctly with the retaining clip

4.4 Clamp the rubber flexible hose

4.6 Prise out the clip and disconnect the fluid pipe

Refitting

7 Clean the release bearing contact surfaces on the release lever and guide sleeve. Do not apply any grease or lubricant to the sliding surfaces of the bearing or guide sleeve.
8 Slide the release lever/bearing assembly into position over the guide sleeve, then push the end of the lever over the pivot, ensuring that the retaining spring clip engages correctly over the end of the release lever **(see illustration)**.
9 Refit the gearbox, referring to Chapter 7A.

4 Hydraulic slave cylinder – removal, inspection and refitting

⚠️ *Warning: Hydraulic fluid is poisonous; wash off immediately and thoroughly in the case of skin contact, and seek immediate medical advice if any fluid is swallowed or gets into the eyes. Certain types of hydraulic fluid are inflammable, and may ignite when allowed into contact with hot components; when servicing any hydraulic system, it is safest to assume that the fluid is inflammable, and to take precautions against the risk of fire as though it is petrol that is being handled. Hydraulic fluid is also an effective paint stripper, and will attack plastics; if any is spilt, it should be washed off immediately, using copious quantities of fresh water. Finally, it is hygroscopic (it absorbs moisture from the air) – old fluid may be contaminated and unfit for further use. When topping-up or renewing the fluid, always use the recommended type, and ensure that it comes from a freshly-opened sealed container.*

Removal

1 Remove the brake fluid reservoir cap, and siphon out sufficient hydraulic fluid so that the fluid level is below the level of the reservoir fluid hose connection to the clutch master cylinder (the brake fluid reservoir feeds both the brake and clutch hydraulic systems). Do not empty the reservoir, as this will draw air into the brake hydraulic circuits.

2 To improve access, jack up the vehicle, and support it securely on axle stands (see *Jacking and vehicle support*).
3 Release the bolts and remove the underbody shield (where fitted) for access to the gearbox bellhousing.
4 Apply a clamp to the slave cylinder flexible rubber pipe to prevent fluid loss **(see illustration)**.
5 Undo the two securing nuts and withdrawn the slave cylinder from the mounting studs on the transmission.
6 Prise out the retaining clip, and disconnect the fluid pipe from the cylinder **(see illustration)**.

Inspection

7 Inspect the slave cylinder for fluid leaks and damage, and renew if necessary. At the time of writing, no spare parts are available for the slave cylinder, and if faulty, the complete unit must be renewed. Check with your dealer or specialist.

Refitting

8 Press the piston into the cylinder, then reconnect the fluid pipe. Refill the fluid reservoir, then extend and compress the piston in the cylinder five times whilst holding the cylinder vertical.
9 The remainder of refitting is a reversal of removal, bearing in mind the following points.
a) Before refitting, clean and then lightly grease the end of the slave cylinder pushrod.
b) Tighten the mounting nuts to the specified torque.
c) On completion, top-up the hydraulic fluid level and bleed the clutch hydraulic circuit as described in Section 6.

5 Hydraulic master cylinder – removal, inspection and refitting

⚠️ *Warning: Hydraulic fluid is poisonous; wash off immediately and thoroughly in the case of skin contact, and seek immediate medical advice if any fluid is swallowed or gets into*

the eyes. Certain types of hydraulic fluid are inflammable, and may ignite when allowed into contact with hot components; when servicing any hydraulic system, it is safest to assume that the fluid is inflammable, and to take precautions against the risk of fire as though it is petrol that is being handled. Hydraulic fluid is also an effective paint stripper, and will attack plastics; if any is spilt, it should be washed off immediately, using copious quantities of fresh water. Finally, it is hygroscopic (it absorbs moisture from the air) – old fluid may be contaminated and unfit for further use. When topping-up or renewing the fluid, always use the recommended type, and ensure that it comes from a freshly-opened sealed container.

Removal

1 Release fasteners and remove the trim panel above the driver's pedals **(see illustration)**. Disconnect any wiring plugs as the panel is withdrawn.
2 Release the clips, remove the plastic cover, then remove the brake fluid reservoir cap, and siphon out sufficient hydraulic fluid so that the fluid level is below the level of the reservoir fluid hose connection to the clutch master cylinder (the brake fluid reservoir feeds both the brake and clutch hydraulic systems). Do not empty the reservoir, as this will draw air into the brake hydraulic circuits.
3 Disconnect the clutch master cylinder hose from the brake fluid reservoir. Be prepared for fluid spillage, and plug the open end of the hose to prevent dirt entry.

5.1 Panel retaining bolts

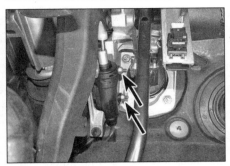

5.4 Undo the nuts and push the bolts to the left

5.5a Pushrod pivot pin location

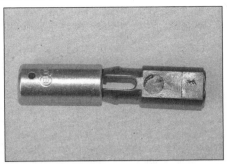

5.5b Push an 8.0 mm socket onto the end of the pin to compress the retaining clips, and push the pin from place

4 Unscrew the two nuts and push back the two bolts securing the master cylinder to the pedal bracket in the footwell **(see illustration)**.
5 Using an 8 mm socket, squeeze together the ends of the pin, then press out the master cylinder pushrod pivot pin from the clutch pedal **(see illustrations)**.
6 Using a small screwdriver, prise out the retaining clip and then pull the master cylinder from the hydraulic pressure pipe **(see illustration)**. Withdraw the master cylinder, and ease the fluid supply hose through the bulkhead grommet a little, taking care not to strain the pipe. Do not pull the hose completely through the grommet. Be prepared for fluid leaks.
7 Pull the supply hose from the top of the master cylinder, and leave the hose in place in the bulkhead grommet for reassembly. Be prepared for fluid spillage.
8 Depress the locking tab, and disconnect the master cylinder switch wiring plug (where fitted). If required, carefully release the clips and detach the switch from the cylinder.

Inspection

9 Inspect the master cylinder for fluid leaks and damage, and renew if necessary. At the time of writing, no spare parts were available for the master cylinder, and if faulty the complete unit must be renewed. Check with your local dealer or parts supplier.

Refitting

10 Refitting is a reversal of removal, bearing in mind the following points.
a) *Take care not to strain the master cylinder fluid pipe during refitting.*

b) *On completion, top-up the level in the brake fluid reservoir, then bleed the clutch hydraulic system (see Section 6).*

6 Hydraulic system – bleeding

⚠️ *Warning: Hydraulic fluid is poisonous; wash off immediately and thoroughly in the case of skin contact, and seek immediate medical advice if any fluid is swallowed or gets into the eyes. Certain types of hydraulic fluid are inflammable, and may ignite when allowed into contact with hot components; when servicing any hydraulic system, it is safest to assume that the fluid is inflammable, and to take precautions against the risk of fire as though it is petrol that is being handled. Hydraulic fluid is also an effective paint stripper, and will attack plastics; if any is spilt, it should be washed off immediately, using copious quantities of fresh water. Finally, it is hygroscopic (it absorbs moisture from the air) – old fluid may be contaminated and unfit for further use. When topping-up or renewing the fluid, always use the recommended type, and ensure that it comes from a freshly-opened sealed container.*

Note: *BMW recommend that pressure-bleeding equipment is used to bleed the clutch hydraulic system.*

General

1 The correct operation of any hydraulic system is only possible after removing all air from the components and circuit; this is achieved by bleeding the system.
2 During the bleeding procedure, add only clean, unused hydraulic fluid of the recommended type; never re-use fluid that has already been bled from the system. Ensure that sufficient fluid is available before starting work.
3 If there is any possibility of incorrect fluid being already in the system, the brake and clutch components and circuit must be flushed completely with uncontaminated, correct fluid, and new seals should be fitted to the various components.
4 If hydraulic fluid has been lost from the system, or air has entered because of a leak, ensure that the fault is cured before proceeding further.
5 To improve access, apply the handbrake, then jack up the front of the vehicle, and support it securely on axle stands (see *Jacking and vehicle support*).
6 Undo the bolts and remove the underbody shield (where fitted) for access to the gearbox bellhousing.
7 Check that the clutch hydraulic pipe(s) and hose(s) are secure, that the unions are tight, and that the bleed screw on the rear of the clutch slave cylinder (mounted under the vehicle on the lower left-hand side of the gearbox bellhousing) is closed. Clean any dirt from around the bleed screw **(see illustration)**.
8 Release the clips, remove the plastic cover over the reservoir **(see illustration)**, then unscrew the brake fluid reservoir cap, and

5.6 Prise out the clip and detach the pipe

6.7 Clutch slave cylinder bleed screw

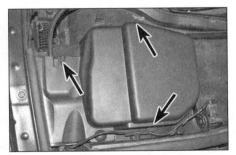

6.8 Release the clips, and remove the plastic cover from the right-hand side of the engine compartment

top the fluid up to the MAX level line; refit the cap loosely, and remember to maintain the fluid level at least above the MIN level line throughout the procedure, or there is a risk of further air entering the system. Note that the brake fluid reservoir feeds both the brake and clutch hydraulic systems.

9 It is recommended that pressure-bleeding equipment is used to bleed the system. Alternatively, there are a number of one-man, do-it-yourself brake bleeding kits currently available from motor accessory shops. These kits greatly simplify the bleeding operation, and also reduce the risk of expelled air and fluid being drawn back into the system. If such a kit is not available, the basic (two-man) method must be used, which is described in detail below.

10 If pressure-bleeding equipment or a one-man kit is to be used, prepare the vehicle as described previously, and follow the equipment/kit manufacturer's instructions, as the procedure may vary slightly according to the type being used; generally, they are as outlined below in the relevant sub-section.

11 Whichever method is used, the same basic process must be followed to ensure that the removal of all air from the system.

Bleeding

Basic (two-man) method

12 Collect a clean glass jar, a suitable length of plastic or rubber tubing which is a tight fit over the bleed screw, and a ring spanner to fit the screw. The help of an assistant will also be required.

13 Where applicable, remove the dust cap from the bleed screw. Fit the spanner and tube to the screw, place the other end of the tube in the jar, and pour in sufficient fluid to cover the end of the tube.

14 Ensure that the reservoir fluid level is maintained at least above the MIN level line throughout the procedure.

15 Have the assistant fully depress the clutch pedal several times to build-up pressure, then maintain it on the final downstroke.

16 While pedal pressure is maintained, unscrew the bleed screw (approximately one turn) and allow the compressed fluid and air to flow into the jar. The assistant should maintain pedal pressure, following it down to the floor if necessary, and should not release it until instructed to do so. When the flow stops, tighten the bleed screw again, have the assistant release the pedal slowly, and recheck the reservoir fluid level.

17 Repeat the steps given in paragraphs 15 and 16 until the fluid emerging from the bleed screw is free from air bubbles.

18 When no more air bubbles appear, tighten the bleed screw securely. Do not overtighten the bleed screw.

19 Temporarily disconnect the bleed tube from the bleed screw, and move the container of fluid to one side.

20 Unscrew the two securing nuts, and withdraw the slave cylinder from the bellhousing, taking care not to strain the fluid hose.

21 Reconnect the bleed tube to the bleed screw, and submerge the end of the tube in the container of fluid.

22 With the bleed screw pointing vertically upwards, unscrew the bleed screw (approximately one turn), and slowly push the slave cylinder pushrod into the cylinder until no more air bubbles appear in the fluid.

23 Hold the pushrod in position, then tighten the bleed screw.

24 Slowly allow the pushrod to return to its rest position. Do not allow the pushrod to return quickly, as this will cause air to enter the slave cylinder.

25 Remove the tube and spanner, and refit the dust cap to the bleed screw.

26 Refit the slave cylinder to the bellhousing, and tighten the securing nuts to the specified torque.

Using a one-way valve kit

27 As their name implies, these kits consist of a length of tubing with a one-way valve fitted, to prevent expelled air and fluid being drawn back into the system; some kits include a translucent container, which can be positioned so that the air bubbles can be more easily seen flowing from the end of the tube.

28 The kit is connected to the bleed screw, which is then opened. The user returns to the driver's seat, depresses the clutch pedal with a smooth, steady stroke, and slowly releases it; this is repeated until the expelled fluid is clear of air bubbles.

29 Note that these kits simplify work so much that it is easy to forget the reservoir fluid level; ensure that this is maintained at least above the MIN level line at all times.

Using a pressure-bleeding kit

30 These kits are usually operated by the reservoir of pressurised air contained in a tyre. However, note that it will probably be necessary to reduce the pressure to a lower level than normal; refer to the instructions supplied with the kit.

31 By connecting a pressurised, fluid-filled container to the fluid reservoir, bleeding can be carried out simply by opening the bleed screw, and allowing the fluid to flow out until no more air bubbles can be seen in the expelled fluid.

32 This method has the advantage that the large reservoir of fluid provides an additional safeguard against air being drawn into the system during bleeding.

All methods

33 If after following the instructions given, it is suspected that air is still present in hydraulic system, remove the slave cylinder (Section 4) without disconnecting the hydraulic pipes, push the cylinder piston all the way in, and holding the cylinder with the bleed screw uppermost, bleed the system again. **Note:** *Steps must be taken to ensure that the slave cylinder piston is prevented from extending during the bleeding procedure. If necessary,* *use a metal strip and two threaded bars to fabricate a tool to hold the piston in.*

34 When bleeding is complete, and firm pedal feel is restored, wash off any spilt fluid, check that the bleed screw is tightened securely, and refit the dust cap.

35 Check the hydraulic fluid level in the reservoir, and top-up if necessary (see *Weekly checks*). Refit the plastic cover over the reservoir.

36 Discard any hydraulic fluid that has been bled from the system; it will not be fit for re-use.

37 Check the feel of the clutch pedal. If it feels at all spongy, air must still be present in the system, and further bleeding is required. Failure to bleed satisfactorily after a reasonable repetition of the bleeding procedure may be due to worn master or slave cylinder seals.

38 On completion, refit the underbody shield (where fitted) and lower the vehicle to the ground.

7 Clutch pedal – removal and refitting

Removal

1 Remove the steering column as described in Chapter 10.

2 Squeeze together the ends of the pin, then press out the master cylinder pushrod pivot pin from the clutch pedal **(see illustrations 5.5a and 5.5b)**.

3 Prise off the clip securing the pedal to the pivot shaft, then slide the pedal from the shaft. Recover the pivot bushes if they are loose. Where fitted, release the return coil spring. **Note:** *It is possible to remove the return spring with the pedal in place. Use a length of wire/cable to pull the spring lower end from the pedal, then detach it from the bracket* **(see illustration).**

Refitting

4 Before refitting the pedal to the pivot shaft, check the condition of the pivot bushes, and renew if necessary. Apply a little grease to the bushes.

5 Refitting is a reversal of removal. Ensure that the clutch switch plunger is fully extended prior to refitment.

7.3 Clutch pedal return spring

Chapter 7 Part A:
Manual gearbox

Contents

Degrees of difficulty

Easy, suitable for novice with little experience	Fairly easy, suitable for beginner with some experience	Fairly difficult, suitable for competent DIY mechanic	Difficult, suitable for experienced DIY mechanic	Very difficult, suitable for expert DIY or professional

Specifications

Type
Petrol engines	GS6-17BG
4-cylinder diesel engine	GS6-17DG, 37DZ or 45DZ
6-cylinder diesel engines	GS6-53DZ

Torque wrench settings

	Nm	lbf ft
Gearbox crossmember-to-body bolts:		
M8	21	15
M10	42	31
Gearbox mounting-to-gearbox nuts:		
M8	21	15
M10	42	31
Gearbox-to-engine bolts:		
Hexagon-head bolts:		
M8	25	18
M10	49	36
M12	74	55
Torx-head bolts:		
M8	22	16
M10	43	32
M12	72	53
Oil filler/level and drain plugs:		
GS6-17 transmission	45	33
GS6-37/45 transmission:		
M12	25	18
M18	35	26
GS6-53 transmission	35	26
Output flange-to-output shaft nut: *		
GS6-17, GS6-37 and GS6-45 transmissions:		
Stage 1	170	125
Stage 2	Fully loosen nut	
Stage 3	120	89
GS6-53 transmission:		
Stage 1	200	148
Stage 2	Fully loosen nut	
Stage 3	140	103
Reversing light switch	16	11
Zero-gear sensor	5	3

Coat the threads of the nut with locking compound

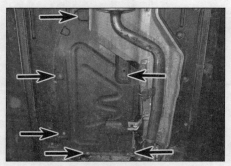

2.1 Transmission undershield fasteners

2.2 Oil level/filler plug

3.3 Oil drain plug

1 General Information

1 The gearbox is a 6-speed unit, and is contained in a cast-alloy casing bolted to the rear of the engine.
2 Drive is transmitted from the crankshaft via the clutch to the input shaft, which has a splined extension to accept the clutch friction disc. The output shaft transmits the drive via the propeller shaft to the rear differential.
3 The input shaft runs in line with the output shaft. The input shaft and output shaft gears are in constant mesh with the layshaft gear cluster. Selection of gears is by sliding synchromesh hubs, which lock the appropriate output shaft gears to the output shaft.
4 Gear selection is via a floor-mounted lever and selector mechanism or, depending on model, switches mounted on the steering wheel. A Sequential Manual Gearbox (SMG) option is available for some models, where the gearchanges can be performed sequentially using the floor-mounted lever, or the 'paddle' shift switches on the steering wheel. On models so equipped, the gearchanges can be performed automatically, with the electronic control module (ECM) controlling gearchange and clutch operation (via hydraulic controls) dictated by driving style and road conditions. A 'launch control' is available on some models, where at the press of a button, the ECM will control engine speed, clutch operation and gearchange functions, to achieve maximum acceleration – consult your owner's handbook for further details.
5 The selector mechanism causes the appropriate selector fork to move its respective synchro-sleeve along the shaft, to lock the gear pinion to the synchro-hub. Since the synchro-hubs are splined to the output shaft, this locks the pinion to the shaft, so that drive can be transmitted. To ensure that gearchanging can be made quickly and quietly, a synchromesh system is fitted to all forward gears, consisting of baulk rings and spring-loaded fingers, as well as the gear pinions and synchro-hubs. The synchromesh

cones are formed on the mating faces of the baulk rings and gear pinions.
6 The transmission is filled during production, and is then considered 'filled for life', with BMW making no recommendations concerning the changing of the fluid.

2 Manual gearbox oil level check

1 To improve access, jack up the vehicle and support on axle stands (see *Jacking and vehicle support*). Ensure that the car is level. Undo the fasteners and remove the undershield beneath the transmission (where fitted) **(see illustration)**.
2 Unscrew the gearbox oil level/filler plug from the right-hand side of the gearbox casing **(see illustration)**.
3 The oil level should be up to the bottom of the level/filler plug hole.
4 If necessary, top-up the level, using the correct type of fluid (see *Lubricants and fluids*) until the oil overflows from the filler/level plug hole.
5 Wipe away any spilt oil, then refit the filler/level plug, and tighten to the specified torque.
6 Refit the transmission undershield (where fitted) and lower the vehicle to the ground.

3 Manual gearbox oil renewal

Note: *New gearbox oil drain plug and oil filler/level plug sealing rings may be required on refitting.*
1 The gearbox oil should be drained with the gearbox at normal operating temperature. If the car has just been driven at least 20 miles the gearbox can be considered warm.
2 Immediately after driving the car, park it on a level surface, apply the handbrake. If desired, jack up the car and support on axle stands (see *Jacking and vehicle support*) to improve access, but make sure that the car

is level. Remove the transmission undershield (where fitted).
3 Working under the car, slacken the gearbox oil drain plug about half a turn **(see illustration)**. Position a draining container under the drain plug, then remove the plug completely. If possible, try to keep the plug pressed into the gearbox while unscrewing it by hand the last couple of turns.

> **HAYNES HiNT** *As the plug releases from the threads, move it away sharply so the stream of fluid from the gearbox runs into the container, not up your sleeve.*

4 Where applicable, recover the sealing ring from the drain plug.
5 Refit the drain plug, using a new sealing ring where applicable, and tighten to the specified torque.
6 Unscrew the oil filler/level plug from the side of the gearbox, and recover the sealing ring, where applicable **(see illustration 2.2)**.
7 Fill the gearbox through the filler/level plug hole with the specified quantity and type of oil (see Chapter 1A or 1B), until the oil overflows from the filler/level plug hole.
8 Refit the filler/level plug, using a new sealing ring where applicable, and tighten to the specified torque.
9 Where applicable, lower the car to the ground.

4 Gearchange components – removal and refitting

Manual gear lever assembly

Note: *A new gear lever bearing will be required on refitting.*
1 Jack up the car and support securely on axle stands (see *Jacking and vehicle support*). Undo the fasteners and remove the undershield beneath the transmission (where fitted) **(see illustration 2.1)**.
2 Undo the fasteners, and remove the

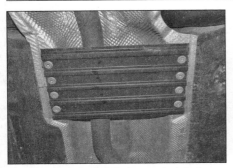

4.2 Remove the reinforcement plate from below the exhaust system

4.4 Squeeze together the sides, and remove the gear lever gaiter

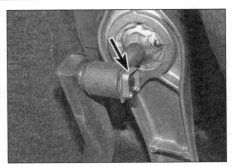

4.6 Slide the retaining clip from the selector rod pin

reinforcement plate from beneath the vehicle **(see illustration)**.

3 Undo the fasteners and remove the heat shield from beneath the propeller shaft.

4 Starting at the front left-hand edge, push in the sides and free the gear lever gaiter from the centre console. Note that the gaiter is integral with the gear lever knob **(see illustration)**.

5 Support the transmission with a trolley/transmission jack, then undo the bolts/nuts and remove the crossmember and mounting assembly from the rear of the transmission.

6 Prise the securing clip from the end of the gear selector rod pin. Withdraw the selector rod pin from the eye on the end of the gear lever **(see illustration)**.

7 It is now necessary to release the gear lever lower bearing retaining ring from the gear selector arm. A special tool is available for this purpose, but two screwdrivers, with the tips engaged in opposite slots in the bearing ring, can be used instead. To unlock the bearing ring, turn it a quarter-turn anti-clockwise **(see illustration)**.

8 The bearing can now be pushed up through the housing, and the gear lever can be withdrawn from inside the vehicle.

9 If desired, the bearing can be removed from the gear lever ball by pressing it downwards. To withdraw the bearing over the lever eye, rotate the bearing until the eye passes through the slots provided in the bearing.

10 Fit a new bearing using a reversal of the removal process. Ensure that the bearing is

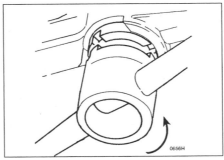

4.7 Turn the bearing ring anti-clockwise – special tool shown

pressed securely into position on the gear lever ball.

11 Refit the lever using a reversal of the removal process, bearing in mind the following points.

a) Grease the contact faces of the bearing before refitting.

b) Lower the gear lever into position, ensuring that the arrow on the gear lever grommet points towards the front of the vehicle.

c) Make sure that the gear lever grommet is correctly engaged with the gear selector arm and with the opening in the vehicle floor **(see illustration)**.

d) When engaging the bearing with the selector arm, make sure that the arrows or tabs (as applicable) on the top of the bearing point towards the rear of the vehicle.

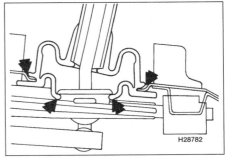

4.11 Gear lever grommet correctly engaged with the selector arm and vehicle floor

e) To lock the bearing in position in the selector arm, press down on the top of the bearing retaining tab locations until the tabs are heard to click into position.

f) Grease the selector rod pin before engaging it with the gear lever eye.

Automatic gearchange (SMG)

12 No information was available at the time of writing.

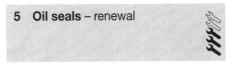

5   Oil seals – renewal

Input shaft oil seal

1 With the gearbox removed as described in Section 8, proceed as follows.

2 Remove the clutch release bearing and lever as described in Chapter 6.

3 Unscrew the securing bolts and withdraw the clutch release bearing guide sleeve from the gearbox bellhousing **(see illustration)**.

4 Note the fitted depth of the now-exposed input shaft oil seal.

5 Drill small holes in the oil seal (two small pilot holes should be provided at opposite points on the seal). Coat the end of the drill bit with grease to prevent any swarf from the holes entering the gearbox **(see illustration)**.

6 Using a small drift, tap one side of the seal (opposite to the hole) into the bellhousing as far as the stop.

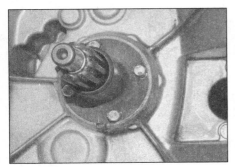

5.3 Undo the bolts securing the release bearing guide sleeve

5.5 Drill a small hole in the oil seal

5.7 Insert a self-tapping screw in to the hole, and pull the seal from place with pliers

5.17 Counterhold the output flange and undo the nut using a deep socket

5.18 Use a three-legged puller to remove the output flange

7 Screw a small self-tapping screw into the opposite side of the seal, and use pliers to pull out the seal **(see illustration)**.

8 Clean the oil seal seating surface.

9 Lubricate the lips of the new oil seal with a little clean gearbox oil, then carefully slide the seal over the input shaft into position in the bellhousing.

10 Tap the oil seal into the bellhousing to the previously-noted depth.

11 Refit the guide sleeve to the gearbox housing, tighten the retaining bolts securely, using a drop of locking compound on the threads of the bolts.

12 Refit the clutch release lever and bearing as described in Chapter 6.

13 Refit the gearbox as described in Section 8, then check the gearbox oil level as described in Section 2.

Output flange oil seal

Note: *Thread-locking compound will be required for the gearbox flange nut on refitting.*

14 Jack up the vehicle and support securely on axle stands (see *Jacking and vehicle support*).

15 Disconnect the propeller shaft from the gearbox flange, and support it clear of the gearbox using wire or string. See Chapter 8 for details.

16 Where applicable, prise the gearbox flange nut cover plate from the flange using a screwdriver. Discard the cover plate – it is

not required on refitting. If necessary, support the transmission and remove the transmission crossmember to improve access.

17 Counterhold the gearbox flange by bolting a forked or two-legged tool to two of the flange bolt holes, then unscrew the flange securing nut using a deep socket and extension bar **(see illustration)**.

18 Using a puller, draw the flange from the end of the gearbox output shaft **(see illustration)**. Be prepared for oil spillage.

19 Note the fitted depth of the oil seal then, then using an oil seal puller or remover (take care to avoid damage to the gearbox output shaft), pull/prise the oil seal from the gearbox casing **(see illustration)**.

20 Clean the oil seal seating surface.

21 Lubricate the lips of the new oil seal with a little clean gearbox oil, then carefully tap the seal into the gearbox casing to the to the previously-noted depth using a suitable tubular spacer or socket **(see illustration)**.

22 Refit the flange to the output shaft. **Note:** *To ease refitment of the flange, immerse it in hot water for a few minutes, then install it on the shaft.*

23 Tighten the flange nut to the Stage one torque setting, then slacken and remove the nut (Stage two). Coat the threads of the flange nut with thread-locking compound, then tighten the nut to the Stage three torque as specified. Counterhold the flange as during removal.

24 If a flange nut cover plate was originally

fitted, discard it. There is no need to fit a cover plate on refitting.

25 Reconnect the propeller shaft to the gearbox flange as described in Chapter 8, then check the gearbox oil level as described in Section 2, and lower the vehicle to the ground.

Gear selector shaft oil seal

Note: *A new selector shaft eye securing roll-pin will be required on refitting.*

26 Jack up the vehicle and support securely on axle stands (see *Jacking and vehicle support*).

27 Disconnect the propeller shaft from the gearbox flange, and support it clear of the gearbox using wire or string. Refer to Chapter 8 for details. For improved access, support the transmission, and remove the transmission crossmember.

28 Slide back the locking collar, then slide out the pin securing the gear selector shaft eye to the end of the gear selector shaft.

29 Pull the gear selector shaft eye (complete with gear linkage) off the end of the selector shaft, and move the linkage clear of the selector shaft.

30 Using a small flat-bladed screwdriver, prise the selector shaft oil seal from the gearbox casing.

31 Clean the oil seal seating surface, then tap the new seal into position using a small socket or tube of the correct diameter **(see illustration)**.

5.19 Carefully pull the seal from place

5.21 Tap the seal into place using a tubular spacer or socket which bears only on the hard outer edge of the seal

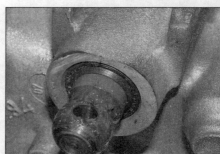

5.31 Tap the new selector shaft oil seal into position

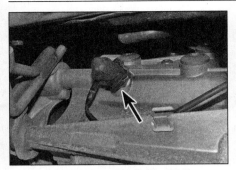

6.4 The reversing light switch

8.6 Prise up the clips, and slide the pin each side from the casing

8.10 Adapter plate retaining bolt

32 Check the condition of the rubber washer in the end of the selector shaft eye and renew if necessary.

33 Push the selector shaft eye back onto the end of the selector shaft, then align the holes in the eye and shaft and secure the eye to the shaft using the pin.

34 Slide the locking collar into position over the roll-pin.

35 Reconnect the propeller shaft to the gearbox flange as described in Chapter 8.

36 Check the gearbox oil level as described in Section 2, then lower the vehicle to the ground.

6 Reversing light switch – testing, removal and refitting

Testing

1 The reversing light circuit is controlled by a plunger-type switch screwed into the right-hand side (GS-17DG and 37DG) or left-hand side (GS-45DZ) of the gearbox casing. If a fault develops in the circuit, first ensure that the circuit fuse has not blown.

2 To test the switch, disconnect the wiring connector, and use a multimeter (set to the resistance function) or a battery-and-bulb test circuit to check that there is continuity between the switch terminals only when reverse gear is selected. If this is not the case, and there are no obvious breaks or other damage to the wires, the switch is faulty, and must be renewed.

Removal

3 Jack up the vehicle and support securely on axle stands (see *Jacking and vehicle support*).

4 Disconnect the wiring connector, then unscrew the switch from the gearbox casing **(see illustration)**.

Refitting

5 Screw the switch back into position in the gearbox housing and tighten it securely. Reconnect the wiring connector, and test the operation of the circuit.

6 Lower the vehicle to the ground.

7 Zero-Gear sensor – removal and refitting

1 On models equipped with Stop-Start system, a Zero-Gear sensor is fitted to the top of the gearbox casing. In order to access the sensor, remove the gearbox as described in Section 8.

2 Undo the 2 retaining bolts and remove the sensor.

3 Refitting is a reversal of removal, tightening the retaining bolts to their specified torque. **Note:** *If a new sensor has been fitted, it must be calibrated using BMW diagnostic equipment. Entrust this task to a BMW dealer or suitably equipped repairer.*

8 Manual gearbox – removal and refitting

Note: *This is an involved operation. Read through the procedure thoroughly before starting work, and ensure that adequate lifting tackle and/or jacking/support equipment is available.*

Removal

1 Disconnect the battery negative lead (see Chapter 5A).

2 Jack up the car and support securely on axle stands (see *Jacking and vehicle support*). Note that the car must be raised sufficiently to allow clearance for the gearbox to be removed from under the car. Undo the bolts and remove the engine/transmission undershields.

3 Remove the starter motor as described in Chapter 5A.

4 Remove the propeller shaft as described in Chapter 8.

5 Undo the nut and remove the undershield bracket from alongside the transmission.

6 Working under the car, prise up the retaining clips and extract the pin each side securing the gear lever support bracket to the transmission casing **(see illustration)**. Similarly, disconnect the selector rod pin from the end of the gear lever **(see illustration 4.6)**.

7 Working at the gearbox bellhousing, unscrew the nuts, and withdraw the clutch slave cylinder from the studs on the bellhousing. Support the slave cylinder clear of the working area, but do not strain the hose.

8 Note their fitted locations, then disconnect all wiring plugs, and release any wiring harnesses from the gearbox casing. Where applicable, disconnect the Zero-gear sensor wiring plug from the top of the gearbox housing.

9 On some diesel models, remove the exhaust mounting bracket from the rear of the transmission casing.

10 Where applicable, unscrew the bolt securing the engine/gearbox adapter plate to the right-hand side of the gearbox bellhousing and/or remove the flywheel lower cover plate **(see illustration)**.

11 Place a suitable block of wood between the front of the engine sump and the steering rack. Once the transmission is removed, the engine will tend to tip forwards.

12 Place a trolley jack under the gearbox casing, just behind the bellhousing. Use a block of wood to spread the load, then raise the jack to just take the weight of the gearbox.

13 Remove the crossmember and mountings from the rear of the transmission, and allow the transmission/engine assembly to lower slightly.

14 Unscrew the engine-to-gearbox bolts.

15 Slide the gearbox rearwards to disengage the input shaft from the clutch. Take care during this operation to ensure that the weight of the gearbox is not allowed to hang on the input shaft.

Refitting

16 Commence refitting by checking that the clutch friction disc is centralised as described in Chapter 6 (Clutch assembly – removal, inspection and refitting).

17 Before refitting the gearbox, it is advisable to inspect the clutch release bearing and lever as described in Chapter 6.

18 The remainder of the refitting procedure is a reversal of removal, bearing in mind the following points.

a) *Check that the gearbox positioning dowels are securely in place at the rear of the engine.*
b) *Tighten all fixings to the specified torque.*
c) *Lightly grease the gear selector arm pivot pin and the gear selector rod pin before refitting.*
d) *Reconnect the propeller shaft to the gearbox flange as described in Chapter 8.*
e) *Refit the starter motor as described in Chapter 5A.*

9 Manual gearbox overhaul – general information

1 Overhauling a manual gearbox is a difficult and involved job for the DIY home mechanic. In addition to dismantling and reassembling many small parts, clearances must be precisely measured and, if necessary, changed by selecting shims and spacers. Internal gearbox components are also often difficult to obtain, and in many instances, extremely expensive. Because of this, if the gearbox develops a fault or becomes noisy, the best course of action is to have the unit overhauled by a specialist repairer, or to obtain an exchange reconditioned unit. Be aware that some gearbox repairs can be carried out with the gearbox in the car.

2 Nevertheless, it is not impossible for the more experienced mechanic to overhaul the gearbox, provided the special tools are available, and the job is done in a deliberate step-by-step manner, so that nothing is overlooked.

3 The tools necessary for an overhaul include internal and external circlip pliers, bearing pullers, a slide hammer, a set of pin punches, a dial test indicator, and possibly a hydraulic press. In addition, a large, sturdy workbench and a vice will be required.

4 During dismantling of the gearbox, make careful notes of how each component is fitted, to make reassembly easier and more accurate.

5 Before dismantling the gearbox, it will help if you have some idea what area is malfunctioning. Certain problems can be closely related to specific areas in the gearbox, which can make component examination and renewal easier. Refer to the Fault finding Section at the end of this manual for more information.

Chapter 7 Part B:
Automatic transmission

Contents

Degrees of difficulty

Easy, suitable for novice with little experience	Fairly easy, suitable for beginner with some experience	Fairly difficult, suitable for competent DIY mechanic	Difficult, suitable for experienced DIY mechanic	Very difficult, suitable for expert DIY or professional

Specifications

Transmission type

Petrol engines	GA6HP19Z
4-cylinder diesel engines	GA6HP19Z
6-cylinder diesel engines	GA6HP26Z

Torque wrench settings

Note: On some fixings different grades of bolt can be used; the grade of each bolt is stamped on the bolt head. Ensure that each bolt is tightened to the correct torque for its grade.

	Nm	lbf ft
Engine-to-transmission bolts:		
All engines:		
Hexagon bolts:		
M8	24	18
M10	45	33
M12	82	61
Torx bolts:		
M8	21	15
M10	42	31
M12	72	53
Output flange nut: *		
Stage 1	190	140
Stage 2	Slacken 360°	
Stage 3	120	89
Torque-converter-to-driveplate bolts:		
M8	26	19
M10:		
8.8	49	36
10.9	56	41
Transmission crossmember-to-body bolts:		
M8	21	15
M10	42	31
Transmission mounting-to-gearbox nuts:		
M8	21	15
M10	42	31
Transmission oil drain plug*	8	6
Transmission oil filler/level plug:		
M18	35	26
M30	80	59
*Do not re-use		

Caution: All aluminium fastenings must be renewed. If in doubt, try to attract the bolt/stud with a magnet. Aluminium is not magnetic.

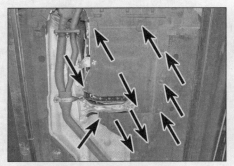

2.2 Undo the fasteners and remove the undershield

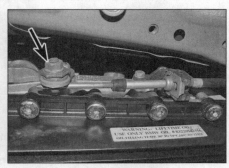

2.3a Undo the cable clamping nut

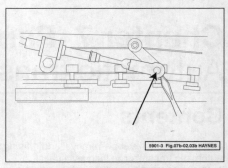

2.3b Prise the cable end fitting from the transmission lever

1 General Information

1 A six-speed automatic transmission is fitted, consisting of a torque converter, an epicyclic geartrain and hydraulically-operated clutches and brakes.

2 The torque converter provides a fluid coupling between engine and transmission, which acts as a clutch, and also provides a degree of torque multiplication when accelerating.

3 The epicyclic geartrain provides either of the five/six forward or one reverse gear ratio, according to which of its component parts are held stationary or allowed to turn. The components of the geartrain are held or released by brakes and clutches which are activated by a hydraulic control unit. A fluid pump within the transmission provides the necessary hydraulic pressure to operate the brakes and clutches.

4 Driver control of the transmission is by a four-position selector lever, incorporating a Steptronic function. The transmission has 'park', 'reverse', 'neutral' and 'drive' positions. The Drive position (D) provides automatic changing throughout the range of all forward gear ratios, and is the position selected for normal driving. An automatic kickdown facility shifts the transmission down a gear if the accelerator pedal is fully depressed.

5 Certain models are available with Steptronic gearchange where the driver is able to induce gearchanges with a simple movement of the lever – forward to change up, and back to change down.

6 Due to the complexity of the automatic transmission, any repair or overhaul work must be left to a BMW dealer or specialist with the necessary special equipment for fault diagnosis and repair. The contents of the following Sections are therefore confined to supplying general information, and any service information and instructions that can be used by the owner.

2 Gear selector lever – removal and refitting

Removal

1 Jack up the car and support securely on axle stands (see *Jacking and vehicle support*). Ensure the gear lever is in position P.

2 Working underneath the vehicle, undo the fasteners and remove the transmission undershield **(see illustration)**.

3 The selector cable is secured to the transmission lever either by a nut or a push-on clip. Either slacken the clamping nut, or prise the cable end fitted from the lever as applicable **(see illustrations)**.

4 Prise out the clip securing the selector cable

to the transmission bracket, or unbolt the bracket from the transmission as applicable.

5 Remove the centre console as described in Chapter 11.

6 Note their fitted positions, then disconnect any wiring plugs attached to the gear lever assembly.

7 Undo the three bolts securing the lever assembly to the floor, manoeuvre the assembly up from its location **(see illustration)**. Note that the lever assembly is only available complete with the selector cable. No further dismantling is recommended.

Refitting

8 Refitting is a reversal of removal, noting the following points:

a) *Prior to refitting the gear knob, push the gaiter down the lever until the locking groove in the lever is exposed.*

b) *On completion, adjust the selector cable as described in Section 3.*

3 Gear selector cable – removal, refitting and adjustment

Removal and refitting

1 The selector cable can only be renewed complete with the selector lever assembly. Removal is described in Section 2.

Adjustment

2 Move the selector lever to position P. To move the lever when the battery is disconnected, prise up the lever gaiter and depress the release catch **(see illustration)**.

Selector cable with clamp nut

3 If not already done, loosen the clamp nut securing the cable to the end fitting (the car should be raised for access).

4 Push the operating lever on the transmission away from the cable bracket on the transmission (towards the Park position).

5 Press the end of the cable in the opposite

2.7 Undo the 3 bolts

3.2 Depress the catch to release the lever when the battery is disconnected

3.5a Gently press the cable towards the bracket...

3.5b... and tighten the clamping nut

3.6 Slacken the cable end fitting bolt

direction (ie, towards the cable bracket), then release the cable, counterhold the clamp and tighten the clamp nut (see illustrations).

Selector cable with push-on clip

6 Slacken the adjustment bolt on the cable end fitting, then push the lever on the transmission forwards in to the Park position (see illustration).

7 Ensure the lever inside the vehicle is in the 'P' position, then pull the inner cable towards the rear of the vehicle slightly, and tighten the adjustment bolt securely.

All models

8 Check that the cable is correctly adjusted by starting the engine, applying the brakes firmly, and moving the selector lever through all the selector positions.

---

4 Fluid seals – renewal

Torque converter seal

1 Remove the transmission and the torque converter as described in Section 5.

2 Using a hooked tool, prise the old oil seal from the transmission bellhousing. Alternatively, drill a small hole, then screw a self-tapping screw into the seal and use pliers to pull out the seal.

3 Lubricate the lip of the new seal with clean fluid, then carefully drive it into place using a large socket or tube.

4 Remove the old O-ring seal from the input shaft, and slide a new one into place. Apply a smear of petroleum jelly to the new O-ring.

5 Refit the torque converter and transmission as described in Section 5.

Output flange oil seal

6 Renewal of the oil seal involves partial dismantling of the transmission, which is a complex operation – see Section 6. Oil seal renewal should be entrusted to a BMW dealer or specialist.

---

5 Automatic transmission – removal and refitting

Note: *This is an involved operation. Read through the procedure thoroughly before starting work, and ensure that adequate lifting tackle and/or jacking/support equipment is available. A suitable tool will be required to align the torque converter when refitting the transmission, and new fluid pipe O-rings may be required.*

Removal

1 Disconnect the battery negative lead – see Chapter 5A.

2 Jack up the car and support securely on axle stands (see *Jacking and vehicle support*). Note that the car must be raised sufficiently to allow clearance for the transmission to be removed from under the car. Undo the bolts and remove the engine/transmission undershield from the vehicle.

3 Undo the bolts and remove the front reinforcement brace/plate from under the transmission.

4 Remove the starter motor as described in Chapter 5A.

5 Remove the exhaust system and heat shield (see Chapter 4A or 4B), then unbolt the exhaust mounting crossmember from under the car.

6 Remove the propeller shaft as described in Chapter 8.

7 Disconnect the selector cable from the transmission with reference to Section 3.

8 Disconnect the wiring plugs under the front of the transmission bellhousing, unclip the wiring harness, then undo the 3 bolts and remove the cover plate (see illustrations).

9 Unscrew the three torque converter bolts, turning the crankshaft using a spanner or socket on the pulley hub bolt for access to each bolt in turn (see illustration).

10 Undo the nuts and remove the brackets from the right-hand side of the transmission sump pan, then undo the 3 bolts and remove

5.8a Unclip the wiring harness and plugs...

5.8b... then undo the bolts and remove the cover plate

5.9 Undo the torque converter bolts

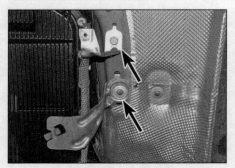

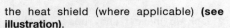

5.10 Remove the brackets adjacent to the transmission

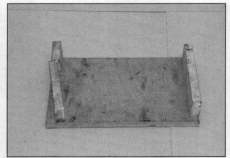

5.11a We made a wooden platform...

5.11b... which supported the transmission on the sump pan flange each side

the heat shield (where applicable) **(see illustration)**.

11 Support the transmission using a trolley jack and interposed blocks of wood **(see illustrations)**. The transmission sump is plastic – ensure the transmission is supported around the edge of the sump pan.

Caution: The transmission is heavy, so ensure that it is adequately supported.

12 Undo the bolts/nuts and remove the crossmember from the rear of the transmission **(see illustration)**.

13 Place a suitable block of wood between the engine sump casing and the steering rack, as once the transmission is removed, the engine will be front-heavy.

14 Lower the transmission a little, then rotate the collar anti-clockwise and pull the wiring plug from the transmission casing **(see**

illustration). Release the wiring harness clips on the transmission casing.

15 Unbolt the fluid cooler pipe brackets and clamps. Undo the clamp bolt and disconnect the fluid pipes – be prepared for fluid spillage **(see illustration)**. Plug/seal the openings to prevent contamination.

16 Unscrew the engine-to-transmission bolts, and recover the washers, then slide the transmission rearwards. Ensure the torque converter comes away from the driveplate, and stays in place in the transmission.

17 Insert a suitable metal or wooden lever through the slot in the bottom of the bellhousing to retain the torque converter. As the transmission is released from the engine, check to make sure that the engine is adequately supported, and no hoses are trapped.

18 Lower the transmission and carefully withdraw it from under the car, making sure that the torque converter is held in position. If the transmission is to be removed for some time, ensure that the engine is adequately supported in the engine compartment. Take measures to ensure the torque converter is prevented from sliding forwards **(see illustration)**.

Refitting

19 Ensure that the transmission locating dowels are in position on the engine.

20 Before mating the transmission with the engine, it is essential that the torque converter is perfectly aligned with the driveplate.

21 Turn the driveplate to align one of the torque converter-to-driveplate bolt holes.

22 Ensure that the transmission is adequately supported, and manoeuvre it into position under the car.

23 Refit and tighten the engine-to-transmission bolts.

24 Refit the torque converter-to-driveplate bolt. Tighten the bolt to the specified torque.

25 Turn the crankshaft as during removal for access to the remaining two torque converter-to-driveplate bolt locations. Refit and tighten the bolts.

26 Further refitting is a reversal of removal, bearing in mind the following points.

a) *Tighten all fixings to the specified torques, where applicable.*

b) *Check the condition of the transmission fluid pipe O-rings and renew if necessary.*

c) *Refit the propeller shaft (see Chapter 8).*

d) *Refit the starter motor (see Chapter 5A).*

e) *Reconnect and adjust the selector cable as described in Section 3.*

f) *On completion, check the transmission fluid as described in Section 8.*

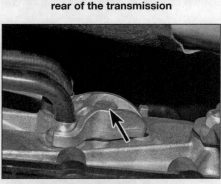

5.12 Remove the crossmember from the rear of the transmission

5.14 Rotate the collar anti-clockwise and plug the wiring plug from the casing

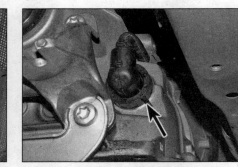

5.15 Fluid cooler pipe clamp bolt

5.18 We bolted a metal bar over the bellhousing opening to prevent the torque converter sliding forwards

6 Automatic transmission overhaul – general information

1 In the event of a fault occurring with the transmission, it is first necessary to determine whether it is of an electrical, mechanical or hydraulic nature, and to do this special test equipment is required. It is therefore essential to have the work carried out by a BMW dealer or suitably-equipped specialist if a transmission fault is suspected.

2 Do not remove the transmission from the car for possible repair before professional fault diagnosis has been carried out, since most tests require the transmission to be in the car.

7 Electronic components/ sensors – removal and refitting

1 The turbine speed sensor, output speed sensor, transmission range switch and electronic control module (ECM) are all contained within the transmission casing. Removal of the components involves removal and the sump and partial dismantling of the transmission. Therefore renewal of these components should be entrusted to a BMW dealer or suitably equipped specialist.

8 Automatic transmission fluid level check

Note: *There is no recommendation in the BMW service schedule for the transmission fluid to be checked, or renewed. However, it may be prudent to check the fluid level every few years – especially if the vehicle is used on mostly short journeys or for towing. The fluid level can only be accurately checked using BMW diagnostic equipment. The following procedure will ensure the transmission has sufficient fluid for the vehicle to be gently driven to a BMW dealer or suitably-equipped specialist, where the level can be accurately checked.*

1 The fluid level is checked by removing the filler/level plug from the side of the transmission casing. If desired, jack up the car and support on axle stands (see *Jacking and vehicle support*) to improve access, but make sure that the car is level.

2 Undo the bolts and remove the undershield beneath the transmission **(see illustration 2.1).**

3 Place a container under the transmission fluid pan, then unscrew the filler/level plug **(see illustration)**. Recover the sealing ring (where fitted).

4 The fluid level should be up to the lower edge of the filler/level plug hole.

5 If necessary, top-up the fluid until it overflows from the plug hole.

6 Start the engine and allow it to idle. With

8.3 Filler plug is located at the left-hand rear of the transmission

the brake pedal depressed, shift through the gears, and return it to Park. The oil level must be checked with the engine running and the transmission oil up to the temperature indicated on a sticker affixed to the transmission casing, adjacent to the filler hole. On the vehicles we examined, the temperature range was between 30° C and 50° C. This temperature is determined by plugging in suitable diagnostic equipment into the vehicles EOBD connector, located in the driver's footwell side panel (see Chapter 4A or 4B). In the absence of suitable equipment, err on the side of caution – check the level before the engine/transmission gets to normal operating temperature, then get the level checked again by a BMW dealer or suitably-equipped specialist.

7 Add oil until it begins to run out of the filler hole. Depress the brake pedal and check the level again.

8 Refit the filler/level plug, using a new sealing ring (where fitted); tighten to the specified torque.

9 Automatic transmission fluid renewal

Note: *There is no recommendation in the BMW service schedule for the transmission fluid to be checked, or renewed. However, it may be prudent to renew the fluid level every few years – especially if the vehicle is used on mostly short journeys or for towing.*

1 The transmission fluid should be drained with the transmission at operating temperature. If the car has just been driven at least 20 miles, the transmission can be considered warm.

2 Immediately after driving the car, park it on a level surface, apply the handbrake. If desired, jack up the car and support on axle

9.4 Transmission fluid drain plug

stands (see *Jacking and vehicle support*) to improve access, but make sure that the car is level.

3 Undo the bolts and remove the undershield beneath the transmission **(see illustration 2.1).**

4 Slacken the transmission fluid pan drain plug about half a turn **(see illustration)**. Position a draining container under the drain plug, then remove the plug completely. If possible, try to keep the plug pressed into the fluid pan while unscrewing it by hand the last couple of turns.

> **HAYNES HiNT**
> *As the plug releases from the threads, move it away sharply so the stream of fluid issuing from the fluid pan runs into the container, not up your sleeve.*

5 Discard the drain plug – BMW insist that a new one is fitted.

6 Fit the new drain plug and tighten to the specified torque.

7 With reference to Section 8, fill the transmission with the specified quantity of the correct type of fluid (see Chapter 1A or 1B) – fill the transmission through filler/level plug hole.

8 Check the fluid level as described in Section 8, bearing in mind that the new fluid will not yet be at operating temperature.

9 With the handbrake applied, and the transmission selector lever in position P, start the engine and run it at idle for a few minutes to warm-up the new fluid, then recheck the fluid level as described in Section 8. Note that it may be necessary to drain off a little fluid once the new fluid has reached operating temperature.

Chapter 8
Final drive, driveshafts and propeller shaft

Contents

Degrees of difficulty

Easy, suitable for novice with little experience	**Fairly easy,** suitable for beginner with some experience	**Fairly difficult,** suitable for competent DIY mechanic	**Difficult,** suitable for experienced DIY mechanic	**Very difficult,** suitable for expert DIY or professional

Specifications

Final drive
Type . . . . Unsprung, attached to rear suspension crossmember

Driveshaft
Type . . . . Steel shafts with ball-and-cage type constant velocity joints at each end

Constant velocity joint grease capacity . . . . 80g in each joint

Propeller shaft
Type . . . . Two-piece tubular shaft with centre bearing, centre and rear universal joint. Front joint is either rubber coupling or universal joint (depending on model)

Torque wrench settings

Note: *On some fixings different grades of bolt can be used; the grade of each bolt is stamped on the bolt head. Ensure that each bolt is tightened to the correct torque for its grade.*

	Nm	lbf ft
Final drive unit		
Mounting bolts:		
Front bolt	100	74
Rear bolts	165	122
Oil filler plug	60	44
Vibration damper on bracket (where fitted)	68	50
Driveshaft		
Driveshaft retaining nut: *		
M24	250	185
M27	300	221
Shaft to final drive flange bolts: *		
M8	52	38
M10	70	52
M12	120	89

Torque wrench settings (continued)

	Nm	lbf ft
Propeller shaft		
Flexible disc to transmission: *		
M10:		
8.8...	48	35
10.9..	64	47
ZNS (external Torx) bolts/nuts:		
M10:		
Stage 1	20	15
Stage 2	Angle-tighten a further 90°	
M12:		
Stage 1	55	41
Stage 2	Angle-tighten a further 90°	
Shaft/coupling to final drive: *		
M10:		
With ribbed teeth under head:		
Stage 1	40	30
Stage 2	Angle-tighten a further 45°	
Without ribbed teeth under head:		
Stage 1	20	15
Stage 2	Angle-tighten a further 90°	
M12:		
Stage 1	55	41
Stage 2	Angle-tighten a further 90°	
Support bearing bracket nuts/bolts	21	15
Roadwheels		
Wheel bolts......................................	120	89

Do not re-use

1 General Information

1 Power is transmitted from the transmission to the rear axle by a two-piece propeller shaft, joined behind the centre bearing by a 'slip joint,' a sliding, splined coupling. The slip joint allows slight fore-and-aft movement of the propeller shaft. The forward end of the propeller shaft is attached to the output flange of the transmission by a flexible rubber coupling. On some models, a vibration damper is mounted between the front of the propeller shaft and coupling. The middle of the propeller shaft is supported by the centre bearing which is bolted to the vehicle body. Universal joints are located at the centre bearing and at the rear end of the propeller shaft, to compensate for movement of the transmission and differential on their mountings and for any flexing of the chassis.

2 The final drive assembly includes the drive pinion, the ring gear, the differential and the output flanges. The drive pinion, which drives the ring gear, is also known as the differential input shaft and is connected to the propeller shaft via an input flange. The differential is bolted to the ring gear and drives the rear wheels through a pair of output flanges bolted to driveshafts with constant velocity (CV) joints at either end. The differential allows the wheels to turn at different speeds when cornering.

3 The driveshafts deliver power from the final drive unit output flanges to the rear wheels.

The driveshafts are equipped with constant velocity (CV) joints at each end. The inner CV joints are bolted to the differential flanges, and the outer CV joints engage the splines of the wheel hubs, and are secured by a large nut.

4 Major repair work on the differential assembly components (drive pinion, ring-and-pinion and differential) requires many special tools and a high degree of expertise, and therefore should not be attempted by the home mechanic. If major repairs become necessary, we recommend that they be performed by a BMW service department or other suitably-equipped automotive engineer.

2 Final drive unit – removal and refitting

Note: *New propeller shaft rear coupling nuts and driveshaft retaining bolts will be required on refitting.*

Removal

1 Chock the front wheels. Jack up the rear of the vehicle and support it on axle stands (see *Jacking and vehicle support*). Remove both rear wheels.

2 On 6-cylinder diesel models, remove the rear exhaust system.

3 Using paint or a suitable marker pen, make alignment marks between the propeller shaft and final drive unit flange. Unscrew the bolts/nuts securing the propeller shaft to the final drive unit and discard them; new ones must be used on refitting.

4 Slacken and remove the retaining bolts and plates securing the right-hand driveshaft to the final drive unit flange and support the driveshaft by tying it to the vehicle underbody using a piece of wire. **Note:** *Do not allow the driveshaft to hang under its own weight as the CV joint may be damaged. Discard the bolts, new ones should be used on refitting.*

5 Disconnect the left-hand driveshaft from the final drive as described in Paragraph 4.

6 Undo the nuts/bolts and remove the heat shield panel from the left-hand end of the tension strut beneath the final drive input shaft flange.

7 Move a jack and interposed block of wood into position and raise it so that it is supporting the weight of the final drive unit.

8 Making sure the final drive unit is safely supported, slacken and remove the two bolts securing the front of the unit in position and the single bolt securing the rear of the unit in position.

9 Carefully lower the final drive unit out of position and remove it from underneath the vehicle. Examine the final drive unit mounting rubbers for signs of wear or damage and renew if necessary.

Refitting

10 Refitting is a reversal of removal noting the following.
a) *Raise the final drive unit into position and engage it with the propeller shaft rear joint, making sure the marks made prior to removal are correctly aligned.*
b) *Insert the final drive unit front mounting bolts, then the rear bolt.*

c) Tighten the final drive unit front mounting bolts to the specified torque setting, followed by the rear one.
d) Fit the new propeller shaft joint bolts/nuts and tighten them to the specified torque.
e) Fit the new driveshaft joint retaining bolts and plates and tighten them to the specified torque.
f) On completion, refill/top-up the final drive unit with oil as described in Section 10.

3 Final drive unit oil seals – renewal

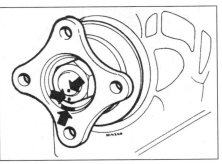

3.2 Make alignment marks on the flange, the pinion shaft and nut to ensure proper reassembly

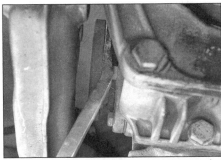

3.11 Use a suitable lever to remove the driveshaft flange from the final drive unit

Propeller shaft flange oil seal

Note: A new flange nut retaining plate will be required.
1 Remove the final drive unit as described in Section 2 and secure the unit in a vice.
2 Remove the retaining plate and make alignment marks between the propeller flange nut, the drive flange and pinion (see illustration). Discard the retaining plate a new one must be used on refitting.
3 Hold the drive flange stationary by bolting a length of metal bar to it, then unscrew the nut noting the exact number of turns necessary to remove it.
4 Using a suitable puller, draw the drive flange from the pinion and remove the dust cover. If the dust cover shows signs of wear, renew it.
5 Lever the oil seal from the final drive casing with a screwdriver. Wipe clean the oil seal seating.
6 Smear a little oil on the sealing lip of the new oil seal, then press it squarely into the casing until flush with the outer face. If necessary the seal can be tapped into position using a metal tube which bears only on its hard outer edge.
7 Fit the dust cover and locate the drive

flange on the pinion aligning the marks made on removal. Refit the flange nut, screwing it on by the exact number of turns counted on removal, so that the alignment marks align.
Caution: Do not overtighten the flange nut. If the nut is overtightened, the collapsible spacer behind the flange will be deformed necessitating its renewal. This is a complex operation requiring the final drive unit to be dismantled.
8 Secure the nut in position with the new retaining plate, tapping it squarely into position.
9 Refit the final drive unit as described in Section 2 and refill it with oil as described in Section 10.

Driveshaft flange oil seal

Note: New driveshaft joint retaining bolts and a driveshaft flange circlip will be required.
10 Slacken and remove the bolts securing the driveshaft constant velocity joint to the final drive unit and recover the retaining plates. Position the driveshaft clear of the flange and tie it to the vehicle underbody using a piece of wire. Note: Do not allow the driveshaft to hang under its own weight as the CV joint may be damaged.
11 Using a suitable lever, carefully prise the driveshaft flange out from the final drive unit taking care not to damage the dust seal or casing (see illustration). Remove the flange and recover the dust seal. If the dust seal shows signs of damage, renew it.
12 Carefully lever the oil seal out from the

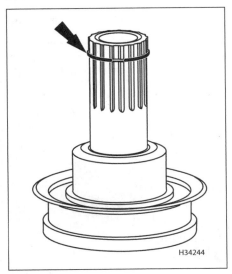

3.13 Renew the output flange circlip

3.15 Install the new seal using a socket which bears only on the hard outer edge of the seal

final drive unit. Wipe clean the oil seal seating.
13 With the flange removed, prise out the circlip from the end of the splined shaft (see illustration).
14 Fit a new circlip, making sure it is correctly located in the splined shaft groove.
15 Smear a little final drive oil on the sealing lip of the new oil seal, then press it squarely into the casing until it reaches its stop. If necessary the seal can be tapped into position using a metal tube which bears only on its hard outer edge (see illustration).
16 Fit the dust cover and insert the drive flange. Push the drive flange fully into position and check that it is securely retained by the circlip.
17 Align the driveshaft with the flange and refit the new retaining bolts and plates, tightening them to the specified torque.
18 Refill the final drive unit with oil as described in Section 10.

4 Driveshaft – removal and refitting

Note: A new driveshaft retaining nut and bolts will be required on refitting.

Removal

1 Remove the wheel trim/hub cap (as applicable) and slacken the driveshaft retaining nut with the vehicle resting on its wheels. Also slacken the wheel bolts.
2 Chock the front wheels, then jack up the rear of the vehicle and support it on axle stands (see Jacking and vehicle support).
3 Remove the relevant rear roadwheel.
4 If the left-hand driveshaft is to be removed, remove the exhaust system tailpipe to improve access (see the relevant Part of Chapter 4A).
5 Slacken and remove the left- and right-hand anti-roll bar mountings and pivot the bar downwards (see Chapter 10).
6 Unscrew and remove the driveshaft nut.
7 Make alignment marks, then slacken and remove the bolts securing the driveshaft constant velocity joint to the final drive unit

4.7 Make alignment marks then remove the Torx bolts

4.10 When the driveshaft nut has been tightened, stake the nut using a punch

and recover the retaining plates (where fitted) **(see illustration)**. Position the driveshaft clear of the flange and tie it to the vehicle underbody using a piece of wire. **Note:** *Do not allow the driveshaft to hang under its own weight as the CV joint may be damaged.*

8 Withdraw the driveshaft outer constant velocity joint from the hub assembly. The outer joint will be very tight, tap the joint out of the hub using a soft-faced mallet. If this fails to free it from the hub, the joint will have to be pressed out using a suitable tool which is bolted to the hub.

9 Remove the driveshaft from underneath the vehicle.

Refitting

10 Refitting is the reverse of removal noting the following points.

a) Lubricate the nut-to-wheel bearing contact

area and tighten the nut to the specified torque. Do not oil the threads. If necessary, wait until the vehicle is lowered to the ground and then tighten the nut to the specified torque. Once tightened, use a hammer and punch to stake the nut **(see illustration)**.

b) Fit new inner joint retaining bolts and plates (where fitted) and tighten to the specified torque.

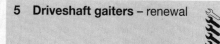

5   Driveshaft gaiters – renewal

1 Remove the driveshaft (see Section 4).
2 Clean the driveshaft and mount it in a vice.
3 Release the two inner joint gaiter retaining

clips and free the gaiter and dust cover from the joint **(see illustration)**.

4 Lever off the sealing cover from the end of the inner constant velocity (CV) joint **(see illustration)**.

5 Scoop out excess grease and remove the inner joint circlip from the end of the driveshaft **(see illustration)**.

6 Securely support the joint inner member and tap the driveshaft out of position using a hammer and suitable drift **(see illustration)**. If the joint is a tight fit, a suitable puller will be required to draw off the joint. Do not dismantle the inner joint.

7 With the joint removed, slide the inner gaiter and dust cover off from the end of the driveshaft **(see illustration)**.

8 Release the outer joint gaiter retaining clips then slide the gaiter along the shaft and remove it.

9 Thoroughly clean the constant velocity joints using paraffin, or a suitable solvent, and dry thoroughly. Carry out a visual inspection as follows.

10 Move the inner splined driving member from side-to-side to expose each ball in turn at the top of its track. Examine the balls for cracks, flat spots or signs of surface pitting.

11 Inspect the ball tracks on the inner and outer members. If the tracks have widened, the balls will no longer be a tight fit. At the same time check the ball cage windows for wear or cracking between the windows.

12 If on inspection any of the constant velocity joint components are found to be worn or damaged, it must be renewed. The inner joint is available separately but if the outer joint is worn it will be necessary to renew the complete joint and driveshaft assembly. If the joints are in satisfactory condition, obtain new gaiter repair kits which contain gaiters, retaining clips, an inner constant velocity joint circlip and the correct type and quantity of grease required.

13 Tape over the splines on the end of the driveshaft.

14 Slide the new outer gaiter onto the end of the driveshaft.

15 Pack the outer joint with the grease supplied in the gaiter kit. Work the grease well into the bearing tracks whilst twisting the joint, and fill the rubber gaiter with any excess.

5.3 Release the gaiter retaining clips and slide the gaiter down the shaft

5.4 Carefully remove the sealing cover from the inner end of the joint

5.5 Remove the inner joint circlip from the driveshaft

5.6 Support the inner joint inner member then tap the driveshaft out of position...

5.7... and slide off the gaiter

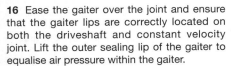

5.20a Fill the inner joint with the grease supplied...

5.20b... and work it into the bearing tracks

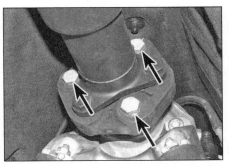

6.3 Undo the three bolts/nuts (arrowed)

16 Ease the gaiter over the joint and ensure that the gaiter lips are correctly located on both the driveshaft and constant velocity joint. Lift the outer sealing lip of the gaiter to equalise air pressure within the gaiter.

17 Fit the large metal retaining clip to the gaiter. Pull the retaining clip tight then bend it back to secure it in position and cut off any excess clip. Secure the small retaining clip using the same procedure.

18 Engage the new inner gaiter with its dust cover and slide the assembly onto the driveshaft.

19 Remove the tape from the driveshaft splines and fit the inner constant velocity joint. Press the joint fully onto the shaft and secure it in position with a new circlip.

20 Work the grease supplied fully into the inner joint and fill the gaiter with any excess **(see illustrations)**.

21 Slide the inner gaiter into position and press the dust cover onto the joint, making sure the retaining bolt holes are correctly aligned. Lift the outer sealing lip of the gaiter, to equalise air pressure within the gaiter, and secure it in position with the retaining clips.

22 Apply a smear of suitable sealant (BMW recommend BMW sealing gel) and press the new sealing cover fully onto the end of the inner joint.

23 Check that both constant velocity joints are free to move easily then refit the driveshaft as described in Section 4.

6 Propeller shaft – removal and refitting

Removal

1 Chock the front wheels. Jack up the rear of the vehicle and support it on axle stands (see *Jacking and vehicle support*).

2 Remove the exhaust system and heat shield as described in the relevant Part of Chapter 4. Where necessary, unbolt the exhaust system mounting bracket(s) in order to gain the necessary clearance required to remove the propeller shaft.

3 Make alignment marks between the shaft, transmission flange and rubber coupling.

Slacken and remove the nuts and bolts securing the coupling to the transmission **(see illustration)**. Discard the bolts and nuts – new ones should be used on refitting.

4 Using paint or a suitable marker pen, make alignment marks between the propeller shaft (or rubber coupling on diesel models) and final drive unit flange. Unscrew the bolts securing the propeller shaft (or rubber coupling on diesel models) to the final drive unit and discard them; new ones must be used on refitting **(see illustrations)**.

5 With the aid of an assistant, support the propeller shaft then unscrew the centre support bearing bracket retaining bolts **(see illustration)**. Lower the centre of the shaft and disengage it from the transmission and final drive unit. Remove the shaft from underneath the vehicle. **Note:** *Do not separate*

the two halves of the shaft without first making alignment marks. If the shafts are incorrectly joined, the propeller shaft assembly may become imbalanced, leading to noise and vibration during operation.

6 Inspect the rubber coupling (where fitted), the support bearing and shaft universal joints as described in Sections 7, 8 and 9. Inspect the transmission flange locating pin and propeller shaft bush for signs of wear or damage and renew as necessary.

Refitting

7 Apply a smear of molybdenum disulphide grease (BMW recommend Molykote Longterm 2) to the transmission pin and shaft bush and manoeuvre the shaft into position **(see illustration)**.

8 Align the marks made prior to removal and

6.4a Undo the bolts securing the final drive flange to the propeller shaft

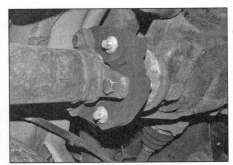

6.4b On diesel models, a rubber coupling is fitted between the propeller shaft and the final drive flange

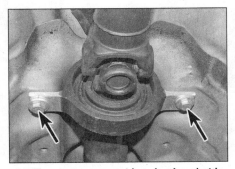

6.5 The centre support bearing bracket is secured by two bolts (arrowed)

6.7 Apply molybdenum disulphide grease to the transmission pin

7.4 Coupling-to-propeller shaft retaining bolts (arrowed)

engage the shaft with the transmission and final drive unit flanges. With the marks correctly aligned, refit the support bracket retaining bolts, tightening them lightly only at this stage.
9 Fit new retaining bolts to the rear coupling of the propeller shaft and tighten them to the specified torque.
10 Insert the new bolts and fit the new retaining nuts. Tighten them to the specified torque, noting that the nut/bolt should only be rotated on the flange side to avoid stressing the rubber coupling.
11 Tighten the support bracket bolts to the specified torque.
12 Refit the exhaust system and associated components as described in Chapter 4A or 4B.

7	Propeller shaft rubber coupling – check and renewal

Check

1 Firmly apply the handbrake, then jack up the front of the vehicle and support it on axle stands (see *Jacking and vehicle support*).
2 Closely examine the rubber coupling linking the propeller shaft to the transmission, looking

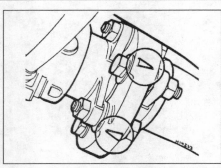

7.5 If the coupling has directional arrows, make sure the arrows are pointing towards the propeller shaft/transmission flanges and not the bolts heads

for signs of damage such as cracking or splitting or for signs of general deterioration. If necessary, renew the coupling as follows.

Renewal

3 Remove the propeller shaft as described in Section 6.
4 Slacken and remove the nuts securing the coupling to the shaft and remove it **(see illustration)**.
5 Fit the new rubber coupling noting that the arrows on the side of the coupling must point towards the propeller shaft/transmission flanges **(see illustration)**. Fit the new retaining nuts and tighten them to the specified torque.
6 Refit the propeller shaft as described in Section 6.

8	Propeller shaft support bearing – check and renewal

Check

1 Wear in the support bearing will lead to noise and vibration when the vehicle is driven. The bearing is best checked with the propeller shaft removed (see Section 6). To gain access

to the bearing with the shaft in position, remove the exhaust system and heat shields as described in the relevant Part of Chapter 4.
2 Rotate the bearing and check that it turns smoothly with no sign of freeplay; if it's difficult to turn, or if it has a gritty feeling, renew it. Also inspect the rubber portion. If it's cracked or deteriorated, renew it.

Renewal

3 Remove the propeller shaft as described in Section 6.
4 Make alignment marks between the front and rear sections of the propeller shaft then detach the rubber gaiter from the groove on the shaft, and pull the two halves of the shaft apart. Recover the damper ring from the end of the shaft **(see illustrations)**.
5 Release the rubber gaiter from the groove on the bearing support.
6 Draw the bearing and support bracket off from the propeller shaft using a suitable puller and a hydraulic press.
7 Firmly support the support bearing bracket and press out the bearing with a suitable tubular spacer.
8 Fit the new bearing to the bracket and press it into position using a tubular spacer which bears only on the bearing outer race.
9 Press the bearing and support fully onto the propeller shaft using a tubular spacer which bears only on the bearing inner race. The collar must point in the direction of travel.
10 Fit the smaller diameter of the rubber gaiter into the groove on the centre bearing.
11 Apply a smear of molybdenum disulphide grease (BMW recommend Molykote Longterm 2) to the splines and ensure the damper ring is in place.
12 Align the marks made prior to separation and joint the front and rear sections of the propeller shaft. Refit the rubber gaiter to the groove on the propeller shaft.
13 Refit the propeller shaft as described in Section 6.

8.4a Pull back the gaiter, then pull the halves of the shaft apart

8.4b Recover the damper ring (arrowed)

9 Propeller shaft universal joints – check and renewal

Check

1 Wear in the universal joints is characterised by vibration in the transmission, noise during acceleration, and metallic squeaking and grating sounds as the bearings disintegrate. The joints can be checked with the propeller shaft still fitted noting that it will be necessary to remove the exhaust system and heat shields (see Chapter 4A or 4B) to gain access.
2 If the propeller shaft is in position on the vehicle, try to turn the propeller shaft while holding the transmission/final drive flange. Free play between the propeller shaft and the front or rear flanges indicates excessive wear.
3 If the propeller shaft is already removed, you can check the universal joints by holding the shaft in one hand and turning the yoke or flange with the other. If the axial movement is excessive, renew the propeller shaft.

Renewal

4 At the time of writing, no spare parts were available to enable renewal of the universal joints to be carried out. Therefore, if any joint shows signs of damage or wear the complete propeller shaft assembly must be renewed. Consult your BMW dealer for latest information on parts availability.
5 If renewal of the propeller shaft is necessary, it may be worthwhile seeking the advice of an automotive engineering specialist. They may be able to repair the original shaft assembly or supply a reconditioned shaft on an exchange basis.

10 Final drive oil level check

1 BMW described the final drive as 'filled for life'. There is no requirement in the service schedule to check or change the final drive oil. However, it may be prudent to check the fluid level every few years as follows:

10.2 Final drive filler plug

2 With the vehicle level, unscrew the filler plug from the rear of the final drive casing **(see illustration)**.
3 The oil level should be upto the lower edge of the filler hole. If it's not, add the specified fluid until the level is up to the bottom of the filler hole.
4 Refit the oil filler plug and tighten it to the specified torque.

Chapter 9
Braking system

Contents

Degrees of difficulty

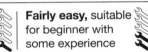

Easy, suitable for novice with little experience	**Fairly easy,** suitable for beginner with some experience	**Fairly difficult,** suitable for competent DIY mechanic	**Difficult,** suitable for experienced DIY mechanic	**Very difficult,** suitable for expert DIY or professional

Specifications

General

Caliper type	Teves floating caliper
Brake pad friction material minimum thickness.	2.0 mm
Disc diameter.	292 to 348 mm (according to model)

Disc thickness:
New:

292 mm diameter	22.0 mm
300, 312 and 330 mm diameter	24.0 mm
338 mm diameter	26.0 mm
348 mm diameter	30.0 mm
Minimum.	2.4 mm thinner than new
Maximum disc run-out	0.2 mm

Rear disc brakes

Disc diameter:

Solid disc	296 mm
Ventilated disc	300 to 336 mm (according to model)

Disc thickness:
New:

Solid disc	10.0 mm

Ventilated disc:

300 mm diameter	20.0 mm
324 and 336 mm diameter	22.0 mm
Minimum.	1.6 mm thinner than new
Maximum disc run-out	0.2 mm
Brake pad friction material minimum thickness.	2.0 mm

Handbrake

Drum diameter . . . . 160 to 180 mm (according to model)
Shoe friction material minimum thickness . . . . 1.5 mm

Torque wrench settings

	Nm	lbf ft
ABS pressure sensors to master cylinder	19	14
ABS wheel sensor retaining bolts.	8	6
Brake disc retaining bolt.	16	12
Brake hose unions:		
M10 thread	17	13
M12 thread	19	14
Front brake caliper:		
Guide pins:		
Socket head	30	22
Hexagon head	35	26
Mounting bracket bolts: *		
M10.	65	48
M12.	110	81
Master cylinder mounting nuts*	26	19
Rear brake caliper:		
Guide pin bolts	35	26
Mounting bracket bolts*	67	49
Roadwheel bolts.	120	89
Servo unit mounting nuts*	22	16

Do not re-use

---

1 General Information

1 The braking system is of the servo-assisted, dual-circuit hydraulic type. Under normal circumstances, both circuits operate in unison. However, if there is hydraulic failure in one circuit, full braking force will still be available at two wheels.

2 All models are fitted with front and rear disc brakes. ABS is fitted as standard to all models (refer to Section 19 for further information on ABS operation). **Note:** *On models equipped with Dynamic Stability Control (DSC), the ABS system also operates the traction control side of the system.*

3 The front disc brakes are actuated by single-piston sliding type calipers, which ensure that equal pressure is applied to each disc pad.

4 All models are fitted with rear disc brakes, actuated by single-piston sliding calipers, whilst a separate drum brake arrangement is fitted in the centre of the brake disc to provide a separate means of handbrake application. **Note:** *When servicing any part of the system, work carefully and methodically; also observe scrupulous cleanliness when overhauling any part of the hydraulic system. Always renew components (in axle sets, where applicable) if in doubt about their condition, and use only genuine BMW parts, or at least those of known good quality. Note the warnings given in 'Safety first' and at relevant points in this Chapter concerning the dangers of asbestos dust and hydraulic fluid.*

2 Hydraulic system – bleeding

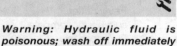

⚠️ *Warning: Hydraulic fluid is poisonous; wash off immediately and thoroughly in the case of skin contact, and seek immediate medical advice if any fluid is swallowed or gets into the eyes. Certain types of hydraulic fluid are flammable, and may ignite when allowed into contact with hot components; when servicing any hydraulic system, it is safest to assume that the fluid is flammable, and to take precautions against the risk of fire as though it is petrol that is being handled. Hydraulic fluid is also an effective paint stripper, and will attack plastics; if any is spilt, it should be washed off immediately, using copious quantities of fresh water. Finally, it is hygroscopic (it absorbs moisture from the air) – old fluid may be contaminated and unfit for further use. When topping-up or renewing the fluid, always use the recommended type, and ensure that it comes from a freshly-opened sealed container.*

⚠️ *Warning: If the high-pressure hydraulic system linking the master cylinder, hydraulic unit and (where fitted) accumulator has been disturbed, then bleeding of the brakes should be entrusted to a BMW dealer or specialist. They will have access to the special service tester which is needed to operate the ABS modulator pump and bleed the high-pressure hydraulic system safely.*

General

1 The correct operation of any hydraulic system is only possible after removing all air from the components and circuit; this is achieved by bleeding the system.

2 During the bleeding procedure, add only clean, unused hydraulic fluid of the recommended type; never re-use fluid that has already been bled from the system. Ensure that sufficient fluid is available before starting work.

3 If there is any possibility of incorrect fluid being already in the system, the brake components and circuit must be flushed completely with uncontaminated, correct fluid, and new seals should be fitted to the various components.

4 If hydraulic fluid has been lost from the system, or air has entered because of a leak, ensure that the fault is cured before continuing further.

5 Park the vehicle on level ground, switch off the engine and select first or reverse gear, then chock the wheels and release the handbrake.

6 Check that all pipes and hoses are secure, unions tight and bleed screws closed. Clean any dirt from around the bleed screws.

7 Unscrew the master cylinder reservoir cap, and top the master cylinder reservoir up to the MAX level line; refit the cap loosely, and remember to maintain the fluid level at least above the MIN level line throughout the procedure, or there is a risk of further air entering the system.

8 There are a number of one-man, do-it-yourself brake bleeding kits currently available from motor accessory shops. It is recommended that one of these kits is used whenever possible, as they greatly simplify the bleeding operation, and reduce the risk of expelled air and fluid being drawn back into the system. If such a kit is not available, the basic (two-man) method must be used, which is described in detail below.

9 If a kit is to be used, prepare the vehicle as described previously, and follow the kit manufacturer's instructions, as the procedure may vary slightly according to the type being used; generally, they are as outlined below in the relevant sub-section.

10 Whichever method is used, the same sequence must be followed (paragraphs 11 and 12) to ensure the removal of all air from the system.

Bleeding sequence

11 If the system has been only partially disconnected, and suitable precautions were taken to minimise fluid loss, it should be necessary only to bleed that part of the system.

12 If the complete system is to be bled, then it should be done working in the following sequence:
a) Right-hand rear brake.
b) Left-hand rear brake.
c) Right-hand front brake.
d) Left-hand front brake.

⚠️ Warning: After bleeding, on models with Dynamic Stability Control (DSC), the operation of the braking system should be checked by a BMW dealer or suitably-equipped specialist.

Bleeding

Basic (two-man) method

13 Collect a clean glass jar, a suitable length of plastic or rubber tubing which is a tight fit over the bleed screw, and a ring spanner to fit the screw. The help of an assistant will also be required.

14 Remove the dust cap from the first screw in the sequence. Fit the spanner and tube to the screw, place the other end of the tube in the jar, and pour in sufficient fluid to cover the end of the tube.

15 Ensure that the master cylinder reservoir fluid level is maintained at least above the MIN level line throughout the procedure.

16 Have the assistant fully depress the brake pedal several times to build-up pressure, then maintain it on the final downstroke.

17 While pedal pressure is maintained, unscrew the bleed screw (approximately one turn) and allow the compressed fluid and air to flow into the jar. The assistant should maintain pedal pressure, following it down to the floor if necessary, and should not release it until instructed to do so. When the flow stops, tighten the bleed screw again, have the assistant release the pedal slowly, and recheck the reservoir fluid level.

18 Repeat the steps in paragraphs 16 and 17 until the fluid emerging from the bleed screw is free from air bubbles. If the master cylinder has been drained and refilled, and air is being bled from the first screw in the sequence, allow about 5 seconds between cycles for the master cylinder passages to refill.

19 When no more air bubbles appear, tighten the bleed screw securely, remove the tube and spanner, and refit the dust cap. Do not overtighten the bleed screw.

20 Repeat the procedure on the remaining screws in the sequence, until all air is removed from the system and the brake pedal feels firm again.

Using a one-way valve kit

21 As their name implies, these kits consist of a length of tubing with a one-way valve fitted, to prevent expelled air and fluid being drawn back into the system; some kits include a translucent container, which can be positioned so that the air bubbles can be more easily seen flowing from the end of the tube **(see illustration)**.

22 The kit is connected to the bleed screw, which is then opened. The user returns to the driver's seat, depresses the brake pedal with a smooth, steady stroke, and slowly releases it; this is repeated until the expelled fluid is clear of air bubbles.

23 Note that these kits simplify work so much that it is easy to forget the master cylinder reservoir fluid level; ensure that this is maintained at least above the MIN level line at all times.

Using a pressure-bleeding kit

24 These kits are usually operated by the reservoir of pressurised air contained in a tyre. However, note that it will probably be necessary to reduce the pressure to a lower level than normal; refer to the instructions supplied with the kit. **Note:** BMW specify that a pressure of 2 bar should not be exceeded in the brake hydraulic system.

25 By connecting a pressurised, fluid-filled container to the master cylinder reservoir, bleeding can be carried out simply by opening each screw in turn (in the specified sequence), and allowing the fluid to flow out until no more air bubbles can be seen in the expelled fluid.

26 This method has the advantage that the large reservoir of fluid provides an additional safeguard against air being drawn into the system during bleeding.

27 Pressure-bleeding is particularly effective when bleeding 'difficult' systems, or when bleeding the complete system at the time of routine fluid renewal.

All methods

28 When bleeding is complete, and firm pedal feel is restored, wash off any spilt fluid, tighten the bleed screws securely, and refit their dust caps.

29 Check the hydraulic fluid level in the master cylinder reservoir, and top-up if necessary (see Weekly checks).

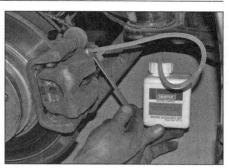

2.21 Bleeding a rear brake caliper using a one-way valve kit

30 Discard any hydraulic fluid that has been bled from the system; it will not be fit for re-use.

31 Check the feel of the brake pedal. If it feels at all spongy, air must still be present in the system, and further bleeding is required. Failure to bleed satisfactorily after a reasonable repetition of the bleeding procedure may be due to worn master cylinder seals.

3 Hydraulic pipes and hoses – renewal

⚠️ Warning: Under no circumstances should the hydraulic pipes/hoses linking the master cylinder, hydraulic unit and (where fitted) the accumulator be disturbed. If these unions are disturbed and air enters the high-pressure hydraulic system, bleeding of the system can only be safely carried out by a BMW dealer or suitably-equipped specialist using the special service tester.

Note: Before starting work, refer to the warnings at the beginning of Section 2.

1 If any pipe or hose is to be renewed, minimise fluid loss by first removing the master cylinder reservoir cap, then tightening it down onto a piece of polythene to obtain an airtight seal. Alternatively, flexible hoses can be sealed, if required, using a proprietary brake hose clamp; metal brake pipe unions can be plugged (if care is taken not to allow dirt into the system) or capped immediately they are disconnected. Place a wad of rag under any union that is to be disconnected, to catch any spilt fluid.

2 If a flexible hose is to be disconnected, unscrew the brake pipe union nut before removing the spring clip which secures the hose to its mounting bracket.

3 To unscrew the union nuts, it is preferable to obtain a brake pipe spanner of the correct size; these are available from most large motor accessory shops. Failing this, a close-fitting open-ended spanner will be required, though if the nuts are tight or corroded, their flats may be rounded-off if the spanner slips. In such a case, using self-locking pliers is often the only way to unscrew a stubborn union, but it follows that the pipe and the damaged nuts must be renewed on reassembly. Always clean a union and surrounding area before disconnecting it. If disconnecting a component with more than one union, make a careful note of the connections before disturbing any of them.

4 If a brake pipe is to be renewed, it can be obtained, cut to length and with the union nuts and end flares in place, from BMW dealers. All that is then necessary is to bend it to shape, following the line of the original, before fitting it to the car. Alternatively, most motor accessory shops can make up brake pipes from kits, but this requires very careful measurement of the original, to ensure that the replacement is of the correct length. The safest answer is usually to take the original to the shop as a pattern.

5 On refitting, do not overtighten the union nuts. It is not necessary to exercise brute force to obtain a sound joint.

6 Ensure that the pipes and hoses are correctly routed, with no kinks, and that they are secured in the clips or brackets provided. After fitting, remove the polythene from the reservoir, and bleed the hydraulic system as described in Section 2. Wash off any spilt fluid, and check carefully for fluid leaks.

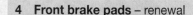

4 Front brake pads – renewal

⚠ *Warning: Renew both sets of front brake pads at the same time – never renew the pads on only one wheel, as uneven braking may result. Note that the dust created by wear of the pads may contain asbestos, which is a health hazard. Never blow it out with compressed air, and don't inhale any of it. An approved filtering mask should be worn when working on the brakes. DO NOT use petrol or petroleum-based solvents to clean brake parts; use brake cleaner or methylated spirit only.*

1 Apply the handbrake, then slacken the front roadwheel bolts. Jack up the front of the vehicle and support it on axle stands (see *Jacking and vehicle support*). Remove both front roadwheels.

2 Follow the relevant accompanying photos **(illustrations 4.2a to 4.2z)** for the pad renewal procedure. Be sure to stay in order and read the caption under each illustration, and note the following points:

a) *New pads may have an adhesive foil on the backplates. Remove this foil prior to installation.*

b) *Clean the caliper guide surfaces with non-abrasive cleaners only, and apply a little brake assembly grease (BMW pad paste 83 23 9 407 830 or Copperslip).*

c) *When pushing the caliper piston back to accommodate new pads, keep a close eye on the fluid level in the reservoir.*

d) *BMW insist that the brake pad wear sensor must be renewed if it's been removed.*

e) *On vehicles over 2 years old, BMW recommend that a new retaining spring is fitted.*

3 Depress the brake pedal repeatedly, until the pads are pressed into firm contact with the brake disc, and normal (non-assisted) pedal pressure is restored.

4 Repeat the above procedure on the remaining front brake caliper.

5 Apply the little anti-seize grease to the hub surface, then refit the roadwheels, lower the vehicle to the ground and tighten the roadwheel bolts to the specified torque.

6 Check the hydraulic fluid level as described in.

Caution: New pads will not give full braking efficiency until they have bedded-in. Be prepared for this, and avoid hard braking as far as possible for the first hundred miles or so after pad renewal.

4.2a Using a screwdriver between the edge of the disc and the caliper body, lever the caliper outwards a little, forcing the piston to retract. This provides clearance for the pads to be removed from a worn disc

4.2b Open the plastic box on the inner wing (retaining clip arrowed)...

4.2c... and disconnect the pad wear sensor wiring plug (white)

4.2d Prise up the bleed screw plastic cap and release the pad wear sensor wiring loom

4.2e Pull the wear sensor from the inner pad. Note that BMW insist the sensor is not re-used, as the retaining clip distorts during removal

4.2f Using a screwdriver, compress the spring and remove it from the caliper

4.2g Prise out the rubber caps...

4.2h... and unscrew the guide pins using a 7.0 mm Allen key/bit

4.2i Slide the caliper and pads from the mounting bracket/disc

4.2j Pull the outer pad from the caliper...

4.2k... then pull the inner pad from the caliper piston

4.2l To avoid straining the rubber hose, suspend the caliper from the coil spring

4.2m Use brake cleaner and a soft brush to clean the caliper/bracket mounting surfaces

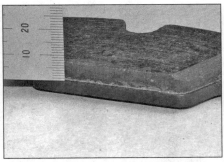

4.2n Measure the thickness of the pads friction material – if it's less than 2.0 mm on any pad, all the front pads must be renewed

4.2o If new pads are to be fitted, push the piston back into the caliper body using a retraction tool. Keep an eye on the brake fluid level whilst pushing the piston back

4.2p Apply a very thin smear of brake assembly grease (supplied with genuine pad kits) to the mounting edges of the pads backing plate

4.2q Fit the outer pad to the mounting bracket, ensuring the friction material is against the disc surface

4.2r Press the inner pad clip into the caliper piston...

4.2s... then slide the caliper into place

4.2t Tighten the guide pins to the specified torque...

4.2u... and refit the rubber caps

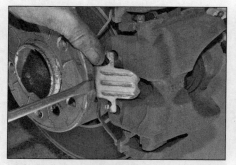

4.2v Use a screwdriver to manoeuvre the retaining spring...

4.2w... back into place

4.2x Slide the new pad wear sensor into the inner pad groove...

4.2y... clip the wear sensor wiring loom back under the bleed screw cap strap...

4.2z... and reconnect the sensor wiring plug

5 Rear brake pads – renewal

⚠ **Warning: Renew both sets of rear brake pads at the same time – never renew the pads on only one wheel, as uneven braking may result. Note that the dust created by wear of the pads may contain asbestos, which is a health hazard. Never blow it out with compressed air, and don't inhale any of it. An approved filtering mask should be worn when working on the brakes. DO NOT use petrol or petroleum-based solvents to clean brake parts; use brake cleaner or methylated spirit only.**

1 Apply the handbrake, then slacken the rear roadwheel bolts. Jack up the rear of the vehicle and support it on axle stands (see *Jacking and vehicle support*). Remove both rear roadwheels.

Teves caliper

2 Follow the relevant accompanying photos **(illustrations 5.2a to 5.2y)** for the pad renewal procedure. Be sure to stay in order and read the caption under each illustration, and note the following points:

a) New pads may have an adhesive foil on the backplates. Remove this foil prior to installation.

b) Clean the caliper guide surfaces with non-abrasive cleaners only, and apply a little brake assembly grease (BMW pad paste 83 23 9 407 830 or Copperslip).

c) When pushing the caliper piston back to accommodate new pads, keep a close eye on the fluid level in the reservoir.

d) BMW insist that the brake pad wear sensor must be renewed if it's been removed.

e) On vehicles over 2 years old, BMW recommend that a new retaining spring is fitted.

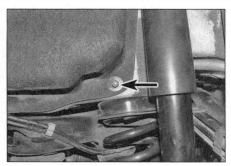

5.2a Using a screwdriver between the edge of the disc and the caliper body, lever the caliper outwards a little, forcing the piston to retract. This provides clearance for the pads to be removed from a worn disc

5.2b Undo the nut...

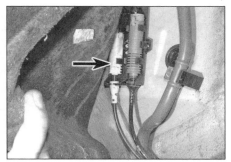

5.2c... pull back the wheel arch liner, and disconnect the pad wear sensor wiring plug

5.2d Pull off the bleed screw rubber cap to release the pad wear sensor wiring loom

5.2e Pull the wear sensor from the inner pad. Note that BMW insist the sensor is not re-used, as the retaining clip distorts during removal

5.2f Using a screwdriver, compress the spring and remove it from the caliper

5.2g Prise out the rubber caps...

5.2h... unscrew the guide pins with a 7.0 mm Allen key/bit...

5.2i... and slide the caliper with pads from the mounting bracket

5.2j Prise away the outer brake pad...

5.2k... and pull the inner brake pad clip from the caliper piston

5.2l To avoid straining the rubber hose, suspend the caliper from the vehicle body

5.2m Measure the thickness of the pads friction material – if it's less than 2.0 mm on any pad, all the rear pads must be renewed

5.2n Use brake cleaner and a soft brush to clean the caliper/bracket mounting surfaces

5.2o If new pads are to be fitted, push the piston back into the caliper body using a retraction tool. Keep an eye on the brake fluid level whilst pushing the piston back

5.2p Apply a very thin smear of brake assembly grease (supplied with genuine pad kits) to the mounting edges of the pads backing plate

5.2q Fit the outer brake pad to the caliper mounting bracket, ensuring the friction material is against the disc surface

5.2r Press the inner brake pad retaining clip into the caliper piston...

5.2s... and slide the caliper into position

5.2t Tighten the guide pins to the specified torque...

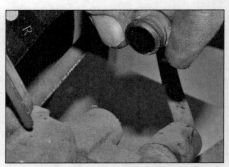

5.2u... and refit the rubber caps

5.2v Slide the new pad wear sensor into the inner pad groove...

5.2w... clip the wear sensor wiring loom back under the bleed screw cap strap and reconnect the sensor wiring plug

5.2x Use a screwdriver to lever the retaining spring...

5.2y... back into position

TRW caliper

3 Follow the relevant accompanying photos **(illustrations 5.3a to 5.3z)** for the pad renewal procedure. Be sure to stay in order and read the caption under each illustration, and note the following points:

a) *New pads may have an adhesive foil on the backplates. Remove this foil prior to installation.*

b) *Clean the caliper guide surfaces with non-abrasive cleaners only, and apply a little brake assembly grease (BMW pad paste 83 23 9 407 830 or Copperslip).*

c) *When pushing the caliper piston back to accommodate new pads, keep a close eye on the fluid level in the reservoir.*

d) *BMW insist that the brake pad wear sensor must be renewed if it's been removed.*

All calipers

4 Depress the brake pedal repeatedly, until the pads are pressed into firm contact with the brake disc, and normal (non-assisted) pedal pressure is restored.

5 Repeat the above procedure on the remaining rear brake caliper.

6 Apply the little anti-seize grease to the

5.3a Using a screwdriver between the edge of the disc and the caliper body, lever the caliper outwards a little, forcing the piston to retract. This provides clearance for the pads to be removed from a worn disc

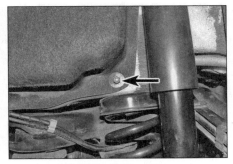

5.3b Undo the nut...

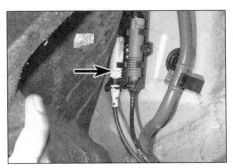

5.3c... pull back the wheel arch liner, and disconnect the pad wear sensor wiring plug

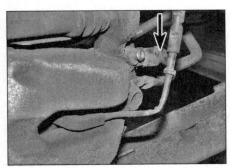

5.3d Pull off the bleed screw rubber cap to release the pad wear sensor wiring loom

5.3e Pull the wear sensor from the inner pad. Note that BMW insist the sensor is not re-used, as the retaining clip distorts during removal

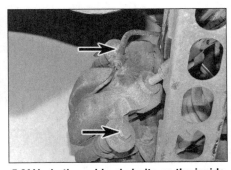

5.3f Undo the guide pin bolts on the inside of the caliper...

5.3g... counterhold the guide pins with an open-ended spanner as the bolts are slackened

5.3h Slide the caliper from the mounting bracket...

5.3i... and suspend it from the vehicle body to prevent straining the rubber fluid hose

5.3j Pull the outer brake pad from the mounting bracket...

5.3k... followed by the inner pad

5.3l Remove the lower pad shim...

5.3m... and the upper pad shim

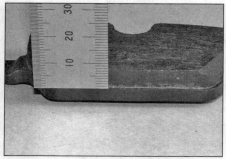

5.3n Measure the thickness of the pads friction material – if it's less than 2.0 mm on any pad, all the rear pads must be renewed

5.3o Use brake cleaner and a soft brush to clean the caliper/bracket mounting surfaces

5.3p Refit the upper...

5.3q... and lower pad shims

5.3r Apply a very thin smear of brake assembly grease (supplied with genuine pad kits) to the mounting edges of the pads backing plate

5.3s Fit the inner brake pad to the mounting bracket...

5.3t... and the outer brake pad. Ensure the friction material is against the disc surface

5.3u If new pads are to be fitted, push the piston back into the caliper body using a retraction tool. Keep an eye on the brake fluid level whilst pushing the piston back

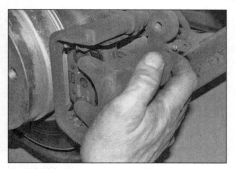

5.3v Manoeuvre the caliper back into position

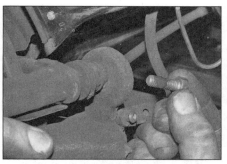

5.3w Apply a little thread locking compound to the guide pin bolts...

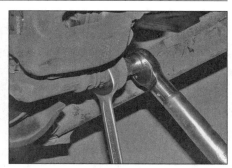

5.3x... and tighten them to the specified torque

hub surface, then refit the roadwheels, lower the vehicle to the ground and tighten the roadwheel bolts to the specified torque.

7 Check the hydraulic fluid level as described in *Weekly checks*.

Caution: New pads will not give full braking efficiency until they have bedded-in. Be prepared for this, and avoid hard braking as far as possible for the first hundred miles or so after pad renewal.

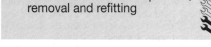

6 Front brake disc – inspection, removal and refitting

Note: *Before starting work, refer to the note at the beginning of Section concerning the dangers of asbestos dust.*

Inspection

Note: *If either disc requires renewal, BOTH should be renewed at the same time, to ensure even and consistent braking. New brake pads should also be fitted.*

1 Apply the handbrake, then jack up the front of the car and support it on axle stands. Remove the appropriate front roadwheel.

2 Slowly rotate the brake disc so that the full area of both sides can be checked; remove the brake pads if better access is required to the inboard surface (see Section 4). Light scoring is normal in the area swept by the brake pads, but if heavy scoring or cracks are found, the disc must be renewed.

3 It is normal to find a lip of rust and brake

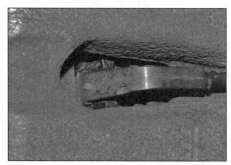

5.3y Slide the new pad wear sensor into the slot in the inner brake pad backplate...

dust around the disc's perimeter; this can be scraped off if required. If, however, a lip has formed due to excessive wear of the brake pad swept area, then the disc's thickness must be measured using a micrometer **(see illustration)**. Take measurements at several places around the disc, at the inside and outside of the pad swept area; if the disc has worn at any point to the specified minimum thickness or less, the disc must be renewed.

4 If the disc is thought to be warped, it can be checked for run-out. Either use a dial gauge mounted on any convenient fixed point, while the disc is slowly rotated, or use feeler blades to measure (at several points all around the disc) the clearance between the disc and a fixed point, such as the caliper mounting bracket. If the measurements obtained are at the specified maximum or beyond, the disc is excessively warped, and must be renewed;

5.3z... reconnect the sensor wiring plug, refit the wheel arch liner, and secure the wiring loom with the retaining clips

however, it is worth checking first that the hub bearing is in good condition (Chapters 1A or 1B and/or 10). If the run-out is excessive, the disc must be renewed.

5 Check the disc for cracks, especially around the wheel bolt holes, and any other wear or damage, and renew if necessary.

Removal

6 Unscrew the two bolts securing the brake caliper mounting bracket to the hub carrier, then slide the caliper assembly off the disc **(see illustration)**. Using a piece of wire or string, tie the caliper to the front suspension coil spring, to avoid placing any strain on the hydraulic brake hose.

7 Use chalk or paint to mark the relationship of the disc to the hub, then remove the bolt securing the brake disc to the hub, and remove the disc **(see illustration)**. If it is tight,

6.3 Measure the thickness of the disc with a micrometer

6.6 Caliper mounting bracket bolts

6.7 Disc retaining bolt

lightly tap its rear face with a hide or plastic mallet.

Refitting

8 Refitting is the reverse of the removal procedure, noting the following points:

a) *Ensure that the mating surfaces of the disc and hub are clean and flat.*

b) *Align (if applicable) the marks made on removal, and tighten the disc retaining bolt to the specified torque.*

c) *If a new disc has been fitted, use a suitable solvent to wipe any preservative coating from the disc, before refitting the caliper.*

d) *Slide the caliper into position over the disc, making sure the pads pass either side of the disc. Tighten the caliper mounting bolts to the specified torque setting.*

e) *Refit the roadwheel, then lower the vehicle to the ground and tighten the roadwheel bolts to the specified torque. On completion, repeatedly depress the brake pedal until normal (non-assisted) pedal pressure returns.*

7 Rear brake disc – inspection, removal and refitting

Note: *Before starting work, refer to the note at the beginning of Section concerning the dangers of asbestos dust.*

Inspection

Note: *If either disc requires renewal, BOTH should be renewed at the same time, to ensure even and consistent braking. New brake pads should also be fitted.*

1 Firmly chock the front wheels, then jack up the rear of the car and support it on axle stands. Remove the appropriate rear roadwheel. Release the handbrake

2 Inspect the disc as described in Section 6.

Removal

3 Remove the brake pads as described in Section.

4 Undo the 2 bolts and remove the caliper mounting bracket. Discard the bolts – new ones must be fitted.

5 Slacken and remove the brake disc retaining bolt **(see illustration 6.7)**.

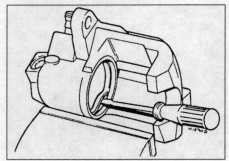

8.8 Extracting the piston seal – take care not to scratch the surface of the bore

6 It should now be possible to withdraw the brake disc from the stub axle by hand. If it is tight, lightly tap its rear face with a hide or plastic mallet. If the handbrake shoes are binding, first check that the handbrake is fully released, then continue as follows.

7 Referring to Section 14 for further details, fully slacken the handbrake adjustment, to obtain maximum free play in the cable.

 If the piston cannot be withdrawn by hand, it can be pushed out by applying compressed air to the brake hose union hole. Only low pressure should be required, such as is generated by a foot pump. As the piston is expelled, take great care not to trap your fingers between the piston and caliper.

8 Insert a screwdriver through one of the wheel bolt holes in the brake disc, and rotate the adjuster knurled wheel on the upper pivot to retract the shoes **(see illustration 14.6)**. The brake disc can then be withdrawn.

Refitting

9 If a new disc is been fitted, use a suitable solvent to wipe any preservative coating from the disc. Ensure the disc mounting surface on the hub is free from dirt and corrosion.

10 Align (if applicable) the marks made on removal, then fit the disc and tighten the retaining bolt to the specified torque.

11 Refit the caliper mounting bracket, and tighten the new bolts to the specified torque.

12 Adjust the handbrake shoes and cable as described in Section 14.

13 Refit the roadwheel, then lower the car to the ground, and tighten the roadwheel bolts to the specified torque. On completion, repeatedly depress the brake pedal until normal (non-assisted) pedal pressure returns. Recheck the handbrake adjustment.

8 Front brake caliper – removal, overhaul and refitting

Note: *Before starting work, refer to the note at the beginning of Section 2 concerning the dangers of hydraulic fluid, and to the warning at the beginning of Section concerning the dangers of asbestos dust.*

Removal

1 Apply the handbrake, then jack up the front of the vehicle and support it on axle stands. Remove the appropriate roadwheel.

2 Minimise fluid loss by using a brake hose clamp, a G-clamp or a similar tool to clamp the flexible hose.

3 Clean the area around the union, then slacken the brake hose union nut.

4 Remove the brake pads (see Section 4).

5 Unscrew the caliper from the end of the brake hose and remove it from the vehicle.

Overhaul

6 With the caliper on the bench, wipe away all traces of dust and dirt, but avoid inhaling the dust, as it is a health hazard.

7 Withdraw the partially-ejected piston from the caliper body, and remove the dust seal.

8 Using a small screwdriver, extract the piston hydraulic seal, taking great care not to damage the caliper bore **(see illustration)**.

9 Thoroughly clean all components, using only methylated spirit, isopropyl alcohol or clean hydraulic fluid as a cleaning medium. Never use mineral-based solvents such as petrol or paraffin, as they will attack the hydraulic system's rubber components. Dry the components immediately, using compressed air or a clean, lint-free cloth. Use compressed air to blow clear the fluid passages.

10 Check all components, and renew any that are worn or damaged. Check particularly the cylinder bore and piston; these should be renewed (note that this means the renewal of the complete body assembly) if they are scratched, worn or corroded in any way. Similarly check the condition of the guide pins and their bushes; both pins should be undamaged and (when cleaned) a reasonably tight sliding fit in the bushes. If there is any doubt about the condition of any component, renew it.

11 If the assembly is fit for further use, obtain the appropriate repair kit; the components are available from BMW dealers in various combinations. All rubber seals should be renewed as a matter of course; these should never be re-used.

12 On reassembly, ensure that all components are clean and dry.

13 Soak the piston and the new piston (fluid) seal in clean hydraulic fluid. Smear clean fluid on the cylinder bore surface.

14 Fit the new piston (fluid) seal, using only your fingers (no tools) to manipulate it into the cylinder bore groove.

15 Fit the new dust seal to the piston. Locate the rear of the seal in the recess in the caliper body, and refit the piston to the cylinder bore using a twisting motion. Ensure that the piston enters squarely into the bore, and press it fully into the bore.

Refitting

16 Screw the caliper fully onto the flexible hose union.

17 Refit the brake pads (see Section 4).

18 Securely tighten the brake pipe union nut.

19 Remove the brake hose clamp, and bleed the hydraulic system as described in Section 2. Note that, providing the precautions described were taken to minimise brake fluid loss, it should only be necessary to bleed the relevant front brake.

20 Refit the roadwheel, then lower the vehicle to the ground and tighten the roadwheel bolts to the specified torque. On completion, check the hydraulic fluid level as described in *Weekly checks*.

9 Rear brake caliper – removal, overhaul and refitting

Note: *Before starting work, refer to the note at the beginning of Section 2 concerning the dangers of hydraulic fluid, and to the warning at the beginning of Section concerning the dangers of asbestos dust.*

Removal

1 Chock the front wheels, then jack up the rear of the vehicle and support on axle stands. Remove the relevant rear wheel.
2 Minimise fluid loss by using a brake hose clamp, a G-clamp or a similar tool to clamp the flexible hose.
3 Clean the area around the union, then loosen the brake hose union nut.
4 Remove the brake pads as described in Section 5.
5 Unscrew the caliper from the end of the flexible hose, and remove it from the vehicle.

Overhaul

6 Refer to Section 8.

Refitting

7 Screw the caliper fully onto the flexible hose union.
8 Refit the brake pads (refer to Section 5).
9 Securely tighten the brake pipe union nut.

10 Remove the brake hose clamp, and bleed the hydraulic system as described in Section 2. Note that, providing the precautions described were taken to minimise brake fluid loss, it should only be necessary to bleed the relevant rear brake.
11 Refit the roadwheel, then lower the vehicle to the ground and tighten the roadwheel bolts to the specified torque. On completion, check the hydraulic fluid level as described in *Weekly checks*.

10 Master cylinder – removal, overhaul and refitting

Removal

Note: *Although it is possible for the home mechanic to remove the master cylinder, if the hydraulic unions are disconnected from the master cylinder, air will enter the high-pressure hydraulic system linking the master cylinder and hydraulic unit. Bleeding of the high pressure system can only be safely carried out by a BMW dealer or specialist who has access to the service tester (see Section 2). Consequently, once the master cylinder has been refitted, the vehicle must be taken on a trailer or transporter to a suitably-equipped BMW dealer or specialist.*

Note: *Before starting work, refer to the warning at the beginning of Section 2 concerning the dangers of hydraulic fluid.*
Note: *New master cylinder retaining nuts will be required on refitting.*

1 Working at the rear of the engine compartment, undo the bolts and remove the pollen filter cover **(see illustration)**. Slide the filter from the housing. If necessary, refer to Chapter 1A or 1B.
2 Release the catches and remove the left- and right-hand plastic covers from behind the suspension turret each side of the engine compartment. Unclip the wiring where applicable **(see illustration)**.
3 Depress the clips and pull the cable guide forwards from the pollen filter lower housing **(see illustration)**.
4 Release the catch and undo the bolt each side, then slide the pollen filter lower housing forwards and manoeuvre it from place **(see illustrations)**.
5 Remove the master cylinder reservoir cap, and siphon the hydraulic fluid from the reservoir. **Note:** *Do not siphon the fluid by mouth, as it is poisonous; use a syringe or a hand-held vacuum pump. Alternatively, open any convenient bleed screw in the system, and gently pump the brake pedal to expel the fluid through a plastic tube connected to the screw until the level of fluid drops below that of the reservoir (see Section 2).* Disconnect

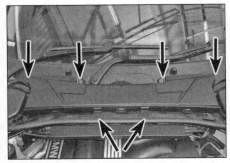
10.1 Undo the bolts and remove the pollen filter cover

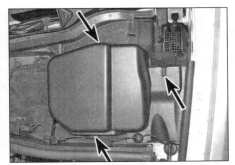
10.2 Release the and remove the plastic cover each side behind the suspension turrets

10.3 Depress the clips and slide forwards the cable guide(s)

10.4a Rotate the temperature sensor anti-clockwise and pull it from the bracket on the lower pollen filter cover

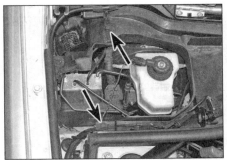
10.4b Release the catch and undo the bolt each side...

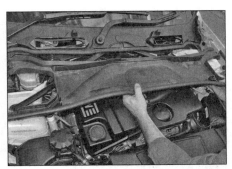
10.4c... then pull the lower pollen filter cover forwards

10.5 Disconnect the wiring plug from the fluid level sensor

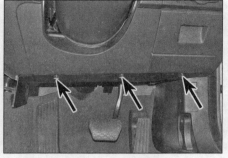

11.7 Undo the 3 bolts securing the panel above the pedals

11.8 Pushrod pin retaining clip

the wiring connector(s) from the brake fluid reservoir **(see illustration)**.

6 Disconnect the fluid hose(s) from the side of the reservoir, and plug the hose end(s) to minimise fluid loss.

7 Unclip, and pull out the master cylinder reservoir locking pin.

8 Carefully ease the fluid reservoir out from the top of the master cylinder. Recover the reservoir seals, and plug the cylinder ports to prevent dirt entry.

9 Working under the facia, undo the 3 bolts and remove the trim panel above the driver's pedals. Disconnect any wiring plugs as the panel is withdrawn.

10 Prise off the clip and remove the pin securing the servo pushrod to the brake pedal **(see illustration 11.8)**. The servo must be slackened so the master cylinder can be removed and installed.

11 Undo the servo retaining nuts. Note that new nuts must be fitted.

12 Wipe clean the area around the brake pipe unions on the on the pipes from the master cylinder to the ABS modulator/hydraulic unit, and place absorbent rags beneath the pipe unions to catch any surplus fluid. Make a note of the correct fitted positions of the unions, then unscrew the union nuts and carefully withdraw the pipes. The pipes must not be bent. Plug or tape over the pipe ends and master cylinder orifices to minimise the loss of brake fluid and to prevent the entry of dirt into the system. Wash off any spilt fluid immediately with cold water.

13 Slacken and remove the two nuts and

washers securing the master cylinder to the vacuum servo unit, then withdraw the unit from the engine compartment. Remove the O-ring from the rear of the master cylinder. Discard the retaining nuts, new ones should be used on refitting.

Overhaul

14 If the master cylinder is faulty, it must be renewed. Repair kits are not available from BMW dealers so the cylinder must be treated as a sealed unit. Renew the master cylinder O-ring seal and reservoir seals regardless of their apparent condition.

Refitting

15 Remove all traces of dirt from the master cylinder and servo unit mating surfaces, and fit a new O-ring to the groove on the master cylinder body.

16 Fit the master cylinder to the servo unit, ensuring that the servo unit pushrod enters the master cylinder bore centrally. Fit the new master cylinder retaining nuts and washers, and tighten them to the specified torque.

17 Wipe clean the brake pipe unions, then refit them to the master cylinder/hydraulic unit ports and tighten them securely.

18 Press the new reservoir seals firmly into the master cylinder ports, then ease the reservoir into position. Refit the reservoir locking pin securely. Reconnect the fluid hose(s) to the reservoir, and reconnect the wiring connector(s).

19 The remainder of refitting is a reversal of removal, noting the following points:

a) Tighten all fasteners to their specified torque where given.
b) Refill the master cylinder reservoir with new fluid, and bleed the complete hydraulic system as described in Section 2.

11 Brake pedal – removal and refitting

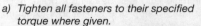

Removal

Manual transmission

1 Remove the clutch pedal as described in Chapter 6.

2 Undo the 2 bolts and move the clutch master cylinder to one side.

3 Remove the stop-light switch as described in Section 18.

4 Slide off the retaining clip and remove the clevis pin securing the brake pedal to the servo unit pushrod.

5 Undo the 3 nuts and manoeuvre the brake pedal bracket assembly from under the facia. Discard the self-locking nuts – new ones must be fitted.

6 If required, unhook the return spring and slide the pedal from the pivot.

Automatic transmission

7 Working under the facia, undo the 3 bolts and remove the trim panel above the driver's pedals **(see illustration)**. Disconnect any wiring plugs as the panel is withdrawn.

8 Prise off the clip and remove the pin securing the servo pushrod to the brake pedal **(see illustration)**.

9 Remove the stop-light switch as described in Section 18.

10 Undo the 3 nuts and manoeuvre the pedal and bracket assembly from under the facia **(see illustrations)**. Discard the self-locking nuts – new ones must be fitted. Note that at the time of writing, the pedal was only available as part of the complete bracket assembly. Consult your BMW dealer.

Refitting

11 Refitting is the reverse of removal. Apply a smear of multipurpose grease to the pedal pivot and clevis pin.

11.10a Pedal bracket lower nuts...

11.10b... and upper nut

14.3 Squeeze together the sides and remove the handbrake lever gaiter from the centre console

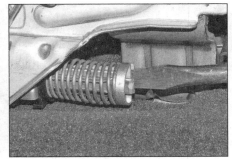

14.4 Push the spring stop back until it engages with the hook

14.6 Rotate the adjuster knurled ring (shown with the disc removed)

12 Vacuum servo unit – testing

1 To test the operation of the servo unit, depress the footbrake several times to exhaust the vacuum, then start the engine whilst keeping the pedal firmly depressed. As the engine starts, there should be a noticeable 'give' in the brake pedal as the vacuum builds-up. Allow the engine to run for at least two minutes, then switch it off. If the brake pedal is now depressed it should feel normal, but further applications should result in the pedal feeling firmer, with the pedal stroke decreasing with each application.

2 If the servo unit fails to operate satisfactorily, the fault lies within the unit itself. Repairs to the unit are not possible – if faulty, the servo unit must be renewed. **Note:** *Removal of the servo unit involves removal of the ABS/DSC modulator/hydraulic unit. Due to the need for special diagnostic equipment, this task should only be carried out be a BMW dealer or suitably-equipped specialist.*

13 Vacuum servo unit check valve – removal, testing and refitting

1 Removal of the servo unit check valve, requires the removal of the ABS/DSC modulator/hydraulic unit. Due to the need for special diagnostic equipment, this task should only be carried out be a BMW dealer or suitably-equipped specialist.

14 Handbrake – adjustment

1 Applying normal moderate pressure, pull the handbrake lever to the fully applied position, counting the number of clicks emitted from the handbrake ratchet mechanism. If adjustment is correct, there should be approximately 7 or 8 clicks before the handbrake is fully applied. If there are more than 10 clicks, adjust as follows.

2 Slacken and remove one wheel bolt from each rear wheel then chock the front wheels, jack up the rear of the vehicle and support it on axle stands.

3 Access to the handbrake cable adjuster can be gained by removing the handbrake lever gaiter from the centre console **(see illustration)**. If greater access is required, the rear section of the centre console will have to be removed (Chapter 11).

4 Release the handbrake, then use a screwdriver to push the spring stop back until the retaining hook engages with the stop **(see illustration)**.

5 Starting on the right-hand rear wheel, rotate the wheel so the adjuster knurled ring is visible through the hole.

6 Insert a screwdriver in through the bolt hole and fully expand the handbrake shoes by rotating the adjuster knurled ring. When the wheel/disc can no longer be turned, back the knurled ring off by 8 notches (185 mm diameter drum) or 9 notches (160 mm diameter drum) so that the wheel is free to rotate easily **(see illustration)**.

7 Repeat paragraph 5 and 6 on the left-hand wheel.

8 Unlock the cable adjuster unit by levering out the retaining hook from the spring stop with a screwdriver **(see illustration)**.

9 Fully release the handbrake lever, and check that the wheels rotate freely. Slowly apply the handbrake, and check that the brake shoes start to contact the drums when the handbrake is set to the third notch of the ratchet mechanism. Check the adjustment by applying the handbrake fully, counting the clicks emitted from the handbrake ratchet and, if necessary, re-adjust.

10 Once adjustment is correct, check the operation of the handbrake warning light switch, then refit the centre console section/handbrake lever gaiter (as applicable). Refit the roadwheels, then lower the vehicle to the ground and tighten the wheel bolts to the specified torque.

15 Handbrake lever – removal and refitting

Removal

1 Remove the centre console as described in Chapter 11, then remove the airbag control unit as described in Chapter 12.

2 Release the handbrake, then use a screwdriver to push the spring stop back until the retaining hook engages with the stop **(see illustration 14.4)**.

3 Disconnect the handbrake warning switch, then release the clips and move the cable guide/bracket to one side.

4 Press the cable retainer each side forwards, and slide the ends of the handbrake cables upwards from the balance arm **(see illustration)**.

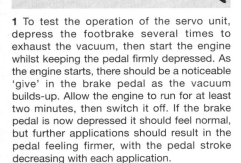

14.8 Lever the retaining hook from the cable stop

14.8 Lever the retaining hook from the cable stop

15.4 Slide the cable end fittings up from the balance arm

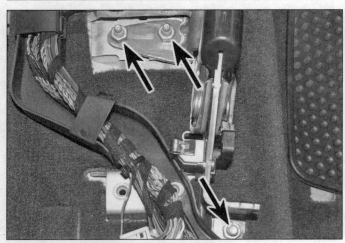

15.5 Handbrake lever assembly retaining nuts

16.3 Undo the bolt and remove the retaining bracket

5 Undo the 3 retaining nuts and remove the lever from the vehicle **(see illustration)**.

Refitting

6 Refitting is a reversal of the removal. Prior to refitting the centre console, adjust the handbrake as described in Section 14.

16 Handbrake cables –
removal and refitting

Removal

1 Detach the front ends of the cables from the lever balance arm as described in Section 15.

16.4a Unfold the expander, then withdraw the pin...

17.4a Using pliers, unhook and remove the handbrake shoe front...

2 Remove the rear brake discs as described in Section 7.
3 Undo the bolt and remove the cable retaining bracket from the inboard face of the hub carrier **(see illustration)**.
4 Slide the cable core in the direction of the expander lock up to the stop, depress the nipple and pull out the cable core from the expander **(see illustrations)**.
5 Working back along the length of the cable, noting its correct routing, and free it from all the relevant retaining clips.

Refitting

6 Insert the cable into the brake carrier/guard

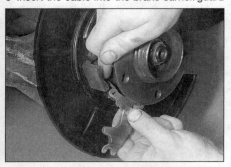

16.4b... and detach the expander from the end of the handbrake cable

17.4b... and rear return springs

plate, and push it in up to the stop on the cable outer sleeve.
7 Grip the sleeve of the cable end, and push it into the expander until it snaps into place.
8 Refitting is a reversal of the removal procedure. Prior to refitting the centre console, adjust the handbrake as described in Section 14.

17 Handbrake shoes –
removal and refitting

Removal

1 Carefully prise up the handbrake lever gaiter from the centre console. If greater access is required, the rear section of the centre console will have to be removed (Chapter 11).
2 Apply the handbrake, then use a screwdriver to push the spring stop back until the retaining hook engages with the stop **(see illustration 14.4)**.
3 Remove the rear brake disc as described in Section 7, and make a note of the correct fitted position of all components.
4 Using a pair of pliers, carefully unhook and remove the handbrake shoe return springs **(see illustrations)**.
5 Release the shoe retaining pins using pliers by depressing them and rotating them

17.5a Rotate the retainer pins through 90°...

17.5b... then remove the pins, springs...

17.6... and handbrake shoes

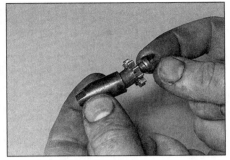

17.8 Clean the adjuster assembly and coat it with fresh brake assembly grease

through 90°, then remove the pins and springs **(see illustrations)**.

6 Remove both handbrake shoes, and recover the shoe adjuster mechanism, noting which way around it is fitted **(see illustration)**.

7 Inspect the handbrake shoes for wear or contamination, and renew if necessary. It is recommended that the return springs are renewed as a matter of course.

8 While the shoes are removed, clean and inspect the condition of the shoe adjuster and expander mechanisms, renew them if they show signs of wear or damage. If all is well, apply a fresh coat of brake grease (BMW recommend Molykote Paste G) to the threads of the adjuster and sliding surfaces of the expander mechanism **(see illustration)**. Do not allow the grease to contact the shoe friction material.

Refitting

9 Prior to installation, clean the backplate, and apply a thin smear of high-temperature brake grease or anti-seize compound to all those surfaces of the backplate which bear on the shoes. Do not allow the lubricant to foul the friction material.

10 Offer up the handbrake shoes, and secure them in position with the retaining pins and springs.

11 Make sure the lower ends of the shoes are correctly engaged with the expander, then slide the adjuster mechanism into position between the upper ends of the shoes **(see illustration)**.

12 Check all components are correctly fitted, and fit the upper and lower return springs using a pair of pliers.

13 Centralise the handbrake shoes, and refit the brake disc as described in Section 7.

14 Prior to refitting the roadwheel, adjust the handbrake as described in Section 14.

18 Stop-light switch – removal and refitting

Removal

1 The stop-light switch is located on the pedal bracket behind the facia.

2 Slacken and remove the retaining bolts securing the driver's side lower facia panel. Unclip the panel and remove it from the vehicle. Disconnect any wiring plugs as the panel is withdrawn.

3 Reach up behind the facia and disconnect the wiring connector from the switch

4 Pull the switch from the mounting. If required, depress the clips and withdraw the switch mounting from the pedal bracket **(see illustrations)**.

Refitting

5 Fully depress the brake pedal and hold it down, refit the mounting, then manoeuvre the switch into position. Push the switch fully into position, then slowly release the brake pedal and allow it to return to its stop. This

will automatically adjust the stop-light switch. **Note:** *If the pedal is released too quickly, the switch will be incorrectly adjusted.*

6 Reconnect the wiring connector, and check the operation of the stop-lights. The stop-lights should illuminate after the brake pedal has travelled approximately 5 mm. If the switch is not functioning correctly, it is faulty and may need to be renewed; no other adjustment is possible.

7 On completion, refit the driver's side lower facia panel.

19 Anti-lock braking system (ABS) – general information

Note: *On all models the ABS unit is a dual function unit, and works both the anti-lock braking system (ABS) and traction control function of the Dynamic Stability Control (DSC) system.*

1 ABS is fitted to all models as standard. The system comprises a hydraulic block which contains the hydraulic solenoid valves and the electrically-driven return pump, the four roadwheel sensors (one fitted to each wheel), and the electronic control module (ECM). The purpose of the system is to prevent the wheel(s) locking during heavy braking. This is achieved by automatic release of the brake on the relevant wheel, followed by re-application of the brake.

2 The solenoids are controlled by the ECM,

17.11 Refit the adjuster assembly, making sure it's correctly engaged with both handbrake shoes

18.4a Pull the switch from the switch mounting

18.4b Press the retaining clips and remove the switch mounting

which itself receives signals from the four wheel sensors (one fitted on each hub), which monitor the speed of rotation of each wheel. By comparing these signals, the ECM can determine the speed at which the vehicle is travelling. It can then use this speed to determine when a wheel is decelerating at an abnormal rate, compared to the speed of the vehicle, and therefore predicts when a wheel is about to lock. During normal operation, the system functions in the same way as a non-ABS braking system. In addition to this, the brake pedal position sensor (which is fitted to the vacuum servo unit) also informs the ECM of how hard the brake pedal is being depressed.

3 If the ECM senses that a wheel is about to lock, it operates the relevant solenoid valve in the hydraulic unit, which then isolates the brake caliper on the wheel which is about to lock from the master cylinder, effectively sealing-in the hydraulic pressure.

4 If the speed of rotation of the wheel continues to decrease at an abnormal rate, the ECM switches on the electrically-driven return pump, and pumps the hydraulic fluid back into the master cylinder, releasing pressure on the brake caliper so that the brake is released. Once the speed of rotation of the wheel returns to an acceptable rate, the pump stops; the solenoid valve opens, allowing the hydraulic master cylinder pressure to return to the caliper, which then re-applies the brake. This cycle can be carried out at up to 10 times a second.

5 The action of the solenoid valves and return pump creates pulses in the hydraulic circuit. When the ABS system is functioning, these pulses can be felt through the brake pedal.

6 The operation of the ABS system is entirely dependent on electrical signals. To prevent the system responding to any inaccurate signals, a built-in safety circuit monitors all signals received by the ECM. If an inaccurate signal or low battery voltage is detected, the ABS system is automatically shut down, and the warning light on the instrument panel is illuminated to inform the driver that the ABS system is not operational. Normal braking should still be available, however.

7 If a fault does develop in the ABS system, the vehicle must be taken to a BMW dealer or suitably-equipped specialist for fault diagnosis and repair.

8 An accumulator is also incorporated into the hydraulic system. As well as performing the ABS function as described above, the hydraulic unit also works the traction/stability control side of the DSC system. If the ECM senses that the wheels are about to lose traction under acceleration, the hydraulic unit momentarily applies the rear brakes to prevent the wheel(s) spinning. If the system senses that the lateral acceleration/yaw rate of the vehicle is about to exceed a predetermined threshold – resulting in oversteer or understeer, the system can apply the brake of each individual wheel to maintain stability and prevent/control a skid.

9 The DSC system can also control the steering of the vehicle to maintain stability in an oversteer or understeer situation – known as Active steering. With conventional systems, the driver has to actively steer the vehicle in a straight line if the brakes are applied on a road surface with varying traction levels. In these situations, the DSC control unit calculates the yaw rate with the brake pressure sensors on the front axle, then the DSC control unit transmits to the Active Steering control unit the yaw-moment compensation correction angle needed for stabilisation.

10 Should a fault develop with the ABS/DSC system, the vehicle must be taken to a BMW dealer or suitably-equipped specialist who will be able to interrogate the systems self-diagnosis capacity, and pin-point the fault.

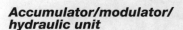

20 Anti-lock braking system (ABS) components – removal and refitting

Accumulator/modulator/ hydraulic unit

1 Although it is possible for the home mechanic to remove the hydraulic unit, the unit's self-diagnosis system must be interrogated by dedicated test equipment before and after removal, and the unit must be bled by BMW service test equipment. Consequently, we recommend that removal and refitting the hydraulic unit should be entrusted to a BMW dealer or suitably-equipped specialist.

Electronic control module (ECM)

2 In order to remove the ECM, the hydraulic unit must first be removed, as the ECM is screwed to the side of the hydraulic unit. Consequently, we recommend that removal and refitting of the ECM is entrusted to a BMW dealer or suitably-equipped specialist.

Front wheel sensor

Removal

3 Chock the rear wheels, then firmly apply the handbrake, jack up the front of the vehicle and support on axle stands. Remove the appropriate front roadwheel. Trace the wiring back from the sensor to the connector which is situated in a protective plastic box. Unclip the lid, then free the wiring connector and disconnect it from the main harness (see illustration).

4 Slacken and remove the bolt securing the sensor to the hub carrier, and remove the sensor and lead assembly from the vehicle (see illustration).

Refitting

5 Prior to refitting, apply a thin coat of multi-

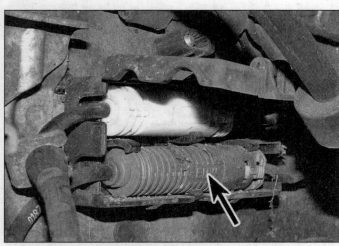

20.3 Open the connector box on the inner wing, and disconnect the ABS sensor wiring plug

20.4 Undo the bolt and pull the ABS sensor from the hub carrier

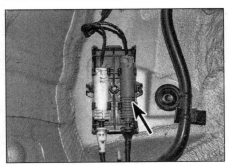

20.10a Fold back the wheel arch liner, open the connector box, and disconnect the ABS sensor wiring plug

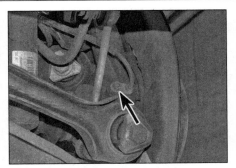

20.10b Undo the bolt and pull the sensor from the hub carrier

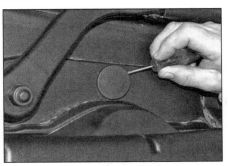

21.2 Remove the cap from the centre of the scuttle panel

purpose grease to the sensor tip (BMW recommend the use of Staburags NBU 12/k).

6 Ensure that the sensor and hub carrier sealing faces are clean, then fit the sensor to the hub. Refit the retaining bolt and tighten it to the specified torque.

7 Ensure that the sensor wiring is correctly routed and retained by all the necessary clips, and reconnect it to its wiring connector. Refit the sensor connector into the box and securely clip the lid in position.

8 Refit the roadwheel, then lower the vehicle to the ground and tighten the roadwheel bolts to the specified torque.

Rear wheel sensor

Removal

9 Chock the front wheels, then jack up the rear of the vehicle and support it on axle stands. Remove the appropriate roadwheel.

10 Remove the sensor as described in paragraphs 3 and 4. Note that the sensor wiring connector is located behind the wheel arch liner. Undo the bolts and pull the rear section of the liner forwards to access the connector **(see illustrations)**.

Refitting

11 Refit the sensor as described above in paragraphs 5 to 8.

Front reluctor rings

12 The front reluctor rings are fixed onto the rear of wheel hubs. Examine the rings for

damage such as chipped or missing teeth. If renewal is necessary, the complete hub assembly must be dismantled and the bearings renewed, with reference to Chapter 10.

Rear reluctor rings

13 The rear reluctor rings are pressed onto the driveshaft outer joints. Examine the rings for signs of damage such as chipped or missing teeth, and renew as necessary. If renewal is necessary, the driveshaft assembly must be renewed (see Chapter 8).

21 Vacuum pump – removal and refitting

Petrol engines

1 The vacuum pump is located on the rear of the cylinder head, and is driven by the exhaust camshaft.

Models with suspension turret braces

2 Remove the plastic cap from the centre of the scuttle trim panel. Two different types of the cap are fitted: one with a central slot, removed by rotating it 45° anti-clockwise, and one without a central slot, which is prised from place **(see illustration)**. Note, if the cap or seal are damaged, they must be renewed. Failure to do so may result in water ingress.

3 Undo the bolt in the centre of the scuttle, exposed by the cap removal **(see illustration)**. Discard the bolt – a new one must be fitted.

Version A

4 Undo the bolt at each outer end of the braces, then hold the rubber grommet in place and slide the braces outwards from place **(see illustration)**. Do not allow the grommet to be displaced. Discard the bolts – new ones must be fitted.

Version B

5 Undo the nuts securing the brace bracket to the suspension turrets, and carefully slide the braces from place **(see illustration)**.

All models

6 Working at the rear of the engine compartment, undo the bolts and remove the pollen filter cover **(see illustration 10.1)**. Slide the filter from the housing. If necessary, refer to Chapter 1A or 1B.

7 Release the catches and remove the left- and right-hand plastic covers from behind the suspension turret each side of the engine compartment. Unclip the hose from the left-hand cover **(see illustration 10.2)**.

8 Depress the clips and pull the cable guide forwards from the pollen filter lower housing **(see illustration 10.3)**.

9 Release the catch and undo the bolt each side, then slide the pollen filter lower housing forwards and manoeuvre it from place **(see illustrations 10.4a and 10.4b)**.

10 Pull the ignition coil plastic cover from the rubber retaining grommets.

11 Disconnect the vacuum hose from the

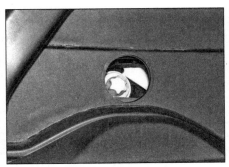

21.3 Undo the bolt beneath the cap

21.4 Undo the bolt at the end of each brace

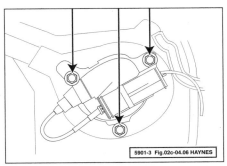

21.5 Strut brace bracket retaining nuts

21.11 Undo the 3 bolts and remove the vacuum pump

21.12 Ensure the pump drive engages with the slot in the end of the camshaft

21.17 Undo the bolt and pull the hose connection from the pump

pump, undo the three bolts and remove the pump **(see illustration)**. Discard the O-ring seal, a new one must be fitted.

12 Refitting is a reversal of removal, ensuring the drive lug of the pump engages correctly with the slot in the camshaft **(see illustration)**. Tighten the pump retaining bolts securely.

4-cylinder diesel engines

N47 engines

13 On these engines, the vacuum pump is integral with the oil pump. Refer to Chapter 2C for the oil pump removal procedure.

6-cylinder diesel engines

M57T2 engines

14 Undo the 2 bolts and remove the plastic cover from the top of the engine.
15 The vacuum pump is located at the front of the engine, and is driven by the camshaft.
16 Remove the EGR pipe/cooler as described in Chapter 4C Section 3. There is no need to drain the coolant or disconnect the coolant pipes – pull the pipe/cooler forwards slightly to facilitate vacuum pump removal. **Note:** *If the vacuum pump is being removed as part of the camshaft removal procedure, the EGR pipe/cooler must be completely removed.*

17 Undo the bolt and disconnect the hose connection from the vacuum pump **(see illustration)**. Renew the connection O-ring seal.
18 Undo the bolt and remove the vacuum pump. Renew the O-ring seal **(see illustrations)**.
19 Refitting is a reversal of removal, ensuring the drive lug of the pump engages correctly with the slot in the camshaft **(see illustration)**. Tighten the pump retaining bolts securely.

N57 engines

20 On these engines, the vacuum pump is integral with the oil pump. Refer to Chapter 2C for the oil pump removal procedure.

21.18a Undo the bolt and pull the pump from the cylinder head

21.18b Renew the pump O-ring seal

21.19 The pump drive engages with the slot in the end of the camshaft

Chapter 10
Suspension and steering

Contents

Degrees of difficulty

Easy, suitable for novice with little experience	Fairly easy, suitable for beginner with some experience	Fairly difficult, suitable for competent DIY mechanic	Difficult, suitable for experienced DIY mechanic	Very difficult, suitable for expert DIY or professional

Specifications

Front suspension
Type . . . . Independent, with MacPherson struts incorporating coil springs and telescopic shock absorbers. Anti-roll bar fitted to all models

Rear suspension
Type . . . . Independent, trailing arms located by upper and lower control arms with coil springs and shock absorbers. Anti-roll bar fitted to all models

Steering
Type . . . . Rack and pinion. Power assistance standard on all models

Wheel alignment and steering angles
Note: *Vehicle must be laden to simulate front and rear passengers, and a full fuel tank.*
Front wheel:
  Camber angle:
    Standard suspension . . . . -18' ± 25'
    Sports suspension . . . . -33' ± 30'
    Maximum difference between sides . . . . 30'
  Castor angle:
    Standard suspension . . . . Not available
    Sports suspension . . . . Not available
    Maximum difference between sides . . . . 30'
  Toe setting (total) . . . . 0° 14' ± 12'
Rear wheel:
  Camber angle:
    Standard suspension . . . . -1° 30' ± 25'
    Sports suspension . . . . -1° 50' ± 25'
    Maximum difference between sides . . . . 30'
  Toe setting (total) . . . . 0° 18' ± 12'

Torque wrench settings

	Nm	lbf ft

Note: *On some fixings different grades of bolt can be used; the grade of each bolt is stamped on the bolt head. Ensure that each bolt is tightened to the correct torque for its grade.*

Front suspension	Nm	lbf ft
Anti-roll bar connecting link nuts*	58	43
Anti-roll bar mounting clamp nuts*	22	16
Control arm balljoint nut*	165	122
Control arm-to-subframe nut: *		
M12:		
8.8:		
Stage 1	68	50
Stage 2	Angle-tighten a further 90°	
12.9:		
Stage 1	100	74
Stage 2	Angle-tighten a further 90°	
DSC sensor bolts	8	6
Hub/bearing assembly*	110	81
Strut piston rod nut*	64	47
Strut-to-hub carrier nut: *		
M10	45	33
M12	81	60
Strut mounting-to-body nuts*	34	25
Tension strut balljoint nut*	165	122
Tension strut-to-subframe nut: *		
M12:		
8.8:		
Stage 1	68	50
Stage 2	Angle-tighten a further 90°	
10.9:		
Stage 1	100	74
Stage 2	Angle-tighten a further 90°	

Rear suspension	Nm	lbf ft
Anti-roll bar clamps	21	15
Anti-roll bar link:		
Bolt	21	15
Nut*	58	43
Camber arm-to-hub carrier nut*	165	122
Camber arm-to subframe nut*	165	122
Control arm-to-hub carrier bolt: *		
Stage 1	100	74
Stage 2	Angle-tighten a further 90°	
Control arm-to-subframe nut*	100	74
Shock absorber upper mounting nut: *		
M10	27	20
M14	37	27
Shock absorber lower mounting bolts: *		
M10	60	44
M12	100	74
Shock absorber lower mounting nut*	37	27
Subframe	100	74
Toe arm-to-hub carrier	100	74
Toe arm-to-subframe nut*	100	74
Traction strut-to-hub carrier bolt: *		
Stage 1	100	74
Stage 2	Angle-tighten a further 90°	
Traction strut-to-subframe nut*	100	74
Trailing arm-to-hub carrier nut*	100	74
Trailing arm-to-subframe nut*	100	74

Steering	Nm	lbf ft
Lateral acceleration sensor	8	6
Power steering pipe union bolts:		
M10 union bolt	12	9
M14 union bolt	35	26
M16 union bolt	40	30
M18 union bolt	45	33

Torque wrench settings (continued)

	Nm	lbf ft
Steering (continued)		
Power steering pump bolts:		
Diesel engines	22	16
Petrol engines.	19	14
Steering column bolts	22	16
Steering column universal joint clamp/pinch-bolt*.	22	16
Steering rack mounting bolts/nuts: *		
Stage 1	56	41
Stage 2	Angle-tighten a further 90°	
Steering wheel	63	46
Track rod end balljoint retaining nut*	165	122
Track rod end clamp bolt*	40	30
Track rod to steering rack.	110	81
Roadwheels		
Roadwheel bolts.	120	89

* Do not re-use

1 General Information

1 The independent front suspension is of the MacPherson strut type, incorporating coil springs and integral telescopic shock absorbers. The MacPherson struts are located by transverse lower suspension arms, which use rubber inner mounting bushes, and incorporate a balljoint at the outer ends. The front hub carriers, which carry the brake calipers and the hub/disc assemblies, are bolted to the MacPherson struts, and connected to the lower arms through balljoints. A front anti-roll bar is fitted to all models. The anti-roll bar is rubber-mounted and is connected to both suspension struts/ lower arms (as applicable) by connecting links **(see illustration)**.

2 The rear suspension is of the fully independent type consisting of trailing arms, which are linked to the rear axle carrier by various control arms/struts. Coil springs are fitted between the upper control arms and vehicle body, and shock absorbers are connected to the vehicle body and trailing arms. A rear anti-roll bar is fitted on all

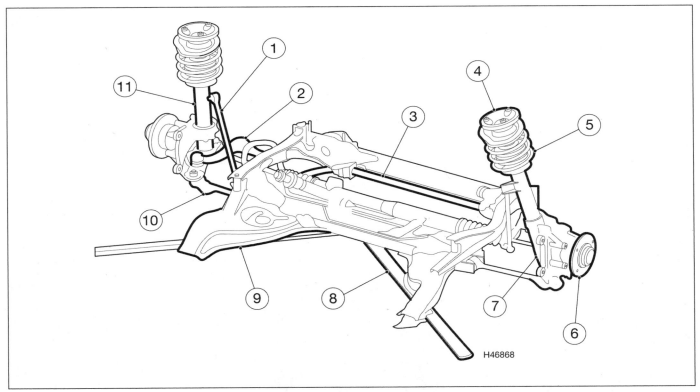

H46868

1.1 Front axle details

1 Anti-roll bar link
2 Tension strut
3 Front anti-roll bar
4 Strut top mounting
5 Coil spring
6 Wheel bearing
7 Hub carrier
8 Reinforcement strut/ brace
9 Front subframe
10 Control arm
11 Shock absorber strut

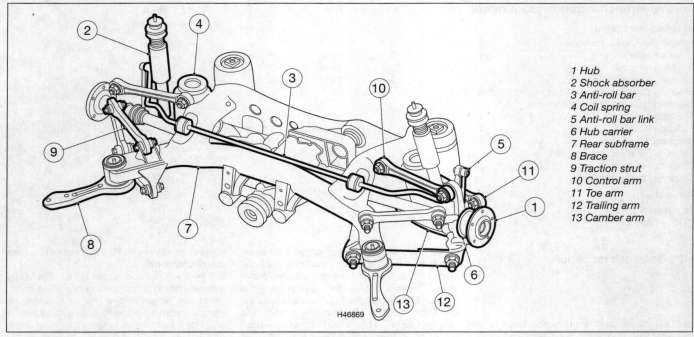

1 Hub
2 Shock absorber
3 Anti-roll bar
4 Coil spring
5 Anti-roll bar link
6 Hub carrier
7 Rear subframe
8 Brace
9 Traction strut
10 Control arm
11 Toe arm
12 Trailing arm
13 Camber arm

1.2 Rear axle details

models. The anti-roll bar is rubber-mounted, and is connected to the upper control arms by connecting links **(see illustration)**.

3 The steering column is connected to the steering rack by an intermediate shaft, which incorporates a universal joint.

4 The steering rack is mounted onto the front subframe, and is connected by two track rods to the steering arms projecting forwards from the hub carriers. The track rod ends are threaded, to facilitate adjustment.

5 Power-assisted steering is fitted as standard to all models. The hydraulic steering system is powered by a belt-driven pump, which is driven off the crankshaft pulley, whilst on some models a fully-electronic system is available, which has a rack-mounted electric motor to provide the power assistance.
Note: *The information contained in this Chapter is applicable to the standard suspension set-up. On models with M-Technic sports suspension, slight differences will be found. Refer to your BMW dealer for details.*

2 Front hub assembly – removal and refitting

Removal

1 Remove the front brake disc (Chapter 9).
2 Undo the 4 retaining bolts and remove the hub and bearing assembly **(see illustration)**. Discard the bolts, new ones must be fitted. Note that the hub and bearing is only available as a complete assembly.

Refitting

3 Ensure the mating surfaces of the hub and hub carrier are clean, then position the hub on the carrier.
4 Fit the new retaining bolts and tighten them to the specified torque.
5 Refit the brake disc as described in Chapter 9.

3 Front hub carrier – removal and refitting

Note: *New suspension strut-to-hub, tension strut balljoint and control arm balljoint nuts will be required on refitting.*

Removal

1 Firmly apply the handbrake, then jack up the front of the car and support it on axle stands. Remove the relevant front roadwheel, then undo the fasteners and remove the engine undershield **(see illustration)**.
2 If the hub carrier is to be renewed, remove the hub assembly (see Section 2).
3 If the hub carrier assembly is to be refitted, remove the brake disc and ABS wheel speed sensor as described in Chapter 9.
4 On models with Xenon headlights, release the clamp and detach the ride height sensor rod from the control arm **(see illustration)**.

2.2 Front hub retaining bolts

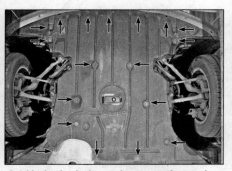

3.1 Undo the bolts and remove the engine undershield

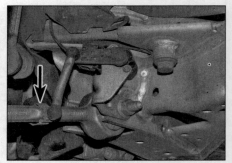

3.4 Release the clamp and detach the sensor rod

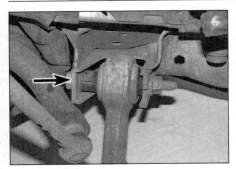

3.5 Control arm-to-subframe bolt

3.8a Note that the bolt is inserted from the front

3.8b Using an Allen key to slightly spread the hub carrier clamp

5 Slacken the bolt securing the control arm to the front subframe **(see illustration)**. This is to prevent damage to the mounting bush as the hub carrier is removed.

6 Detach the control arm and tension strut from the hub carrier as described in Section 5 **(see illustrations 5.3 and 5.6)**.

7 Undo the nut and detach the track rod end from the hub carrier as described in Section 25.

8 Slacken and remove the bolt securing the suspension strut to the hub carrier. Note that the bolt is inserted from the front. Slide the hub carrier down and off from the end of the strut. Discard the nut, a new one must be fitted. To ease removal, insert a large screwdriver or Allen key into the slot on the back of the hub carrier and slightly spread the hub carrier clamp **(see illustrations)**. Take care to spread the carrier clamp only as much as absolutely necessary, as excessive force will cause damage.

9 Examine the hub carrier for signs of wear or damage, and renew if necessary.

Refitting

10 Prior to refitting, clean the threads of the strut-to-hub carrier bolt hole by running a tap of the correct thread size and pitch down it.

11 Locate the hub carrier correctly with the suspension strut, ensuring that the locating

> **HAYNES HINT** *If a suitable tap is not available, clean out the holes using the old bolt with slots cut in its threads.*

pins on the strut slide into the slot in the hub carrier clamp **(see illustration)**. Slide the hub carrier up until it contacts the 'stop' on the strut. Fit the bolt from the front and tighten the new nut to the specified torque.

12 Engage the hub carrier with the control arm balljoint stud, and fit the new retaining nut. Tighten the nut to the specified torque.

13 Engage the tension strut balljoint with the hub carrier, fit the new nut and tighten it to the specified torque.

14 Engage the track rod balljoint in the hub carrier, then fit a new retaining nut and tighten it to the specified torque.

15 Fit the new hub assembly (see Section 2) where applicable.

16 On models where the hub was not disturbed, refit the ABS wheel speed sensor and disc (see Chapter 9).

17 Refit the roadwheel and the undershield, then lower the car to the ground and tighten the wheel bolts to the specified torque.

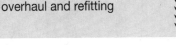

4 Front strut – removal, overhaul and refitting

Removal

1 Chock the rear wheels, apply the handbrake, then jack up the front of the car and support on axle stands. Remove the appropriate roadwheel. Undo the fasteners and remove the engine undershield.

2 Remove the brake disc as described in Chapter 9.

3 Trace the wiring back to the connectors, and disconnect the ABS wheel speed sensor and the brake pad wear sensor. Unclip the wiring from any retaining clips.

4 On models with Xenon headlights, release the clamp and detach the ride height sensor rod from the control arm **(see illustration 3.4)**.

5 Slacken the bolt/nut securing the control arm to the front subframe **(see illustration 3.5)**. This is to prevent damage to the mounting bush as the hub carrier is removed.

6 Detach the control arm and tension strut from the hub carrier as described in Section 5 **(see illustrations 5.3 and 5.6)**.

7 Undo the nut and detach the track rod end from the hub carrier as described in Section 25.

8 Counterhold using the flats on the balljoint shank, then undo the nut securing the anti-roll bar link to the strut **(see illustration)**. Discard the nut – a new one must be fitted. Note that the brake hose bracket is also retained by the nut.

9 Place a trolley jack under the hub carrier to prevent it falling as the upper mounting nuts are removed.

Models with suspension turret braces

10 Remove the plastic cap from the centre of the scuttle trim panel. Two different types of the cap are fitted: one with a central slot, removed by rotating it 45° anti-clockwise, and one without a central slot, which is prised from place **(see illustration)**. Note, if the cap

3.11 Ensure the locating pins slide into the slot

4.8 Counterhold the balljoint, and undo the anti-roll bar link nut

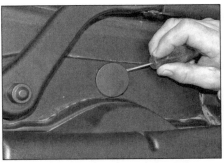

4.10 Remove the cap from the centre of the scuttle trim panel...

4.11... then undo the bolt

4.12 Undo the bolts each side at the end of the braces

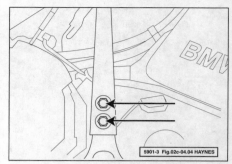

4.13 Undo the strut-to-bracket nuts

or seal are damaged, they must be renewed. Failure to do so may result in water ingress.

11 Undo the bolt in the centre of the scuttle, exposed by the cap removal **(see illustration)**. Discard the bolt – a new one must be fitted.

Version A

12 Undo the bolt at each outer end of the braces, then hold the rubber grommet in place and slide the braces outwards from place **(see illustration)**. Do not allow the grommet to be displaced. Discard the bolts – new ones must be fitted.

Version B

13 Undo the nuts securing the braces to the brackets on top of the suspension strut towers **(see illustration)**.

14 Undo the nuts and remove the brace

brackets to the top of the suspension strut towers **(see illustration)**.

All models

15 From within the engine compartment, unscrew the strut upper mounting nuts, then carefully lower the strut assembly out from underneath the wing. **Note:** *On some models, a centring pin fixed to the strut upper mounting plate, aligns with a corresponding hole in the vehicle body work* **(see illustration)**. On models where no centring pin is fitted, make alignment marks between the mounting plate and vehicle body. It is essential that the mounting plate is fitted to its original location to preserve the strut camber angle. Recover the sealing washer and mounting shim from between the strut and the wing **(see illustration)**.

Overhaul

⚠️ *Warning: Before attempting to dismantle the front suspension strut, a suitable tool to hold the coil spring in compression must be obtained. Adjustable coil spring compressors are readily available, and are recommended for this operation. Any attempt to dismantle the strut without such a tool is likely to result in damage or personal injury.*

16 With the strut removed from the car, clean away all external dirt, then mount it upright in a vice.

17 Slacken and remove the bolt securing the suspension strut to the hub carrier. Remove the brake ABS sensor wiring bracket, then slide the hub carrier down and off from the end of the strut. Discard the nut, a new one must be fitted. To ease removal, insert a suitably-sized Allen key into the slot on the back of the hub carrier and slightly spread the hub carrier clamp **(see illustrations 3.8a and 3.8b)**. Take care to spread the carrier clamp only as much as absolutely necessary, as excessive force will cause damage.

18 Fit the spring compressor, and compress the coil spring until all tension is relieved from the upper spring seat **(see illustration)**.

19 Remove the cap from the top of the strut to gain access to the strut upper mounting retaining nut. Slacken the nut whilst retaining

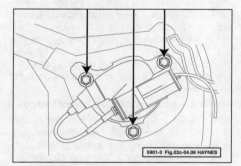

4.14 If required, undo the nuts and remove the brackets

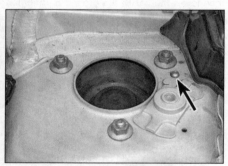

4.15a Note the centring pin

4.15b Recover the sealing washer...

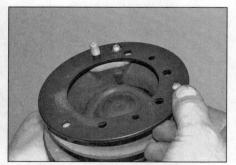

4.15c... and mounting shim

4.18 Compress the spring until the upper seat is no longer under tension

4.19a Prise off the cap

4.19b Use an Allen bit to prevent the piston rod rotating...

4.19c... then undo the nut using a socket and hollow ratchet

the strut piston with a suitable Allen bit **(see illustrations)**.

20 Remove the mounting nut, and lift off the mounting plate complete with thrust bearing, shim, washer and supporting ring/seat.

21 Lift off the coil spring, followed by the bump stop, gaiter and lower spring seat.

22 With the strut assembly now completely dismantled, examine all the components for wear, damage or deformation, and check the upper mounting bearing for smoothness of operation. Renew any of the components as necessary.

23 Examine the strut for signs of fluid leakage. Check the strut piston for signs of pitting along its entire length, and check the strut body for signs of damage.

24 If any doubt exists about the condition of the coil spring, carefully remove the spring compressors, and check the spring for distortion and signs of cracking. Renew the

4.26a Refit the lower spring seat...

4.26b... followed by the gaiter and bump stop

spring if it is damaged or distorted, or if there is any doubt as to its condition.

25 Inspect all other components for damage or deterioration, and renew any that are suspect.

26 Refit the lower spring seat, and slide the

bump stop and gaiter onto the strut piston **(see illustrations)**.

27 Fit the coil spring onto the strut, making sure the rubber seat and spring are correctly located **(see illustration)**.

28 Fit the support ring/seat, shim, washer and upper mounting plate, so that the spring end is against the seat stop **(see illustrations)**.

29 Fit the new mounting plate nut and tighten it to the specified torque.

30 Ensure the spring ends and seats are correctly located, then carefully release the compressor and remove it from the strut. Refit the cap to the top of the strut.

Refitting

31 Refitting is a reversal of removal, noting the following points:

a) Tighten all fasteners to their specified torque where given.

4.27 Ensure the spring end and seat are correctly located

4.28a Fit the support ring/seat, aligning the spring end with the seat

4.28b Refit the shim...

4.28c... washer...

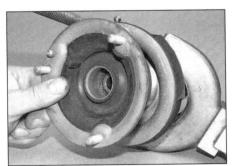

4.28d... and upper mounting plate

b) *Renew all self-locking nuts.*
c) *We recommend the front wheel alignment is checked at the earliest opportunity. On models with active steering, have the steering angle sensor calibration checked using BMW diagnostic equipment. Entrust this task to a BMW dealer or suitably-equipped specialist.*

5 Front arms/strut – removal, overhaul and refitting

Note: *New control arm front balljoint nuts will be required on refitting.*

Removal

1 Chock the rear wheels, firmly apply the handbrake, then jack up the front of the car and support on axle stands. Remove the appropriate front roadwheel. Undo the fasteners and remove the engine undershield **(see illustration 3.1)**.

Control arm

2 On models fitted with suspension ride height sensors, release the clamp and disconnect the sensor link bracket from the arm.

3 Unscrew the control arm balljoint nut to the point where the edge of the nut is flush with the end of the balljoint shank, then release the arm from the hub carrier by gently tapping the end of the balljoint shank with a soft-faced hammer **(see illustrations)**. There is no need to use a balljoint separator.

4 Undo the nut and pull the inner mounting bolt from the control arm **(see illustration 3.5)**. Note that the bolt is inserted from the rear. Discard the nut – a new one must be fitted.

5 Remove the lower arm assembly from underneath the car. Note that the balljoint may be a tight fit in the crossmember and may need to be tapped out of position.

Tension strut

6 Undo the tension strut balljoint nut. If necessary, use a Torx bit in the end of the balljoint shank to counterhold the nut, then release the arm from the hub carrier by gently

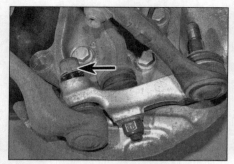

5.3a Undo the control arm balljoint nut...

5.3b ... and tap the balljoint from the hub carrier

tapping the end of the balljoint shank with a soft-faced hammer **(see illustration)**. There is no need to use a balljoint separator.

7 Undo the inner mounting bolt and remove the strut from the subframe **(see illustration)**. Discard the nut – a new one must be fitted.

Overhaul

8 Thoroughly clean the arm or strut and the area around the mountings, removing all traces of dirt and underseal if necessary, then check carefully for cracks, distortion or any other signs of wear or damage, paying particular attention to the mounting bushes and balljoint. Note that the balljoints are integral with both the arm and the strut. If the tension strut bush requires renewal, the strut should be taken to a BMW dealer or suitably-equipped garage. A hydraulic press and suitable spacers are required to press the bush out of position and install the new one.

Refitting

Control arm

9 Locate the inner end of the control arm with the subframe, insert the bolt from the rear, then fit the new nut – do not tighten the nut at this stage. On models with height sensors, refit the bracket before fitting the retaining nut.

10 Ensure the balljoint studs and mounting holes are clean and dry, then offer up the control arm, and engage the balljoint with the hub carrier. If necessary, press the inner

balljoint stud into position using a jack positioned beneath the arm.

11 Fit a new nut to the outer balljoint stud, and tighten it to the specified torque setting.

12 On models equipped with suspension ride height sensors, refit the sensor link bracket to the control arm and secure the clamp.

13 Refit the roadwheel, then lower the car to the ground and tighten the wheel bolts to the specified torque.

14 With the weight of the vehicle on the wheels, tighten the control arm inner bolt/nut to the specified torque.

15 Refit the engine undershield.

16 On models with active steering, it may be necessary to have the steering angle sensor calibration carried out using BMW diagnostic equipment. Entrust this task to a BMW dealer or suitably-equipped specialist.

17 We recommend that the front wheel alignment is checked at the earliest opportunity. On models with active steering, have the steering angle sensor calibration checked using BMW diagnostic equipment. Entrust this task to a BMW dealer or suitably-equipped specialist.

Tension strut

18 Locate the inner end of the strut in the subframe bracket, then insert the bolt and fit the new nut. Do not tighten the nut at this stage.

19 Engage the strut balljoint with the hub carrier, fit the new nut and tighten it to the specified torque.

20 Refit the roadwheel, then lower the car to the ground and tighten the wheel bolts to the specified torque.

21 With the weight of the vehicle on the wheels, tighten the strut inner bolt/nut to the specified torque.

22 Refit the engine undershield.

6 Front arm balljoint – renewal

1 The balljoints on both the tension strut and control arm are integral, and cannot be renewed separately. If defective, the complete arm/strut must be renewed, as described in Section 5.

5.6 Use a Torx bit to counterhold the tension strut balljoint shank nut

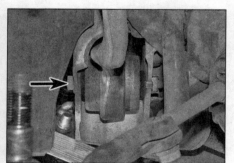

5.7 Tension strut-to-subframe bolt

7 Front anti-roll bar – removal and refitting

Removal

1 Chock the rear wheels, firmly apply the handbrake, then jack up the front of the car and support on axle stands. Undo the fasteners and remove the engine undershield, then remove both front roadwheels.

2 Unscrew the retaining nuts, and free the connecting link from each end of the anti-roll bar using a second spanner to counterhold the balljoint stud (**see illustration**).

3 Make alignment marks between the mounting bushes and anti-roll bar, then slacken the anti-roll bar mounting clamp retaining nuts (**see illustration**).

4 Undo the nuts and remove both clamps from the subframe, and manoeuvre the anti-roll bar out from underneath the car. Remove the mounting bushes from the bar. Discard the self-locking nuts – new ones must be fitted.

5 Carefully examine the anti-roll bar components for signs of wear, damage or deterioration, paying particular attention to the mounting bushes. Renew worn components as necessary.

Refitting

6 Fit the rubber mounting bushes to the anti-roll bar, aligning them with the marks made prior to removal. Rotate each bush so that its flat surface is uppermost, and the split side on the rear.

7 Offer up the anti-roll bar, and manoeuvre it into position. Refit the mounting clamps, and fit the new retaining nuts. Ensure that the bush markings are still aligned with the marks on the bars, then tighten the mounting clamp retaining nuts to the specified torque.

8 Engage the anti-roll bar connecting links with the bar. Make sure the flats on the balljoint shank are correctly located against the lugs on the bar then fit the new retaining nuts and tighten to the specified torque.

9 Refit the brackets to the centre of the anti-roll bar and tighten the bolts securely.

10 Refit the undershield, then refit the roadwheels, lower the car to the ground and tighten the wheel bolts to the specified torque.

8 Front anti-roll bar connecting link – removal and refitting

Note: *New connecting link nuts will be required on refitting.*

Removal

1 Firmly apply the handbrake, then jack up the front of the car and support it on axle stands.

2 Unscrew the retaining nut, and free the

7.2 Use a second spanner to counterhold the anti-roll bar balljoint stud

connecting link from the anti-roll bar using a second spanner to counterhold the link balljoint stud.

3 Slacken and remove the nut securing the link to the suspension strut, using a second spanner to counterhold the link balljoint stud (**see illustration 4.8**).

4 Check the connecting link balljoints for signs of wear. Check that each balljoint is free to move easily, and that the rubber gaiters are undamaged. If necessary renew the connecting link.

Refitting

5 Refitting is a reverse of the removal sequence, using new nuts and tightening them to the specified torque setting.

9 Rear hub assembly – removal and refitting
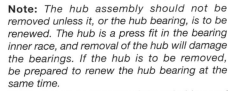

Note: *The hub assembly should not be removed unless it, or the hub bearing, is to be renewed. The hub is a press fit in the bearing inner race, and removal of the hub will damage the bearings. If the hub is to be removed, be prepared to renew the hub bearing at the same time.*

Note: *A long bolt/length of threaded bar and suitable washers will be required on refitting.*

Removal

1 Remove the relevant driveshaft as described in Chapter 8.

2 Remove the brake disc as described in Chapter 9.

3 Bolt a slide hammer to the hub surface, and use the hammer to draw the hub out from the bearing. If the bearing inner race stays attached to the hub, a puller will be required to draw it off.

4 With the hub removed, renew the bearing as described in Section 10.

Refitting

5 Apply a smear of oil to the hub surface, and locate it in the bearing inner race.

6 Draw the hub into position using a long bolt or threaded length of bar and two nuts. Fit a large washer to either end of the bolt/bar, so the inner one bears against the bearing

7.3 Note that the split-side of the anti-roll bar bush is at the rear

inner race, and the outer one against the hub. Slowly tighten the nut(s) until the hub is pulled fully into position. **Note:** *Do not be tempted to knock the hub into position with a hammer and drift, as this will almost certainly damage the bearing.*

7 Remove the bolt/threaded bar and washers (as applicable), and check that the hub bearing rotates smoothly and easily.

8 Refit the brake disc as described in Chapter 9.

9 Refit the driveshaft, referring to Chapter 8.

10 Rear hub bearings – renewal

1 Remove the rear hub as described in Section 9.

2 Remove the hub bearing retaining circlip from the trailing arm.

3 Tap the hub bearing out from the hub carrier using a hammer and suitable punch.

4 Thoroughly clean the hub carrier bore, removing all traces of dirt and grease, and polish away any burrs or raised edges which might hinder reassembly. Renew the circlip if there is any doubt about its condition.

5 On reassembly, apply a light film of clean engine oil to the bearing outer race to aid installation.

6 Locate the bearing in the hub carrier and tap it fully into position, ensuring that it enters the carrier squarely, using a suitable tubular spacer which bears only on the bearing outer race.

7 Secure the bearing in position with the circlip, making sure it is correctly located in the hub carrier groove.

8 Fit the rear hub as described in Section 9.

11 Rear shock absorber – removal, overhaul and refitting

Removal

1 Check the front wheels, then jack up the rear of the car and support it on axle stands. To improve access, remove the rear roadwheel.

11.4 Rear shock absorber lower mounting nut

11.5a When refitting the rubber cap above the shock absorber mounting, the arrow must point upwards

11.5b Rear shock absorber upper mounting nut

2 Remove the luggage compartment side trim panel as described in Chapter 11.
3 Position a jack underneath the hub carrier, and raise the jack so that it is supporting the weight of the carrier. This will prevent the hub carrier dropping when the shock absorber is unbolted.
4 Slacken and remove the nut securing the shock absorber to the lower mounting **(see illustration)**. Counterhold the shock absorber shaft with a spanner.
5 From within the luggage compartment, prise up the rubber cap, then unscrew the upper mounting nut, counterholding the shock absorber shaft with a spanner **(see illustrations)**. Lower the shock absorber out from underneath the car.
6 If required, undo the two bolts and remove the mounting from the suspension arm **(see illustrations)**.

Overhaul
7 Remove the trim cap, bump stop and protective tube.
8 Examine the shock absorber for signs of fluid leakage. Check the piston for signs of pitting along its entire length, and check the body for signs of damage. While holding it in an upright position, test the operation of the shock absorber by moving the piston through a full stroke, and then through short strokes of 50 to 100 mm. In both cases, the resistance felt should be smooth and continuous. If the resistance is jerky, or uneven, or if there is any visible sign of wear or damage, renewal is necessary.

11.6a Undo the shock absorber mounting bolts...

9 Inspect all other components for signs of damage or deterioration, and renew any that are suspect.
10 Slide the tube, bump stop and cap onto the shock absorber.

Refitting
11 If removed, refit the lower mounting to the suspension arm, and tighten the bolts to the specified torque.
12 Ensure the upper mounting and body contact surfaces are clean and dry.
13 Manoeuvre the shock absorber into position, and fit the new upper mounting nut.
14 Engage the lower end of the shock absorber with the mounting, then fit the nut, tightening it to the specified torque.
15 Tighten the upper mounting nut to the specified torque setting then refit the rubber cap over the upper mounting, noting that the arrow must point upwards.
16 Refit the luggage compartment trim panel.
17 Refit the roadwheel and lower the car to the ground.

12 Rear coil spring – removal and refitting

Removal
1 Chock the front wheels, then jack up the rear of the car and support it on axle stands. Remove the relevant roadwheel.
2 The coil spring must be removed

11.6b... and manoeuvre the mounting from place

using a special BMW tool Nos 33 5 011/ 012/013/014/015/016. Do not attempt to remove the coil spring without this tool.
3 Insert the lower collar of the special tool (No 33 5 012) above the lowest coil of the spring, ensuring it makes the maximum contact with the spring, and locates correctly.
4 Insert the guide spindles (Nos 33 5 013, 33 5 014 and 33 5 015) through the base of the spring, and up through the lower collar.
5 Insert the upper collar of the special tool (No 33 5 011) below the highest coil of the spring, ensuring it makes the maximum contact with the spring, and locates correctly with the upper end of the guide spindles.
6 Fit the tool No 33 5 016 over the lower end of the guide spindles, then tighten the spindles and compress the spring just enough to remove it. Do not fully compress the spring or it will be damaged.
7 Inspect the spring closely for signs of damage, such as cracking, and check the spring seats for signs of wear. Renew worn components as necessary.

Refitting
8 Manoeuvre the compressed spring into place, ensuring the ends of the coils and the seats are correctly aligned.
9 Gradually release the tension on the spring, ensuring it locates correctly with the spring seats as it extends.
10 Refit the roadwheel then lower the car to the ground. Tighten the wheel bolts to the specified torque.

13 Rear hub carrier – removal, overhaul and refitting

Removal
1 Chock the front wheels, then jack up the rear of the car and support it on axle stands. Remove the relevant roadwheel.
2 Remove the relevant driveshaft (see Chapter 8).
3 Remove the brake disc and ABS wheel speed sensor as described in Chapter 9.
4 Referring to Chapter 9, disconnect the handbrake cable from the rear wheel.

13.8 Anti-roll bar link bolt

5 Remove the coil spring as described in Section 12.
6 Position a jack underneath the hub carrier, and support the weight of the arm.
7 Slacken and remove the shock absorber lower mounting nut, then undo the 2 bolts and remove the shock absorber mounting – refer to Section 11.
8 Undo the bolt and detach the anti-roll bar link from the hub carrier **(see illustration)**.
9 Disconnect the trailing arm, traction strut, tow arm, control arm and camber arm from the hub carrier as described in Section 14, then remove the hub carrier.

Overhaul

10 Thoroughly clean the hub carrier and the area around the carrier mountings, removing all traces of dirt and underseal if necessary. Check carefully for cracks, distortion or any other signs of wear or damage, paying

particular attention to the mounting bushes and balljoint. If either bushes or balljoint requires renewal, the hub carrier should be taken to a BMW dealer or suitably-equipped garage. A hydraulic press and suitable spacers are required to press the bushes/ balljoint out of position and install the new ones. Inspect the pivot bolts for signs of wear or damage and renew as necessary.

Refitting

11 Refitting is a reversal of removal, noting the following points:
a) *Renew all self locking nuts.*
b) *Only tighten the trailing arm, traction strut, toe arm, control arm and camber arm bolts/nuts when the weight of the vehicle is back on the wheels.*
c) *Tighten all fasteners to their specified torque where given.*
d) *Have the rear wheel alignment checked at the earliest opportunity.*

14 Rear arms/strut – removal, overhaul and refitting

Removal

1 Chock the front wheels, then jack up the rear of the car and support it on axle stands (see *Jacking and vehicle support*). Remove the relevant roadwheel.

Control arm

2 Undo the bolt securing the control arm to

the hub carrier **(see illustration)**. Discard the bolt – a new one must be fitted.
3 Undo the nut, and pull out the bolt securing the arm to the rear subframe **(see illustration)**. Note that the bolt is inserted from the front. Discard the nut – a new one must be fitted.

Trailing arm

4 Undo the bolts and detach the trailing arm from the hub carrier and rear subframe **(see illustration)**. Note that the inner bolt is inserted from the rear, whilst the outer bolt is inserted from the front. Discard the nuts – new ones must be fitted.

Camber arm

5 Remove the rear coil spring as described in Section 12.
6 Undo the 2 bolts and remove the shock absorber lower mounting from the camber arm **(see illustration 11.6a)**. Note that the nuts must be renewed.
7 Support the hub carrier with a trolley jack.
8 Make alignment marks between the camber arm and the inner eccentric bolt head, then undo the nuts and remove the arm retaining bolts **(see illustrations)**. Note that the inner bolt is inserted from the front, whilst the outer bolt is inserted from the rear. Renew the self-locking nuts.
9 Manoeuvre the camber arm from position.

Traction strut

10 Undo the bolt and detach the anti-roll bar link from the hub carrier **(see illustration 13.8)**.
11 Undo the bolt securing the traction strut to the hub carrier **(see illustration)**. Discard

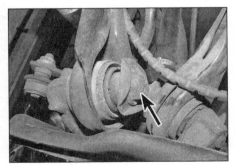

14.2 Control arm-to-hub carrier bolt

14.3 Control arm-to-subframe bolt

14.4 Undo the bolts and remove the trailing arm

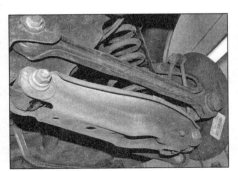

14.8a Camber arm

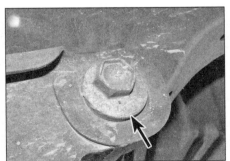

14.8b Make alignment marks between the eccentric bolt head and the arm

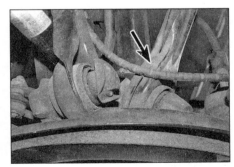

14.11 Hub carrier end of the traction strut

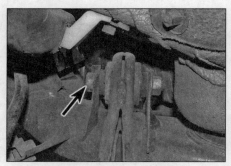

14.12 Traction strut-to-subframe bolt

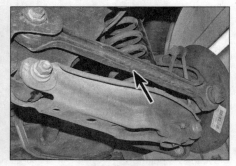

14.15 Toe arm

the bolt – a new one must be fitted. Note that the tapered side of the strut bushing must fit against the hub carrier.

12 Undo the nut and pull the inner mounting bolt from the bracket **(see illustration)**. Discard the nut – a new one must be fitted.

13 Manoeuvre the traction strut from position.

Toe arm

14 Make alignment marks between the toe arm inner eccentric bolt head and the subframe.

15 Undo the bolt securing the toe arm to the hub carrier **(see illustration)**.

16 Undo the nut, then pull the inner eccentric bolt from the subframe. On some models, it's necessary to unclip the plastic cover from the bolt head. Note that the bolt is inserted from the front. Discard the self-locking nut – a new one must be fitted.

Overhaul

17 Thoroughly clean the arms/strut and the area around the mountings, removing all traces of dirt and underseal if necessary. Check for cracks, distortion or any other wear or damage, paying particular attention to the mounting bushes. If the bushes require renewal, the arm/strut should be taken to a BMW dealer or suitably-equipped garage. A hydraulic press and suitable spacers are required to press the bushes out of position and fit the new ones.

18 Inspect the pivot bolts for signs of wear or damage, and renew as necessary.

Refitting

19 Refitting is a reversal of removal, noting the following points:

a) Renew all self-locking nuts.

b) Only tighten the trailing arm, traction strut,

toe arm, control arm and camber arm bolts/nuts when the weight of the vehicle is back on the wheels.

c) Tighten all fasteners to their specified torque where given.

d) Have the rear wheel alignment checked at the earliest opportunity.

15 Rear anti-roll bar – removal and refitting

Removal

1 Remove both rear coils springs as described in Section 12.

2 Remove the control arm from the left-hand side and both traction struts as described in Section 14.

3 Undo the nuts and detach both anti-roll bar links from the anti-roll bar **(see illustration)**.

4 It's now necessary to lower the rear subframe a little to enable the anti-roll bar to be removed. Begin by undoing the rear exhaust section mountings and heat shield.

5 Disconnect the wiring for the rear ABS sensors and brake pads wear sensors at the junction on the rear subframe.

6 Undo the bolts securing the braces each side at the front of the subframe to the vehicle body **(see illustration)**.

7 Use clamps on the rear brake flexible hoses, then disconnect the hoses from the rigid pipes **(see illustration)**.

8 Support the rear subframe with a trolley jack and suitable sections of wood, then slacken the subframe mounting bolts and lower the subframe as much as possible without placing any strain on the brake hoses **(see illustration)**.

9 Make alignment marks between the mounting bushes and anti-roll bar, then slacken the anti-roll bar mounting clamp retaining bolts **(see illustration)**.

10 Remove both clamps from the subframe, and manoeuvre the anti-roll bar out from underneath the car. Remove the mounting bushes from the bar.

11 Carefully examine the anti-roll bar components for signs of wear, damage or

15.3 Use a slim spanner to counterhold the anti-roll bar link balljoint shank

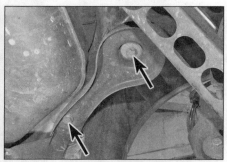

15.6 Undo the bolts and remove the brace each side

15.7 Clamp the flexible hoses

15.8 Subframe mounting bolt

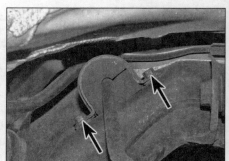

15.9 Anti-roll bar clamp bolts

deterioration, paying particular attention to the mounting bushes. Renew any worn components as necessary.

Refitting

12 Fit the rubber mounting bushes to the anti-roll bar, aligning them with the marks made prior to removal.
13 Offer up the anti-roll bar, and manoeuvre it into position.
14 Refit the mounting clamps, and fit the bolts. Ensure that the bush markings are still aligned with the marks on the bars, then securely tighten the mounting clamp retaining bolts.
15 Refitting is a reversal of removal, noting the following points:
a) Renew all self-locking nuts.
b) Only tighten the traction strut, and control arm bolts/nuts when the weight of the vehicle is back on the wheels.
c) Tighten all fasteners to their specified torque where given.
d) Reconnect the brake hoses and bleed the hydraulic system as described in Chapter 9.
e) Have the rear wheel alignment checked at the earliest opportunity.

16 Steering wheel – removal and refitting
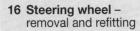

Removal

1 Set the front wheels in the straight-ahead position, and set the steering lock.
2 Remove the airbag unit from the centre of the steering wheel, referring to Chapter 12.
3 Slacken and remove the steering wheel retaining bolt. Disconnect the steering wheel wiring plug(s) **(see illustration)**.
4 Mark the steering wheel and steering column shaft in relation to each other, then lift the steering wheel off the column splines. If it is tight, tap it up near the centre, using the palm of your hand, or twist it from side-to-side, whilst pulling upwards to release it from the shaft splines **(see illustration)**. The airbag contact unit will automatically be locked in position as the wheel is removed; do not attempt to rotate it whilst the wheel is removed.

Refitting

5 Refitting is the reverse of removal, noting the following points.
a) If the contact unit has been rotated with the wheel removed, centralise it by pressing down on the white button and rotating its centre fully anti-clockwise. From this position, rotate the centre back through three complete rotations in a clockwise direction.
b) Engage the wheel with the column splines,

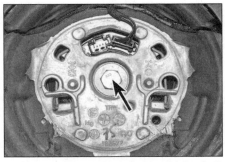
16.3 Undo the steering wheel retaining bolt

aligning the marks made on removal, and tighten the steering wheel retaining bolt to the specified torque.
c) Refit the airbag unit (see Chapter 12).

17 Steering column – removal, inspection and refitting

Note: New steering column shear-bolts, and an intermediate shaft clamp bolt/nut, will be required on refitting.

Removal

1 Disconnect the battery negative terminal (see Chapter 5A).
2 Undo the 3 Torx bolts and remove the lower facia panel above the driver's pedals **(see**

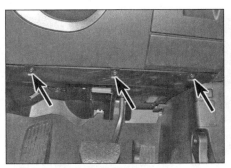
17.2 Undo the 3 bolts and remove the panel above the pedals

17.5a Unclip the column upper shroud

16.4 Make alignment marks between the steering wheel and the shaft

illustration). Disconnect any wiring plugs as the panel is withdrawn.
3 Reach up behind the facia, and pull the footwell heating duct downwards from the driver's side lower facia, and detach it from the heater distribution housing **(see illustration)**. Release the wiring harness from the duct as it's withdrawn.
4 Fully extend, and set the wheel in the lowest position. Remove the steering wheel as described in Section 16.
5 Using a blunt, flat-bladed tool, carefully prise the column upper shroud from the lower shroud, set the column in the highest position, then press the retaining clip each side outwards a little, and pull the lower column shroud downwards. If required, unclip the upper shroud from the gap cover **(see illustrations)**.

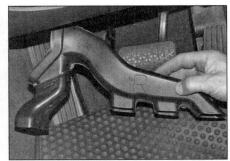
17.3 Unclip the right-hand footwell heating duct

17.5b Squeeze together the clips and detach the upper shroud from the gaiter

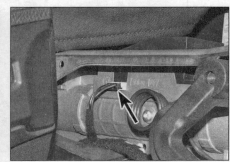

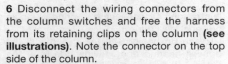
17.6a Disconnect the switch gear wiring plugs...

17.6b... and the plug on the top of the column

17.7 Pull up the gaiter at the base of the column

6 Disconnect the wiring connectors from the column switches and free the harness from its retaining clips on the column **(see illustrations)**. Note the connector on the top side of the column.

7 Slide up the rubber gaiter at the base of the column **(see illustration)**.

8 Slacken and remove the clamp bolt, and disengage the shaft from the column **(see illustration)**. Discard the bolt – a new one must be fitted.

9 Undo the 4 mounting bolts and pull the column to the rear **(see illustrations)**.

Inspection

10 The steering column incorporates a telescopic safety feature. In the event of a front-end crash, the shaft collapses and prevents the steering wheel injuring the driver. Before refitting the steering column, examine the column and mountings for damage and deformation, and renew as necessary.

11 Check the steering shaft for signs of free play in the column bushes. If any damage or wear is found on the steering column bushes, the column should be overhauled. Overhaul of the column is a complex task requiring several special tools, and should be entrusted to a BMW dealer.

Refitting

12 Manoeuvre the column into position and engage it with the intermediate shaft splines, aligning the marks made prior to removal.

13 Locate the column in position and screw in the mounting bolt. Tighten them to the specified torque.

14 Reconnect the wiring connectors to the ignition switch and column switches, and secure the wiring to the column, ensuring it is correctly routed.

15 Ensure the intermediate shaft and column marks are correctly aligned, and insert the column into the shaft. Fit the new clamp bolt and tighten it to the specified torque.

16 Refit the rubber gaiter to the bulkhead at the base of the column. Note that the arrow on the gaiter must point to the mounting stud.

17 Refit the lower and upper steering column shrouds.

18 Refit the steering wheel as described in Section 16.

19 Refit the footwell air duct.

20 Reconnect the battery negative lead as described in Chapter 5A.

21 If a new column has been fitted, it will be necessary to recalibrate the steering angle sensor using BMW diagnostic equipment. Entrust this task to a BMW dealer or suitably-equipped specialist.

18 Steering column lock – general information

1 At the time of writing, it would appear that the electrically-operated steering column lock is only available as a complete unit with the steering column. Check with a BMW dealer or parts specialist..

19 Steering column intermediate shaft – removal and refitting

Removal

1 Chock the rear wheels, firmly apply the handbrake, then jack up the front of the car and support on axle stands. Set the front wheels in the straight-ahead position. Undo the bolts and remove the engine undershield **(see illustration 3.1)**.

2 Undo the fasteners and remove the lower facia panel above the driver's pedals **(see illustration 17.2)**.

3 Prise the rubber gaiter upwards from the base of the column **(see illustration 17.7)**.

4 Using paint or a suitable marker pen, make

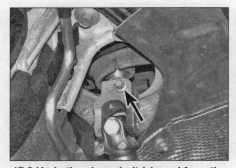
17.8 Undo the clamp bolt (viewed from the engine compartment)

17.9a Undo the upper mounting bolts...

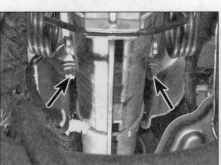
17.9b... the lower mounting bolts...

17.9c... and manoeuvre the column rearwards

20.3a Counterhold the track rod end ball-joint shank with a Torx bit. Undo the nut...

20.3b... and tap the balljoint from the hub carrier

20.5 Steering rack pinion coupling pinch-bolt

alignment marks between the intermediate shaft universal joint and the steering column, the shaft and flexible coupling, and the flexible coupling and the steering rack pinion (see illustration 17.8).

5 Slacken and remove the clamp bolts, then slide the two halves of the shaft together and remove the shaft assembly from the car.

6 Inspect the intermediate shaft universal joint for signs of roughness in its bearings and ease of movement. Also examine the shaft rubber coupling for signs of damage or deterioration, and check that the rubber is securely bonded to the flanges. If the universal joint or rubber coupling are suspect, the complete intermediate shaft should be renewed.

Refitting

7 Check that the front wheels are still in the straight-ahead position, and that the steering wheel is correctly positioned.

8 Align the marks made on removal, and engage the intermediate shaft joint with the steering column and the coupling with the steering rack.

9 Insert the new clamp bolts, and tighten them to the specified torque setting.

10 The remainder of refitting is a reversal of removal. If a new shaft has been fitted, it will be necessary to recalibrate the steering angle sensor using BMW diagnostic equipment. Entrust this task to a BMW dealer or suitably-equipped specialist.

20 Steering rack assembly – removal, overhaul and refitting

Removal

1 Chock the rear wheels, firmly apply the handbrake, then jack up the front of the car and support on axle stands. Remove both front roadwheels, undo the fasteners and remove the engine undershield.

2 Set the steering in the 'straight-ahead' position and engage the steering lock. On models with electric power steering, disconnect the battery negative lead as described in Chapter 5A.

3 Undo the nuts securing the steering rack track rod balljoints to the hub carriers, and unscrew them until the edge of the nuts are flush with the ends of the balljoint shanks. Release the balljoints by gently tapping the ends of the shanks with a soft-faced hammer (see illustrations). There is no need to use a universal balljoint separator.

4 Using paint or a suitable marker pen, make alignment marks between the intermediate shaft coupling and the steering rack pinion. Note: On some models an alignment mark is already provided on the pinion flange, which aligns with a mark cast into the pinion housing.

5 Slacken and remove the coupling pinch-bolt (see illustration).

Conventional power steering

6 Using brake hose clamps, clamp both

the supply and return hoses near the power steering fluid reservoir. This will minimise fluid loss. Mark the unions to ensure they are correctly positioned on reassembly, then slacken and remove the feed and return pipe union bolts from the steering rack pinion housing, and recover the sealing washers – remove the heat shield if necessary. Be prepared for fluid spillage, and position a suitable container beneath the pipes whilst unscrewing the bolts (see illustration). Plug the pipe ends and steering rack orifices to prevent fluid leakage and to keep dirt out of the hydraulic system.

7 Release the power steering pipes from the retaining clips on the steering rack.

Electric power steering

8 Release the steering rack wiring harness from the cable ties, then disconnect the wiring plug from the rack motor (see illustration).

All types

9 Slacken and remove the steering rack mounting bolts, and remove the steering rack from underneath the car (see illustration). Discard the nuts and bolts – new ones must be fitted.

Overhaul

10 Examine the steering rack assembly for signs of wear or damage, and check that the rack moves freely throughout the full length of its travel, with no signs of roughness or excessive free play between the steering rack pinion and rack. It is not possible to overhaul the steering rack assembly housing

20.6 Undo the bolts and detach the pipes from the rack pinion

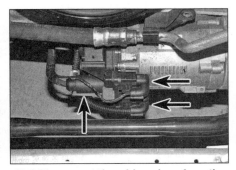

20.8 Disconnect the wiring plugs from the electric power steering rack

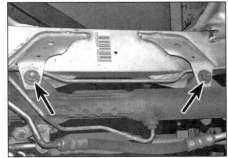

20.9 Steering rack mounting bolts

components; if it is faulty, the assembly must be renewed. The only components which can be renewed individually are the steering rack gaiters, the track rod balljoints and the track rods. These procedures are covered later in this Chapter.

Refitting

11 Offer up the steering rack, and insert the mounting bolts. Fit new nuts and bolts, and tighten them to the specified torque setting.

Conventional power steering

12 Position a new sealing washer on each side of the pipe hose unions and refit the union bolts. Tighten the union bolts to the specified torque.

Electric power steering

13 Reconnect the motor wiring plug, and secure the harness in its original position using cable ties.

All types

14 Align the marks made on removal, and connect the intermediate shaft coupling to the steering rack. Insert the new clamp bolt then tighten it to the specified torque.
15 Locate the track rod balljoints in the hub carriers, then fit the new nuts and tighten them to the specified torque.
16 Refit the roadwheels, and the engine under-shield, then lower the car to the ground and tighten the wheel bolts to the specified torque.

Conventional power steering

17 Bleed the hydraulic system as described in Section 22.
18 We recommend that the front wheel alignment is checked at the earliest opportunity. On models with active steering, have the steering angle sensor calibration checked using BMW diagnostic equipment. Entrust this task to a BMW dealer or suitably-equipped specialist.

Electric power steering

19 If a new steering rack has been fitted, it must be programmed/calibrated using BMW diagnostic equipment. Entrust this task to a BMW dealer or suitably-equipped specialist.
20 We recommend that the front wheel alignment is checked at the earliest opportunity. On models with active steering, have the steering

21.7 Power steering pump mounting bolts

angle sensor calibration checked using BMW diagnostic equipment. Entrust this task to a BMW dealer or suitably-equipped specialist.

21 Power steering pump – removal and refitting

Note: *This procedure applies only to models with conventional power steering. On models with electric power steering, the motor is integral with the rack assembly. Consult a BMW dealer or parts specialist with regard to parts availability.*

Removal

1 Chock the rear wheels, then jack up the front of the car and support it on axle stands (see *Jacking and vehicle support*). Undo the fasteners and remove the engine undershield.

Diesel engines

2 On 6-cylinder N57 engines, remove the cooling fan shroud as described in Chapter 3 Section 6.
3 Working as described in Chapter 1A or 1B, release the drivebelt tension and unhook the drivebelt from the pump pulley, noting that on 4-cylinder engines the steering pump pulley retaining bolts should be slackened prior to releasing the tension.
4 On 4-cylinder engines, unscrew the retaining bolts and remove the pulley from the power steering pump, noting which way around it is fitted.
5 On all models, using brake hose clamps, clamp both the supply and return hoses near the power steering fluid reservoir. This will minimise fluid loss during subsequent operations.
6 Mark the unions to ensure they are correctly positioned on reassembly, then slacken and remove the feed and return pipe union bolts and recover the sealing washers. Be prepared

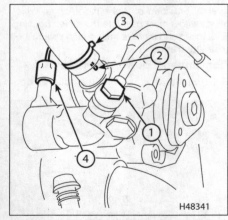

21.13 Steering pump connections

1 *Pressure pipe*
2 *These marks must align*
3 *Suction pipe*
4 *Wiring plug*

for fluid spillage, and position a suitable container beneath the pipes whilst unscrewing the bolts. Plug the pipe ends and steering pump orifices, to keep dirt out of the hydraulic system.
7 Slacken and remove the mounting bolts and remove the pump **(see illustration)**.
8 If the power steering pump is faulty, seek the advice of your BMW dealer as to the availability of spare parts. If spares are available, it may be possible to have the pump overhauled by a suitable specialist, or alternatively obtain an exchange unit. If not, the pump must be renewed.

Petrol engines

9 Remove the coolant thermostat as described in.
10 Slacken the steering pump pulley bolts, then remove the auxiliary drivebelt as described in.
11 Completely undo the retaining bolts and remove the pulley.
12 Using brake hose clamps, clamp both the supply and return hoses near the power steering fluid reservoir. This will minimise fluid loss during subsequent operations.
13 Mark the unions to ensure they are correctly positioned on reassembly, then slacken and remove the feed and return pipe union bolts, and recover the sealing washers **(see illustration)**. Be prepared for fluid spillage, and position a suitable container beneath the pipes whilst unscrewing the bolts. Plug the pipe ends and steering pump orifices, to prevent fluid leakage and to keep dirt out of the hydraulic system.
14 Disconnect the wiring plug from the rear of the pump.
15 Undo the outer pump retaining bolt and remove the spacer **(see illustration)**.
16 Undo the remaining bolts and manoeuvre the pump from position.

Refitting

17 Where necessary, transfer the rear mounting bracket to the new pump, and securely tighten its mounting bolts.
18 Prior to refitting, ensure that the pump is primed by injecting the specified type of fluid

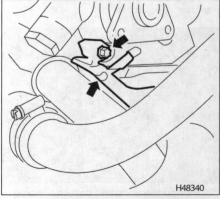

21.15 Pump outer bolt and spacer

in through the supply hose union and rotating the pump shaft.

19 Manoeuvre the pump into position and refit the pivot bolts, tightening them to the specified torque.

20 Position a new sealing washer on each side of the pipe hose unions and refit the union bolts. Tighten the union bolts to the specified torque.

21 Remove the hose clamps and refit the pump pulley (where applicable). Ensure the pulley is the right way around, and securely tighten its retaining bolts.

22 Refit the auxiliary drivebelt and tension it as described in Chapter 1A or 1B.

23 On N57 engines, refit the cooling fan and shroud as described in Chapter 3 Section 6.

24 On completion, lower the car to the ground and bleed the hydraulic system as described in Section 22.

22 Power steering system – bleeding

1 With the engine stopped, fill the fluid reservoir right up to the top with the specified type of fluid.

2 With the engine running, slowly move the steering from lock-to-lock twice to purge out the trapped air, then stop the engine and top-up the level in the fluid reservoir. Repeat this procedure until the fluid level in the reservoir does not drop any further.

3 If, when turning the steering, an abnormal noise is heard from the fluid lines, it indicates that there is still air in the system. Check this by turning the wheels to the straight-ahead position and switching off the engine. If the fluid level in the reservoir rises, then air is present in the system and further bleeding is necessary.

23 Active Steering control unit – removal and refitting

1 Disconnect the battery negative lead as described in Chapter 5A.

2 Release the fasteners and remove the rear section of the front left-hand wheel arch liner.

3 Undo the bolt and disconnect the earth cable from the bracket, then disconnect the wiring plugs from the control unit.

4 Undo the mounting nut and bolt, then manoeuvre the control unit from place.

5 Refitting is a reversal of removal, noting that if a new unit is fitted, it must be programmed/coded using BMW diagnostic equipment. Entrust this task to a BMW dealer or suitably-equipped specialist.

24 Steering rack rubber gaiters – renewal

1 Raise the front of the vehicle and support it securely on axle stands (see *Jacking and vehicle support*). Undo the fasteners and remove the engine undershield.

2 Undo the track rod end clamp bolt **(see illustration)**. Discard the bolt – a new one must be fitted.

3 Release the clip securing the rubber gaiter to the track rod **(see illustration)**. Note the fitted position of the gaiter on the track rod.

4 Mark the position of the track rod end on the threaded portion of the track rod, or count the number of turns and unscrew the track rod from the track rod end.

5 Release the clamp securing the gaiter to the steering rack, and pull the gaiter over the track rod **(see illustration)**.

6 Thoroughly clean the track rod and the steering rack housing, using fine abrasive paper to polish off any corrosion, burrs or sharp edges which might damage the new gaiter's sealing lips on installation. Scrape off all the grease from the old gaiter, and apply it to the track rod inner balljoint. (This assumes that grease has not been lost or contaminated as a result of damage to the old gaiter. Use fresh grease if in doubt – consult a BMW dealer or parts specialist).

7 Apply a little grease to the track rod so the gaiter will slide, then carefully slide the new gaiter (with the retaining clips in place) over the track rod, and locate it on the steering rack housing. Position the outer edge of the gaiter on the track rod.

8 Secure the gaiter to the rack with the retaining clamp.

9 Thread the track rod into the track rod end, aligning the marks made previously, or counting the number of turns, so the track rod and end are in their original positions.

10 Insert the new track rod end clamp bolt and tighten it to the specified torque.

11 Ensure the outer end of the gaiter is still in the correct position, then secure it with the retaining clip.

12 Refit the engine undershield and lower the vehicle to the ground.

13 Upon completion, it is recommended that the front wheel alignment is checked at the earliest opportunity. On models with active steering, have the steering angle sensor calibration checked using BMW diagnostic equipment. Entrust this task to a BMW dealer or suitably-equipped specialist.

25 Track rod end/balljoint – removal and refitting

Removal

1 Apply the handbrake, then jack up the front of the car and support it on axle stands (see *Jacking and vehicle support*). Remove the appropriate front roadwheel.

2 Make a mark on the track rod and measure the distance from the mark to the centre of the balljoint. Note this measurement down, as it will be needed to ensure the wheel alignment remains correctly set when the balljoint is installed.

3 Unscrew the track rod end clamp bolt **(see illustration 24.2)**. Discard the bolt – a new one must be fitted.

4 Undo the nut securing the track rod balljoint to the hub carrier, and unscrew it until the edge of the nut is flush with the end of the balljoint shank. Release the balljoint by gently tapping the end of the shank with a soft-faced hammer **(see illustration 20.3a and 20.3b)**. There is no need to use a balljoint separator tool – a new one must be fitted.

5 Counting the exact number of turns necessary to do so, unscrew the balljoint from the track rod end.

6 Carefully clean the balljoint and the threads. Renew the balljoint if its movement is sloppy or too stiff, if excessively worn, or if damaged in any way; carefully check the stud taper and

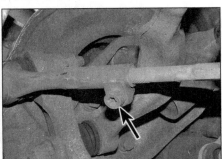

24.2 Undo the track rod end clamp bolt

24.3 Release the gaiter outer clip

24.5 Release the clip securing the gaiter to the rack

threads. If the balljoint gaiter is damaged, the complete balljoint assembly must be renewed; it is not possible to obtain the gaiter separately.

Refitting

7 Screw the balljoint onto the track rod by the number of turns noted on removal. This should position the balljoint at the relevant distance from the track rod mark that was noted prior to removal.

8 Refit the balljoint shank to the hub carrier, then fit a new retaining nut and tighten it to the specified torque.

9 Insert the new track rod end clamp bolt, and tighten it to the specified torque.

10 Refit the roadwheel, then lower the car to the ground and tighten the roadwheel bolts to the specified torque.

11 Upon completion, it is recommended that the front wheel alignment is checked at the earliest opportunity. On models with active steering, have the steering angle sensor calibration checked using BMW diagnostic equipment. Entrust this task to a BMW dealer or suitably-equipped specialist.

26 Track rod – renewal

1 Remove the steering rack gaiter as described in Section 24.

2 Move the rack in as far as possible, then unscrew the track rod nut from the end of the steering rack.

3 Position the track rod on the end of the rack and tighten the retaining nut to the specified torque.

4 Refit the steering gaiter as described in Section 24.

27 Dynamic Stability Control – general information and component renewal

General information

1 Dynamic Stability Control (DSC) is standard on most models, and available as an option on all other models. Strictly speaking, DSC includes ABS and Traction control, but this Section is concerned with Cornering Brake Control (CBC). By monitoring steering wheel movements, suspension ride heights, road speed and lateral acceleration the system controls the pressure in the brake lines to each of the four brake calipers during braking, reducing the possibility of understeer or oversteer.

Component renewal

Steering angle sensor

2 The steering angle sensor is integral with the steering column switch module – refer to Chapter 12.

Front ride height sensor

3 Undo the nut securing the control rod to the sensor arm **(see illustration)**.

4 Remove the two retaining bolts, and withdraw the ride sensor **(see illustration)**. Disconnect the wiring plug as the sensor is removed.

5 Refitting is a reversal of removal. Have the headlight alignment check on completion.

Rear ride height sensor

6 Undo the nut securing the jointed rod to the sensor **(see illustration)**.

7 Undo the bolt securing the sensor mounting bracket to the subframe, and disconnect the sensor wiring plug.

8 If required, undo the 2 bolts and separate the sensor from the mounting bracket.

9 Refitting is a reversal of removal.

DSC control unit

10 The DSC control unit is integral with the ABS control unit, renewal of which should be entrusted to a BMW dealer or suitably-equipped specialist – see Chapter 9.

28 Wheel alignment and steering angles – general information

Definitions

1 A car's steering and suspension geometry is defined in four basic settings – all angles are usually expressed in degrees; the steering axis is defined as an imaginary line drawn through the axis of the suspension strut, extended where necessary to contact the ground.

2 Camber is the angle between each roadwheel and a vertical line drawn through its centre and tyre contact patch, when viewed from the front or rear of the car. Positive camber is when the roadwheels are tilted outwards from the vertical at the top; negative camber is when they are tilted inwards.

3 The front camber angle is not adjustable, and is given for reference only (see paragraph 5). The rear camber angle is adjustable and can be adjusted using a camber angle gauge.

4 Castor is the angle between the steering axis and a vertical line drawn through each roadwheel's centre and tyre contact patch, when viewed from the side of the car. Positive castor is when the steering axis is tilted so that it contacts the ground ahead of the vertical; negative castor is when it contacts the ground behind the vertical.

5 Castor is not adjustable, and is given for reference only; while it can be checked using a castor checking gauge, if the figure obtained is significantly different from that specified, the car must be taken for careful checking by a professional, as the fault can only be caused by wear or damage to the body or suspension components.

6 Toe is the difference, viewed from above, between lines drawn through the roadwheel centres and the car's centre-line. 'Toe-in' is when the roadwheels point inwards, towards each other at the front, while 'toe-out' is when they splay outwards from each other at the front.

7 The front wheel toe setting is adjusted by screwing the right-hand track rod in or out of its balljoint, to alter the effective length of the track rod assembly.

8 Rear wheel toe setting is also adjustable. The toe setting is adjusted by slackening the trailing arm mounting bracket bolts and repositioning the bracket.

Checking and adjustment

9 Due to the special measuring equipment necessary to check the wheel alignment, and the skill required to use it properly, the checking and adjustment of these settings is best left to a BMW dealer or similar expert. Note that most tyre-fitting shops now possess sophisticated checking equipment.

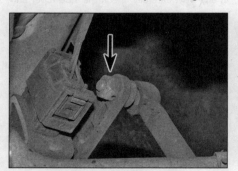

27.3 Undo the nut securing the rod to the arm

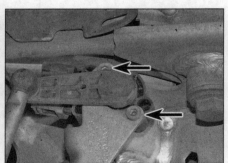

27.4 Ride height sensor retaining bolts

27.6 A nut secures the rod to the sensor arm

Chapter 11
Bodywork and fittings

Contents

Degrees of difficulty

Easy, suitable for novice with little experience	**Fairly easy,** suitable for beginner with some experience	**Fairly difficult,** suitable for competent DIY mechanic	**Difficult,** suitable for experienced DIY mechanic	**Very difficult,** suitable for expert DIY or professional

Specifications

Torque wrench settings	Nm	lbf ft
Seat belt:		
Front anchorage mounting bolts	44	32
All other mountings	36	27
Seat mounting bolts*	42	31

*Do not re-use

1 General Information

1 The bodyshell is made of pressed-steel sections. Most components are welded together, but some use is made of structural adhesives.

2 The bonnet, door and some other vulnerable panels are made of zinc-coated metal, and are further protected by being coated with an anti-chip primer before being sprayed.

3 Extensive use is made of plastic materials, mainly in the interior, but also in exterior components. The bumpers and front grille are injection-moulded from a synthetic material that is very strong and yet light. Plastic components, such as wheel arch liners, are fitted to the underside of the vehicle to improve the body's resistance to corrosion.

2 Maintenance – bodywork and underframe

1 The condition of a vehicle's bodywork is the one thing that significantly affects its value. Maintenance is easy, but needs to be regular. Neglect, particularly after minor damage, can lead quickly to further deterioration and costly repair bills. It is important also to keep watch on those parts of the vehicle not immediately visible, for instance the underside, inside all the wheel arches, and the lower part of the engine compartment.

2 The basic maintenance routine for the bodywork is washing – preferably with a lot of water, from a hose. This will remove all the loose solids which may have stuck to the vehicle. It is important to flush these off in such a way as to prevent grit from scratching the finish. The wheel arches and underframe need washing in the same way, to remove any accumulated mud which will retain moisture and tend to encourage rust. Oddly enough, the best time to clean the underframe and wheel arches is in wet weather, when the mud is thoroughly wet and soft. In very wet weather, the underframe is usually cleaned of large accumulations automatically, and this is a good time for inspection.

3 Periodically, except on vehicles with a wax-based underbody protective coating, it is a good idea to have the whole of the underframe of the vehicle steam-cleaned, engine compartment included, so that a thorough inspection can be carried out to see what minor repairs and renovations are necessary. Steam cleaning is available at many garages, and is necessary for the

removal of the accumulation of oily grime, which sometimes is allowed to become thick in certain areas. If steam-cleaning facilities are not available, there are some excellent grease solvents available which can be brush-applied; the dirt can then be simply hosed off. Note that these methods should not be used on vehicles with wax-based underbody protective coating, or the coating will be removed. Such vehicles should be inspected annually, preferably just before Winter, when the underbody should be washed down, and repair any damage to the wax coating. Ideally, a completely fresh coat should be applied. It would also be worth considering the use of such wax-based protection for injection into door panels, sills, box sections, etc, as an additional safeguard against rust damage, where such protection is not provided by the vehicle manufacturer.

4 After washing paintwork, wipe off with a chamois leather to give an unspotted clear finish. A coat of clear protective wax polish will give added protection against chemical pollutants in the air. If the paintwork sheen has dulled or oxidised, use a cleaner/polisher combination to restore the brilliance of the shine. This requires a little effort, but such dulling is usually caused because regular washing has been neglected. Care needs to be taken with metallic paintwork, as special non-abrasive cleaner/polisher is required to avoid damage to the finish. Always check that the door and ventilator opening drain holes and pipes are completely clear, so that water can be drained out. Brightwork should be treated in the same way as paintwork. Windscreens and windows can be kept clear of the smeary film which often appears, by proprietary glass cleaner. Never use any form of wax or other body or chromium polish on glass.

3 Maintenance – upholstery and carpets

1 Mats and carpets should be brushed or vacuum-cleaned regularly, to keep them free of grit. If they are badly stained, remove them from the vehicle for scrubbing or sponging, and make quite sure they are dry before refitting. Seats and interior trim panels can be kept clean by wiping with a damp cloth and a proprietary brand of cleaner. If they do become stained (which can be more apparent on light-coloured upholstery), use a little liquid detergent and a soft nail brush to scour the grime out of the grain of the material. Do not forget to keep the headlining clean in the same way as the upholstery. When using liquid cleaners inside the vehicle, do not over-wet the surfaces being cleaned. Excessive damp could get into the seams and padded interior, causing stains, offensive odours or even rot. If the inside of the vehicle gets wet accidentally, it is worthwhile taking some trouble to dry it out properly, particularly where carpets are involved. Do not leave oil or electric heaters inside the vehicle for this purpose.

4 Minor body damage – repair

Minor scratches in bodywork

1 If the scratch is very superficial, and does not penetrate to the metal of the bodywork, repair is very simple. Lightly rub the area of the scratch with a paintwork renovator, or a very fine cutting paste, to remove loose paint from the scratch, and to clear the surrounding bodywork of wax polish. Rinse the area with clean water.

2 Apply touch-up paint to the scratch using a fine paint brush; continue to apply fine layers of paint until the surface of the paint in the scratch is level with the surrounding paintwork. Allow the new paint at least two weeks to harden, then blend it into the surrounding paintwork by rubbing the scratch area with a paintwork renovator or a very fine cutting paste. Finally, apply wax polish.

3 Where the scratch has penetrated right through to the metal of the bodywork, causing the metal to rust, a different repair technique is required. Remove any loose rust from the bottom of the scratch with a penknife, then apply rust-inhibiting paint to prevent the formation of rust in the future. Using a rubber or nylon applicator, fill the scratch with bodystopper paste. If required, this paste can be mixed with cellulose thinners to provide a very thin paste which is ideal for filling narrow scratches. Before the stopper-paste in the scratch hardens, wrap a piece of smooth cotton rag around the top of a finger. Dip the finger in cellulose thinners, and quickly sweep it across the surface of the stopper-paste in the scratch; this will ensure that the surface of the stopper-paste is slightly hollowed. The scratch can now be painted over as described earlier in this Section.

Dents in bodywork

4 When deep denting of the vehicle's bodywork has taken place, the first task is to pull the dent out, until the affected bodywork almost attains its original shape. There is little point in trying to restore the original shape completely, as the metal in the damaged area will have stretched on impact, and cannot be reshaped fully to its original contour. It is better to bring the level of the dent up to a point which is about 3 mm below the level of the surrounding bodywork. In cases where the dent is very shallow anyway, it is not worth trying to pull it out at all. If the underside of the dent is accessible, it can be hammered out gently from behind, using a mallet with a wooden or plastic head. Whilst doing this, hold a suitable block of wood firmly against the outside of the panel, to absorb the impact from the hammer blows and thus prevent a large area of the bodywork from being 'belled-out'.

5 Should the dent be in a section of the bodywork which has a double skin, or some other factor making it inaccessible from behind, a different technique is called for. Drill several small holes through the metal inside the area – particularly in the deeper section. Then screw long self-tapping screws into the holes, just sufficiently for them to gain a good purchase in the metal. Now the dent can be pulled out by pulling on the protruding heads of the screws with a pair of pliers.

6 The next stage of the repair is the removal of the paint from the damaged area, and from an inch or so of the surrounding 'sound' bodywork. This is accomplished most easily by using a wire brush or abrasive pad on a power drill, although it can be done just as effectively by hand, using sheets of abrasive paper. To complete the preparation for filling, score the surface of the bare metal with a screwdriver or the tang of a file, or alternatively, drill small holes in the affected area. This will provide a really good 'key' for the filler paste.

7 To complete the repair, see the Section on filling and respraying.

Rust holes or gashes in bodywork

8 Remove all paint from the affected area, and from an inch or so of the surrounding 'sound' bodywork, using an abrasive pad or a wire brush on a power drill. If these are not available, a few sheets of abrasive paper will do the job most effectively. With the paint removed, you will be able to judge the severity of the corrosion, and therefore decide whether to renew the whole panel (if this is possible) or to repair the affected area. New body panels are not as expensive as most people think, and it is often quicker and more satisfactory to fit a new panel than to attempt to repair large areas of corrosion.

9 Remove all fittings from the affected area, except those which will act as a guide to the original shape of the damaged bodywork (e.g. headlight shells etc). Then, using tin snips or a hacksaw blade, remove all loose metal and any other metal badly affected by corrosion. Hammer the edges of the hole inwards, in order to create a slight depression for the filler paste.

10 Wire-brush the affected area to remove the powdery rust from the surface of the remaining metal. Paint the affected area with rust-inhibiting paint, if the back of the rusted area is accessible, treat this also.

11 Before filling can take place, it will be necessary to block the hole in some way. This can be achieved by the use of aluminium or plastic mesh, or aluminium tape.

12 Aluminium or plastic mesh, or glass-fibre matting, is probably the best material to use for a large hole. Cut a piece to the approximate size and shape of the hole to be filled, then position it in the hole so that its edges are below the level of the surrounding bodywork. It can be retained in position by several blobs of filler paste around its periphery.

13 Aluminium tape should be used for small or very narrow holes. Pull a piece off the roll, trim it to the approximate size and shape required, then pull off the backing paper (if used) and stick the tape over the hole; it can be overlapped if the thickness of one piece is insufficient. Burnish down the edges of the tape with the handle of a screwdriver or similar, to ensure that the tape is securely attached to the metal underneath.

Filling and respraying

14 Before using this Section, see the Sections on dent, deep scratch, rust holes and gash repairs.

15 Many types of bodyfiller are available, but generally speaking, those proprietary kits which contain a tin of filler paste and a tube of resin hardener are best for this type of repair. A wide, flexible plastic or nylon applicator will be found invaluable for imparting a smooth and well-contoured finish to the surface of the filler.

16 Mix up a little filler on a clean piece of card or board – measure the hardener carefully (follow the maker's instructions on the pack), otherwise the filler will set too rapidly or too slowly. Using the applicator, apply the filler paste to the prepared area; draw the applicator across the surface of the filler to achieve the correct contour and to level the surface. As soon as a contour that approximates to the correct one is achieved, stop working the paste – if you carry on too long, the paste will become sticky and begin to 'pick-up' on the applicator. Continue to add thin layers of filler paste at 20-minute intervals, until the level of the filler is just proud of the surrounding bodywork.

17 Once the filler has hardened, the excess can be removed using a metal plane or file. From then on, progressively-finer grades of abrasive paper should be used, starting with a 40-grade production paper, and finishing with a 400-grade wet-and-dry paper. Always wrap the abrasive paper around a flat rubber, cork, or wooden block – otherwise the surface of the filler will not be completely flat. During the smoothing of the filler surface, the wet-and-dry paper should be periodically rinsed in water. This will ensure that a very smooth finish is imparted to the filler at the final stage.

18 At this stage, the 'dent' should be surrounded by a ring of bare metal, which in turn should be encircled by the finely 'feathered' edge of the good paintwork. Rinse the repair area with clean water, until all of the dust produced by the rubbing-down operation has gone.

19 Spray the whole area with a light coat of primer – this will show up any imperfections in the surface of the filler. Repair these imperfections with fresh filler paste or bodystopper, and once more smooth the surface with abrasive paper. Repeat this spray-and-repair procedure until you are satisfied that the surface of the filler, and the feathered edge of the paintwork, are perfect. Clean the repair area with clean water, and allow to dry fully.

20 The repair area is now ready for final spraying. Paint spraying must be carried out in a warm, dry, windless and dust-free atmosphere. This condition can be created artificially if you have access to a large indoor working area, but if you are forced to work in the open, you will have to pick your day very carefully. If you are working indoors, dousing the floor in the work area with water will help to settle the dust which would otherwise be in the atmosphere. If the repair area is confined to one body panel, mask off the surrounding panels; this will help to minimise the effects of a slight mis-match in paint colours. Bodywork fittings (e.g. chrome strips, door handles etc) will also need to be masked off. Use genuine masking tape, and several thicknesses of newspaper, for the masking operations.

21 Before commencing to spray, agitate the aerosol can thoroughly, then spray a test area (an old tin, or similar) until the technique is mastered. Cover the repair area with a thick coat of primer; the thickness should be built up using several thin layers of paint, rather than one thick one. Using 400-grade wet-and-dry paper, rub down the surface of the primer until it is really smooth. While doing this, the work area should be thoroughly doused with water, and the wet-and-dry paper periodically rinsed in water. Allow to dry before spraying on more paint.

22 Spray on the top coat, again building up the thickness by using several thin layers of paint. Start spraying at one edge of the repair area, and then, using a side-to-side motion, work until the whole repair area and about 2 inches of the surrounding original paintwork is covered. Remove all masking material 10 to 15 minutes after spraying on the final coat of paint.

23 Allow the new paint at least two weeks to harden, then, using a paintwork renovator, or a very fine cutting paste, blend the edges of the paint into the existing paintwork. Finally, apply wax polish.

Plastic components

24 With the use of more and more plastic body components by the vehicle manufacturers (e.g. bumpers. spoilers, and in some cases major body panels), rectification of more serious damage to such items has become a matter of either entrusting repair work to a specialist in this field, or renewing complete components. Repair of such damage by the DIY owner is not really feasible, owing to the cost of the equipment and materials required for effecting such repairs. The basic technique involves making a groove along the line of the crack in the plastic, using a rotary burr in a power drill. The damaged part is then welded back together, using a hot-air gun to heat up and fuse a plastic filler rod into the groove. Any excess plastic is then removed, and the area rubbed down to a smooth finish. It is important that a filler rod of the correct plastic is used, as body components can be made of a variety of different types (e.g. polycarbonate, ABS, polypropylene).

25 Damage of a less serious nature (abrasions, minor cracks etc) can be repaired by the DIY owner using a two-part epoxy filler repair material. Once mixed in equal proportions, this is used in similar fashion to the bodywork filler used on metal panels. The filler is usually cured in twenty to thirty minutes, ready for sanding and painting.

26 If the owner is renewing a complete component himself, or if he has repaired it with epoxy filler, he will be left with the problem of finding a suitable paint for finishing which is compatible with the type of plastic used. At one time, the use of a universal paint was not possible, owing to the complex range of plastics encountered in body component applications. Standard paints, generally speaking, will not bond to plastic or rubber satisfactorily. However, it is now possible to obtain a plastic body parts finishing kit which consists of a pre-primer treatment, a primer and coloured top coat. Full instructions are normally supplied with a kit, but basically, the method of use is to first apply the pre-primer to the component concerned, and allow it to dry for up to 30 minutes. Then the primer is applied, and left to dry for about an hour before finally applying the special-coloured top coat. The result is a correctly-coloured component, where the paint will flex with the plastic or rubber, a property that standard paint does not normally possess.

5 Major body damage – repair

1 Where serious damage has occurred, or large areas need renewal due to neglect, it means that complete new panels will need welding-in, and this is best left to professionals. If the damage is due to impact, it will also be necessary to check completely the alignment of the bodyshell, and this can only be carried out accurately by a BMW dealer using special jigs. If the body is left misaligned, it is primarily dangerous, as the car will not handle properly, and secondly, uneven stresses will be imposed on the steering, suspension and possibly transmission, causing abnormal wear, or complete failure, particularly to such items as the tyres.

6 Front bumper – removal and refitting

Removal

1 Apply the handbrake, then jack up the front of the vehicle and support it on axle stands (see *Jacking and vehicle support*).

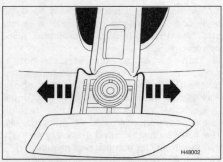

6.2 Pull out the retaining clips and remove the cover

6.3 Undo the 4 bolts

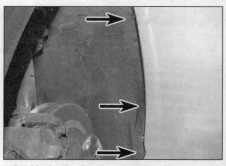

6.4 Undo the 3 bolts securing the wheel arch liner

2 On models with headlight washers, pull the washer jet covers forwards, then gently pull the retaining clips apart slightly, and remove the covers **(see illustration)**.

3 Undo the 4 bolts at the upper edge of the bumper **(see illustration)**.

4 Undo the 3 bolts each side securing the wheel arch liner to the bumper **(see illustration)**.

5 Undo the 7 bolts on the bumper underside **(see illustration)**.

6 Pull back the wheel arch liner, and undo the 2 bolts each side securing the bumper to the wing **(see illustration)**.

7 Pull the rear edges of the bumper out slightly, then pull the bumper forward a little, note their fitted locations, and disconnect the various wiring plugs.

8 Remove the bumper forwards and away from the vehicle with the help of an assistant.

Refitting

9 Refitting is a reverse of the removal procedure.

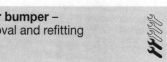

7 Rear bumper –
removal and refitting

Removal

1 To improve access, chock the front wheels, then jack up the rear of the vehicle and support it on axle stands (see *Jacking and vehicle support*).

2 Remove the body-mounted rear light units as described in Chapter 12.

3 Prise out the caps and remove the bolt each side in the corner of the boot lid/tailgate aperture **(see illustrations)**.

4 Undo the bolts each side securing the wheel arch liner to the bumper **(see illustration)**.

5 Pull the wheel arch liner forward and undo the bolt each side securing the bumper to the rear wing **(see illustration)**.

6 Undo the bolts on the lower edges of the bumper **(see illustration)**.

7 Gently prise up the black plastic holders in the rear light apertures, and with the help of an assistant, push the bumper rearwards to release the retaining clips. Strike the front edge of the bumper each side with the palm of your hand to help release the clips.

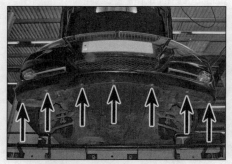

6.5 Undo the 7 bolts on the bumper underside

6.6 Undo the 2 bolts securing the bumper to the wing each side

7.3a Prise out the cap...

7.3b... and undo the bolt each side of the boot lid/tailgate aperture

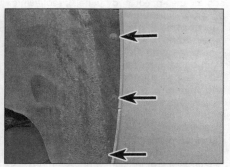

7.4 Undo the bolts securing the wheel arch liner to the bumper

7.5 Undo the bolt each side securing the bumper to the wing

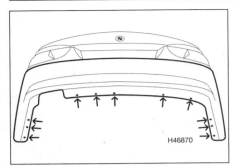

7.6 Undo the bolts at the lower edge of the bumper

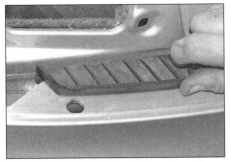

7.7a Prise up the plastic holders a little...

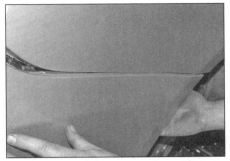

7.7b... then strike the front edge of the bumper each side to release the clips

Disconnect the parking sensor wiring plugs (where applicable) as the bumper is withdrawn (see illustrations).

Refitting

8 Refitting is a reverse of the removal procedure ensuring that the bumper ends are correctly engaged with their slides. Apply locking compound to the bumper mounting bolts and tighten them securely.

8 Bonnet – removal, refitting and adjustment

Removal

1 Open the bonnet and have an assistant support it. Using a pencil or felt tip pen, mark the outline of each bonnet hinge relative to the bonnet to use as a guide on refitting.
2 With the aid of an assistant, support the bonnet in the open position then remove the retaining clips and detach the support struts from the bonnet (see illustration).
3 Slacken and remove the left and right-hand hinge-to-bonnet rear bolts and loosen the front bolts (see illustration). Slide the bonnet forwards to disengage it from the hinges and remove it from the vehicle. Recover any shims which are fitted between the hinge and bonnet.
4 Inspect the bonnet hinges for signs of wear and free play at the pivots, and if necessary renew. Each hinge is secured to the body by two bolts. Mark the position of the hinge on the body then undo the retaining bolts and remove it from the vehicle. On refitting, align the new hinge with the marks and securely tighten the retaining bolts.

Refitting and adjustment

5 Fit the shims (where fitted) to the hinge and, with the aid of an assistant, engage the bonnet with the hinges. Refit the rear bolts and tighten them by hand only. Align the hinges with the marks made on removal, then tighten the retaining bolts securely. Note the earth strap attached to the base of the left-hand side hinge.

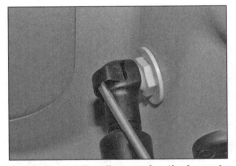

8.2 Prise out the clip securing the bonnet support strut

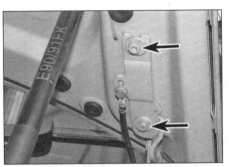

8.3 Remove the lower hinge bolt, and slacken the upper

6 Close the bonnet, and check for alignment with the adjacent panels. If necessary, slacken the hinge bolts and re-align the bonnet to suit. Once the bonnet is correctly aligned, securely tighten the hinge bolts. Once the bonnet is correctly aligned, check that the bonnet fastens and releases satisfactorily.

9 Bonnet release cable – removal and refitting

Removal

1 The bonnet release cable is in three sections, the main first cable from the release

lever to the connection at the right-hand side inner wing (adjacent to the windscreen washer reservoir), the second from the connection to the right-hand bonnet lock, and the third one linking the two bonnet locks.

Release lever-to-connection cable

2 Open the driver's door, and carefully pull up the door sill trim panel.
3 Undo the fasteners and remove the lower facia panel above the pedals. Disconnect any wiring plugs as the panel is withdrawn.
4 Undo the bolt and remove the bonnet release handle, then undo the bolt and remove the footwell kick panel (see illustrations).
5 Undo the bolts and pull the release lever

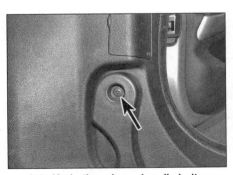

9.4a Undo the release handle bolt...

9.4b... then undo the kick panel bolt

9.5a Undo the bolts...

9.5b... and detach the cable from the lever

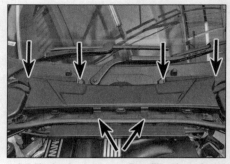

9.6 Undo the upper pollen filter housing bolts

assembly from the A-pillar, then separate the cable inner end fitting from the release lever **(see illustrations)**.

6 Undo the bolts and remove the upper

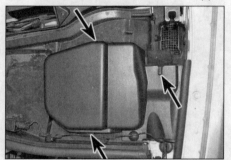

9.7 Release the clips and remove the plastic cover each side

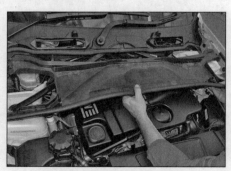

9.9a Rotate the temperature sensor anti-clockwise and detach it from the bracket

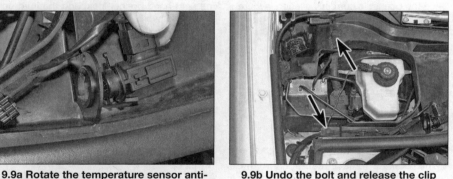

9.9c... then slide the pollen filter lower housing forwards

section of the pollen filter housing **(see illustration)**.

7 Release the catches and remove the left- and right-hand plastic covers from behind

9.8 Release the clips and pull the cable guide forwards

9.9b Undo the bolt and release the clip each side...

9.12a Prise open the housing...

the suspension turret each side of the engine compartment. Unclip the hose from the left-hand cover **(see illustration)**.

8 Depress the clips and pull the cable guide forwards from the pollen filter lower housing **(see illustration)**.

9 Release the catch and undo the bolt each side, then slide the pollen filter lower housing forwards and manoeuvre it from place **(see illustrations)**.

10 Remove the plastic expansion rivet and nut, then remove the water channel on the right-hand side.

11 Push/pull the outer release cable grommet from the engine compartment bulkhead, and pull the cable into the engine compartment.

12 Unclip the connection housing from the inner wing. Prise open the connection housing and disconnect the inner and outer cables **(see illustrations)**.

Connection-to-bonnet lock cable

13 Unclip the connection housing from the inner wing. Prise open the housing and disconnect the inner and outer cables **(see illustrations 9.12a and 9.12b)**.

14 Remove the bonnet lock as described in Section 10. To improve access, remove the intake hood from the bonnet slam panel.

Refitting

15 Refitting is the reverse of removal ensuring that the cable is correctly routed, and secured to all the relevant retaining clips. Check that the bonnet lock operates correctly before closing the bonnet.

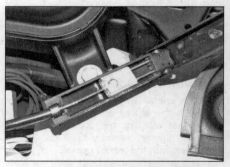

9.12b... and disconnect the cables

10.4 Undo the bolts securing the bonnet lock

11.2 Door check link Torx bolt

11.3 Undo the hinge nuts

10 Bonnet lock – removal and refitting

Removal

1 Unclip the connection housing from the inner wing. Prise open the housing and disconnect the inner and outer cables **(see illustrations 9.12a and 9.12b)**.
2 Undo the 3 bolts at the top edge of the bumper **(see illustration 6.3)**.
3 Make alignment marks between the lock(s) and crossmember to aid refitting.
4 Slacken and remove the lock retaining bolts then lift the lock from place. Free the release outer cable from the lock, then detach the inner cable from the lock **(see illustration)**. Remove the lock from the vehicle.

Refitting

5 Locate the bonnet release inner cable in the lock and reconnect the outer cable to the lever. Seat the lock on the crossmember.
6 Align the lock with the marks made prior to removal then refit the bolts and tighten them securely.
7 Check that the locks operate smoothly when the release lever is moved, without any sign of undue resistance. Check that the bonnet fastens and releases satisfactorily.
8 Once the locks are operating correctly, refit the bumper bolts.

11 Door – removal, refitting and adjustment

Removal

1 Disconnect the battery negative terminal (see Chapter 5A).
2 Undo the Torx bolt securing the door check link to the pillar **(see illustration)**.
3 Unscrew the hinge nuts from both the upper and lower door hinges **(see illustration)**.
4 Have an assistant support the door, undo the retaining bolt and withdraw the door wiring connector from the pillar. Pull out the locking element and unplug the connector as the door is withdrawn. If necessary the hinge pins can be unscrewed from the hinges.

Refitting

5 Manoeuvre the door into position and reconnect the wiring plug. Push the connector into the pillar and secure it in place with the bolt.
6 Engage the hinges with the studs on the door, and tighten the nuts securely. Note that if necessary, the position of the door can be adjusted by inserting or removing shims between the hinge and the door (available from BMW dealers).
7 Align the check link with the pillar, fit and tighten the securing bolt.

Adjustment

8 Close the door and check the door alignment with surrounding body panels. If necessary, slight adjustment of the door position can be made by slackening the hinge retaining nuts and repositioning the hinge/door as necessary. Once the door is correctly positioned, securely tighten the hinge nuts. If

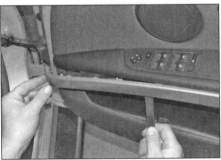

12.1 Carefully prise the decorative trim from the panel

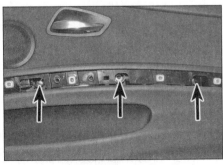

12.3a Undo the bolts securing the door panel – driver's side...

the paint work around the hinges has been damaged, paint the affected area with a suitable touch-in brush to prevent corrosion.

12 Door inner trim panel – removal and refitting

Removal

Front door

1 Starting at the front of the trim, using a trim clip releasing tool or flat-bladed screwdriver, carefully prise the decorative trim from the door panel, then unhook it from the rear **(see illustration)**.
2 If removing the passenger's door trim panel, starting at the lower edge, carefully prise the interior door handle trim from place **(see illustration)**.
3 Undo the Torx bolts securing the door trim **(see illustrations)**.

12.2 Prise the interior door handle trim from the passenger's door panel

12.3b... and passenger's side

12.4 Pull the panel inwards, before lifting it over the locking knob

12.5 Unclip the rear edge, and disconnect the release handle cable

12.7 Use a sharp knife to cut through the insulation panel sealant

12.8 Prise the decorative trim from the panel

12.9 Prise the cover from the door handle...

13 Disconnect the various wiring plugs as the panel is withdrawn.

14 If required, carefully prise the sound insulation panel away from the door, using a flat-bladed tool to cut through the sealant.

Refitting

15 Refitting of the trim panel is the reverse of removal. Before refitting, check whether any of the trim panel retaining clips were broken on removal, and renew them as necessary. Ensure that where removed, the sound insulation panel is sealed into its original location. If the sound insulation panel is damaged on removal it must be renewed.

4 Release the door trim panel clips, carefully levering between the panel and door with a flat-bladed screwdriver. Work around the outside of the panel, including the top edge, and when all the studs are released, ease the panel away from the top of the door, then lift it over the locking knob **(see illustration)**.

5 Holding the panel away from the door, disconnect the interior handle release cable from the door lock **(see illustration)**.

6 Disconnect the various wiring plugs as the panel is withdrawn.

7 If required, carefully prise the sound insulation panel away from the door, using a flat-bladed tool to cut through the sealant **(see illustration)**.

Rear door

8 Starting at the rear, carefully prise the

decorative trim form the door panel, then unhook it from the front **(see illustration)**.

9 Starting at the base of the trim, using a trim clip releasing tool or flat-bladed screwdriver, carefully prise the cover from the door pull handle **(see illustration)**.

10 Undo the panel retaining Torx bolts **(see illustration)**.

11 Release the door trim panel clips, carefully levering between the panel and door with a flat-bladed screwdriver. Work around the outside of the panel, including the top edge, and when all the studs are released, ease the panel away from the top of the door, then lift it over the locking knob **(see illustration)**.

12 Holding the panel away from the door, disconnect the interior handle release cable from the door lock **(see illustration 12.5)**.

---

13 Door handle and lock components – removal and refitting

Removal

Interior door handle

1 Remove the interior door trim panel as described in Section 12.

2 Operate the interior handle lever, prise out the locking clip and detach the cable from the handle **(see illustration 12.5)**.

3 Undo the retaining bolt, then release the clips and remove the handle from the door trim **(see illustration)**.

Front door lock assembly

4 Remove the window regulator assembly

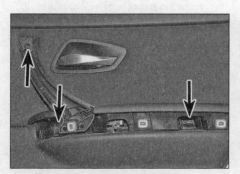

12.10... and undo the panel retaining bolts

12.11 Lever between the panel and the door with a blunt, flat-bladed tool to release the clips

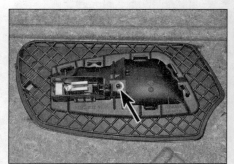

13.3 Undo the bolt, then release the clips around the circumference and pull the handle from the panel

13.7a Pull the outer cable from the bracket, and disengage the inner cable

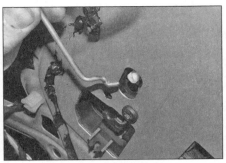

13.7b Pull the lock button control rod from the lock

13.8 Pull the release cable from the door lock

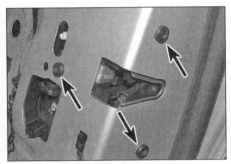

13.9a Undo the door lock bolts...

13.9b... and manoeuvre it from the door

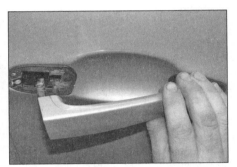

13.11 Pull the handle rearwards, then outwards

as described in Section 14. Note that it's not necessary to completely remove the window – slide it to the top of the channel and secure it in place with adhesive tape.

5 If working on the driver's door, remove the lock cylinder as described in Paragraphs 13 and 14.

6 Release the lock assembly wiring retaining clips and disconnect the wiring connector(s).

7 Disconnect the interior release cable from the lock, then unclip the lock button control rod from the lock (see illustrations).

8 Unclip the release cable from the door lock by pulling the cable from the clips. Note the routing of the cable – it must be refitted in the original position (see illustration).

9 Slacken and remove the lock assembly retaining screws then manoeuvre it from the door (see illustrations).

Front door exterior handle

10 If working on the driver's door, remove the lock cylinder as described in Paragraphs 13 and 14. If working on the passenger's door, prise out the grommet in the door end panel to expose the outer handle rear cover retaining bolt – remove the bolt, and pull out the cover. Note: On models with handle lighting, lift the lighting element from place and position it in the handle aperture to prevent accidental damage as the handle is removed.

11 Pull the outer handle rearwards, then outwards to disengage the front locator (see illustration).

12 To remove the handle operating frame, remove the door lock, then remove the rubber gasket from the front handle mounting, undo the Torx bolt, and pull the frame forwards from place. Disconnect any wiring plugs as the frame is removed (see illustrations).

Front door lock cylinder

13 Prise out the grommet in the door end panel to expose the lock cylinder retaining bolt (see illustration).

14 Undo the retaining bolt, insert the key,

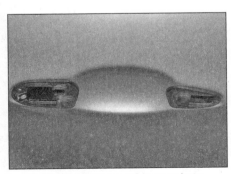

13.12a Remove the rubber gaskets...

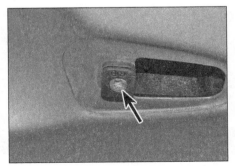

13.12b... and undo the retaining bolt

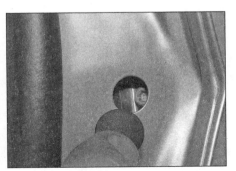

13.13 Remove the rubber grommet and undo the bolt

13.14 Pull the lock cylinder from place

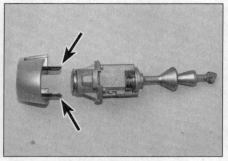

13.15 Release the two clips and separate the cover from the cylinder

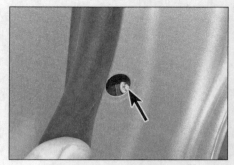

13.20a Undo the retaining bolt...

and pull the lock cylinder from the door **(see illustration)**.

15 If required, release the two retaining clips and separate the cylinder from the plastic cover **(see illustration)**.

Rear door lock

16 Remove the door inner trim panel and sound insulation material as described in Section 12. Disconnect the door lock wiring plug(s).

17 Disconnect the release cable from the lock, then unclip the lock button control rod **(see illustration 13.7a and 13.7b)**.

18 Unclip the outer handle release cable from the door lock by pulling the cable from the clips. Note the routing of the cable – it's essential it's refitted in the original position **(see illustration 13.8)**.

19 Slacken and remove the lock assembly retaining Torx bolts, release the wiring harness from the retaining clips, then manoeuvre it from the door **(see illustration 13.9a and 13.9b)**.

Rear door exterior handle

20 Prise out the grommet in the door end panel to expose the outer handle rear cover retaining bolt. Undo the bolt and remove the rear cover from the outer handle **(see illustrations)**.

21 Pull the outer handle rearwards, then outwards to disengage the front locator **(see illustration)**. **Note:** *On models with handle lighting, lift the lighting element from place and position it in the handle aperture to prevent accidental damage as the handle is removed.*

22 To remove handle operating frame, remove the door lock as described in this Section, then remove the rubber gasket from the front handle mounting, undo the Torx bolt, and pull the frame forwards from place. Disconnect any wiring plugs as the frame is removed **(see illustration 13.12a and 13.12b)**.

Refitting

Interior door handle

23 Clip the door handle into the trim and refit the retaining bolt.

24 Reconnect the release cable to the handle.

25 Refit the door trim panel as described in Section 12.

Front door lock assembly

26 Ensure that the seal on the door lock is undamaged.

27 Manoeuvre the lock assembly into position, refit the bolts, but don't tighten them at this stage.

28 Force the lock fully into the corner of the door frame. The lock seal must fully contact the door frame to prevent water ingress. Tighten the retaining bolts securely.

29 Reconnect the release cable and wiring plugs to the lock.

30 Clip the lock button control rod and interior release cable into place on the lock.

31 On the driver's door, refit the lock cylinder as described in paragraphs 39 and 40.

32 Refit the window regulator assembly as described in Section 14.

33 Do not close the door until the operation of the lock has been set-up and checked as follows:
a) *Using a screwdriver 'close' the door lock by pushing in the lock lever.*
b) *Using the key, unlock the door.*
c) *Using the outside handle, 'open' the lock.*

Front door exterior handle

34 Ensure that the lock lever is positioned as shown **(see illustration)**. If not, pull the lever outwards until it engages with the retaining clip.

35 Insert the front of the handle into the corresponding hole in the door skin, followed by the rear of the handle. Hold the handle gently again the door and push it forward until it 'clicks' into place.

36 If refitting the driver's door handle, refit the lock cylinder as described in Paragraphs 39 and 40. If refitting the passenger's handle, fit the outer handle rear cover into place, and tighten the retaining bolt securely. Refit the grommet to the door end panel.

37 Do not close the door until the operation of the lock has been set-up and checked as described in Paragraph 33.

Front door lock cylinder

38 If separated, clip the plastic cover back onto the cylinder.

39 Lubricate the outside of the lock cylinder with a suitable grease.

40 Refit the lock cylinder into the door lock, and tighten the retaining bolt securely. Refit the plastic grommet into the door end panel. Before closing the door, check the lock operation as described in Paragraph 33.

13.20b... and pull the rear cover from place

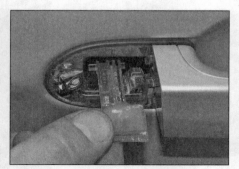

13.21 Place the handle lighting element in the aperture to prevent damage

13.34 Position the lock lever so the retaining clip holds it outwards

14.5a Use a screwdriver...

14.5b... to push out the window clamp catch

14.6 Lift the rear first, and remove the window

Rear door lock

41 Ensure that the seal on the door lock is undamaged.

42 Manoeuvre the lock assembly into position, refit the bolts, but don't tighten them at this stage.

43 Force the lock fully into the corner of the door frame. The lock seal must fully contact the door frame to prevent water ingress. Tighten the retaining bolts securely.

44 Reconnect the release cable and wiring plugs to the lock.

45 Clip the lock button control rod into place on the lock.

46 Do not close the door until the operation of the lock has been set-up and checked as follows:

a) *Using a screwdriver 'close' the door lock by pushing in the lock lever.*

b) *Using the key, unlock the door.*

c) *Using the outside handle, 'open' the lock.*

47 Reseal the plastic sound insulation panel to the door. Refit the trim panel as described in Section 12.

Rear door exterior handle

48 Ensure that the lock lever is positioned as shown **(see illustration 13.34)**. If not, pull the lever outwards until it engages with the retaining clip.

49 Insert the front of the handle into the corresponding hole in the door skin, followed by the rear of the handle. Hold the handle gently against the door and push it forward until it 'clicks' into place.

50 Fit the outer handle rear cover into place, and tighten the retaining bolt securely. Refit the grommet to the door end panel.

51 Do not close the door until the operation of the lock has been set-up and checked as described in Paragraph 33.

14 Door windows and regulator
– removal and refitting

Removal

Front door window

1 Fully open the window then raise it approximately 105 mm (measured at the rear of the glass), to access the window catches.

2 Disconnect the battery negative lead (see Chapter 5A).

3 Remove the inner trim panel and the sound insulation panel (Section 12).

4 Starting at the rear using a wide, flat-bladed tool, carefully lever up the window inner sealing strip from the base of the window.

5 Lever out the window clamp catches, and slide the window upwards **(see illustrations)**.

6 Lifting the rear first, remove the window from the vehicle **(see illustration)**.

Front door window regulator

7 Release the door window from the clamp catches as described earlier in this Section. Note that there is no need to remove the window from the door, simply use adhesive tape, or rubber wedges, to secure the window in the fully-closed position.

8 Disconnect the window motor wiring plug.

9 Undo the 5 regulator mounting nuts, release any retaining clips, and manoeuvre the regulator from the door **(see illustrations)**.

10 Where applicable, undo the retaining bolts and separate the motor from the regulator **(see illustration)**.

Rear door window

11 Fully lower the window, then remove the door inner trim panel and sound insulation panel as described in Section 12.

12 Using a wide, flat-bladed tool, carefully lever up the window inner sealing strip from the door skin **(see illustration)**.

13 Carefully pull the rubber weatherstrip from the front edge of the door window frame, pull the plastic window frame trim from the front of the frame, then peel back the window sealing strip from the front edge of the window opening to gain access to the window trim

14.9a Undo the regulator mounting nuts...

14.9b... and manoeuvre the regulator from the door

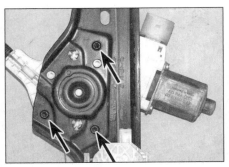

14.10 Window motor retaining bolts

14.12 Lever up the inner sealing strip from the door

14.13a Pull the rubber strip from the front edge of the door

14.13b Pull the plastic trim from the front of the frame

14.13c Prise the sealing strip from the front of the window aperture

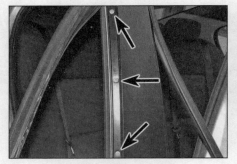

14.13d Undo the 3 bolts...

14.13e... and remove the panel

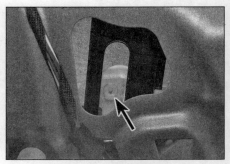

14.15 Press the window clamp catch outwards...

panel bolts. Undo the retaining bolts, and lift the panel from the door **(see illustrations)**.

14 Fully close the window, then lower it approximately 120 mm, measured at the front edge.

15 Press the window clamp catch outwards, and slide the window upwards **(see illustration)**.

16 Lifting the rear first, remove the window from the vehicle **(see illustration)**.

Rear door fixed window

17 As the rear door fixed window is bonded in place, renewal of the window should be entrusted to a BMW dealer or automotive window specialist.

Rear door window regulator

18 Release the door window from the clamp catches as described earlier in this Section, slide it upwards and secure it in position with adhesive tape.

19 Disconnect the battery negative lead as described in Chapter 5A.

20 Disconnect the regulator motor wiring plug, and release the harness from any retaining clips.

21 Undo the regulator securing nuts, release any retaining clips, lift out the lower end of the assembly, and manoeuvre it from the door **(see illustration)**.

22 Where applicable, undo the retaining bolts, and remove the motor from the regulator **(see illustration)**.

Rear side fixed window

23 As the rear side fixed window is bonded in place, renewal of the window should be entrusted to a BMW dealer or automotive window specialist.

Refitting

Front door window

24 Refitting is the reverse of removal.

Renew the window clamp catches if they are damaged.

Front door window regulator

25 Refitting is the reverse of removal. Once the regulator has been refitted, operate the button to fully close the window, then continue to hold the button for at least 1 second to 'normalise' the anti-trapping function.

Rear door window glass

26 Refitting is the reverse of removal. Renew the window clamp catch if they are damaged.

Rear door window regulator

27 Refitting is the reverse of removal. Once the regulator has been refitted, operate the button to fully close the window, then continue to hold the button for at least 1 second to 'normalise' the anti-trapping function.

14.16... and lift the window from the door

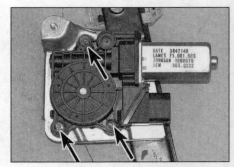

14.21 Window regulator retaining nuts

14.22 Regulator motor retaining bolts

15.1a Prise out the centre pins, lever out the plastic expansion rivets...

15.1b... and remove the boot lid trim panel

15.6 Raise the spring clip and pull the strut from the mounting

15 Boot lid/tailgate and support struts – removal and refitting

Removal

Boot lid

1 Open the boot, prise up the centre pins a little and remove the plastic expanding rivets, then remove the trim panel from the boot lid (see illustrations).

2 Disconnect the wiring connectors from the number plate lights and boot lid lock, and tie a piece of string to the end of the wiring. Noting the correct routing of the wiring harness, release the harness rubber grommets from the boot lid and withdraw the wiring. When the end of the wiring appears, untie the string and leave it in position in the boot lid; it can then be used on refitting to draw the wiring into position.

3 Draw around the outline of each hinge with a suitable marker pen then slacken the hinge upper bolt, remove the lower bolt and remove the boot lid from the vehicle.

4 Inspect the hinges for signs of wear or damage and renew if necessary; the hinges are secured to the vehicle by bolts.

Tailgate

5 Removal and refitting of the tailgate requires special BMW body work tools, and the experience to use them. Consequently, we recommend that this task be entrusted to a BMW dealer or suitably-equipped specialist.

Support struts

6 Support the boot lid/tailgate in the open position. Using a small flat-bladed screwdriver raise the spring clip, and pull the support strut off its upper mounting (see illustration). Repeat the procedure on the lower strut mounting and remove the strut from the vehicle.

Refitting

Boot lid

7 Refitting is the reverse of removal, aligning the hinges with the marks made before removal.

8 On completion, close the boot lid and check its alignment with the surrounding panels. If necessary slight adjustment can be made by slackening the retaining bolts and repositioning the boot lid on its hinges.

If the paint work around the hinges has been damaged, paint the affected area with a suitable touch-in brush to prevent corrosion.

Support struts

9 Refitting is a reverse of the removal procedure, ensuring that the strut is securely retained by its retaining clips.

16 Boot lid/tailgate lock components – removal and refitting

Removal

Boot lid lock

1 Open the boot, prise up the centre pins and remove the plastic expanding rivets, then remove the trim panel from the boot lid – see Section 15.

2 Disconnect the lock wiring plug.

3 Undo the three bolts, and manoeuvre the lock from the boot lid. Disconnect the cable from the lock cylinder as the lock is withdrawn (see illustrations).

4 To disconnect the operating cable, release the clip and slide off the plastic outer cable

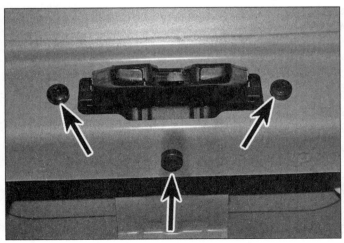

16.3a Boot lid lock retaining bolts

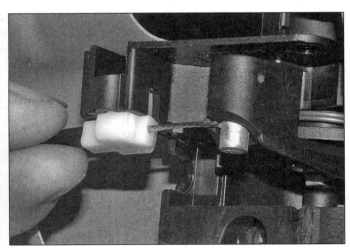

16.3b Slide the outer fitting from the bracket, and slide the end fitting from the lever

16.4a Release the clip and slide off the outer cable fitting...

16.4b... prise out the centre pin...

16.4c... and lever the inner cable end fitting from the lever

16.7 Lock cylinder retaining bolts

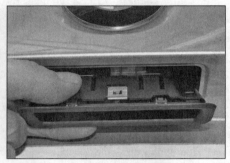

16.9 Squeeze together the sides and push the button from the lid

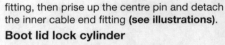

fitting, then prise up the centre pin and detach the inner cable end fitting **(see illustrations)**.

Boot lid lock cylinder

5 Remove the trim panel from the boot lid as described in Section 15.
6 Disconnect the operating cable from the lock cylinder **(see illustration 16.3b)**.
7 Undo the two retaining bolts, then pull the lock from panel **(see illustration)**.

Boot lock release button

8 Remove the trim panel (see Section 15).
9 Reach up behind the button, squeeze the sides and push the assembly from place **(see illustration)**. Disconnect the wiring plug as the button is withdrawn.

Tailgate lock

10 Pull the rear window side trims inwards to release the retaining clips, and disengage them from the upper trim **(see illustration)**.
11 Release the 3 clips, then fold down and remove the trim insert on the tailgate rear panel.
12 Open the rear window, pull the plastic trim at the top of the rear panel rearwards to release the clips, then undo the 2 bolts at the top of the panel **(see illustrations)**.
13 Prise out the cover, then undo the bolt in the handle recess each side **(see illustration)**.
14 Pull the rear trim panel away from the tailgate to release the retaining clips **(see illustration)**. Disconnect the luggage compartment light as the panel is withdrawn.

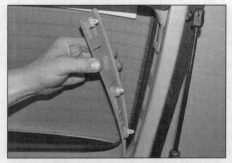

16.10 Pull the side trims inwards to release the clips

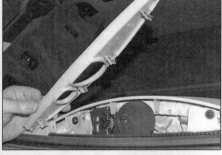

16.12a Pull the plastic trim rearwards...

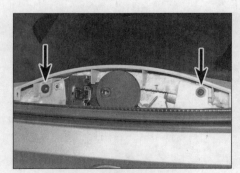

16.12b... and undo the 2 bolts

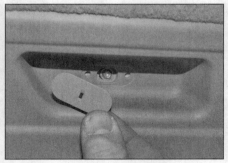

16.13 Prise out the cover and undo the bolt each side

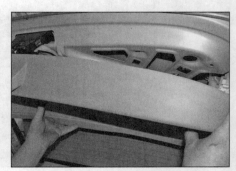

16.14 Pull the panel from the tailgate

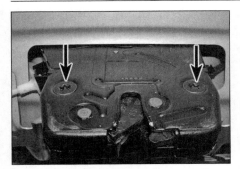
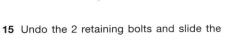

16.15 Undo the 2 bolts and remove the tailgate lock

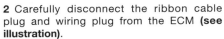

16.16 Slide the outer cable fitting from the bracket and disconnect the release cable

16.19 Tailgate window lock bolts

15 Undo the 2 retaining bolts and slide the lock from place **(see illustration)**.
16 Disconnect the release cable and wiring plug as the lock is withdrawn **(see illustration)**.

Rear window lock

17 Remove the tailgate lower trim panel as described in Paragraphs 10 to 14 of this Section.
18 Disconnect the lock wiring plug.
19 Undo the 2 retaining bolts and withdraw the lock from the tailgate **(see illustration)**.

Refitting

20 Refitting is a reversal of removal, noting the following points:
a) *Reconnect all wiring plugs, and secure the wiring harnesses using the retaining clips (where applicable).*
b) *Match-up any previously-make alignment marks.*
c) *Check the operation of the locks/cylinders before refitting the trim panels.*
d) *Tighten all fasteners securely.*

17 Central locking components – removal and refitting

Note: *The central locking system is highly complex, and is equipped with a sophisticated self-diagnosis capability. Before removing any of the central locking components, have the system interrogated by a BMW dealer or suitably-equipped specialist to pin-point any fault.*

Removal

Electronic control module (ECM)

1 The central locking system is controlled by the Footwell Module and the Car Access System (CAS) ECM. Removal of the Footwell Module is described in the next Section. The CAS ECM is located behind the passenger side glovebox. To access the control module, undo the 3 bolts and remove the trim panel above the driver's pedals **(see illustration)**. Disconnect any wiring plugs as the panel is withdrawn.

2 Carefully disconnect the ribbon cable plug and wiring plug from the ECM **(see illustration)**.
3 Undo the retaining bolts and manoeuvre the module from place. **Note:** *If a new ECM is fitted, it must be programmed and initialised using dedicated diagnostic equipment. Entrust this task to a BMW dealer or suitably-equipped specialist.*

Door lock actuator

4 The actuator is integral with the door lock assembly. Remove the door lock as described in Section 13.

Boot lock actuator

5 The boot lid actuator is integral with the boot lock assembly. Remove the boot lid as described in Section 16.

Tailgate lock actuator

6 Remove the tailgate lock as described in Section 16.
7 Undo the two retaining bolts and remove the actuator from the lock.

Fuel filler flap solenoid

8 Open the filler cap, then peel away the rubber grommet from the actuator rod.
9 Squeeze together the retaining clips and pull the solenoid from place.
10 Disconnect the wiring connector as the solenoid is withdrawn.

Refitting

11 Refitting is the reverse of removal. Prior to

refitting any trim panels removed for access thoroughly check the operation of the central locking system.

18 Electric window components – removal and refitting

Note: *The electric window system is equipped with a sophisticated self-diagnosis capability. Should a fault develop, before removing any of the electric window electronics, have the system interrogated by a BMW dealer or suitably-equipped specialist to pin-point any fault.*

Window switches

1 Refer to Chapter 12.

Electric window motors

2 Remove the window regulator as described in Section 14.
3 Slacken and remove the retaining bolts and remove the motor from the regulator.
4 On refitting, fit the motor to the regulator and securely tighten its retaining bolts.
5 Refit the regulator assembly as described in Section 14.

Electronic control module (ECM)

6 Disconnect the battery negative lead as described in Chapter 5A.
7 The electric window system is controlled by

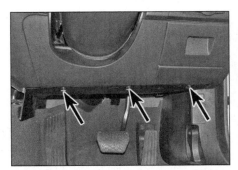

17.1 Undo the 3 bolts and remove the trim panel above the pedals

17.2 Disconnect the ribbon cable, then lever over the catch and disconnect the wiring plug

the Footwell module, which is located behind the driver's footwell side trim panel. To access the ECM, remove the footwell side trim panel as described in Section 26.

8 Disconnect the ECM wiring plugs **(see illustration).**

9 Undo the upper and lower retaining nuts, then remove the ECM.

10 Refitting is a reversal of removal. **Note:** *If a new ECM is fitted, it must be programmed and initialised using dedicated diagnostic equipment. Entrust this task to a BMW dealer or suitably-equipped specialist.*

19 Mirrors and associated components – removal and refitting

Exterior mirror assembly

1 Remove the door inner trim panel as described in Section 12.

2 Carefully pull the plastic trim away from the front inner edge of the door frame **(see illustration).**

3 Disconnect the mirror wiring plug, then undo the retaining Torx bolts and remove the mirror from the door. Recover the rubber seal which is fitted between the door and mirror; if the seal is damaged it must be renewed **(see illustration).**

4 Refitting is the reverse of removal, tightening the mirror bolts securely.

Exterior mirror glass

Note: *If the mirror glass is removed when the mirror is cold the retaining clips are likely to break.*

5 Tilt the mirror glass fully inwards.

6 Insert a wide plastic or wooden wedge in between the outer edge of the mirror glass and mirror housing and carefully prise the glass from the motor **(see illustration).** Take great care when removing the glass; do not use excessive force as the glass is easily broken.

7 Remove the glass from the mirror and, where necessary, disconnect the wiring connectors from the mirror heating element.

8 On refitting, reconnect the wiring to the glass and clip the glass onto the motor, taking great care not to break it.

18.8 The footwell module is located to the right of the pedals

Exterior mirror switch

9 Refer to Chapter 12.

Exterior mirror motor

10 Remove the mirror glass as described above.

11 Undo the single retaining bolt and pull the motor from position **(see illustration).** Disconnect the wiring plug as the motor is withdrawn.

12 Refitting is the reversal of removal.

Exterior mirror housing cover

13 Remove the mirror glass as described above.

14 Release the four retaining clips and remove the mirror housing cover to the front **(see illustrations).**

15 Refitting is a reversal of removal.

19.3 Exterior mirror retaining bolts

19.2 Pull away the plastic trim from the front inner edge of the door

Interior mirror

16 There are essentially two different types of mirror arms and mountings. One type has a plastic cover over the plug connection, and the other type has a mirror arm which splits in two to reveal the wiring plug.

Plastic cover type arm

17 Carefully lever out the plastic cover, and disconnect the mirror wiring plug (where applicable).

18 Strike the lower part of the mirror forwards with the ball of your hand to unclip the arm from the mounting.

Caution: Do not twist the arm whilst attempting removal as the clip will be damaged, and do not pull the arm to the rear as the windscreen may be damaged.

19.6 Carefully prise the mirror from place

19.11 Undo the bolt and remove the motor

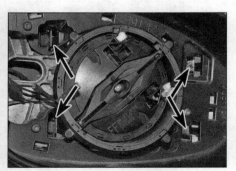

19.14a Release the 4 clips...

19.14b... and remove the cover

Split cover mirror arm

19 Prise apart the two sides of the mirror base cover apart **(see illustration)**.
20 Note their fitted positions, then disconnect the various wiring plugs from the mirror and rain sensor (where fitted).
21 Rotate the mirror arm 60° anti-clockwise and remove it **(see illustration)**.

All types

22 To refit the mirrors, position the mirror arm over the mounting at an angle of 60° to the vertical. Push the arm to the vertical and check that it engages correctly. Where applicable, refit the covers and reconnect the wiring plug(s).

---

20 Windscreen and rear screen/tailgate glass – general information

Windscreen and Saloon rear screen

1 These areas of glass are secured by the tight fit of the weatherstrip in the body aperture, and are bonded in position with a special adhesive. Renewal of such fixed glass is a difficult, messy and time-consuming task, which is beyond the scope of the home mechanic. It is difficult, unless one has plenty of practise, to obtain a secure, waterproof fit. Furthermore, the task carries a high risk of breakage; this applies especially to the laminated glass windscreen. In view of this, owners are strongly advised to have this sort of work carried out by one of the many specialist windscreen fitters.

Touring rear screen

2 Although on these models the rear screen opens independently of the tailgate, to remove the screen the rear spoiler must be removed. This is a complex task requiring specialist bodywork tools and experience. Any attempt to remove the spoiler without the necessary equipment is very likely to result in damage. Consequently, we recommend that this work is entrusted to a BMW dealer or suitably-equipped specialist.

19.19 Prise apart the two halves of the cover

21 Sunroof – general information, motor renewal and initialisation

General information

1 Due to the complexity of the sunroof mechanism, considerable expertise is needed to repair, renew or adjust the sunroof components successfully. Removal of the roof first requires the headlining to be removed, which is a complex and tedious operation, and not a task to be undertaken lightly. Therefore, any problems with the sunroof (except motor renewal) should be referred to a BMW dealer or specialist.
2 On models with an electric sunroof, if the sunroof motor fails to operate, first check the relevant fuse. If the fault cannot be traced and rectified, the sunroof can be opened and closed manually using an Allen key to turn the motor spindle (a suitable key is supplied with the vehicle tool kit). To gain access to the motor, unclip the cover from the headlining. Remove the Allen key from the tool kit and insert it into the motor spindle. Disconnect the motor wiring connector and rotate the key to move the sunroof to the required position.

Motor renewal

3 Disconnect the battery negative lead as described in Chapter 5A.
4 Starting at the front edge, carefully prise the interior light lens unit from between the sunvisors.
5 Release the clips at the front edge, and remove

19.21 Rotate the mirror arm 60° anti-clockwise

the interior light unit from the headlining between the sunvisors **(see illustrations)**. Disconnect the wiring plug(s) as the unit is withdrawn.
6 Undo the 3 retaining bolts, and pull the motor from its location. Disconnect the wiring plug as the motor is removed **(see illustration)**.
7 Refitting is a reversal of removal, but carry out the initialisation procedure as described next.

Initialisation

8 Upon completion, initialise the sunroof as follows:
a) *Press and hold the switch in the 'tilt' position.*
b) *After reaching the 'end of tilt' position, keep the switch pressed for a further 30 seconds. The 'normalisation' is complete when the sunroof rear end lifts briefly.*
c) *Keep the switch pressed in the 'tilt' position, after approximately 5 seconds, the sunroof will move to the closed position, back to the open position, then finally back to the closed position.*
d) *Release the switch.*

---

22 Body exterior fittings – removal and refitting

Wheel arch liners and body underpanels

1 The various plastic covers fitted to the underside of the vehicle are secured in position by a mixture of bolts, nuts and

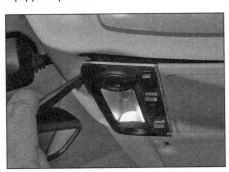

21.5a Use a flat-bladed tool to release the clips...

21.5b... at the front edge of the interior light unit

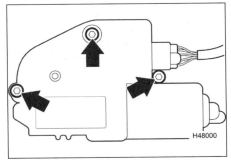

21.6 Sunroof motor retaining bolts

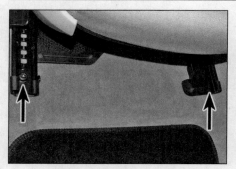

23.2 Front seat rail mounting bolts

23.3 Pull the trim panel from the side of the seat base

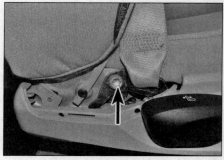

23.4 Seat belt lower anchorage retaining bolt

retaining clips, and removal will be fairly obvious on inspection. Work methodically around, removing its retaining bolts and releasing its retaining clips until the panel is free and can be removed from the underside of the vehicle. Most clips used on the vehicle are simply prised out of position. Other clips can be released by unscrewing/prising out the centre pins and then removing the clip.
2 Where fitted, disconnect the tyre pressure transmitter wiring plug as the wheel arch liner is withdrawn.
3 On refitting, renew any retaining clips that may have been broken on removal, and ensure that the panel is securely retained by all the relevant clips and bolts.

Body trim strips and badges

4 The various body trim strips and badges are held in position with a special adhesive tape. Removal requires the trim/badge to be heated, to soften the adhesive, and then cut away from the surface. Due to the high risk of damage to the vehicle's paintwork during this operation, it is recommended that this task should be entrusted to a BMW dealer or suitably-equipped specialist.

Rear spoiler

5 This is a complex task requiring specialist bodywork tools and experience. Any attempt to remove the spoiler without the necessary equipment is very likely to result in damage. Consequently, we recommend that this work is entrusted to a BMW dealer or suitably-equipped specialist.

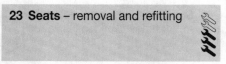

23 Seats – removal and refitting

Front seat removal

1 Fully raise the seat cushion and slide the seat fully rearwards.
2 Slacken and remove the bolts securing the front of the seat rails to the floor **(see illustration)**. Discard the bolts – new ones must be fitted.
3 Move the seat fully forwards, depress the clip and remove the seat belt lower anchorage trim panel from the seat base **(see illustration)**.
4 Undo the retaining bolt and detach the seat belt lower anchorage from the seat base **(see illustration)**.
5 Slacken and remove the bolts securing the rear of the seat rails to the floor **(see illustration)**. Discard the bolts – new ones must be fitted.
6 Disconnect the battery negative lead as described in Chapter 5A.
7 Working under the front of the seat, slide out the locking element, and disconnect the seat wiring plug **(see illustration)**.
8 With the help of an assistant, manoeuvre the seat out from the vehicle.
Caution: The seat is heavy!

Folding rear seat removal

Saloon models

9 The trim panel between the seat backrest and the door aperture must be removed.

Pull the top of the trim forward to release the retaining clip, and then pull the trim panel upwards to remove it. Repeat this procedure on the remaining trim panel on the other side.
10 Pull up on the front of the seat cushion to release the left- and right-hand retaining clips, and remove it forwards and out from the vehicle. Disconnect the seat heating wiring connectors (where applicable) as the seat is withdrawn.
11 Release the rear seat back rest, and fold it forward.
12 Undo the bolt each side at the outer hinges, then pull the backrests from the centre mountings.

Touring models

13 Pull up on the front of the seat cushion to release the left- and right-hand retaining clips, and remove it forwards.
14 Undo the centre seat belt lower anchorage bolt, and lift the cushion out from the vehicle. Disconnect the seat heating wiring connectors (where applicable) as the seat is withdrawn.
15 Release the rear seat back rest, and fold it forward.
16 The trim panel between the seat backrest and the door aperture must be removed. Pull the top of the trim forward to release the retaining clip, and then pull the trim panel upwards to remove it **(see illustration)**. Repeat this procedure on the remaining trim panel on the other side.
17 Undo the bolt each side securing the

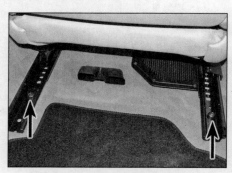

23.5 Front seat rear mounting bolts

23.7 Slide out the locking element and disconnect the wiring plug

23.16 Pull the top edge forwards, then lift the trim panel upwards

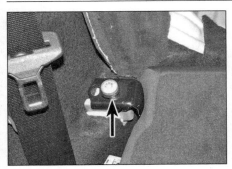

23.17 Undo the bolt each side...

23.18... then pull the backrests outwards to disengage the centre mounting

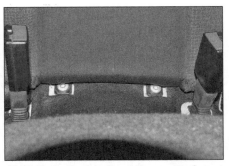

23.20 Undo the 2 bolts at the centre, lower edge of the backrest

backrest outer brackets to the vehicle body **(see illustration)**.

18 Lift each backrest assembly at the outer edges, and pull them outwards to disengage the centre mounting **(see illustration)**. Manoeuvre the seats from the vehicle.

Fixed rear seat removal

19 Pull up on the front edge of the seat base cushion to release the left- and right-hand retaining clips and remove it from the vehicle.

20 Undo the 2 retaining bolts at the centre, lower edge of the backrest **(see illustration)**.

21 Working in the luggage compartment, use a large flat-bladed screwdriver to release the catches, then slide the seat upwards to release its lower retaining pins and remove it from the vehicle **(see illustration)**.

Refitting

Front seat

22 Refitting is the reverse of removal, noting the following points.

a) On manually-adjusted seats, fit the new seat retaining bolts and tighten them by hand only. Slide the seat fully forwards and then slide it back by two stops of the seat locking mechanism. Rock the seat to ensure that the seat locking mechanism is correctly engaged then tighten the mounting bolts to the specified torque.

b) On electrically-adjusted seats, ensure that the wiring is connected and correctly

routed then tighten the seat mounting bolts securely.

c) Tighten the seat belt mounting bolt to the specified torque.

d) Reconnect the battery negative lead as described in Chapter 5A.

Folding rear seat

23 Refitting is the reverse of removal. Tighten the seat belt lower mounting bolts to the specified torque setting.

Fixed rear seat

24 Refitting is the reverse of removal making sure the seat back lower locating pegs are correctly engaged with the body, and the seat belt buckles and lap belt are fed through the intended openings.

24 Seat belt tensioning mechanism – general information

1 All models are fitted with a seat belt tensioner system. The system is designed to instantaneously take up any slack in the seat belt in the case of a sudden frontal impact, therefore reducing the possibility of injury to the seat occupants. Each front seat is fitted with its tensioner on the inside of the seat cushion, whilst the rear seat tensioners are fitted at the outer anchorages.

2 The seat belt tensioner is triggered by a frontal impact above a predetermined force.

Lesser impacts, including impacts from behind, will not trigger the system.

3 When the system is triggered, a pyrotechnic device is detonated which acts on the seat belt anchorage, and keeps the occupant in position in the seat. Once the tensioner has been triggered, the seat belt will be permanently locked and the assembly must be renewed.

4 There is a risk of injury if the system is triggered inadvertently when working on the vehicle. If any work is to be carried out on the seat/seat belt disable the tensioner by disconnecting the battery negative lead (see Chapter 5A), and waiting at least 60 seconds before proceeding.

5 Also note the following warnings before contemplating any work on the front seat.

⚠ *Warning: If the tensioner mechanism is dropped, it must be renewed, even it has suffered no apparent damage.*

• *Do not allow any solvents to come into contact with the tensioner mechanism.*

• *Do not subject the seat to any form of shock as this could accidentally trigger the seat belt tensioner.*

• *Check for any deformation of the seat belt stalk tensioner, and anchorage brackets. Renew any that are damaged.*

25 Seat belt components – removal and refitting

⚠ *Warning: Read Section 24 before proceeding.*

Front belt removal

1 Remove the B-pillar trim panel as described in Section 26.

2 Prise the belt anchorage trim from the seat **(see illustration 23.3)**.

3 Undo the belt anchorage bolt from the seat frame, and detach the belt.

4 Undo the bolts and remove the seat belt guide from the pillar.

5 Undo the bolt securing the upper seat belt mounting **(see illustration)**.

6 Unscrew the inertia reel retaining bolt and

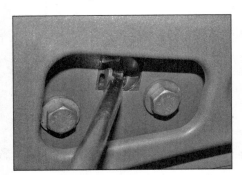

23.21 Use a screwdriver to release the catches in the luggage compartment

25.5 Seat belt upper mounting bolt

25.6 Seat belt inertia reel retaining bolt

25.9a Slide the connector from the bracket...

25.9b... and prise out the wiring plugs until the relevant plug is released

remove the seat belt from the door pillar (see illustration).

7 If necessary (where fitted), undo the retaining bolts and remove the height adjustment mechanism from the door pillar.

Front stalk removal

8 Remove the seat as described in Section 23.

9 Release the tensioner wiring harness from the retaining clips, slide the connector from the mounting bracket, then release the clips/cable tie and prise out the wiring plugs one at a time until the relevant plug is released (see illustrations).

10 Slacken and remove the stalk assembly retaining bolt and remove the assembly from the side of the seat (see illustration). Note that the bolt must be renewed.

Rear side belt removal

Saloon models

11 Remove the rear seat as described in Section 23.

12 Remove the parcel shelf as described in Section 26.

13 Undo the retaining bolt and remove the inertia reel unit. Note how the mounting bracket engages with the lug on the pillar (see illustration).

14 Undo the seat belt lower mounting bolt (see illustration).

Touring models

15 Remove the rear seat as described in Section 23.

16 Remove the D-pillar trim panel as described in Section 26.

17 Remove the luggage compartment side panel as described in Section 26.

18 Undo the 4 bolts and remove the cover over the inertia reel (see illustrations).

19 Slacken and remove the Torx bolt securing the lower end of the belt to the body (see illustration).

20 The inertia reel is secured by one Torx bolt. Slacken and remove the bolt and washer.

21 Manoeuvre the assembly from the mounting bracket and withdraw it from the vehicle.

Rear stalk removal

22 Remove the rear seat cushion as described in Section 23.

23 Disconnect the wiring plug (where applicable) then slacken and remove the bolt and washer and remove the stalk from the

25.10 Remove the stalk assembly retaining bolt

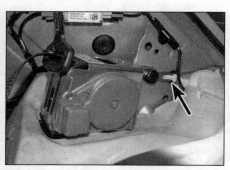

25.13 Note the lug at the rear of the inertia reel bracket

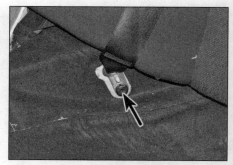

25.14 Rear side seat belt lower mounting bolt

25.18a Undo the 2 bolts at the front...

25.18b... and the 2 at the rear

25.19 Inertia reel retaining bolt

25.23a Prise up the locking catch and disconnect the wiring plug

25.23b Seat belt stalk mounting bolt

25.25 Rear centre belt inertia reel bolt

vehicle. Note the mounting bracket locating pin **(see illustrations)**.

Rear centre belt and buckle removal

Saloon models

24 Remove the rear seat as described in Section 23.
25 Undo the retaining bolt and remove the inertia reel unit **(see illustration)**.
26 Undo the seat belt lower mounting bolt **(see illustration)**.

Touring models

27 The centre belt inertia reel unit is not available separately from the backrest. Check with your BMW dealer or parts specialist.

Refitting

28 Refitting is a reversal of the removal procedure, ensuring that all fasteners are tightened to their specified torque where given. Apply a little thread-locking compound to the mounting bolts.

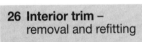

26 Interior trim –
removal and refitting

General

1 The interior trim panels are secured using either bolts or various types of trim fasteners, usually studs or clips.

2 Check that there are no other panels overlapping the one to be removed; usually there is a sequence that has to be followed that will become obvious on close inspection.
3 Remove all obvious fasteners, such as bolts. If the panel will not come free, it is held by hidden clips or fasteners. These are usually situated around the edge of the panel and can be prised up to release them; note, however, that they can break quite easily so new ones should be available. The best way of releasing such clips without the correct type of tool is to use a large flat-bladed screwdriver. Note that some panels are secured by plastic expanding rivets, where the centre pin must be prised up before the rivet can be removed. Note in many cases that the adjacent sealing strip must be prised back to release a panel.
4 When removing a panel, never use excessive force or the panel may be damaged; always check carefully that all fasteners have been removed or released before attempting to withdraw a panel.
5 Refitting is the reverse of the removal procedure; secure the fasteners by pressing them firmly into place and ensure that all disturbed components are correctly secured to prevent rattles.

A-pillar trim

6 Due to the head impact airbag fitted in the area, disconnect the battery as described in Chapter 5A.
7 Pull the rubber weatherstrip from the door pillar in the area of the pillar trim.
8 Using a wooden or plastic flat-bladed lever,

25.26 Rear centre belt lower mounting bolt

carefully prise out the trim insert from the A-pillar trim **(see illustration)**.
9 Undo the retaining Torx bolt, and pull the trim to the centre of the vehicle, starting at the top **(see illustration)**.
10 Refitting is the reverse of the removal procedure; secure the fasteners by pressing them firmly into place and ensure that all disturbed components are correctly secured to prevent rattles.

B-pillar trim

11 Begin by carefully prising up the front door sill trim panel from its retaining clips.
12 Pull away the rubber weatherstrip each side of the B-pillar **(see illustration)**.
13 The lower edge of the lower trim is secured by two plastic clips. Pull the lower edge of the trim inwards, then pull it downwards to disengage it from the upper trim panel **(see**

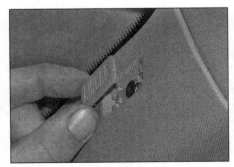

26.8 Prise out the insert, and undo the bolt

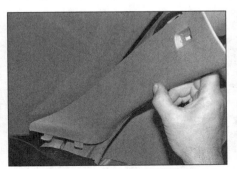

26.9 Note how the base of the A-pillar trim engages with the facia

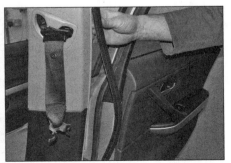

26.12 Pull away the weatherstrip each side of the B-pillar

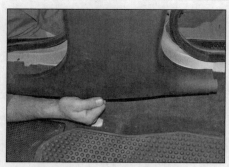

26.13 Pull the lower edge of the trim panel inwards

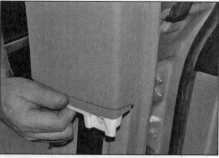

26.14a Pull the lower edge of the trim inwards to release the clips

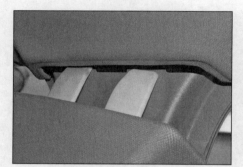

26.14b The two lugs of the upper trim engage with the headlining

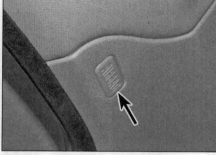

26.17 Prise out the cap and remove the bolt beneath

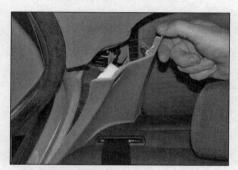

26.18 Pull the C-pillar trim inwards to release the clips

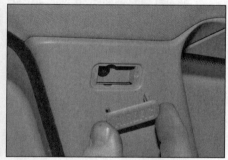

26.20 Prise out the cap and undo the bolt

illustration). Note how the trim engages with the rear door sill trim panel.

14 Pull the lower edge of the upper trim inwards to release the retaining clips, then pull the it downwards. Note how the upper edge of the trim engages with the headlining moulding **(see illustrations)**. Feed the seat belt through the trim panel as it's with- drawn.

15 Refitting is the reverse of the removal procedure; secure the fasteners by pressing them firmly into place and ensure that all disturbed components are correctly secured to prevent rattles. Prise the retaining clips from the door sill and refit them to the sill trim prior to refitting.

C-pillar trim

Saloon models

16 Pull the door weatherstrip away from the area adjacent to the pillar trim.

17 Prise out the cap at the top edge of the trim and undo the Torx bolt beneath **(see illustration)**.

18 Pull the pillar trim upwards from place **(see illustration)**.

19 Refitting is the reverse of the removal procedure; secure the fasteners by pressing them firmly into place and ensure that all disturbed components are correctly secured to prevent rattles.

Touring models

20 Prise out the cap and undo the bolt beneath **(see illustration)**.

21 Pull the trim panel upwards and inwards to release the clips **(see illustration)**.

22 Refitting is a reversal of removal.

D-pillar trim

23 Lift out the luggage compartment floor panel, then rotate the fastener anti-clockwise and lift out the side panel above the battery.

24 Remove the C-pillar trim panel as described previously in this Section.

25 Prise out the clip at the front edge, and pull the upper pillar trim panel downwards to release the retaining clips **(see illustration)**.

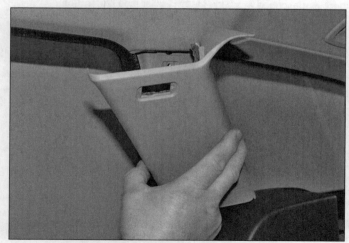

26.21 Pull the C-pillar trim panel upwards

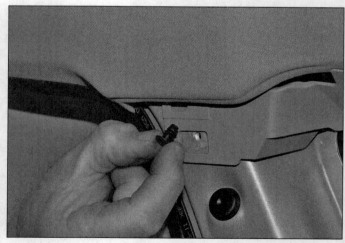

26.25 Prise out the clip at the front edge of the upper pillar trim

26.28a Prise up the centre pins and remove the plastic expansion rivets

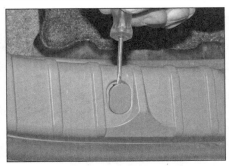

26.28b Prise up the caps and remove the bolts beneath

26.29 Remove the warning triangle holder

26.30 Undo the Torx bolt securing the stowage anchor

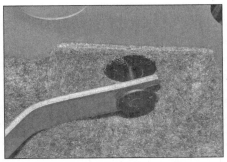

26.31a Prise up the centre pins...

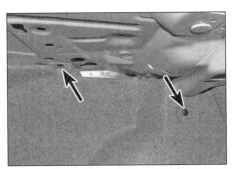

26.31b... and remove the plastic expansion rivets

26 Undo the 5 retaining bolts, then pull the lower pillar trim panel inwards to release the retaining clips. Disconnect any wiring plugs as the trim is removed.

27 Refitting is a reversal of removal.

Luggage area trim panel – Saloon models

28 Lift out the luggage compartment floor panel, prise up the centre pins, lever out the 4 expansion rivets, then prise out the caps, undo the 2 bolts and remove the boot lid sill trim panel (see illustrations).

29 Remove the warning triangle from the holders (where applicable), then rotate the holders anti-clockwise and remove them (see illustration).

30 Undo the Torx bolt securing the luggage stowage anchor (see illustration).

31 Prise up the centre pin and lever out the retaining clips (see illustrations).

32 Remove the panel.

33 Refitting is a reversal of removal.

Luggage area trim panel – Touring models

34 Fold the rear seat backrest forwards.

35 Remove the luggage compartment floor panel.

36 Pull up the plastic cover over the seat belt inertia reel, and feed the seat belt though the slot (see illustration).

Left-hand panel

37 Operate the release handle, open the access panel in front of the rear lights, and lift it from place.

38 Remove the 2 bolts, and prise out the expansion rivet at the top edge of the luggage compartment side trim panel (see illustration).

39 Disconnect the power outlet wiring plug (where applicable), prise out the expansion rivet and undo the bolt securing the stowage hook (see illustration). Lift the panel from place.

Right-hand panel

40 Rotate the fasteners anti-clockwise and lift out the panel above the battery.

41 Prise up the centre pin, remove the plastic expansion rivet, then undo the stowage hook

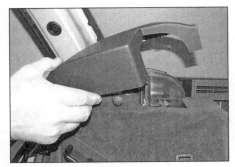

26.36 Pull up the cover over the inertia reel

26.38 Undo the 2 bolts and prise out the plastic expansion rivet

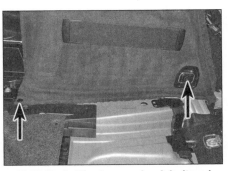

26.39 Undo the stowage hook bolt and prise out the plastic expansion rivet

26.41 Prise out the expansion rivets and undo the stowage hook bolt

26.42 Undo the bolt and remove the expansion rivet

26.45 Using a blunt, flat-bladed tool, carefully prise the cup holders surround trim from the facia

Torx bolt at the lower section of the side panel **(see illustration)**.
42 Undo the 2 bolts at the top of the panel, prise up the centre pin and remove the plastic expansion rivet **(see illustration)**.
43 Lift the side panel from place.

Both sides

44 Refitting is a reversal of removal.

Glovebox

45 Using a blunt, flat-bladed tool, carefully prise the cup holders surround trim from place **(see illustration)**.
46 Undo the retaining bolts and remove the cup holder assemblies above the glovebox **(see illustration)**.

47 Open the glovebox, undo the retaining bolts, and remove the glovebox complete with hinge and bracket **(see illustration)**. Disconnect and wiring plugs as the glovebox is withdrawn.
48 Refitting is the reverse of the removal procedure.

Glovebox lock

49 Open the glovebox lid, undo the two retaining bolts and remove the lock.

Carpets

50 The passenger compartment floor carpet is in one piece, secured at its edges by bolts or clips, usually the same fasteners used to secure the various adjoining trim panels.

51 Carpet removal and refitting is reasonably straightforward but very time-consuming because all adjoining trim panels must be removed first, as must components such as the seats, the centre console and seat belt lower anchorages.

Headlining

52 The headlining is clipped to the roof and can be withdrawn only once all fittings such as the grab handles, sunvisors, sunroof (if fitted), windscreen and rear quarter windows and related trim panels have been removed and the door, tailgate and sunroof aperture sealing strips have been prised clear.
53 Note that headlining removal requires considerable skill and experience if it is to be carried out without damage and is therefore best entrusted to an expert.

Cup holders

54 Using a blunt, flat-bladed tool, carefully prise the decorative trim strip above the glovebox from the facia **(see illustration 26.45)**.
55 Undo the 2 retaining bolts and remove the cup holder assembly above the glovebox **(see illustration 26.46)**.
56 Refitting is a reversal of removal.

Parcel shelf

57 Remove the rear seats (see Section 23).
58 Remove both C-pillar trim panels as described earlier in this Section.
59 Prise up the grille, then undo the bolts and remove the speakers from the rear parcel shelf **(see illustration)**. Disconnect the speaker wiring plugs as they are withdrawn.
60 Undo the bolts and detach the seat belt lower anchorages as described in Section 25.
61 Prise up the centre pins, and remove the plastic expansion rivets at the front edge of the parcel shelf **(see illustration)**.
62 On models with folding rear seats, remove the side cushion on each side by pulling the top edge forwards, then lifting from place.
63 Prise up the trims around the seat belts where they pass through the parcel shelf.

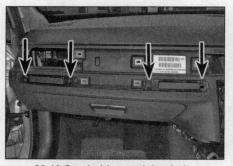

26.46 Cup holder retaining bolts

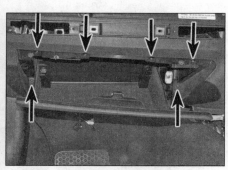

26.47 Undo the bolts and withdraw the glovebox

26.59 Prise up the speaker grille

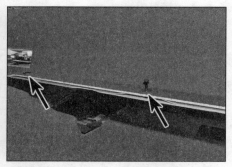

26.61 Prise up the centre pins and remove the plastic expansion rivets

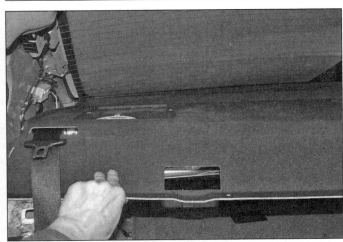
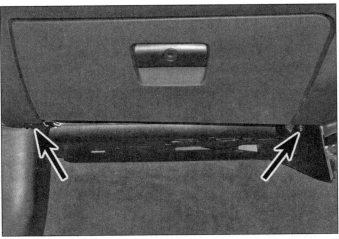

26.64 Pull the parcel shelf forwards and feed the seat belts through

26.68 Undo the 2 bolts and pull the trim panel rearwards

64 Pull the parcel shelf forwards and remove it (see illustration). Feed the seat belts through the parcel shelf as it's withdrawn.
65 Refitting is a reversal of removal.

Footwell side trim panel

66 Pull away the rubber weatherstrip in the area of the trim panel.
67 Pull the door sill trim panel upwards to release the clips at the front.

Passenger's side

68 Undo the 2 bolts and pull the lower

facia panel rearwards (see illustration). Disconnect the wiring plugs as the panel is withdrawn.
69 Pull the footwell side trim panel inwards to release the retaining clips.

Driver's side

70 Undo the bolts and remove the panel above the pedals (see illustration 17.1). Disconnect any wiring plugs as the panel is withdrawn.
71 Undo the bolt and pull the bonnet release handle from place (see illustration 9.4a).

72 Undo the retaining bolt, then pull the footwell panel inwards/rearwards to release the retaining clips (see illustration 9.4b). Disconnect any wiring plugs as the panel is withdrawn.

Both sides

73 Refitting is a reversal of removal.

Sunvisors

74 To remove the sunvisor, undo the 2 Torx bolts securing the outer mounting, and lower it from place (see illustration). Disconnect the vanity mirror switch wiring plug as the sunvisor is withdrawn.
75 To remove the inner mounting, prise open the plastic cover, and undo the mounting Torx bolt (see illustration).
76 Refitting is a reversal of removal.

Grab handles

77 Prise down the plastic covers and undo the retaining Torx bolts (see illustration).
78 Refitting is a reversal of removal.

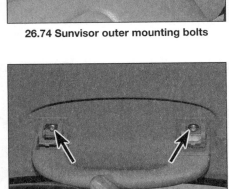
26.74 Sunvisor outer mounting bolts

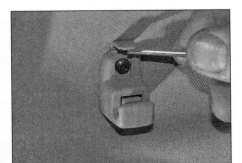
26.75 Prise open the cover and undo the inner mounting bolt

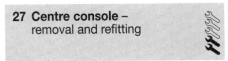
27 Centre console – removal and refitting

Removal

1 On manual transmission models, carefully squeeze the sides of the gear lever gaiter inwards, then pull it upwards from the centre console trim (see illustration).
2 On automatic transmission models, pull the selector lever knob from place with a sharp, upwards pull. Don't twist the knob or the mechanism will be damaged. Squeeze the sides of the gear lever gaiter inwards, then pull it upwards from the centre console trim, then prise up the gaiter surround trim. Disconnect

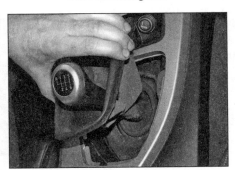
27.1 Squeeze together the sides and pull up the gear lever gaiter

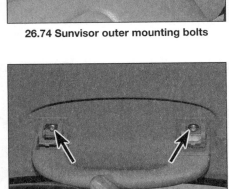
26.77 Grab handle bolts

27.2a Pull the selector lever knob sharply upwards

27.2b Squeeze together the sides and pull the gaiter upwards

27.2c Prise up the gaiter surround trim

27.3 Prise up the trim from the top of the centre console

27.4a Remove the caps...

27.4b... and undo the two bolts

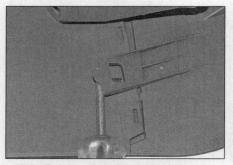

27.5a Release the clips each side at the lower part of the rear section (shown from the inside of the console)...

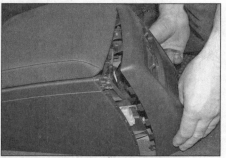

27.5b... and pull the rear section from place

the wiring plug as the trim is removed (**see illustrations**).

3 Open the storage compartment lid, then using a blunt, flat-bladed tool, carefully prise up the trim from the top of the centre console (**see illustration**). Disconnect any wiring plugs as the trim is removed.

4 Prise out the caps and remove the 2 bolts at the front of the console (**see illustrations**).

5 Carefully release the clips at the rear/sides of the console, then pull the rear section away to release the clips at the top (**see illustrations**). Disconnect any wiring plugs as it's withdrawn.

6 Undo the 2 nuts securing the rear of the console (**see illustrations**). Disconnect any

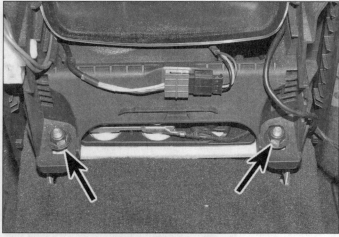

27.6a Undo the nuts...

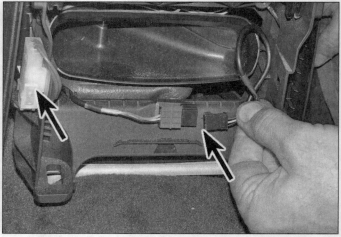

27.6b... and disconnect the wiring plugs

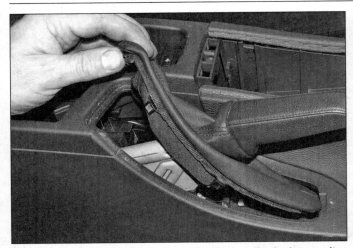

27.7a Squeeze in the sides and remove the handbrake lever gaiter from the console

27.7b Rotate the locking lever, and disconnect the wiring plug in the aperture

wiring plugs accessible through the rear section.

7 Carefully prise the handbrake lever gaiter from the console, and disconnect the wiring plugs exposed in the aperture **(see illustrations)**. To improve access, cut the cable tie and pull the gaiter from the lever. Ensure the handbrake lever is fully raised.

8 Raise the rear of the console, then pull it rearwards a little to disengage the guides at the front **(see illustration)**. Note their fitted locations, then disconnect any wiring plugs as the console is withdrawn. Manoeuvre the centre console over the handbrake lever.

Refitting

9 Manoeuvre the centre console over the handbrake lever, and ensure the front guides and vent engage correctly. The remainder of refitting is the reverse of removal making sure all fasteners are securely tightened.

---

28 Facia panel assembly – removal and refitting

Removal

1 Remove the centre console as described in Section 27.

2 Disconnect the battery negative lead as described in Chapter 5A.

3 Remove the steering column as described in Chapter 10.

4 Remove both A-pillar trim panels as described in Section 26.

5 Undo the bolts and remove the lower trim panel from the passenger's side of the facia **(see illustration 26.68)**. Disconnect any wiring plugs as the panel is withdrawn.

6 Remove the instrument panel as described in Chapter 12.

7 Remove the facia display unit (where fitted) as described in Chapter 12 Section 18.

8 Remove the light control unit/switch as described in Chapter 12.

9 Using a blunt, flat-bladed tool, carefully prise the decorative trim panel from the passenger's side of the facia **(see illustration)**. Disconnect any wiring plugs as the panel is withdrawn.

10 Remove the heating/air conditioning control panel as described in Chapter 3.

11 Using a blunt, flat-bladed tool, carefully prise the surround trim from the driver's side of the facia, then undo the 2 bolts and remove the ignition switch **(see illustrations)**. Disconnect any wiring plugs as the switch is withdrawn.

12 Remove the facia-mounted audio unit as described in Chapter 12.

27.8 Raise the rear of the console and manoeuvre it over the handbrake lever

28.11a Prise the surround trim away...

13 Remove the passenger's side glovebox as described in Section 26.

14 Disconnect the passenger's side airbag wiring plugs, with reference to Chapter 12. Undo the bolt securing the airbag support bracket to the facia **(see illustration)**.

15 Where fitted, remove the centre speaker from the facia as described in Chapter 12. On models without a speaker, prise up the vent grille, and undo the bolts revealed **(see illustrations)**.

16 Carefully prise the solar sensor from the centre of the facia, and disconnect the wiring plug **(see illustration)**.

17 Pull the rear cabin centre vent duct from the lower facia.

28.9 Carefully prise the decorative trim panel from the facia

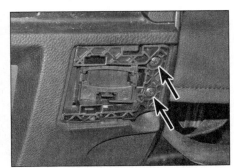

28.11b... and undo the ignition switch bolts

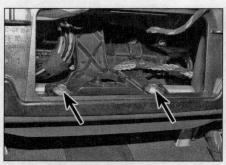

28.14 Airbag support bracket bolts

28.15a Prise up the centre grille...

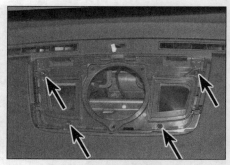

28.15b... and undo the bolts

28.16 Push the solar sensor from the facia

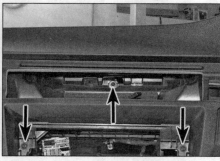

28.18a The facia is secured by 3 bolts in the centre...

18 The facia is now secured by 3 bolts in the centre, and 2 at each end. Undo the bolts, and with the aid of an assistant, pull the facia rearwards, note their fitted positions and disconnect any wiring plugs as necessary. Manoeuvre the facia from the passenger cabin (see illustrations).

> **HAYNES HINT** *Label each wiring connector as it is disconnected from its relevant component. The labels will prove useful on refitting, when routing the wiring and feeding the wiring through the facia apertures.*

Refitting

19 Refitting is a reversal of the removal procedure, noting the following points:
a) Manoeuvre the facia into position and ensure that the wiring is correctly routed and securely retained by its facia clips.
b) Clip the facia back into position, ensure the locating lugs at the front edge of the facia engage correctly, making sure all the wiring connectors are fed through their respective apertures, then refit all the facia fasteners, and tighten them securely.
c) On completion, reconnect the battery and check that all the electrical components and switches function correctly.

28.18b... 2 bolts at the passenger's end...

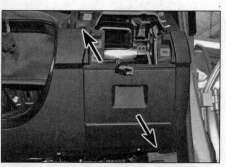

28.18c... and 2 bolts at the driver's end

Chapter 12
Body electrical systems

Contents

Degrees of difficulty

| **Easy,** suitable for novice with little experience | **Fairly easy,** suitable for beginner with some experience | **Fairly difficult,** suitable for competent DIY mechanic | **Difficult,** suitable for experienced DIY mechanic | **Very difficult,** suitable for expert DIY or professional |

Specifications

System type .... 12 volt negative earth

Bulbs

Wattage

Exterior lights

Directional indicator:
   Rear indicator.. LED
   Front indicator PY24
Direction indicator side repeater .... 5 WY or ST
Foglight:
   Front .... 55 (H11 type)
   Rear H21
Headlight:
   Halogen (dipped and main beam) .... 55 (H7 type)
   Xenon DS1
High-level stop-light.................................... LED
Number plate light .... LED
Reversing light .... 16 capless
Sidelight 5
Stop-light 21
Taillight .... LED

Interior light

Courtesy lights 6
Footwell lights 5
Glovebox light 5
Luggage compartment light............................. 5 capless
Vanity mirror 10

Torque wrench settings

	Nm	lbf ft
Airbag system fixings:		
Passenger's side airbag retaining nuts.	7	5
Impact sensor mounting bolts	8	6
Suspension turret braces: *		
M10:		
Stage 1	40	30
Stage 2	Angle-tighten a further 60°	
M12:		
Stage 1	100	74
Stage 2	Angle-tighten a further 100°	
Wiper arm-to-wiper spindle nut	30	22
Tyre pressure transmitter Torx bolt	4	3

*Do not re-use

1 General information and precautions

⚠️ **Warning: Before carrying out any work on the electrical system, read through the precautions given in 'Safety first!' at the beginning of this manual and Chapter 5A.**

1 The electrical system is of the 12 volt negative earth type. Power for the lights and all electrical accessories is supplied by a lead-acid type battery which is charged by the alternator.

2 This Chapter covers repair and service procedures for the various electrical components not associated with engine. Information on the battery, alternator and starter motor can be found in Chapter 5A.

3 It should be noted that prior to working on any component in the electrical system, the battery negative terminal should first be disconnected to prevent the possibility of electrical short circuits and/or fires.

2 Electrical fault finding – general information

Note: *Refer to the precautions given in 'Safety first!' and in Section 1 of this Chapter before starting work. The following tests relate to testing of the main electrical circuits, and should not be used to test delicate electronic circuits (such as anti-lock braking systems), particularly where an electronic control module (ECM) is used.*

Caution: The BMW 3-Series electrical system is extremely complex. Many of the ECMs are connected via a 'Databus' system, where they are able to share information from the various sensors, and communicate with each other. For instance, as the automatic gearbox approaches a gear ratio shift point, it signals the engine management ECM via the Databus. As the gearchange is made by the transmission ECM, the engine management ECM retards the ignition timing, momentarily reducing engine output to ensure a smoother transition from one gear ratio to the next. Due to the design of the Databus system, it is not advisable to backprobe the ECMs with a multimeter in the traditional manner. Instead, the electrical systems are equipped with a sophisticated self-diagnosis system which can interrogate the various ECMs to reveal stored fault codes, and help pin-point faults. In order to access the self-diagnosis system, specialist test equipment (fault code reader/scanner) is required.

General

1 A typical electrical circuit consists of an electrical component, any switches, relays, motors, fuses, fusible links or circuit breakers related to that component, and the wiring and connectors which link the component to both the battery and the chassis. To help to pin-point a problem in an electrical circuit, wiring diagrams are included at the end of this Chapter.

2 Before attempting to diagnose an electrical fault, first study the appropriate wiring diagram to obtain a complete understanding of the components included in the particular circuit concerned. The possible sources of a fault can be narrowed down by noting if other components related to the circuit are operating properly. If several components or circuits fail at one time, the problem is likely to be related to a shared fuse or earth connection.

3 Electrical problems usually stem from simple causes, such as loose or corroded connections, a faulty earth connection, a blown fuse, a melted fusible link, or a faulty relay (refer to Section 3 for details of testing relays). Visually inspect the condition of all fuses, wires and connections in a problem circuit before testing the components. Use the wiring diagrams to determine which terminal connections will need to be checked in order to pin-point the trouble spot.

4 The basic tools required for electrical fault finding include a circuit tester or voltmeter (a 12 volt bulb with a set of test leads can also be used for certain tests); a self-powered test light (sometimes known as a continuity tester); an ohmmeter (to measure resistance); a battery and set of test leads; and a jumper wire, preferably with a circuit breaker or fuse incorporated, which can be used to bypass suspect wires or electrical components. Before attempting to locate a problem with test instruments, use the wiring diagram to determine where to make the connections.

5 To find the source of an intermittent wiring fault (usually due to a poor or dirty connection, or damaged wiring insulation), a 'wiggle' test can be performed on the wiring. This involves wiggling the wiring by hand to see if the fault occurs as the wiring is moved. It should be possible to narrow down the source of the fault to a particular section of wiring. This method of testing can be used in conjunction with any of the tests described in the following sub-Sections.

6 Apart from problems due to poor connections, two basic types of fault can occur in an electrical circuit – open circuit, or short circuit.

7 Open circuit faults are caused by a break somewhere in the circuit, which prevents current from flowing. An open circuit fault will prevent a component from working, but will not cause the relevant circuit fuse to blow.

8 Short circuit faults are caused by a 'short' somewhere in the circuit, which allows the current flowing in the circuit to 'escape' along an alternative route, usually to earth. Short circuit faults are normally caused by a breakdown in wiring insulation, which allows a feed wire to touch either another wire, or an earthed component such as the bodyshell. A short circuit fault will normally cause the relevant circuit fuse to blow.

Finding an open circuit

9 To check for an open circuit, connect one lead of a circuit tester or voltmeter to either the negative battery terminal or a known good earth.

10 Connect the other lead to a connector in

2.20a Typical earth connections: between the left-hand engine mounting and body...

2.20b... cylinder head to inner wing (petrol models)...

2.20c... front inner wing – both sides...

2.20d... right-hand side of the rear panel...

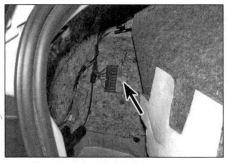

2.20e... left-hand side of the luggage compartment...

2.20f... behind the rear seats

the circuit being tested, preferably nearest to the battery or fuse.

11 Switch on the circuit, bearing in mind that some circuits are live only when the ignition switch is moved to a particular position.

12 If voltage is present (indicated either by the tester bulb lighting or a voltmeter reading, as applicable), this means that the section of the circuit between the relevant connector and the battery is problem-free.

13 Continue to check the remainder of the circuit in the same fashion.

14 When a point is reached at which no voltage is present, the problem must lie between that point and the previous test point with voltage. Most problems can be traced to a broken, corroded or loose connection.

Finding a short circuit

15 To check for a short circuit, first disconnect the load(s) from the circuit (loads are the components which draw current from a circuit, such as bulbs, motors, heating elements, etc).

16 Remove the relevant fuse from the circuit, and connect a circuit tester or voltmeter to the fuse connections.

17 Switch on the circuit, bearing in mind that some circuits are live only when the ignition switch is moved to a particular position.

18 If voltage is present (indicated either by the tester bulb lighting or a voltmeter reading, as applicable), this means that there is a short circuit.

19 If no voltage is present, but the fuse

still blows with the load(s) connected, this indicates an internal fault in the load(s).

Finding an earth fault

20 The battery negative terminal is connected to 'earth' – the metal of the engine/transmission and the car body – and most systems are wired so that they only receive a positive feed, the current returning through the metal of the car body **(see illustrations)**. This means that the component mounting and the body form part of that circuit. Loose or corroded mountings can therefore cause a range of electrical faults, ranging from total failure of a circuit to a puzzling partial fault. In particular, lights may shine dimly (especially when another circuit sharing the same earth point is in operation), motors (eg, wiper motors or the radiator cooling fan motor) may run slowly, and the operation of one circuit may have an apparently unrelated effect on another. Note that on many vehicles, earth straps are used between certain components, such as the engine/transmission and the body, usually where there is no metal-to-metal contact between components due to flexible rubber mountings, etc.

21 To check whether a component is properly earthed, disconnect the battery and connect one lead of an ohmmeter to a known good earth point. Connect the other lead to the wire or earth connection being tested. The resistance reading should be zero; if not, check the connection as follows.

22 If an earth connection is thought to be

faulty, dismantle the connection and clean back to bare metal both the bodyshell and the wire terminal or the component earth connection mating surface. Be careful to remove all traces of dirt and corrosion, then use a knife to trim away any paint, so that a clean metal-to-metal joint is made. On reassembly, tighten the joint fasteners securely; if a wire terminal is being refitted, use serrated washers between the terminal and the bodyshell to ensure a clean and secure connection. When the connection is remade, prevent the onset of corrosion in the future by applying a coat of petroleum jelly.

3 Fuses and relays – general information

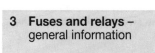

Main fuses

1 The fuses are located behind the passenger's side glovebox.

2 To remove the fusebox cover, open the glovebox, turn the two quick-release fasteners and pull down the cover.

3 A list of the circuits each fuse protects is given on the label attached to the inside of the main fusebox cover. A pair of tweezers for removing the fuses is also clipped to the fusebox. Note that the vertical fuses are active, and the horizontal fuses are spare. High amperage 'fusible links' are located on

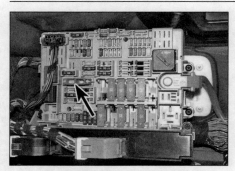

3.3 The fusebox is located behind the passenger's side glovebox. Note the tweezers for removing the fuses (arrowed)

3.4 Use the tweezers provided to pull the relevant fuse

3.7 Some relays are located in the electrical box in the left-hand corner of the engine compartment

the top face of the fusebox **(see illustration)**.
4 To remove a fuse, first switch off the circuit concerned (or the ignition), then pull the fuse out of its terminals using the tweezers which are clipped to the fusebox **(see illustration)**. The wire within the fuse should be visible; if the fuse is blown it will be broken or melted.
5 Always renew a fuse with one of an identical rating; never use a fuse with a different rating from the original or substitute anything else. Never renew a fuse more than once without tracing the source of the trouble. The fuse rating is stamped on top of the fuse; note that the fuses are also colour-coded for easy recognition.
6 If a new fuse blows immediately, find the cause before renewing it again; a short to earth as a result of faulty insulation is most

likely. Where a fuse protects more than one circuit, try to isolate the defect by switching on each circuit in turn (if possible) until the fuse blows again. Always carry a supply of spare fuses of each relevant rating on the vehicle, a spare of each rating should be clipped into the base of the fusebox.

Relays

7 The majority of relays are located behind the passenger's side glovebox **(see illustration)**, whilst other relays are located in the 'E-box' in the left-hand corner of the engine compartment.
8 If a circuit or system controlled by a relay develops a fault and the relay is suspect, operate the system; if the relay is functioning it should be possible to hear it click as it is

energised. If this is the case the fault lies with the components or wiring of the system. If the relay is not being energised then either the relay is not receiving a main supply or a switching voltage, or the relay itself is faulty. Testing is by the substitution of a known good unit but be careful; while some relays are identical in appearance and in operation, others look similar but perform different functions.
9 To renew a relay first ensure that the ignition switch is off. The relay can then simply be pulled out from the socket and the new relay pressed in.

---

4   Switches – removal and refitting

Note: *Disconnect the battery negative lead (see Chapter 5A) before removing any switch, and reconnect the lead after refitting the switch.*

Ignition switch

1 Carefully prise the switch surround from place **(see illustration)**.
2 Undo the 2 bolts and pull the switch from the facia **(see illustration)**. Disconnect the wiring plug as the switch is withdrawn.
3 Refitting is a reversal of removal.

4.1 Prise the switch surround from the facia

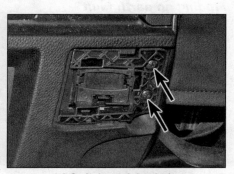

4.2 Switch retaining bolts

Engine start switch

4 Using a blunt, flat-bladed tool, carefully prise the decorative trim strip/air vents from the facia **(see illustration)**. Disconnect any wiring plugs as the trim is removed.
5 Squeeze together the clips and push the engine start switch from the trim **(see illustration)**.
6 Refitting is a reversal of removal.

Steering column switch module

7 Place the steering column in the fully lowered and extended position. Remove the steering wheel as described in Chapter 10.
8 Note that as the steering wheel is removed, the airbag rotary contact unit is automatically locked to prevent any accidental rotation.

4.4 Carefully prise the decorative trim strip from the facia

4.5 Squeeze together the clips and push the start switch from the trim

4.9a Unclip the column upper shroud...

4.9b... and lower column shroud...

4.9c... if required, squeeze together the clips and detach the upper shroud from the gaiter

9 Unclip the upper and lower steering column shrouds **(see illustrations)**.
10 Undo the 4 bolts and slide the module up the steering column **(see illustration)**.
11 Disconnect the various wiring plugs from the module as it's withdrawn. **Note:** *The steering column switch module has very few mechanical elements, as the operating components are optical switches. The module also incorporates the steering angle sensor. Handle the module with great care.*
12 If required, release the clips and separate the airbag rotary contact unit **(see illustration)**. No further dismantling of the module is recommended.
13 Refitting is a reversal of the removal procedure, ensuring that the wiring is correctly routed. Note that if a new module has been fitted, it must be coded/calibrated using BMW diagnostic equipment. Entrust this

task to a BMW dealer or suitably-equipped specialist.

Lighting switch

14 Using a blunt, flat-bladed tool, carefully prise the decorative trim strip/air vent from the right-hand side of the facia **(see illustration)**. Disconnect any wiring plugs as the trim is removed.
15 Carefully prise the switch and surround trim from the facia. Unlock and disconnect the wiring plug from the switch as it's withdrawn **(see illustrations)**.
16 If required, release the catches and detach the switch from the surround trim **(see illustration)**.
17 Refitting is the reverse of removal.

Hazard warning/ central locking/ DTC switches

18 Using a blunt, flat-bladed tool, carefully

prise the decorative trim strip/air vents from the facia **(see illustration 4.4)**. Disconnect any wiring plugs as the trim is removed.
19 Press the switch block from the strip **(see illustration)**.
20 Refitting is the reverse of removal.

4.10 Undo the switch module retaining bolts

4.12 Release the clips around the outer edge of the contact unit (upper clips arrowed)

4.14 Prise the decorative trim strip/air vent from the facia

4.15a Pull the switch and surround from place...

4.15b... then lever over the locking catch and disconnect the wiring plug

4.16 Release the clips and detach the switch from the surround

4.19 Press the switch block from place

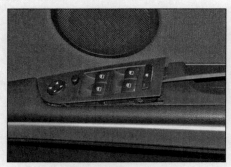

4.21 Carefully prise the electric window switch panel from the armrest

4.30 Release the clips and detach the switch cluster

4.34 Handbrake warning light switch bolt

Electric window switches

21 Using a blunt, flat-bladed tool, carefully lever the switch panel from the armrest **(see illustration)**. If necessary, use a piece of card to protect the armrest material.
22 Disconnect the wiring plugs as the switch panel is removed.
23 Refitting is the reversal of removal.

Exterior mirror switches

24 The mirror adjustment switch is integral with the electric window switch. Remove the switch assembly as previously described in this Section.

Clutch pedal position switch

25 Undo the driver's side lower facia panel retaining bolts then unclip the panel and remove it from the vehicle. Note their fitted positions and disconnect any wiring plugs as the panel is withdrawn.
26 Disconnect the wiring plug from the switch.
27 Using a screwdriver, unclip the switch from the side of the master cylinder.
28 Refitting is the reverse of removal.

Central facia switch cluster

29 Remove the heating/air conditioning/climate control panel as described in Chapter 3.
30 Disconnect the wiring plug, then release the clips and detach the switch cluster (where fitted) from the control panel **(see illustration)**.
31 Refitting is a reversal of removal.

Heated rear window/blower/ air conditioning switches

32 The switches are an integral part of the control unit and cannot be renewed. If a switch is faulty seek the advice of a BMW dealer or parts specialist.

Handbrake warning light switch

33 Remove the centre console as described in Chapter 11 to gain access to the handbrake lever.
34 Disconnect the wiring connector from the warning light switch then undo the bolt and remove the switch **(see illustration)**.
35 Refitting is the reverse of removal. Check the operation of the switch before refitting the centre console, the warning light should illuminate between the first and second clicks of the ratchet mechanism.

Stop-light switch

36 Refer to Chapter 9.

Courtesy light switches

37 The function of the courtesy light switches is incorporated into the door/boot lid/tailgate lock assembly. To remove the relevant lock, refer to Chapter 11.

Steering wheel switches

38 Two different types of steering wheels are fitted to the 3-Series range. Either a Multifunction steering wheel, or a Sports steering wheel. To remove the switches, remove the driver's airbag as described in Section 25, then proceed under the relevant heading.

Multifunction steering wheel

39 Disconnect the switches wiring plug from the centre of the steering wheel. Note that the switches are wired together.
40 Carefully prise the switches from the steering wheel **(see illustration)**. Note that the horn switch is integral with the airbag unit.

Sports steering wheel

41 Undo the 3 retaining bolts on the front face of the steering wheel (two securing the upper section and one securing the lower section), and unclip the switch carrier panel from the steering wheel. Disconnect the wiring plug as the panel with withdrawn.
42 If required, undo the bolts and detach the switches from the panel **(see illustration)**.

Sunroof/interior light switches

43 Using a blunt, flat-bladed tool, carefully prise the interior light lens from place **(see illustration 6.4)**.
44 Release the clips, and prise the switch/panel assembly from the headlining **(see illustrations 6.5a and 6.5b)**. Disconnect the wiring plugs as the panel is withdrawn.
45 No further dismantling of the assembly is recommended. The switches are not available separately. Consult a BMW dealer or parts specialist.
46 Refitting is the reverse of removal. If a new switch/panel assembly has been fitted, the switch module for the sunroof will need to be programmed using BMW diagnostic equipment. Entrust this task to a BMW dealer or suitably-equipped specialist.
47 Upon completion, initialise the sunroof as follows:
a) *Press and hold the switch in the 'tilt' position.*
b) *After reaching the 'end of tilt' position, keep the switch pressed for a further 30 seconds. The 'normalisation' is complete when the sunroof rear end lifts briefly.*
c) *Keep the switch pressed in the 'tilt' position, after approximately 5 seconds, the sunroof will move to the closed position, back to the open position, then finally back to the closed position.*
d) *Release the switch.*

Boot lid/tailgate release switches

48 Unclip the diagnostic plug socket cover on the driver's side footwell panel.

4.40 Prise the switch block from the steering wheel – multifunction steering wheel

4.42 Each steering wheel switch is secured by a bolt

5.3 Fold up the clip and remove the cover

5.5 Press the top of the clip forwards, the move it to the side to release it

5.10 Pull the catch rearwards and remove the cover

49 Push the release switch from the panel. Disconnect the wiring plug as the switch is removed.

50 Refitting is a reversal of removal.

iDrive controller

51 Remove the upper section of the centre console as described in Chapter 11 Section 27.

52 Release the catches on each side, and press the controller upwards from the panel.

53 Refitting is a reversal of removal. Note that if a new controller is fitted, it may need to be programmed using BMW diagnostic equipment (or equivalent).

Automatic transmission shift paddles

54 Remove the driver's airbag as described in Section 25.

55 Disconnect the shift paddles wiring plugs, then undo the 2 bolts and pull the paddles from the steering wheel.

56 Refitting is a reversal of removal.

5 Bulbs (exterior lights) – renewal

General

1 Whenever a bulb is renewed, note the following points.

a) *Remember that if the light has just been in use the bulb may be extremely hot.*
b) *Always check the bulb contacts and holder, ensuring that there is clean metal-to-metal contact between the bulb and its live(s) and earth. Clean off any corrosion or dirt before fitting a new bulb.*
c) *Wherever bayonet-type bulbs are fitted ensure that the live contact(s) bear firmly against the bulb contact.*
d) *Always ensure that the new bulb is of the correct rating and that it is completely clean before fitting it; this applies particularly to headlight/foglight bulbs (see below).*

Halogen headlights

Main beam

2 Two different types of covers may be fitted to the rear of the headlight, and the bulbs secured by two different fasteners. Proceed according to version fitted:

Version 1

3 Reach behind the headlight, fold the wire retaining clip to upwards, and remove the cover upwards from the headlight **(see illustration)**.

4 Pull the wiring plug from the bulb.

5 Release the retaining clip and pull the bulb from the reflector **(see illustration)**.

6 When handling the new bulb, use a tissue or clean cloth to avoid touching the glass with the fingers; moisture and grease from the skin can cause blackening and rapid failure of

this type of bulb. If the glass is accidentally touched, wipe it clean using methylated spirit.

7 Push the new bulb into the reflector, ensuring that the bulb's locating lugs align with the corresponding slots in the reflector.

8 Secure the bulb in place with the retaining clip, and reconnect the wiring plug.

9 Refit the cover.

Version 2

10 Reach behind the headlight, pull the catch on the side of the cover rearwards, and open the cover **(see illustration)**.

11 Push the bulb at the plug upwards against the holder, the pull it backwards and remove it **(see illustration)**.

12 Disconnect the wiring plug.

13 Insert the new bulb into the holder at the top, then push it forwards to engage it with the reflector.

14 When handling the new bulb, use a tissue or clean cloth to avoid touching the glass with the fingers; moisture and grease from the skin can cause blackening and rapid failure of this type of bulb. If the glass is accidentally touched, wipe it clean using methylated spirit.

15 Refit the cover.

Dipped beam

16 The dipped beam bulb is accessed through a flap in the wheel arch liner. Turn the wheel inwards, then use a coin to rotate the fasteners anti-clockwise and open the flap **(see illustrations)**.

17 Two different types of covers are fitted to the rear of the headlight to access the dipped

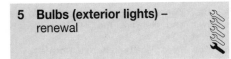
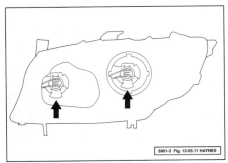

5.11 Push the bulbholder upwards and pull it rearwards

5.16a Rotate the fasteners...

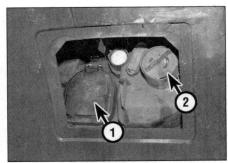

5.16b... and remove the flap to access the dipped beam cover (1) or indicator bulbholder (2)

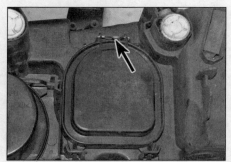

5.17 Release the clip (arrowed) at the top of the dipped beam cover

beam. Either unclip the cover, or rotate it anti-clockwise to remove it (see illustration).

18 The bulb removal procedure is identical to the main beam bulb removal procedure as described previously in this Section.

19 Close the flap in the wheel arch liner, and rotate the fastener clockwise to secure it.

Xenon headlights

Dipped beam

20 On models equipped with Xenon high-intensity dipped beam bulbs, due to the potential high voltages involved, disconnect the battery negative lead as described in Chapter 5A.

21 Remove wheel arch liner as described in Chapter 11, or remove the headlight as described in Section 7.

5.35a Pull the sidelight bulbholder from place...

5.38 Twist the directional indicator bulb holder anti-clockwise and remove it

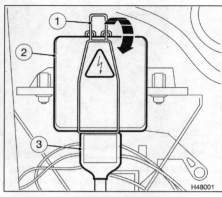

5.24 Xenon headlight ignitor details

1 Retaining clip 2 Ignitor 3 Wiring plug

22 Unclip the plastic cover from the rear of the headlight.

23 Disconnect the ignitor unit wiring plug.

24 Unclip the retaining wire clip and fold it downwards (see illustration).

25 Pull the ignitor and bulb assembly from the reflector.

26 Refitting is a reversal of removal.

Main beam

27 Proceed as described in Paragraphs 20 to 23 of this Section.

28 Pull the wiring plug from the bulb.

29 Release the retaining clip and pull the bulb from the reflector.

30 When handling the new bulb, use a tissue

5.35b... then pull the capless bulb from the holder

5.39 Squeeze together the clips and rotate the bulb assembly anti-clockwise

or clean cloth to avoid touching the glass with the fingers; moisture and grease from the skin can cause blackening and rapid failure of this type of bulb. If the glass is accidentally touched, wipe it clean using methylated spirit.

31 Push the new bulb into the reflector, ensuring that the bulb's locating lugs align with the corresponding slots in the reflector.

32 Secure the bulb in place with the retaining clip, and reconnect the wiring plug.

33 The remainder of refitting is a reversal of removal.

Front sidelight

Note: Not fitted to all models

34 Unclip the plastic cover from the rear of the main beam bulb.

35 Pull the bulbholder from the headlight unit. The bulb is of the capless type and is a push-fit in the holder (see illustrations).

36 Refitting is a reversal of removal.

Direction indicator

37 The indicator bulb is accessed through a flap in the wheel arch liner. Turn the wheel inwards, then use a coin to rotate the fasteners and open the flap (see illustration 5.16a and 5.16b).

38 Twist the bulbholder anti-clockwise to remove it from the light unit (see illustration).

39 The PY24 bulb is separated from the holder by squeezing together the clips and twisting anti-clockwise a little (see illustration).

40 Refitting is a reverse of the removal.

'Angel eyes' side lights

41 Unclip the plastic cover from the rear of the main beam bulb.

42 Disconnect the wiring plug, then undo the screws and remove the bulb unit (see illustration).

43 Pull the capless bulb from the holder.

44 Refitting is a reversal of removal.

Direction indicator side repeater

45 Using finger pressure, push the side repeater lens gently rearwards. Pull out the

5.42 Undo the screws and remove the bulb/holder

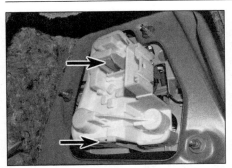

5.45 Push the side repeater rearwards and pull out the front edge

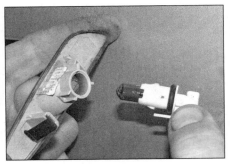

5.46 Rotate the bulbholder anti-clockwise

5.50 The foglight bulb is integral with the holder

front edge of the lens and withdraw it from the wing **(see illustration)**.

46 Rotate the bulbholder anti-clockwise and pull it from the lens, pull the capless bulb from the holder **(see illustration)**.

47 Refitting is a reversal of removal.

Front foglight

48 Remove the front section of the wheel arch liner.

49 Disconnect the wiring plug, then rotate the bulbholder anti-clockwise and remove it from the light.

50 The bulb is integral with the bulbholder **(see illustration)**.

51 When handling the new bulb, use a tissue or clean cloth to avoid touching the glass with the fingers; moisture and grease from the skin can cause blackening and rapid failure of this type of bulb. If the glass is accidentally touched, wipe it clean using methylated spirit.

52 Refitting is a reversal of removal. If necessary, adjust the aim of the light by rotating the adjusting screw adjacent to the lens **(see illustration)**.

Body-mounted rear lights

Note: *The tail lights, directional indicators and parking lights are non-replaceable LEDs.*

Saloon models

53 From inside the vehicle luggage compartment, release the retaining clip or undo the fastener and open the access flap behind the light unit.

54 Release the retaining clips and pull the bulbholder from the rear of the light unit **(see illustration)**.

55 Press the relevant bulb in slightly, twist it anti-clockwise, and remove it from the bulbholder.

56 Refitting is a reversal of removal.

Touring models

57 Open the flap in the luggage compartment to expose the bulbholder (left-hand lights) or lift out the floor panel, undo the 2 fasteners and lift out the side panel (right-hand lights).

58 Release the retaining clip, and pull the bulbholder assembly from the rear of the light **(see illustration)**.

59 Press the relevant bulb in slightly, twist it anti-clockwise, and remove it from the bulbholder.

60 Refitting is a reversal of removal.

Boot lid-mounted rear lights

61 Prise out the centre pins, lever out the expansion clips and partially release the boot lid trim panel behind the light cluster **(see illustration)**.

62 Release the retaining clip, and remove the bulbholder from the boot lid **(see illustration)**.

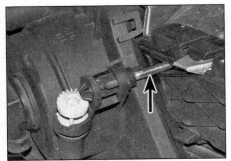

5.52 Insert an Allen key through the hole in the corner of the front, lower grille

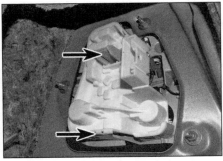

5.54 Depress the retaining clips and pull the bulbholder from place

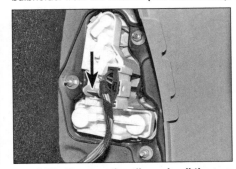

5.58a Depress the clip and pull the bulbholder from the light unit

5.58b Press in the bulb, rotate it anti-clockwise and remove it

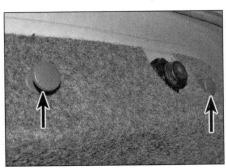

5.61 Prise up the centre pins from the expansion clips

5.62 Press the retaining clip and pull the bulbholder from the boot lid

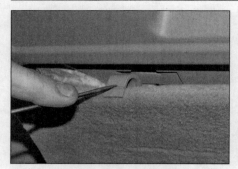

5.65 Release the 3 clips and fold down the tailgate panel

63 Press the relevant bulb in slightly, twist it anti-clockwise, and remove it from the bulbholder.
64 Refitting is a reversal of removal.

Tailgate-mounted rear lights

65 Open the tailgate. Carefully release the 3 retaining clips at the lower edge of the tailgate trim panel and fold the panel downwards **(see illustration)**.
66 Move the insulation material to one side, then release the retaining clip, and remove the bulbholder from the tailgate **(see illustration)**.
67 Press the relevant bulb in slightly, twist it anti-clockwise, and remove it from the bulbholder.
68 Refitting is a reversal of removal.

High-level stop-light

69 The high-level stop-light is an LED strip.

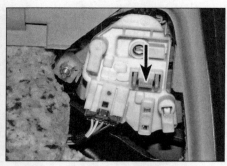

5.66 Press the retaining clip and pull the bulbholder from the tailgate

If a fault develops, consult your local BMW dealer or specialist.

Number plate light

70 The number plate lights are illuminated by non-replaceable LEDs. If a fault develops, consult your local BMW dealer or specialist.
71 Refitting is the reverse of removal, making sure the bulb is securely held in position by the contacts.

6   Bulbs (interior lights) – renewal

General

1 Refer to Section 5, paragraph 1.

Courtesy/interior lights

Centre light unit

2 Push the light unit rearwards, then pull down the front edge. Rotate the bulbholder anti-clockwise, and pull the capless bulb from the holders **(see illustrations)**.
3 Push the new bulb(s) into the holder(s), and refit them in to the light unit. Refit the light unit. Note that the front edge of the light unit must be fitted first, then push the rear edge into place.

Front light unit

4 Using a blunt, flat-bladed tool, carefully prise the light lens from place **(see illustration)**.
5 Using the same tool, depress the clips at the front edge, and pull the unit downwards. The clips are exactly in line with the centre line of each reading light **(see illustrations)**.
6 Rotate the bulbholder anti-clockwise and pull the capless bulb from the holder.
7 Push the new bulb(s) into the holder(s), and refit them in to the light unit. Clip the lens back into place before refitting the light unit. Note that the rear edge of the light unit must be fitted first, then push the front edge into place.

Footwell light

8 Carefully lever the light out from the panel. Disconnect the wiring plug as the light unit is withdrawn.
9 Release the catch, remove the cover, and remove the bulb.
10 Fit the new bulb into position, refit the cover, and refit the light to the panel.

6.2a Push the light unit rearwards, and pull down the front edge

6.2b Rotate the bulbholders anti-clockwise...

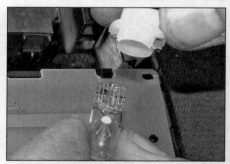

6.2c... and pull the capless bulb from the holder

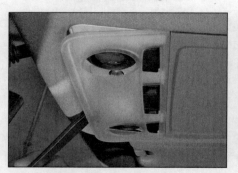

6.4 Carefully prise the lens from the light unit

6.5a Depress the clips at the front edge of the light unit

6.5b Use a blunt tool to press the clips rearwards

Luggage compartment light

11 Carefully lever the light out from the panel **(see illustration)**. Disconnect the wiring plug as the light unit is withdrawn.

12 Rotate the bulbholder anti-clockwise, and pull the capless bulb from the contacts **(see illustration)**.

Warning/instrument panel lights

13 The instrument panel is illuminated by a series of LEDs, which are not renewable.

Glovebox illumination light bulb

14 Open up the glovebox. Using a small flat-bladed screwdriver carefully prise the top of the light assembly and withdraw it. Release the bulb from its contacts.

15 Install the new bulb, ensuring it is securely held in position by the contacts, and clip the light unit back into position.

Heater/air conditioning control panel illumination

16 The control panel is illuminated by LEDs which are not serviceable. If a fault develops, have the system checked by a BMW dealer or suitably-equipped specialist.

Switch illumination bulbs

17 All of the switches are fitted with illuminating LEDs; some are also fitted with a LED to show when the circuit concerned is operating. On all switches, these LEDs are an integral part of the switch assembly and cannot be obtained separately. LED renewal will therefore require the renewal of the complete switch assembly.

Vanity lights

18 Prise down the front edge of the light unit, and pull the festoon bulb from the contacts **(see illustrations)**.

| 7 | Exterior light units – removal and refitting |

Headlight

1 Remove the front bumper as described in Chapter 11.

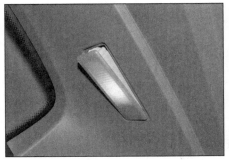

6.11 Carefully prise the light from place

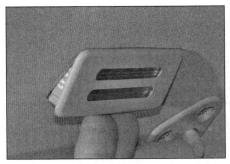

6.18a Pull the down the front edge of the vanity light

2 Where applicable, carefully lever out the headlight washer jet from the trim below the headlamp, and pull it out to its stop. With a sharp tug, separate the jet from the washer tube.

3 Undo the 5 bolts and pull the headlight forwards slightly **(see illustrations)**.

4 Note their fitted positions, and disconnect all wiring plugs/harnesses from the rear of the headlight.

5 Remove the headlight unit from the vehicle.

6 Refitting is a direct reversal of the removal procedure. Once the light unit is correctly positioned, securely tighten the retaining bolts and check the headlight beam alignment using the information given in Section 8.

Xenon headlight control unit

7 Remove the relevant headlight as described earlier in this Section.

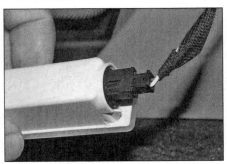

6.12 Rotate the bulbholder anti-clockwise

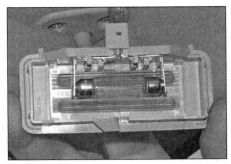

6.18b Pull the festoon bulb from the contacts

8 Undo the 3 retaining bolts, slide the control unit to the rear of the headlight remove it.

9 Disconnect the wiring plugs as the unit is withdrawn.

10 Refitting is a reversal of removal.

Adaptive headlight control unit

11 Remove the left-hand front wheel arch liner as described in Chapter 11.

12 Undo the 4 bolts and remove the control unit from the base of the headlight.

13 Refitting is a reversal of removal. Note that if a new unit has been fitted, it must be programmed using BMW diagnostic equipment. Entrust this task to a BMW dealer or suitably-equipped specialist.

Direction indicator

14 The front direction indicators are integral with the headlights.

7.3a Undo the bolts at the top of the headlight...

7.3b... two bolts at the inner edge...

7.3c... and one behind the headlight

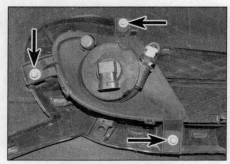

7.19 Foglight retaining bolts

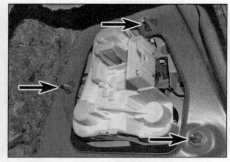

7.23 Rear light retaining nuts – Saloon models

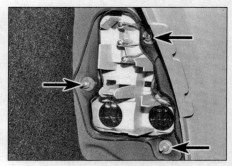

7.27 Rear light retaining nuts – Touring models

Direction indicator side repeater

15 Using finger pressure, push the side repeater lens gently forwards. Pull out the rear edge of the lens and withdraw it from the wing **(see illustration 5.41)**. Disconnect the wiring plug as the unit is withdrawn.
16 Refitting is a reversal of removal.

Front foglight

17 Undo the fasteners and pull back the front section of the wheel arch liner.
18 Disconnect the foglight wiring plug.
19 Undo the 3 bolts and pull the foglight from the bumper **(see illustration)**.
20 Refitting is a reversal of removal.

Body-mounted rear lights

Saloon models

21 From inside the luggage compartment, prise open the access panel behind the rear lights.

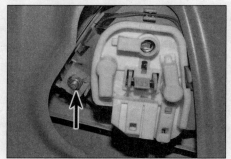

7.31 Undo the nut, and remove the plastic retainer

7.38 Pull down the rear edge of the brake light cover

22 Disconnect the wiring plug, release the clip and pull the bulbholder assembly from the rear light **(see illustration 5.54)**.
23 Undo the three retaining nuts and remove the cluster form the wing **(see illustration)**.
24 Refitting is a reversal of removal.

Touring models

25 Operate the release catch and lift out the access panel (left-hand rear lights) or lift out the floor panel, undo the two fasteners and lift out the panel in front of the rear lights (right-hand lights). To improve access to the left-hand light, remove the warning triangle from its location.
26 Disconnect the wiring plug, release the retaining clip, and pull the bulbholder assembly from the rear light **(see illustration 5.58a)**.
27 Undo the three retaining nuts, and remove the light cluster **(see illustration)**.

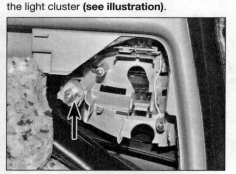

7.36 Slacken the retaining nut

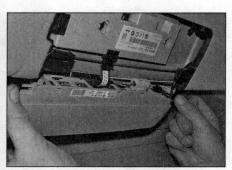

7.39 Slide out the catches and remove the light unit

28 Refitting is a reversal of removal. Note how the outer light unit guide engages with the pin on the vehicle body.

Boot lid-mounted rear lights

29 Prise up the centre pins, then lever out the clips and partially release the boot lid trim panel behind the light cluster **(see illustration 5.61)**.
30 Disconnect the wiring plug, release the retaining clip, and remove the bulbholder from the boot lid **(see illustration 5.62)**.
31 Undo the securing nut, remove the plastic retainer, and remove the light cluster **(see illustration)**. Note that the edge of the light unit wraps around the edge of the boot lid.
32 Refitting is a reversal of removal.

Tailgate-mounted rear lights

33 Release the 3 clips and fold down the tailgate trim panel behind the rear lights **(see illustration 5.65)**.
34 Pull away the section of insulation behind the rear lights.
35 Disconnect the rear light cluster wiring plug, release the retaining clip and remove the bulbholder **(see illustration 5.66)**.
36 Slacken the securing nut, press the clamping lever in the direction of the light cluster and remove it **(see illustration)**.
37 Refitting is a reversal of removal.

High-level stop-light

Saloon models

38 Pull down the rear edge of the cover in front of the high-level stop-light **(see illustration)**.
39 Disconnect the wiring plug, pull out the locking catches and remove the light unit **(see illustration)**.
40 Refitting is a reversal of removal.

Touring models

41 Removal of the high-level stop-light involves removal of the rear spoiler. This is a complex task requiring specialist bodywork tools and experience. Any attempt to remove the spoiler without the necessary equipment is very likely to result in damage. Consequently, we recommend that this work is entrusted to a BMW dealer or suitably-equipped specialist.

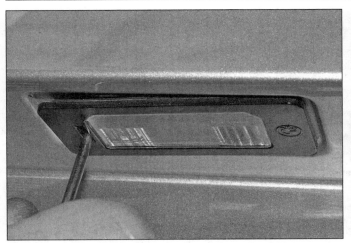

7.42 Push the number plate unit to the side to compress the clip, and remove it

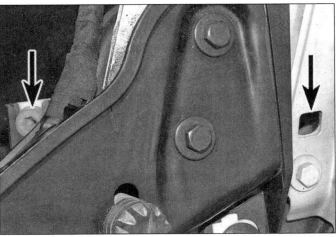

8.2 The headlight vertical adjustment screw is accessed from behind the headlight, whilst the horizontal screw is accessed through a hole in the inner wing

Number plate light

42 Using a small screwdriver in the slot provided, push the light unit to the right-hand side, and pull it from place **(see illustration)**. Disconnect the wiring plug as the unit is withdrawn.

43 Refitting is the reverse of removal.

8 Headlight beam alignment – general information

1 Accurate adjustment of the headlight beam is only possible using optical beam setting equipment and this work should therefore be carried out by a BMW dealer or suitably-equipped workshop.

2 For reference, the headlights can be adjusted by rotating the adjuster screws on the top of the headlight unit **(see illustration)**. The outer adjuster alters the horizontal position of the beam whilst the inner adjuster alters the vertical aim of the beam.

3 Some models have an electrically-operated headlight beam adjustment system which is controlled through the switch in the facia. On these models ensure that the switch is set to the 'off' position before adjusting the headlight aim.

9 Instrument panel – removal and refitting

Removal

1 Disconnect the battery negative terminal (see Chapter 5A).

2 Move the steering column down as far as it will go, and extend it completely.

3 Slacken and remove the two retaining Torx bolts from the top of the instrument panel, and carefully pull the top of the panel from the facia **(see illustrations)**.

4 Lever over the retaining catches then disconnect the wiring connectors and remove the instrument panel from the vehicle **(see illustration)**.

Refitting

5 Refitting is the reverse of removal making sure the instrument panel wiring is correctly reconnected and securely held in position by any retaining clips. On completion reconnect the battery and check the operation of the panel warning lights to ensure that they are functioning correctly. **Note:** *If the instrument cluster has been renewed, the new unit must be coded to match the vehicle. This can only be carried out by a BMW dealer or suitably-equipped specialist.*

10 Instrument panel components – removal and refitting

1 At the time of writing, no individual components are available for the instrument panel and therefore the panel must be treated as a sealed unit. If there is a fault with one of the instruments, remove the panel as described in Section 9 and take it to your BMW dealer for testing. They have access to a special diagnostic tester which will be able to locate the fault and will then be able to advise you on the best course of action.

11 Rain sensor – removal and refitting

1 The rain sensor is incorporated into the front face of the interior mirror mounting base. Press up on the lower end of the mounting

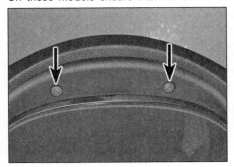

9.3a Undo the two bolts...

9.3b... and pull the top of the instrument cluster rearwards

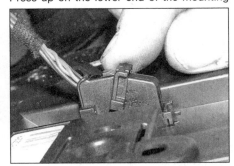

9.4 Lever over the retaining catches to disconnect the wiring plugs

11.1 Prise apart the two halves of the trim

11.3 Pull down the sensor retaining clips

trim, and press the two halves of the mounting trim apart at the base, and release the trim retaining clips **(see illustration)**.

2 With the trim removed, disconnect the sensor wiring plug

3 Pull down the two sensor retaining clips, and pull the sensor to the rear **(see illustration)**.

4 Refitting is a reversal of removal.

12 Suspension height sensor – removal and refitting

1 Vehicles equipped with Xenon headlights are also equipped with automatic headlight adjustment. Ride sensors fitted to the front and rear suspension provide information on

the suspension ride height, whilst the headlight range control motors alter the headlight beam angle as necessary. The sensors are fitted between the suspension subframes and lower arms. Removal and refitting of these sensors is described in Chapter 10, Section 27.

13 Tyre run flat indicator system – general information

1 This system monitors the pressures of the tyres whilst it's being driven. As a tyre deflates, the weight of the vehicle caused the tyre carcass to deform, resulting in a reduction of the tyres rolling circumference, and an increase in that wheel's rotational speed in comparison to the other wheels. The

system monitors the pressures by comparing the wheels' speeds, and alerts the driver if the pressure drops approximately 30%.

2 The software for the system is contained within the ABS/DSC control unit. Wheel speed data is provided by the sensors used by the ABS/DSC system – refer to Chapter 9 for information on these components.

14 Horn(s) – removal and refitting

Removal

1 The horn(s) is/are located behind the left- and right-hand ends of the front bumper.

2 To gain access to the horn(s) from below, apply the handbrake then jack up the front of the vehicle and support it on axle stands (see *Jacking and vehicle support*). Undo the retaining bolts and remove the lower front section of the wheel arch liner. Unclip and remove the brake disc cooling duct (where applicable).

3 Undo the retaining nut and remove the horn, disconnecting its wiring connectors as they become accessible **(see illustration)**.

Refitting

4 Refitting is the reverse of removal.

15 Wiper arm – removal and refitting

14.3 Horn retaining nut

15.3a Undo the wiper arm spindle nut

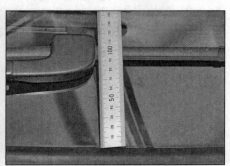

15.3b If using a puller, refit the nut so it's level with the end of the spindle to prevent thread damage

15.4 The distance from the windscreen surround trim to the lower edge of the arm-to-blade pivot point is 88 ± 3 mm (driver's side) or 95 ± 3 mm (passenger's side)

Removal

1 Operate the wiper motor then switch it off so that the wiper arm returns to the at rest position.

2 Stick a piece of masking tape along the edge of the wiper blade to use as an alignment aid on refitting.

3 Prise off the wiper arm spindle nut cover then slacken and remove the spindle nut. Lift the blade off the glass and pull the wiper arm off its spindle. If necessary the arm can be levered off the spindle using a suitable flat-bladed screwdriver or suitable puller **(see illustrations)**. **Note:** *If both windscreen wiper arms are to be removed at the same time mark them for identification; the arms are not interchangeable.*

Refitting

4 Ensure that the wiper arm and spindle splines are clean and dry then refit the arm to the spindle, aligning the wiper blade with the tape fitted on removal. Note that if the knurled-tapered sleeves fitted to the arms are loose, they must be renewed. Refit the spindle nut, tightening it to the specified torque setting, and clip the nut cover back in position. If the wipers are being refitted to a new windscreen, position the wipers arms as shown **(see illustration)**.

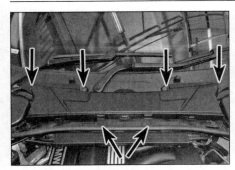

16.1 Upper pollen filter housing bolts

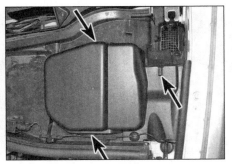

16.2 Release the clips and remove the plastic covers behind the suspension turrets

16.3 Release the clips and pull the cable guide forwards

---

16 Wiper motor and linkage – removal and refitting

Removal

Front wiper motor

1 Working at the rear of the engine compartment, undo the bolts and remove the pollen filter cover **(see illustration)**. Slide the filter from the housing.
2 Release the catches and remove the left- and right-hand plastic covers from behind the suspension turret each side of the engine compartment. Unclip the hose from the left-hand cover **(see illustration)**.
3 Depress the clips and pull the cable guide forwards from the pollen filter lower housing **(see illustration)**.
4 Release the catch and undo the bolt each side, then slide the pollen filter lower housing forwards and manoeuvre it from place **(see illustrations)**.
5 Remove the wiper arms as described in the previous Section.

6 Disconnect the washer hose, pull away the sealing strip and pull the scuttle trim panel upwards from the base of the windscreen. Manoeuvre the scuttle trim panel from position **(see illustrations)**. Disconnect the heated washer jet wiring plugs as the panel is withdrawn.
7 On models with strut braces, slacken the centre bolt, undo the outer bolts and carefully pull both struts from place. Note that new bolts must be fitted upon reassembly **(see illustration)**. Take care not to displace the braces' grommets.

16.4a On the driver's side, rotate the air temperature sensor and detach it from the panel. On the passenger's side, disconnect the bonnet switch

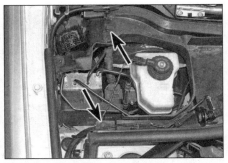

16.4b Undo the bolt, and release the clip each side...

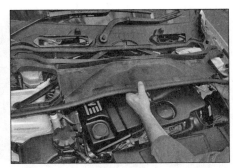

16.4c... then pull the lower pollen filter housing forwards

16.6a Pull the scuttle trim panel upwards from the base of the windscreen

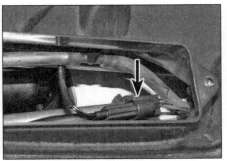

16.6b Disconnect the heated washer jet wiring plug

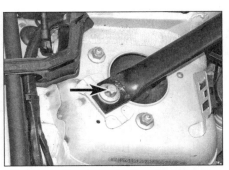

16.7 Undo the centre bolt and outer bolts, then remove the strut braces

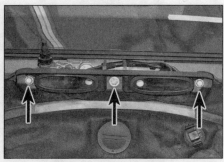

16.8a Undo the bolts (arrowed) and remove the bulkhead centre panel

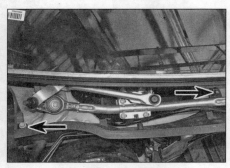

16.8b Undo the nut/bolt...

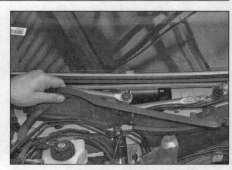

16.8c... and remove the right-hand panel

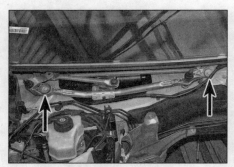

16.10 Wiper linkage retaining bolts

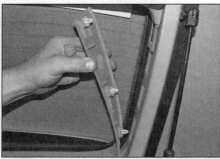
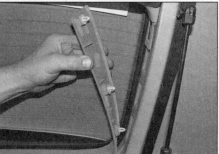

16.12 Pull the window side trims inwards to release the clips

8 Undo the bolts/nut and remove the bulkhead centre and right-hand panels (see illustrations).

9 Unclip the wiring harness from the linkage bracket.

10 Undo the wiper linkage retaining bolts, and lift the linkage assembly from position (see illustration). Disconnect the wiper motor wiring plug as it's withdrawn.

11 No further dismantling is recommended. The motor is only available as a complete assembly with the linkage.

Rear wiper motor

12 Pull the rear window side trims inwards to release the retaining clips, and disengage them from the upper trim (see illustration).

13 Release the 3 clips, then fold down and remove the trim insert on the tailgate rear panel (see illustration 5.65).

14 Open the rear window, pull the plastic trim at the top of the rear panel rearwards to release the clips, then undo the 2 bolts at the top of the panel (see illustrations).

15 Prise out the cover, then undo the bolt in the handle recess each side (see illustration).

16 Pull the rear trim panel away from the tailgate to release the retaining clips (see illustration). Disconnect the luggage compartment light as the panel is withdrawn.

17 Disconnect the wiper motor wiring plug.

18 Undo the 5 retaining bolts and remove the wiper motor (see illustration).

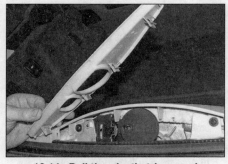

16.14a Pull the plastic trim panel rearwards...

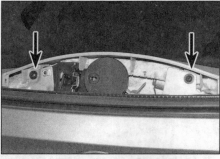

16.14b... then undo the 2 bolts

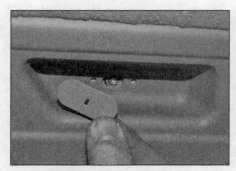

16.15 Prise out the cover in each handle recess, and undo the bolt

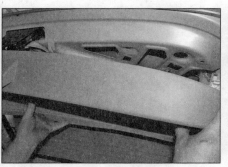

16.16 Pull the panel from the tailgate

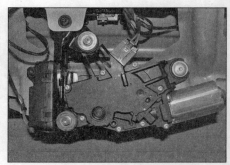

16.18 Undo the bolts and remove the wiper motor

16.19 Tailgate lock bolts

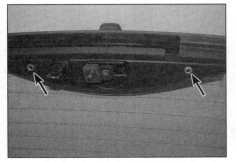

16.21 Prise out the plastic caps and undo the 2 nuts

16.22 Slacken and remove the wiper spindle nut

19 If required, the window lock can be separated from the wiper motor by undoing the two retaining bolts **(see illustration)**.

Rear wiper arm spindle and housing

20 Remove the rear wiper arm as described in the previous Section.
21 Open the tailgate, prise out the two plastic caps, and undo the two nuts securing the plastic cover over the spindle **(see illustration)**. Remove the cover.
22 On the outside of the screen, slacken and remove the wiper arm spindle nut. Recover any washers **(see illustration)**.
23 On the inside of the screen, disconnect the rear window button wiring plug, undo the retaining nut, and manoeuvre the housing and spindle from position **(see illustration)**. No further dismantling is recommended.

Refitting

24 Refitting is the reverse of removal. On completion refit the wiper arms as described in Section 15.

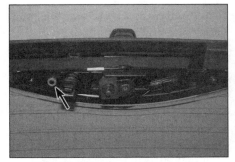

16.23 Undo the nut and remove the housing complete with the spindle

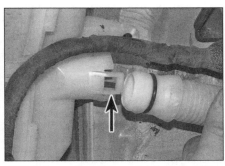

17.2 Release the clips and detach the filler hose

the reservoir clips, then disconnect the filler hose **(see illustration)**. Be prepared for fluid spillage.
3 Undo the bolt and manoeuvre the reservoir from position **(see illustration)**. Note their fitted positions, then disconnect the wiring plugs and hoses from the reservoir components.
4 Refitting is a reversal of removal. Ensure the locating lugs on the rear edge of the reservoir engage correctly with the corresponding slots in the inner wing. Refill the reservoir and check for leakage.

Washer pumps

5 Remove the reservoir as previously described in this Section. On Touring models, two pumps are fitted – one for the front screen and one for the rear.

6 Disconnect the wiring connector(s) and hose(s) from the washer pump(s). Carefully rotate the pump(s) clockwise, and pull them up from the reservoir. Inspect the pump sealing grommet(s) for signs of damage or deterioration and renew if necessary **(see illustration)**.
7 Refitting is the reverse of removal, using a new sealing grommet if the original one shows signs of damage or deterioration. Refill the reservoir and check the pump grommet for leaks.

Washer reservoir level switch

8 Remove the reservoir as described earlier in this Section.
9 Rotate the level switch anti-clockwise and remove it from the reservoir **(see illustration)**.
10 Refitting is the reverse of removal, using a

| 17 | **Windscreen/headlight washer system components** – removal and refitting |

Washer reservoir

1 The reservoir is located behind the right-hand front wheel arch. Remove the wheel arch liner as described in Chapter 11.
2 Unclip the wiring harness and hose from

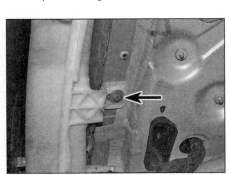

17.3 Washer fluid reservoir retaining bolt

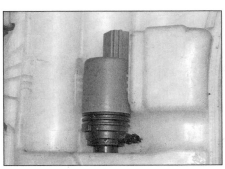

17.6 Rotate the pump clockwise and pull it up from the reservoir

17.9 Rotate the level switch anti-clockwise and pull it from the reservoir

17.13 Press the jet rearwards, then pull up the front edge

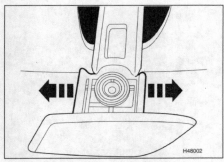

17.16 Spread the clips and detach the cover

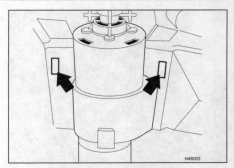

17.20 Release the clips on the underside of the jet

new sealing grommet if the original one shows signs of damage or deterioration. Refill the reservoir and check for leaks.

Washer jets

Windscreen

11 Working at the rear of the engine compartment, undo the bolts and remove the pollen filter cover. Slide the filter from the housing **(see illustration 16.1)**.
12 Reach through the apertures, disconnect the hoses and, where applicable, the heated jet wiring plugs **(see illustration 16.6b)**.
13 Press the washer jet rearwards, pull up the front edge, and manoeuvre it from the panel **(see illustration)**.
14 Refitting is a reversal of removal.

Headlight

15 Using a wooden or plastic lever, carefully prise out the washer jet cover from below the

headlight, and pull it out to its stop.
16 Pull out the clips and detach the cover from the jet **(see illustration)**.
17 Remove the front bumper as described in Chapter 11.
18 Where applicable disconnect the jet heater wiring plug.
19 Disconnect the hose from the jet. Be prepared for fluid spillage.
20 Release the 2 clips and manoeuvre the jet from place **(see illustration)**.
21 Refitting is a reversal of removal.

Rear screen

22 Remove the high-level stop-light as described in Section 7.
23 Release the clip, disconnect the hose and pull the jet from the high-level stop-light.
24 Refitting is a reversal of removal. Aim the jet to an area 100 mm from the top, and 320 mm from the edge of the window.

Wash/wipe system control module

25 The wash/wipe system is controlled by the central control module assembly, integral with the main fusebox as described in Section 3.

18 Infotainment units – removal and refitting

Note: *The following removal and refitting procedure is for the range of audio units which BMW fit as standard equipment. Removal and refitting procedures of non-standard will differ slightly.*

Removal

Facia-mounted audio unit

1 Using a blunt, flat-bladed tool, carefully lever the decorative trim from the passenger's side of the facia **(see illustrations)**. Disconnect any wiring plugs as the trim is removed. Renew any damaged trim clips.
2 Remove the heater/air conditioning/climate control panel as described in Chapter 3.
3 Undo the two bolts and pull the unit slightly from the facia **(see illustration)**.
4 Note their fitted positions, and disconnect the wiring plugs from the rear of the unit (slide out the locking element on the main plug) **(see illustrations)**.

CD autochanger

5 Disconnect the battery negative lead as described in Chapter 5A.

18.1a Carefully prise the decorative trim...

18.1b... from the passenger's side of the facia

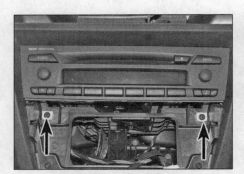

18.3 Audio unit retaining bolts

18.4a Lever over the locking catch and disconnect the main wiring plug...

18.4b... followed by the aerial connection

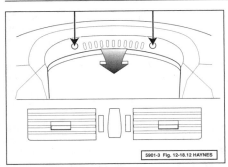

18.12 Undo the screws and pull the upper edge of the display unit rearwards

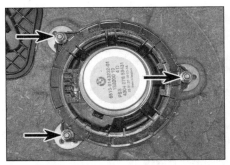

19.2 Door speaker retaining nuts

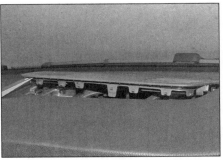

19.10 Prise up the facia speaker grille

6 Remove the left-hand side luggage compartment trim panel as described in Chapter 11.
7 Undo the four mounting bolts, and lift the unit from position. Disconnect the wiring plugs as the unit is withdrawn.

Amplifier

8 Disconnect the battery negative lead as described in Chapter 5A.
9 The amplifier (where fitted) is located behind the left-hand side luggage compartment trim panel. Open the flap and lift out the storage tray.
10 Disconnect the amplifier wiring plugs, undo the retaining bolts and remove the unit. Note that on Saloon models, the amplifier is under the CD autochanger (where fitted).

Facia display unit

11 Disconnect the battery negative lead as described in Chapter 5A Section 4.
12 Undo the 2 screws at the top and pull the upper edge of the display unit rearwards, and manoeuvre it from the facia **(see illustration)**. Disconnect the wiring plugs as the unit is withdrawn.

Refitting

13 Refitting is a reversal of removal.

19 Loudspeakers –
removal and refitting

Note: *Not all components are fitted to all models.*

Door panel speaker(s)

1 Remove the door inner trim panel as described in Chapter 11.
2 Unscrew the 3 nuts and remove the speaker from the door trim **(see illustration)**.
3 Where fitted, unscrew the large retaining collar and remove the small speaker from the trim panel.
4 Refitting is the reverse of removal.

Door upper loudspeaker

5 Remove the door inner trim panel as described in Chapter 11.

6 Carefully unclip the plastic panel from the front inner edge of the door.
7 Remove the foam wedge from the door frame.
8 Disconnect the speaker wiring plug, release the catches and remove the speaker.
9 Refitting is a reversal of removal.

Facia loudspeaker

10 Carefully prise up the speaker grille from the facia **(see illustration)**.
11 Undo the retaining bolts, pull the speaker from place, and disconnect the wiring plug.
12 Refitting is a reversal of removal.

Rear loudspeaker

13 Carefully prise the speaker grille out from the rear parcel shelf **(see illustration)**.
14 Undo the retaining bolts and lift the

19.13 Prise up the parcel shelf speaker grille

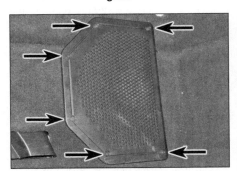

19.18 Undo the bolts and remove the speaker grille

speaker **(see illustration)**. Disconnect the wiring plug as the speaker is withdrawn.
15 Refitting is the reverse of removal.

Floor speakers

16 The floor speakers are located under the front seats. Remove the relevant front seat as described in Chapter 11.
17 Pull the front door sill trim panel upwards to release the retaining clips.
18 Undo the bolts and remove the speaker grille **(see illustration)**.
19 Fold back the carpet, disconnect the wiring plug, undo the 2 nuts and lift the speaker assembly from place **(see illustration)**.
20 If required, undo the bolts and detach the speaker from the housing.
21 Refitting is a reversal of removal. Prise the retaining clips from the door sill and refit them to the sill trim panel prior to refitting.

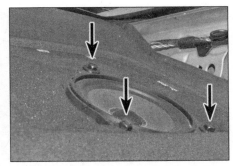

19.14 Undo the speaker retaining bolts

19.19 Speaker assembly retaining nuts

20.4 Roof-mounted aerial amplifier

20 Radio aerial – general information

Rear window aerial

1 The radio aerial is built into the rear screen. In order to improve reception an amplifier (fitted in front of the high-level stop-light) is fitted to boost the signal to the radio unit.

Roof-mounted aerial

2 The roof-mounted aerial is bonded onto the panel. Successful renewal requires special tools and the experience to use them. Consequently, we recommend this task is entrusted to a BMW dealer or specialist.

3 In order to improve reception an amplifier is fitted to boost the signal to the radio unit. On Saloon models, the amplifier is located above the high-level stop-light – remove the stop-light as described in Section 7. On Touring models, the amplifier is located under the rear spoiler.

4 Disconnect the aerial lead and wiring then undo the retaining bolts and remove the amplifier **(see illustration)**. Refitting is the reverse of removal.

21 Cruise control system – information and component renewal

Information

1 The cruise control function is incorporated into the engine management ECM. The only renewable external components are the clutch pedal switch.

Clutch pedal switch renewal

2 Renewal of the switch is described in Section 4 of this Chapter.

22 Anti-theft alarm system – general information

1 The E90/91 3-Series models are equipped with a sophisticated anti-theft alarm and immobiliser system. Should a fault develop, the system's self-diagnosis facility should be interrogated using dedicated test equipment. Consult your BMW dealer or suitably-equipped specialist.

23 Heated front seat components – removal and refitting

Heater mats

1 On models equipped with heated front seats, a heater pad is fitted to the both the seat back and seat cushion. Renewal of either heater mat involves peeling back the upholstery, removing the old mat, sticking the new mat in position and then refitting the upholstery. Upholstery removal and refitting requires considerable skill and experience if it is to be carried out successfully, and is therefore best entrusted to your BMW dealer or specialist. In practice, it will be very difficult for the home mechanic to carry out the job without ruining the upholstery.

Heated seat switches

2 Refer to Section 4, Central facia switch cluster.

24 Airbag system – general information and precautions

1 The models covered by this manual are equipped with a driver's airbag mounted in the centre of the steering wheel, a passenger's airbag located behind the facia, two head airbags located in each A-pillar/headlining, two airbags located in each front seat. The airbag system comprises of the airbag units, impact sensors, the control unit and a warning light in the instrument panel.

2 The airbag system is triggered in the event of a heavy frontal or side impact above a predetermined force; depending on the point of impact. The airbag(s) is inflated within milliseconds and forms a safety cushion between the cabin occupants and the cabin interior, and therefore greatly reduces the risk of injury. The airbag then deflates almost immediately.

3 Every time the ignition is switched on, the airbag control unit performs a self-test. The self-test takes approximately 2 to 6 seconds and during this time the airbag warning light on the facia is illuminated. After the self-test has been completed the warning light should go out. If the warning light fails to come on, remains illuminated after the initial period or comes on at any time when the vehicle is being driven, there is a fault in the airbag system. The vehicle must be taken to a BMW dealer for examination at the earliest possible opportunity.

 Warning: Before carrying out any operations on the airbag system, disconnect the battery negative terminal, and wait for at least 1 minute. This will allow the capacitors in the system to discharge. When operations are complete, make sure no one is inside the vehicle when the battery is reconnected.
• **Note that the airbag(s) must not be subjected to temperatures in excess of 75°C. When the airbag is removed, ensure that it is stored the correct way up to prevent possible inflation.**
• **Do not allow any solvents or cleaning agents to contact the airbag assemblies. They must be cleaned using only a damp cloth.**
• **The airbags and control unit are both sensitive to impact. If either is dropped or damaged they should be renewed.**
• **Disconnect the airbag control unit wiring plug prior to using arc-welding equipment on the vehicle.**

25 Airbag system components – removal and refitting

Note: *Refer to the warnings in Section 24 before carrying out the following operations.*
1 Disconnect the battery negative terminal (see Chapter 5A), then continue as described under the relevant heading.

Driver's side airbag

2 Two different types of driver's airbags may be fitted. Sports steering wheel airbag, and normal steering wheel airbag.

Sports steering wheel

3 With the steering wheel in the straight-ahead position, insert a T25 Torx screwdriver through the hole in the front-side of the steering wheel at 90 degrees to the steering column, to release the spring clip, and pull that side of the airbag away from the wheel **(see illustrations)**. Repeat this process on the other side of the wheel.

25.3a Insert a screwdriver through the hole/depression in the front of the steering wheel...

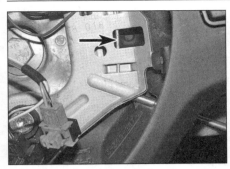

25.3b... and push the clip to release the airbag

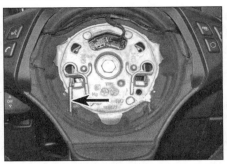

25.4a Insert a Torx screwdriver through the hole in the base of the steering wheel...

25.4b... and push the spring clip towards the centre of the wheel

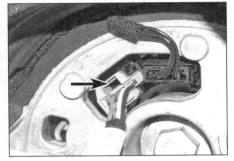

25.5a Prise down the clip and disconnect the airbag wiring plug – standard steering wheel

25.5b Prise up the locking clip...

25.5c... and disconnect the airbag wiring plug – sports steering wheel

Standard steering wheel

4 With the steering wheel in the straight-ahead position, insert a T20 Torx screwdriver straight up, approximately 5.5 cm through the hole in the base of the steering wheel at 90 degrees to the steering column to release the spring clip, and pull that side of the airbag away from the wheel **(see illustrations)**. Repeat this process on the other side of the wheel.

Both steering wheels

5 Disconnect the airbag wiring plug(s) **(see illustrations)**. Note that the airbag must not be knocked or dropped and should be stored the correct way up with its padded surface uppermost.

6 On refitting, reconnect the wiring plugs, and ensure that connectors are locked in place. Note that the connectors are colour-coded to ensure correct refitment. The connector plugs into the socket of the same colour. Position the airbag on the wheel and push the unit home until it locks in place. Reconnect the battery negative terminal.

Passenger's side airbag

7 Remove the passenger's side glovebox as described in Chapter 11.

8 Prise up the locking catch and disconnect the wiring plug at each end of the airbag **(see illustration)**.

9 Undo the retaining nuts and remove the airbag **(see illustration)**.

10 Refitting is a reversal of removal. Tighten the airbag retaining nuts to the specified torque, and reconnect the battery negative terminal as described in Chapter 5A.

25.8 Prise up the locking catch and disconnect the passenger's airbag wiring plugs

25.9 Passenger's airbag retaining nuts

25.14a Remove the insulation cover...

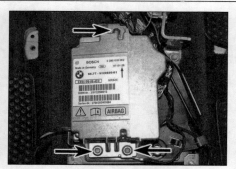

25.14b... then undo the nuts/bolts and remove the airbag control unit

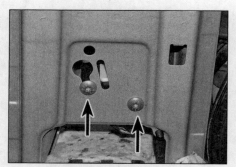

25.20a Slacken the upper bolt, and undo the lower bolt

25.20b Depress the clip and disconnect the sensor wiring plug

Side airbags

11 The side airbags are incorporated into the side of the front and rear seats. Removal of the units requires the seat upholstery to be removed. This is a specialist task, which we recommend should be entrusted to a BMW dealer or specialist.

Head/overhead curtain airbags

12 Renewal of the head airbags/inflatable curtain requires removal of the headlining. This is a specialist task, and should be entrusted to a BMW dealer or specialist.

Airbag control unit

13 Remove the centre console as described in Chapter 11.

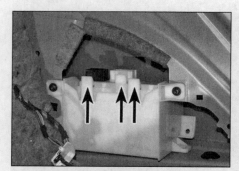

26.4 Parking distance control unit retaining clips

14 Remove the insulation cover, undo the retaining nuts and bolts, then and lift the module. Note the earth strap fitted under one of the mounting nuts. Disconnect the wiring plug as the unit is withdrawn (see illustrations).
15 Refitting is the reverse of removal. Note that the control unit must be installed with the arrow pointing towards the front of the vehicle, and that the earth strap is fitted under one of the module mounting nuts. If a new control unit is fitted, it must be programmed using BMW diagnostic equipment. Entrust this task to a BMW dealer or suitably-equipped specialist.

Impact sensors

16 There may be two impact sensors each

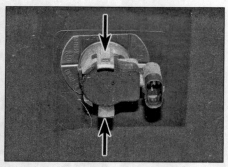

26.7 Release the sensor clips

side of the vehicle – one in each front door, one at the base of the B-pillars, and a sensor built into the control unit.

Door sensors

Note: *Not fitted to all models*
17 Remove the door inner trim panel and sound insulation material as described in Chapter 11.
18 Undo the two retaining bolts, and remove the sensor. Disconnect the wiring plug as the sensor is withdrawn.

B-pillar sensors

19 Remove the B-pillar trim panel as described in Chapter 11.
20 Slacken the upper bolt, and remove the lower bolt, then manoeuvre the sensor from position. Disconnect the wiring plug as the sensor is withdrawn (see illustrations).

All sensors

21 Refitting is a reversal of removal. Tighten the fasteners to their specified torque.

---

26 Parking distance control (PDC) – information and component removal and refitting

General information

1 In order to aid parking, all models in the 3-Series range can be equipped with a system that informs the driver of the distance between the rear or front of the vehicle, and any vehicle/obstacle behind or in front whilst parking. The system consists of several ultrasonic sensors mounted in the bumpers which measure the distance between themselves and the nearest object. The distance is indicated by an audible signal in the passenger cabin. The closer the object, the more frequent the signals, until at less the 30 cm the signal becomes continuous.

Component removal and refitting

PDC electronic control module

2 Remove the right-hand side luggage compartment side panel as described in Chapter 11.
3 Unclip the wiring harness and remove the insulation mat.
4 Note their fitted positions, and disconnect the unit's wiring plugs. Release the clip and lift out the control unit (see illustration).
5 Refitting is a reversal of removal.

Ultrasonic sensors

6 Remove the bumper (see Chapter 11).
7 Disconnect the sensor wiring plugs, release the retaining clips and remove the sensors from the bumper (see illustration).
8 Refitting is the reverse of removal.

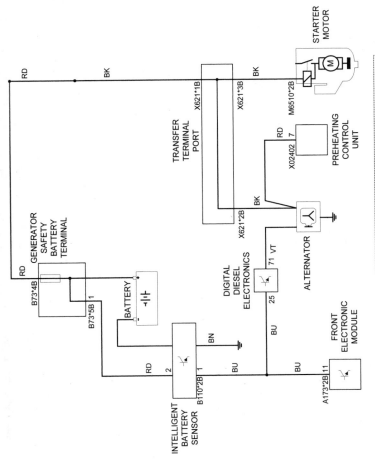

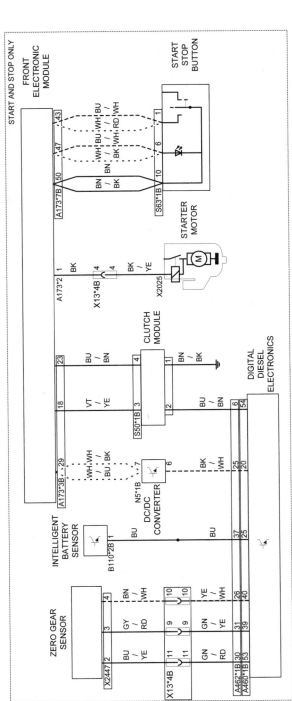

Starting and charging

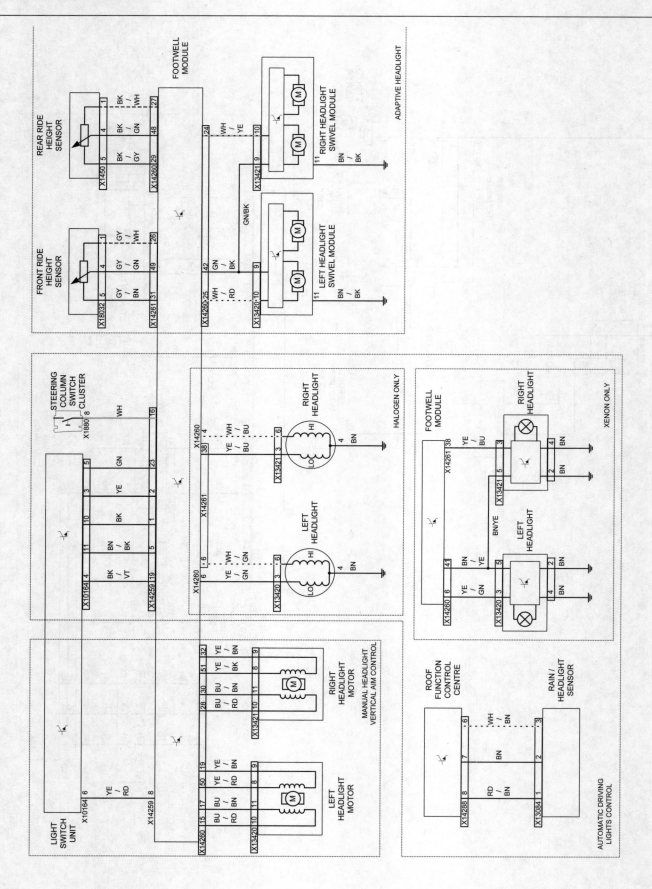

Manual, auto and adaptive lights control

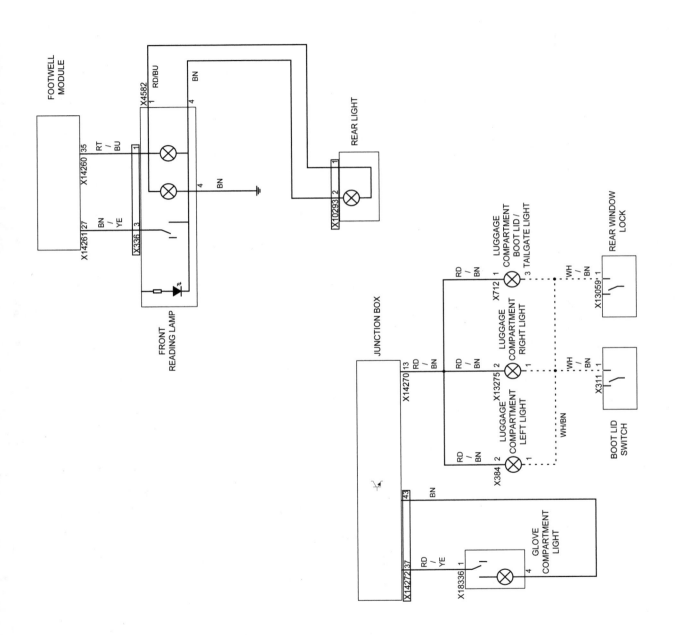

Interior lights

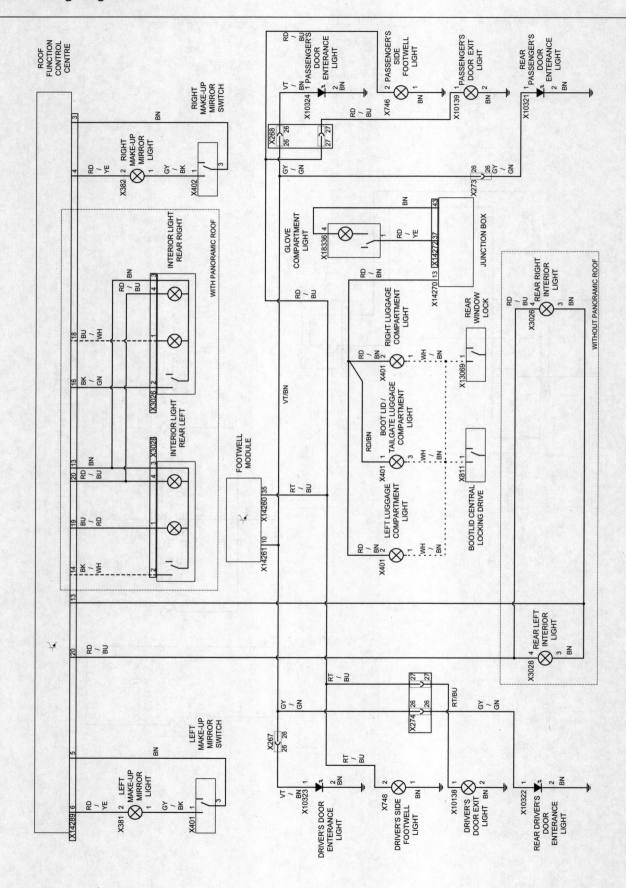

Interior lights Hi level trim

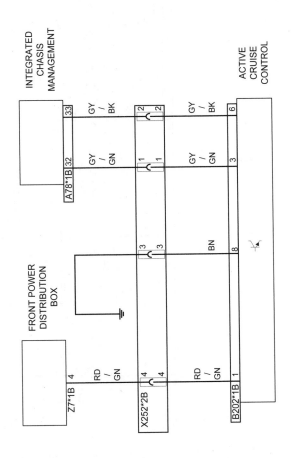

Cruise control

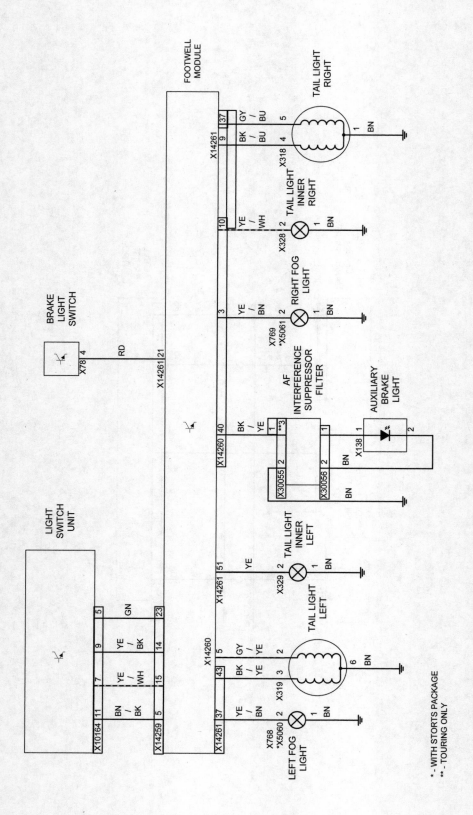

Front and rear fog and brake lights

* - WITH STORTS PACKAGE
** - TOURING ONLY

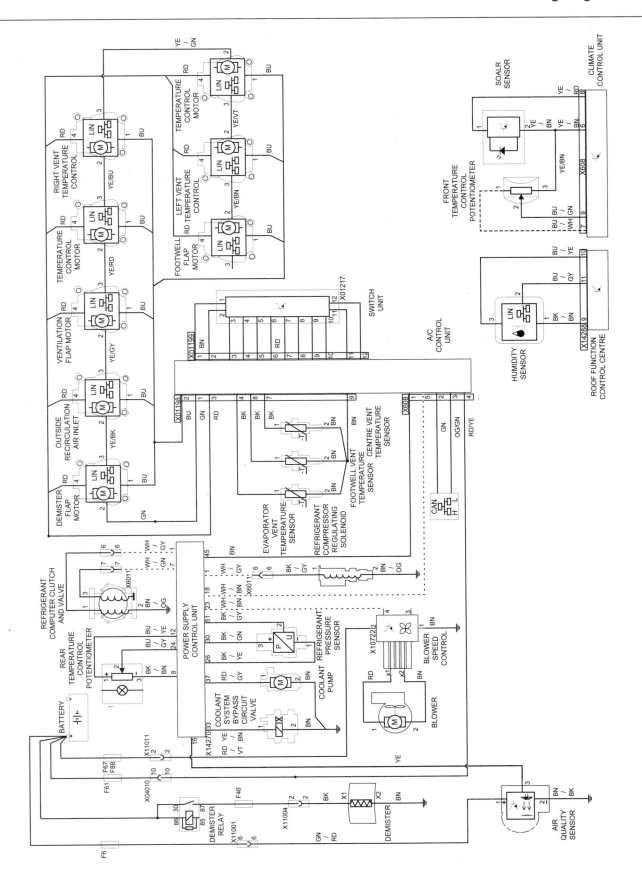

AC dual zone

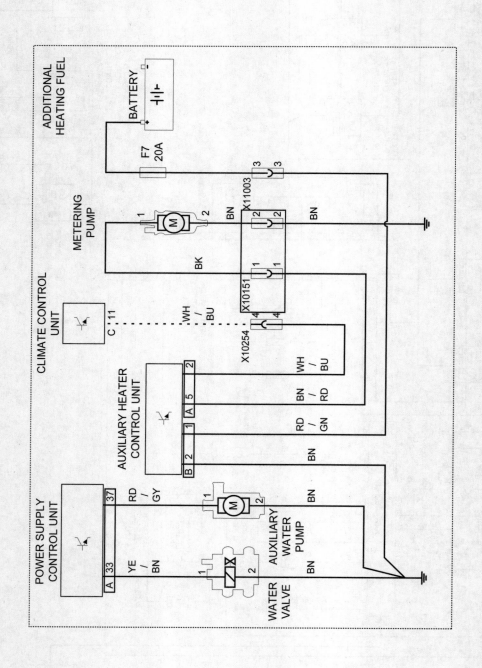

Additional fuel fired heating

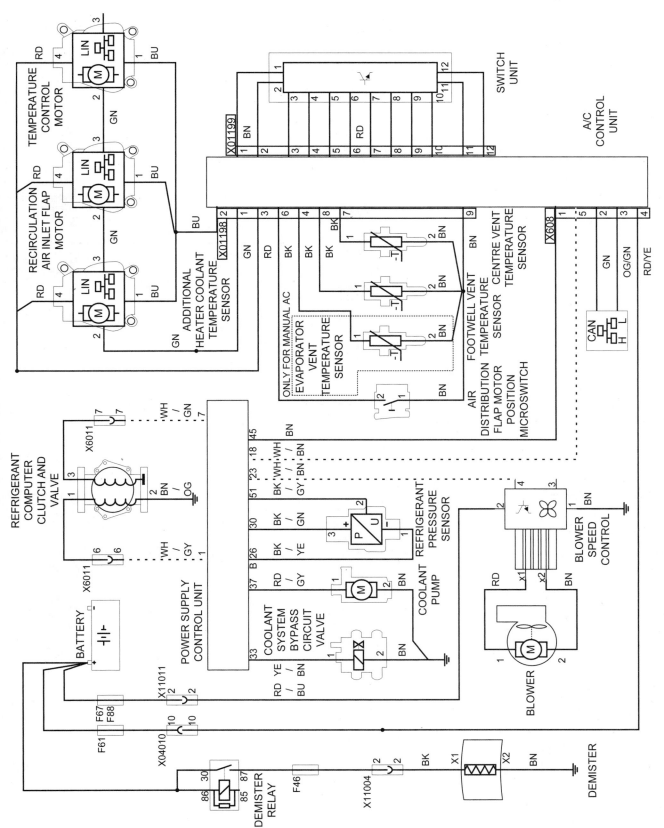

Basic heating

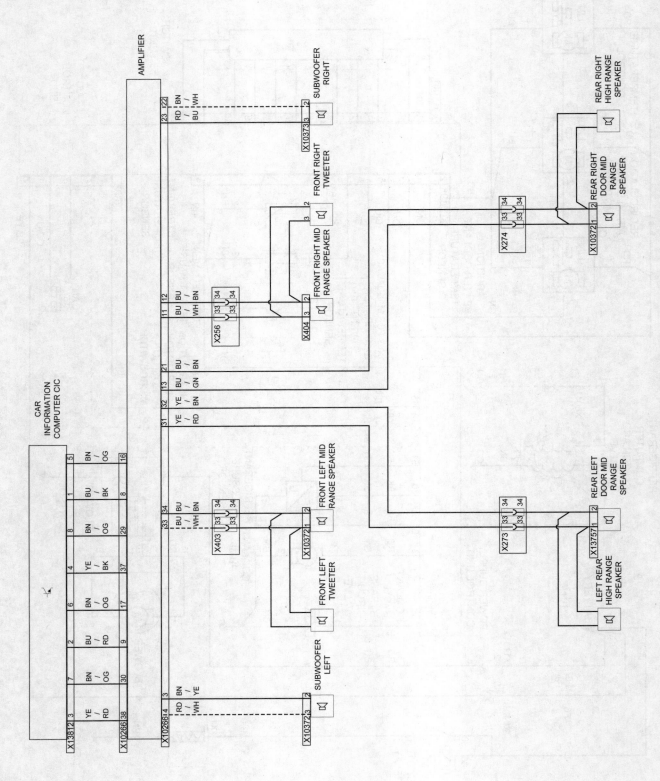

Sound – Amplifier

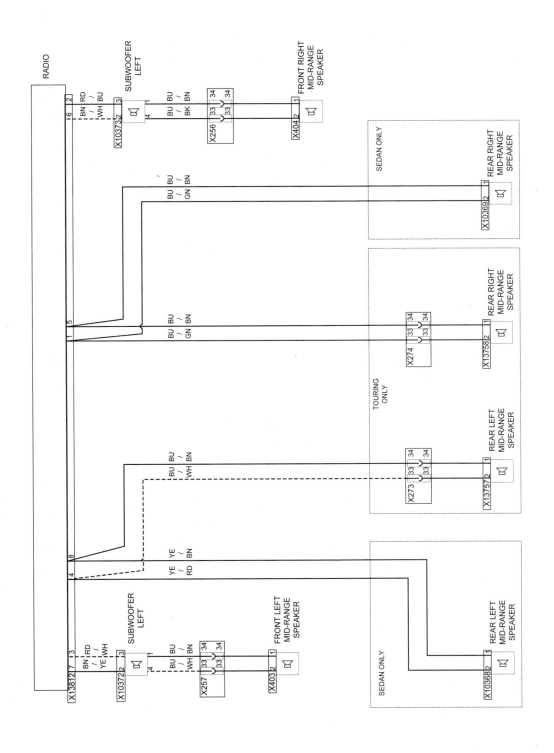

Sound – Radio

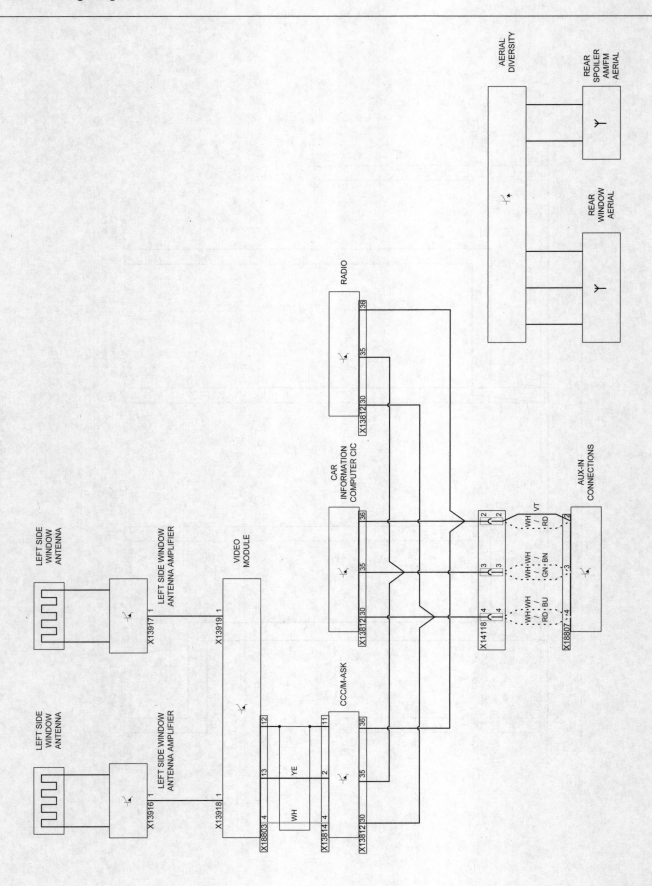

Sound – Video, Antenna and AUX

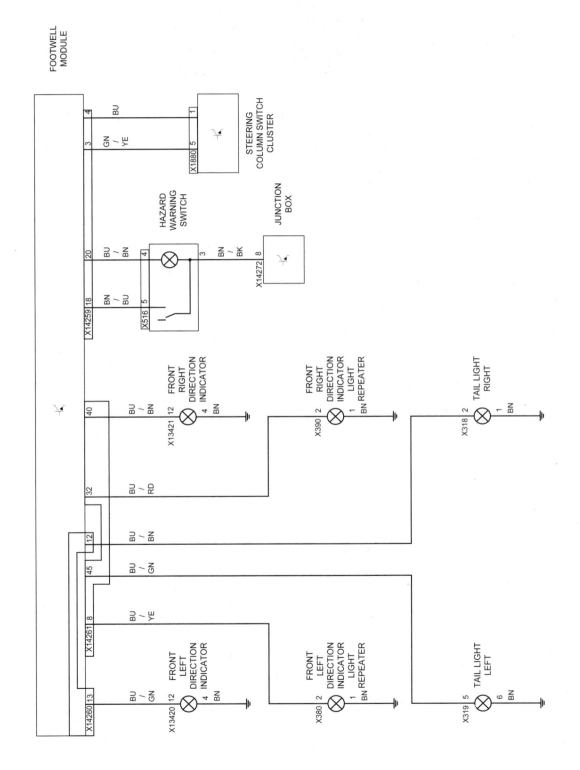

Directional indicator and hazard lights

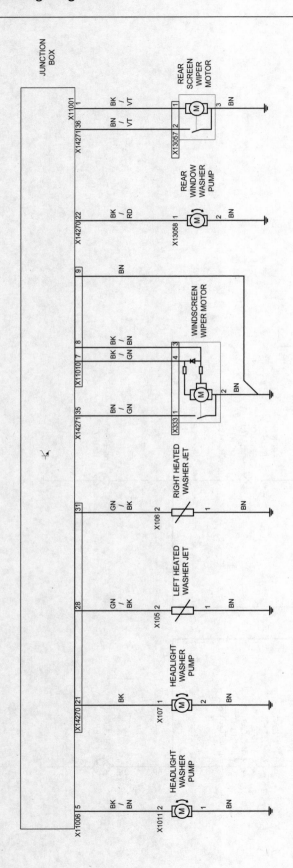

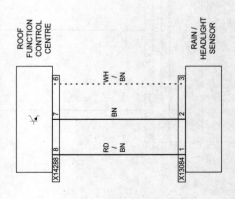

Wipers and washers

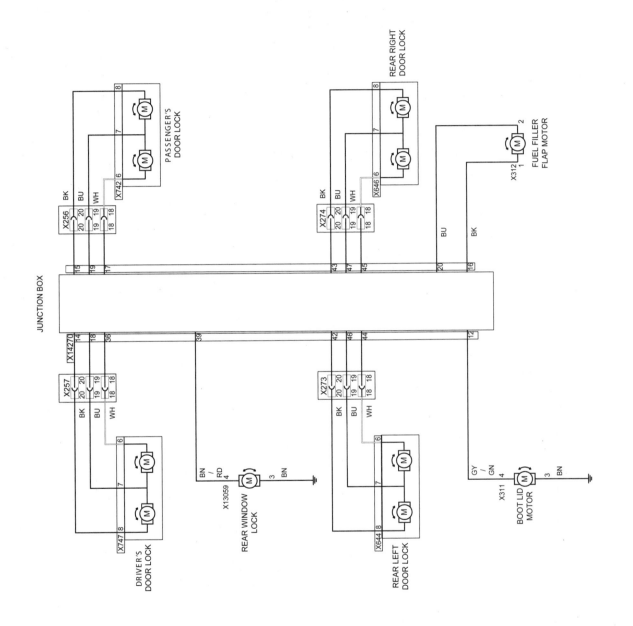

Power door locks

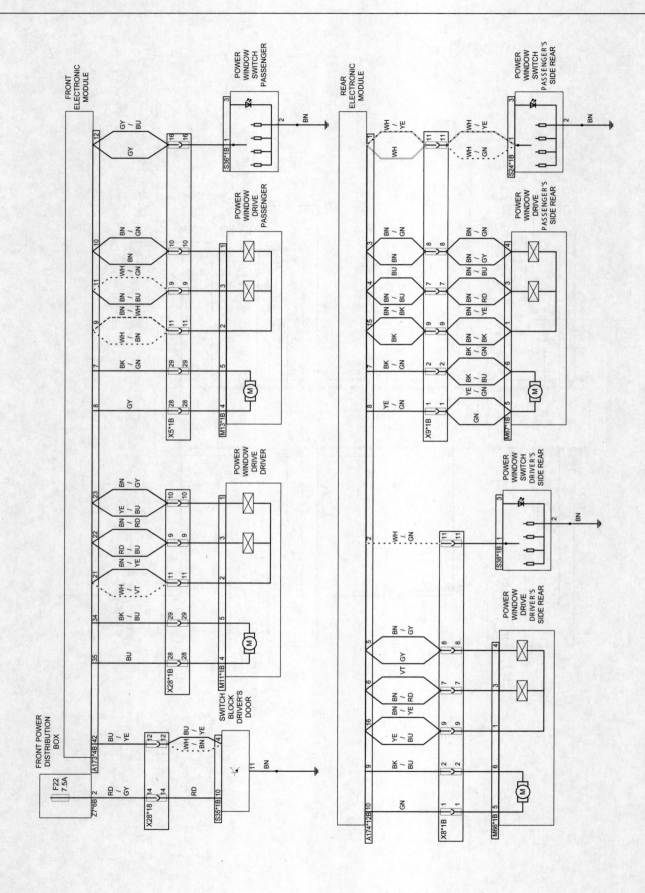

Power windows

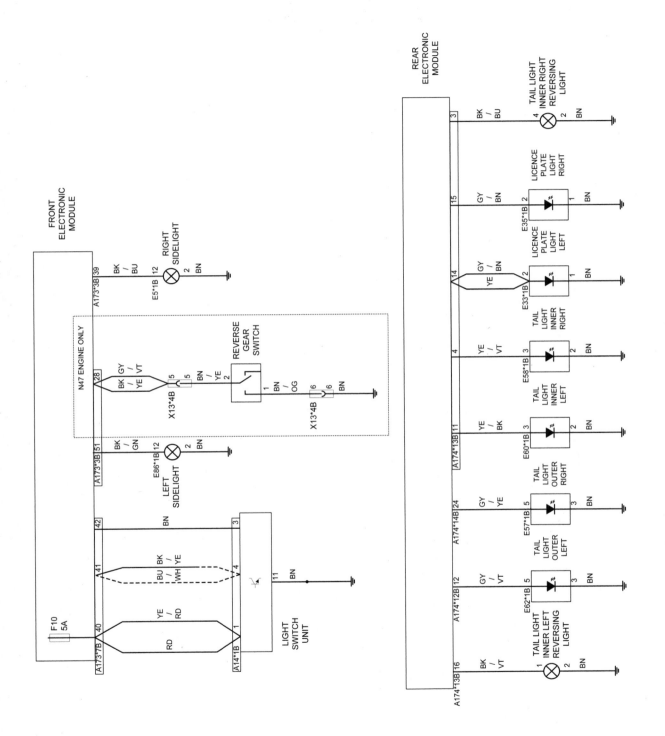

Reversing and side lights

Notes

Dimensions and weights

Note: *All figures are approximate, and may vary according to model. Refer to manufacturer's data for exact figures.*

Dimensions

Overall length:
Saloon . . . . 4531 mm
Touring . . . . 4527 mm
Overall width (inc. mirrors):
Saloon . . . . 1989 mm
Touring . . . . 1989 mm
Overall height:
Saloon . . . . 1421 mm
Touring . . . . 1418 mm
Wheelbase:
Saloon . . . . 2760 mm
Touring . . . . 2760 mm

Weights

Kerb weight (depending on model) . . . . 1425 kg to 1610 kg
Maximum roof rack load . . . . 75 kg

Fuel economy

Although depreciation is still the biggest part of the cost of motoring for most car owners, the cost of fuel is more immediately noticeable. These pages give some tips on how to get the best fuel economy.

Working it out

Manufacturer's figures

Car manufacturers are required by law to provide fuel consumption information on all new vehicles sold. These 'official' figures are obtained by simulating various driving conditions on a rolling road or a test track. Real life conditions are different, so the fuel consumption actually achieved may not bear much resemblance to the quoted figures.

How to calculate it

Many cars now have trip computers which will

display fuel consumption, both instantaneous and average. Refer to the owner's handbook for details of how to use these.

To calculate consumption yourself (and maybe to check that the trip computer is accurate), proceed as follows.

1. Fill up with fuel and note the mileage, or zero the trip recorder.
2. Drive as usual until you need to fill up again.
3. Note the amount of fuel required to refill the tank, and the mileage covered since the previous fill-up.
4. Divide the mileage by the amount of fuel used to obtain the consumption figure.

For example:

Mileage at first fill-up (a) = 27,903
Mileage at second fill-up (b) = 28,346
Mileage covered (b - a) = 443
Fuel required at second fill-up = 48.6 litres

The half-completed changeover to metric units in the UK means that we buy our fuel

in litres, measure distances in miles and talk about fuel consumption in miles per gallon. There are two ways round this: the first is to convert the litres to gallons before doing the calculation (by dividing by 4.546, or see Table 1). So in the example:

48.6 litres ÷ 4.546 = 10.69 gallons
443 miles ÷ 10.69 gallons = 41.4 mpg

The second way is to calculate the consumption in miles per litre, then multiply that figure by 4.546 (or see Table 2).

So in the example, fuel consumption is:

443 miles ÷ 48.6 litres = 9.1 mpl
9.1 mpl x 4.546 = 41.4 mpg

The rest of Europe expresses fuel consumption in litres of fuel required to travel 100 km (l/100 km). For interest, the conversions are given in Table 3. In practice it doesn't matter what units you use, provided you know what your normal consumption is and can spot if it's getting better or worse.

Table 1: conversion of litres to Imperial gallons

litres	1	2	3	4	5	10	20	30	40	50	60	70
gallons	0.22	0.44	0.66	0.88	1.10	2.24	4.49	6.73	8.98	11.22	13.47	15.71

Table 2: conversion of miles per litre to miles per gallon

miles per litre	5	6	7	8	9	10	11	12	13	14
miles per gallon	23	27	32	36	41	46	50	55	59	64

Table 3: conversion of litres per 100 km to miles per gallon

litres per 100 km	4	4.5	5	5.5	6	6.5	7	8	9	10
miles per gallon	71	63	56	51	47	43	40	35	31	28

Maintenance

A well-maintained car uses less fuel and creates less pollution. In particular:

Filters

Change air and fuel filters at the specified intervals.

Oil

Use a good quality oil of the lowest viscosity specified by the vehicle manufacturer (see *Lubricants and fluids*). Check the level often and be careful not to overfill.

Spark plugs

When applicable, renew at the specified intervals.

Tyres

Check tyre pressures regularly. Under-inflated tyres have an increased rolling resistance. It is generally safe to use the higher pressures specified for full load conditions even when not fully laden, but keep an eye on the centre band of tread for signs of wear due to over-inflation.

When buying new tyres, consider the 'fuel saving' models which most manufacturers include in their ranges.

Driving style

Acceleration

Acceleration uses more fuel than driving at a steady speed. The best technique with modern cars is to accelerate reasonably briskly to the desired speed, changing up through the gears as soon as possible without making the engine labour.

Air conditioning

Air conditioning absorbs quite a bit of energy from the engine – typically 3 kW (4 hp) or so. The effect on fuel consumption is at its worst in slow traffic. Switch it off when not required.

Anticipation

Drive smoothly and try to read the traffic flow so as to avoid unnecessary acceleration and braking.

Automatic transmission

When accelerating in an automatic, avoid depressing the throttle so far as to make the transmission hold onto lower gears at higher speeds. Don't use the 'Sport' setting, if applicable.

When stationary with the engine running, select 'N' or 'P'. When moving, keep your left foot away from the brake.

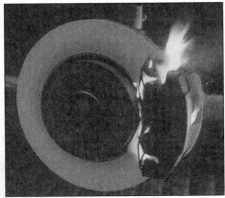

Braking

Braking converts the car's energy of motion into heat – essentially, it is wasted. Obviously some braking is always going to be necessary, but with good anticipation it is surprising how much can be avoided, especially on routes that you know well.

Carshare

Consider sharing lifts to work or to the shops. Even once a week will make a difference.

Electrical loads

Electricity is 'fuel' too; the alternator which charges the battery does so by converting some of the engine's energy of motion into electrical energy. The more electrical accessories are in use, the greater the load on the alternator. Switch off big consumers like the heated rear window when not required.

Freewheeling

Freewheeling (coasting) in neutral with the engine switched off is dangerous. The effort required to operate power-assisted brakes and steering increases when the engine is not running, with a potential lack of control in emergency situations.

In any case, modern fuel injection systems automatically cut off the engine's fuel supply on the overrun (moving and in gear, but with the accelerator pedal released).

Gadgets

Bolt-on devices claiming to save fuel have been around for nearly as long as the motor car itself. Those which worked were rapidly adopted as standard equipment by the vehicle manufacturers. Others worked only in certain situations, or saved fuel only at the expense of unacceptable effects on performance, driveability or the life of engine components.

The most effective fuel saving gadget is the driver's right foot.

Journey planning

Combine (eg) a trip to the supermarket with a visit to the recycling centre and the DIY store, rather than making separate journeys.

When possible choose a travelling time outside rush hours.

Load

The more heavily a car is laden, the greater the energy required to accelerate it to a given speed. Remove heavy items which you don't need to carry.

One load which is often overlooked is the contents of the fuel tank. A tankful of fuel (55 litres / 12 gallons) weighs 45 kg (100 lb) or so. Just half filling it may be worthwhile.

Lost?

At the risk of stating the obvious, if you're going somewhere new, have details of the route to hand. There's not much point in achieving record mpg if you also go miles out of your way.

Parking

If possible, carry out any reversing or turning manoeuvres when you arrive at a parking space so that you can drive straight out when you leave. Manoeuvering when the engine is cold uses a lot more fuel.

Driving around looking for free on-street parking may cost more in fuel than buying a car park ticket.

Premium fuel

Most major oil companies (and some supermarkets) have premium grades of fuel which are several pence a litre dearer than the standard grades. Reports vary, but the consensus seems to be that if these fuels improve economy at all, they do not do so by enough to justify their extra cost.

Roof rack

When loading a roof rack, try to produce a wedge shape with the narrow end at the front. Any cover should be securely fastened – if it flaps it's creating turbulence and absorbing energy.

Remove roof racks and boxes when not in use – they increase air resistance and can create a surprising amount of noise.

Short journeys

The engine is at its least efficient, and wear is highest, during the first few miles after a cold start. Consider walking, cycling or using public transport.

Speed

The engine is at its most efficient when running at a steady speed and load at the rpm where it develops maximum torque. (You can find this figure in the car's handbook.) For most cars this corresponds to between 55 and 65 mph in top gear.

Above the optimum cruising speed, fuel consumption starts to rise quite sharply. A car travelling at 80 mph will typically be using 30% more fuel than at 60 mph.

Supermarket fuel

It may be cheap but is it any good? In the UK all supermarket fuel must meet the relevant British Standard. The major oil companies will say that their branded fuels have better additive packages which may stop carbon and other deposits building up. A reasonable compromise might be to use one tank of branded fuel to three or four from the supermarket.

Switch off when stationary

Switch off the engine if you look like being stationary for more than 30 seconds or so. This is good for the environment as well as for your pocket. Be aware though that frequent restarts are hard on the battery and the starter motor.

Windows

Driving with the windows open increases air turbulence around the vehicle. Closing the windows promotes smooth airflow and

reduced resistance. The faster you go, the more significant this is.

And finally . . .

Driving techniques associated with good fuel economy tend to involve moderate acceleration and low top speeds. Be considerate to the needs of other road users who may need to make brisker progress; even if you do not agree with them this is not an excuse to be obstructive.

Safety must always take precedence over economy, whether it is a question of accelerating hard to complete an overtaking manoeuvre, killing your speed when confronted with a potential hazard or switching the lights on when it starts to get dark.

Conversion factors

Length (distance)
Inches (in)	x 25.4	= Millimetres (mm)	x 0.0394	= Inches (in)
Feet (ft)	x 0.305	= Metres (m)	x 3.281	= Feet (ft)
Miles	x 1.609	= Kilometres (km)	x 0.621	= Miles

Volume (capacity)
Cubic inches (cu in; in³)	x 16.387	= Cubic centimetres (cc; cm³)	x 0.061	= Cubic inches (cu in; in³)
Imperial pints (Imp pt)	x 0.568	= Litres (l)	x 1.76	= Imperial pints (Imp pt)
Imperial quarts (Imp qt)	x 1.137	= Litres (l)	x 0.88	= Imperial quarts (Imp qt)
Imperial quarts (Imp qt)	x 1.201	= US quarts (US qt)	x 0.833	= Imperial quarts (Imp qt)
US quarts (US qt)	x 0.946	= Litres (l)	x 1.057	= US quarts (US qt)
Imperial gallons (Imp gal)	x 4.546	= Litres (l)	x 0.22	= Imperial gallons (Imp gal)
Imperial gallons (Imp gal)	x 1.201	= US gallons (US gal)	x 0.833	= Imperial gallons (Imp gal)
US gallons (US gal)	x 3.785	= Litres (l)	x 0.264	= US gallons (US gal)

Mass (weight)
Ounces (oz)	x 28.35	= Grams (g)	x 0.035	= Ounces (oz)
Pounds (lb)	x 0.454	= Kilograms (kg)	x 2.205	= Pounds (lb)

Force
Ounces-force (ozf; oz)	x 0.278	= Newtons (N)	x 3.6	= Ounces-force (ozf; oz)
Pounds-force (lbf; lb)	x 4.448	= Newtons (N)	x 0.225	= Pounds-force (lbf; lb)
Newtons (N)	x 0.1	= Kilograms-force (kgf; kg)	x 9.81	= Newtons (N)

Pressure
Pounds-force per square inch (psi; lbf/in²; lb/in²)	x 0.070	= Kilograms-force per square centimetre (kgf/cm²; kg/cm²)	x 14.223	= Pounds-force per square inch (psi; lbf/in²; lb/in²)
Pounds-force per square inch (psi; lbf/in²; lb/in²)	x 0.068	= Atmospheres (atm)	x 14.696	= Pounds-force per square inch (psi; lbf/in²; lb/in²)
Pounds-force per square inch (psi; lbf/in²; lb/in²)	x 0.069	= Bars	x 14.5	= Pounds-force per square inch (psi; lbf/in²; lb/in²)
Pounds-force per square inch (psi; lbf/in²; lb/in²)	x 6.895	= Kilopascals (kPa)	x 0.145	= Pounds-force per square inch (psi; lbf/in²; lb/in²)
Kilopascals (kPa)	x 0.01	= Kilograms-force per square centimetre (kgf/cm²; kg/cm²)	x 98.1	= Kilopascals (kPa)
Millibar (mbar)	x 100	= Pascals (Pa)	x 0.01	= Millibar (mbar)
Millibar (mbar)	x 0.0145	= Pounds-force per square inch (psi; lbf/in²; lb/in²)	x 68.947	= Millibar (mbar)
Millibar (mbar)	x 0.75	= Millimetres of mercury (mmHg)	x 1.333	= Millibar (mbar)
Millibar (mbar)	x 0.401	= Inches of water (inH$_2$O)	x 2.491	= Millibar (mbar)
Millimetres of mercury (mmHg)	x 0.535	= Inches of water (inH$_2$O)	x 1.868	= Millimetres of mercury (mmHg)
Inches of water (inH$_2$O)	x 0.036	= Pounds-force per square inch (psi; lbf/in²; lb/in²)	x 27.68	= Inches of water (inH$_2$O)

Torque (moment of force)
Pounds-force inches (lbf in; lb in)	x 1.152	= Kilograms-force centimetre (kgf cm; kg cm)	x 0.868	= Pounds-force inches (lbf in; lb in)
Pounds-force inches (lbf in; lb in)	x 0.113	= Newton metres (Nm)	x 8.85	= Pounds-force inches (lbf in; lb in)
Pounds-force inches (lbf in; lb in)	x 0.083	= Pounds-force feet (lbf ft; lb ft)	x 12	= Pounds-force inches (lbf in; lb in)
Pounds-force feet (lbf ft; lb ft)	x 0.138	= Kilograms-force metres (kgf m; kg m)	x 7.233	= Pounds-force feet (lbf ft; lb ft)
Pounds-force feet (lbf ft; lb ft)	x 1.356	= Newton metres (Nm)	x 0.738	= Pounds-force feet (lbf ft; lb ft)
Newton metres (Nm)	x 0.102	= Kilograms-force metres (kgf m; kg m)	x 9.804	= Newton metres (Nm)

Power
Horsepower (hp)	x 745.7	= Watts (W)	x 0.0013	= Horsepower (hp)

Velocity (speed)
Miles per hour (miles/hr; mph)	x 1.609	= Kilometres per hour (km/hr; kph)	x 0.621	= Miles per hour (miles/hr; mph)

Fuel consumption*
Miles per gallon, Imperial (mpg)	x 0.354	= Kilometres per litre (km/l)	x 2.825	= Miles per gallon, Imperial (mpg)
Miles per gallon, US (mpg)	x 0.425	= Kilometres per litre (km/l)	x 2.352	= Miles per gallon, US (mpg)

Temperature
Degrees Fahrenheit = (°C x 1.8) + 32   Degrees Celsius (Degrees Centigrade; °C) = (°F - 32) x 0.56

It is common practice to convert from miles per gallon (mpg) to litres/100 kilometres (l/100km), where mpg x l/100 km = 282

Spare parts are available from many sources, including maker's appointed garages, accessory shops, and motor factors. To be sure of obtaining the correct parts, it may sometimes be necessary to quote the vehicle identification number. If possible, it can also be useful to take the old parts along for positive identification. Items such as starter motors and alternators may be available under a service exchange scheme – any parts returned should always be clean.

Our advice regarding spare part sources is as follows:

Officially-appointed garages

This is the best source of parts which are peculiar to your car, and are not otherwise generally available (eg, badges, interior trim, certain body panels, etc). It is also the only place at which you should buy parts if the vehicle is still under warranty.

Accessory shops

These are very good places to buy materials and components needed for the maintenance of your car (oil, air and fuel filters, spark plugs, light bulbs, drivebelts, oils and greases, brake pads, touch-up paint, etc). Parts like this sold by a reputable shop are of the same standard as those used by the car manufacturer.

Motor factors

Good factors will stock all the more important components which wear out comparatively quickly and can sometimes supply individual components needed for the overhaul of a larger assembly. They may also handle work such as cylinder block reboring, crankshaft regrinding and balancing, etc.

Tyre and exhaust specialists

These outlets may be independent or members of a local or national chain. They frequently offer competitive prices when compared with a main dealer or local garage, but it will pay to obtain several quotes before making a decision. Also ask what 'extras' may be added to the quote – for instance, fitting a new valve and balancing the wheel are both often charged on top of the price of a new tyre.

Other sources

Beware of parts of materials obtained from market stalls, car boot sales or similar outlets. Such items are not always sub-standard, but there is little chance of compensation if they do prove unsatisfactory. In the case of safety-critical components such as brake pads there is the risk not only of financial loss but also of an accident causing injury or death.

Second-hand components or assemblies obtained from a car breaker can be a good buy in some circumstances, but this sort of purchase is best made by the experienced DIY mechanic.

Vehicle identification numbers

Modifications are a continuing and unpublicised process in vehicle manufacture, quite apart from major model changes. Spare parts manuals and lists are compiled upon a numerical basis, the individual vehicle identification numbers being essential to correct identification of the component concerned.

When ordering spare parts, always give as much information as possible. Quote the vehicle type and year, vehicle identification number (VIN), and engine number, as appropriate.

The vehicle identification number (VIN) is stamped into the right-hand suspension turret in the engine compartment, and is repeated on the model plate affixed to the base of the drivers door central pillar (see illustrations).

The model plate also gives vehicle loading details, engine type, and various trim and colour codes.

The engine number is stamped on the right-hand end of the cylinder block.

The transmission identification numbers are located on a plate attached to the top of the transmission casing, or cast into the casing itself.

The VIN plate is stamped onto the right-hand suspension turret in the engine compartment

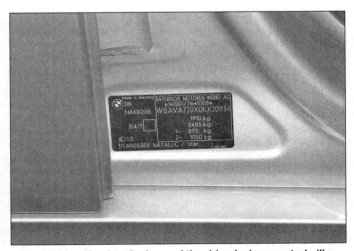

The VIN is affixed to the base of the driver's door central pillar

Whenever servicing, repair or overhaul work is carried out on the car or its components, observe the following procedures and instructions. This will assist in carrying out the operation efficiently and to a professional standard of workmanship.

Joint mating faces and gaskets

When separating components at their mating faces, never insert screwdrivers or similar implements into the joint between the faces in order to prise them apart. This can cause severe damage which results in oil leaks, coolant leaks, etc upon reassembly. Separation is usually achieved by tapping along the joint with a soft-faced hammer in order to break the seal. However, note that this method may not be suitable where dowels are used for component location.

Where a gasket is used between the mating faces of two components, a new one must be fitted on reassembly; fit it dry unless otherwise stated in the repair procedure. Make sure that the mating faces are clean and dry, with all traces of old gasket removed. When cleaning a joint face, use a tool which is unlikely to score or damage the face, and remove any burrs or nicks with an oilstone or fine file.

Make sure that tapped holes are cleaned with a pipe cleaner, and keep them free of jointing compound, if this is being used, unless specifically instructed otherwise.

Ensure that all orifices, channels or pipes are clear, and blow through them, preferably using compressed air.

Oil seals

Oil seals can be removed by levering them out with a wide flat-bladed screwdriver or similar implement. Alternatively, a number of self-tapping screws may be screwed into the seal, and these used as a purchase for pliers or some similar device in order to pull the seal free.

Whenever an oil seal is removed from its working location, either individually or as part of an assembly, it should be renewed.

The very fine sealing lip of the seal is easily damaged, and will not seal if the surface it contacts is not completely clean and free from scratches, nicks or grooves. If the original sealing surface of the component cannot be restored, and the manufacturer has not made provision for slight relocation of the seal relative to the sealing surface, the component should be renewed.

Protect the lips of the seal from any surface which may damage them in the course of fitting. Use tape or a conical sleeve where possible. Lubricate the seal lips with oil before fitting and, on dual-lipped seals, fill the space between the lips with grease.

Unless otherwise stated, oil seals must be fitted with their sealing lips toward the lubricant to be sealed.

Use a tubular drift or block of wood of the appropriate size to install the seal and, if the seal housing is shouldered, drive the seal down to the shoulder. If the seal housing is unshouldered, the seal should be fitted with its face flush with the housing top face (unless otherwise instructed).

Screw threads and fastenings

Seized nuts, bolts and screws are quite a common occurrence where corrosion has set in, and the use of penetrating oil or releasing fluid will often overcome this problem if the offending item is soaked for a while before attempting to release it. The use of an impact driver may also provide a means of releasing such stubborn fastening devices, when used in conjunction with the appropriate screwdriver bit or socket. If none of these methods works, it may be necessary to resort to the careful application of heat, or the use of a hacksaw or nut splitter device.

Studs are usually removed by locking two nuts together on the threaded part, and then using a spanner on the lower nut to unscrew the stud. Studs or bolts which have broken off below the surface of the component in which they are mounted can sometimes be removed using a stud extractor. Always ensure that a blind tapped hole is completely free from oil, grease, water or other fluid before installing the bolt or stud. Failure to do this could cause the housing to crack due to the hydraulic action of the bolt or stud as it is screwed in.

When tightening a castellated nut to accept a split pin, tighten the nut to the specified torque, where applicable, and then tighten further to the next split pin hole. Never slacken the nut to align the split pin hole, unless stated in the repair procedure.

When checking or retightening a nut or bolt to a specified torque setting, slacken the nut or bolt by a quarter of a turn, and then retighten to the specified setting. However, this should not be attempted where angular tightening has been used.

For some screw fastenings, notably cylinder head bolts or nuts, torque wrench settings are no longer specified for the latter stages of tightening, "angle-tightening" being called up instead. Typically, a fairly low torque wrench setting will be applied to the bolts/nuts in the correct sequence, followed by one or more stages of tightening through specified angles.

Locknuts, locktabs and washers

Any fastening which will rotate against a component or housing during tightening should always have a washer between it and the relevant component or housing.

Spring or split washers should always be renewed when they are used to lock a critical component such as a big-end bearing retaining bolt or nut. Locktabs which are folded over to retain a nut or bolt should always be renewed.

Self-locking nuts can be re-used in non-critical areas, providing resistance can be felt when the locking portion passes over the bolt or stud thread. However, it should be noted that self-locking stiffnuts tend to lose their effectiveness after long periods of use, and should then be renewed as a matter of course.

Split pins must always be replaced with new ones of the correct size for the hole.

When thread-locking compound is found on the threads of a fastener which is to be re-used, it should be cleaned off with a wire brush and solvent, and fresh compound applied on reassembly.

Special tools

Some repair procedures in this manual entail the use of special tools such as a press, two or three-legged pullers, spring compressors, etc. Wherever possible, suitable readily-available alternatives to the manufacturer's special tools are described, and are shown in use. In some instances, where no alternative is possible, it has been necessary to resort to the use of a manufacturer's tool, and this has been done for reasons of safety as well as the efficient completion of the repair operation. Unless you are highly-skilled and have a thorough understanding of the procedures described, never attempt to bypass the use of any special tool when the procedure described specifies its use. Not only is there a very great risk of personal injury, but expensive damage could be caused to the components involved.

Environmental considerations

When disposing of used engine oil, brake fluid, antifreeze, etc, give due consideration to any detrimental environmental effects. Do not, for instance, pour any of the above liquids down drains into the general sewage system, or onto the ground to soak away. Many local council refuse tips provide a facility for waste oil disposal, as do some garages. If none of these facilities are available, consult your local Environmental Health Department, or the National Rivers Authority, for further advice.

With the universal tightening-up of legislation regarding the emission of environmentally-harmful substances from motor vehicles, most vehicles have tamperproof devices fitted to the main adjustment points of the fuel system. These devices are primarily designed to prevent unqualified persons from adjusting the fuel/air mixture, with the chance of a consequent increase in toxic emissions. If such devices are found during servicing or overhaul, they should, wherever possible, be renewed or refitted in accordance with the manufacturer's requirements or current legislation.

OIL CARE
FOLLOW THE CODE
OIL BANK LINE
0800 66 33 66
www.oilbankline.org.uk

Note: It is antisocial and illegal to dump oil down the drain. To find the location of your local oil recycling bank, call this number free.

The jack supplied with the vehicle tool kit should **only** be used for changing the roadwheels in an emergency – see *Wheel changing* at the front of this book. When carrying out any other kind of work, raise the vehicle using a heavy-duty hydraulic (or 'trolley') jack, and always supplement the jack with axle stands positioned under the vehicle jacking points. If the roadwheels do not have to be removed, consider using wheel ramps – if wished, these can be placed under the wheels once the vehicle has been raised using a hydraulic jack, and the vehicle lowered onto the ramps so that it is resting on its wheels.

Only ever jack the vehicle up on a solid, level surface. If there is even a slight slope, take great care that the vehicle cannot move as the wheels are lifted off the ground. Jacking up on an uneven or gravelled surface is not recommended, as the weight of the vehicle will not be evenly distributed, and the jack may slip as the vehicle is raised.

As far as possible, do not leave the vehicle unattended once it has been raised, particularly if children are playing nearby.

Before jacking up the front of the car, ensure that the handbrake is firmly applied. When jacking up the rear of the car, place wooden chocks in front of the front wheels, and engage first gear (or P).

When using a hydraulic jack or axle stands, always position the jack head or axle stand head under the relevant rubber lifting blocks. These are situated directly underneath the vehicle jack location holes in the sill – the vehicle can also be raised with a trolley jack positioned under the jacking point on the front reinforcement strut, and under the rear differential (not the end cover) **(see illustration)**.

The jack supplied with the vehicle locates in the holes provided in the sill. Ensure that the jack head is correctly engaged before attempting to raise the vehicle.

Never work under, around, or near a raised

vehicle, unless it is adequately supported in at least two places.

When jacking or supporting the vehicle at these points, always use a block of wood between the jack head or axle stand, and the vehicle body. It is also considered good practice to use a large block of wood when supporting under other areas, to spread the load over a wider area, and reduce the risk of damage to the underside of the car (it also helps to prevent the underbody coating from being damaged by the jack or axle stand). **Do not** jack the vehicle under any other part of the sill, engine sump, floor pan, subframe, or directly under any of the steering or suspension components.

Never work under, around, or near a raised vehicle, unless it is adequately supported on stands. Do not rely on a jack alone, as even a hydraulic jack could fail under load. Makeshift methods should not be used to lift and support the car during servicing work.

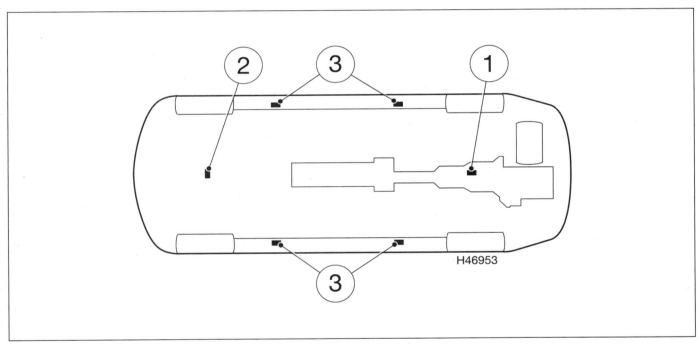

H46953

Vehicle jacking points

1 Rear differential   2 Jacking point on front reinforcement strut   3 Side jacking points

Introduction

A selection of good tools is a fundamental requirement for anyone contemplating the maintenance and repair of a motor vehicle. For the owner who does not possess any, their purchase will prove a considerable expense, offsetting some of the savings made by doing-it-yourself. However, provided that the tools purchased meet the relevant national safety standards and are of good quality, they will last for many years and prove an extremely worthwhile investment.

To help the average owner to decide which tools are needed to carry out the various tasks detailed in this manual, we have compiled three lists of tools under the following headings: *Maintenance and minor repair*, *Repair and overhaul*, and *Special*. Newcomers to practical mechanics should start off with the *Maintenance and minor repair* tool kit, and confine themselves to the simpler jobs around the vehicle. Then, as confidence and experience grow, more difficult tasks can be undertaken, with extra tools being purchased as, and when, they are needed. In this way, a *Maintenance and minor repair* tool kit can be built up into a *Repair and overhaul* tool kit over a considerable period of time, without any major cash outlays. The experienced do-it-yourselfer will have a tool kit good enough for most repair and overhaul procedures, and will add tools from the *Special* category when it is felt that the expense is justified by the amount of use to which these tools will be put.

Maintenance and minor repair tool kit

The tools given in this list should be considered as a minimum requirement if routine maintenance, servicing and minor repair operations are to be undertaken. We recommend the purchase of combination spanners (ring one end, open-ended the other); although more expensive than open-ended ones, they do give the advantages of both types of spanner.

☐ *Combination spanners:*
Metric - 8 to 19 mm inclusive
☐ *Adjustable spanner - 35 mm jaw (approx.)*
☐ *Spark plug spanner (with rubber insert) - petrol models*
☐ *Spark plug gap adjustment tool - petrol models*
☐ *Set of feeler gauges*
☐ *Brake bleed nipple spanner*
☐ *Screwdrivers:*
Flat blade - 100 mm long x 6 mm dia
Cross blade - 100 mm long x 6 mm dia
Torx - various sizes (not all vehicles)
☐ *Combination pliers*
☐ *Hacksaw (junior)*
☐ *Tyre pump*
☐ *Tyre pressure gauge*
☐ *Oil can*
☐ *Oil filter removal tool*
☐ *Fine emery cloth*
☐ *Wire brush (small)*
☐ *Funnel (medium size)*
☐ *Sump drain plug key (not all vehicles)*

Repair and overhaul tool kit

These tools are virtually essential for anyone undertaking any major repairs to a motor vehicle, and are additional to those given in the *Maintenance and minor repair* list. Included in this list is a comprehensive set of sockets. Although these are expensive, they will be found invaluable as they are so versatile - particularly if various drives are included in the set. We recommend the half-inch square-drive type, as this can be used with most proprietary torque wrenches.

The tools in this list will sometimes need to be supplemented by tools from the *Special* list:

☐ *Sockets (or box spanners) to cover range in previous list (including Torx sockets)*
☐ *Reversible ratchet drive (for use with sockets)*
☐ *Extension piece, 250 mm (for use with sockets)*
☐ *Universal joint (for use with sockets)*
☐ *Flexible handle or sliding T "breaker bar" (for use with sockets)*
☐ *Torque wrench (for use with sockets)*
☐ *Self-locking grips*
☐ *Ball pein hammer*
☐ *Soft-faced mallet (plastic or rubber)*
☐ *Screwdrivers:*
Flat blade - long & sturdy, short (chubby), and narrow (electrician's) types
Cross blade – long & sturdy, and short (chubby) types
☐ *Pliers:*
Long-nosed
Side cutters (electrician's)
Circlip (internal and external)
☐ *Cold chisel - 25 mm*
☐ *Scriber*
☐ *Scraper*
☐ *Centre-punch*
☐ *Pin punch*
☐ *Hacksaw*
☐ *Brake hose clamp*
☐ *Brake/clutch bleeding kit*
☐ *Selection of twist drills*
☐ *Steel rule/straight-edge*
☐ *Allen keys (inc. splined/Torx type)*
☐ *Selection of files*
☐ *Wire brush*
☐ *Axle stands*
☐ *Jack (strong trolley or hydraulic type)*
☐ *Light with extension lead*
☐ *Universal electrical multi-meter*

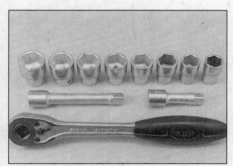
Sockets and reversible ratchet drive

Brake bleeding kit

Torx key, socket and bit

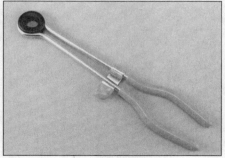
Hose clamp

Angular-tightening gauge

Special tools

The tools in this list are those which are not used regularly, are expensive to buy, or which need to be used in accordance with their manufacturers' instructions. Unless relatively difficult mechanical jobs are undertaken frequently, it will not be economic to buy many of these tools. Where this is the case, you could consider clubbing together with friends (or joining a motorists' club) to make a joint purchase, or borrowing the tools against a deposit from a local garage or tool hire specialist. It is worth noting that many of the larger DIY superstores now carry a large range of special tools for hire at modest rates.

The following list contains only those tools and instruments freely available to the public, and not those special tools produced by the vehicle manufacturer specifically for its dealer network. You will find occasional references to these manufacturers' special tools in the text of this manual. Generally, an alternative method of doing the job without the vehicle manufacturers' special tool is given. However, sometimes there is no alternative to using them. Where this is the case and the relevant tool cannot be bought or borrowed, you will have to entrust the work to a dealer.

☐ *Angular-tightening gauge*
☐ *Valve spring compressor*
☐ *Valve grinding tool*
☐ *Piston ring compressor*
☐ *Piston ring removal/installation tool*
☐ *Cylinder bore hone*
☐ *Balljoint separator*
☐ *Coil spring compressors (where applicable)*
☐ *Two/three-legged hub and bearing puller*
☐ *Impact screwdriver*
☐ *Micrometer and/or vernier calipers*
☐ *Dial gauge*
☐ *Stroboscopic timing light*
☐ *Dwell angle meter/tachometer*
☐ *Fault code reader*
☐ *Cylinder compression gauge*
☐ *Hand-operated vacuum pump and gauge*
☐ *Clutch plate alignment set*
☐ *Brake shoe steady spring cup removal tool*
☐ *Bush and bearing removal/installation set*
☐ *Stud extractors*
☐ *Tap and die set*
☐ *Lifting tackle*
☐ *Trolley jack*

Buying tools

Reputable motor accessory shops and superstores often offer excellent quality tools at discount prices, so it pays to shop around.

Remember, you don't have to buy the most expensive items on the shelf, but it is always advisable to steer clear of the very cheap tools. Beware of 'bargains' offered on market stalls or at car boot sales. There are plenty of good tools around at reasonable prices, but always aim to purchase items which meet the relevant national safety standards. If in doubt, ask the proprietor or manager of the shop for advice before making a purchase.

Care and maintenance of tools

Having purchased a reasonable tool kit, it is necessary to keep the tools in a clean and serviceable condition. After use, always wipe off any dirt, grease and metal particles using a clean, dry cloth, before putting the tools away. Never leave them lying around after they have been used. A simple tool rack on the garage or workshop wall for items such as screwdrivers and pliers is a good idea. Store all normal spanners and sockets in a metal box. Any measuring instruments, gauges, meters, etc, must be carefully stored where they cannot be damaged or become rusty.

Take a little care when tools are used. Hammer heads inevitably become marked, and screwdrivers lose the keen edge on their blades from time to time. A little timely attention with emery cloth or a file will soon restore items like this to a good finish.

Working facilities

Not to be forgotten when discussing tools is the workshop itself. If anything more than routine maintenance is to be carried out, a suitable working area becomes essential.

It is appreciated that many an owner-mechanic is forced by circumstances to remove an engine or similar item without the benefit of a garage or workshop. Having done this, any repairs should always be done under the cover of a roof.

Wherever possible, any dismantling should be done on a clean, flat workbench or table at a suitable working height.

Any workbench needs a vice; one with a jaw opening of 100 mm is suitable for most jobs. As mentioned previously, some clean dry storage space is also required for tools, as well as for any lubricants, cleaning fluids, touch-up paints etc, which become necessary.

Another item which may be required, and which has a much more general usage, is an electric drill with a chuck capacity of at least 8 mm. This, together with a good range of twist drills, is virtually essential for fitting accessories.

Last, but not least, always keep a supply of old newspapers and clean, lint-free rags available, and try to keep any working area as clean as possible.

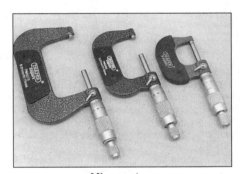
Micrometers

Dial test indicator ("dial gauge")

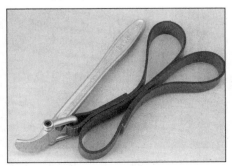
Strap wrench

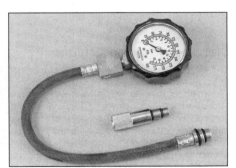
Compression tester

Fault code reader

This is a guide to getting your vehicle through the MOT test. Obviously it will not be possible to examine the vehicle to the same standard as the professional MOT tester. However, working through the following checks will enable you to identify any problem areas before submitting the vehicle for the test.

It has only been possible to summarise the test requirements here, based on the regulations in force at the time of printing. Test standards are becoming increasingly stringent, although there are some exemptions for older vehicles.

An assistant will be needed to help carry out some of these checks.

The checks have been sub-divided into four categories, as follows:

1 Checks carried out **FROM THE DRIVER'S SEAT**

2 Checks carried out **WITH THE VEHICLE ON THE GROUND**

3 Checks carried out **WITH THE VEHICLE RAISED AND THE WHEELS FREE TO TURN**

4 Checks carried out on **YOUR VEHICLE'S EXHAUST EMISSION SYSTEM**

---

1 Checks carried out **FROM THE DRIVER'S SEAT**

Handbrake

☐ Test the operation of the handbrake. Excessive travel (too many clicks) indicates incorrect brake or cable adjustment.
☐ Check that the handbrake cannot be released by tapping the lever sideways. Check the security of the lever mountings.

Footbrake

☐ Depress the brake pedal and check that it does not creep down to the floor, indicating a master cylinder fault. Release the pedal, wait a few seconds, then depress it again. If the pedal travels nearly to the floor before firm resistance is felt, brake adjustment or repair is necessary. If the pedal feels spongy, there is air in the hydraulic system which must be removed by bleeding.

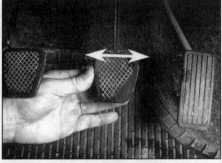

☐ Check that the brake pedal is secure and in good condition. Check also for signs of fluid leaks on the pedal, floor or carpets, which would indicate failed seals in the brake master cylinder.
☐ Check the servo unit (when applicable) by operating the brake pedal several times, then keeping the pedal depressed and starting the engine. As the engine starts, the pedal will move down slightly. If not, the vacuum hose or the servo itself may be faulty.

Steering wheel and column

☐ Examine the steering wheel for fractures or looseness of the hub, spokes or rim.
☐ Move the steering wheel from side to side and then up and down. Check that the steering wheel is not loose on the column, indicating wear or a loose retaining nut. Continue moving the steering wheel as before, but also turn it slightly from left to right.
☐ Check that the steering wheel is not loose on the column, and that there is no abnormal

movement of the steering wheel, indicating wear in the column support bearings or couplings.

Windscreen, mirrors and sunvisor

☐ The windscreen must be free of cracks or other significant damage within the driver's field of view. (Small stone chips are acceptable.) Rear view mirrors must be secure, intact, and capable of being adjusted.

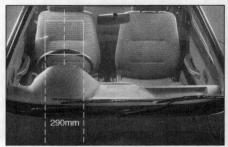

☐ The driver's sunvisor must be capable of being stored in the "up" position.

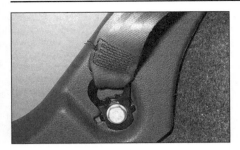

Seat belts and seats

Note: *The following checks are applicable to all seat belts, front and rear.*

☐ Examine the webbing of all the belts (including rear belts if fitted) for cuts, serious fraying or deterioration. Fasten and unfasten each belt to check the buckles. If applicable, check the retracting mechanism. Check the security of all seat belt mountings accessible from inside the vehicle.
☐ Seat belts with pre-tensioners, once activated, have a "flag" or similar showing on the seat belt stalk. This, in itself, is not a reason for test failure.
☐ The front seats themselves must be securely attached and the backrests must lock in the upright position.

Doors

☐ Both front doors must be able to be opened and closed from outside and inside, and must latch securely when closed.

2 Checks carried out WITH THE VEHICLE ON THE GROUND

Vehicle identification

☐ Number plates must be in good condition, secure and legible, with letters and numbers correctly spaced – spacing at (A) should be at least twice that at (B).

☐ The VIN plate and/or homologation plate must be legible.

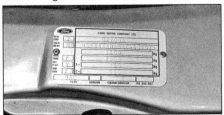

Electrical equipment

☐ Switch on the ignition and check the operation of the horn.
☐ Check the windscreen washers and wipers, examining the wiper blades; renew damaged or perished blades. Also check the operation of the stop-lights.

☐ Check the operation of the sidelights and number plate lights. The lenses and reflectors must be secure, clean and undamaged.
☐ Check the operation and alignment of the headlights. The headlight reflectors must not be tarnished and the lenses must be undamaged.
☐ Switch on the ignition and check the operation of the direction indicators (including the instrument panel tell-tale) and the hazard warning lights. Operation of the sidelights and stop-lights must not affect the indicators - if it does, the cause is usually a bad earth at the rear light cluster.
☐ Check the operation of the rear foglight(s), including the warning light on the instrument panel or in the switch.
☐ The ABS warning light must illuminate in accordance with the manufacturers' design. For most vehicles, the ABS warning light should illuminate when the ignition is switched on, and (if the system is operating properly) extinguish after a few seconds. Refer to the owner's handbook.

Footbrake

☐ Examine the master cylinder, brake pipes and servo unit for leaks, loose mountings, corrosion or other damage.

☐ The fluid reservoir must be secure and the fluid level must be between the upper (**A**) and lower (**B**) markings.

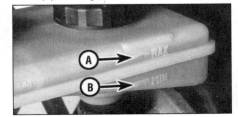

☐ Inspect both front brake flexible hoses for cracks or deterioration of the rubber. Turn the steering from lock to lock, and ensure that the hoses do not contact the wheel, tyre, or any part of the steering or suspension mechanism. With the brake pedal firmly depressed, check the hoses for bulges or leaks under pressure.

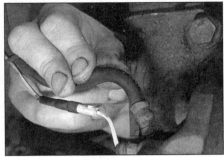

Steering and suspension

☐ Have your assistant turn the steering wheel from side to side slightly, up to the point where the steering gear just begins to transmit this movement to the roadwheels. Check for excessive free play between the steering wheel and the steering gear, indicating wear or insecurity of the steering column joints, the column-to-steering gear coupling, or the steering gear itself.
☐ Have your assistant turn the steering wheel more vigorously in each direction, so that the roadwheels just begin to turn. As this is done, examine all the steering joints, linkages, fittings and attachments. Renew any component that shows signs of wear or damage. On vehicles with power steering, check the security and condition of the steering pump, drivebelt and hoses.
☐ Check that the vehicle is standing level, and at approximately the correct ride height.

Shock absorbers

☐ Depress each corner of the vehicle in turn, then release it. The vehicle should rise and then settle in its normal position. If the vehicle continues to rise and fall, the shock absorber is defective. A shock absorber which has seized will also cause the vehicle to fail.

Exhaust system

☐ Start the engine. With your assistant holding a rag over the tailpipe, check the entire system for leaks. Repair or renew leaking sections.

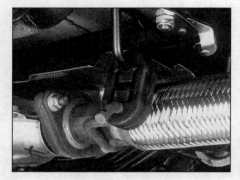

3 Checks carried out
WITH THE VEHICLE RAISED AND THE WHEELS FREE TO TURN

Jack up the front and rear of the vehicle, and securely support it on axle stands. Position the stands clear of the suspension assemblies. Ensure that the wheels are clear of the ground and that the steering can be turned from lock to lock.

Steering mechanism

☐ Have your assistant turn the steering from lock to lock. Check that the steering turns smoothly, and that no part of the steering mechanism, including a wheel or tyre, fouls any brake hose or pipe or any part of the body structure.
☐ Examine the steering rack rubber gaiters for damage or insecurity of the retaining clips. If power steering is fitted, check for signs of damage or leakage of the fluid hoses, pipes or connections. Also check for excessive stiffness or binding of the steering, a missing split pin or locking device, or severe corrosion of the body structure within 30 cm of any steering component attachment point.

Front and rear suspension and wheel bearings

☐ Starting at the front right-hand side, grasp the roadwheel at the 3 o'clock and 9 o'clock positions and rock gently but firmly. Check for free play or insecurity at the wheel bearings, suspension balljoints, or suspension mountings, pivots and attachments.
☐ Now grasp the wheel at the 12 o'clock and 6 o'clock positions and repeat the previous inspection. Spin the wheel, and check for roughness or tightness of the front wheel bearing.

☐ If excess free play is suspected at a component pivot point, this can be confirmed by using a large screwdriver or similar tool and levering between the mounting and the component attachment. This will confirm whether the wear is in the pivot bush, its retaining bolt, or in the mounting itself (the bolt holes can often become elongated).

☐ Carry out all the above checks at the other front wheel, and then at both rear wheels.

Springs and shock absorbers

☐ Examine the suspension struts (when applicable) for serious fluid leakage, corrosion, or damage to the casing. Also check the security of the mounting points.
☐ If coil springs are fitted, check that the spring ends locate in their seats, and that the spring is not corroded, cracked or broken.
☐ If leaf springs are fitted, check that all leaves are intact, that the axle is securely attached to each spring, and that there is no deterioration of the spring eye mountings, bushes, and shackles.

☐ The same general checks apply to vehicles fitted with other suspension types, such as torsion bars, hydraulic displacer units, etc. Ensure that all mountings and attachments are secure, that there are no signs of excessive wear, corrosion or damage, and (on hydraulic types) that there are no fluid leaks or damaged pipes.
☐ Inspect the shock absorbers for signs of serious fluid leakage. Check for wear of the mounting bushes or attachments, or damage to the body of the unit.

Driveshafts (fwd vehicles only)

☐ Rotate each front wheel in turn and inspect the constant velocity joint gaiters for splits or damage. Also check that each driveshaft is straight and undamaged.

Braking system

☐ If possible without dismantling, check brake pad wear and disc condition. Ensure that the friction lining material has not worn excessively, (A) and that the discs are not fractured, pitted, scored or badly worn (B).

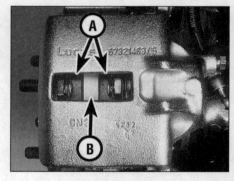

☐ Examine all the rigid brake pipes underneath the vehicle, and the flexible hose(s) at the rear. Look for corrosion, chafing or insecurity of the pipes, and for signs of bulging under pressure, chafing, splits or deterioration of the flexible hoses.
☐ Look for signs of fluid leaks at the brake calipers or on the brake backplates. Repair or renew leaking components.
☐ Slowly spin each wheel, while your assistant depresses and releases the footbrake. Ensure that each brake is operating and does not bind when the pedal is released.

☐ Examine the handbrake mechanism, checking for frayed or broken cables, excessive corrosion, or wear or insecurity of the linkage. Check that the mechanism works on each relevant wheel, and releases fully, without binding.

☐ It is not possible to test brake efficiency without special equipment, but a road test can be carried out later to check that the vehicle pulls up in a straight line.

Fuel and exhaust systems

☐ Inspect the fuel tank (including the filler cap), fuel pipes, hoses and unions. All components must be secure and free from leaks.

☐ Examine the exhaust system over its entire length, checking for any damaged, broken or missing mountings, security of the retaining clamps and rust or corrosion.

Wheels and tyres

☐ Examine the sidewalls and tread area of each tyre in turn. Check for cuts, tears, lumps, bulges, separation of the tread, and exposure of the ply or cord due to wear or damage. Check that the tyre bead is correctly seated on the wheel rim, that the valve is sound and properly seated, and that the wheel is not distorted or damaged.

☐ Check that the tyres are of the correct size for the vehicle, that they are of the same size

and type on each axle, and that the pressures are correct.

☐ Check the tyre tread depth. The legal minimum at the time of writing is 1.6 mm over at least three-quarters of the tread width. Abnormal tread wear may indicate incorrect front wheel alignment.

Body corrosion

☐ Check the condition of the entire vehicle structure for signs of corrosion in load-bearing areas. (These include chassis box sections, side sills, cross-members, pillars, and all suspension, steering, braking system and seat belt mountings and anchorages.) Any corrosion which has seriously reduced the thickness of a load-bearing area is likely to cause the vehicle to fail. In this case professional repairs are likely to be needed.

☐ Damage or corrosion which causes sharp or otherwise dangerous edges to be exposed will also cause the vehicle to fail.

4 Checks carried out on YOUR VEHICLE'S EXHAUST EMISSION SYSTEM

Petrol models

☐ The engine should be warmed up, and running well (ignition system in good order, air filter element clean, etc).

☐ Before testing, run the engine at around 2500 rpm for 20 seconds. Let the engine drop to idle, and watch for smoke from the exhaust. If the idle speed is too high, or if dense blue or black smoke emerges for more than 5 seconds, the vehicle will fail. Typically, blue smoke signifies oil burning (engine wear); black smoke means unburnt fuel (dirty air cleaner element, or other fuel system fault).

☐ An exhaust gas analyser for measuring carbon monoxide (CO) and hydrocarbons (HC) is now needed. If one cannot be hired or borrowed, have a local garage perform the check.

CO emissions (mixture)

☐ The MOT tester has access to the CO limits for all vehicles. The CO level is measured at idle speed, and at 'fast idle' (2500 to 3000 rpm). The following limits are given as a general guide:
At idle speed – Less than 0.5% CO
At 'fast idle' – Less than 0.3% CO
Lambda reading – 0.97 to 1.03

☐ If the CO level is too high, this may point to poor maintenance, a fuel injection system problem, faulty lambda (oxygen) sensor or catalytic converter. Try an injector cleaning treatment, and check the vehicle's ECU for fault codes.

HC emissions

☐ The MOT tester has access to HC limits for all vehicles. The HC level is measured at 'fast idle' (2500 to 3000 rpm). The following limits are given as a general guide:
At 'fast idle' – Less then 200 ppm

☐ Excessive HC emissions are typically caused by oil being burnt (worn engine), or by a blocked crankcase ventilation system ('breather'). If the engine oil is old and thin, an oil change may help. If the engine is running badly, check the vehicle's ECU for fault codes.

Diesel models

☐ The only emission test for diesel engines is measuring exhaust smoke density, using a calibrated smoke meter. The test involves accelerating the engine at least 3 times to its maximum unloaded speed.

Note: *On engines with a timing belt, it is VITAL that the belt is in good condition before the test is carried out.*

☐ With the engine warmed up, it is first purged by running at around 2500 rpm for 20 seconds. A governor check is then carried out, by slowly accelerating the engine to its maximum speed. After this, the smoke meter is connected, and the engine is accelerated quickly to maximum speed three times. If the smoke density is less than the limits given below, the vehicle will pass:
Non-turbo vehicles: 2.5m-1
Turbocharged vehicles: 3.0m-1

☐ If excess smoke is produced, try fitting a new air cleaner element, or using an injector cleaning treatment. If the engine is running badly, where applicable, check the vehicle's ECU for fault codes. Also check the vehicle's EGR system, where applicable. At high mileages, the injectors may require professional attention.

Engine

- [ ] Engine fails to rotate when attempting to start
- [ ] Engine rotates, but will not start
- [ ] Engine difficult to start when cold
- [ ] Engine difficult to start when hot
- [ ] Starter motor noisy or excessively-rough in engagement
- [ ] Engine starts, but stops immediately
- [ ] Engine idles erratically
- [ ] Engine misfires at idle speed
- [ ] Engine misfires throughout the driving speed range
- [ ] Engine hesitates on acceleration
- [ ] Engine stalls
- [ ] Engine lacks power
- [ ] Engine backfires
- [ ] Oil pressure warning light illuminated with engine running
- [ ] Engine runs-on after switching off
- [ ] Engine noises

Cooling system

- [ ] Overheating
- [ ] Overcooling
- [ ] External coolant leakage
- [ ] Internal coolant leakage
- [ ] Corrosion

Fuel and exhaust systems

- [ ] Excessive fuel consumption
- [ ] Fuel leakage and/or fuel odour
- [ ] Excessive noise or fumes from exhaust system

Clutch

- [ ] Pedal travels to floor – no pressure or very little resistance
- [ ] Clutch fails to disengage (unable to select gears)
- [ ] Clutch slips (engine speed increases, with no increase in vehicle speed)
- [ ] Judder as clutch is engaged
- [ ] Noise when depressing or releasing clutch pedal

Manual transmission

- [ ] Noisy in neutral with engine running
- [ ] Noisy in one particular gear
- [ ] Difficulty engaging gears
- [ ] Jumps out of gear
- [ ] Vibration
- [ ] Lubricant leaks

Automatic transmission

- [ ] Fluid leakage
- [ ] Transmission fluid brown, or has burned smell
- [ ] General gear selection problems
- [ ] Transmission will not downshift (kickdown) with accelerator pedal fully depressed
- [ ] Engine will not start in any gear, or starts in gears other than Park or Neutral
- [ ] Transmission slips, shifts roughly, is noisy, or has no drive in forward or reverse gears

Differential and propshaft

- [ ] Vibration when accelerating or decelerating
- [ ] Low-pitched whining; increasing with road speed

Braking system

- [ ] Vehicle pulls to one side under braking
- [ ] Noise (grinding or high-pitched squeal) when brakes applied
- [ ] Excessive brake pedal travel
- [ ] Brake pedal feels spongy when depressed
- [ ] Excessive brake pedal effort required to stop vehicle
- [ ] Judder felt through brake pedal or steering wheel when braking
- [ ] Brakes binding
- [ ] Rear wheels locking under normal braking

Suspension and steering

- [ ] Vehicle pulls to one side
- [ ] Wheel wobble and vibration
- [ ] Excessive pitching and/or rolling around corners, or during braking
- [ ] Wandering or general instability
- [ ] Excessively-stiff steering
- [ ] Excessive play in steering
- [ ] Lack of power assistance
- [ ] Tyre wear excessive

Electrical system

- [ ] Battery will not hold a charge for more than a few days
- [ ] Ignition/no-charge warning light remains illuminated with engine running
- [ ] Ignition/no-charge warning light fails to come on
- [ ] Lights inoperative
- [ ] Instrument readings inaccurate or erratic
- [ ] Horn inoperative, or unsatisfactory in operation
- [ ] Windscreen wipers inoperative, or unsatisfactory in operation
- [ ] Windscreen washers inoperative, or unsatisfactory in operation
- [ ] Electric windows inoperative, or unsatisfactory in operation
- [ ] Central locking system inoperative, or unsatisfactory in operation

Introduction

The vehicle owner who does his or her own maintenance according to the recommended service schedules should not have to use this section of the manual very often. Modern component reliability is such that, provided those items subject to wear or deterioration are inspected or renewed at the specified intervals, sudden failure is comparatively rare. Faults do not usually just happen as a result of sudden failure, but develop over a period of time. Major mechanical failures in particular are usually preceded by characteristic symptoms over hundreds or even thousands of miles. Those components which do occasionally fail without warning are often small and easily carried in the vehicle.

With any fault finding, the first step is to decide where to begin investigations. Sometimes this is obvious, but on other occasions, a little detective work will be necessary. The owner who makes half a dozen haphazard adjustments or replacements may be successful in curing a fault (or its symptoms), but will be none the wiser if the fault recurs, and ultimately may have spent more time and money than was necessary. A calm and logical approach will be found to be more satisfactory in the long run. Always take into account any warning signs or abnormalities that may have been noticed in the period preceding the fault – power loss, high or low gauge readings, unusual smells,

etc – and remember that failure of components such as fuses or spark plugs may only be pointers to some underlying fault.

The pages which follow provide an easy-reference guide to the more common problems which may occur during the operation of the vehicle. These problems and their possible causes are grouped under headings denoting various components or systems, such as Engine, Cooling system, etc. The general Chapter which deals with the problem is also shown in brackets; refer to the relevant part of that Chapter for system-specific information. Whatever the fault, certain basic principles apply. These are as follows:

Verify the fault. This is simply a matter of

being sure that you know what the symptoms are before starting work. This is particularly important if you are investigating a fault for someone else, who may not have described it very accurately.

Don't overlook the obvious. For example, if the vehicle won't start, is there fuel in the tank? (Don't take anyone else's word on this particular point, and don't trust the fuel gauge either). If an electrical fault is indicated, look for loose or broken wires before digging out the test gear.

Cure the disease, not the symptom. Substituting a flat battery with a fully-charged one will get you off the hard shoulder, but if the underlying cause is not attended to, the new battery will go the same way. Similarly, changing oil-fouled spark plugs for a new set will get you moving again, but remember that the reason for the fouling (if it wasn't simply an incorrect grade of plug) will have to be established and corrected.

Don't take anything for granted. Particularly, don't forget that a 'new' component may itself be defective (especially if it's been rattling

around in the boot for months), and don't leave components out of a fault diagnosis sequence just because they are new or recently-fitted. When you do finally diagnose a difficult fault, you'll probably realise that all the evidence was there from the start.

Consider what work, if any, has recently been carried out. Many faults arise through careless or hurried work. For instance, if any work has been performed under the bonnet, could some of the wiring have been dislodged or incorrectly routed, or a hose trapped? Have all the fasteners been properly tightened? Were new, genuine parts and new gaskets used? There is often a certain amount of detective work to be done in this case, as an apparently-unrelated task can have far-reaching consequences.

Diesel fault diagnosis

The majority of starting problems on small diesel engines are electrical in origin. The mechanic who is familiar with petrol engines but less so with diesel may be inclined to view the diesel's injectors and pump in the same

light as the spark plugs and distributor, but this is generally a mistake.

When investigating complaints of difficult starting for someone else, make sure that the correct starting procedure is understood and is being followed. Some drivers are unaware of the significance of the preheating warning light – many modern engines are sufficiently forgiving for this not to matter in mild weather, but with the onset of winter, problems begin. Glow plugs in particular are often neglected – just one faulty plug will make cold-weather starting very difficult.

As a rule of thumb, if the engine is difficult to start but runs well when it has finally got going, the problem is electrical (battery, starter motor or preheating system). If poor performance is combined with difficult starting, the problem is likely to be in the fuel system. The low-pressure (supply) side of the fuel system should be checked before suspecting the injectors and high-pressure pump. The most common fuel supply problem is air getting into the system, and any pipe from the fuel tank forwards must be scrutinised if air leakage is suspected.

Engine

Engine fails to rotate when attempting to start

- [ ] Battery terminal connections loose or corroded (see *Weekly checks*)
- [ ] Battery discharged or faulty (Chapter 5A)
- [ ] Broken, loose or disconnected wiring in the starting circuit (Chapter 5A)
- [ ] Defective starter solenoid or ignition switch (Chapter 5A or 12)
- [ ] Defective starter motor (Chapter 5A)
- [ ] Starter pinion or flywheel ring gear teeth loose or broken (Chapter 2A, 2B, 2C or 5A)
- [ ] Engine earth strap broken or disconnected (Chapter 12)
- [ ] Engine suffering 'hydraulic lock' (eg, from water ingested after traversing flooded roads, or from a serious internal coolant leak) – consult a BMW dealer or specialist for advice
- [ ] Automatic transmission not in position P or N (Chapter 7B)

Engine rotates, but will not start

- [ ] Fuel tank empty
- [ ] Battery discharged (engine rotates slowly) (Chapter 5A)
- [ ] Battery terminal connections loose or corroded (see *Weekly checks*)
- [ ] Ignition components damp or damaged – petrol models (Chapter 1A or 5B)
- [ ] Immobiliser fault, or 'uncoded' ignition key being used (Chapter 12 or *Roadside repairs*)
- [ ] Crankshaft sensor fault (Chapter 4A or 4B)
- [ ] Broken, loose or disconnected wiring in the ignition circuit – petrol models (Chapter 1A or 5B)
- [ ] Worn, faulty or incorrectly-gapped spark plugs – petrol models (Chapter 1A)
- [ ] Preheating system faulty – diesel models (Chapter 5A)
- [ ] Fuel injection system fault (Chapter 4A or 4B)
- [ ] Air in fuel system – diesel models (Chapter 4B)
- [ ] Major mechanical failure (eg, timing chain snapped) (Chapter 2A, 2B, 2C or 2D)

Engine difficult to start when cold

- [ ] Battery discharged (Chapter 5A)
- [ ] Battery terminal connections loose or corroded (see *Weekly checks*)

- [ ] Worn, faulty or incorrectly-gapped spark plugs – petrol models (Chapter 1A)
- [ ] Other ignition system fault – petrol models (Chapter 1A or 5B)
- [ ] Preheating system faulty – diesel models (Chapter 5A)
- [ ] Fuel injection system fault (Chapter 4A or 4B)
- [ ] Wrong grade of engine oil used (*Weekly checks*, Chapter 1A or 1B)
- [ ] Low cylinder compression (Chapter 2A, 2B or 2C)

Engine difficult to start when hot

- [ ] Air filter element dirty or clogged (Chapter 1A or 1B)
- [ ] Fuel injection system fault (Chapter 4A or 4B)
- [ ] Low cylinder compression (Chapter 2A, 2B or 2C)

Starter motor noisy or excessively-rough in engagement

- [ ] Starter pinion or flywheel ring gear teeth loose or broken (Chapter 2A, 2B, 2C or 5A)
- [ ] Starter motor mounting bolts loose or missing (Chapter 5A)
- [ ] Starter motor internal components worn or damaged (Chapter 5A)

Engine starts, but stops immediately

- [ ] Loose or faulty electrical connections in the ignition circuit – petrol models (Chapter 1A or 5B)
- [ ] Vacuum leak at the throttle body or intake manifold – petrol models (Chapter 4A)
- [ ] Blocked injectors/fuel injection system fault (Chapter 4A or 4B)
- [ ] Air in fuel, possibly due to loose fuel line connection – diesel models (Chapter 4B)

Engine idles erratically

- [ ] Air filter element clogged (Chapter 1A or 1B)
- [ ] Vacuum leak at the throttle body, intake manifold or associated hoses – petrol models (Chapter 4A)
- [ ] Worn, faulty or incorrectly-gapped spark plugs – petrol models (Chapter 1A)
- [ ] Uneven or low cylinder compression (Chapter 2A, 2B, 2C or 2D)
- [ ] Camshaft lobes worn (Chapter 2A, 2B or 2C)
- [ ] Blocked injectors/fuel injection system fault (Chapter 4A or 4B)
- [ ] Air in fuel, possibly due to loose fuel line connection – diesel models (Chapter 4B)

Engine (continued)

Engine misfires at idle speed

- [ ] Worn, faulty or incorrectly-gapped spark plugs – petrol models (Chapter 1A)
- [ ] Vacuum leak at the throttle body, intake manifold or associated hoses – petrol models (Chapter 4A)
- [ ] Blocked injectors/fuel injection system fault (Chapter 4A or 4B)
- [ ] Faulty injector(s) – diesel models (Chapter 4B)
- [ ] Uneven or low cylinder compression (Chapter 2A, 2B or 2C)
- [ ] Disconnected, leaking, or perished crankcase ventilation hoses (Chapter 4C)

Engine misfires throughout the driving speed range

- [ ] Fuel filter choked (Chapter 1A or 1B)
- [ ] Fuel pump faulty, or delivery pressure low – (Chapter 4A or 4B)
- [ ] Fuel tank vent blocked, or fuel pipes restricted (Chapter 4A or 4B)
- [ ] Vacuum leak at the throttle body, intake manifold or associated hoses – petrol models (Chapter 4A)
- [ ] Worn, faulty or incorrectly-gapped spark plugs – petrol models (Chapter 1A)
- [ ] Faulty injector(s) – diesel models (Chapter 4B)
- [ ] Faulty ignition coils – petrol models (Chapter 5B)
- [ ] Uneven or low cylinder compression (Chapter 2A, 2B or 2C)
- [ ] Blocked injector/fuel injection system fault (Chapter 4A or 4B)
- [ ] Blocked catalytic converter (Chapter 4C)
- [ ] Engine overheating – petrol models (Chapter 3)
- [ ] Fuel tank level low

Engine hesitates on acceleration

- [ ] Worn, faulty or incorrectly-gapped spark plugs – petrol models (Chapter 1A)
- [ ] Vacuum leak at the throttle body, intake manifold or associated hoses – petrol models (Chapter 4A)
- [ ] Blocked injectors/fuel injection system fault (Chapter 4A or 4B)
- [ ] Faulty injector(s) – diesel models (Chapter 4B)
- [ ] Faulty clutch pedal switch (Chapter 6)

Engine stalls

- [ ] Vacuum leak at the throttle body, intake manifold or associated hoses – petrol models (Chapter 4A)
- [ ] Fuel filter choked (Chapter 1A or 1B)
- [ ] Fuel pump faulty, or delivery pressure low (Chapter 4A or 4B)
- [ ] Fuel tank vent blocked, or fuel pipes restricted (Chapter 4A or 4B)
- [ ] Blocked injectors/fuel injection system fault (Chapter 4A or 4B)
- [ ] Faulty injector(s) – diesel models (Chapter 4B)

Engine lacks power

- [ ] Air filter element blocked (Chapter 1A or 1B)
- [ ] Fuel filter choked (Chapter 1A or 1B)
- [ ] Fuel pipes blocked or restricted (Chapter 4A or 4B)
- [ ] Worn, faulty or incorrectly-gapped spark plugs – petrol models (Chapter 1A)
- [ ] Engine overheating – petrol models (Chapter 4A)
- [ ] Fuel tank level low – diesel models (Chapter 4B)
- [ ] Accelerator position sensor faulty (Chapter 4A or 4B)
- [ ] Vacuum leak at the throttle body, intake manifold or associated hoses – petrol models (Chapter 4A)
- [ ] Blocked injectors/fuel injection system fault (Chapter 4A or 4B)
- [ ] Faulty injector(s) – diesel models (Chapter 4B)
- [ ] Fuel pump faulty, or delivery pressure low – petrol models (Chapter 4A)
- [ ] Uneven or low cylinder compression (Chapter 2A, 2B or 2C)
- [ ] Blocked catalytic converter (Chapter 4C)

- [ ] Brakes binding (Chapter 1A, 1B or 9)
- [ ] Clutch slipping (Chapter 6)

Engine backfires

- [ ] Vacuum leak at the throttle body, intake manifold or associated hoses – petrol models (Chapter 4A)
- [ ] Blocked injectors/fuel injection system fault (Chapter 4A or 4B)
- [ ] Blocked catalytic converter (Chapter 4C)
- [ ] Ignition coil unit faulty – petrol models (Chapter 5B)

Oil pressure warning light illuminated with engine running

- [ ] Low oil level, or incorrect oil grade (see Weekly checks)
- [ ] Faulty oil pressure sensor, or wiring damaged (Chapter 12)
- [ ] Worn engine bearings and/or oil pump (Chapter 2A, 2B or 2C)
- [ ] High engine operating temperature (Chapter 3)
- [ ] Oil pump pressure relief valve defective (Chapter 2A, 2B or 2C)
- [ ] Oil pump pick-up strainer clogged (Chapter 2A, 2B or 2C)

Engine runs-on after switching off

- [ ] Excessive carbon build-up in engine (Chapter 2A, 2B or 2C)
- [ ] High engine operating temperature (Chapter 3)
- [ ] Fuel injection system fault (Chapter 4A or 4B)

Engine noises

Pre-ignition (pinking) or knocking during acceleration or under load

- [ ] Ignition timing incorrect/ignition system fault – petrol models (Chapter 1A or 5B)
- [ ] Incorrect grade of spark plug – petrol models (Chapter 1A)
- [ ] Incorrect grade of fuel
- [ ] Knock sensor faulty – petrol models (Chapter 4A)
- [ ] Vacuum leak at the throttle body, intake manifold or associated hoses – petrol models (Chapter 4A)
- [ ] Excessive carbon build-up in engine (Chapter 2A, 2B or 2C)
- [ ] Blocked injector/fuel injection system fault (Chapter 4A or 4B)
- [ ] Faulty injector(s) – diesel models (Chapter 4B)

Whistling or wheezing noises

- [ ] Leaking intake manifold or throttle body gasket – petrol models (Chapter 4A)
- [ ] Leaking exhaust manifold gasket or pipe-to-manifold joint (Chapter 4A or 4B)
- [ ] Leaking vacuum hose (Chapter 4A, 4B, 5B or 9)
- [ ] Blowing cylinder head gasket (Chapter 2A, 2B or 2C)
- [ ] Partially blocked or leaking crankcase ventilation system (Chapter 4C)

Tapping or rattling noises

- [ ] Worn valve gear or camshaft (Chapter 2A, 2B or 2C)
- [ ] Ancillary component fault (coolant pump, alternator, etc) (Chapter 3, 5A, etc)

Knocking or thumping noises

- [ ] Worn big-end bearings (regular heavy knocking, perhaps less under load) (Chapter 2D)
- [ ] Worn main bearings (rumbling and knocking, perhaps worsening under load) (Chapter 2D)
- [ ] Piston slap – most noticeable when cold, caused by piston/bore wear (Chapter 2D)
- [ ] Ancillary component fault (coolant pump, alternator, etc) (Chapter 3, 5A, etc)
- [ ] Engine mountings worn or defective (Chapter 2A, 2B or 2C)
- [ ] Front suspension or steering components worn (Chapter 10)

Cooling system

Overheating

- ☐ Insufficient coolant in system (see *Weekly checks*)
- ☐ Thermostat faulty (Chapter 3)
- ☐ Radiator core blocked, or grille restricted (Chapter 3)
- ☐ Cooling fan faulty (Chapter 3)
- ☐ Inaccurate coolant temperature sender (Chapter 3)
- ☐ Airlock in cooling system (Chapter 3)
- ☐ Expansion tank pressure cap faulty (Chapter 3)
- ☐ Engine management system fault (Chapter 4A or 4B)

Overcooling

- ☐ Thermostat faulty (Chapter 3)
- ☐ Inaccurate coolant temperature sender (Chapter 3)
- ☐ Cooling fan faulty (Chapter 3)
- ☐ Engine management system fault (Chapter 4A or 4B)

External coolant leakage

- ☐ Deteriorated or damaged hoses or hose clips (Chapter 1A or 1B)
- ☐ Radiator core or heater matrix leaking (Chapter 3)
- ☐ Expansion tank pressure cap faulty (Chapter 1A or 1B)
- ☐ Coolant pump internal seal leaking (Chapter 3)
- ☐ Coolant pump gasket leaking (Chapter 3)
- ☐ Boiling due to overheating (Chapter 3)
- ☐ Cylinder block core plug leaking (Chapter 2D)

Internal coolant leakage

- ☐ Leaking cylinder head gasket (Chapter 2A, 2B or 2C)
- ☐ Cracked cylinder head or cylinder block (Chapter 2D)

Corrosion

- ☐ Infrequent draining and flushing (Chapter 1A or 1B)
- ☐ Incorrect coolant mixture or inappropriate coolant type (see *Weekly checks*)

Fuel and exhaust systems

Excessive fuel consumption

- ☐ Air filter element dirty or clogged (Chapter 1A or 1B)
- ☐ Fuel injection system fault (Chapter 4A or 4B)
- ☐ Engine management system fault (Chapter 4A or 4B)
- ☐ Crankcase ventilation system blocked (Chapter 4C)
- ☐ Tyres under-inflated (see *Weekly checks*)
- ☐ Brakes binding (Chapter 1A, 1B or 9)
- ☐ Fuel leak, causing apparent high consumption (Chapter 1A, 1B, 4A or 4B)

Fuel leakage and/or fuel odour

- ☐ Damaged or corroded fuel tank, pipes or connections (Chapter 4A or 4B)
- ☐ Evaporative emissions system fault – petrol models (Chapter 4C)

Excessive noise or fumes from exhaust system

- ☐ Leaking exhaust system or manifold joints (Chapter 1A, 1B, 4A or 4B)
- ☐ Leaking, corroded or damaged silencers or pipe (Chapter 1A, 1B, 4A or 4B)
- ☐ Broken mountings causing body or suspension contact (Chapter 1A or 1B)

Clutch

Pedal travels to floor – no pressure or very little resistance

- [ ] Air in hydraulic system/faulty master or slave cylinder (Chapter 6)
- [ ] Faulty hydraulic release system (Chapter 6)
- [ ] Clutch pedal return spring detached or broken (Chapter 6)
- [ ] Broken clutch release bearing or fork (Chapter 6)
- [ ] Broken diaphragm spring in clutch pressure plate (Chapter 6)

Clutch fails to disengage (unable to select gears)

- [ ] Air in hydraulic system/faulty master or slave cylinder (Chapter 6)
- [ ] Faulty hydraulic release system (Chapter 6)
- [ ] Clutch disc sticking on transmission input shaft splines (Chapter 6)
- [ ] Clutch disc sticking to flywheel or pressure plate (Chapter 6)
- [ ] Faulty pressure plate assembly (Chapter 6)
- [ ] Clutch release mechanism worn or incorrectly assembled (Chapter 6)

Clutch slips (engine speed increases, with no increase in vehicle speed)

- [ ] Faulty hydraulic release system (Chapter 6)

- [ ] Clutch disc linings excessively worn (Chapter 6)
- [ ] Clutch disc linings contaminated with oil or grease (Chapter 6)
- [ ] Faulty pressure plate or weak diaphragm spring (Chapter 6)

Judder as clutch is engaged

- [ ] Clutch disc linings contaminated with oil or grease (Chapter 6)
- [ ] Clutch disc linings excessively worn (Chapter 6)
- [ ] Faulty or distorted pressure plate or diaphragm spring (Chapter 6).
- [ ] Worn or loose engine or transmission mountings (Chapter 2A, 2B or 2C)
- [ ] Clutch disc hub or transmission input shaft splines worn (Chapter 6)

Noise when depressing or releasing clutch pedal

- [ ] Worn clutch release bearing (Chapter 6)
- [ ] Worn or dry clutch pedal bushes (Chapter 6)
- [ ] Worn or dry clutch master cylinder piston (Chapter 6)
- [ ] Faulty pressure plate assembly (Chapter 6)
- [ ] Pressure plate diaphragm spring broken (Chapter 6)
- [ ] Broken clutch disc cushioning springs (Chapter 6)

Manual transmission

Noisy in neutral with engine running

- [ ] Lack of oil (Chapter 7A)
- [ ] Input shaft bearings worn (noise apparent with clutch pedal released, but not when depressed) (Chapter 7A)*
- [ ] Clutch release bearing worn (noise apparent with clutch pedal depressed, possibly less when released) (Chapter 6)

Noisy in one particular gear

- [ ] Worn, damaged or chipped gear teeth (Chapter 7A)*

Difficulty engaging gears

- [ ] Clutch fault (Chapter 6)
- [ ] Worn or damaged gearchange cables (Chapter 7A)
- [ ] Lack of oil (Chapter 7A)
- [ ] Worn synchroniser units (Chapter 7A)*

Jumps out of gear

- [ ] Worn or damaged gearchange cables (Chapter 7A)
- [ ] Worn synchroniser units (Chapter 7A)*
- [ ] Worn selector forks (Chapter 7A)*

Vibration

- [ ] Lack of oil (Chapter 7A)
- [ ] Worn bearings (Chapter 7A)*

Lubricant leaks

- [ ] Leaking driveshaft or selector shaft oil seal (Chapter 7A)
- [ ] Leaking housing joint (Chapter 7A)*
- [ ] Leaking input shaft oil seal (Chapter 7A)*

Although the corrective action necessary to remedy the symptoms described is beyond the scope of the home mechanic, the above information should be helpful in isolating the cause of the condition, so that the owner can communicate clearly with a professional mechanic.

Automatic transmission

Fluid leakage

☐ Automatic transmission fluid is usually brown in colour. Fluid leaks should not be confused with engine oil, which can easily be blown onto the transmission by airflow.

☐ To determine the source of a leak, first remove all built-up dirt and grime from the transmission housing and surrounding areas using a degreasing agent, or by steam-cleaning. Drive the vehicle at low speed, so airflow will not blow the leak far from its source. Raise and support the vehicle, and determine where the leak is coming from. The following are common areas of leakage:
a) *Fluid pan.*
b) *Drain or filler plugs.*
c) *Transmission-to-fluid cooler unions (Chapter 7B).*

Transmission fluid has burned smell

☐ Transmission fluid level low (Chapter 7B)

General gear selection problems

☐ Chapter 7B deals with checking the selector cable on automatic transmissions. The following are common problems which may be caused by a faulty cable or sensor:
a) *Engine starting in gears other than Park or Neutral.*
b) *Indicator panel indicating a gear other than the one actually being used.*
c) *Vehicle moves when in Park or Neutral.*
d) *Poor gear shift quality or erratic gear changes.*

Transmission will not downshift (kickdown) with accelerator pedal fully depressed

☐ Low transmission fluid level (Chapter 7B)
☐ Engine management system fault (Chapter 4A)
☐ Faulty transmission sensor or wiring (Chapter 7B)
☐ Faulty selector cable (Chapter 7B)

Engine will not start in any gear, or starts in gears other than Park or Neutral

☐ Faulty transmission sensor or wiring (Chapter 7B)
☐ Engine management system fault (Chapter 4A)
☐ Faulty selector cable (Chapter 7B)

Transmission slips, shifts roughly, is noisy, or has no drive in forward or reverse gears

☐ Transmission fluid level low (Chapter 7B)
☐ Faulty transmission sensor or wiring (Chapter 7B)
☐ Engine management system fault (Chapter 4A)

Note: *There are many probable causes for the above problems, but diagnosing and correcting them is considered beyond the scope of this manual. Having checked the fluid level and all the wiring as far as possible, a dealer or transmission specialist should be consulted if the problem persists.*

Differential and propshaft

Vibration when accelerating or decelerating

☐ Worn universal joint (Chapter 8)
☐ Bent or distorted propeller shaft (Chapter 8)

Low-pitched whining; increasing with roadspeed

☐ Worn differential (Chapter 8)

Braking system

Note: *Before assuming that a brake problem exists, make sure that the tyres are in good condition and correctly inflated, that the front wheel alignment is correct, and that the vehicle is not loaded with weight in an unequal manner. Apart from checking the condition of all pipe and hose connections, any faults occurring on the anti-lock braking system should be referred to a BMW dealer or specialist for diagnosis.*

Vehicle pulls to one side under braking

☐ Worn, defective, damaged or contaminated brake pads on one side (Chapter 1A, 1B or 9)
☐ Seized or partially-seized brake caliper piston (Chapter 1A, 1B or 9)
☐ A mixture of brake pad lining materials fitted between sides (Chapter 1A, 1B or 9)
☐ Brake caliper mounting bolts loose (Chapter 9)
☐ Worn or damaged steering or suspension components (Chapter 1A, 1B or 10)

Noise (grinding or high-pitched squeal) when brakes applied

☐ Brake pad friction lining material worn down to metal backing (Chapter 1A, 1B or 9)
☐ Excessive corrosion of brake disc (may be apparent after the vehicle has been standing for some time) (Chapter 1A, 1B or 9)
☐ Foreign object (stone chipping, etc) trapped between brake disc and shield (Chapter 1A, 1B or 9)

Excessive brake pedal travel

☐ Faulty master cylinder (Chapter 9)
☐ Air in hydraulic system (Chapter 1A, 1B, 6 or 9)
☐ Faulty vacuum servo unit (Chapter 9)

Brake pedal feels spongy when depressed

☐ Air in hydraulic system (Chapter 1A, 1B, 6 or 9)
☐ Deteriorated flexible rubber brake hoses (Chapter 1A, 1B or 9)
☐ Master cylinder mounting nuts loose (Chapter 9)
☐ Faulty master cylinder (Chapter 9)

Excessive brake pedal effort required to stop vehicle

☐ Faulty vacuum servo unit (Chapter 9)
☐ Faulty vacuum pump – diesel models (Chapter 9)
☐ Disconnected, damaged or insecure brake servo vacuum hose (Chapter 9)
☐ Primary or secondary hydraulic circuit failure (Chapter 9)
☐ Seized brake caliper piston (Chapter 9)
☐ Brake pads incorrectly fitted (Chapter 9)
☐ Incorrect grade of brake pads fitted (Chapter 9)
☐ Brake pad linings contaminated (Chapter 1A, 1B or 9)

Judder felt through brake pedal or steering wheel when braking

Note: *On models equipped with ABS, vibration may be felt through the brake pedal under heavy braking. This is a normal feature of ABS operation, and does not constitute a fault.*

☐ Excessive run-out or distortion of discs (Chapter 1A, 1B or 9)
☐ Brake pad linings worn (Chapter 1A, 1B or 9)
☐ Brake caliper mounting bolts loose (Chapter 9)
☐ Wear in suspension or steering components or mountings (Chapter 1A, 1B or 10)
☐ Front wheels out of balance (see *Weekly checks*)

Brakes binding

☐ Seized brake caliper piston (Chapter 9)
☐ Incorrectly-adjusted handbrake mechanism (Chapter 9)
☐ Faulty master cylinder (Chapter 9)

Rear wheels locking under normal braking

☐ Rear brake pad linings contaminated or damaged (Chapter 1A, 1B or 9)
☐ Rear brake discs warped (Chapter 1A, 1B or 9)

Suspension and steering

Note: *Before diagnosing suspension or steering faults, be sure that the trouble is not due to incorrect tyre pressures, mixtures of tyre types, or binding brakes.*

Vehicle pulls to one side

- ☐ Defective tyre (see *Weekly checks*)
- ☐ Excessive wear in suspension or steering components (Chapter 1A, 1B or 10)
- ☐ Incorrect front wheel alignment (Chapter 10)
- ☐ Accident damage to steering or suspension components (Chapter 1A or 1B)

Wheel wobble and vibration

- ☐ Front wheels out of balance (vibration felt mainly through the steering wheel) (see *Weekly checks*)
- ☐ Rear wheels out of balance (vibration felt throughout the vehicle) (see *Weekly checks*)
- ☐ Roadwheels damaged or distorted (see *Weekly checks*)
- ☐ Faulty or damaged tyre (see *Weekly checks*)
- ☐ Worn steering or suspension joints, bushes or components (Chapter 1A, 1B or 10)
- ☐ Wheel bolts loose (Chapter 1A or 1B)

Excessive pitching and/or rolling around corners, or during braking

- ☐ Defective shock absorbers (Chapter 1A, 1B or 10)
- ☐ Broken or weak spring and/or suspension component (Chapter 1A, 1B or 10)
- ☐ Worn or damaged anti-roll bar or mountings (Chapter 1A, 1B or 10)

Wandering or general instability

- ☐ Incorrect front wheel alignment (Chapter 10)
- ☐ Worn steering or suspension joints, bushes or components (Chapter 1A, 1B or 10)
- ☐ Roadwheels out of balance (see *Weekly checks*)
- ☐ Faulty or damaged tyre (see *Weekly checks*)
- ☐ Wheel bolts loose
- ☐ Defective shock absorbers (Chapter 1A, 1B or 10)

Excessively-stiff steering

- ☐ Seized steering linkage balljoint or suspension balljoint (Chapter 1A, 1B or 10)

- ☐ Broken or incorrectly-adjusted auxiliary drivebelt (Chapter 1A or 1B)
- ☐ Incorrect front wheel alignment (Chapter 10)
- ☐ Steering rack damaged (Chapter 10)

Excessive play in steering

- ☐ Worn steering column/intermediate shaft joints (Chapter 10)
- ☐ Worn track rod balljoints (Chapter 1A, 1B or 10)
- ☐ Worn steering rack (Chapter 10)
- ☐ Worn steering or suspension joints, bushes or components (Chapter 1A, 1B or 10)

Lack of power assistance

- ☐ Broken or incorrectly-adjusted auxiliary drivebelt (Chapter 1A or 1B)
- ☐ Incorrect power steering fluid level (see *Weekly checks*)
- ☐ Restriction in power steering fluid hoses (Chapter 1A or 1B)
- ☐ Faulty power steering pump (Chapter 10)
- ☐ Faulty steering rack (Chapter 10)

Tyre wear excessive

Tyres worn on inside or outside edges

- ☐ Tyres under-inflated (wear on both edges) (see *Weekly checks*)
- ☐ Incorrect camber or castor angles (wear on one edge only) (Chapter 10)
- ☐ Worn steering or suspension joints, bushes or components (Chapter 1A, 1B or 10)
- ☐ Excessively-hard cornering or braking
- ☐ Accident damage

Tyre treads exhibit feathered edges

- ☐ Incorrect toe-setting (Chapter 10)

Tyres worn in centre of tread

- ☐ Tyres over-inflated (see *Weekly checks*)

Tyres worn on inside and outside edges

- ☐ Tyres under-inflated (see *Weekly checks*)

Tyres worn unevenly

- ☐ Tyres/wheels out of balance (see *Weekly checks*)
- ☐ Excessive wheel or tyre run-out
- ☐ Worn shock absorbers (Chapter 1A, 1B or 10)
- ☐ Faulty tyre (see *Weekly checks*)

Electrical system

Note: *For problems associated with the starting system, refer to the faults listed under 'Engine' earlier in this Section.*

Battery will not hold a charge for more than a few days

- ☐ Battery defective internally (Chapter 5A)
- ☐ Battery terminal connections loose or corroded (see *Weekly checks*)
- ☐ Auxiliary drivebelt worn or incorrectly adjusted (Chapter 1A or 1B)
- ☐ Alternator not charging at correct output (Chapter 5A)
- ☐ Alternator or voltage regulator faulty (Chapter 5A)
- ☐ Short-circuit causing continual battery drain (Chapter 5A or 12)

Ignition/no-charge warning light remains illuminated with engine running

- ☐ Auxiliary drivebelt broken, worn, or incorrectly adjusted (Chapter 1A or 1B)
- ☐ Internal fault in alternator or voltage regulator (Chapter 5A)
- ☐ Broken, disconnected, or loose wiring in charging circuit (Chapter 5A or 12)

Ignition/no-charge warning light fails to come on

- ☐ Broken, disconnected, or loose wiring in warning light circuit (Chapter 5A or 12)
- ☐ Alternator faulty (Chapter 5A)

Lights inoperative

- ☐ Bulb blown (Chapter 12)
- ☐ Corrosion of bulb or bulbholder contacts (Chapter 12)
- ☐ Blown fuse (Chapter 12)
- ☐ Faulty relay (Chapter 12)
- ☐ Broken, loose, or disconnected wiring (Chapter 12)
- ☐ Faulty switch (Chapter 12)

Instrument readings inaccurate or erratic

Fuel or temperature gauges give no reading

- ☐ Faulty gauge sender unit (Chapter 3, 4A or 4B)
- ☐ Wiring open-circuit (Chapter 12)
- ☐ Faulty instrument cluster (Chapter 12)

Fuel or temperature gauges give continuous maximum reading

- ☐ Faulty gauge sender unit (Chapter 3, 4A or 4B)
- ☐ Wiring short-circuit (Chapter 12)
- ☐ Faulty instrument cluster (Chapter 12)

Horn inoperative, or unsatisfactory in operation

Horn operates all the time

- ☐ Horn push either earthed or stuck down (Chapter 12)
- ☐ Horn cable-to-horn push earthed (Chapter 12)

Horn fails to operate

- ☐ Blown fuse (Chapter 12)
- ☐ Cable or connections loose, broken or disconnected (Chapter 12)
- ☐ Faulty horn (Chapter 12)

Horn emits intermittent or unsatisfactory sound

- ☐ Cable connections loose (Chapter 12)
- ☐ Horn mountings loose (Chapter 12)
- ☐ Faulty horn (Chapter 12)

Electrical system (continued)

Windscreen wipers inoperative, or unsatisfactory in operation

Wipers fail to operate, or operate very slowly

- ☐ Wiper blades stuck to screen, or linkage seized or binding (Chapter 12)
- ☐ Blown fuse (Chapter 12)
- ☐ Battery discharged (Chapter 5A)
- ☐ Cable or connections loose, broken or disconnected (Chapter 12)
- ☐ Faulty wiper motor (Chapter 12)

Wiper blades sweep over too large or too small an area of the glass

- ☐ Wiper blades incorrectly fitted, or wrong size used (see *Weekly checks*)
- ☐ Wiper arms incorrectly positioned on spindles (Chapter 12)
- ☐ Excessive wear of wiper linkage (Chapter 12)
- ☐ Wiper motor or linkage mountings loose or insecure (Chapter 12)

Wiper blades fail to clean the glass effectively

- ☐ Wiper blade rubbers dirty, worn or perished (see *Weekly checks*)
- ☐ Wiper blades incorrectly fitted, or wrong size used (see *Weekly checks*)
- ☐ Wiper arm tension springs broken, or arm pivots seized (Chapter 12)
- ☐ Insufficient windscreen washer additive to adequately remove road film (see *Weekly checks*)

Windscreen washers inoperative, or unsatisfactory in operation

One or more washer jets inoperative

- ☐ Blocked washer jet
- ☐ Disconnected, kinked or restricted fluid hose (Chapter 12)
- ☐ Insufficient fluid in washer reservoir (see *Weekly checks*)

Washer pump fails to operate

- ☐ Broken or disconnected wiring or connections (Chapter 12)
- ☐ Blown fuse (Chapter 12)
- ☐ Faulty washer switch (Chapter 12)
- ☐ Faulty washer pump (Chapter 12)

Washer pump runs for some time before fluid is emitted from jets

- ☐ Faulty one-way valve in fluid supply hose (Chapter 12)

Electric windows inoperative, or unsatisfactory in operation

Window glass will only move in one direction

- ☐ Faulty switch (Chapter 12)

Window glass slow to move

- ☐ Battery discharged (Chapter 5A)
- ☐ Regulator seized or damaged, or in need of lubrication (Chapter 11)
- ☐ Door internal components or trim fouling regulator (Chapter 11)
- ☐ Faulty motor (Chapter 11)

Window glass fails to move

- ☐ Blown fuse (Chapter 12)
- ☐ Faulty relay (Chapter 12)
- ☐ Broken or disconnected wiring or connections (Chapter 12)
- ☐ Faulty motor (Chapter 11)
- ☐ Faulty control module (Chapter 11)

Central locking system inoperative, or unsatisfactory in operation

Complete system failure

- ☐ Remote handset battery discharged, where applicable
- ☐ Blown fuse (Chapter 12)
- ☐ Defective control module (Chapter 12)
- ☐ Broken or disconnected wiring or connections (Chapter 12)
- ☐ Faulty motor (Chapter 11)

Latch locks but will not unlock, or unlocks but will not lock

- ☐ Remote handset battery discharged, where applicable
- ☐ Faulty master switch (Chapter 12)
- ☐ Broken or disconnected latch operating rods or levers (Chapter 11)
- ☐ Faulty control module (Chapter 12)
- ☐ Faulty motor (Chapter 11)

One solenoid/motor fails to operate

- ☐ Broken or disconnected wiring or connections (Chapter 12)
- ☐ Faulty operating assembly (Chapter 11)
- ☐ Broken, binding or disconnected latch operating rods or levers (Chapter 11)
- ☐ Fault in door latch (Chapter 11)

A

ABS (Anti-lock brake system) A system, usually electronically controlled, that senses incipient wheel lockup during braking and relieves hydraulic pressure at wheels that are about to skid.

Air bag An inflatable bag hidden in the steering wheel (driver's side) or the dash or glovebox (passenger side). In a head-on collision, the bags inflate, preventing the driver and front passenger from being thrown forward into the steering wheel or windscreen.

Air cleaner A metal or plastic housing, containing a filter element, which removes dust and dirt from the air being drawn into the engine.

Air filter element The actual filter in an air cleaner system, usually manufactured from pleated paper and requiring renewal at regular intervals.

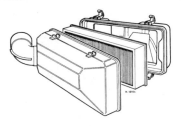

Air filter

Allen key A hexagonal wrench which fits into a recessed hexagonal hole.

Alligator clip A long-nosed spring-loaded metal clip with meshing teeth. Used to make temporary electrical connections.

Alternator A component in the electrical system which converts mechanical energy from a drivebelt into electrical energy to charge the battery and to operate the starting system, ignition system and electrical accessories.

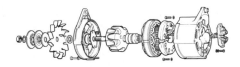

Alternator (exploded view)

Ampere (amp) A unit of measurement for the flow of electric current. One amp is the amount of current produced by one volt acting through a resistance of one ohm.

Anaerobic sealer A substance used to prevent bolts and screws from loosening. Anaerobic means that it does not require oxygen for activation. The Loctite brand is widely used.

Antifreeze A substance (usually ethylene glycol) mixed with water, and added to a vehicle's cooling system, to prevent freezing of the coolant in winter. Antifreeze also contains chemicals to inhibit corrosion and the formation of rust and other deposits that would tend to clog the radiator and coolant passages and reduce cooling efficiency.

Anti-seize compound A coating that reduces the risk of seizing on fasteners that are subjected to high temperatures, such as exhaust manifold bolts and nuts.

Anti-seize compound

Asbestos A natural fibrous mineral with great heat resistance, commonly used in the composition of brake friction materials. Asbestos is a health hazard and the dust created by brake systems should never be inhaled or ingested.

Axle A shaft on which a wheel revolves, or which revolves with a wheel. Also, a solid beam that connects the two wheels at one end of the vehicle. An axle which also transmits power to the wheels is known as a live axle.

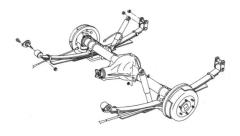

Axle assembly

Axleshaft A single rotating shaft, on either side of the differential, which delivers power from the final drive assembly to the drive wheels. Also called a driveshaft or a halfshaft.

B

Ball bearing An anti-friction bearing consisting of a hardened inner and outer race with hardened steel balls between two races.

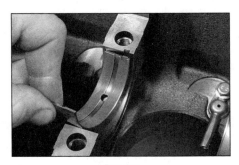

Bearing

Bearing The curved surface on a shaft or in a bore, or the part assembled into either, that permits relative motion between them with minimum wear and friction.

Big-end bearing The bearing in the end of the connecting rod that's attached to the crankshaft.

Bleed nipple A valve on a brake wheel cylinder, caliper or other hydraulic component that is opened to purge the hydraulic system of air. Also called a bleed screw.

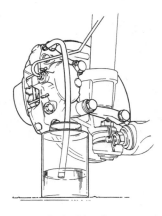

Brake bleeding

Brake bleeding Procedure for removing air from lines of a hydraulic brake system.

Brake disc The component of a disc brake that rotates with the wheels.

Brake drum The component of a drum brake that rotates with the wheels.

Brake linings The friction material which contacts the brake disc or drum to retard the vehicle's speed. The linings are bonded or riveted to the brake pads or shoes.

Brake pads The replaceable friction pads that pinch the brake disc when the brakes are applied. Brake pads consist of a friction material bonded or riveted to a rigid backing plate.

Brake shoe The crescent-shaped carrier to which the brake linings are mounted and which forces the lining against the rotating drum during braking.

Braking systems For more information on braking systems, consult the *Haynes Automotive Brake Manual*.

Breaker bar A long socket wrench handle providing greater leverage.

Bulkhead The insulated partition between the engine and the passenger compartment.

C

Caliper The non-rotating part of a disc-brake assembly that straddles the disc and carries the brake pads. The caliper also contains the hydraulic components that cause the pads to pinch the disc when the brakes are applied. A caliper is also a measuring tool that can be set to measure inside or outside dimensions of an object.

Camshaft A rotating shaft on which a series of cam lobes operate the valve mechanisms. The camshaft may be driven by gears, by sprockets and chain or by sprockets and a belt.

Canister A container in an evaporative emission control system; contains activated charcoal granules to trap vapours from the fuel system.

Canister

Carburettor A device which mixes fuel with air in the proper proportions to provide a desired power output from a spark ignition internal combustion engine.

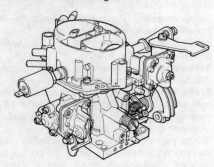

Carburettor

Castellated Resembling the parapets along the top of a castle wall. For example, a castellated balljoint stud nut.

Castellated nut

Castor In wheel alignment, the backward or forward tilt of the steering axis. Castor is positive when the steering axis is inclined rearward at the top.

Catalytic converter A silencer-like device in the exhaust system which converts certain pollutants in the exhaust gases into less harmful substances.

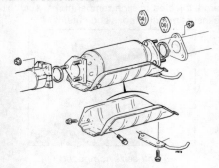

Catalytic converter

Circlip A ring-shaped clip used to prevent endwise movement of cylindrical parts and shafts. An internal circlip is installed in a groove in a housing; an external circlip fits into a groove on the outside of a cylindrical piece such as a shaft.

Clearance The amount of space between two parts. For example, between a piston and a cylinder, between a bearing and a journal, etc.

Coil spring A spiral of elastic steel found in various sizes throughout a vehicle, for example as a springing medium in the suspension and in the valve train.

Compression Reduction in volume, and increase in pressure and temperature, of a gas, caused by squeezing it into a smaller space.

Compression ratio The relationship between cylinder volume when the piston is at top dead centre and cylinder volume when the piston is at bottom dead centre.

Constant velocity (CV) joint A type of universal joint that cancels out vibrations caused by driving power being transmitted through an angle.

Core plug A disc or cup-shaped metal device inserted in a hole in a casting through which core was removed when the casting was formed. Also known as a freeze plug or expansion plug.

Crankcase The lower part of the engine block in which the crankshaft rotates.

Crankshaft The main rotating member, or shaft, running the length of the crankcase, with offset "throws" to which the connecting rods are attached.

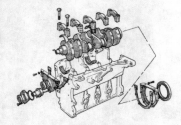

Crankshaft assembly

Crocodile clip See Alligator clip

D

Diagnostic code Code numbers obtained by accessing the diagnostic mode of an engine management computer. This code can be used to determine the area in the system where a malfunction may be located.

Disc brake A brake design incorporating a rotating disc onto which brake pads are squeezed. The resulting friction converts the energy of a moving vehicle into heat.

Double-overhead cam (DOHC) An engine that uses two overhead camshafts, usually one for the intake valves and one for the exhaust valves.

Drivebelt(s) The belt(s) used to drive accessories such as the alternator, water pump, power steering pump, air conditioning compressor, etc. off the crankshaft pulley.

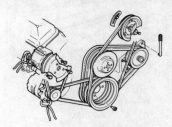

Accessory drivebelts

Driveshaft Any shaft used to transmit motion. Commonly used when referring to the axleshafts on a front wheel drive vehicle.

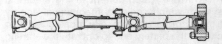

Driveshaft

Drum brake A type of brake using a drum-shaped metal cylinder attached to the inner surface of the wheel. When the brake pedal is pressed, curved brake shoes with friction linings press against the inside of the drum to slow or stop the vehicle.

Drum brake assembly

E

EGR valve A valve used to introduce exhaust gases into the intake air stream.

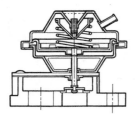

EGR valve

Electronic control unit (ECU) A computer which controls (for instance) ignition and fuel injection systems, or an anti-lock braking system. For more information refer to the *Haynes Automotive Electrical and Electronic Systems Manual*.

Electronic Fuel Injection (EFI) A computer controlled fuel system that distributes fuel through an injector located in each intake port of the engine.

Emergency brake A braking system, independent of the main hydraulic system, that can be used to slow or stop the vehicle if the primary brakes fail, or to hold the vehicle stationary even though the brake pedal isn't depressed. It usually consists of a hand lever that actuates either front or rear brakes mechanically through a series of cables and linkages. Also known as a handbrake or parking brake.

Endfloat The amount of lengthwise movement between two parts. As applied to a crankshaft, the distance that the crankshaft can move forward and back in the cylinder block.

Engine management system (EMS) A computer controlled system which manages the fuel injection and the ignition systems in an integrated fashion.

Exhaust manifold A part with several passages through which exhaust gases leave the engine combustion chambers and enter the exhaust pipe.

Exhaust manifold

F

Fan clutch A viscous (fluid) drive coupling device which permits variable engine fan speeds in relation to engine speeds.

Feeler blade A thin strip or blade of hardened steel, ground to an exact thickness, used to check or measure clearances between parts.

Feeler blade

Firing order The order in which the engine cylinders fire, or deliver their power strokes, beginning with the number one cylinder.

Flywheel A heavy spinning wheel in which energy is absorbed and stored by means of momentum. On cars, the flywheel is attached to the crankshaft to smooth out firing impulses.

Free play The amount of travel before any action takes place. The "looseness" in a linkage, or an assembly of parts, between the initial application of force and actual movement. For example, the distance the brake pedal moves before the pistons in the master cylinder are actuated.

Fuse An electrical device which protects a circuit against accidental overload. The typical fuse contains a soft piece of metal which is calibrated to melt at a predetermined current flow (expressed as amps) and break the circuit.

Fusible link A circuit protection device consisting of a conductor surrounded by heat-resistant insulation. The conductor is smaller than the wire it protects, so it acts as the weakest link in the circuit. Unlike a blown fuse, a failed fusible link must frequently be cut from the wire for replacement.

G

Gap The distance the spark must travel in jumping from the centre electrode to the side

Adjusting spark plug gap

electrode in a spark plug. Also refers to the spacing between the points in a contact breaker assembly in a conventional points-type ignition, or to the distance between the reluctor or rotor and the pickup coil in an electronic ignition.

Gasket Any thin, soft material - usually cork, cardboard, asbestos or soft metal - installed between two metal surfaces to ensure a good seal. For instance, the cylinder head gasket seals the joint between the block and the cylinder head.

Gasket

Gauge An instrument panel display used to monitor engine conditions. A gauge with a movable pointer on a dial or a fixed scale is an analogue gauge. A gauge with a numerical readout is called a digital gauge.

H

Halfshaft A rotating shaft that transmits power from the final drive unit to a drive wheel, usually when referring to a live rear axle.

Harmonic balancer A device designed to reduce torsion or twisting vibration in the crankshaft. May be incorporated in the crankshaft pulley. Also known as a vibration damper.

Hone An abrasive tool for correcting small irregularities or differences in diameter in an engine cylinder, brake cylinder, etc.

Hydraulic tappet A tappet that utilises hydraulic pressure from the engine's lubrication system to maintain zero clearance (constant contact with both camshaft and valve stem). Automatically adjusts to variation in valve stem length. Hydraulic tappets also reduce valve noise.

I

Ignition timing The moment at which the spark plug fires, usually expressed in the number of crankshaft degrees before the piston reaches the top of its stroke.

Inlet manifold A tube or housing with passages through which flows the air-fuel mixture (carburettor vehicles and vehicles with throttle body injection) or air only (port fuel-injected vehicles) to the port openings in the cylinder head.

J

Jump start Starting the engine of a vehicle with a discharged or weak battery by attaching jump leads from the weak battery to a charged or helper battery.

L

Load Sensing Proportioning Valve (LSPV) A brake hydraulic system control valve that works like a proportioning valve, but also takes into consideration the amount of weight carried by the rear axle.

Locknut A nut used to lock an adjustment nut, or other threaded component, in place. For example, a locknut is employed to keep the adjusting nut on the rocker arm in position.

Lockwasher A form of washer designed to prevent an attaching nut from working loose.

M

MacPherson strut A type of front suspension system devised by Earle MacPherson at Ford of England. In its original form, a simple lateral link with the anti-roll bar creates the lower control arm. A long strut - an integral coil spring and shock absorber - is mounted between the body and the steering knuckle. Many modern so-called MacPherson strut systems use a conventional lower A-arm and don't rely on the anti-roll bar for location.

Multimeter An electrical test instrument with the capability to measure voltage, current and resistance.

N

NOx Oxides of Nitrogen. A common toxic pollutant emitted by petrol and diesel engines at higher temperatures.

O

Ohm The unit of electrical resistance. One volt applied to a resistance of one ohm will produce a current of one amp.

Ohmmeter An instrument for measuring electrical resistance.

O-ring A type of sealing ring made of a special rubber-like material; in use, the O-ring is compressed into a groove to provide the sealing action.

O-ring

Overhead cam (ohc) engine An engine with the camshaft(s) located on top of the cylinder head(s).

Overhead valve (ohv) engine An engine with the valves located in the cylinder head, but with the camshaft located in the engine block.

Oxygen sensor A device installed in the engine exhaust manifold, which senses the oxygen content in the exhaust and converts this information into an electric current. Also called a Lambda sensor.

P

Phillips screw A type of screw head having a cross instead of a slot for a corresponding type of screwdriver.

Plastigage A thin strip of plastic thread, available in different sizes, used for measuring clearances. For example, a strip of Plastigage is laid across a bearing journal. The parts are assembled and dismantled; the width of the crushed strip indicates the clearance between journal and bearing.

Plastigage

Propeller shaft The long hollow tube with universal joints at both ends that carries power from the transmission to the differential on front-engined rear wheel drive vehicles.

Proportioning valve A hydraulic control valve which limits the amount of pressure to the rear brakes during panic stops to prevent wheel lock-up.

R

Rack-and-pinion steering A steering system with a pinion gear on the end of the steering shaft that mates with a rack (think of a geared wheel opened up and laid flat). When the steering wheel is turned, the pinion turns, moving the rack to the left or right. This movement is transmitted through the track rods to the steering arms at the wheels.

Radiator A liquid-to-air heat transfer device designed to reduce the temperature of the coolant in an internal combustion engine cooling system.

Refrigerant Any substance used as a heat transfer agent in an air-conditioning system. R-12 has been the principle refrigerant for many years; recently, however, manufacturers have begun using R-134a, a non-CFC substance that is considered less harmful to the ozone in the upper atmosphere.

Rocker arm A lever arm that rocks on a shaft or pivots on a stud. In an overhead valve engine, the rocker arm converts the upward movement of the pushrod into a downward movement to open a valve.

Rotor In a distributor, the rotating device inside the cap that connects the centre electrode and the outer terminals as it turns, distributing the high voltage from the coil secondary winding to the proper spark plug. Also, that part of an alternator which rotates inside the stator. Also, the rotating assembly of a turbocharger, including the compressor wheel, shaft and turbine wheel.

Runout The amount of wobble (in-and-out movement) of a gear or wheel as it's rotated. The amount a shaft rotates "out-of-true." The out-of-round condition of a rotating part.

S

Sealant A liquid or paste used to prevent leakage at a joint. Sometimes used in conjunction with a gasket.

Sealed beam lamp An older headlight design which integrates the reflector, lens and filaments into a hermetically-sealed one-piece unit. When a filament burns out or the lens cracks, the entire unit is simply replaced.

Serpentine drivebelt A single, long, wide accessory drivebelt that's used on some newer vehicles to drive all the accessories, instead of a series of smaller, shorter belts. Serpentine drivebelts are usually tensioned by an automatic tensioner.

Serpentine drivebelt

Shim Thin spacer, commonly used to adjust the clearance or relative positions between two parts. For example, shims inserted into or under bucket tappets control valve clearances. Clearance is adjusted by changing the thickness of the shim.

Slide hammer A special puller that screws into or hooks onto a component such as a shaft or bearing; a heavy sliding handle on the shaft bottoms against the end of the shaft to knock the component free.

Sprocket A tooth or projection on the periphery of a wheel, shaped to engage with a chain or drivebelt. Commonly used to refer to the sprocket wheel itself.

Starter inhibitor switch On vehicles with an automatic transmission, a switch that prevents starting if the vehicle is not in Neutral or Park.

Strut See MacPherson strut.

T

Tappet A cylindrical component which transmits motion from the cam to the valve stem, either directly or via a pushrod and rocker arm. Also called a cam follower.

Thermostat A heat-controlled valve that regulates the flow of coolant between the cylinder block and the radiator, so maintaining optimum engine operating temperature. A thermostat is also used in some air cleaners in which the temperature is regulated.

Thrust bearing The bearing in the clutch assembly that is moved in to the release levers by clutch pedal action to disengage the clutch. Also referred to as a release bearing.

Timing belt A toothed belt which drives the camshaft. Serious engine damage may result if it breaks in service.

Timing chain A chain which drives the camshaft.

Toe-in The amount the front wheels are closer together at the front than at the rear. On rear wheel drive vehicles, a slight amount of toe-in is usually specified to keep the front wheels running parallel on the road by offsetting other forces that tend to spread the wheels apart.

Toe-out The amount the front wheels are closer together at the rear than at the front. On front wheel drive vehicles, a slight amount of toe-out is usually specified.

Tools For full information on choosing and using tools, refer to the *Haynes Automotive Tools Manual.*

Tracer A stripe of a second colour applied to a wire insulator to distinguish that wire from another one with the same colour insulator.

Tune-up A process of accurate and careful adjustments and parts replacement to obtain the best possible engine performance.

Turbocharger A centrifugal device, driven by exhaust gases, that pressurises the intake air. Normally used to increase the power output from a given engine displacement, but can also be used primarily to reduce exhaust emissions (as on VW's "Umwelt" Diesel engine).

U

Universal joint or U-joint A double-pivoted connection for transmitting power from a driving to a driven shaft through an angle. A U-joint consists of two Y-shaped yokes and a cross-shaped member called the spider.

V

Valve A device through which the flow of liquid, gas, vacuum, or loose material in bulk may be started, stopped, or regulated by a movable part that opens, shuts, or partially obstructs one or more ports or passageways. A valve is also the movable part of such a device.

Valve clearance The clearance between the valve tip (the end of the valve stem) and the rocker arm or tappet. The valve clearance is measured when the valve is closed.

Vernier caliper A precision measuring instrument that measures inside and outside dimensions. Not quite as accurate as a micrometer, but more convenient.

Viscosity The thickness of a liquid or its resistance to flow.

Volt A unit for expressing electrical "pressure" in a circuit. One volt that will produce a current of one ampere through a resistance of one ohm.

W

Welding Various processes used to join metal items by heating the areas to be joined to a molten state and fusing them together. For more information refer to the *Haynes Automotive Welding Manual.*

Wiring diagram A drawing portraying the components and wires in a vehicle's electrical system, using standardised symbols. For more information refer to the *Haynes Automotive Electrical and Electronic Systems Manual.*

Note: *References throughout this index are in the form* **"Chapter number"** • **"Page number"**. *So, for example, 2C•15 refers to page 15 of Chapter 2C.*

Note: *References throughout this index are in the form* **"Chapter number"** • **"Page number"**. *So, for example, 2C•15 refers to page 15 of Chapter 2C.*

Preserving Our Motoring Heritage

< The Model J Duesenberg Derham Tourster. Only eight of these magnificent cars were ever built – this is the only example to be found outside the United States of America

Almost every car you've ever loved, loathed or desired is gathered under one roof at the Haynes Motor Museum. Over 300 immaculately presented cars and motorbikes represent every aspect of our motoring heritage, from elegant reminders of bygone days, such as the superb Model J Duesenberg to curiosities like the bug-eyed BMW Isetta. There are also many old friends and flames. Perhaps you remember the 1959 Ford Popular that you did your courting in? The magnificent 'Red Collection' is a spectacle of classic sports cars including AC, Alfa Romeo, Austin Healey, Ferrari, Lamborghini, Maserati, MG, Riley, Porsche and Triumph.

A Perfect Day Out

Each and every vehicle at the Haynes Motor Museum has played its part in the history and culture of Motoring. Today, they make a wonderful spectacle and a great day out for all the family. Bring the kids, bring Mum and Dad, but above all bring your camera to capture those golden memories for ever. You will also find an impressive array of motoring memorabilia, a comfortable 70 seat video cinema and one of the most extensive transport book shops in Britain. The Pit Stop Cafe serves everything from a cup of tea to wholesome, home-made meals or, if you prefer, you can enjoy the large picnic area nestled in the beautiful rural surroundings of Somerset.

John Haynes O.B.E., Founder and Chairman of the museum at the wheel of a Haynes Light 12. >

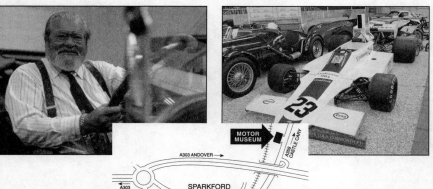

< Graham Hill's Lola Cosworth Formula 1 car next to a 1934 Riley Sports.

The Museum is situated on the A359 Yeovil to Frome road at Sparkford, just off the A303 in Somerset. It is about 40 miles south of Bristol, and 25 minutes drive from the M5 intersection at Taunton.
Open 9.30am - 5.30pm (10.00am - 4.00pm Winter) 7 days a week, *except Christmas Day, Boxing Day and New Years Day*
Special rates available for schools, coach parties and outings Charitable Trust No. 292048